Royal Air Force

BOMBER COMMAND
LOSSES

Volume 7
Operational Training Units
1940-1947

Royal Air Force
BOMBER COMMAND LOSSES
Volume 7

Operational Training Units
1940-1947

W R CHORLEY

Royal Air Force Bomber Command Losses
Volume 7:
Operational Training Units 1940-1947

Copyright © 2002 W R Chorley

First published in 2002 by
Midland Publishing
4 Watling Drive, Hinckley, LE10 3EY, UK.
Tel: 01455 254490   Fax: 01455 233737
E-mail: midlandbooks@compuserve.com

ISBN 1 85780 132 6

Midland Publishing is an
imprint of Ian Allan Publishing Ltd.

Printed and bound in England by
Bookcraft
First Avenue
Midsomer Norton, BA3 4BS, UK

Contents

An eight-page photo-section (i-viii)
illustrating many of the aircraft types
operated by the Bomber OTUs
is situated between pages 350 and 351.

Acknowledgements

Without any shadow of doubt, this volume has proven the most difficult to compile and its outcome has only been made possible by the assistance and encouragement generously provided by various departments and individuals who have gone out of their way to answer the many questions put to them.

First and foremost, Mike Hatch and his staff at the Air Historical Branch have, on numerous occasions, guided me in the right direction, after I had trawled the multitude of unit records held at the Public Record Office. But for their generous help, this book would have been much the poorer. I am also indebted to the Commonwealth War Graves Commission, the Australian War Museum, the Royal Air Force Museum Hendon, and Salisbury Library, all providers of professional help and support, so necessary in bringing about a successful conclusion to the project.

Invaluable aid has been forthcoming from Hugh Wheeler who, in the earliest days of my research into the losses, provided me with material garnered, along with Graham Warner, in respect of the many Blenheims lost from 13 and 17 Operational Training Units. Likewise, Eric Kaye, aided by Gerry V Tyack MBE, John Pratley and Chris Pointon, all experts in respect of the units based at Moreton-in-Marsh, Wellesbourne Mountford and Lichfield, plus their respective satellites, have saved me countless hours of labour, for which I am eternally grateful. Hans de Haan, too, has been a mine of knowledge, answering numerous letters and meticulously checking tables of submitted data.

Although mentioned in my introduction, the help provided by Errol Martyn of New Zealand deserves further recognition. Not only has Errol allowed me to extract material from his two remarkable volumes commemorating the airmen of the Royal New Zealand Air Force who have given their lives from 1915 to the present day, but has put at my disposal many items of correspondence, relevant to my research. Similarly, Oliver Clutton-Brock, has advised me on all matters pertaining to the one hundred and seventy-seven airmen known to have been made captive, thus allowing me to present a very detailed appendix on this subject.

Betty Clements has willingly looked at my notes concerning Polish Air Force casualties sustained by 18 Operational Training Unit, while Rod Priddle and Bob Collis have provided much worthwhile detail regarding air accidents over Wiltshire and East Anglia respectively.

Brian Walker (and Eric Kaye) have delved into various newspaper archives, securing copies of reports concerning training aircraft that fell onto civilian property in the Balderton and Banbury areas (a shade over fifty civilians lost their lives as a direct result of Operational Training Unit accidents).

Many others have provided me with useful snippets of information; hopefully, I have acknowledged their help, either by way of a footnote, or by direct reference in the appropriate summary. Thus, for any omissions on my part, I hereby humbly apologise.

Last, but by no means least, I pay tribute to my family and to my publishers for all their support during the three years it has taken to prepare the book that follows.

Bill Chorley, January 2002

Introduction

During the compilation of the first six volumes of this series of Royal Air Force Bomber Command Losses of the Second World War, I was able to present a certain amount of, mainly, statistical data pertaining to the losses reported from the Operational Training Units (OTUs) and other supporting formations within the command structure.

Since then, a more exhaustive study of the training units has enabled me to expand on this initial research and the purpose of this volume is to report in substantially more detail the casualties sustained by those OTUs that came under the bright shield of Bomber Command.

Between April 1940 and the end of the war, the majority of crews posted to the operational squadrons passed through the portals of the OTU system. Subsequently, of those who were fortunate to survive their period of front line service many found themselves back where they started, this time as rather reluctant instructors! Sadly, a few would not survive this second spell, such being the demands of the training syllabus. Most fatalities, of course, occurred amongst the trainee aircrews struggling to master the intrinsic difficulties of operational flying and such was the vociferous nature of Bomber Command that from a humble beginning of just eight training establishments, the number of OTUs serving the Command peaked in the high summer of 1944 at twenty-two.

Administering to the demands of the OTUs came under the umbrella of No. 6 Group, with its headquarters at Abingdon. In mid-July 1940, a second group came into being at Brampton Grange and to No. 7 Group fell the responsibilities of attending to the Hampden and Blenheim OTUs.

Two years on, a revision of the training headquarters resulted in No. 6 Group being redesignated No. 91 Group, while No. 7 Group was retitled No. 92 Group. At the same time Lichfield became the base for No. 93 Group, the new formation taking over the husbandry of five OTUs, all equipped with Wellingtons of various Marks. For a complete picture of the formation of the OTUs and their parent groups, readers should refer to the first of the appendices.

The principal sources consulted during the period of research have been the Operational Record Books (ORBs) and their appendices, the aircraft accident cards (AM Form 1180), the aircraft movement cards (AM Form 78) and extracts taken from aircrew flying log books that have passed through my hands in years past. The AM Form 78s have enabled me to clear up the few anomalies that materialised while trawling the Air-Britain aircraft serial registers (meticulously compiled over several decades by James J Halley MBE) which have been so useful in establishing the aircraft and units which form the backbone of this volume. Where OTU aircraft were lost on operational sorties, I have, again, referred to the Bomber Command loss cards and, as the summaries will show, further information has come to light in several cases. Unit ORBs have provided additional data, particularly where the aircraft concerned came down over the United Kingdom or in the coastal waters surrounding our island home. Rarely were loss cards raised for these crews and, thus, the statistics shown in previous volumes will be significantly altered.

Other prime sources of reference have been the Commonwealth War Graves Commission cemetery registers and the Commission's invaluable website, the Australian War Museum website, the Allied Air Forces prisoner of war file (AIR20/2336) (supplemented by much useful advice and help from Oliver Clutton-Brock) and the magnificent tributes to the fallen from the Royal Canadian Air Force (RCAF), Royal New Zealand Air Force (RNZAF) and the Polish Air Force (PAF). In order, these tributes are titled They Shall Grow Not Old, For Your Tomorrow and Ksiega Lotnikow Polskich (the latter kindly loaned by Graham Warrener). To their respective authors, Les Allison and Harry Hayward, Errol W Martyn and Olgierd Cumft and Hubert Kazimierz Kujawa, I am eternally indebted.

The presentation of the summaries follow the established pattern of dates and units appearing in chronological sequence. In a handful of cases, I have been able to show the aircraft's respective Flight but rarely have I been able to establish, beyond doubt, the unit's code combination or individual letter. Such detail frequently escaped the attention of most ORB compilers! The term "Training" is deemed sufficient to complete the majority of key entry lines, though in the summaries I have often elaborated on the purpose of the training detail.

The order in which the crews are reported varies considerably, principally because sorties were often undertaken with a hotchpotch of trades. For example, air gunnery details were often flown with three or more air gunners aboard, while navigation training, oft as not, required the presence of a navigator instructor. However, to the best of my knowledge, the first name shown in the matrix identifies the airman at the controls when the aircraft took off. In most cases, standard crew complements for Fairey Battle single-engined light bombers were pilot, navigator and wireless operator/air gunner. Hampden losses showing four members of crew can be assumed to be pilot, navigator and two wireless operator/air gunners. (In the early war years, navigation and air bombing were the responsibilities of one man and, in general, his aircrew category was referred to as an observer. Similarly, throughout the war wireless operators often attended an air gunnery course as part of their training).

Whitley and Wellington crews are likely to be pilot, navigator, air bomber, wireless operator and air gunner, though bearing in mind the statement in parenthesis the second named might well be a co-pilot. Where six names appear, then it is likely the aircraft was operating with two air gunners.

Ansons were issued to nineteen of the 22 bomber OTUs and four, 16, 19, 20 and 26 OTUs retained the type into 1945. Used primarily as a navigation trainer, fatal accidents involving the Anson robbed the services of at least one qualified navigator as well as taking the lives of several trainees.

Throughout the existence of the OTUs, a myriad of aircraft types were issued in the support role. Lysanders and Martinets were assigned for target towing duties with the Martinet also being employed to assist in fighter affiliation training. By around mid-1944, Hurricanes had mainly taken over these duties, while other types employed included Tomahawks and a handful of Spitfires. Also on the inventory of most OTUS were Magisters and Masters, Tiger Moths and Oxfords (the last named being particularly well used by 14 OTU). Crew compilations for these sundry aircraft need little explanation, except to say that the second named in a target towing accident summary usually held the category of drogue operator.

There are, however, many entries where it has been impossible to ascertain complete crew details. This is particularly the case where no fatalities occurred. Frequently, OTUs failed to record such matters in their diaries and, thus, I have had to rely on the evidence presented on the AM Form 1180.

As has been indicated, most summaries will attempt to explain the purpose of the flight and because the vast majority of flying accidents occurred over the United Kingdom, a reasonable degree of accuracy has been achieved in reporting the crash location and its cause.

Additional information has been forthcoming from private sources and, where it is deemed appropriate, due recognition has been accorded by way of a footnote.

Distances within the United Kingdom are shown in miles, while kilometres are used in all summaries pertaining to losses over the continent of Europe. When describing crashes that occurred within the British Isles, the name of the county, if quoted, will be appropriate to the county boundaries then in force. Thus, losses in the vicinity of Cottesmore will be described as occurring in Rutland and not Leicestershire. Times are shown in the twenty-four hour clock system and are likely to be in Greenwich Mean Time.

One major change occurs in the reporting of ranks. Previously, I recorded the rank as shown on the loss card, but as these cards are in the minority as far as most OTU accidents are concerned, I have resorted to reporting the rank finally held by the airman in question. Commissioning details were often omitted from the ORBs, but the CWGC cemetery registers and AIR20/2336 show the outcome of successful applications.

It has not been possible to identify every casualty, principally because of a paucity of such detail in unit records. However, I am reasonably confident that I have established the names of all RCAF, RNZAF and PAF airmen who fell in the final stages of their training. Finally, due to the fact that training methods ran a well ordered course throughout the period covered by this volume the text that heralds the beginning of each chapter is relatively brief. To compensate, I have included a resumé at the end of each year (less 1945 and 1946) which expands on matters not covered by the summaries.

Sources & Bibliography

Air Historical Branch:
Aircraft Accident Cards
Aircraft Movement Cards
Bomber Command Loss Cards

Australian War Museum:
Roll of Honour website

Commonwealth War Graves Commission:
Cemetery & Memorial Registers and website

Public Record Office Kew:
Allied Air Forces Prisoner of War File
Escape & Evasion Reports
OTU Operational Record Books and Appendices

Air-Britain (Historians) Ltd:
Royal Air Force Aircraft K1000 to K9999, James J Halley
Royal Air Force Aircraft L1000 to N9999, James J Halley
Royal Air Force Aircraft P1000 to P9999, James J Halley
Royal Air Force Aircraft R1000 to R9999, James J Halley
Royal Air Force Aircraft T1000 to V9999, James J Halley
Royal Air Force Aircraft X1000 to Z9999, James J Halley
Royal Air Force Aircraft AA100 to AZ999, James J Halley
Royal Air Force Aircraft BA100 to BZ999, James J Halley
Royal Air Force Aircraft DA100 to DZ999, James J Halley
Royal Air Force Aircraft EA100 to EZ999, James J Halley
Royal Air Force Aircraft FA100 to FZ999, James J Halley
Royal Air Force Aircraft HA100 to HZ999, James J Halley
Royal Air Force Aircraft JA100 to JA999, James J Halley
Royal Air Force Aircraft KA100 to KZ999, James J Halley
Royal Air Force Aircraft LA100 to LZ999, James J Halley
Royal Air Force Aircraft MA100 to MZ999, James J Halley
Royal Air Force Aircraft NA100 to NZ999, James J Halley
Royal Air Force Aircraft PA100 to RZ999, James J Halley
Royal Air Force Aircraft SA100 to VZ999, James J Halley
Royal Air Force Flying Training and Support Units, Ray Sturtivant, John Hamlin and
    James J Halley
The Anson File, Ray Sturtivant
The Battle File, Sidney Shail
The Hampden File, Harry Moyle
The Whitley File, R N Roberts

Aviation in Leicestershire and Rutland, Roy Bonser, Midland Publishing, 2001
Bomber Squadron of the RAF and their Aircraft, Philip Moyes, Macdonald, 1964
De Havilland Mosquito Crash Log, David J Smith, Midland Counties Publications, 1980
Deutsche Nachtjagd, Personalverluste in Ausbildung und Einsatz - fliegendes Personal,
    Michael Balss, Balss, 1997
For Your Tomorrow, Volume One, Errol W Martyn, Volplane Press, 1998
For Your Tomorrow, Volume Two, Errol W Martyn, Volplane Press, 1999
Ksiega Lotnikow Polskich, Poleglych Zmarlych Izaginionych 1939-1946,
    Olgierd Cumft & Hubert Kazimierz Kujawa, Wydawnictwo Ministerstwa Obrony Narodowej, 1989
Royal Air Force Flying Training Losses in Yorkshire 1939-1947, David E Thompson, unpublished
The Bomber Command War Diaries, Martin Middlebrook & Chris Everitt, Midland Publishing, 1996
The Children's Encyclopedia, Edited by Arthur Mees, The Educational Book Company, 1940
The Distinguished Flying Medal, I T Tavender, Hayward, 1990
They Shall Not Grow Old, A Book of Remembrance, Allison & Hayward, CATP Museum, 1992
Vickers Wellington Crash Log, Volume 1 1937-1942, David J Smith, Smith

Glossary of Terms

AFC	Air Force Cross
AFM	Air Force Medal
AM	Air Ministry
AS	Anti-Submarine
ASR	Air Sea Rescue
ATC	Air Training Corps
AC1	Aircraftman First Class
AC2	Aircraftman Second Class
ACW1	Aircraftwoman First Class
ACW2	Aircraftwoman Second Class
BEM	British Empire Medal
Capt	Captain
Cdt	Cadet
Cpl	Corporal
CWGC	Commonwealth War Graves Commission
Det	Detachment
DFC	Distinguished Flying Cross
DFM	Distinguished Flying Medal
DSO	Distinguished Service Order
EA	Enemy Aircraft
Evd	Evader
FFAF	Free French Air Force
Flt	Flight
Fw	Feldwebel
F/L	Flight Lieutenant
F/O	Flying Officer
F/S	Flight Sergeant
GM	George Medal
Grnd	Ground
G/C	Group Captain
HCU	Heavy Conversion Unit
Hptm	Hauptmann
Inj	Injured
Int	Interned
LAC	Leading Aircraftman
LACW	Leading Aircraftwoman
Lt	Leutnant/Lieutenant
Lt(A)	Lieutenant (Air)
Maj	Major
MBE	Member of the Order of the British Empire
MC	Military Cross
MID	Mentioned in Dispatches
Misc	Miscellaneous
MM	Military Medal
Mid(A)	Midshipman (Air)
NJG	Nachtjagdgeschwader

Oblt	Oberleutnant
OC	Officer Commanding
OM	Order of Merit
ORB	Operations Record Books
OTU	Operational Training Unit
Op:	Operation
PAF	Polish Air Force
POW	Prisoner of War
Pte	Private
P/O	Pilot Officer
QDM	International Q-code Signal for Magnetic Course to Steer
QGH	International Q-code Signal for Controlled Descent through Cloud
RA	Royal Artillery
RAAF	Royal Australian Air Force
RAF	Royal Air Force
RCAF	Royal Canadian Air Force
RIAF	Royal Indian Air Force
RN	Royal Navy
RNAF	Royal Norwegian Air Force
RNVR	Royal Naval Volunteer Reserve
RNZAF	Royal New Zealand Air Force
RAF(VR)	Royal Air Force (Volunteer Reserve)
SAAF	South African Air Force
Sqn	Squadron
S/L	Squadron Leader
S/O	Section Officer
S/S	Staff Sergeant
S/Lt(A)	Sub-Lieutenant (Air)
T/S	Technical Sergeant
Uffz	Unteroffizier
Unkn	Unknown
USA	United States of America
VSAAF	United States Army Air Force
VC	Victoria Cross
WAAF	Women's Auxiliary Air Force
W/C	Wing Commander
W/O	Warrant Officer
WO1	Warrant Officer First Class
WO2	Warrant Officer Second Class
1Lt	First Lieutenant
2Lt	Second Lieutenant
+	Fatal Casualty

Chapter 1

Early Days

8 April to 9 May 1940

Monday, the 8th of April 1940, was a reasonably fine spring day, certainly quite suited for flying training. At Bicester, D Flight of the newly established 13 OTU was ordered to prepare for a formation flying exercise that would take the twin-engined Blenheims on a northwesterly route from their pleasant Oxfordshire base to Ronaldsway on the Isle of Man before turning south on an equally long leg, across Wales, to Hartland Point on Devon's northern coast, west of Bideford.

Having made landfall, the formation would then head eastwards for home, arriving in time for lunch. With the weather set fair, few problems were expected in completing the exercise.

Amongst the crews attending the pre-flight briefing was one captained by a twenty-two year old Londoner, Sergeant Alfred Ernest Hall of Putney. Similar to so many of the airmen passing through the training system, Hall was a product of the pre-war Volunteer Reserve scheme and now after over six months of wartime flying experience, he was almost fit to be posted to an operational squadron.

His observer, Sergeant Fred Graham, just nineteen, had joined the regular air force a few years previous and he likely viewed the flight with some excitement hoping, perhaps, to catch a fleeting glimpse of his home town of Blackpool as the formation sped across the Irish Sea. The third member of the crew was Leading Aircraftman Geoffrey Halstead James, a Devonian and, like his skipper, a pre-war Volunteer Reserve airman. Indeed, his service number suggests he may have commenced training as a pilot, but now his function was that of a wireless operator/air gunner.

From what evidence is available, the first leg of the flight passed off without undue incident but as the Blenheims headed south increasing amounts of cloud blocked their path and at roughly 1120 hours, Sergeant Hall's aircraft was observed to leave the formation. Eye witnesses suggested he might have been dazzled by the sun, after emerging from a particularly dense billow of cloud, but whatever the reason his Blenheim, banking gently, was soon lost from sight.

When next reported, it was a telephone message to say the bomber had been found, smashed to smithereens on Carnedd Llewelyn in North Wales. All three airmen had died instantly.

In the days that followed, burial services were held in their home towns, the grieving parents unaware that their loved ones had been the first fatal casualties sustained by the newly established OTUs.

Before the day was over, five more lives had been taken. Four had died at around five in the afternoon when a Whitley, enroute to Jurby on the Isle of Man from its base at Abingdon, crashed near Stratford-upon-Avon and in the hour before midnight a cherry red glow in the sky a mile east of Benson marked the funeral pyre of a New Zealand born Battle pilot.

Not an auspicious beginning for the embryo OTUs. To trace the origins of these units, it is necessary to go back to the last days of peace. As Europe moved closer to war, Bomber Command could boast a total of fifty-five squadrons. However, a closer inspection of this quite impressive figure shows that twenty were either Reserve or Group Pool squadrons, while the entire strength of No.1 Group, ten squadrons of Fairey Battle light bombers, had been hurriedly despatched to France where they would operate as the Advanced Air Striking Force under the control of Air Marshal Sir Arthur Barratt. Joining the Battles across the channel were two squadrons of Blenheims, both assigned for reconnaissance duties with the Air Component of the British Expeditionary Force.

Thus, the effective strength of Bomber Command was nowhere near as impressive as a first glance might suggest. The expansion years of the late 1930s had witnessed an upsurge in the reformation of squadrons that had lain dormant since the armistice of 1918 but while it had been relatively simple to reestablish the numerical strength of the air force, the task of providing the new squadrons with operationally proficient crews had been a quite different matter, hence the necessity for so many training squadrons. Within the confines of Bomber Command, this dire situation was not lost on its commander, the astute Air Chief Marshal Sir Edgar Ludlow-Hewitt.

Although not destined to lead his Command beyond the spring of 1940, Ludlow-Hewitt was determined to husband his forces. He was aided in some measure by the narrow margins imposed by the War Cabinet on Bomber Command during the first months of the war, but these limitations apart, Sir Edgar likely regarded the training squadrons of No.6 Group to be equal in importance to those that formed the backbone of his four operational groups.

As the first volume in this series shows all too plainly, the much vaunted strength of Bomber Command was found wanting in many respects. Acknowledging the shortcomings of the Command and its operating procedures was the first painful step along the road that by the spring of 1945 would result in Air Chief Marshal Sir Arthur Harris directing one of the most powerful air fleets in the Western world.

And so it came to pass that in early April 1940, fifteen squadrons, domicile on eight bomber stations, were disbanded and their equipment and staff merged with the head-quarters of their parent stations to form the first eight Operational Training Units.

Not surprisingly, the establishments of these new units was quite considerable and, on paper at least, the amalgamation of 215 Squadron and SHQ Bassingbourn to form 11 OTU resulted in a muster of fifty-two Wellington and seventeen Anson aircraft, while No. 14 OTU at Cottesmore had call upon thirty-nine Hampden/Hereford types, plus an equal amount of Anson navigation trainers.

No less exacting was the administrative work necessary to ensure the smooth running of the new units and this was to lead to a spate of in-house posting of senior staff. At Abingdon, home to the Whitleys of No. 10 OTU that until recently had flown under the banners of 97 Squadron and 166 Squadron, Wing Commander J C Foden was appointed OC Training Wing on 12 April, but within seven days had been transferred to head the unit's Maintenance Wing. Meanwhile, the post of Chief Ground Instructor changed hands three times in as many months; Squadron Leader R W M Clark being moved to take over Wing Commander Foden's chair at the Training Wing while his successor, Squadron Leader A V 'Tom' Sawyer lasted a mere six weeks before he was appointed B Flight Commander in succession to Flight Lieutenant R B Harvey.

For the rank and file members of the now defunct squadrons, life carried on much as normal but the news on 9 April, announcing the invasion of neutral Denmark and Norway could have left little doubt in the minds of many of Hitler's true intentions.

Bomber Command responded immediately to this latest act of German aggression with sorties directed at trying to hinder the military advance (all defence in Denmark had been swept aside in hours but Allied forces were being rushed to Norway as a counter to the invasion), but no relaxation was forth-coming in respect of the limitations imposed in September 1939, that effectively tied the hands of Bomber Command as far as targets on the German mainland were concerned. For the present, Adolf Hitler was not going to be overly inconvenienced by the activities of the Royal Air Force.

With squadron wastage gradually increasing in all commands, the success of the OTUs was of paramount importance to the entire war effort. Pre-war flying training standards ensured that the quality of pilots entering the system was reasonably good, but whereas in peacetime instruction could be given at a relatively measured pace, needs now demanded that course times be pared to the minimum in order to produce the maximum amount of trained aircrew.

Thus, trainees and instructors alike were being obliged to adapt to methods of flying training that were demanding in the extreme. Not surprisingly, casualties soon began to mount as crews were pressed ever harder to absorb the complexities of navigation and bombing, wireless procedures and gunnery and the mechanical mysteries of variable pitch propellers, hydraulic systems and other such recent innovations peculiar to modern aircraft.

Sadly, for more than a few, the task set was too severe.

8 Apr 1940	10 OTU C Flt	Whitley III	K8957	Transit

F/O A L McSherry   +   T/o Abingdon and set course for Jurby on the
P/O K R B Ainsworth   +   Isle of Man. While flying at 8,000 feet, lost
P/O J M Davies   +   control and crashed circa 1700 near the railway
LAC M H Costello   +   station at Northcote, not far distant from
P/O G W Salzgeber   Stratford-upon-Avon. P/O Salzgeber
parachuted safely. F/O McSherry is buried in Burstwick (All Saints) Churchyard; P/O Ainsworth was taken to Woodchurch (Holy Cross) Churchyard at Birkenhead, while P/O Davies and LAC Costello were brought for interment in Abingdon Cemetery.

12 OTU		Battle I	P2273	Training

P/O M E F Barnett   +   T/o 2310 Benson to practice night circuits and landings but after climbing to between 500 and 600 feet, the Battle yawed to starboard, lost height and crashed at Ewelme, roughly a mile E of the airfield and burst into flames. Eighteen year old P/O Barnett, born in London but educated in New Zealand where he qualified as a pilot, is buried in the extension to Benson (St. Helen) Churchyard. He was the first New Zealander to lose his life at a bomber OTU.

Note. The bibliographic details for P/O Barnett have been taken from Errol Martyn's first volume of For Your Tomorrow and I cannot stress too strongly the worth of this book, and his second volume, in all matters relating to the fate of New Zealand airmen. It is a work of significant importance.

8 Apr
1940

| 13 OTU D Flt | **Blenheim IV** | L9039 | **Training** |

Sgt A E Hall   +   T/o Bicester for a formation cross country;
Sgt F Graham   +   base-Ronaldsway-Hartland Point-base. Left the
LAC G H James   +   formation, in cloud, banking gently and crashed
                                        circa 1120 on Carnedd Llewelyn, some 6 miles SSE
of Bethesda, Caernarvon. All rest in cemeteries within the United Kingdom. It
is thought Sgt Hall may have been dazzled by the sun as he emerged from the
overcast.

Note. Part of the information pertaining to the Blenheim loss has been taken
from notes prepared in respect of 13 OTU by Roger Peacock and Hugh Wheeler. I
am indebted to them both.

14 Apr
1940

| 11 OTU | **Wellington I** | L4390 | **Training** |

P/O I A McDiarmid   T/o Bassingbourn for night flying practice.
                                       Crashed 2230 while trying to make an emergency
landing a mile or so N of Bletchley in Buckinghamshire. No injuries reported.

Note. This incident, like so many non-fatal accidents, has not been recorded
in unit records and, therefore, the names of his crew are not known.

| 17 OTU | **Blenheim I** | L1264 | **Training** |

S/L H F Chester   T/o Upwood. Damaged beyond repair, after landing
                                       safely at 1420, when the undercarriage was raised
in mistake for the flaps. No one was hurt and, subsequently, the airframe was
salvaged for instructional purposes. S/L Chester had accumulated 3,070 flying
hours, 235 of these being on Blenheims. Tragically, within three months of this
incident he was killed while flying with 82 Squadron (see Bomber Command Losses,
Volume 1, page 84) to attack targets along the Dortmund-Ems Kanal.

15 Apr
1940

| 14 OTU | **Hampden I** | L4197 | **Training** |

P/O R R Sandford   T/o Cottesmore for night circuits and landings.
                                       Crash-landed 2245, wheels retracted, due to
hydraulic failure. No injuries reported. P/O Sandford later served with 44
Squadron and lost his life during operations to Augsburg on 17 April 1942 (see
Bomber Command Losses, Volume 3, page 72).

17 Apr
1940

| 15 OTU | **Wellington I** | L4291 | **Training** |

F/L T W Piper   inj   T/o 0320 Harwell for night dual, including
F/O Harris   inj   instrument flying and single-engined landings.
                                       Lost power and forced-landed in a field near
West Ilsley, 16 miles NE of Reading. A fire broke out and the Wellington was
totally destroyed. Both pilots were admitted to SSQ Harwell. F/L Piper made
a good recovery from his injuries and by the summer of 1941, he was flying
Stirlings with 15 Squadron. On 19 July of that year, he was shot down by
flak near Dunkerque and became a prisoner of war (see Bomber Command Losses,
Volume 2, page 94), ending up in Stalag Luft III.

21 Apr
1940

| 14 OTU | **Hampden I** | L4200 | **Training** |

P/O T A Freke   T/o Cottesmore for night circuits and landings.
                                       Wrecked 2140, while trying to overshoot the
runway, finishing up in a hedge. No injuries reported.

22 Apr
1940

| 15 OTU | **Wellington I** | L4236 | **Training** |

Sgt G F Heayes   T/o Harwell for dual circuits and landings.
                                     Landed 1450, but bounced back into the air,
the force of the impact jamming the control column. On its second arrival,
the bomber caught fire. No injuries reported. A Staff Pilot, Sgt Heayes
was destined to survive a number of nasty accidents, as the following pages
will duly show.

| 16 OTU | **Hampden I** | L4148 | **Air Test** |

F/L B P Jones   inj   T/o Upper Heyford but the ailerons proved to
LAC R Holt   +   be ineffective and the order to bale out was
LAC J F Dobson   +   given. Moments later, at 1620, the Hampden
                                       plunged into a field between Souldern and
Fritwell, villages close to the Northamptonshire border and some 7 and 8 miles
SE respectively of Banbury, Oxfordshire. LAC Holt rests in Sheffield (Tinsley
Park) Cemetery; his fellow passenger, LAC Dobson, lies in East Retford Cemetery.

25 Apr
1940

16 OTU		**Hampden I**	P1181	**Training**
W/C K H R Elliott				
F/S E G Crouch				

T/o 1044 Upper Heyford on the pilot's first solo on type but a minute later an engine cut and a crash-landing was made near the airfield. No serious injuries reported. It is believed F/S Crouch was attending to the duties of wireless operator.

29 Apr
1940

15 OTU		**Wellington I**	L4267	**Training**
P/O C I Rolfe				

T/o Harwell to practice emergency landing procedures. Lost power and forced-landed at about 1550 in the vicinity of Swindon, Wiltshire. No injuries reported. Subsequently, P/O Rolfe became a Stirling pilot and was shot down during a raid to Berlin (see Bomber Command Losses, Volume 2, page 107), ending up in Stalag Luft III as a prisoner of war.

5 May
1940

10 OTU		**Whitley III**	K9007	**Training**
P/O W T Davies				

T/o Abingdon to practice night circuits and landings. During the exercise, the port under-carriage leg jammed and all attempts to free the unit failed. P/O Davies gained height, baling out his co-pilot and wireless operator, before returning to base for a successful crash-landing at 0230. Unfortunately, before coming to a stop, the Whitley skidded into a machine-gun emplacement and caught fire.

6 May
1940

14 OTU		**Hampden I**	P1274	**Training**
Sgt O Beck	+			
P/O K A Ramsay	+			
LAC E O Backshall	+			
AC1 J Foster	+			

T/o Cottesmore for night flying practice. Overshot the runway, following a heavy landing, and while trying to go round again crashed 0050 some 2 miles NNE of the airfield. The first two named rest in the extension to Cottesmore (St. Nicholas) Churchyard, while LAC Backshall and AC1 Foster were taken for burial in their home towns.

7 May
1940

16 OTU		**Hampden I**	P1251	**Training**
S/L G H Sheehan	inj			
Sgt Stilwell	inj			
P/O E R Appleton	inj			
LAC Browne	inj			
AC1 Clarke	inj			

T/o 2135 Upper Heyford but the port engine cut and being unable to maintain height, the bomber smashed into a tree near Fritwell, 8 miles SE of Banbury, Oxfordshire. A fire broke out on impact. S/L Sheehan and Sgt Stilwell were very badly injured; both owe their lives to the bravery of LAC Browne and AC1 Clarke who between them dragged the two airman to safety. P/O Appleton, too, received very severe burns but he managed to get clear, unaided. On 25 August 1942, S/L Sheehan, now flying Lancasters with 61 Squadron, failed to return from a sortie to Frankfurt (see Bomber Command Losses, Volume 3, page 189).

9 May
1940

10 OTU		**Whitley II**	K7227	**Training**
F/O D M Strong				

T/o Abingdon. Reported to have crash-landed, wheels retracted, circa 1820 close to Pershore airfield. No injuries reported. F/O Strong was an experienced pilot with 1,100 hours to his credit, 200 of these on Whitleys. On 4 June 1941, now promoted to S/L, he was appointed Officer Commanding A Flight, handing over these duties to S/L G P Seymour-Price on 16 July 1941. Posted to 104 Squadron as a Flight Commander, S/L Strong AFC failed to return from operations to Torino on 10-11 September 1941 (see Bomber Command Losses, Volume 2, page 143).

14 OTU		**Hereford I**	L6016	**Training**
Sgt D J Fielder				
LAC D Sharpe	inj			
LAC J L Brooks				
LAC A C Wright				

T/o Cottesmore. During the exercise, an engine failed and the aircraft began to lose height. It is likely the order to abandon, or prepare to bale out, was given as LAC Sharpe left the aircraft and was slightly injured as a result of his parachute descent. At around 1100 the bomber crash-landed, wheels up, in a field near Tugby, 11 miles ESE of Leicester.

Chapter Two

Increasing Strength

10 May 1940 to 30 May 1942

Few, I doubt, could have accurately forecast the collapse of the French army and with it the near catastrophic situation that faced the British Expeditionary Force within days of the German "Blitzkreig" on 10 May 1940.

In less than three weeks from the leading elements of the Wehrmacht crossing into the Benelux countries, until then apprehensive observers, Operation Dynamo was in full swing as the Royal Navy and their French counterparts, magnificently aided by a flotilla of little ships that had put out from harbours in Southern England, strove to evacuate thousands of bewildered servicemen from the beaches at Dunkerque.

Now, rightly, celebrated as a triumph over seemingly impossible odds, in June 1940 the events of Dunkerque were viewed very differently. England really was alone (though let it never be forgotten just how many of our Allies made their way from the cauldron of a broken Europe to join forces with those who were coming forth from all corners of our Empire and Dominions) and it seemed a mere matter of time before the full weight of Germany's military might would be across the Channel and put our island to the sword.

As Fighter Command joined daily battle to deny the Luftwaffe control over the Channel, Bomber Command, now freed of all previous restraints, took the first steps in its long and strength-sapping campaign to destroy the enemy's industrial base.

For the two years covered by this chapter, little impression would be made, but the die was cast and the OTUs would work to ensure its temper would never be broken for want of human resources.

As will be seen from the summaries that follow, many fell at the final hurdle but sufficient trainees were always available to take their place in the system.

10 May 1940	**13 OTU** Sgt K C Hobday	**Blenheim IV**	L8795	**Training**

T/o Bicester. Crashed circa 1220, as a result of engine failure, at Launton some 2 miles E of the airfield. No injuries reported.

	17 OTU P/O G M McFarland	**Blenheim IV**	L4889 +	**Training**

T/o Upwood. On return to base, stalled and came down 2240 at a spot known locally as Green Dyke. Until recently P/O McFarland, a New Zealander, had been head prefect at Nelson College, He rests in Bury Cemetery, Huntingdonshire.

12 May 1940	**15 OTU** P/O P A Clarke	**Wellington I**	L4231	**Training**

T/o Harwell. Crash-landed at approximately 1635 near Aldergrove airfield, Antrim, after overshooting the runway with unserviceable flaps. Salvaged by 4 MU, the airframe was struck off charge on 31 May 1940.

13 May 1940	**11 OTU** P/O G G Heathcote	**Wellington I**	L4378	**Training**

T/o 0654 Bassingbourn but an engine cut and in the ensuing emergency landing, the Wellington hit a tree and caught fire. No injuries reported. Until as recently as 7 May, P/O Heathcote had been serving with 9 Squadron at Honington, participating in one sortie as a second pilot and eleven as captain of his own crew.

15 OTU	**Wellington IA**	N2901	**Training**
P/O T T MacDonald	inj		
P/O W M A Davies	+		
P/O V U L Clarke	inj		
Sgt S C L Brewer	inj		
AC2 A M Pulfrey	+		
AC2 F Eccles	inj		

T/o Harwell for a combined navigation and practice bombing detail. Lost power and crashed at around 1120 some 2 miles from Axminster in Devon. P/O Davies, a King's Scholar Eton and Exhibitioner King's College, Cambridge, was brought back for burial in Harwell Cemetery, while AC2 Pulfrey rests in Grimsby (Scartho Road) Cemetery. It is believed that the survivors recovered from their injuries and, thankfully, went on to survive the war.

| 23 May 1940 | 12 OTU | Battle I L4965 | Training |

P/O D A Dadswell — T/o Benson. Returned to base at 1130 and, inadvertently, landed with the wheels still retracted. The Battle languished, unrepaired, until 20 December when it was allotted the serial 2433M and disposed of as a training aid. Subsequently, it was reduced to scrap on 30 June 1943. P/O Dadswell, meanwhile, converted to Wellingtons and while serving with 214 Squadron, was posted missing from operations on 7-8 December 1940 (see Bomber Command Losses, Volume 1, page 137).

| 24 May 1940 | 12 OTU | Battle I K9481 | Training |

P/O W D Finlayson + T/o Benson for a navigation exercise; base-
Sgt E Wigham + Frome-Tiverton-Holsworthy-Exeter-Lyme Regis-
AC2 A W A Coull + Frome-base. Encountered bad visibility and at around 1140 crashed into a hillside, which was shrouded by cloud, near Sidmouth on the south Devonshire coast. P/O Finlayson of Dunedin, New Zealand, who had joined the RAF on a Short Service Commission, is buried in Plymouth Old Cemetery (Pennycomequick); Sgt Wigham lies at Darlington West Cemetery and eighteen year old AC2 Coull was taken to Scotland and interred in Dunnotter Cemetery.

| | 12 OTU | Battle I L4977 | Training |

P/O P K Sigley + T/o Benson similar tasked. Flew into high ground
Sgt G M Stephens + at Bowd Croft, about a mile NNW of Sidmouth. P/O
AC1 R R Lamont + Sigley of Palmerston North rests with his fellow countryman in Plymouth Old Cemetery, as does his crew. P/O Sigley and P/O Finlayson had graduated from the same flying course in New Zealand. AC1 Lamont was aged eighteen.

| | 12 OTU | Battle I N2026 | Training |

P/O E Trumper inj T/o Penrhos for an air firing exercise over Caernarvon Bay but lost power and crash-landed 1700 in a field, about a mile NW of the airfield. It is believed the crew escaped serious injury.

| | 17 OTU | Blenheim IV P4907 | Training |

P/O I A Mead inj T/o Upwood for a navigation exercise; base-
Sgt A R Jackson + Pershore-Fishguard-Criccieth-Aberystwyth-base.
AC2 R South + Crashed 1155 in Tremadog Bay at the eastern end of the Lleyn Peninsular, The bodies of Sgt Jackson and AC2 South were recovered on 11 and 26 June 1940 respectively; Sgt Jackson lies at Pwllheli Borough Cemetery and AC2 South rests in Adwick-le-Street Cemetery. F/O Mead recovered from his injuries but lost his life on 2 June 1941, while flying with 18 Squadron (see Bomber Command Losses, Volume 2, page 61).

| 27 May 1940 | 16 OTU | Hampden I L4156 | Training |

P/O N G Dryburgh + T/o in company with Hampden I L4158, both crews
LAC T Baird + being part of the unit's detached Armament Flt
LAC R S Aitken + and set course for the Bristol Channel and an air firing detail. Collided with each other off Ilfracombe, Devon. P/O Dryburgh, he was 38 years of age, is buried in Edinburgh (Dean or Western) Cemetery; his crew, both of whom were from Glasgow, are perpetuated on panel 22 of the Runnymede Memorial.

| | 16 OTU | Hampden I L4158 | Training |

P/O R C Frost inj T/o in company with Hampden I L4156, tasked as
P/O T A Nixon + above and lost in the manner described. P/O Frost
LAC H Sharpe + was alive when recovered from the sea, but died
LAC J Whyte + soon after admission to hospital. He rests in Upper Heyford Cemetery. P/O Nixon, whose parents were from Surrey, is buried in Scotland at the Vale of Leven Cemetery at Bonhill. LAC Sharpe of Falkirk is commemorated on panel 24 of the Runnymede Memorial, while LAC Whyte rests in Glasgow Western Necropolis.

| 29 May 1940 | 14 OTU | Hampden I P1275 | Training |

F/O A B Lennie — T/o Cottesmore for a night exercise. Crashed 0030 into trees while approaching the runway. It is noted that F/O Lennie became a Test Pilot and lost his life on 8 December 1942. He is buried in Fettercairn Cemetery, Kincardineshire.

1 Jun
1940
14 OTU
P/O G V Eason
Hampden I P1281   **Training**
T/o 0045 Cottesmore for night flying practice but stalled and crashed, almost immediately. It is believed the crew escaped serious injury.

2 Jun
1940
16 OTU
P/O B Simpson
Hampden I P1179   **Training**
+ T/o 1700 Upper Heyford for the pilot's first Hampden solo but while banking to the left flew into a tree near the airfield and burst into flames. P/O Simpson, a regular service officer, is buried in Upper Heyford Cemetery.

3 Jun
1940
12 OTU
P/O A G McIntyre RNZAF   inj
Sgt G H Hudson   +
Sgt D L Leonard   +
Battle I P2269   **Training**
T/o Benson for a night navigation exercise but became lost and, unwittingly, strayed into the Portsmouth defence zone. Engaged by AA, the Battle was hit and abandoned at 0056, crashing near Ryde on the Isle of Wight. Sgt Hudson of Chorlton-cum-Hardy, Manchester, is buried in Bembridge (Holy Trinity) Churchyard, while panel 16 of the Runnymede Memorial commemorates Sgt Leonard. His second Christian name matched his surnames. P/O McIntyre RNZAF is thought to have survived the war. He was the first RNZAF airman to be involved in the loss of a Bomber Command OTU aircraft.

4 Jun
1940
16 OTU
Sgt G E Cowan
Hampden I P4295   **Training**
T/o Brackley for a two hour exercise in night circuits and landings. While landing at 0010, held off too high and in the ensuing heavy landing the starboard engine and undercarriage was torn from the mainplane. No one was hurt and soon afterwards Sgt Cowan was posted to 61 Squadron. On 16-17 December 1940, he failed to return from Mannheim (see Bomber Command Losses, Volume 1, page 140). Subsequently, he was awarded a Distinguished Flying Medal.

5 Jun
1940
17 OTU
Sgt M H Farmer
Anson I N5112   **Training**
T/o Upwood for a W/T exercise, involving the taking of loop bearings. Forced-landed 1130 in a rough field, due to engine failure, near Towcester, 9 miles SSW from Northampton and was wrecked after swinging into a hedge.

8 Jun
1940
14 OTU
P/O G T R Johns   inj
Anson I N5037   **Training**
T/o Cottesmore for night circuits and landings. At approximately 0015, undershot the flare-path and crashed into the station's bomb dump. It is thought P/O Johns may have been distracted by searchlights flickering across his field of vision.

9 Jun
1940
13 OTU
Blenheim I L1211   **Unknown**
Reported as damaged beyond repair on this date but no details of an accident have been discovered. Form AM 78 indicates that the Blenheim had been taken on charge at 13 OTU on 18 April 1940 and was written off on 9 June 1940. No indication of flying hours appended.

10 Jun
1940
12 OTU
P/O M C Pettit   inj
Battle I L5282   **Training**
T/o 0015 Benson and crashed almost immediately, coming down a mile E of the airfield. A fire broke out and the Battle was destroyed. Eyewitnesses stated that the Battle seemed to be pulling out of dive, or gliding at high speed. The propeller was found 20 to 30 yards away from the wreckage and it is thought the engine was running at high speed up to the moment of impact. P/O Pettit, who was badly hurt, had logged 48 hours on the type and a 141 in total.

13 OTU TTFlt
F/O A Chalmers   +
AC1 B B C Smith   +
AC1 H B Bennett   +
Battle I L4951   **Training**
T/o Squires Gate. At 1523, while circling the airfield, the Battle was seen to bank steeply as if to avoid entering low cloud. It then appeared to side slip, hitting a wall before cartwheeling across a railway track and ending up entangled in telegraph wires. F/O Chalmers (who was OC the Towed Target Flight) of Greenwich was buried in Blackpool (Carleton) Cemetery. Of his 528 flying hours, 325 had been logged on Battles. His crew were claimed by their next-of-kin. It is noted that AC1 Bennett's second Christian name was Bapaume.

11 Jun **12 OTU**   **Battle I**   **K9463**   **Training**
1940   P/O B P Thomson   +   T/o 0205 Benson and crashed almost immediately,
       Sgt D J Craven   +   due to engine failure, spinning into the ground
       LAC P A Lewis   +   SW of the airfield. P/O Thomson of Whangarei,
                                       New Zealand, who had joined the Royal Air Force
on a Short Service Commission, and Sgt Craven rest in the extension to Benson
(St. Helen) Churchyard, while LAC Lewis lies in Southampton (South Stoneham)
Cemetery. A pre-war regular, he was twenty years of age.

12 Jun **14 OTU**   **Hampden I**   **P1280**   **Training**
1940   P/O E B Liddell   T/o Cottesmore to practice night flying. At
                                       2140 the Hampden landed heavily and was damaged
beyond economical repair. No injuries reported. Posted to 50 Squadron, P/O
Liddell (who was known to his family and friends as Squibs) failed to return
from Mannheim on 10-11 December 1940 (see Bomber Command Losses, Volume 1,
page 138).

17 OTU   **Blenheim IV**   **L9172**   **Training**
       Sgt V A Bain   T/o Upwood for a navigation exercise; base-
       Sgt W H Wheeler   +   Lundy Island-Exmouth-base. At 1223, while
       AC2 S Boulton   +   flying at 20,000 feet, the pilot radioed
                                       "breaking up" and soon afterwards eyewitnesses
saw the Blenheim falling in a series of uneven rolls and slowly disintegrating.
The main debris fell into the tinplate works area at Cwmafan, 8 miles ESE of
Swansea. All three crew were pitched from the aircraft, Sgt Bain parachuting
virtually unscathed. His crew were not so fortunate; Sgt Wheeler is buried in
Bushey (St. James) Churchyard, while AC2 Boulton was taken to Hatfield (Woodhouse) Cemetery, near Doncaster.

Note. Sgt Wheeler's son, Hugh, born after this tragic accident, has served
as Archivist for the Blenheim Society. As has likely become clear, checks
are being carried out, through various channels, in respect of some of the
survivors and it is noted that a F/O V A Bain is buried in France, having
been killed while flying Dakota transport aircraft with 525 Squadron on 30
January 1946. He may not, however, be the same person as summarised above.

13 Jun **11 OTU Det**   **Wellington IA**   **N3012**   **Training**
1940   P/O W Gilmour   inj   T/o Jurby for an air firing exercise. Lost
       Sgt R L Culley   inj   engine power and ditched circa 1500 in the
       P/O L Swan   inj   Irish Sea off Orrisdale Head on the Isle of
       P/O P E Hindmarsh   inj   Man's west coast, a few miles N from Kirk
       Sgt A G Askham   inj   Michael. P/O Gilmour, subsequently gained
       LAC J C Somerville   inj   a Distinguished Flying Cross before losing
       AC2 L M W Griffin   inj   his life while flying with 156 Squadron (see
                                       Bomber Command Losses, Volume 3, page 199).
He is buried in Belgium at Heverlee War Cemetery.

Note. Neither the main Operational Record Book, or the appendices for 11 OTU,
refer to this accident and the details, as summarised, have been taken from the
Form AM 1180 and other records lodged with the Air Historical Branch. Omissions
of this nature are common in respect of training unit establishments.

14 OTU   **Hampden I**   **P4309**   **Training**
       Sgt A P Linsdell   T/o Cottesmore for local flying practice. On
                                       return to base at around 1830, overshot the
runway and crashed, heavily. No one was hurt. On 18-19 September 1940, Sgt
Linsdell, now commissioned, lost his life while serving with 83 Squadron (see
Bomber Command Losses, Volume 1, page 111).

16 OTU   **Hampden I**   **L4138**   **Training**
       P/O A C Rowe   inj   T/o 1200 Upper Heyford but at 20 feet was hit by
       P/O M S Blythe   inj   a 61 Squadron Hampden I P4339 QR-H (captained by
       LAC Evitt   P/O D A Helsby) which had taken off on what
                                       proved to be a converging course. P/O Rowe and
P/O Blythe were rushed to hospital, very seriously injured, but LAC Evitt escaped
relatively lightly. From the wreckage of the 61 Squadron machine, two were found
dead but two were still alive, albeit badly hurt (see Bomber Command Losses,
Volume 1, page 77, which erroneously reports Cottesmore as the aerodrome).

13 Jun	16 OTU	Hampden I	P4297	Training

13 Jun
1940

16 OTU   **Hampden I**   P4297   **Training**

F/O J E S MacAlister   +   T/o Upper Heyford to practice instrument flying.
P/O E A E Sedgley   +   At around 1000, while orbiting a boys' school at
AC2 J Lennon   +   Iwerne Minster, 5 miles NNW of Blandford Forum,
     Dorset, the Hampden spiralled out of control.
F/O MacAlister, the son of Sir George MacAlister and Lady MacAlister of Tonbridge
in Kent, is buried in Upper Heyford Cemetery; P/O Sedgley, a New Zealander, and
AC2 Lennon lie nearby at Middleton Stoney (All Saints) Churchyard. F/O MacAlister
was a Bachelor of Arts (Honours) graduate from Oxford University. His brother,
P/O Peter Donald MacAlister (who took the name Farragut), died on active service
(see Bomber Command Losses, Volume 2, page 80) while flying with 12 Squadron.

15 Jun
1940

14 OTU   **Hereford I**   L6008   **Training**

Sgt D S Matthews   T/o Cottesmore for a bombing exercise, the
     detail to be flown at 1,000 feet. As a result
of engine failure, forced-landed 1325 to the SW of Pickworth, 8 miles SSW of
Sleaford, Lincolnshire. No injuries. Soon after this incident, Sgt Matthews
was posted to 144 Squadron. On 7 March 1941, the London Gazette published
details of an award of the DFM. Subsequently he was commissioned and while
serving with 61 Squadron was killed when his Manchester crashed in Wiltshire
(see Bomber Command Losses, Volume 3, page 16).

Note. 14 OTU had the dubious distinction of being the first of the Bomber
Command OTUs to lose ten aircraft; seven Hampdens, two Herefords and an
Anson general purpose trainer.

16 Jun
1940

15 OTU   **Wellington I**   L4366   **Ground**

     Destroyed by fire at Harwell airfield.

20 Jun
1940

12 OTU   **Battle I**   K9420   **Training**

P/O F G Denman   T/o Benson for a gunnery exercise over Lyme Bay.
     At approximately 1430, the engine caught fire
and the crew ditched their Battle off Seaton, on the south Devonshire coast. It
is believed the crew escaped serious injury.

21 Jun
1940

16 OTU   **Hampden I**   P1268   **Training**

Sgt H Woolstencroft   inj   T/o Upper Heyford for night circuits and
     landings. Undershot the runway and crashed
circa 2340, smashing into a fuel bowser. No serious injuries reported.

22 Jun
1940

15 OTU   **Wellington I**   L4282   **Training**

S/L A H Smythe   T/o Harwell for night dual circuits and
     landings. The pupil pilot, who is not named,
overshot the flare-path, whereupon S/L Smythe took over the controls and
raised the undercarriage. However, the bomber ran on for at least 150 yards
before veering sharply and finishing up amongst a pile of sandbags.

25 Jun
1940

11 OTU   **Wellington I**   L4222   **Training**

P/O H R Bjelke-Petersen   T/o Bassingbourn to practice night circuits
     and landings. Landed 0030, in the midst of an
enemy air raid alert, striking at least one of the Glim lamps. Moments later
the undercarriage gave way. P/O Bjelke-Petersen became a prisoner of war
following operations to Hanau on 28-29 September 1940 (see Bomber Command
Losses, Volume 1, page 114).

28 Jun
1940

13 OTU   **Blenheim I**   L9212   **Training**

Sgt T G J Pascoe   +   T/o Bicester for a formation cross country. At
Sgt N R A Hawthorne   +   around 1740, while over Pembrokeshire, an engine
     inj   failed and the Blenheim was forced-landed in a
     field near Bosherston, 5 miles S of Pembroke.
Unfortunately, a concealed bank lay in its path and in the ensuing impact two
members of the crew were killed and a third airman was very seriously injured.
The two who died rest in Pembroke (Llanion) Cemetery. Sgt Pascoe was from Cape
Town; his observer hailed from Belfast.

4 Jul
1940

11 OTU   **Wellington IA**   N3003   **Training**

P/O R Beer   inj   T/o 1200 Bassingbourn but an escape hatch blew
Sgt T G Moore   inj   out and upon completing a circuit, the port oleo
     inj   collapsed, a fire starting almost immediately.

7 Jul   **11 OTU**   **Wellington I**   **L4331**   **Training**
1940   F/O P L B Morgan   T/o Bassingbourn for a night exercise. At 0130,
       P/O A L T Todd   while making ready to land, an engine cut causing
                                    the Wellington to swing towards the floodlighting
stands. F/O Morgan reacted by pulling back on the control column and in doing so
the bomber stalled and from around 40 feet side slipped, wing first, to the
ground. Posted soon after to 9 Squadron, F/O Morgan flew 31 sorties between
1 September and 25 April 1941, before becoming an instructor at 21 OTU.

13 OTU   **Blenheim I**   **L6773**   **Training**
Sgt S L Bennett   T/o Bicester. Landed downwind at 1545 and ran
                                    into some fencing. No injuries reported. For
reasons unknown, Sgt Bennett transferred to 16 OTU and commenced Hampden flying.
However, on 23 August he was to be involved in a very nasty night flying crash
at Brackley (see page 27). On the last day of 1940, he failed to return from
Blenheim operations in the Middle East. By this time he was serving with 211
Squadron. Panel 239 of the Alamein Memorial now perpetuates his name.

14 OTU   **Hampden I**   **P1309**   **Training**
P/O C O Dunkels   T/o Cottesmore for night flying practice.
                                    Overshot the runway and crashed 2340 into
a pillbox. No injuries reported. On 29-30 August 1940, P/O Dunkels, now with
44 Squadron, was posted missing following a raid on Gelsenkirchen (see Bomber
Command Losses, Volume 1, page 104).

9 Jul   **13 OTU**   **Blenheim I**   **L1249**   **Training**
1940   F/L D C Smythe   T/o 1450 Bicester with a pupil pilot at the
                                    controls for "blind" circuits and landings.
As the Blenheim climbed away from the airfield, an engine cut and F/L Smythe
took over the controls, successfully avoiding an obstruction. In doing so,
however, he lost flying speed and a wing brushed the ground. Seconds later,
the bomber went through a hedge and ended up on the main road, just S of the
airfield. Neither pilot was hurt, despite their aircraft going up in flames,
but a civilian who was in the vicinity was very seriously injured.

10 Jul   **13 OTU**   **Anson I**   **N5156**   **Unknown**
1940   Missing.

13 OTU   **Anson I**   **N5172**   **Unknown**
                                     Missing.

Note. The AM Form 78 for each of these aircraft indicates both were allotted
to 13 OTU on 18 April 1940 and were classed as missing on 10 July 1940. This
is supported by the entries in the Air-Britain serial register, L1000-N9999
and The Anson File, also published by Air-Britain. The latter, however, adds
"on operations" in respect of N5156. However, no AM Form 1180 has yet been
traced for either aircraft and, unfortunately, the unit records for the first
four months of its existence are incomplete. Avro historian, Harry Holmes,
has a note to the effect that both aircraft collided on 10 July 1940 but no
information pertaining to the identity of the two crews.

15 OTU   **Anson I**   **N5019**   **Training**
Sgt A C Smith   inj   T/o 2220 Harwell for a night navigation sortie.
P/O T C Watson   +   Became lost and just over an hour into the
Sgt C J Dent   +   exercise, flew into the slopes of Y Gamrhiw near
Sgt A Williams   +   Llanwrthwl, 3 miles S of Rhayder, Radnor. Of
Sgt H Hannan   +   those who died, two (P/O Watson and Sgt Dent)
                         inj   were buried in Shawbury (St. Mary) Churchyard
                                   and two were taken to their home towns. Despite
being badly hurt, Sgt Smith managed to make his way to Ty Coch Farm, where he
was tended by a Mr Pugh until an ambulance arrived to take him to Builth Wells
Cottage Hospital. On 24 November 1941, now with 97 Squadron, his Manchester I
R5792 was involved in a midair collision with a 56 OTU Hurricane I V6864, flown
by Sgt G A Johnstone, and all were killed in the resultant crash at Walpole St.
Andrew, Norfolk (see Bomber Command Losses, Volume 2, page 184).

Note. I am indebted to Terry Hill, author of "Down in Wales 2" for material
used in this summary.

| 14 Jul 1940 | 12 OTU | Battle I L4966 | Air Test |

14 Jul 1940   **12 OTU**   **Battle I L4966**   **Air Test**
Sgt G W Schoon   inj   T/o Benson for a height test. While approaching the airfield, at 1240, the engine failed and the cockpit promptly filled with fumes. Smashing into trees, the Battle caught fire, trapping Sgt Schoon who, but for the heroic actions of Sgt D Jobson RAF and Pte E D Gurnham RASC, would have surely perished. For their actions, his saviours each received a George Medal, this being duly noted by the unit's diarist on 11 January 1941.

15 Jul 1940   **17 OTU**   **Blenheim IV L9171**   **Training**
F/O W H Powdrell   T/o Upwood. Crash-landed 0625, prompted by engine failure, at Great Raveley, about 6 miles NNE from Huntingdon. The instructional serial 2161M was allocated to the salvaged airframe which, on 5 June 1942, was handed over to 13 OTU before being disposed of to scrap on 21 February 1944. F/O Powdrell, a New Zealander, subsequently became a Flight Commander with 103 Squadron, failing to return from operations to Milano on 14-15 February 1943 (see Bomber Command Losses, Volume 4, page 42).

Note. Errol Martyn's invaluable books on New Zealanders who have given their lives in nearly a century of flying show that S/L Powdrell, who came from Hawerna, Taranaki, but was serving with the regular Royal Air Force, had achieved 1,120 flying hours and had flown at least 22 operational sorties.

16 Jul 1940   **20 OTU**   **Wellington IA N2896**   **Training**
Sgt K J Douglas   T/o Lossiemouth. Landed 1336, whereupon the undercarriage collapsed. A Volunteer Reserve pilot, Sgt Douglas had logged 533 flying hours, 274 of these at the controls of Wellingtons. He is thought to have survived the war.

Note. Until the loss of this aircraft, all OTU accidents had involved aircraft from the units that formed on 8 April 1940. Since then, three more bomber OTUs had been established; 18 OTU on 15 June 1940, preceded by 19 OTU and 20 OTU on 27 May 1940.

19 Jul 1940   **12 OTU**   **Battle I P2270**   **Training**
Sgt A F Forster   T/o Benson. At 1310 the pilot landed in a field adjacent to the airfield. Realising his mistake, Sgt Forster opened the throttle and almost in the same instant saw that he was heading for a wire fence. Pulling back the control column, he cleared the fence but stalled and crashed. Salvaged as a training aid with the serial 2143M allotted, the Battle was shipped in September 1940 to Canada, where it became A164.

15 OTU   **Anson I N5186**   **Training**
F/L F N Hughes   +   T/o Harwell for formation flying practice, during the course of which a midair collision occurred. Three members of the crew managed to bale out but F/L Hughes died when the Anson hit the ground, 2 miles SW of the airfield. He is buried in Prestatyn (Coed Bell) Cemetery.

16 OTU   **Hereford I L6026**   **Training**
Sgt W W Huggins   T/o Upper Heyford but was obliged to force-land on Weston-on-the-Green airfield with one engine ablaze. Prompt action by the Bicester Fire Party detachment saved the airframe which, subsequently, became a training aid with the serial 2968M.

20 Jul 1940   **12 OTU**   **Battle I L4959**   **Training**
P/O A V Fisher   T/o Benson for a navigation exercise; base-South Cerney-Peterborough-base. Forced-landed with engine trouble, 1453, some 2 miles E of South Cerney airfield. P/O Fisher and his crew escaped unhurt but a few weeks later, during a solo night flying detail, he was killed in a crash near Benson (see page 24).

17 OTU   **Blenheim IV L8844**   **Training**
Sgt E Kibble   inj   T/o Upwood on a navigation exercise; base-
        inj   Hungerford-Worcester-base. During the flight,
        inj   an engine failed and Sgt Kibble, while trying to stretch his glide, stalled and crashed 1230 in a wheat field near Newnham Courtney, 1 mile SSE of Daventry, Northamptonshire.

21 Jul   **12 OTU**   **Battle I**   P2272   **Training**
1940   S/Lt(A) E A Moore RN   T/o Benson for a low-level navigation exercise
which ended in engine failure and a forced-
landing at Boro Corner near Tiverton, Devon. No one was hurt, despite the fact
that the Battle hit a tree. The airframe was later salvaged and as a training
aid bore the serial 2159M.

22 Jul   **15 OTU**   **Wellington I**   L4369   **Training**
1940   F/L R Sawrey-Cookson   T/o 2205 Harwell with the flaps fully extended
and following a steep climb to 50 feet, stalled
and hit the ground on or near the airfield. A fire broke out on impact. At this
stage in his flying career, F/L Sawrey-Cookson had logged 1,305 hours, 571 of
these on Wellingtons. Subsequently, he commanded 75 Squadron, losing his life
on operations to Köln in April 1942 (see Bomber Command Losses, Volume 3, page
61). At the time of his death he had been awarded a DSO and a DFC.

24 Jul   **12 OTU**   **Battle I**   L5482   **Training**
1940   Mid(A) C G Mortimer RN   +   T/o Benson for a low-level navigation exercise.
     Sgt E P Wood   +   Flew into high tension cables and crashed circa
     Sgt M V Everitt   +   1250 near North Stoke, 14 miles ESE of Oxford.
                                  Mid Mortimer RN, aged eighteen and the only
naval pilot to lose his life at a Bomber Command OTU, is buried in Finchley at
St. Pancras Cemetery. Sgt Everitt rests in the extension to Benson (St. Helen)
Churchyard, while Sgt Wood was taken to Conisbrough Cemetery. Mid Mortimer had
been attached from HMS Daedalus.

       16 OTU   **Hampden I**   L4190   **Training**
     Sgt L R Adams   inj   T/o Upper Heyford for night high-level bombing
     P/O G Hall   practice. At 0100, Sgt Adams came in to land,
     P/O S C Wise   touching down at high speed thus causing the
     Sgt F Jowett   Hampden to run beyond the runway and end up on
                                    a road, having gone through two hedges. A fire
broke out but no one was too badly hurt, though the pilot required attention to
his head injuries.

26 Jul   **16 OTU**   **Hampden I**   L4139   **Training**
1940   P/O K R K Smettem   T/o Finningley and while landing here at 2300,
the undercarriage gave way. The airframe, which
had accumulated 151 flying hours, was salvaged and, subsequently, became 2170M.
P/O Smettem, meanwhile, was posted to 50 Squadron and lost his life during
operations to Mönchengladbach on 30-31 August 1940 (see Bomber Command Losses,
Volume 1, page 104).

27 Jul   **16 OTU**   **Hampden I**   P1180   **Training**
1940   P/O D M March   inj   T/o 2310 Brackley on his first night solo but
                                    clipped a tree and crashed soon afterwards at
King's Sutton, a Northamptonshire village, 4 miles SSE of Banbury, Oxfordshire.
It is thought P/O Marsh sustained very serious injuries.

       20 OTU   **Anson I**   R9583   **Training**
     Sgt T W Newberry   inj   T/o Lossiemouth on a night navigation exercise;
     Sgt C B G Knight   inj   base-Brechin-Kinnainds Head-Forres-Peterhead-
     Sgt R H Bird   inj   Kinloss-base. At 0035, having reduced height
     Sgt W J Westwater   inj   in order to pick up the coast line, flew into
     Sgt L M Peterson   inj   high ground near Carnan-tri-tighearnen, Nairn.

27-28 Jul   **11 OTU Z Sqn**   **Wellington IA**   N3002   -O   **Op: Nickel**
1940   S/L R H Maw   inj   T/o 2150 Bassingbourn using call sign 6RHO and
     P/O D W E Sharpe   inj   making for Beauvais-Meaux-Melun-Evreux. On return
     P/O E H G Brooks   inj   the starboard engine failed and while trying to
     Sgt C D Chenier   inj   force -land, at 0305, the Wellington hit some
     Sgt A Patterson   trees on Clop Hill near Henlow, Bedfordshire.
     Sgt S G Keatley   S/L Maw sustained a double leg fracture while
                                    Sgt Chenier was treated for rib fractures.
The others were less seriously hurt. This was the first loss reported from
an Operational Training Unit engaged on such operations.

Note. The appendices for 11 OTU contain many examples of the Nickels dropped
from their aircraft, as well as numerous course photographs.

28 Jul
1940

17 OTU   **Blenheim IV** **L4869**   **Training**
P/O A B Smith   T/o Upwood. Forced-landed, wheels retracted, due to engine failure, 0745, near Whitchurch, 5 miles NNW of Aylesbury, Buckinghamshire. The Blenheim was salvaged and in time became a training aid with the serial 2171M applied.

29 Jul
1940

12 OTU   **Battle I** **L5091**   **Training**
Sgt R Hanna   + T/o Benson for a night exercise only to dive
Sgt R C Thomson   + back to the ground, near Wallingford, Berkshire.
Sgt W Robb   + Eighteen year old Sgt Robb of Tealing in Angus was buried locally in the extension to Benson (St. Helen) Churchyard; his skipper lies in Aldershot Civil Cemetery, while Sgt Thomson rests at Bawtry Cemetery.

30 Jul
1940

16 OTU   **Hampden I** **L4169**   **Air Test**
P/O G E Weston   T/o Upper Heyford following the fitting of a new tail bay. At approximately 1500, while in the vicinity of Bishop's Itchington, 7 miles SE of Royal Leamington Spa, Warwickshire, the flying controls locked in both fore and aft travel and the Hampden rolled on to its back. With little time to waste, P/O Weston slid back the canopy, unfastened his straps, dropped out and parachuted safely. Fortunately, he was the sole occupant. Born in New Zealand, he rose to S/L rank, gaining a DFC, before being killed on 1 October 1942, when his 61 Squadron Lancaster crashed while taking off for Wismar (see Bomber Command Losses, Volume 3, page 230). His brother, F/S Godfrey Randal Weston RNZAF died in a 1657 HCU Stirling crash at Stradishall in April 1944. Both brothers now rest side by side in Hemblington (All Saints) Churchyard, Norfolk, next to the graves of their paternal grandparents.

1 Aug
1940

16 OTU   **Hampden I** **P1266**   **Training**
P/O F R W Palmer   T/o Upper Heyford for a night navigation flight; base-Worcester-Andover-Weston Zoyland-base. During the final leg of the exercise, the port engine failed but for the next hour, P/O Palmer managed to keep going on his starboard engine. However, at 0115 he was obliged to land at Babdown Farm airfield in Gloucestershire, where his aircraft swung onto soft ground and was damaged beyond repair.

16 OTU   **Hereford I** **L6067**   **Training**
Sgt O G Day   + T/o Upper Heyford for a low-level formation
F/O G H Thevenard   + exercise, in the course of which an engine
Sgt S N Baker   + failed. At 1510, eye witnesses observed the
AC2 G W Rhodes   + bomber to stall and plunge into the ground in a banked vertical dive near Souldern, 7 miles NNW of Bicester, Oxfordshire. F/O Thevenard, who came from Hull, is buried in Middleton Stoney (All Saints) Churchyard; Sgt Day rests at Leicester (Gilroes) Cemetery; Sgt Baker lies in Dordon (St. Leonard) Churchyard, while AC2 Rhodes, shown as a passenger, was taken to Sheffield (Crookes) Cemetery.

2 Aug
1940

12 OTU   **Battle I** **L4971**   **Training**
P/O R O Shuttleworth   + T/o Benson for solo night flying practice but crashed 0015 at Ewelme, about a mile E of the airfield. P/O Shuttleworth is buried in Old Warden (St. Leonard) Churchyard. Before the war, he had been a racing driver and founder of the now famous collection of vintage aircraft that bears his name. His father was Col Frank Shuttleworth of Biggleswade, Bedfordshire.

3 Aug
1940

17 OTU   **Blenheim IV** **L8846**   **Training**
Sgt N C Green   T/o 0609 Upwood and crashed a minute later following loss of power from an engine.

4 Aug
1940

16 OTU   **Hampden I** **P4294**   **Training**
P/O C G Llewellyn   + T/o Upper Heyford for solo night circuits and landings. Stalled on the approach, crashing 2210 into Tusmore Park, near the airfield. P/O Llewellyn is buried in Cardiff (Cathays) Cemetery.

5 Aug
1940

12 OTU   **Battle I** **P2271**   **Training**
P/O L E F Parry   T/o Benson. Abandoned 2250, crashing at South Moreton, 3 miles WSW of Wallingford, Berkshire.

5 Aug　　**15 OTU**　　　　**Wellington I** L4264　　　　　　　　　　**Training**
1940　　　P/O E J Lester　　　　　　　　+　T/o Harwell for dual circuits and landings. At
　　　　　F/L J L Rees　　　　　　　　 +　1445, stalled while turning finals and dived to
　　　　　P/O P D Arup　　　　　　　　 +　the ground. Harrow born, P/O Lester, a Bachelor
　　　　　　　　　　　　　　　　　　　　of Laws graduate from London University, rests
in Harwell Cemetery; F/L Rees was taken to Merionethshire where it is possible
his father, the Revd Nathaniel Rees, conducted the funeral service at Arthog (St.
Catherine) Churchyard, Llangelynin, while P/O Arup is commemorated on panel 1 of
Woking (St. John's) Crematorium.

6 Aug　　**10 OTU**　　　　　**Whitley III** K9015　　　　　　　　　　**Training**
1940　　　P/O H H J Miller　　　　　　　　T/o Abingdon to practice night flying. On the
　　　　　　　　　　　　　　　　　　　　approach to land, at around 2350, held off too
high and as his flying speed decayed, P/O Miller was unable to prevent a wing
from hitting the ground, with some force, causing considerable damage to the
aircraft. Removed to Airwork, Gatwick, on 17 August, the Whitley was deemed
to be beyond economical repair.

12 OTU　　　　　**Battle I** L4943　　　　　　　　　　　　　**Training**
P/O A V Fisher　　　　　　　　+　T/o 2314 Benson for solo night flying practice.
　　　　　　　　　　　　　　　　Climbed to between 800 and 1,000 feet before
swinging first to the right and then to the left. Out of control, the Battle
dived into the ground near Watlington, 13 miles SE of Oxford. Hailing from
Paeroa in New Zealand, P/O Fisher rests in the extension to Benson (St. Helen)
Churchyard. It will be recalled he had forced-landing on 20 July (see page 21).

12 OTU　　　　　**Battle I** L5275　　　　　　　　　　　　　**Training**
S/L(A) W H Johnstone RN　　　　T/o Benson for formation flying practice. Crash-
　　　　　　　　　　　　　　　　landed, due to engine failure, 1115 at Little
Milton, 7 miles SE of Oxford. The Battle was later used as an instructional
airframe with the serial 2201M applied.

16 OTU　　　　**Hereford I** L6053　　　　　　　　　　　　**Training**
Sgt A J Fetherston　　　　　　+　T/o Upper Heyford for the pilot's first solo on
　　　　　　　　　　　　　　　　type. At 0955, while approaching the airfield
with the undercarriage down and flaps fully extended, stalled and came down on
the Upper Heyford to Kirtlington road near the village of Caulcott, 5 miles WNW
of Bicester, Oxfordshire. Sgt Fetherston was laid to rest locally in Middleton
Stoney (All Saints) Churchyard.

7 Aug　　**10 OTU**　　　　　**Whitley V** N1507　　　　　　　　　　**Training**
1940　　　Sgt G B Clarke　　　　　　　　　T/o 0100 Harwell (having landed here in mistake
　　　　　　　　　　　　　　　　　　　　for Abingdon) but in raising the tail pushed too
far forward on the control column and the propellers dug in as a result. Taken
to the Armstrong Whitworth repair facility at Coventry on 14 August, the bomber
was found to be beyond economical repair. Sgt Clarke was posted to 77 Squadron
and became a prisoner-of-war following a raid on Bremen in September 1940 (see
Bomber Command Losses, Volume 1, page 109).

16 OTU　　　　**Hampden I** P2110　　　　　　　　　　　　**Training**
Sgt W W Huggins　　　　　　　　　T/o 0750 Upper Heyford for a navigation exercise
　　　　　　　　　　　　　　　　　but the brakes failed to release completely, thus
causing the Hampden to swing violently to the right. Having come to a stop, the
port engine burst into flames.

17 OTU　　　　**Blenheim IV** P4902　　　　　　　　　　　**Training**
F/L E P Mortimer　　　　　　　+　T/o Upwood. Spun and crashed near North Crawley,
Sgt D A Gibbs　　　　　　　　　+　3 miles ENE of Newport Pagnell, Buckinghamshire.
Sgt D F Alves　　　　　　　　　+　F/L Mortimer and Sgt Alves, both regulars, rest
　　　　　　　　　　　　　　　　in Bury Cemetery, while Devonian, Sgt Gibbs was
　　　　　　　　　　　　　　　　taken home to lie in Paignton Cemetery.

8 Aug　　**16 OTU**　　　　**Hampden I** P2131　　　　　　　　　　**Training**
1940　　　Sgt J H Morphett　　　　　　　　T/o Upper Heyford. During the flight, a serious
　　　　　　　　　　　　　　　　　　　　oil leak in the starboard engine resulted in the
reduction gear breaking off. As he was in the circuit, Sgt Morphett attempted to
land across the wind but was unable to lower the flaps. At 1230 he touched down
but ran off the airfield. On 8 April 1942, he was killed while flying Manchesters
with 83 Squadron (see Bomber Command Losses, Volume 3, page 62).

| 8– 9 Aug
1940 | 13 OTU | Blenheim I | L1191 | Training |

Sgt W Nelson + T/o Bicester for a night reconnaissance sortie.
Sgt S Sanderson + At 0001 the Blenheim was seen making an approach
Sgt C A Smith + to the airfield at Weston-on-the-Green when it
dived suddenly to the ground and burst into
flames. Sgt Nelson, a member of the Auxiliary Air Force, lies in Stockton-on-Tees
(Oxbridge Lane) Cemetery; Sgt Sanderson is buried in Belfast City Cemetery, while
Sgt Smith was taken to the City of London Cemetery at Manor Park, East Ham.

| 9 Aug
1940 | 10 OTU | Whitley V | N1495 | Training |

P/O L Williams + T/o Abingdon for night flying practice. While
Sgt C W McKenzie + nearing the airfield at 0240, smashed into trees
Sgt A G Allen + and burst into flames. An experienced pilot with
735 hours to his credit (but only fourteen on
the Whitley), P/O Williams was cremated at St. John's Wood Crematorium at Woking.
His observer was taken to Selby Cemetery where, it is noted, that although a man
of Selby, he had married Ivy McKenzie of Chestfield, in Kent. Sgt Allen lies in
Blanchland (St. Mary) Churchyard, Shotley High Quarter where his is the sole
service grave for the Second World War.

| | 14 OTU | Hereford I | L6052 | Training |

Sgt M F Hughes inj T/o 0929 Cottesmore for a shallow dive-bombing
Sgt J Grant + task but having reached a mere 500 feet an
engine cut and within a minute the Hereford
had smashed into a tree and crashed just to the W of the airfield, bursting
into flames on impact. Sgt Grant, he was nineteen years of age, is buried
in Scotland at Loanhead Cemetery, Lasswade.

| 11 Aug
1940 | 19 OTU | Whitley IV | K9023 | Unknown |

Reported in several publications to have been
destroyed while taking off from Kinloss (an engine failing at a crucial moment)
but no AM Form 1180 has been traced. However, it is believed the airframe was
taken to an Airworks facility, eventually becoming a training aid as 3302M.

| 13 Aug
1940 | 11 OTU | Wellington I | L4286 | Unknown |

Although reported as destroyed in a take off
accident, I consider it most likely that this is the aircraft referred to in
the next summary. As yet, no accident card has been traced, but Form AM 78
shows the Wellington was written off on this date with 149.45 flying hours
recorded. It had served with 11 OTU since 31 May.

| | 11 OTU | Wellington I | L4387 | Training |

F/O F A H Lambart + T/o 2215 Bassingbourn but swung out of control
Sgt H H Boulter + and struck another aircraft. On impact, the
Sgt P B F Pryke + Wellington burst into flames. Three are buried
Sgt D O Rewa RNZAF + in Bassingbourn cum Kneesworth Cemetery; Sgt
Sgt S Robinson + Pryke was taken to Cambridge City Cemetery;
Sgt D L Jones + Sgt Robinson lies in Middleton (St. Mary)
Churchyard, Leeds, while Sgt Jones rests in
his native Wales at Criccieth Burial Ground. F/O Lambart of Ottawa had served
twixt 1932 and 1937 as a constable with the Royal Canadian Mounted Police. Sgt
Rewa RNZAF had trained as an observer in New Zealand and was the first from his
course to be killed outside of his country. Sgt Boulter's brother, F/L John
Clifford Boulter DFC, a regular service officer flying Spitfires with 603 (City
of Edinburgh) Squadron was killed on 17 February 1941; he is buried in Dirleton
Cemetery, East Lothian.

| | 13 OTU | Blenheim IV | L9038 | Training |

Sgt H A G Miller RNZAF inj T/o 1430 Bicester but an engine cut and the
Blenheim stalled and crashed, as the pilot tried
desperately to avoid flying into trees. Critically injured, Sgt Miller RNZAF
died a few hours later. He rests in Caversfield (St. Laurence) Churchyard.

| 14 Aug
1940 | 15 OTU | Wellington I | L4294 | Unknown |

The aircraft accident card for this aircraft
has yet to be found, but its movements records indicate acceptance by 15 OTU
on 18 April, followed by serious damage on the date here shown. Eleven days
later, it was struck off charge.

14 Aug 1940	15 OTU	Wellington I	L4308	Training

Sgt R L Peacock + T/o Harwell for a navigation exercise; base-
Sgt H W Sabin + Salisbury-Barnstaple-Lundy Island-base. At
Sgt J Brooke + approximately 1125, the Wellington was seen
Sgt A Morgan + diving towards the waters of the Bristol Channel
Sgt J E Fuller RNZAF + with flames streaming from its port engine.
Sgt C J A Ive + A search was made of the area, some 5 miles
E of Lundy Island, and an Admiralty yacht
recovered the body of Sgt Sabin; he was brought back for interment in Harwell
Cemetery. Of his five companions, no trace was found and all are commemorated
on the Runnymede Memorial.

15 OTU   Wellington I   L7770   Unknown
No accident record traced but AM Form 78
indicates that the Wellington was written off on this date, having been taken
on unit charge on 27 April 1940. No flying totals recorded.

17 OTU   Blenheim IV   L8839   Training
F/S T J Watkins   T/o Upwood. Wrecked after crash-landing at
base with a jammed undercarriage.

16 Aug 1940   10 OTU   Whitley III   K8940   Enemy Action
Badly damaged when the Luftwaffe attacked the
airfield at Stanton Harcourt. The next day, a Marshalls repair team inspected
the Whitley and two days later it was struck off charge.

15 OTU   Wellington IA   N2895   Enemy Action
Destroyed on the ground at Harwell airfield in
the course of a bombing attack by the Luftwaffe.

15 OTU   Wellington IA   N3018   Enemy Action
Destroyed in the circumstances described above.

Note. As a result of this attack, the following casualties were reported:

AC1 E N Pitt   + Buried in Hastings Cemetery.
AC2 E J Saunders   + Buried in Nunhead (All Saints) Cemetery. A
Cpl W Lockerbie   inj member of the Royal Air Force (Volunteer
AC1 W Dicks   inj Reserve), his service number indicates he
AC2 K Apps   inj had been called up in July 1939 under the
AC2 E Goff   inj terms of the Military Training Act.
AC2 T Johnson   inj

19 Aug 1940   14 OTU   Hampden I   P1305   Training
P/O W E King   + T/o Cottesmore for a navigation exercise.
Sgt S Britnor   + Emerged from the cloud base, diving almost
Sgt J Bishop   + vertically, and crashed at Sharnbrook,
Sgt J A Jackson   + 8 miles NNW of Bedford. All were taken to
Cardington (St. Mary) Church Cemetery for
burial in a collective grave. Sgt Bishop was the son of the Revd L Cornewall
Bishop, of South Kensington. The first three named are described as pilots.

15 OTU   Wellington I   L4280   Enemy Action
Destroyed on the ground at Harwell airfield by
enemy bombing.

15 OTU   Wellington I   L4289   Enemy Action
Destroyed in the manner described above.

15 OTU   Wellington I   L4347   Enemy Action
Destroyed in the manner described above.

21 Aug 1940   11 OTU   Wellington I   L4335   Training
F/L R W Turner   inj T/o Bassingbourn for dual circuits and landings.
Sgt A R Ward   inj Landed 1125, but ballooned back into the air,
stalled and hit the ground with the control
column jammed in the neutral position. A fire broke out almost immediately.
Sgt Ward later served with 57 Squadron and became a prisoner of war following
a raid on Hamburg in March 1941 (see Bomber Command Losses, Volume 2, page 31).

23 Aug
1940

16 OTU   **Hampden I**   P2132   **Training**

Sgt S L Bennett   inj   T/o Brackley for night flying practice. At 2210 overshot the runway, ran through a stone wall and hit a farmhouse. Both the aircraft and the building were set alight, the Hampden being completely destroyed. Fortunately, the local fire brigade were able to save the farmhouse, while Sgt Bennett escaped with only minor cuts and abrasions. It will be recalled (see page 20) that he trained on Blenheims at 13 OTU and in the aftermath of this accident, he reverted to that type.

24 Aug
1940

11 OTU   **Wellington IA**   N2945   **Training**

Sgt R T Richardson   +   T/o Bassingbourn and set course for the Isle of
Sgt E G Turner   +   Man and an air gunnery exercise over the Irish
Sgt R S Hartnell   +   Sea. At approximately 1100 the Wellington went
Sgt H G Ives   +   into the sea off Bradda Head, 2 miles WNW from
Sgt F A E Gates   +   Castletown. Apart from the two pilots, the
Sgt C A V Attwood   +   entire crew were made up of air gunners. Four
Sgt E R Eastoe   +   are commemorated on the Runnymede Memorial; two,
Sgt E J Stephens   +   Sgt Hartnell and Sgt Gates, are buried on the
island in Jurby (St. Patrick) Churchyard and two, Sgt Ives and Sgt Eastoe, were brought back to the mainland and laid to rest in Tonbridge Cemetery and Walthamstow (Queen's Road) Cemetery respectively.

14 OTU   **Anson I**   R9752   **Training**

P/O P A Haggerty   inj   T/o Cottesmore for a navigation exercise; base-
P/O W E Fruitiger   inj   Abbotsinch-West Freugh-Yeadon-Goole-base. While
P/O S Carter   inj   flying on the leg Wigtown to Yeadon, developed
Sgt S K Coates   inj   engine trouble and ditched 1250 some 3 miles SE
Sgt Martin   of Burrow Head on the Wigtown coast.

20 OTU   **Anson I**   R9663   **Training**

F/L V Mitchell   inj   T/o 0015 Lossiemouth for a night navigation
Sgt R H Bird   inj   flight; base-Brechin-Kinnainds Head-Forres-
Sgt F C Smith   inj   Peterhead-base. An hour into the exercise, the
Sgt S A Fawcett   inj   Anson came to grief on high ground (that was
Sgt S Clark   inj   hidden by cloud) in the Bridge of Buchat area.

28 Aug
1940

12 OTU   **Battle I**   K9419   **Training**

P/O O P Davies RNZAF   T/o Benson for a navigation exercise. Wrecked circa 1420 while force -landing in the aftermath of engine failure, clipping trees near Milton Lilbourne, 2 miles E of Pewsey, Wiltshire. This particular Battle had force -landed on 14 July at Shillingford in Oxfordshire. P/O Davies RNZAF is believed to have survived the war.

17 OTU   **Blenheim IV**   L8843   **Training**

P/O H M Hoadley RNZAF   +   T/o 2145 Upwood for solo night flying practice and crashed almost immediately, bursting into flames. P/O Hoadley RNZAF is buried locally in Bury Cemetery. It is reported that the night was extremely dark and, thus, it is possible the pilot became disorientated while making a climbing turn.

29 Aug
1940

11 OTU   **Anson I**   K8754   **Training**

F/S N B Buckley   T/o Bassingbourn for a night navigation sortie. Undershot the flare path and hit a haystack at around 2145, while trying to land at Windrush Reserve Landing Ground. At the time, this Gloucestershire airfield was being used by 6 FTS and 15 FTS.

12 OTU   **Battle I**   L5283   **Training**

P/O N Paterson   T/o Benson for, it is believed, a flight to Kemble but due to engine failure an emergency landing was made on Aston Down airfield, in the process of which the Battle ran into a stone wall.

3 Sep
1940

17 OTU   **Blenheim IV**   R3621   **Training**

Sgt J W Turner   +   T/o Upwood but was in trouble immediately and
Sgt M Tanner   +   crashed at Bury, 7 miles NNE of Huntingdon.
Sgt W Parker   inj   Sgt Turner is buried in Nottingham Southern Cemetery; his observer, Sgt Tanner, was taken to Clydach-on-Tawe (St. John The Baptist) Churchyard, Rhyndwycldach. His brother F/O Samuel Arthur Raymond Tanner of 98 Squadron was killed on 21 September 1943.

4 Sep 1940	**17 OTU**	**Blenheim I**	**L8682**	**Training**

P/O D Rockel   T/o 2138 Upwood for night flying practice but within two minutes P/O Rockel was obliged to parachute, leaving his Blenheim to crash and burn near Warboys airfield.

12 Sep 1940	**12 OTU**	**Battle I**	**N2148**	**Training**

Sgt R A Jooris   +   T/o Benson for an evening cross country; base-
Sgt L G Mitchell   +   Launceston-Hartland Point-Wincanton-Brize
Sgt H E M Long   +   Norton-base. Encountered very poor visibility and it is assumed that while pulling up to avoid high ground, the Battle stalled. This tragedy occurred at 1840 near Cadeleigh, 3 miles SSW of Tiverton, Devon. Sgt Jooris of Wembley was taken to Exeter Higher Cemetery; his crew were claimed by their next-of-kin. It is noted that Sgt Long was a Fellow of the Royal College of Organists. Their aircraft had been taken on unit charge nine days previous, having spent over eighteen months in storage at 8 MU Little Rissington.

	15 OTU	**Wellington I**	**L4215**	**Training**

Sgt G F Heayes   T/o 0300 Harwell for night circuits and landings but the starboard tyre burst, sending the bomber crashing out of control. It will be recalled that Sgt Heayes had crashed during a training flight the previous April (see page 13); at the time of that accident he had logged 295 hours on Wellingtons; now he had 450 hours on type, while his overall flying totals had increased from 755 to 1,100 hours.

16 Sep 1940	**19 OTU**	**Magister I**	**T9814**	**Transit**

S/L C W McK Thompson   +   T/o Kinloss with the intention of flying to Manby in Lincolnshire. Crashed 1638 into high ground roughly 6 miles S of Dalwhinnie, an isolated Inverness-shire village at the NE end of Loch Ericht. S/L Thompson lies in Kinloss Abbey Burial Ground. His age is not given in the CWGC register, but his service number suggests he joined the air force in the 1920s. A crash investigation revealed that the Magister had not been fitted with a full blind flying panel.

	20 OTU	**Wellington IA**	**N2900**	**Unknown**

Alleged to have been destroyed in a take-off accident at Lossiemouth but, to date, no evidence has been traced to support this report. Form AM 78 merely shows that the Wellington was allotted to 20 OTU on 9 July 1940 and written off on the date, here given.

17 Sep 1940	**12 OTU**	**Battle I**	**N2164**	**Training**

P/O S Boczkowski PAF   T/o Benson for a local photo reconnaissance exercise. Became lost and while making a precautionary landing on Fairoaks airfield, ran into a pillbox. P/O Boczkowski was the first Polish air force pilot to be involved in a serious Bomber Command OTU aircraft accident. It is believed he survived the war.

	14 OTU Det	**Hampden I**	**P4311**	**Training**

P/O B Y Sowter   +   T/o Pembrey and headed out over the Bristol
Sgt D J Blair   +   Channel for an air firing detail. Crashed 1050,
Sgt G W Brown   +   trying to make a forced-landing, at Kidwelly,
Sgt J D L Cooper   +   a little over 8 miles S of Carmarthen. All are buried in Pembrey (St. Illtyd) Churchyard. Both air gunners were from Scotland and their service numbers suggest they joined the Volunteer Reserve on the same day.

19 Sep 1940	**19 OTU**	**Whitley IV**	**K9051**	**Training**

F/L D Nolan-Neylan   T/o Kinloss for dual night flying but lost power and was force -landed, straight ahead. However, it was 21 November 1941 before the Whitley was finally struck off charge. F/L Nolan-Neylan had reported for instructional duties on 24 July.

	20 OTU	**Wellington IA**	**N2883**	**Training**

P/O P G V Jarvis   +   T/o Lossiemouth for a combined bombing and
P/O H R Stothard   +   navigation exercise. Crashed at around 1700
P/O D L Parker   +   on high ground near Glen Moriston, Inverness-
Sgt A L Cameron   +   shire. All are buried in Lossiemouth Burial
Sgt A C Dandridge   +   Ground, Drainie.
Sgt G H Gratton   +

22 Sep
1940

17 OTU	Blenheim I	L8610		Training
Sgt H H Wilson		+		
P/O A D Coplestone		+		
Sgt J November		+		

T/o Upwood for a navigation exercise. Smashed into the summit of Garn Wen at around 1510, this being in the SE corner of the Brecon Beacons, near Abersychan, 4 miles NNW of Pontypool. Sgt Wilson was brought back to Upwood for burial in Bury Cemetery; P/O Coplestone, whose parents are believed to have been trapped following the German occupation of Jersey, is buried in Hampshire at Boldre (St. John) Churchyard (he was a Barrister and a Member of Inner Temple), while Sgt November lies in Yardley Wood (Christ Church) Churchyard, Birmingham.

23 Sep
1940

17 OTU	Blenheim IV	L8797		Training
F/L R G Coventry		+		
Sgt J Lane		inj		
Sgt G Wilson		inj		

T/o Upwood for live bombing practice over Cardigan Bay. Crash-landed, due to engine problems, at approximately 1430 near Tuffley on the southern outskirts of Gloucester. The son of The Hon. Thomas George Coventry and Alice Coventry of nearby Bath, F/L Coventry rests in Down Hatherley (St. Mary and Corpus Christi) Churchyard.

18 OTU	Battle I	K9480		Training
LAC E V Rozmiarek PAF		+		
Mr A Evans		+		
Mrs A Evans		+		
Mstr R Evans		+		
Miss A Evans		+		

T/o Hucknall for circuits and landings practice, completing three circuits successfully. On the fourth he climbed away to port, gaining height, but then stalled and crashed onto a council house at the junction of Ruffs Drive and Laughton Crescent, Hucknall. LAC Rozmiarek PAF is buried in Hucknall Cemetery, his being one of thirteen Polish service burials located here. He was also the first of his countrymen to be killed in a Bomber Command OTU accident, while Mr Albert Evans and his family were, likewise, the first civilian fatalities.

Note. I am extremely indebted to Brian Walker for turning out the details pertaining to the loss of this aircraft, particularly in identifying the family who perished. It is also appropriate for me to thank Bill Baguley for his ever-ready help in answering questions regarding aircraft losses in the Nottingham area.

24 Sep
1940

15 OTU	Wellington I	L4281		Unknown

Form AM 78 indicates that this Wellington was destroyed by fire, following a flying accident, and that the airframe had logged a total of 476.00 hours. As yet, no aircraft accident card has been found, though a minor incident at Harwell, involving F/S W R Kelly, on 19 June 1940 has come to light.

19 OTU	Whitley V	P5006		Training
F/S C H Ashley		+		
Sgt D S Proudfoot		+		
Sgt N R Foley		+		
Sgt E S Millard		+		
Sgt P H Lucas DFM		+		
Sgt I D S E Hay		+		

T/o Kinloss for a navigation exercise. At circa 1640, the Whitley emerged from the cloud cover, the base being given as 1,500 feet above ground level, and crashed on Ben Aigen, Moray. Three, F/S Ashley, Sgt Proudfoot and Sgt Millard, rest in Kinloss Abbey Burial Ground, the others were taken to their home towns. Sgt Lucas had flown a tour of duty with 77 Squadron and his DFM was published on 22 October 1940.

25 Sep
1940

13 OTU	Blenheim IV	T1796		Training
F/L H I Edwards		inj		
P/O L A E Osbon		inj		
Sgt Raisbeck		inj		

T/o Bicester for a night reconnaissance sortie but having become lost made a force-landing at around 0015, about a mile NW of Litchfield and 4 miles NW of Overton, Hampshire. F/L Edwards, born in Freemantle, Australia, but serving with the Royal Air Force, was destined to become a recipient of the Victoria Cross for his outstanding leadership of 105 Squadron during a hazardous daylight raid by Blenheims against Bremen on 4 July 1941 (see Bomber Command Losses, Volume 2, page 72). Almost a year later and by sheer coincidence, P/O Osbon (now flying Wellingtons with 101 Squadron) became a prisoner of war whilst attacking Bremen (see Bomber Command Losses, Volume 3, page 116).

Note. For further details regarding F/L Edward's VC, please refer to "For Valour, The Air VCs" by Chaz Bowyer, published by William Kimber (1978).

27 Sep **14 OTU** **Hampden I** P4308 **Training**
1940 P/O J S H Lupton + T/o Cottesmore for his second Hampden solo but
at 0930 he flew into a tree at Squires Farm,
Langham, 2 miles or so NNW of Oakham. P/O Lupton, whose father was the Revd
Albert Horner Lupton of Gussage St. Michael in Dorset lies in the neighbouring
county of Wiltshire at Idmiston (All Saints) Churchyard.

28 Sep **13 OTU** **Blenheim I** L6781 **Training**
1940 F/O P D Sharp T/o 2150 Weston-on-the-Green for his first
night solo in a Blenheim. On becoming airborne
he climbed at too steep an angle, stalled and crashed amongst some trees close
to the airfield. A fire broke out on impact, but F/O Sharp escaped the flames
without serious injury.

30 Sep **12 OTU** **Battle I** L5079 **Training**
1940 Sgt O Odstrcilek + T/o Benson for his first solo on type but at
around 1145 he crashed at Streatley, 10 miles
to the NW of Reading, bursting into flames. The accident was attributed to
engine failure. Sgt Odstrcilek was the first Czechoslovakian airman to be
killed at a Bomber Command OTU. He is buried in the extension to Benson (St.
Helen) Churchyard. It is further noted that he had accumulated 749 hours of
flying experience.

14 OTU Det **Hereford I** L6036 **Transet**
F/L N W Timmerman T/o Cottesmore and set course for Pembrey. At
1910 an engine failed and he was obliged to
force -land in Monmouthshire.

1 Oct **10 OTU B Flt** **Anson I** R3304 **Training**
1940 Sgt C F Gibbons T/o 0950 Abingdon for a combined air firing and
navigation exercise; base-Beaumaris-Aberystwyth-
base, the air firing phase to take place over Cardigan Bay. Reported ditched at
circa 1450 in the Irish Sea. Unconfirmed reports indicate one member of crew was
killed and one was injured.

12 OTU **Battle I** K9416 **Training**
P/O J M R Sokolowski + T/o Benson for solo night flying. Crashed 2030
de Jenko PAF into a wood at Heath End on the SE side of the
Oxfordshire village of Checkendon, 6 miles SE
from Wallingford, Berkshire. P/O Sokolowski de Jenko PAF is buried in the
extension to Benson (St. Helen) Churchyard, his being one of four Polish air
force graves in this churchyard. All had been posted to 12 OTU.

3 Oct **16 OTU** **Anson I** N9749 **Transit**
1940 P/O E J Spencer inj T/o Upper Heyford and set course for Brackley.
Arriving here, at around 0900, P/O Spencer made
a low pass above the airfield and in doing so, flew into the Watch Office (it
seems without hurting any of the occupants) and crash-landed. On being helped
from the cockpit, he was taken to St. Hugh's Hospital in Oxford suffering from
concussion and a broken nose. He was the sole occupant of the aircraft.

19 OTU **Whitley IV** K9031 **Training**
Sgt J A Smith + T/o Kinloss for night dual training. At 2230,
Sgt E F Cryer + distress flares were seen from the direction of
Sgt E A Dancer + Findhorn Bay, off the Moray coast. Subsequently,
the Whitley was found but all attempts to lift
the bomber from the seabed were thwarted by silting and the prevailing inclement
autumn weather. Two bodies were recovered and taken for burial but Sgt Smith is
commemorated on panel 19 of the Runnymede Memorial.

5 Oct **14 OTU** **Hampden I** P2072 **Training**
1940 P/O D J Fielder T/o Cottesmore for a night navigation sortie.
Sgt Hawes inj In failing visibility, P/O Fielder descended in
Sgt White an attempt to verify his position and by doing
Sgt Gray inj so crash-landed 2000 on high ground near Richmond
in Yorkshire. This was his second bad accident
at 14 OTU (see page 14 for details) and not long after this latest incident he
was posted to 83 Squadron. On 27-28 December 1940, his Hampden failed to return
from a raid on Lorient (see Bomber Command Losses, Volume 1, page 142).

8 Oct 1940	13 OTU	Blenheim I L6783	Training

F/O P D Sharp   +   T/o Bicester for a formation flight and was
P/O C C M Gauldie   +   totally destroyed following a midair collision
Sgt G E Ancliffe   +   with another of the unit's aircraft. The three
airmen now rest in various cemeteries across the
United Kingdom. It will be recalled that F/O Sharp had narrowly escaped with his
life a fortnight previous when his Blenheim crashed at Weston-on-the-Green (see
the previous page).

	13 OTU	Blenheim IV L4883	Training

F/L S F Coutts-Wood DFC   +   T/o Bicester similarly tasked and destroyed in
Sgt S Chambers   +   the circumstances described above. F/L Coutts-
Sgt D W Wordsworth   +   Wood was cremated in Nottingham Crematorium West
Sgt W J Brett   +   Bridgford; his crew were taken to cemeteries in
the north of England.

	15 OTU	Wellington I L7773	Training

Sgt G F Heayes   T/o 2104 Harwell for a night navigation flight
but within a minute of becoming airborne, the
Wellington was on the ground, and on fire, some 3 miles SW of the airfield. No
one was badly hurt and for Sgt Heayes this was his third serious crash in less
than six months of flying instructing (see pages 13 and 28).

	16 OTU	Hampden I P1271	Training

P/O A F Jefferys   +   T/o Upper Heyford for instrument flying practice.
Sgt J D Shiels   +   Emerged from a cloud base of 1,300 feet, diving,
Sgt R T Bowtell   +   and broke up at 1230 over Home Farm, Highnam,
Sgt R A W Keeling   +   some 3 miles NW from the centre of Gloucester.
Sgt Shiels was taken to Mill Hill (St. Paul)
Churchyard, Hendon, but the rest of the crew lie in Gloucester Old Cemetery.
Sgt Keeling was a Canadian from Camper, Manitoba, while Sgt Bowtell was a
member of the pre-war Auxiliary Air Force.

11 Oct 1940	10 OTU	Whitley V N1526	Training

F/L J E Riepenhausen   +   T/o Abingdon for a night exercise but crashed
P/O L F East DFM   +   circa 2300 near the Akeman Street landing ground.
Sgt W R Small   +   It is believed the accident was caused by a large
Sgt J Fletcher   +   area of fabric stripping from the mainplanes. Sgt
Sgt P P McKee   +   McKee was buried in Abingdon (SS Mary and Edmund)
Sgt F D Phoenix   +   Roman Catholic Churchyard, while the others were
claimed by their relatives. P/O East had served
with 78 Squadron; his award being Gazetted eleven days after his death. A few
weeks previous he had displayed airmanship of the highest order when he forced-
landed a Whitley (without damage, or hurt to its crew) in a field near St. Neots.

12 Oct 1940	16 OTU	Hampden I P2140	Training

Sgt R B Hanmer   T/o Upper Heyford for flying training. Landed
Sgt H Johnson   1330 at high speed and while trying to avoid a
road that was under construction, he applied the
brakes with such force that the Hampden swung through 90 degrees and lost its
undercarriage. On 20-21 April 1941, he lost his life while on operations with
83 Squadron (see Bomber Command Losses, Volume 2, page 44).

	17 OTU	Blenheim IV L4866	Training

F/L C E Harris   inj   T/o Upwood but while only about 30 feet off the
runway, an engine cut and the Blenheim hit the
ground, wing first, and cartwheeled.

15 Oct 1940	15 OTU	Wellington IA P2523	Unknown

What documentation survives indicates this
aircraft was destroyed, by fire, on this date, following a flying accident.

16 Oct 1940	14 OTU	Anson I L7924	Training

Sgt S J Howard   +   T/o Cottesmore for a training flight to Carlisle
Sgt A Hurst   +   and return. Reported crashed at approximately
Sgt S R Sumner   +   1515 after a wing clipped a tree at Hartford Hill
Sgt T H Todd   +   Flats, Gilling West, 3 miles NNE from Richmond,
Sgt C Murray   +   Yorkshire. All are buried in cemeteries across
the United Kingdom.

17 Oct
1940

15 OTU		Wellington I	L4259		Training

F/O W S Munday   +   T/o Hampstead Norris for circuit practice. At

Sgt G T Watt   +   1105, while on the downwind leg of the circuit,
the port engine burst into flames and shortly
afterwards the Wellington stalled and dived into the ground. Both pilots lie
in Harwell Cemetery. F/O Munday was an Australian serving with the Royal Air
Force on a Short Service Commission. He had married Hilda Pauline Munday of
Lee-on-Solent in Hampshire.

20 Oct
1940

15 OTU		Wellington I	L4220		Training

F/O B Statham   inj   T/o Hampstead Norris for night circuits and

                         inj   landings. While in the circuit, F/O Statham
distracted by glare from the cockpit lighting
reflecting on the windscreen. Having adjusted the system, he came into land
but overshot the flare path and crashed 1935 into a tree. It is believed he
misread his air speed indicator.

21 Oct
1940

11 OTU		Wellington IA	N2905	-R	Training

P/O R J Cooper   inj   T/o Bassingbourn tasked for night bombing

                         inj   practice. Lost power and while trying to
land overshot the runway and ran into one
of the airfield's defence posts. This was the unit's first serious flying
accident since late August.

13 OTU		Blenheim IV	L8871		Training

Sgt L H Hillelson   +   T/o 1420 Weston-on-the-Green but an engine cut

Sgt J F F Kerr   +   causing the Blenheim to swing out of control.

Sgt W A Dismore   inj   In the ensuing crash, a fire broke out and the
bomber was totally destroyed. Sgt Dismore died
two days later; he is buried in Ilford Cemetery. Sgt Hillelson rests in Grimsby
Hebrew Congregation Cemetery, while Belfast born Sgt Kerr was taken home to lie
in the city's Dundonald Cemetery.

22 Oct
1940

14 OTU		Hampden I	P1343		Training

Sgt H Irving   T/o Cottesmore for local instrument flying

Sgt Eastwood   practice and wireless procedures training.

Sgt Robertson   At 1630, with the weather deteriorating fast,

Sgt Williams   inj   the crew made an approach to the runway at
Wittering, but failed to see some trees in
the overcast and crashed, heavily. Not long after this incident, Sgt Irving
was posted to 49 Squadron only to be killed during operations to the port of
Wilhelmshaven on 12 January 1941 (see Bomber Command Losses, Volume 2, page 14).

24 Oct
1940

20 OTU		Wellington IA	L7775		Training

P/O D V Gilmour   inj   T/o Lossiemouth for a night navigation sortie;

P/O H M Coombs   +   base-Brechin-Kinnairds Head-Inverness-base. At

Sgt A W Milroy   inj   roughly 2100 crashed into a hillside on Bruach

Sgt K W Bordycott   inj   Moor, 4 miles NW of Braemar, Aberdeenshire. It

Sgt G R Lyon   inj   is thought P/O Gilmour mistook the snow covered

Sgt F Hutson   +   moorland for cloud. P/O Coombs, a Bachelor of

Sgt J A Sparks   inj   Science graduate from Bristol University, lies
in Dyce Old Churchyard, while Sgt Hutson rests
in Sheffield (Crookes) Cemetery. Of the survivors, three were destined to lose
their lives; P/O Gilmour with 24 Squadron on 16 December 1941; Sgt Bordycott
(see Bomber Command Losses, Volume 4, page 114) and Sgt Sparks (see Bomber
Command Losses, Volume 3, page 188). A substantial amount of the wreckage,
including an engine nacelle complete with landing gear, was recovered during
May and June 1986, by the South Yorkshire Air Museum and by 1998 this material
had been deposited in a Nissen-type shed at East Kirkby Aviation Heritage Centre.
Further details of this accident were reported by Fly Past in March 1987.

25 Oct
1940

13 OTU		Blenheim IV	Z5804		Training

Sgt D R Weir   T/o Weston-on-the-Green for bombing practice.
Undershot the runway and crashed 2030.

19 OTU		Whitley IV	K9023		Training

Sgt R S Williams   T/o Kinloss for night dual training but wrecked
after landing, downwind, at 1940. Sgt Williams
had flown a tour of operations with 102 Squadron; his Whitley became 3302M.

29 Oct   **17 OTU**   **Blenheim IV**   **N3572**   **Training**
1940   P/O F Windram   T/o Upwood for a cross country flight. Lost
                                     engine power and forced-landed, 1100, in a
       field at Oakley, 4 miles NW of Bedford. No injuries reported.

31 Oct   **20 OTU**   **Wellington IC**   **R3223**   **Training**
1940   Sgt J D Loach   inj   T/o Lossiemouth for night flying practice.
       P/O F C D Winser   inj   Landed 2105, heavily, and bounced back into
       Sgt S Robinson DFM   inj   the air. Before the situation could be
       Sgt J V Hooker   inj   rectified, the Wellington hit the ground
       Sgt H Brown   inj   and almost immediately commenced to burn.
       Sgt J H Willis   inj   Rescue services were quickly to the scene
       Sgt A R Clough   inj   to assist the crew. Sgt Robinson had recently
       Sgt D N Beal   inj   completed a tour of duty with 38 Squadron and
                                       his DFM had been Gazetted on 22 October 1940.

3 Nov   **19 OTU**   **Whitley V**   **P5088**   **Training**
1940   P/O J G Walker   T/o Kinloss for a three hour night navigation
                                     exercise. Landed 2115, but none too successfully
and P/O Walker attempted to go round again. Unfortunately, having become airborne, he was rather premature in raising the flaps and the Whitley crash-landed
amongst some lighting poles. Subsequently, the airframe became 2332M. Just
over a year later, and while serving with 102 Squadron, P/O Walker failed to
return from Kiel (see Bomber Command Losses, Volume 2, page 188).

6 Nov   **15 OTU B Flt**   **Wellington IA**   **P2529**   **Training**
1940   Sgt P M Smith   inj   T/o 0930 Harwell but downwind by mistake and
                         inj   never became airborne. Travelling at high speed
                                   the bomber went through the boundary fence and
       Sgt V A Harris   crossed a road, hitting the Horse and Jockey
                                   Inn. This removed the tail section, but did
little to halt the momentum as the Wellington ran into a field, where it began
to burn. Amazingly, only one member of crew was seriously hurt. Sgt Smith,
was making his first flight without the guiding influence of a screened pilot,
was posted, at least with Sgt Harris, to 15 Squadron but while making a second
pilot sortie on 15 February 1941, failed to return (see Bomber Command Losses,
Volume 2, page 22). Sgt Harris was re-crewed and went on to participate in at
least forty-five operations, serving with four Bomber Command squadrons. It is
thought that while flying with 51 Squadron, between May 1943 and January 1944,
he was performing the duties of Signals Leader as his five operational sorties
were flown with either the Squadron commander or one of the Flight Commanders.
His last four months of active service were spent at Nuneaton with 105 OTU and
on leaving the RAF in October 1945, his log book shows 1,043.10 flying hours.

Note. I am grateful to Dr. Robert Kirby, author of "Avro Manchester" (Midland
Publishing Limited), for much of the detail used in this summary.

7 Nov   **19 OTU**   **Whitley V**   **N1440**   **Training**
1940   F/O J F Painter DFC   +   T/o Kinloss with a screened pilot, three pupil
       Sgt H D Gaywood   +   pilots and two wireless operators. While flying
       Sgt R E Rolison   +   at 1,200 feet, near Forres, Moray, the nose of
       Sgt F S Legge   +   the bomber dropped suddenly and diving steeply
       Sgt S P Gallagher   +   it smashed into the ground and burst into
       Sgt F W Lewis   +   flames. Sgt Gaywood rests in Kinloss Abbey
                                   Burial Ground; the others rest in cemeteries
                                   scattered across the United Kingdom.

13 Nov   **17 OTU**   **Blenheim IV**   **L4898**   **Training**
1940   Sgt F H Miller   inj   T/o Upwood for a formation exercise but at
                                   1500, while flying near Keyston, 12 miles WNW
of Huntingdon, a bird came through the windscreen and hit Sgt Miller in the
face. Badly stunned, and aided by his crew, he very skilfully force -landed.

16 Nov   **10 OTU**   **Whitley V**   **N1482**   **Training**
1940   Sgt F Gibbs   T/o Abingdon for night flying practice. Landed
                                   at 1922 but ran beyond the limits of the runway
and into a ditch, smashing the undercarriage. Visibility was poor. Rather
unusually, of his 145 hours of flying experience, Sgt Gibbs had logged 95 of
these on Whitley types.

21 Nov
1940

12 OTU   **Battle I** **N2022**   **Training**
Sgt S Kuropatwa PAF   T/o 1649 Benson but the engine cut and the
                                       Battle was badly damaged in the ensuing forced
landing that followed a minute later. Taken for repair in works by Rosenfield
the airframe was struck off charge on 5 December 1940 and reduced to scrap. On
18 August 1941, Sgt Kuropatwa lost his life in a Wellington crash while flying
with 300 Squadron (see Bomber Command Losses, Volume 2, page 123).

22 Nov
1940

12 OTU   **Battle I** **L5500**   **Training**
F/O S Wolski PAF   T/o Benson with the intention of flying to
                                       Penrhos and return. Lost engine power and
force -landed some 2 miles W of Llanbedrog on the Lleyn Peninsula, 4 miles
SW of Pwllheli, Caernarvon. At first it was thought the damage could be
repaired and the Battle was taken to one of Fairey's repair facilities.
On closer inspection, however, it was decided to scrap the airframe and this
was officially notified on 13 January 1941.

24 Nov
1940

14 OTU   **Anson I** **R3398**   **Training**
P/O R D Fraser   T/o Cottesmore for a night exercise. It is
Sgt Buck   assumed that the Anson received some form of
                                       challenge as at around 2005 P/O Fraser tried
to fire off the colours of the day. While doing so, the Verey pistol discharged
inside the cockpit, the flash temporarily blinding the crew and inflicting
lacerations to one of the pilot's eyes. Soon afterwards, a forced-landing
was carried out at Castle Bytham, 12 miles SSE of Grantham, Lincolnshire. P/O
Fraser became a prisoner of war early in 1942, while flying Manchesters with
61 Squadron (see Bomber Command Losses, Volume 3, page 27).

26 Nov
1940

12 OTU   **Battle I** **L5071**   **Training**
P/O W Makarewicz PAF   +   T/o 1932 Mount Farm but after climbing to about
P/O A Ignaszak PAF   +   1,000 feet, dived and crashed 1934 roughly a
Sgt F Blyskal PAF   +   mile NW of the airfield and burst into flames.
                                       All are buried in the extension to Benson (St.
Helen) Cemetery, their graves, along with that of P/O Sokolowski de Jenko PAF
(see page 30), making up the Polish Air Force contingent buried here.

Note. As an example of the difficulties facing anyone researching the work
of the training establishments, the crew, summarised above, are the first to
be mentioned by name in the Operational Record Book for 12 OTU (AIR 29/646).

13 OTU   **Anson I** **N5114**   **Training**
Sgt W S Chubb   T/o Bicester for a navigation and wireless
                                       procedures exercise. Forced-landed 1420 with
engine failure and damaged beyond repair after crashing through a hedge near
Launton, 2 miles ESE of Bicester, Oxfordshire. No injuries reported.

15 OTU   **Wellington I** **L4326**   **Training**
F/L G E Langdon   +   T/o Hampstead Norris for circuit training and
Sgt R Burns   +   pre-solo checks. Turning at ninety degrees to
Sgt H Woodward   +   the runway and flying at only around 200 feet,
                                       the Wellington stalled and dived into the
ground. On impact, which occurred at 1525, a fierce fire broke out completely
destroying the Wellington. F/L Langdon was laid to rest in Harwell Cemetery;
his crew, both pupil pilots, were taken to their home towns in Cheshire and
Nottinghamshire respectively.

16 OTU   **Magister I** **L5944**   **Air Test**
F/O P G Sooby   inj   On 24 November, with P/O C A Alldis as his
                                       passenger, F/O Sooby was carrying out authorised
aerobatics near Amersham, Buckinghamshire. Flying at 3,500 feet, he looped the
Magister and then, closing the throttle, executed a stall turn to port. Upon
levelling out, the engine failed to pick up, necessitating a forced-landing.
Two days later, having attended to the carburettor, F/O Sooby was briefed to
fly the trainer back to base. Late in the afternoon, and in failing light, he
took off but while banking to the left, at 150 feet, the engine cut and he was
unable to prevent the Magister from crashing into a tree. Apart from minor cuts
and abrasions, F/O Sooby was unhurt.

26 Nov
1940

17 OTU	Blenheim IV	R2792	Training

F/O E B Morse + T/o Upwood for a navigation exercise; base-
Sgt R L Thorn + Bicester-South Cerney-Northampton-base. Ran
Sgt B Wilson-North + into bad weather and at around 1855, crashed
into a wood at High Lodge near Eriswell, 11
miles NW of Bury St. Edmunds, Suffolk. Two are buried in their home towns but
Sgt Thorn of Thornton Heath is interred in Beck Row (St. John) Churchyard.

17 OTU	Blenheim IV	T1854	Training

Sgt V K Hobbs + T/o Upwood similarly tasked. Became lost and at
Sgt G Davies + around 1900 eyewitnesses report seeing a flare.
Sgt A Robinson . + Soon afterwards, the Blenheim flew into high
ground near Kettering, Northamptonshire. Two
were claimed by their next-of-kin but Sgt Robinson of Marple in Cheshire was
brought back to Upwood and laid to rest in Bury Cemetery. It is noted that
Sgt Davies, who is buried in Monmouthshire, had married Gwyneth Mary Davies
who, by the late 1950s, lived at Burnham-on-Sea, Somerset.

28 Nov
1940

10 OTU E Flt	Magister I	L5958	Training

S/L R Bickford DFC   T/o Abingdon. On return to base at around 1545,
the Magister touched down in the slipstream of
another aircraft and the turbulent air caused the light trainer to cartwheel out
of control. Amazingly, S/L Bickford was little hurt and he continued to serve as
OC E Flight until June 1941, when he left on posting to 76 Squadron. Tragically,
he died when his parachute became entangled in the tail structure of his Halifax,
abandoned at low altitude on 30 August 1941 (see Bomber Command Losses, Volume 2,
page 132). On 8 September 1939, as a F/O, he had taken part in 10 Squadron's
first operational sorties of the war when eight Whitleys, headed by W/C Staton,
carried out a combined Nickel and Reconnaissance of north-west Germany.

20 OTU	Wellington IA	N2884	Training

F/O C D Birch DFC + T/o Lossiemouth for a night navigation exercise
P/O R Vevers + over the North Sea. Last heard on W/T sending
Sgt B Butler + SOS and indicating the port engine had failed
Sgt J C Dickson MID + and height could not be maintained. It is assumed
Sgt N Gaskell + that shortly after 1806, the Wellington went into
Sgt T Graham + the sea in position 5718N 0108E (some 70 miles E
Sgt D G Johnson + of Peterhead, Aberdeenshire). All are perpetuated
Sgt M Ward + by the Runnymede Memorial. Other crews who were
Sgt D Williamson + in the exercise area at the time report extremely
inclement weather, coupled with heavy seas. The
loss of nine lives in a single incident was the most grievous since the formation
of the Bomber Command OTUs. F/O Birch's father was the Revd Arthur Pershore Birch
of Weston-super-Mare in Somerset. Sgt Ward came from Brisbane in Queensland.

29 Nov
1940

13 OTU	Blenheim IV	R3705	Training

Sgt M G Ham + T/o 0949 Bicester for a local formation flying
P/O R L Verity + exercise but as the aircraft climbed, so the
inj port engine faltered and moments later the
Blenheim hit the ground. Sgt Ham rests in
Dethick Lea and Holloway Cemetery, Derbyshire, while P/O Verity was taken to
Lytham St. Anne's (Park) Cemetery. Both had attained Bachelor of Arts degrees;
Sgt Ham, whose father was the Very Revd Herbert Ham MA FRCO, was a graduate of
Worcester College, Oxford, while P/O Verity had attended Leeds University.

2 Dec
1940

12 OTU	Battle I	L5432	Training

P/O E B Topp   T/o Benson for local low-level flying practice.
clipped a tree and forced-landed 1250 at Cuxham
some 11 miles SE of Oxford. P/O Topp had had the misfortune to write off the
twenty-ninth, and last, Fairey Battle from 12 OTU. Already, these obsolete
machines were being replaced within the unit by Wellingtons and it would be
nearly three months before the next serious flying accident would be reported.

3 Dec
1940

19 OTU	Whitley III	K9000	Training

Sgt D E McCoubray inj T/o Kinloss for a night dual and instrument
inj flying practice. At 2200, the Whitley flew
inj into the waters of Nairn harbour. In his report,
Sgt McCoubray (he had recently completed a tour
of duty with 10 Squadron) stated his altimeter had been registering 550 feet.

4 Dec   **11 OTU**   **Wellington IA**   **N2991**   **Unknown**
1940
No accident record card traced; AM Form 78
shows delivery to the unit on 2 September 1940, and when written off had flown
a total of 161.05 hours.

7 Dec   **14 OTU**   **Hampden I**   **P1276**   **Training**
1940   Sgt E W Lovejoy   inj   T/o 1714 Cottesmore for dusk and dark landing
Sgt Clarke   inj   practice but an engine failed and a minute later
the crew crash-landed, coming down between the
airmans' mess and some married quarters.

7 Dec   **16 OTU**   **Hampden I**   **P4292**   **Training**
1940   Sgt A J Coad DFM   +   T/o Upper Heyford for night flying practice.
S/L H D Beck   +   At approximately 1835, an engine failed and the
Sgt M R Dards   +   crew were given priority clearance to return to
Sgt T Hadfield   +   base. Tragically, at 300 feet, the Hampden was
Sgt G A Binks   +   observed to roll onto its back and dive into
the ground between Weston-on-the-Green airfield
and Chesterton village, a mile or so SW of Bicester, Oxfordshire. All rest in
various churchyards, Sgt Dards of Southall being interred locally at Upper
Heyford Cemetery. Sgt Coad had, until recently, served on 50 Squadron and on
24 December, seventeen days after his death, the London Gazette carried the
details of his Distinguished Flying Medal.

10 Dec   **15 OTU**   **Wellington I**   **L4230**   **Training**
1940   S/L G Learner   T/o Harwell for a cross-country flight, during
Sgt Earl   which an engine failed and the Wellington came
Sgt Morley   down at New Radnor, 7 miles WSW of Presteigne,
Sgt Doull   Radnor. It is believed the crew escaped any
Sgt Martin   serious injury, though their aircraft was a
Sgt Mullen   write off.

           17 OTU   **Blenheim IV**   **L4844**   **Training**
Sgt G W Penman   +   T/o Upwood to practice flying in cloud. Crashed
Sgt A Ferguson   +   1255 between Sinton Green and Grimley, 4 miles
Sgt J Roberts   +   NNW and N respectively of Worcester. All were
taken back to their native Scotland for burial
in cemeteries located in Fife, Renfrewshire and the County and City of Edinburgh.
Their service numbers show they had joined the pre-war Volunteer Reserve for
training in their respective trades of pilot, observer and wireless operator.

           18 OTU   **Anson I**   **R3402**   **Training**
S/Lt(A) C R Coxon RN   T/o Bramcote for a wireless procedures exercise.
Landed 1215 Staverton, Gloucestershire and while
taxying ran onto to soft ground and became bogged down. Damaged beyond repair.

14 Dec   **17 OTU**   **Blenheim IV**   **L4835**   **Training**
1940   Sgt I M Curror   +   T/o Upwood for a cross-country exercise during
Sgt A J V Secker RNZAF   +   which the weather deteriorated. Flying at 1,200
Sgt J Pinchard   +   feet, the crew smashed into the side of Clee Hill
(1,750 feet above sea level) some 6 miles E of
Ludlow, Shropshire. Sgt Curror was cremated, the service being held at Dry
Drayton, Cambridge Crematorium. Sgt Secker RNZAF, the son of Maj Victor Hart
Secker, is buried in Bury Cemetery, while Sgt Pinchard rests at Newcastle-
upon-Tyne (Byker and Heaton) Cemetery.

22 Dec   **17 OTU**   **Blenheim IV**   **L4896**   **Training**
1940   P/O C S Rombach   +   T/o Upwood. Flew into high-tension cables and
P/O J H Dales   +   crashed 1150 some 2 miles NE of Market Harborough
P/O L F Squire   +   in Leicestershire. P/O Rombach is buried in
Sgt A Cruise   +   Glasgow (Riddrie Park) Cemetery; P/O Dales lies
in Fulford Burial Ground, while P/O Squire and
Sgt Cruise, both from Luton, lie in Luton Church Burial Ground and Luton General
Cemetery respectively.

           20 OTU   **Wellington IA**   **N2907**   **Training**
F/O R T Sturgess   T/o Lossiemouth. During the flight, many of the
instruments failed and while trying to land at
base at 1403 the Wellington overshot the runway and lost its undercarriage.

23 Dec 1940	11 OTU	Wellington IA	N3014	-Z	Training

P/O D R F Haviland   +   T/o Bassingbourn for night flying practice.
Sgt W L Jones   +   The weather deteriorated and on return to base
P/O A F Pennymore   +   at 2020 the Wellington crashed, while over-
Sgt B Q Sheppard   +   shooting for the second time, into Bassingbourn
Sgt J A Carrol   +   village. Three are buried in Bassingbourn cum
Sgt E J Peters RNZAF   +   Kneesworth Cemetery and three, P/O Pennymore,
     Sgt Sheppard and Sgt Carrol, were claimed by
their next-of-kin. P/O Haviland was the son of Capt Wilfred Pollen Haviland MBE.

	16 OTU	Hampden I	P1182		Training

Sgt A Allison   T/o Upper Heyford for circuits and landings but
     an engine failed resulting in a forced-landing
at 1130 near Little Chesterton, 2 miles SW of Bicester, Oxfordshire. The cause
of the accident was traced to a broken connection in the oil system.

	17 OTU	Blenheim I	L8683		Training

Sgt C S H Bayford   T/o Upwood. Stalled, having lost engine power,
     and crash-landed 1130 near the airfield. Almost
a year later, on 20 December, Sgt Bayford died while flying Blenheims with 84
Squadron, then based at Gambut in Libya. He is buried in Tobruk War Cemetery.

29 Dec 1940	17 OTU	Blenheim IV	L4868		Training

P/O V S Reynolds RNZAF   +   T/o 1934 Upwood and crashed about a minute
P/O K W Edwards   +   later. Apparently, the observer called out
     inj   to say he could see a light and the pilot,
     thinking a collision was imminent, banked
steeply and lost control. In retrospect, it is thought P/O Edwards had caught
sight of a bright star. Both are buried in a joint grave at Birmingham (Lodge
Hill) Cemetery.

	20 OTU	Wellington IA	P9206		Training

P/O J H Waite   T/o Lossiemouth for night bombing and air firing
Sgt L Sladen   practice. Although the crew were able to complete
     their task, the return to base was made in quite
atrocious weather and while endeavouring to land, control was lost and the bomber
crashed at 1712. No one was badly hurt, but the Wellington was wrecked.

31 Dec 1940	20 OTU	Wellington IA	N2980		Training

S/L N W D Marwood-Elton   T/o Lossiemouth on a navigation exercise towards
P/O J Slater   Fort Augustus. While over the Monadhliath
P/O Lucton   Mountains, S of Inverness, the crew ran into a
Sgt C Chandler   series of heavy snow showers and soon afterwards
Sgt E Ford   the starboard engine failed. The order to bale
Sgt R Little   out was given, after which S/L Marwood-Elton put
Sgt W Wright   the Wellington down into the waters of Loch Ness
Sgt J S Fensome   +   off Urquhart Castle. Sadly, Sgt Fensome's
     parachute became tangled and failed to deploy.
He is buried in Biscot (Holy Trinity) Churchyard, Luton. In the years that
followed, four other members of the crew lost their lives; Sgt Chandler, Sgt
Ford, Sgt Little and P/O Slater, while S/L Marwood-Elton became a prisoner of
war. On 21 September 1985, he was present for the raising by Oceaneering
International Services of the Wellington, which was conveyed to Weybridge
for an extensive restoration programme. As OJ-R of 149 Squadron, the bomber
had seen active service during 1939 and 1940, before being accepted by 20 OTU
for training purposes. When ditched, it had flown a total of 330.20 hours.

Resumé. The accident, summarised above, brought to a close the losses of a very
eventful nine months of service for the OTUs. Eleven such establishments had
been formed and not one had escaped the toll of flying accidents. The worst
affected, in terms of aircraft destroyed, was 12 OTU at Benson. No less than
twenty-nine of their Battles had been written off and an equal number of deaths
had resulted amongst their trainees. By comparison, 10 OTU at Abingdon had
fared quite well, losing eleven aircraft with fourteen fatalities. Both the
Blenheim and the Hampden OTUs had experienced a torrid nine months; thirty-nine
Blenheims had been destroyed and forty-four Hampden/Herefords had been lost in
the myriad of accidents, already common to the training units. Coping with
quite complex aircraft and frequently being asked to fly in weather conditions
that may best be described as 'marginal', the task had proven too much for the

limited expertise of their crews. Even the experienced hands were finding life difficult and there is little doubt that icing played a major part in the loss of Flying Officer Haviland and his 11 OTU crew on 23 December. As briefly remarked upon, in the summary, the crew had overshot their first approach and when the wreckage of their Wellington was examined, the windscreen was found to be coated with glazed ice, which likely had a direct bearing on the outcome of the accident.

With their proximity to the Moray Firth, coupled with the hostile environment of the unforgiving Scottish Highlands, it is little wonder that 19 OTU and 20 OTU lost a high proportion of their aircraft in the sea, or in the surrounding hills. So far, neither unit had suffered too badly, though 20 OTU's losses were already into double figures, a portent of trying times ahead.

Nonetheless, despite all the trials and tribulations associated with war time operations, the OTUs were producing a steady flow of crews deemed to be operationally proficient and in the year ahead five more such establishments would be formed in order to keep pace with the demands of a steadily expanding Bomber Command.

Already an established feature within the training syllabus was the practice of sending crews on Nickel sorties. Directed mainly at the occupied countries, and in particular those areas of France not controlled by the Vichy French, the first of these operations had been flown within weeks of the evacuation of our forces from Dunkerque. Although beyond the scope of this volume to examine, in depth, the number of such sorties flown, a few remarks concerning the operation mounted from Abingdon by 10 OTU on 21-22 July 1940, will not go amiss. Three Whitleys were prepared (no serial numbers recorded) and in addition to the packages of Nickels, each aircraft was armed with two 250lb general purpose bombs, though crews were told quite emphatically that bombing was a secondary task and that only aerodromes could be considered as suitable targets. In the event, only Pilot Officer Robson, described as making a very determined effort, released his bombs and through a misunderstanding, these were dropped 'safe'.

All crews successfully released their Nickels, the route being described as St. Valery to Abbeville, then to Amiens and Rouen before exiting over the port of Le Havre. Each Whitley had a crew of five, the captains being Pilot Officer Lawson, Pilot Officer Uprichard and the aforementioned Pilot Officer Robson.

There are no indications that the 'raid' attracted a response from the newly arrived invaders and, in general, crews tasked for these missions came through them without too many difficulties.

5 Jan **15 OTU** **Wellington IC R1291** **Training**
1941 F/O C Warren T/o Harwell tasked for Operational Exercise 3.
Encountered icing of such severity that the
airspeed indicator, wireless and intercom system all failed to function. Thus,
at 1735, the bomber was crash-landed, running through a hedge, at Dovers Grange
Farm, near Bletchley, Buckinghamshire.

Note. As yet, I have not been able to trace Dovers Grange Farm, though a Grange
Farm has been located roughly 4 miles NW of Bletchley and west of Shenley Park.

16 OTU **Hampden I P2114** **Training**
Sgt R A Bridgart + T/o Upper Heyford for his first night solo in a
Sgt C A Jones inj Hampden but became hopelessly lost. For several
hours he searched fruitlessly for an airfield
and when eventually he crashed, at 2205, his Hampden was down near Longworth,
a little under 7 miles WNW of Abingdon, Berkshire. Sgt Bridgart was cremated
and his ashes scattered in the Garden of Rest at Oxford Crematorium, Stanton
St. John.

12 Jan **16 OTU** **Hampden I L4123** **Training**
1941 Sgt W M Davies T/o Upper Heyford for wireless procedures
Sgt C J Smith inj training. Returned to base at around 1235, but
while closing on the runway yawed, suddenly, to
port and crashed amongst trees. A fire broke out and though Sgt Davies escaped
more or less unscathed, Sgt Smith was very seriously hurt, sustaining a broken
pelvis.

13 Jan **16 OTU** **Hereford I L6027** **Training**
1941 Sgt P C T Forster T/o Upper Heyford for night training but the
port engine failed, causing the Hereford to
swing off the runway and crash into two of the unit's aircraft. The Hampden
(see below) was wrecked but the Anson (N5267) was repaired and later saw service
with 6 Pilots Advanced Flying Unit until written off at Little Rissington on 29
July 1943. Sgt Forster, sadly, was killed on 17 April 1941 (see page 47) in a
crash over the Ot Moor bombing ranges.

16 OTU **Hampden I P2141** **Ground**
Wrecked in the manner described above.

14 Jan **13 OTU** **Blenheim IV N3563** **Training**
1941 Sgt L P Murphy T/o Hinton-in-the-Hedges with the intention of
carrying out single-engined landings. After one
such landing, the Blenheim sustained a damaged undercarriage but Sgt Murphy took
off and elected to set course for Bicester. However, before he could reach his
intended destination, the aircraft came down circa 1500 near Whitfield, 4 miles
NE of Brackley, Northamptonshire. A fire broke out but Sgt Murphy, whose total
flying experience on type amounted to just ten hours, escaped unharmed.

15 Jan **14 OTU** **Hampden I P1241** **Training**
1941 Sgt F Rowney T/o 1044 Cottesmore on his first Hampden solo
but almost immediately an engine failed and a
forced-landing was carried out, some 2 miles distant from the airfield. No
injuries reported, but the Hampden was deemed to be beyond economical repair.
Posted to 50 Squadron, he was killed on 9 September 1941 (see Bomber Command
Losses, Volume 2, page 143) while returning from a raid on Kassel.

17 Jan **10 OTU** **Whitley V N1494** **Training**
1941 F/O C W Doggett + T/o Abingdon for night bombing practice. Flew
P/O W Fullerton + into a snowstorm and crashed 0131 into Wootton
Sgt R H Freeman + Road, Abingdon. The screened wireless operator
Sgt C R Kemp + and trainee air gunner managed to parachute to
Sgt H Jolly safety, both reporting that the pilot had lost
Sgt P W R Emmett the use an engine due to icing. Those who died
rest in various cemeteries.

Note. Prior to being accepted by 10 OTU on 21 September 1940, this Whitley
had seen operational service with 10 Squadron. For a short period of time,
it had been assigned to Hendon, possibly for modifications.

25 Jan **20 OTU**   **Wellington IC R1164**   **Transit**
1941   F/O J F M Millar   T/o 1500 Kirkbride in the company of other
                                                aircraft and set course for Lossiemouth, the
aircraft having been assigned to 20 OTU. As the formation proceeded on a
northerly course, the weather deteriorated and about an hour into the flight
F/O Millar, the ferry pilot and sole occupant of the Wellington, was observed
to lose contact. It was subsequently reported that he had crashed into Box Law
roughly 3 miles ENE of Largs, Ayrshire. The aircraft was totally destroyed and
the Court of Inquiry recommended that in future a wireless operator should be
tasked to accompany pilots undertaking delivery flights.

3 Feb   **13 OTU**   **Blenheim IV T2287**   **Training**
1941   Sgt F N Scott   T/o Bicester for a cross-country and wireless
                                                exercise. As visibility decreased, the crew
became lost and Sgt Scott elected to force -land. Selecting a field about a
mile E of Marsh Gibbon, 8 miles SSW of Buckingham, he commenced his approach
but throttled back a shade too early and while trying to stretch the glide he
lost flying speed and crashed 1735, fortunately without injury to himself or
his crew.

            18 OTU   **Wellington IA P9221**   **Training**
            P/O G N Parker   T/o Bramcote for dual and single-engined flying
                                                practice. Lost power, in the circuit, and at
around 1140 the Wellington undershot the runway and smashed into a contractor's
crane. At the time of the accident, visibility was much reduced due to snow
showers sweeping across the area.

4 Feb   **16 OTU**   **Hampden I P1332**   **Training**
1941   P/O A Smith   +   T/o Upper Heyford for a cross-country flight
            Sgt L E Clayton   +   during which the crew ran into some heavy snow
            Sgt A H Cunningham   +   showers. At 1130, having been forced beneath
            Sgt H M Pattinson   +   the cloud base, the Hampden's starboard wing
                                                hit the ground while banking steeply near the
village of Conington, 10 miles NW of Cambridge and practically on the border
with Huntingdonshire. P/O Smith lies in Doncaster (Rose Hill) Cemetery; Sgt
Clayton is buried in Long Stanton (All Saints) Churchyard; Sgt Cunningham is
interred at Crail Cemetery, while Sgt Pattinson was taken to Beltingham (St.
Cuthbert) New Churchyard.

            18 OTU   **Wellington IC R1298**   **Training**
            F/O D Warburton   +   T/o Bramcote for a navigation exercise during
            W/O Z J Perkowski PAF   +   which the crew strayed off track. At 1250, or
            F/O A Minkiewicz PAF   +   thereabouts, the Wellington flew into a barrage
            Sgt L Jachna PAF   +   balloon cable and crashed, possibly in the area
            Sgt V C Hill   +   of Church Minshull, 4 miles SW of Middlewich,
            Sgt B T Abbott   +   Cheshire. The six PAF members of crew, along
            Sgt J P Orynek PAF   +   with Sgt Gosden RNZAF, were buried in Nuneaton
            Sgt S J Wojciechowski PAF   +   (Oaston Road) Cemetery, while the others were
            Sgt W L Gosden RNZAF   +   claimed by their next of kin. F/O Warburton
            LAC H R Kwiatkowski PAF   +   was an Exhibitioner of BNC Oxford; his father
                                               was the Revd Robert Warburton MA of Mere. To
date, this was the highest death toll yet in a single OTU accident.

            20 OTU   **Wellington IC R1005**   **Training**
            P/O B I Clausen RNZAF   +   T/o 1830 Lossiemouth for a night cross-country
            Sgt P G Fazakerley   inj   and practice bombing sortie. At around 2205,
            P/O A H C Gibson   +   the crew returned to base, permission to land
            P/O H G Craigmile   +   being given. However, while flying the cross
            Sgt R Oates   +   wind leg, the airfield controller ordered a
            Sgt A W Harris   inj   red Verey cartridge be fired as another air-
                                               craft was blocking the flight path. Observers
on the ground watched the Wellington turn steeply to port before plunging, out
of control, into the sea near the airfield. Of those who died, P/O Clausen RNZAF
was laid to rest in Lossiemouth Burial Ground; P/O Gibson is commemorated on the
Runneymede Memorial; P/O Craigmile is buried in Aberdeen (Grove) Cemetery, while
Sgt Oates was taken south to lie in Manchester's Southern Cemetery. The injured
were treated in Dr. Gray's Hospital at nearby Elgin (it is observed that in some
documents this hospital is referred to as Dr. Grey's).

4 Feb 1941	20 OTU	Wellington IC	R1367		Training

4 Feb 1941   **20 OTU**   **Wellington IC**   **R1367**   **Training**

Sgt D M Walker RNZAF   inj   T/o Lossiemouth for a cross-country and practice
Sgt E G Morris   +   bombing detail. While circling the airfield, at
P/O J G Pidduck RCAF   inj   1040, the Wellington went out of control and
Sgt S Summersgill   +   crashed on the SE side of the aerodrome. Three
Sgt J K Blencoe   +   perished immediately and Sgt Walker RNZAF died
Sgt P G Carvenec   inj   within a few hours from his terrible injuries.
He lies in Lossiemouth Burial Ground, while the others were claimed by their next of kin.

7 Feb 1941   **16 OTU**   **Hampden I**   **P1149**   **Training**

Sgt W Walker   inj   T/o Upper Heyford and immediately flew into
Sgt H James   +   another of the unit's aircraft which was in
the process of landing. Locked together, the two bombers fell onto the airfield where they began to burn. Sgt Walker managed to escape the inferno with a thigh injury and concussion. His wireless operator was nowhere near so lucky and he now rests in Upper Heyford Cemetery.

16 OTU   **Hampden I**   **P1302**   **Training**

F/O S Moxham DFC   inj   T/o Upper Heyford. Destroyed in the manner
Sgt R E Fenton   +   described above. Two officers were quickly at
the scene; W/C W C Sheen DSO and the gunnery officer, P/O J C Cunningham and between them they managed to drag F/O Moxham from his cockpit and beat out the flames that were engulfing his flying suit. Sadly, their heroic actions were to no avail and F/O Moxham died soon after. He lies in Willesden New Cemetery, while Sgt Fenton was taken to Huddersfield (Edgerton) Cemetery.

9 Feb 1941   **14 OTU**   **Hampden I**   **P1342**   **Training**

Sgt J Austin   T/o Cottesmore. Crash-landed 1255, wheels up,
Sgt Rowney   near the airfield having developed a fault on
Sgt Power   the approach. No one was hurt but the Hampden
was burnt out. Soon after this incident, Sgt Austin was posted to 50 Squadron, losing his life in the July while operating to Bremen (see Bomber Command Losses, Volume 2, page 90).

12 Feb 1941   **20 OTU**   **Wellington IA**   **N2908**   **Unknown**

Accident card not traced. According to its AM Form 78, the Wellington was accepted by the unit on 19 June 1940, having flown previously with 38 Squadron. At the time of its loss, the aircraft had logged a total of 378.35 flying hours.

15 Feb 1941   **11 OTU**   **Wellington I**   **L4375**   **Training**

F/S D L H Miles   +   T/o Newmarket for local flying. At 1610, while
Sgt R H Newman   +   approaching the runway, the bomber stalled and
crashed, bursting into flames. It is likely the Wellington had one engine stopped. F/S Miles, a pre-war regular with roughly eight years of service, is buried in Forest Row Cemetery; Sgt Newman of Croydon was taken to Beck Row (St.John) Churchyard, Suffolk.

18 Feb 1941   **19 OTU D Flt**   **Whitley V**   **N1373**   **Training**

P/O J G MacCoubrey DFM   +   T/o Forres but the port engine failed and while
Sgt O Cousins   +   trying to land, stalled and crashed 1045, near
Sgt S G Mowforth   +   the airfield. Sgt Gates was buried in Kinloss
Sgt W Smith   +   Abbey Burial Ground; the others who died were
Sgt J Hayes   +   claimed by their next of kin. Sgt Lawley made
Sgt R W Gates   +   a good recovery from his injuries. Posted to
Sgt E Lawley   inj   10 Squadron, he was killed in action on 27-28
June 1941 (see Bomber Command Losses, Volume 2, page 75). P/O MacCoubrey's DFM had been Gazetted on 30 July 1940.

21 Feb 1941   **16 OTU**   **Anson I**   **R3331**   **Training**

P/O R J Dufty   +   T/o Upper Heyford for a cross-country exercise.
P/O J R Spiers   +   Crashed 1110, while making a forced-landing, at
Sgt R Williams   +   Cotton Hall Farm in Denbighshire. All rest in
Sgt J R King   +   various cemeteries. It is reported that snow
showers were prevalent in the crash area. Six months later, P/O William McNaughton Spiers, brother to P/O Spiers, was killed flying with 10 Squadron (see Bomber Command Losses, Volume 2, page 103).

23 Feb   **14 OTU**   **Hampden I** **P1292**   **Training**
1941   P/O H G Keartland   T/o 1840 Cottesmore for a night exercise but
        Sgt Hammond   due to a considerable accumulation of melting
        Sgt Banham   snow and slush, the Hampden failed to become
        Sgt Everett   airborne and was wrecked after running through
                                      a hedge.

24 Feb   **13 OTU**   **Blenheim I** **L1309**   **Training**
1941   Sgt W D G Bond   + T/o 0005 Bicester for night flying practice but
                                 after climbing to about 400 feet, the Blenheim
entered a steep dive and on hitting the ground, burst into flames. Nineteen
year old Sgt Bond, of Bedhampton in Hampshire, is buried locally in Caversfield
(St. Laurence) Churchyard.

25 Feb   **11 OTU**   **Wellington I** **L4276**   **Training**
1941   F/L A F Riddlesworth DFC   + T/o Bassingbourn for a demonstration in stalling
        P/O W J Shirtcliffe RAAF   + with the flaps and undercarriage down and in a
        Sgt L F De Roeck   + clean configuration. Lost control and crashed
        AC2 F J Holdstock   + circa 1440 at Newnham, 2 miles SSE of Daventry
        AC2 R J Atkinson   + in Northamptonshire. P/O Shirtcliffe RAAF of
                                 Devonport in New Zealand and Sgt De Roeck are
buried in Bassingbourn cum Kneesworth Cemetery; the others were taken to their
home towns.

16 OTU   **Hampden I** **P1288**   **Training**
        P/O H M Macrossan   T/o Upper Heyford for a night exercise. At about
                                 2100, and in the circuit of Kidlington airfield,
P/O Macrossan turned onto finals but on switching on the landing light, he lost
sight of the flare path and finished up in a field adjacent to the airfield. On
5 April 1941, while flying with 50 Squadron, P/O Macrossan, whose father was the
Hon. Hugh Denis Macrossan, Judge of the Supreme Court in Queensland, failed to
return from operations (see Bomber Command Losses, Volume 2, page 37).

17 OTU   **Magister I** **L5951**   **Training**
        F/L T R Manson   + T/o Upwood only to fly into high-tension cables
                        inj and crash 1500 near Sawtry, 9 miles NNW from
                                 Huntingdon. F/L Manson, described as a pilot/
navigator, is buried in Groton (St. Bartholomew) Churchyard.

27 Feb   **12 OTU**   **Wellington IC** **L7814**   **Enemy action**
1941   Sgt E Featherstone   + Destroyed during an attack by the Luftwaffe on
                                 Benson airfield. Sgt Featherstone, a nineteen
year old wireless operator, is buried in Manchester Southern Cemetery. It is
not clear if Sgt Featherstone was in the Wellington, or whether he happened to
be close by when the bomb exploded. It was, however, the first aircraft of its
type to be written off since 12 OTU converted from Fairey Battles.

19 OTU D Flt   **Whitley V** **N1389**   **Training**
        Sgt Sampson   T/o Forres. Overshot while landing at 1230 and
                                  wrecked after running through a wire fence and
                                  into a ditch.

28 Feb   **12 OTU**   **Wellington IC** **R1285**   **Training**
1941   Sgt E F Fry DFM   + T/o Benson for circuit practice. Lost power
        P/O F H S West   + from one engine and while banking spun out of
                                   control, crashing 1100 near Watlington in
Oxfordshire, slight damage to civilian property being noted. Sgt Fry is buried
in Sittingbourne and Milton (Sittingbourne) Cemetery. His entry in the CWGC
register shows 142 Squadron but according to the DFM register, his award,
which was Gazetted on 11 February 1941, was gained with 214 Squadron. P/O
West lies in the extension to Benson (St. Helen) Churchyard. According to
unit records, he had been attached from 142 Squadron.

14 OTU   **Anson I** **R9749**   **Training**
        Sgt G K Hathersich   T/o Cottesmore for a night navigation exercise
        P/O Jeff   during which the starboard engine failed.
        P/O W E Cochrane   Forced-landed at Westwoodside, a community on
        Sgt Tansley   the W side of Haxby, 10 miles SW of Scunthorpe
        Sgt Shadbolt   in Lincolnshire.

3 Mar 1941	**13 OTU**	**Blenheim IV**	**R3751**	**Training**

Sgt J N Gallyon   +
Sgt E E C Phillips   +
Sgt T Randall   +

T/o Bicester for a cross-country flight. At approximately 1130 the Blenheim crashed near Shillingford, a village on the SE fringes of Exmoor and about 7 miles NNE of Tiverton in Devon. Sgt Phillips of Brockley in London was taken to Exeter Higher Cemetery; Sgt Gallyon is buried in Cambridge and Chesterton (St. Andrew) Churchyard and Sgt Randall rests at Kirby Muxloe Cemetery. Eyewitnesses report the Blenheim diving steeply and with its engines running.

	14 OTU	**Hampden I**	**P1283**	**Training**

P/O G E Kerridge
Sgt Hendra
Sgt Rowney
Sgt Baker

T/o 1935 Cottesmore for practice bombing over the Grimsthorpe ranges but swung out of control and crashed into a paint store. Soon after the impact, the flash bombs ignited and the ensuing blaze destroyed the Hampden and the shed. In addition to the local fire services, Oakham Fire Brigade attended. It will be recalled that Sgt Rowney had been involved in a serious crash on 9 February (see page 41) but it is not known if he is the Sgt Rowney mentioned on page 39.

5 Mar 1941	**15 OTU**	**Anson I**	**N5078**	**Training**

Sgt J Canton
Sgt R Dick
Sgt E L Killip
Sgt F Purnell
Sgt J W Wright
Sgt L A C Standen

T/o Harwell for a night exercise. Caught in searchlights and in the confusion to fire off the colours of the day, a Verey pistol round was accidentally discharged inside the Anson. A fire developed and the crew baled out, the trainer crashing near Priors Hardwick, a small Warwickshire village some 12 miles N from Banbury, Oxfordshire.

	17 OTU	**Blenheim IV**	**V5562**	**Training**

Sgt G H Wood   inj
Sgt L C Crossley   inj
Sgt T Collier   inj

T/o 1144 Polebrook but an engine failed and before the crew could return to the airfield the Blenheim lost so much height that a forced-landing, wheels up, became necessary. It is not thought that their injuries were serious.

6 Mar 1941	**16 OTU**	**Hampden I**	**L4151**	**Training**

P/O P D G Hudson

T/o Brackley. At 1400, while banking left at 700 feet, the port engine cut and the Hampden ended up in a ploughed field at Baynard's Green, a hamlet on the NE side of Upper Heyford airfield and just to the NNE of Ardley and E of Fritwell. A fire broke out but P/O Hudson escaped unharmed.

8 Mar 1941	**17 OTU**	**Blenheim I**	**L6692**	**Training**

Sgt J H Tolman

T/o Polebrook for solo flying and crashed.

13 Mar 1941	**18 OTU**	**Magister I**	**L5996**	**Enemy action**

Destroyed when the Luftwaffe attacked Bramcote airfield. During the raid, which commenced at 2322, at least eight bombs were dropped and slight damage was caused to No.2 hangar. No casualties reported.

	18 OTU	**Wellington I**	**L4233**	**Enemy action**

Destroyed in the circumstances described above.

	18 OTU	**Wellington IC**	**R1320**	**Enemy action**

Destroyed in the circumstances described above. The two Wellingtons had flown a total of 208.40 and 3.10 hours respectively, the former having served with 99 Squadron and 11 OTU.

14 Mar 1941	**10 OTU**	**Whitley V**	**P5087**	**Training**

P/O A Bridson DFC   +
P/O G B Chapman   +
Sgt F H Baldwin   +
Sgt D C Craig   +
Sgt J Orr   +
Sgt W J Savage   +

T/o 1045 Abingdon on a navigation exercise; base-Worcester-Strumble Head-Bardsey Island-Jurby-Great Ormes Head-Ludlow-base. Lost without trace but likely came down in the Irish Sea. All are commemorated on the Runnymede Memorial. P/O Bridson was a New Zealander serving in the Royal Air Force on a Short Service Commission. He had gained his DFC during a tour of operations with 10 Squadron.

14 Mar 1941	13 OTU Det F/L R J Hill DFC	Blenheim I	L1263 +	Transit

T/o Bicester to return to Oulton airfield in Norfolk (where the OTU was maintaining a detachment) having brought two air gunners and their kit to the parent unit. On reaching Oulton at around 1830, F/L Hill carried out a very low high speed pass across the airfield before pulling up and joining the circuit. He then dived and began another fast run on a course which was taking him towards a tall tree (many such obstacles had recently been felled). At the last moment, F/O Hill pulled up into a near vertical climb but a wing struck the branches and was torn away. Seconds later, the Blenheim smashed onto the driveway of Green Farm, Oulton village and burst into flames. Brought back to Bicester, he now rests in Caversfield (St. Laurence) Churchyard.

Note. I am grateful to Mr Lawrence F Round (via Bob Collis) of Belbroughton who, as a member of the Royal Air Force Regiment, was stationed at Oulton and witnessed this unhappy sequence of events.

16 Mar 1941	14 OTU P/O S C R Bell P/O Priest Sgt Cheetham Sgt Hendra Sgt Riddell	Hampden I	P1213 inj	Training

T/o Cottesmore for an air firing exercise. While turning to port at 800 feet, lost control and crashed at Thistleton, 7 miles NNE from Oakham. For Sgt Hendra, this was his second escape in less than a fortnight (see page 43).

18 Mar 1941	13 OTU P/O R A Brown	Blenheim IV	N3631	Transit

T/o Wittering and set course for Bicester but due to adverse weather, coupled with failure of the wireless, forced-landed 1900 near Chalfont St. Giles, Buckinghamshire.

23 Mar 1941	10 OTU Sgt M F Woodhams Sgt F P King	Whitley V	P4999 + inj inj	Training

T/o Abingdon for circuit training. Bounced on landing and while attempting to go round again clipped a tree and crashed 2120 into Wootton Road, Abingdon and caught fire. Sgt Woodhams is buried in Sevenoaks (Greatness Park) Cemetery.

	13 OTU Sgt J D McCallum Sgt Redgrave Sgt C F X Leighton	Blenheim IV	T2285 + inj +	Training

T/o Bicester for a night flying detail. Came down at 2236, having overshot the runway and collided with a tree and some wire cables. Sgt McCallum rests in Abbey Cemetery, Thorn, while Sgt Leighton was taken to Hethe (Holy Trinity) Roman Catholic Cemetery.

25 Mar 1941	20 OTU F/L J F Ritchie P/O F S H Ford P/O E W McLeod RAAF Sgt W A Crosswell Sgt H S Murray Sgt H C Salt Sgt A J Turner Sgt G Whittaker Sgt W P Wilkinson	Wellington IC	R1155 + + + + + + + + +	Training

T/o Lossiemouth for a night bombing detail. At approximately 0105, the Wellington was seen by other crews, similarly engaged, to commence an attack from which it failed to recover before hitting the sea some 4 miles N of Kingston, a village overlooking Spey Bay and about 8 miles SE of the airfield. F/L Ritchie is buried in Edzell Churchyard; his crew are commemorated on the Runnymede Memorial. Sgt Wilkinson was an Associate of the Royal College of Music.

	21 OTU W/C N G Mullholland DFC F/L St. John	Wellington IC	T2712 inj	Transit

T/o Dumfries in the company of other aircraft and set course for Moreton-in-Marsh. It seems that this aircraft was forced down because of increasing cloud cover and at around 1615, while flying at 500 feet, the starboard throttle control failed. Unable to maintain height, W/C Mullholland crash-landed at Frizington, 4 miles E of Whitehaven, Cumberland, sustaining severe facial injuries in the process.

26 Mar 1941	15 OTU Sgt W Nicholls	Wellington I	L4242	Training

T/o Hampstead Norris for dual instruction. Landed 1135, heavily, and broke the undercarriage. Subsequently, the airframe became a training aid with the serial 2557M applied on, or about, 6 April 1941.

26 Mar   **15 OTU**   **Wellington IC**   **R1243**   **Training**
1941   Sgt J P Mountney   +   T/o Harwell (No. 5 crew, No. 31 course) tasked

Sgt C T Atkinson   +   for a 4-hour cross-country; base-Worcester-
Sgt R M Neale   inj   Harlech-Peterborough-base and incorporating a
Sgt S H Thomson   +   bombing detail on either sea markers or smoke
Sgt D B Smith   +   floats. At approximately 1130, observers at
Sgt H G Hoad   +   Criccieth, on the southern shores of the Leyn
Peninsula, saw the Wellington coming in from
the E and fly into the sea. Boats were launched immediately and two airmen
were picked up. Sgt Thomson was pronounced dead and Sgt Neale subsequently
died from his injuries. Their four colleagues are commemorated on the Runnymede
Memorial. At the time of the tragedy, visibility was much reduced owing to sea
fog and it was estimated to be down to 500 yards in the area of the crash.

27 Mar   **14 OTU**   **Hampden I**   **P4313**   **-D1**   **Training**
1941   Sgt D McL Barclay   +   T/o 1015 Cottesmore for a navigation exercise

Sgt J H Case   inj   captained by Sgt Barclay who was either attached
Sgt F A L Hankins   inj   from, or awaiting posting to 49 Squadron (con-
Sgt S G H Harper   inj   versely, he may have recently arrived from this
unit on posting in as a screened pilot). At
about 1130, the Hampden was over the Isle of Man, where the visibility was
extremely poor and, possibly, while trying to locate Jurby he flew into the
chimney of a farmhouse belonging to Mr J R Quilleash before colliding with a
pole carrying electricity cables. Out of control, the bomber hit the ground
roughly a mile from Laxey and 6 miles NNE of Douglas. Sgt Barclay was killed
outright, while Sgt Hankins died a few hours later; both rest in Jurby (St.
Patrick) Churchyard. Sgt Case was rushed to Douglas Hospital where he died
thirty minutes after being admitted; he is buried in Stourbridge Cemetery.

16 OTU   **Hampden I**   **P2066**   **Training**
Sgt V M Bidlake   +   T/o Upper Heyford for circuits and landings and
Sgt C H D Frost   +   single-engined overshoot procedures. Stalled and
crashed 1510 just to the SW of Wroxton Heath,
3 miles WNW of Banbury, Oxfordshire. Sgt Bidlake, whose father William Henry
Bidlake was a Fellow of the Royal Institute of British Architects, and Sgt
Frost were cremated at Charing (Kent County) Crematorium.

31 Mar   **14 OTU**   **Hampden I**   **P2062**   **Training**
1941   Sgt K E Holder   +   T/o Woolfox Lodge for night flying practice.

P/O M J West   +   Approaching to land, went out of control and
P/O J E Richmond   +   crashed 0420, close to the airfield. The first
Sgt F S Jessop   +   three named are all shown in the CWGC registers
as pilots and two, including P/O Richmond, who
held a Bachelor of Arts degree, were buried in the extension to St. Nicholas
Churchyard at Cottesmore. Sgt Holder rests at Streatham Park Cemetery, Mitcham
while Sgt Jessop lies in Lepton (St. John) Churchyard, Kirkburton.

25 OTU A Flt   **Anson I**   **N9912**   **Training**
P/O B M Fournier   inj   T/o Finningley for a night navigation flight.
                                inj   Crashed on high ground on Whitwell Moor near
                                inj   Bolsterstone on the southern side of Stocks-
bridge, Yorkshire. It is not thought their
injuries were life threatening. Along with the loss of a 21 OTU Wellington
six days previous, these were the first serious accidents involving OTUs that
had been formed since the turn of the year.

Note. Formed at Finningley on 1 March 1941, 25 OTU was destined to have an
existence of less than two years. However, during that period it operated
a variety of types, including Hampdens, Wellingtons and more than a few of
the none too popular Avro Manchesters.

5 Apr   **11 OTU**   **Wellington I**   **L4216**   **Training**
1941   F/O D G Hayward   T/o 2105 Steeple Morden for night flying but

                                            an engine cut, causing the Wellington to swing
violently. Running at high speed, the bomber careered off the flare path and
on to rough ground, where the undercarriage collapsed. No one was hurt. This
particular Wellington had been on unit charge since 19 June 1940, and had
previously seen service with 99 Squadron. Its total number of flying hours
are not appended.

8 Apr **14 OTU**   **Hampden I** **P1240**   **Training**
1941   P/O E E G Crump   T/o Cottesmore for night bombing practice in
                                       the course of which an engine failed leading
to a crash-landing at 2215 in a field near Little Bytham, 12 miles SSE from
Grantham, Lincolnshire. Some reports indicate that the Hampden finished up
straddling the Grantham to Peterborough railway line. Subsequently, P/O Crump
converted to Manchesters and was killed in a terrible accident at Waddington
on 15 September 1941, in which ten 207 Squadron airmen perished (see Bomber
Command Losses, Volume 2, page 146).

14 OTU   **Hampden I** **P2092**   **Enemy action**
Sgt R J Holborow   + T/o Cottesmore for night flying practice and,
P/O W E Cochrane   + reportedly, shot down by an enemy intruder at
Sgt W J Cunningham   + approximately 0050, the crash location being
                               given as the same as that in the summary above.
Sgt Holborow is buried in Cheltenham Cemetery; his crew lie in the extension
to Cottesmore (St. Nicholas) Churchyard. P/O Cochrane hailed from Dublin. It
will be recalled he had survived a serious crash on 28 February (see page 42).

10 Apr **11 OTU**   **Wellington I** **L4253**   **Enemy action**
1941   Sgt G D H Dutton   T/o Bassingbourn for dual night circuits and
                                       landings. In the course of the exercise, the
Wellington was shot down by Oblt Schulz of I./NJG2. This happened at around
0040, the bomber crash-landing at Ashwell station, 5 miles NE of Letchworth,
Hertfordshire. Although their aircraft was consumed by fire, neither pilot was
hurt. Sadly, Sgt Dutton was destined to lose his life when his 115 Squadron
Wellington crashed on 11 November 1941, during a fuel consumption test, (see
Bomber Command Losses, Volume 2, page 181).

Note. It is believed that in the aftermath of this incident, pilots assigned
for night dual circuit exercises carried an air gunner in the rear turret. As
various summaries will continue to show, enemy intruder activity, especially
over East Anglia, was adding to the strain of almost continuous night training activities.

17 OTU   **Blenheim IV** **N3591**   **Training**
Sgt B C Rowlands   + T/o Upwood for night flying practice. At
Sgt J D Graham   + 2110, probably due to engine failure, the
                               Blenheim crashed about 200 yards N of Warboys
railway station, Huntingdonshire. Sgt Rowlands is buried in Plymouth (Efford)
Cemetery; his air gunner lies in Aberdeen (Springbank) Cemetery, Peterculter.

17 OTU   **Blenheim IV** **V5519**   **Training**
Sgt D G Knight   T/o Upwood, with his wireless operator, to
Sgt Owen   engage in night circuit practice. At 2120,
                               while banking, flew into a lighting pole and
Sgt S McL Wells   inj crashed onto the flare path, bursting into
Cpl Brennan   inj flames. Both crew members managed to scramble
LAC D G Francks   inj clear but the seven airmen on flare path duty
LAC Plaister   inj were not so fortunate. All were rushed to RAF
AC1 G A Firth   inj Hospital Ely (Sgt Wells died in the ambulance)
AC1 L F R Trickett   inj where four succumbed to their injuries within
AC2 J B Tait   inj twenty-four hours. Sgt Wells and LAC Francks
                               were laid to rest in Bury Cemetery, while the
last three named were claimed by their next of kin.

17 OTU   **Blenheim IV** **V5732**   **Training**
Sgt A J Reid   inj T/o Upwood for a night training exercise.
Sgt Perkins   inj Became lost and, eventually, ran out of fuel
Sgt Gibbons   inj and crash-landed 2359, hitting some trees in
                               Boxworth Grounds near Childerlay Hall, some 6
miles WNW from the centre of Cambridge. All were taken to Addenbrooke's Hospital.
Prior to the crash, the Blenheim had been identified by Wyton but all efforts
to attract the attention of the crew went unrewarded. In 1942, now recovered
from his injuries, Sgt Reid was posted missing in action while flying Bostons
with 107 Squadron (see Bomber Command Losses, Volume 3, page 269).

Note. This had been a particularly bad night for 17 OTU with three Blenheims
written off, two aircrew killed and five others mortally injured.

13 Apr	19 OTU		Anson I	N9857	Training

13 Apr 1941 — **19 OTU** — **Anson I** — **N9857** — **Training**

F/O J H Steyn DFC	+ T/o Kinloss for a night navigation sortie.
P/O W E Drew	+ Returning over Cape Wrath the crew encountered
Sgt C McP Mitchell	+ extremely foul weather and soon after making
F/S T B Kenny	+ contact with base, the port engine failed.
Sgt J Emery	+ Height was lost and the Anson crashed near
Sgt H A Tompsett	+ Loch Meall nan Caorach at 2,300 feet and just
	over 2 miles NNW from the summit of Ben More

Assynt, about 3 miles ENE of Inchnadamph, Sutherland. Despite an extensive search, the wreckage of the aircraft was not discovered until 25 May 1941 and due to the remoteness of the crash site, the crew were buried nearby and a cairn erected. Their graves are the highest in the United Kingdom. A memorial has also been placed by CWGC at the entrance to Inchnadamph Old (Kirkton) Churchyard, Assynt. F/O Steyn hailed from Johannesburg in the Transvaal. He had flown a tour of operations with 10 Squadron. In June 1985, cadets from 2489 (Bridge of Don) Squadron Air Training Corps refurbished the cairn.

15 Apr 1941 — **10 OTU** — **Whitley V** — **T4178** — **Unknown**

Reported as burnt. On this day, The Right Honourable Sir Archibald Sinclair Bt CMG MP, Secretary of State for Air, visited Abingdon. He arrived, by air, at 1735 and after tea inspected ground training in progress and a Whitley. He took his departure, by air, at 1840.

17 OTU — **Blenheim IV** — **L4892** — **Training**

P/O A J Taylor	inj T/o Upwood for a low-level bombing exercise.
P/O T E Wooton	inj Lost power and at 0930 crash-landed, hitting
	some telephone wires and a hedge, roughly 2

miles E of Polebrook airfield and about the same distance ESE of Oundle in Northamptonshire. P/O Taylor was very seriously injured; P/O Wooton less so but he still required hospital treatment.

16 Apr 1941 — **13 OTU** — **Blenheim IV** — **V5881** — **Training**

Sgt C W Kerridge	+ T/o Bicester for a night navigation exercise
Sgt P J Cross	+ Crashed, it is reported due to engine failure,
Sgt G E Cook	+ in the Irish Sea between Rhyll and the Isle of
	Man. All are commemorated on the Runnymede
	Memorial.

17 Apr 1941 — **16 OTU** — **Anson I** — **R9653** — **Training**

Sgt R W H Baxter	T/o Upper Heyford for a cross-country but had
	only covered 200 yards when one of the unit's

Hampdens (P1145), which was taking off from a slightly different angle, ran into the rear of the Anson and totally wrecked the tail and rear fuselage. The pilot of the Hampden, P/O A C Potts, who was giving instruction to a trainee, admitted he failed to see the trainer. No one was hurt and the Hampden, which received damage to its nose and starboard wing, was repaired. Modified to torpedo bomber standards, it saw service with 455 Squadron and 5 OTU before being struck off charge on 3 January 1944.

16 OTU — **Hampden I** — **P2115** — **Training**

Sgt P C T Forster DFM	+ T/o Upper Heyford for practice bombing over the
Sgt W W Walker	+ Ot Moor ranges. During the exercise, the Hampden
Sgt K L Clarke	+ was in the process of diving when structural
Sgt B J Lodge	+ failure occurred and at least one wing came off
Sgt F E Hubank	+ as the aircraft plummeted to the ground at 0949
	at Fencott Bridge near Chalton on Ot Moor, some

6 miles NNE of Oxford. It will be recalled that Sgt Forster had recently been involved in a serious crash (see page 39), since when his DFM for service with 83 Squadron had been Gazetted on 11 February. A Bachelor of Science (Honours) graduate, he is buried along with Sgt Walker in Upper Heyford Cemetery; the others were taken to their home towns.

18 Apr 1941 — **11 OTU** — **Wellington I** — **L4302** — **Training**

P/O H H Boler RAAF	+ T/o Steeple Morden for dual night circuits.
Sgt F Fulford	+ Observed to be making an extremely low approach
	when, suddenly, the nose pitched up and the

aircraft stalled and crashed 0215 at Abington Pigotts, 4 miles NW of Royston, Cambridgeshire. Both pilots are buried in Bassingbourn cum Kneesworth Cemetery. It would seem that an air gunner had not, on this occasion, accompanied the crew.

18 Apr
1941

12 OTU   **Wellington IC P9300**   **Training**

P/O T M Couper RCAF	+	T/o Mount Farm to practice night circuits and
Sgt D McLean RCAF	+	landings. While trying to overshoot the run-
Sgt Wanek RCAF	inj	way, lost power; stalled and crashed 0058,
		hitting the corner of a farm building at

Watlington, Oxfordshire. Both Canadians are buried in the extension to Benson
(St. Helen) Churchyard; Sgt Wanek RCAF is noted as being dangerously injured.

Note. The RCAF Roll of Honour book erroneously describes the accident as
taking place in a Miles Master, a twin-seat trainer that was issued to the
unit in a supporting role.

20 OTU   **Wellington IC N2820**   **Training**

Sgt F S Hobden RNZAF	+	T/o Lossiemouth for night circuits and landings.
Sgt A W Hughes	+	During the exercise, visibility deteriorated and
		at 0027, following a low approach, the bomber

crashed into a hangar used by the Aircraft Repair Section. Sgt Hobden RNZAF
rests in Maresfield Church Cemetery, Sussex (his parent resided at Uckfield)
while Sgt Hughes was taken to Brafferton (St. Augustine) Churchyard.

19 Apr
1941

25 OTU   **Hampden I P1248**   **Training**

P/O R A P Allsebrook	inj	T/o Finningley to practice instrument flying.
P/O J B Ranson	+	Strayed into the Sheffield balloon barrage and
		following a collision with a tethering cable,

which took off part of the port wing, crashed 1626 into Concord Park, Rotherham
Road, Sheffield. P/O Allsebrook managed to parachute from the stricken Hampden
but P/O Ranson was not so fortunate and he is buried in Sheffield (City Road)
Cemetery. His second Christian name was unusual; Bohun. P/O Allsebrook made
a good recovery and went on to become an outstanding bomber pilot, gaining a
DSO and a DFC before being killed in action on 16 September 1943, while flying
with 617 Squadron (see Bomber Command Losses, Volume 4, page 321).

21 Apr
1941

10 OTU   **Whitley V N1411**   **Training**

P/O L S Davies	inj	T/o Stanton Harcourt for night circuit training.
	inj	Landed, circa 0100, but bounced and while trying
	inj	to go round again, lost control and crashed about
		a mile WSW of the airfield.

22 Apr
1941

13 OTU   **Blenheim I L1216**   **Training**

| P/O A Sabine | + | T/o Bicester as part of a formation. At the end |
| | | of the exercise, the formation leader signalled, |

by hand, to P/O Sabine indicating he should break off and land at nearby Great
Massingham airfield, Norfolk. When last sighted, the Blenheim was climbing and
it is assumed control was lost soon afterwards as it dived from about 2,000 feet
and crashed 2015 in the centre of the road in Little Massingham village, 11 miles
ENE of King's Lynn, Norfolk. Amazingly, no one on the ground was hurt and damage
was confined to overhead power lines. P/O Sabine, the sole occupant, is buried
in Kent at West Malling (St. Mary) Cemetery.

23 Apr
1941

18 OTU   **Anson I R3408**   **Training**

Sgt J B Molony	+	T/o Bramcote for a night navigation exercise.
P/O O Sablik PAF	+	Strayed approximately 20 miles off its intended
W/O S Ripley	+	course and entered the Midlands barrage balloon
F/S R Hanson	+	defences. At about 2338, the Anson collided
Sgt J Rudlicki PAF	+	with a cable and came down at Stole House,
		Walsgrave on Sowe on the eastern outskirts

of Coventry. The two PAF members of crew are buried in Nuneaton (Oaston Road)
Cemetery, while the rest were claimed by their next of kin. W/O Ripley, whose
trade was that of wireless operator mechanic/air gunner, had joined as a boy
in 1923. His skipper was Victor Ludorum, Wimbledon College in 1931.

24 Apr
1941

10 OTU   **Whitley V N1503**   **Training**

| F/L J O Lalor | | T/o Stanton Harcourt for night dual flying. |
| | | Landed rather heavily at 2215 and while taxying |

back to its dispersal pan, the undercarriage suddenly collapsed. Damaged beyond
repair, the Whitley was given the serial 3067M, later amended to 3073M. Sadly,
F/L Lalor was mortally wounded on 29-30 August 1941 (see Bomber Command Losses,
Volume 2, page 132), while flying with 102 Squadron. At the time of his death,
he had been promoted to S/L and likely held the position of Flight Commander.

24 Apr 1941	11 OTU	Wellington IA	N2912	–G		Enemy action

Sgt F N Alstrom + T/o Bassingbourn for night circuit training and
Sgt P N Nicholls inj while over the airfield, at 0050, was shot down
Sgt R Wilson + by Fw Gieszubel, I./NJG2. Out of control, the
stricken Wellington crashed onto another of the
unit's aircraft. Eighteen year old Sgt Alstrom is buried in Hove New Cemetery,
while Sgt Wilson, who was aged thirty, lies in Great Crosby (St. Luke) Churchyard
at Crosby. Sgt Nicholls is reported to have escaped with relatively minor wounds.

	11 OTU	Wellington IC	R1404		Enemy action

Destroyed, while parked on its dispersal pan, in
the manner described above. Both machines were burnt out.

26 Apr 1941	21 OTU D Flt	Anson I	R9611		Training

P/O J H Wetherly inj T/o Moreton-in-Marsh for a night navigation
P/O J G Brown inj exercise, which took the crew in the direction
of Peterborough. While returning to base, the
crew, comprising of three trainee navigators with their instructor and P/O Brown
who had joined the flight for experience, ran into bad weather. Eventually, with
the fuel gauges registering almost empty and unable to obtain any good responses
to their wireless signals, the order was given circa 0030 to bale out. All did
so and soon afterwards the Anson crashed a mile N from Nantbwych Station near
Tredegar, Monmouthshire. P/O Wetherly sustained a slightly sprained knee, but
P/O Brown suffered a broken leg and was admitted to Brecon Hospital; the rest
were uninjured. P/O Wetherly had recently completed a tour of operations with
214 Squadron; sadly, he was to lose his life in March 1943 while flying Halifaxes
with 76 Squadron (see Bomber Command Losses, Volume 4, page 84). In 1990, his
life was honoured by the book Portrait of a Bomber Pilot by Christopher Jary,
a foreword being contributed by the late Group Captain Leonard Cheshire VC OM.

	25 OTU	Anson I	N9848	–CE	Training

F/L E Coton T/o Finningley to practice night circuits and
Sgt H A Church landings and it was after one such landing that
the Anson ran into part of the Chance lighting
system, sustaining damage that was uneconomical to repair. No one was hurt.

28 Apr 1941	17 OTU	Blenheim IV	L9341		Training

Sgt Francis T/o Upwood. Crashed on return to base. No
Sgt Nullis injuries reported.
Sgt Page

29 Apr 1941	10 OTU	Whitley V	P4939		Training

P/O L S Bradburn + T/o 0115 Abingdon for night flying practice but
Sgt V G Pledge + crashed almost immediately, less than a mile NW
Sgt R N Birkhead + of the airfield. Eyewitnesses state that while
Sgt D F Percival + climbing away, the nose of the Whitley appeared
to drop, but was then pulled up sharply, leading
to loss of flying speed. All rest in various cemeteries. Sgt Birkhead's brother
Sgt George Thomas Birkhead died on 30 October 1940. A pre-war regular airman, he
is buried in Epsom Cemetery.

	18 OTU	Wellington I	L4297		Training

P/O B J Hawkes + T/o Bramcote for night circuit training only to
Sgt J Zwolski PAF + fly into trees and crash 0109 at Weston Hall,
Sgt T Szostak PAF + Bulkington, on the SE outskirts of Bedworth in
Sgt Z P Gaik PAF + Warwickshire. The three PAF members of crew
are buried in Nuneaton (Oaston Road) Cemetery,
while twenty year old P/O Hawkes, described as a pilot instructor, rests in
Brentford and Chiswick (New Brentford) Cemetery, Heston and Isleworth.

30 Apr 1941	11 OTU	Wellington IC	T2905		Training

P/O K G Evans + T/o Bassingbourn for a night navigation flight
Sgt L H Houghton inj but while flying at 2,000 feet, and off course,
Sgt J S Jones inj flew into a barrage balloon cable and crashed
Sgt T L Lever + circa 2150 into St. Andrew's Park, Bristol. P/O
Sgt C J Clarke + Evans lies in Bristol (Canford) Cemetery; the
Sgt E Wish inj others who died rest in their home towns. Sgt
Houghton joined 142 Squadron and was reported
a prisoner of war in March 1942 (see Bomber Command Losses, Volume 3, page 56).

30 Apr 1941	19 OTU F/L B Brooke	Whitley IV	K9045	Training

T/o Kinloss. Caught fire in flight and being unable to maintain height, F/L Brooke ditched the Whitley at 1550 in Findhorn Bay off the Moray coast, one member of crew being injured as a result.

3 May 1941	13 OTU Sgt D A B Statton	Blenheim IV	N6228 +	Training

T/o Bicester for solo circuits and landings. While banking to the left and preparing to line up with the runway, the Blenheim suddenly dived and crashed 1615 just short of the threshold. Sgt Statton, who had married Phyllis Statton (nee Howells) of Hammersmith in London is buried in Wales at Llantrisant (Trane) Cemetery. With his surname spelt as Stratton, he is commemorated in They Shall Grow Not Old, where his Christian names are given as Donald Allan, along with a note to the effect that although serving in the Royal Air Force he had been born in Ottawa.

4 May 1941	10 OTU	Whitley V	N1467 RK-Z	Training
	P/O C N Small		+	
	P/O W A M Halley		+	
	Sgt J A Mochan		+	
	Mr J Hitchcox		inj	
	Mrs F E Hitchcoc		+	
	Mstr K Hitchcox		inj	

T/o Abingdon for circuit training. At 1600 the Whitley crashed into a house at 31 Linton Road, Oxford. P/O Small rests in Brookwood Cemetery; P/O Halley was taken to Edinburgh (Liberton) Cemetery, while Sgt Mochan is buried in Bacup (Fairwell) Cemetery. An account of this awful tragedy, given by Christopher Tolkien, was reported in the April 2000 issue of the Bomber Command Association Newsletter.

	12 OTU Sgt W R Davey	Wellington IC	R1076	Training

T/o 1730 Benson but an engine failed and the Wellington crashed within the confines of the airfield. No injuries reported. Sgt Davey was shot down by a night-fighter in early August 1941 (see Bomber Command Losses, Volume 2, page 107). At the time he was flying with 101 Squadron.

	14 OTU	Hampden I	P4307	Training
	P/O Chase			
	Sgt Cowell			

T/o Cottesmore but the port engine cut, causing the bomber to swerve out of control and collide with Hampden I P4312 of the same unit, before finishing up in a hedge, where it caught fire. Neither airman was badly hurt and the other Hampden was repaired and returned to service.

	20 OTU P/O H S Thomas	Anson I	R3384	Training

T/o Lossiemouth for a night navigation sortie; base-Skerrymore-base. Became lost and despite many attempts to obtain QDMs, no assistance was forthcoming. Running low on fuel, and still unable to recognise any ground features, the crew baled out, leaving the Anson to crash circa 0400 near a bombing range in the Rose Valley, close to Kinloss airfield.

7 May 1941	11 OTU	Wellington IC	R3227	Enemy action
	F/O T J Warner		inj	
	P/O J McNally		inj	
	Sgt L F Stuart		inj	

T/o Bassingbourn for dual circuits. Visibility was clear, with a half-moon, and at around 0210 the flare path party caught sight of the bomber flying N of the airfield and on the downwind leg. To their alarm, they also saw a second aircraft, which was astern and slightly below the Wellington. As they watched, this aircraft opened fire, sending a volley of cannon shells into the bomber's port wing. F/O Warner immediately took over control, while P/O McNally jettisoned the cockpit escape hatch. On fire, the Wellington crash-landed near Wendy, a little over 10 miles SW from Cambridge, Both pilots were thrown out and finished up in a stream. Sgt Stuart was also pitched from his rear turret. F/O Warner was admitted to RAF Hospital Halton with severe burns to his head and neck, while his two companions were treated for their less serious injuries in SSQ Bassingbourn.

12 May 1941	17 OTU	Blenheim IV	V5391	Training
	Sgt K C Belton		+	
	Sgt N R Macmillan		+	
	Sgt W Hunter		+	

T/o Upwood tasked to fly a low-level exercise at less than 250 feet. Lost without trace, but believed to have crashed in the sea. All are commemorated on the Runnymede Memorial.

| 12 May 1941 | 22 OTU | Anson I N9846 | Enemy action |

Destroyed during an attack by the Luftwaffe on Wellesbourne Mountford in Warwickshire, bombs being dropped on the NE edge of the airfield. No casualties reported. This was the first of the unit's aircraft to be written off since its formation on 14 April 1941.

| 15 May 1941 | 16 OTU | Hampden I P1350 | Training |

Sgt M J Hopkins	+	T/o Upper Heyford for bombing practice but the
Sgt W K Clarke RCAF	+	port engine failed and the Hampden stalled and
Sgt J L Newton	+	spun into a field at 1221 to the W of Fritwell
Sgt H Crawford	+	and 6 miles NW of Bicester, Oxfordshire. Two,
AC2 R Robson	+	Sgt Clarke RCAF, who had graduated from the

University of Manitoba with a Bachelor of Arts degree and Sgt Newton lie in Upper Heyford Cemetery. Sgt Hopkins is buried in Keston Churchyard at Bromley; Sgt Crawford was taken back to his native Northern Ireland and Dunboe First Presbyterian Church Cemetery, while AC2 Robson is interred in Newbiggin (St. Bartholomew) Churchyard, Newbiggin-by-the-Sea.

| | 20 OTU | Anson I R3437 | Training |

F/O H S Thomas	+	T/o Lossiemouth for a navigation exercise. Ran
Sgt C N Weller	+	into a snowstorm and crashed 1650 at Stonewall
Sgt C Brissenden RCAF	+	Farm, 3 miles E of Banff. Sgt Brissenden RCAF
Sgt B A Headland	+	and Sgt Weller, who came from Tottenham, were
F/S E Hughes	+	buried in Lossiemouth Burial Ground, Drainie,
Sgt H King	+	while the others were taken to their home towns.

It will be recalled that F/O Thomas had been obliged to bale out from an Anson earlier in the month (see page 50). Since then, he had added a further three hours flying on type and at the time of his death he had flown a total of 496 hours, 58 of these on Ansons.

| 17 May 1941 | 14 OTU | Hereford I L6047 | Transit |

F/L R J Dunlop-Mackenzie		T/o Benson and headed for Cottesmore. When some
LAC Mountain		nine miles from its destination, the Hereford's
		port engine began to vibrate and not long after

it burst into flames. By this time the airfield was in sight and with commendable skill F/L Dunlop-Mackenzie crash-landed 1850, despite the flames having spread from the port mainplane and into his cockpit. F/L Dunlop-Mackenzie was killed on 25 March 1942, while flying Manchesters with 106 Squadron (see Bomber Command Losses, Volume 3, page 51).

| | 17 OTU | Blenheim IV V5565 | Training |

S/L W R Selkirk	inj	T/o Upwood for a cross-country exercise, during
P/O T R Hodgson	+	the course of which the Blenheim crossed the
Sgt P Savage	+	Lancashire coast. When 5 miles WSW of the
		Morecambe Bay Lightship, the port engine cut

in a left hand turn. This caused the bomber to yaw and fly into the sea. Those who died are commemorated on the Runnymede Memorial. S/L Selkirk recovered from his injuries and, having been promoted to W/C, was posted to command 21 Squadron. It is thought he was flying Blenheim IV Z7341 of the Squadron's Malta detachment and which failed to return to Luqa on 4 February 1942. The son of the Revd William Selkirk and Dora Selkirk, he is commemorated on the Malta Memorial.

| | 20 OTU | Wellington IC R3151 -J | Training |

Sgt E R Peacock	+	T/o Lossiemouth for combined gunnery, bombing
Sgt W C Henning	+	and aerial photography, the crews final task
Sgt A E Sanne	+	prior to posting to an operational squadron.
Sgt J F Smith	+	At roughly 1430, the Wellington was seen going
Sgt M J C Craig RCAF	+	into the waters of Spey Bay, 4 miles NNE from
Sgt J Whitbread	+	Buckie, Banff. All are commemorated on the

Runneymede Memorial. Sgt Peacock was the son of Dr. William Henry Peacock CBE and Mary Hamilton Peacock of Church Stretton.

| | 25 OTU | Hampden I L4124 | Training |

Sgt R S K Hickmott	+	T/o Finningley to practice landings using the
Sgt D G Crichton	+	Sandra floodlight system but crashed 0350, soon
Sgt E D Foster	+	after becoming airborne, at Rossington, 4 miles
		SE of Doncaster. Sgt Hickmott lies in Tunbridge

Wells Cemetery; Sgt Crichton is buried in Dundee Western Cemetery, while Sgt Foster rests in Whiston (St. Mary Magdalene) Churchyard.

18 May 1941	10 OTU		**Whitley V**	P5047	**Demonstration**

	Sgt I C A Morris	inj	T/o 1629 Windrush but the port tyre burst,
	F/L H G Dawson	inj	causing the Whitley to swing quite violently.
	Sgt D D Richardson	inj	Nonetheless, the bomber became airborne but a
	Sgt J T Smale	+	minute later stalled and hit the ground, cart-
	Sgt B R Turnidge	inj	wheeling and bursting into flames. Sgt Morris
	LAC P E Flux	inj	is shown as belonging to 10 OTU, but the others
	LAC Q S Moore	inj	belonged to the locally based 6 Flying Training
	LAC J S E Rawcliffe	+	School. Sgt Smale rests in Lydney (St. Mary)
	AC1 L J F Fletcher	inj	Churchyard, while LAC Rawcliffe is buried at
	AC1 A Foster	inj	Chingford Mount Cemetery.

18 May 1941	25 OTU		**Hampden I**	P1233	**Training**

	P/O P Dixon-Spain	+	T/o Finningley for a night navigation flight.
	Sgt B Halbert	+	Lost without trace. All are commemorated on
	Sgt E K Dawson	+	the Runnymede Memorial.
	Sgt T Morgan	+	

21 May 1941	17 OTU		**Blenheim IV**	L9388	**Training**

	Sgt L W Robertson Pryor	+	T/o Upwood for a navigation exercise. Crashed
	P/O G V Wilson	+	1630, while flying at high speed, on high ground
	Sgt J F Harrison	+	near the Peak and Beck reservoir, sighted close

to Dalton-in-Furness, 3 miles NNE of Barrow-in-
Furness, Lancashire. Sgt Robertson Pryor was brought back to Upwood and buried
in Bury Cemetery, but his two companions were claimed by their next of kin.

24 May 1941	17 OTU		**Blenheim IV**	V5750	**Training**

	Sgt A P Ward		T/o Upwood. On approach at 1600, lost power
			and crashed near the runway.

	17 OTU		**Blenheim IV**	Z5948	**Training**

	P/O P B Ashby		T/o Upwood. Overshot and crashed 1310, beyond
			the runway at Wyton, having landed downwind by

mistake. No injuries reported. Soon after this incident, P/O Ashby was posted
to 21 Squadron, losing his life during anti-shipping operations on 23 July
(see Bomber Command Losses, Volume 2, page 99).

29 May 1941	11 OTU		**Wellington IC**	R1299	**Training**

	P/O D M Weston	+	T/o Bassingbourn. Lost control while making
	Sgt W C Kasson RCAF	inj	an approach towards the runway at Cranfield
	P/O A L Walker RAAF	inj	aerodrome in Bedfordshire, crashing circa 0215
	Sgt E R Simpson RAAF	inj	some 2 miles SW of the airfield. P/O Weston,
	Sgt W J P Gibbons	inj	the sole fatality and the son of the Revd Percy
	Sgt P J C Watkins		Moss Weston, rests in Malvern Wells Cemetery,
			while of the injured, P/O Walker RAAF suffered

a compound fracture to one of his legs. The remainder were treated for minor
cuts and abrasions. Sgt Gibbons lost his life on 29 August 1943 while serving
at 29 OTU (see page 244); he lies in Elstree (St. Nicholas) Churchyard.

	17 OTU		**Blenheim I**	L8546	**Unknown**

Reported as crashed on this date, though, as
yet, no supporting evidence has been traced. The Blenheim had been issued to
Upwood on 12 September 1940.

30 May 1941	25 OTU		**Hampden I**	P1220	**Training**

	Sgt K Richardson	inj	T/o Finningley for solo flying practice. On
			return to base, overshot the runway and crashed

at around 1745 onto an airfield defence post. Visibility at the time was awful.

3 Jun 1941	11 OTU		**Wellington IC**	R1405	**Training**

	Sgt D G Ambrose	+	T/o Bassingbourn for night flying training.
	Sgt J G Turnbull	+	At approximately 0110, while preparing to land,
	Sgt J H Cooper RCAF	+	the Wellington went out of control and crashed
	Sgt H I Holroyd	+	near the flare path. Sgt Cooper, a Bachelor of
	Sgt P A L Lowe	+	Science graduate from the University of Toronto,
	Sgt L F Stuart	inj	lies in Bassingbourn cum Kneesworth Cemetery,
			while the others who died were taken to their

home towns. Sgt Stuart, who had just been pronounced fit to fly following his
accident on 7 May (see page 50), was very seriously injured.

4 Jun 1941	20 OTU	Wellington IA	N2885		Training
	F/L A G Griffin		inj		
	P/O A R Fitch		inj		
	Sgt L H Ellis		inj		
	Sgt L T Lawson RCAF		inj		
	AC2 A Learmouth		inj		
	AC2 V L Rose		inj		
	Gnr Aitchison		inj		

T/o Lossiemouth. Lost engine power and ditched at around 1405 in shallow water off Burghead, 7 miles WSW of Lossiemouth. As was customary, no one saw fit to enter any details of this crash in the unit's records, a failing that would continue until 1942, before a gradual increase in accident reporting becomes evident.

5 Jun 1941	10 OTU	Whitley V	P4940		Training
	Sgt G E Halstead RCAF		+		
	Sgt A Carty RCAF		+		
	Sgt J P Taylor RCAF		+		

T/o 1700 Abingdon for circuits and landings practice, in the course of which the weather worsened and the crew became lost. Regional Control, however, managed to make contact with the Whitley but while trying to establish his position, Sgt Halstead RCAF flew into a line of high-tension cables, carrying 132,000 volts, and crashed 1845 to the N of Hinton Waldrist and about 8 miles WNW from the town of Abingdon. All are buried in Brookwood Military Cemetery. It is noted that the CWGC register for Brookwood shows Sgt Carty RCAF as having only one Christian name, Arthur, but in the publication They Shall Grow Not Old, commonly referred to as the RCAF Roll of Honour, a second name, William, has been added.

8 Jun 1941	11 OTU	Wellington IC	R1728		Enemy action
	F/O W A Foster		+		
	P/O C W S Bristow		+		
	Sgt R P Burt RCAF		+		
	Sgt L Parry		+		
	Sgt E G Buckingham		+		
	Sgt W G N Hare		+		

T/o 1510 Steeple Morden for a navigation flight base-Helmsley-5415N 0145E-5320N 0200E-Manby-Wainfleet Sands-Cranwell-base, estimated time of arrival, 2010. Failed to return. On 21 June the Royal Navy Liaison Officer at Humber advised that a dinghy containing the bodies of Sgt Hare and Sgt Burt RCAF had been recovered by an RAF High Speed Launch at 5413N 0131E, but of the rest there was no sign. Their names are commemorated on the Runnymede Memorial. Sgt Burt RCAF, whose parents lived in Kent at Orpington, is buried in Brandesburton (St. Mary) Churchyard, while Sgt Hare of Palmer's Green in Middlesex was laid to rest in Hull Western Synagogue Cemetery, Kingston-upon-Hull. Another crew, similarly tasked, had reported clear weather along the route and in a report sent on 17 June 1941, Bas/1215/144/P1, paragraph 2 states, "It is reasonable to assume that such loss was caused by enemy action."

12 Jun 1941	17 OTU	Blenheim IV	Z5950		Training
	Sgt P Stocks				

T/o 1520 Upwood but an engine cut and Blenheim finished up, wrecked, on a mound near the bomb dump. It is not thought that anyone was hurt. Within a few weeks, Sgt Stocks was flying with 82 Squadron but failed to return from a raid on the Kiel Kanal (see Bomber Command Losses, Volume 2, page 105). He has no known grave.

	25 OTU	Hampden I	P2111		Training
	Sgt W Allison		+		
	Sgt J A Tyrrell		+		
	Sgt G T Corbett		+		
	Sgt H W White		+		

T/o Finningley for a combined navigation, air firing and practice bombing detail over the Bristol Channel. Lost without trace, though it is likely the bomber came down in the range area as the bodies of Sgt Corbett and Sgt White were washed ashore at Burnham-on-Sea. The former was taken to nearby Bridgwater (Quantock Road) Cemetery, while the latter lies in North Stoneham (St. Nicholas) Churchyard, Southampton. Their two companions are commemorated on the Runnymede Memorial, panels 38 and 53 respectively.

13 Jun 1941	15 OTU	Wellington IC	R1286		Training
	P/O G B Bainbridge		+		
	Sgt R G Cosgrave		+		
	Sgt H J Ford		inj		
	F/S W Powell		inj		
	Sgt J A Sellars		inj		
	Sgt W A Breeze		inj		
	Sgt N Scott		inj		

T/o Harwell on a cross-country exercise. While flying near Aberystwyth an engine failed and the crew turned about and headed in the direction of Worcester. Tragically, height could not be held and at around 1730 the bomber crashed into a bog on high ground 6 miles NE of Pontrhydfendigaid, a village on the W side of the Cambrians. F/S Powell was mortally injured and died while being taken to hospital. He is buried in Gretna Cemetery; P/O Bainbridge lies in Redcar Cemetery, while Sgt Cosgrave, the son of Capt Alexander Kilpatrick Cosgrave RAMC, was cremated at Golders Green Crematorium, Hendon.

13 Jun 1941	**25 OTU**	**Wellington IC**	**R1708**	**Enemy action**

F/S W R L Collyer + T/o Finningley for a night flying exercise. On
Sgt J F Markham + return to base at around 0150 and while in the
Sgt J E Jackson + airfield circuit was shot down by an enemy
Sgt J M Taylor + intruder, crashing at Misson, 9 miles NNW from
Sgt G E Blake + Retford, Nottinghamshire. Apart from Sgt Markham
F/S T A Grosvenor + of Stowupland in Suffolk, who was buried in the
extension to Finningley (St. Oswald) Churchyard,
all were claimed by their next of kin or relations as it is noted that the kin
of F/S Grosvenor who rests in Carisbrooke Cemetery, Newport on the Isle of Wight,
lived in India at Katihar, Bihar.

13–14 Jun 1941	**11 OTU**	**Wellington IC**	**R1723**	**Op: Nickel**

F/O A D R White inj T/o 2232 Steeple Morden and headed for France.
P/O E G Dumont inj Turned back, before reaching the south coast,
Sgt J S Parry RNZAF due to the engines overheating and an inability
Sgt T P Duffy RAAF to maintain altitude. The crew also experienced
Sgt C H Kilpatrick inj hydraulic failure and on touching down at 0020,
Sgt A H Bywater inj without flaps and with a negligible headwind,
Sgt F H Crowley RAAF the Wellington ran off the flare path and was
wrecked. The injuries sustained, although not
life threatening, were extremely painful and F/O White and Sgt Kilpatrick had
to be admitted to Adenbrooke Hospital. Soon after this incident, Sgt Parry RNZAF
formed his own crew and proceeded to 99 Squadron. On 28–29 September 1941, he
was posted missing (see Bomber Command Losses, Volume 2, page 153).

16 Jun 1941	**11 OTU**	**Wellington IC**	**R1022**	**Training**

F/S E Mirfin inj T/o Bassingbourn to practice landings with and
inj without the assistance of flaps. Overshot and
crashed 1145, totally wrecking the bomber. F/S
Mirfin was an experienced pilot with 174 of his 1,281 flying hours logged on
Wellington bombers.

	17 OTU	**Blenheim IV**	**T1932**	**Training**

Sgt L T Weston RNZAF T/o 1700 Upwood but an engine cut resulting in
the aircraft swinging out of control and ending
up with a broken undercarriage. No injuries.

	21 OTU	**Wellington IC**	**T2910**	**Training**

Sgt H J D Smiles DFM inj T/o Moreton-in-Marsh for night dual circuits and
landings, Sgt Smiles being the screened pilot.
At 0010, overshot the runway and with the power decaying, stalled and crashed
into trees on the N side of the airfield. A fire broke out and the bomber was
destroyed. This was the first of two accidents for Sgt Smiles (see page 71).

17 Jun 1941	**10 OTU**	**Whitley V**	**N1474**	**Training**

P/O Ali Raza Khan Pasha RIAF + T/o 2335 Abington but having climbed to 150 feet
P/O K P Chaudhury RIAF + dived in a left hand bank and crashed onto East
Sgt W E S Yerbury RCAF + House, Officers' Married Quarters, bursting into
Sgt J C Kenyon + flames. P/O Pasha RIAF who, prior to hostilities,
was an Assistant Surveyor, is buried in Brookwood
Military Cemetery; P/O Chaudhury RIAF was cremated at Golders Green Crematorium;
Sgt Yerbury RCAF also lies in Brookwood Military Cemetery, while Sgt Kenyon was
taken home for burial in Blackpool (Carleton) Cemetery. In the aftermath of this
dreadful accident, the Air Officer Commanding issued a Group Routine Order in
which he expressed his appreciation of the valiant efforts made by the Stations'
Fire Section to rescue the crew from the inferno of their aircraft.

	14 OTU	**Hampden I**	**P2088**	**Training**

F/S H G A Reed + T/o Cottesmore for night flying practice. While
Sgt A M Greenaway + nearing the runway at 2310, stalled and crashed.
Both members of crew are buried in the extension
to Cottesmore (St. Nicholas) Churchyard; Sgt Greenaway was aged eighteen.

18 Jun 1941	**14 OTU**	**Hampden I**	**P1211**	**Transit**

P/O A A Cooke + T/o Woolfox Lodge and headed for Cottesmore. On
Sgt L Dent + arrival, at 0920, the Hampden yawed and dived to
the ground. P/O Cooke rests in the extension to
Cottesmore (St. Nicholas) Churchyard; Sgt Dent was taken to his home town.

18 Jun   **16 OTU**   **Anson I** **R9652**   **Training**
1941   Sgt R W H Baxter   T/o Upper Heyford for a navigation exercise,
during which the port engine failed. While
attempting an emergency landing, his Anson crashed circa 1150 in the general
vicinity of Shipston-on-Stour, Warwickshire. This was Sgt Baxter's second
accident (see page 47) and by an odd quirk of chance the Anson identified in
this summary preceded off the production line the one written off in the April.

17 OTU   **Anson I** **R9643**   **Training**
Sgt G D Jessup   inj T/o Upwood for a navigation detail, in the
Sgt W S Blackadder   inj course of which an engine failed. Forced-landed
P/O F C Ashley   inj at approximately 1030 at Weston Subedge, 2 miles
Sgt A Gordon   inj NW of Chipping Campden, Gloucestershire.
Sgt J S Calderwood RCAF inj

17 OTU   **Blenheim IV** **V5820**   **Training**
Sgt P J Rolt   inj T/o 0215 Upwood for a night navigation exercise
Sgt G P Rake   inj but lost power and flew into a tree in Biggin
Lane while trying to regain the airfield.

20 OTU   **Wellington IC** **R1664**   **Training**
Sgt J F Barron   T/o Lossiemouth for a night cross-country. Lost
engine power and forced-landed 0315 on the coast
roughly a mile W of Kingston and 7 miles ENE of Elgin, Moray. No injuries.

19 Jun   **11 OTU**   **Wellington IC** **R3178**   **Training**
1941   F/S G F H Sayer   T/o Bassingbourn for night flying practice.
Sustained hydraulic failure and though the crew
were able to pump down the undercarriage, they were not so successful with the
flaps and at 0033 the Wellington finished up in the overshoot area, where it
caught fire. F/S Sayers, the screened pilot, had logged 1,210 flying hours,
no less than 700 of these on Wellingtons.

11 OTU   **Wellington IC** **W5706**   **Training**
Sgt K McLeod RCAF   T/o 2305 Bassingbourn but swung off the runway
P/O Kennedy RAAF   and lost its undercarriage. The accident was
attributed to slippage of the starboard engine's
pitch control lever. Having come to a halt, the bomber caught fire.

12 OTU   **Wellington IC** **R3296**   **Training**
Sgt H Ursell   + T/o Benson to practice night circuits and
Sgt H W Parry   + landings. At 0340, following three unsuccessful
Sgt K T Mitchell   + attempts to land, the bomber stalled and spun in
Sgt L O Hodnett   + at Drayton St. Leonard, 8 miles SSE of Oxford.
Sgt Parry was buried in the extension to Benson
(St. Helen) Churchyard; Sgt Ursell was taken to Brookwood Military Cemetery,
while their two companions are interred in cemeteries at their home towns.

16 OTU   **Hampden I** **P1210**   **Training**
P/O R R Michell   inj T/o Upper Heyford for a cross-country exercise.
Sgt E A McD Grange RCAF inj At around 1845, P/O Michell, a Rhodesian, tried
P/O A E Sinclair   + to land at Balderton airfield, Nottinghamshire,
Sgt R A C Connell   + after experiencing engine failure. While doing
so he missed his first approach and while trying
to go round again, the troublesome motor cut completely and the Hampden finished
up in a field near The Hall, with its wheels and flaps still down. A fire broke
out on impact. P/O Sinclair, he was aged 34, rests in Bedlay Cemetery, Cadder,
while Sgt Connell was taken to Lochwinnoch Cemetery. Of the two who were hurt,
P/O Michell sustained serious burns and a fractured leg, while Sgt Grange RCAF,
having made a good recovery from his injuries, was killed while flying with 467
Squadron on 15 August 1943 (see Bomber Command Losses, Volume 4, page 269).

16 OTU   **Hampden I** **AD831**   **Training**
Sgt J Goldman   + T/o Upper Heyford for a bombing detail but came
Sgt C W Davis RCAF   + down at 1545 at Baynard's Green on the NE side
F/O W H Corbett   + of the airfield. All rest in Upper Heyford
Sgt P Lally   + Cemetery. Sgt Goldman was of Bloemfontein in
the Orange Free State; Sgt Davis RCAF hailed
from Carbonear, Newfoundland and Sgt Lally came from Kilbeg, Co. Galway, Eire.

20 Jun 1941	13 OTU	Blenheim IV	L9238		Training

	Sgt T W Caston RCAF	inj	T/o Bicester for a navigation exercise, during
	Sgt J C Fisher RCAF	inj	which an engine failed and the crew were thus
	Sgt A Leigh	inj	obliged to ditch 1427 in the Irish Sea roughly

18 miles NW of The Chickens. All were picked
up by the trawler SS Sard. It is believed Sgt Caston RCAF and Sgt Fisher RCAF
went on to serve with 110 Squadron, both being commissioned. On 28 February
1942, while serving at the A & AEE Boscombe Down, they were killed when their
Albermarle P1368 crashed at Shalbourne in Wiltshire. Both rest in Brookwood
Military Cemetery.

	19 OTU	Whitley IV	K9047		Training

| | F/O R F S Marriott | | T/o Kinloss but the starboard engine cut and |
| | | | the aircraft ditched 1630 in Findhorn Bay off |

the Moray coast and only some 300 yards from the beach, becoming completely
submerged. The accident was witnessed by a number of groundcrew who promptly
launched a home-made raft and brought the entire crew ashore. It is noted that
F/O Marriott had accumulated 599 flying hours on Whitleys and 718 in total.

21 Jun 1941	11 OTU	Wellington IC	R1292		Training

	Sgt J M Thompson	inj	T/o Bassingbourn for a night flying detail.
	P/O R H Orton	inj	While in the circuit, the port engine failed,
	Sgt A W D Rutledge RCAF	inj	thus necessitating a forced-landing at 0215, in
	Sgt E H Garrod	inj	which the aircraft hit some trees to the W of
	Sgt W M Fraser RCAF	inj	Wendy, a little over 10 miles SW of Cambridge.
	Sgt S Oldfield	inj	Five days after the accident, P/O Orton died
	Sgt T St. C Harrison	inj	from his injuries; he is buried in Peterborough
			(Eastfield) Cemetery; Sgt Garrod lived for a

matter of hours and he now lies in Wandsworth Cemetery. Sgt Oldfield, too,
died shortly after the crash and he rests in Newsome (St. John) Churchyard,
Huddersfield. Sgt Fraser RCAF was, subsequently, posted to 57 Squadron but
lost his life on 1-2 April 1942 (see Bomber Command Losses, Volume 3, page 59).

	13 OTU	Blenheim IV	L9035		Training

	Sgt C R Digges RAAF	inj	T/o Bicester for a cross-country exercise. Shed
		inj	the propeller from its port engine and forced-
			landed 1530 near Wrexham, Denbigh. No one was

too seriously hurt and Sgt Digges RAAF went on to fly with 139 Squadron, gaining
a DFC before being killed on 18 December 1941. He is buried in Norwich Cemetery.

	14 OTU	Hampden I	P4316		Training

	Sgt N McLafferty	+	T/o 1114 Cottesmore for high-level bombing
	P/O I M Begbie	+	practice over the Grimsthorpe ranges but crashed
	Sgt A F Leach	+	a minute later about a mile SE from Cottesmore
	Sgt Thompson	inj	village. P/O Begbie was buried in the extension
			to Cottesmore (St. Nicholas) Churchyard, while

the other who died were taken to their home towns. All three are shown in the
registers as pilots.

23 Jun 1941	13 OTU	Blenheim IV	V5751		Training

	Sgt L M Taylor	+	T/o Bicester for local flying. Crashed 1250,
	Sgt L C Botterman	+	believed due to engine failure, to the N of
	Sgt W H K Annetts	+	Ambrosden and a shade over 2 miles SSE of the
			airfield. Sgt Taylor is buried in Southampton

(South Stoneham) Cemetery; Sgt Botterman lies at Potters Bar (St. Mary) Church
Cemetery, while Sgt Annetts was taken to South Tidworth (St. Mary) Church
Cemetery in Hampshire.

26 Jun 1941	19 OTU	Whitley V	N1379		Training

	Sgt H A Colbourne	+	T/o 0854 Kinloss but within a minute had smashed
	P/O K D Brant DFC	+	into the ground 500 yards SW from the local rail
	P/O R Rimmer	+	station. On impact, the bomber burst into flames
	Sgt D I McKiel RCAF	+	from which there was no escape. Both Canadians
	Sgt A W Morrow RCAF	+	and Sgt Colbourne, who was the son of Lt-Col
	F/S L B Tunstall	+	William Anthony Colbourne of the Indian Army,
			are buried in Kinloss Abbey Burial Ground. P/O

Brant rests in Worthing (Durrington) Cemetery; P/O Rimmer lies at Wimbleton
(Gap Road) Cemetery, while F/S Tunstall was taken to Aspatria (St. Kentigern)
Churchyard in Westmorland.

26 Jun
1941

21 OTU   **Wellington IC N2753**   **Training**
Sgt J F B Dawson   T/o Moreton-in-Marsh for a night navigation
                                  flight. Lost power and forced-landed at 0400
about a mile SW from Wolverton, Buckinghamshire. One member of crew (he has
not been named) was hurt.

22 OTU   **Wellington IC R1586**   **Training**
Sgt T L Kirk RCAF   +   T/o Wellesbourne Mountford for night circuit
Sgt F J Venn RCAF   +   practice. Lost power and it is believed the
Sgt D R White RCAF   +   bomber stalled while trying to avoid trees,
F/S A Bush   +   crashing 0210 near Loxley, 4 miles ESE from
Sgt J G Smithson   +   Stratford-upon-Avon, Warwickshire. Four, the
                                  three Canadians and F/S Bush, are buried in
Stratford-upon-Avon Cemetery, while Sgt Smithson was taken to Chapel Allerton
(St. Matthew) Old Churchyard, Leeds.

Note. These RCAF burials were the first of what would eventually total ninety-
seven Royal Canadian Air Force personnel, thus forming the largest contingent
amongst the 120 air force graves in this cemetery which, in total, has 155
servicemen interred. It is worth remarking that a number of the training units
made use of the cemeteries close to their airfields, but as the war progressed
Regional Cemeteries were established and use of the local churchyards declined
to the greater degree. Exceptions were Kinloss Abbey Burial Ground and, just
along the Moray coast, Lossiemouth Burial Ground. Serving the all too frequent
needs of 19 OTU and 20 OTU, these two cemeteries have a total of 151 Royal Air
Force and Commonwealth air forces graves (at Lossiemouth, there are one Polish
and eight Luftwaffe airmen interred).

27 Jun
1941

15 OTU   **Wellington IC N2817**   **Unknown**
                                  Form AM 78 shows allotment to 15 OTU on 11
January 1941 and damaged beyond repair on the date here shown.

23 OTU C Flt   **Wellington IC R1662**   **Training**
F/L B R Ker   T/o Pershore for a cross-country exercise.
Sgt K J Kellough RCAF   inj   At 1215, the Wellington crashed with some
                                  force in a field between RAF Bawtry and RAF
Finningley. Sgt H J Kellough RCAF sustained a broken leg and very serious burns
and he succumbed to his injuries the following day. His grave is in Doncaster
(Rose Hill) Cemetery. F/L Ker had arrived on the unit on 8 May 1941.

29 Jun
1941

13 OTU   **Blenheim IV Z5803**   **Training**
P/O H R Shuttleworth   T/o Bicester. Wrecked 1710, while making an
                                  emergency landing, due to engine trouble, at
Marsh Gibbon, 7 miles SSW of Buckingham. No injuries reported. Soon after
this incident, P/O Shuttleworth went to 82 Squadron only to be shot down in
late August 1941 (see Bomber Command Losses, Volume 2, page 126). He had
married Phyllis Evelyn Shuttleworth of Nairobi, Kenya.

16 OTU   **Hampden I P1148**   **Training**
P/O C D Magyer   T/o Brackley for night circuits and landings
Sgt A S Chantrell   during the course of which the weather became
                                  steadily worse and, eventually, the crew lost
sight of the flare path. At around 0330, the Hampden was abandoned and left
to crash a mile E of the airfield and close to Heath Farm. No one was hurt.
Sgt Chantrell went on to fly with 106 Squadron, failing to return from a mine
laying sortie in January 1942 (see Bomber Command Losses, Volume 3, page 24).

20 OTU   **Wellington I L4360**   **Training**
F/L A G Griffin   T/o Lossiemouth for night flying training.
                                  Crash-landed 0130 on rough ground, beyond the
runway, breaking the undercarriage. For F/L Griffin, this was his second
accident in less than a month (see page 53). His aircraft had been built
for the RNZAF and had been allotted the serial NZ305.

30 Jun
1941

14 OTU   **Hampden I P4300**   **Training**
P/O J S Curl   +   T/o Cottesmore for a night navigation exercise,
P/O J Mares   +   part of which involved the crew flying over the
Sgt C J Shadbolt   +   North Sea. Last heard on w/t at 0103. All are
Sgt A R Tout RNZAF   +   commemorated on the Runnymede Memorial.

5 Jul 1941	10 OTU	Whitley V	Z6667	Training
	F/S A E W Lynch	+	T/o Abingdon for night bombing practice. Broke	
	Sgt F C Adams RCAF	+	up in the air and crashed at approximately 0240	
	Sgt R G Stratton RCAF	+	at Garsington, 5 miles SE from the centre of	
	Sgt W A Bartleman RCAF	+	Oxford. On impact, the debris commenced to burn.	
	Sgt P H Morris	+	Two of the RCAF members of crew were taken to	
	Sgt G C P Sanderson	+	Brookwood Military Cemetery, but it seems likely	

that Sgt Bartleman RCAF of Edmonton, Alberta,
was claimed by a relative as he is buried in Scotland at Inverness (Tomnahurich)
Cemetery. The others who perished were taken to their home towns. F/S Keith
Robinson Stratton RCAF, brother to Sgt Stratton RCAF, was killed in a training
accident on 28 April 1943, when the Anson (N5379 of 3 OAFU) in which he was
flying crashed on Clee Hill, Shropshire. In total, five airmen (two of them
belonging to the RCAF) died. F/S Stratton RCAF was taken to Bridgnorth Cemetery.

7 Jul 1941	10 OTU	Whitley V	Z6476	Training
	F/L D U Lowson DFC	+	T/o Abingdon for a night navigation exercise in	
	P/O N McCarthy	+	moonlight conditions. Strayed from track and,	
	Sgt G E Buckingham RCAF	+	while flying at 2,000 feet, at roughly 0115 ran	
	Sgt G Farbrother	+	into a barrage balloon cable near Quinton, some	
	Sgt S F Drummond	+	6 miles SSW from Stratford-upon-Avon. On hitting	
	P/O J Graney	+	the ground, the Whitley burst into flames. All	

rest in various cemeteries within the United
Kingdom, Sgt Buckingham RCAF being taken to Brookwood Military Cemetery, as
were P/O McCarthy and Sgt Farbrother.

	17 OTU	Blenheim IV	V5532	Training
	Sgt G V Smith	inj	T/o Upwood for his second night solo on type	
	Sgt J Tippett DFM	inj	but at around 0010 overshot the runway and hit	
			a building near the airfield. Seven weeks	

later, while flying with 226 Squadron, Sgt Smith was reported missing (see
Bomber Command Losses, Volume 2, page 126). Sgt Tippett was amongst the first
airmen to win an immediate DFM when, as an LAC, he helped to beat off fighters
that were attacking his formation over the North Sea (see the London Gazette
published on 30 January 1940). Details of his squadron, however, have not been
appended.

	19 OTU	Whitley V	P5076	Training
	P/O H J Cooper RCAF	+	T/o Kinloss for a night cross-country during	
	Sgt G A Crompton	+	which the port engine seized. Crashed 0333 at	
	Sgt J H McInnes	+	Oldmeldrum, Aberdeen. The two RCAF members of	
	Sgt J C Steeves RCAF	+	crew lie in Dyce Old Churchyard; Sgt Crompton	
	P/O W E Merrifield	inj	rests at Ashton-in-Makerfield (Holy Trinity)	
			Churchyard, while Sgt McInnes is buried in	

Dalnottar Cemetery, Old Kilpatrick. P/O Cooper's brother, Sgt John Donald
Cooper RCAF, lost his life on 21 October 1942, while serving with 7 Squadron
(see Bomber Command Losses, Volume 3, page 244). P/O Merrifield was taken to
Kingseat Hospital (as were the bodies of those who perished).

8 Jul 1941	11 OTU	Wellington I	L4355	Training
	Sgt J Gordon RCAF	+	T/o Steeple Morden for night dual circuits and	
	Sgt N H Burnett RCAF	+	landings. After completing several efficient	
	Sgt F Gilliatt	+	circuits, the Wellington was observed at 0130	
			to stall and crash in an almost vertical dive	

near the airfield. Both Canadians lie in Bassingbourn cum Kneesworth Cemetery,
while Sgt Gilliatt was taken to Bedfont Church Cemetery. Sgt Burnett RCAF had
been injured in a flying accident on 7 January 1941, while under training at
Cap de la Madeleine in Quebec. Their aircraft had been intended for the RNZAF
as NZ304; it had flown a total of 321.50 hours.

10 Jul 1941	13 OTU	Blenheim IV	L9211	Training
	Sgt A R J Dick		T/o Bicester. Overshot 1330 the landing area,	
			due to a strong crosswind and wrecked when the	

port oleo dropped into a deep rut. This caused the undercarriage to collapse
and in turn the Blenheim caught fire. Sgt Dick was unhurt but on 26 August
1941, while flying with 82 Squadron, he was shot down by fighters off Heligoland
(see Bomber Command Losses, Volume 2, page 126). Like so many airmen who flew
with the Blenheim squadrons of 2 Group, he is commemorated on the Runnymede
Memorial.

10 Jul
1941
27 OTU   **Wellington IC T2467**   **Training**
Sgt S D L Hood RNZAF   T/o Lichfield but a tyre burst and the bomber
                                 overran the runway and hit an obstruction. No
one was hurt, but the Wellington was damaged beyond repair. Apart from a brief
spell (20 October to 7 November 1940) spent with 311 Squadron, this aircraft
had spent most of its time in storage units and since acceptance at 22 MU
Silloth on 14 June 1940, had logged a mere 25.05 flying hours. Sgt Hood RNZAF
had served with 149 Squadron and by the time of his death with 1656 HCU on
17-18 January 1943 (see Bomber Command Losses, Volume 4, page 23) he had been
commissioned and mentioned in dispatches.

11 Jul
1941
16 OTU   **Hampden I X3003**   **Training**
Sgt C A Snelling   T/o 0029 Upper Heyford for night circuits and
                                 landings but as the Hampden lifted from the
runway, it swung violently to the left. Believing his port engine had failed,
Sgt Snelling closed the throttles, whereupon the Hampden hit the ground and
was destroyed by a fire which broke out from the starboard engine.

16 OTU   **Hampden I AD849**   **Training**
P/O D G L Buckley   +   T/o 1608 Upper Heyford for bombing practice and
P/O P L Nash RCAF   +   crashed almost immediately at Home Farm, S of
Sgt J T Traviss   +   the hamlet of Rousham on the W bank of the River
Sgt L A Webster   +   Cherwell and SW of the airfield. Eyewitnesses
                                 tell of the Hampden performing a series of
dives, followed by steep climbs, and it is thought likely that P/O Buckley (he
came from Pondoland in South Africa's Cape Province where his father, the Revd
Canon Arthur Neil Litt Buckley had a parish) cracked his head against the canopy
and was thus rendered unconscious. With P/O Nash RCAF, he is buried in Upper
Heyford Cemetery. Sgt Traviss lies in Hendon Cemetery, while Sgt Webster was
taken to Ilford Cemetery.

12 Jul
1941
17 OTU   **Blenheim IV Z6360**   **Training**
Sgt R J Smith   +   T/o Wyton to practice landings with wireless
P/O R O Boon   +   assistance. Lost control and failed to recover
Sgt J Tinker   +   from a spin before crashing 1545 at Old Halves,
                                 near Chatteris, Cambridgeshire. Sgt Smith is
buried in Bury Cemetery but Sgt Tinker of Sheffield was taken to nearby Ramsey
Cemetery. P/O Boon rests at Plymstock (St. Mary and all Saints) Churchyard in
his native Devon.

15 Jul
1941
13 OTU   **Blenheim I L6768**   **Training**
Sgt F L Trevillo RCAF   inj   T/o 0100 Hinton-in-the-Hedges for solo night
                                 circuit training. Turned very late onto finals
and as a result lost sight of the flare path. Tightening the bank, he failed to
see some trees and crashed near the airfield. It is said that Sgt Trevillo RCAF
was very seriously injured but it appears he made a good recovery and eventually
returned to Canada.

14 OTU   **Anson I R3386 -W1**   **Training**
F/S Harpham   inj   T/o Cottesmore only to be hit by one of the
Sgt MacCallum   inj   unit's Hampdens, which was landing without
Sgt Lever   inj   first receiving permission. F/S Harpham was
Sgt Hyland   inj   taken to RAF Hospital Rauceby suffering from
                                 shock and with lacerations to his left arm and
                                 forehead, above his left eye.

14 OTU   **Hampden I P1289**   **Training**
                                 Wrecked in the circumstances described above.
The name of the pilot has been omitted from unit records; furthermore, as yet
an accident card has not been traced.

16 Jul
1941
13 OTU   **Blenheim I L6767**   **Training**
Sgt F L Turner RCAF   +   T/o Bicester to practice solo night circuits and
                                 landings but after overshooting the runway, came
down at 0125 in trees near the village of Launton, just over a mile E of Bicester
town centre. Sgt Turner RCAF rests in Caversfield (St. Laurence) Churchyard.
A little less than a year previous, on 8 August, P/O Raymond had crash-landed
this Blenheim while landing at Bicester; he escaped injury.

17 Jul 1941	13 OTU	Blenheim IV	R3805	Training

Sgt D G Calderone RCAF   +   T/o Finmere for a navigation exercise. While in
Sgt G D Davies   +   the circuit, both engines cut and the Blenheim
Sgt Griffiths   inj   crashed 1745 into Shelswell park, SW of the air-
field and near the villages of Cottisford and
Hethe, Oxfordshire. Sgt Calderone RCAF rests in Kensal Green (St. Mary's) Roman
Catholic Cemetery, Hammersmith, while Sgt Davies is interred at Haverfordwest
(Prendergast) Cemetery.

	14 OTU	Hampden I	P1278	Training

P/O J N Bowker   +   T/o 1619 Cottesmore for P/O Bowker's first solo
Sgt J W Rowe   +   on type but as he climbed away from the airfield,
the Hampden smashed into the ground, about a mile SE of the airfield, bursting
into flames. P/O Bowker, a Canadian serving with the Royal Air Force, lies in
Market Overton (St. Peter and Paul) Churchyard, while his wireless operator was
laid to rest in the extension to Cottesmore (St. Nicholas) Churchyard.

19 Jul 1941	27 OTU	Wellington IC	R1366	Training

Sgt R L Cox RCAF   inj   T/o Lichfield for night circuit training. At
0135, an engine failed as the Wellington came
into land and a wing clipped one of the hangars. Sgt Cox RCAF tried to keep
control but was unable to prevent a crash-landing. Posted to 142 Squadron, he
was killed on 2 June 1942 (see Bomber Command Losses, Volume 3, page 113).

20 Jul 1941	19 OTU	Whitley IV	K9036	Training

P/O W B Mackley   T/o 1445 Kinloss but lost engine power and came
Sgt Allen   inj   down a minute later near the airfield. The aircraft was struck off charge on 6 October 1941.

21 Jul 1941	10 OTU	Whitley V	N1527	Training

P/O P M Gray RNZAF   +   T/o Abingdon for night circuits and landings.
P/O H G C Fooks RNZAF   +   Flew into trees and crashed 0130 some 2 miles
Sgt R Harley   +   S of the airfield. Both New Zealanders rest
Sgt K Lunn   +   in Brookwood Military Cemetery. Their three
Sgt A E Williams   +   colleagues were claimed by their next of kin.
On 7 January 1944, F/O Ernest Berjen Fooks RNZAF,
brother to P/O Fooks RNZAF, was killed when his 180 Squadron Mitchell II FR396
collided in the air with a 98 Squadron machine while returning to Dunsfold from
a raid on la Sorellerie in France. He, too, lies in Brookwood Military Cemetery.

22 Jul 41 1941	10 OTU B Flt	Anson I	N5070	Training

F/L J E Carter MID   +   T/o Abingdon for a night navigation exercise.
Sgt F Corlett DFM   +   Crashed at around 0330 on high ground a mile or
Sgt J Neal RAAF   +   so NW of Westbury, Wiltshire. F/L Carter was
F/S E R Lines   +   OC B Flight and was an extremely able pilot with
Sgt T E Comins   +   1,065 of his 1,338 flying hours being logged on
Anson trainers; he rests in Herne Bay Cemetery.
Three were taken to Brookwood Military Cemetery, while Sgt Corlett lies in Kirk
Maughold (St. Maughold) Churchyard on the Isle of Man. His DFM had been Gazetted
on 17 January 1941, following a tour of operations with 77 Squadron.

	11 OTU	Wellington IC	R1334	Enemy action

Sgt F S Houston RCAF   +   T/o Steeple Morden. Destroyed as a result of a
F/S W A Hannah   +   mid-air collision with Ju 88C-4 R4 + Bl Werke Nr,
Sgt B C Thompson RAAF   +   0842 of 3./NJG2 at 0119 over Ashwell, 6 miles NE
Sgt C M S Lewis   +   from the centre of Letchworth, Hertfordshire.
F/S J Stewart   +   All are buried in various cemeteries within the
Sgt R E Hibbert   +   United Kingdom. The Luftwaffe crew, identified
Sgt P T Manning RCAF   +   below, had taken off from Gilze-Rijen in Holland.
Sgt R A McAllister RAAF   +

Lt Heinz Völker   +   As reported in Deutsche Nachtjagd, Personalver-
Fw Andreas Würstl   +   luste in Ausbildung und Einsatz - fliegendes
Uffz Herbert Indenbirken +   Personal - by Michael Balss published in 1997.

	13 OTU	Blenheim IV	L8876	Unknown

Struck off charge on 1 August 1941, with a total
of 921.20 flying hours appended, following a flying accident on this date.

22 Jul   **16 OTU**   **Hampden I** **P5305**   **Training**
1941   P/O M W Major   +   T/o Brackley for a night navigation exercise.

P/O M W Major		+	T/o Brackley for a night navigation exercise.
Sgt Butler		inj	Undershot the runway and came down at 0315 in
Sgt D F Stephen		inj	a field adjacent to the airfield. P/O Major,
Sgt A C Willis		inj	the son of the Revd Henry Dewsbury Alves Major

is buried in Upper Heyford Cemetery. A graduate of Exeter College, Oxford, P/O Major had until recently been Clerk to the High Court of Justice in Southern Rhodesia. Sgt Butler suffered a fractured left arm but Sgt Stephen and Sgt Willis escaped relatively lightly.

17 OTU   **Blenheim IV** **L9412**   **Training**

Sgt C W Andrews RNZAF	+	T/o Upwood for a night navigation sortie; base-
P/O R T Franklin	+	York-Helmsley-5410N 0200E-5320N 0200E-Market
Sgt L R Palmer	+	Rasen-base. Called Upwood on w/t, soon after

departure and three minutes later sent another signal advising that it was switching to the Andover Direction Finding frequency. Nothing further was heard and it is assumed that some catastrophe overtook the crew, while they were over the North Sea. The first two named are commemorated on the Runnymede Memorial, but the body of Sgt Palmer was washed onto a dyke at Bensersiel, opposite the German island of Langeoog, on 14 September 1941. He was buried in the Evangelical Parish Friedhof at Esens (Wittmund), since when his remains have been exhumed and taken to Sage War Cemetery, Oldenburg.

Note. Much of this information has been extracted from a letter, dated 7 April 1949, written by the staff of Headquarters RNZAF at Halifax House in London.

25 OTU   **Hampden I** **AE149**   **Training**

P/O W H Andrews	inj	T/o Finningley for night flying practice. While airborne, Sgt C G Furby crash-landed at 0145,

his Hampden I P1236 finishing up on the flare path with a broken undercarriage. While the clearance of this machine was in progress, P/O Andrews returned and was instructed to orbit. While doing so, his port engine cut and he was obliged to force -land at 0250. His aircraft was damaged beyond repair but Sgt Furby's Hampden was later returned to service.

24 Jul   **11 OTU**   **Wellington IC** **N2747**   **Training**
1941

Sgt J J Mundy RAAF	inj	T/o Bassingbourn for night flying practice.
Sgt A R Mills RAAF	inj	Stalled and crashed 0331 at Whaddon, 10 miles
Sgt J H Overy	+	SW of Cambridge. Sgt Overy was taken to his home town and buried in Lowestoft (Kirkley)

Cemetery. The indications are that both Australians escaped serious injury.

16 OTU   **Hampden I** **P1269**   **Training**

Sgt E W Phillips	inj	T/o Upper Heyford for solo instrument flying. While trying to land at 1715, overshot the

runway and crashed into a hangar. The wreckage caught fire and Sgt Phillips, whose nose had been broken, owes his life to the prompt actions of W/O J B McGinn who pulled the stunned pilot clear of the flames. After making a good recovery, he was posted to 49 Squadron, only to become one of the sixty-four airmen that lost their lives during Operation Fuller on 12 February 1942 (see Bomber Command Losses, Volume 3, pages 30 and 31).

21 OTU   **Wellington IC** **T2458**   **Training**

F/O C F Sutcliffe	+	T/o Moreton-in-Marsh for a combined night
Sgt I R Mackintosh	+	cross-country and bombing practice over the
Sgt J N Snowden	+	Radway ranges. Reported to have completed the
Sgt J F MacMillan RCAF	+	bombing phase when, at 0112, the Wellington
F/S A H Bell	+	went out of control and crashed into Ufton
Sgt E R Kennedy RCAF	+	Wood, NE of the hamlet of Ufton and 5 miles
Sgt K T Robertson RAAF	+	ESE of Royal Leamington Spa, Warwickshire. However, five were taken some distance and

laid to rest at Long Lawford (St. John's Chapel) Churchyard, which is W of Rugby. F/S Bell and Sgt Snowden were claimed by their next of kin. Their skipper, F/O Sutcliffe was a Canadian, serving with the Royal Air Force on a Short Service Commission during which he had wed Blanche Olive Sutcliffe of Cheltenham; it is further noted his father was the Revd Joseph Fletcher Sutcliffe BD. Sgt Mackintosh's parents resided at Estado do Rio, Brazil. Concerning F/S Bell's CWGC register entry, this indicates he belonged to 149 Squadron and, thus, it is likely he had recently been screened.

25 Jul
1941

11 OTU   **Wellington IC** **R1148**   **Training**
P/O R M Hill   +   T/o Bassingbourn for a night cross-country.
P/O C H Brown   +   Came down at 2355 on the W side of Spalding,
Sgt K G Chamberlain   inj   Lincolnshire and burst into flames. Three lie
Sgt E Shipley   +   in Sutton Bridge (St. Matthew) Churchyard (the
P/O C E B Jones   +   majority of the fifty-six airmen buried here
F/S F C Crook   +   lost their lives while undergoing training at
                              6 OTU (later 56 OTU)). Sgt Shipley and P/O
Crook were taken to their home towns. Sgt Chamberlain escaped with no more
then a cut above his right eyebrow and an injury to his right shoulder.

17 OTU   **Blenheim I** **L6800**   **Training**
Sgt A H A Johnson   +   T/o Upwood. Crashed on the airfield boundary.
                              Sgt Johnson is buried in Brookwood Military
Cemetery; he hailed from Lancashire and St. Anne's-on-Sea.

26 Jul
1941

20 OTU   **Wellington I** **L4333**   **Training**
P/O J D Royal   T/o Lossiemouth for dual conversion training.
                              Wrecked, following a misjudged landing. P/O
Royal was a staff pilot who would serve with great distinction until, sadly,
he was killed, still at 20 OTU, in a fatal crash on 18 May 1942.

27 Jul
1941

10 OTU B Flt   **Anson I** **R3306**   **Army Cooperation**
F/O A D Frampton DFC   +   T/o Abingdon for a sortie concerned with an
P/O W H Arnold RCAF   +   exercise "Battle of Reading". Hit trees and came
Sgt G E Fleming RCAF   +   down at approximately 0930, near the army camp at
Sgt R E Woolston   +   Tilehurst in Berkshire. The first three named lie
                              in Brookwood Military Cemetery. Sgt Woolston was
                              taken to Stockport Borough Cemetery.

19 OTU   **Whitley IV** **K9033**   **Training**
F/S Sampson   T/o Kinloss for night circuits and landings.
Sgt K Greene   Ditched 0235 some 2 miles off the Moray coast.
Sgt Walley   All took to their dinghy and were picked up,
Sgt White   unharmed, by an air-sea rescue launch. F/S
Sgt Carmen   Sampson had been involved in a serious crash
Sgt Walker   on 27 February (see page 42).

28 Jul
1941

10 OTU   **Whitley V** **T4323**   **Training**
Sgt C Cawthorne   +   T/o Abingdon for night bombing practice. While
Sgt P P Chapman RCAF   +   overshooting the runway and banking to the left
P/O P C Chappell   +   the Whitley flew into trees and crashed at 0215
Sgt J B Kamedish RCAF   +   near the airfield. Sgt Cawthorne is buried in
Sgt C Pullan RCAF   +   Sheffield (Crookes) Cemetery; the three RCAF
                              members of crew were taken to Brookwood Military
Cemetery, while P/O Chappell rests in Dunstable Cemetery.

21 OTU   **Wellington IC** **X3198**   **Training**
Sgt C G A Christy   +   T/o Moreton-in-Marsh for the captain's first
Sgt G M Scott   +   solo cross-country. This ended on Carn Fadrum
Sgt G S Parry   +   (1,206 feet above sea level) after the crew
Sgt W J Chevers RCAF   +   ran into fog near Llaniestyn, 7 miles WSW from
Sgt W H Hindle RCAF   +   Pwllheli, Caernarvon. Five, the four Canadians
Sgt H B Webster RCAF   +   and Rhodesian born Sgt Scott of Salisbury, are
Sgt C C Ostenfeld RAAF   +   buried in Pwllheli Borough Cemetery; Sgt Christy
                              lies in Hendon Cemetery, while Sgt Parry was
taken to West Wickham (St. John The Baptist) Churchyard, Beckenham.

30 Jul
1941

19 OTU   **Whitley V** **N1426**   **Training**
P/O J H Eastwood   +   T/o Kinloss for a night navigation exercise
Sgt W E Snell RCAF   +   and homing on wireless bearings. Crashed 0245
Sgt L W Harris   +   and caught fire after flying into trees atop a
Sgt A A Rodgers RCAF   +   600 foot hill at Relugas, 7 miles SSW of Forres,
Sgt N D Downie RCAF   inj   Moray. Weather conditions were extremely poor.
                              Of the four killed, two are buried in Kinloss
Abbey Burial Ground; P/O Eastwood, formerly a 2Lt in the RASC and the son of
the Revd John Hastings Eastwood and Jessie Rose Eastwood (née Wallace) from
Wallington in Surrey, was cremated at Aberdeen Crematorium. Sgt Harris was
taken to Harborne (St. Peter) Churchyard, Birmingham.

30 Jul	20 OTU	Wellington IC	N2826 JM-Z		Training

30 Jul 1941 — **20 OTU** — **Wellington IC** — **N2826 JM-Z** — **Training**

P/O R N Rostance — inj
Sgt D P Langley — inj
Sgt J A Redgrave — inj
Sgt Hood
Sgt A L Smith — inj
Sgt C G Leverrier RCAF — +

T/o Lossiemouth for navigation and bombing practice. At around 1715, the Wellington flew into trees while trying to make an emergency landing near Keith, Banffshire. The wreckage caught fire. Sgt Leverrier RCAF is buried in Lossiemouth Burial Ground, Drainie.

20 OTU — **Wellington IC** — **R1093** — **Training**

P/O P B De Normanville — inj
Sgt C F Richards — +
P/O P Alderson DFM — +
Sgt S St. H G Dunn RCAF — +
Sgt C G Crombie RCAF — inj
Sgt K J Seaman — +

T/o Lossiemouth for a night cross-country and while descending through cloud at 0223, hit Carn Garbh near Helmsdale on the Sutherland coast. Of those who died, Sgt Dunn RCAF is buried in Wick Cemetery, while the others were claimed by their next of kin. P/O Alderson gained his award, Gazetted 22 November 1940, while serving with 15 Squadron. After making a good recovery, Sgt Crombie RCAF lost his life when his Wellington crashed in West Africa on 19 October 1942. He rests in Fajara War Cemetery, Gambia.

20 OTU — **Wellington IC** — **R1170** — **Training**

Sgt W J Spicer — +
Sgt C E W Bonser — +
Sgt K F Druhan RCAF — +
Sgt M G Wilson RCAF — +
Sgt W Degg — inj
Sgt J Chivers — inj

T/o Lossiemouth similarly tasked. While heading for base, encountered heavy driving rain which reduced visibility almost to nil. Confident that they were clear of high ground, the crew dropped down to 500 feet, only to fly into the waters of the Moray Firth, some 5 miles NW of the airfield. Of the four who perished, all are commemorated on the Runnymede Memorial. The wreckage of their aircraft was later found by the crew of a local drifter.

31 Jul 1941 — **13 OTU** — **Blenheim I** — **L6680** — **Training**

Sgt Graham — inj

T/o Bicester for a solo exercise. Landed at Chipping Warden and while doing so, collided with a Wellington. It is not thought that Sgt Graham was seriously injured.

14 OTU — **Hampden I** — **P2128** — **Training**

Sgt D Calvert

T/o Cottesmore. Encountered bad visibility and crashed 1130, while attempting to land at Scampton airfield in Lincolnshire.

2 Aug 1941 — **12 OTU** — **Wellington I** — **L4248** — **Unknown**

Reported to be undergoing repairs on site, on this date, but struck off charge on 2 September 1941.

3 Aug 1941 — **25 OTU** — **Wellington IC** — **X3177** — **Training**

F/O H T Gilbert DFC — +
P/O W H Crane RAAF — +
P/O G L Cohen RAAF — +
Sgt H Soar — +
Sgt E J Matthews — +
Sgt W Harrison — +

T/o Finningley for a night training exercise. At some time between 0430 and 0530, the bomber hit the ground, at high speed, roughly 3 miles SW of Bawtry, Nottinghamshire. Three lie in the extension to Finningley (St. Oswald) Churchyard and three were taken to their home towns.

5 Aug 1941 — **20 OTU** — **Wellington IC** — **N2828** — **Training**

P/O H W Griffin — +
Sgt N D Cryer — +
P/O R B Ingalls RCAF — inj
P/O E A Dare — +
Sgt S F McDonnell — inj
Sgt K R Cox — inj

T/o Lossiemouth for air-to-air firing at a towed drogue. On completion of the exercise, the crew returned to base in conditions of high winds and rain, which seriously reduced visibility. Thus, P/O Griffin failed, until the last moment, to see some trees as he made his approach and while taking avoiding action he stalled the Wellington and crashed, heavily, at 1645 near the airfield. Those who perished are buried at various locations within the United Kingdom.

6 Aug 1941 — **20 OTU** — **Wellington IC** — **T2725** — **Training**

P/O J D Royal

T/o Lossiemouth. Crashed 1340, while making an emergency landing, due to engine failure, at Kirktown of Deskford, roughly 4 miles SSW of Cullen, Banff. It will be recalled that P/O Royal, a staff pilot, had crashed as recently as 26 July (see page 62).

6 Aug 1941	25 OTU C Flt	Hampden I	P4342	Training

P/O D S Jackson · T/o Finningley for an air-to-air firing sortie with a Fairey Battle target tug. At about 1215, the Hampden, which was then flying at 600 feet, banked to the left and finished up in a stabilised yaw. With insufficient height in which to recover, the bomber flopped into Bridlington Bay, some 2 miles ESE of the town. Forty minutes later, an RAF Air-Sea Rescue launch plucked the crew from their dinghy, unharmed.

6- 7 Aug 1941	11 OTU	Wellington IC	Z8807	Op: Nickel

F/S J A Walker RCAF	pow	T/o Bassingbourn. Last heard on w/t at 0615, by
W/O R Charlesworth	pow	which time the Wellington was in the vicinity of
W/O T Humphery	pow	Rotterdam. Roughly 15 minutes later, the bomber
W/O R C Mackenzie RAAF	pow	came down near the hamlet of Greup (Zuid Holland)
W/O L E Sparks	pow	5 km SE of Oud Beijerland. Theirs was the first
W/O S J Pryor	pow	crew from a bomber OTU to be posted missing and,
		tragically, five gallant Dutch civilians were to
Bastiaan Arie Barendrecht	+	pay with their lives for trying to assist them
Joris de Heus	+	evade capture. This atrocity was carried out on
Pieter Kruijthoff	+	19 September 1941, while three of their fellow
Arie van Steensel	+	countrymen received long terms of imprisonment.
Arie van der Stel	+	Their gallantry was remembered a year later with
		the release of the film "One of our Aircraft is

Missing", the opening sequences showing a letter from the Dutch Government in exile (in London) which mentioned their names and recording the terrible fact that they had been shot by the Germans.

Note. I am indebted to Henk Noontenboom and Gerrie Zwanenburg MBE for sending me details of the crash location and the identification of the five patriots and their subsequent commemoration in the Pinewood Studios film.

7 Aug 1941	20 OTU	Anson I	R9584 ZT-J	Training

F/O P B Doorly	+	T/o Lossiemouth. It is believed that the
G/C J E Tennant DSO MC	+	Anson's starboard engine failed, shortly before
P/O A G Gill	+	the trainer crashed at 1200 onto high ground in
P/O H E Waite	+	Glen Avon, 6 miles SW of Tomintoul, a village
Sgt T C Gallant	+	roughly 20 miles NW of Ballater, Aberdeen. All
F/S G W Hemsley	+	rest in various cemeteries across the United
Sgt W H Petratos	+	Kingdom, that for 51 year old G/C Tennant being
AC2 J Edgecombe	+	at Innes House Private Burial Ground, Urquhart
		in Moray.

9 Aug 1941	27 OTU	Wellington IC	R1145	Training

P/O J H Wiley RCAF	inj	T/o Lichfield for a night exercise. Landed 0445
P/O G H Temple RCAF	inj	in error at Bramcote's Q site and ran into an
	inj	obstruction. An investigation into the cause
		of this accident reported that the controller

at the Q site should have doused all lights, once it was realised the crew were not responding to the red Verey signals being fired as a warning.

10 Aug 1941	27 OTU	Wellington IC	R1806	Unknown

Form AM 78 indicates that the Wellington was destroyed on this date, but no supporting aircraft accident card has yet been traced. Allotted to 27 OTU on 18 May 1941, unit records show acceptance eight days later. No record of its flying totals have been appended.

11 Aug 1941	25 OTU C Flt	Hampden I	X2916	Training

P/O A W Genth	+	T/o Finningley for a night bombing exercise
P/O T G Boucher RCAF	+	over the Misson ranges. Lost control while
Sgt R J Moss	+	flying 2 miles SW of the range and crashed
Sgt T V G Clarke	+	at 2230. It is reported that the crew had
		been given permission to land. Three rest

in the extension to Finningley (St. Oswald) Churchyard, while Sgt Moss was taken to Birmingham (Yardley) Cemetery. P/O Boucher RCAF had attended St. Patrick's College, Ottawa, where he had won the Doran Trophy. Although to all intents and purposes a Yorkshire airfield, Finningley's burial ground comes within the boundaries of Nottinghamshire and laid to rest here are forty-two airmen who gave their lives in the Second World War, sixteen, at least, being aircrew who died while training with the resident Operational Training Unit.

12 Aug	17 OTU	Blenheim I	L1245		Enemy action

1941 P/O W E A Wand + T/o Upwood for night flying practice. Shot down
P/O R P Bell RNZAF + by an intruder and crashed 2350 at Crow Farm,
Sgt E A Davies + Wilburton, 5 miles SW of Ely, Cambridgeshire.
Eyewitnesses describe the enemy fighter making
three attacks before delivering the coup de grace. P/O Wand is buried in Mill
Hill (St. Paul) Churchyard, Hendon, while his crew were interred at Bury and
Ramsey cemeteries respectively, both being local to Upwood.

12 Aug	25 OTU	Hampden I	X2970		Training

1941 Sgt E F Grove inj T/o 1544 Balderton but climbed at too steep an
inj angle, stalled and crashed within a minute. A
inj strong gusting wind was a contributory factor.

13 Aug	11 OTU				Enemy action

1941 At 0057, an unidentified enemy aircraft (thought
to have been a Ju88) came in from the SE and attacked Bassingbourn airfield,
dropping four high explosive bombs and some incendiaries. Those who witnessed
the raid estimate the bomber as travelling at 200 m.p.h and flying at between
300 and 400 feet. Bursts of machine-gun fire was also heard. Blast from the
high explosives collapsed one wing of a barrack block, causing considerable
loss of life and serious injury; two, marked * thus, dying from their wounds:

Cpl L W Clutterham inj
AC1 J W Booth inj
AC1 J L Favell inj
AC1 G S Hilton + Abram (St. John) Churchyard, Lancashire
AC1 W F Hunt* + Billericay (Wickford) Cemetery, Essex
AC1 W Morley + Normanton upper Cemetery, Yorkshire
AC1 L J F O'Donovan inj
AC1 F G Phillips + Cardiff (Cathays) Cemetery, Glamorgan
AC1 A Sherman inj
AC1 D Smith* + Ballingry Cemetery, Fifeshire
AC2 V E Canton + Bassingbourn cum Kneesworth Cemetery, Cambridge
AC2 G C Crowder inj
AC2 I John inj
AC2 J Jose inj
AC2 W McMahon + Wallsend (Holy Cross) Cemetery, Northumberland
AC2 R W Reid + Newcastle-upon-Tyne (St. John's Westgate and
AC2 A A Richardson inj Elswick) Cemetery, Northumberland
AC2 W J Talbot + Nottingham Southern Cemetery
AC2 F C Tate inj
AC2 S H Valance inj
AC2 S C Waldon inj
AC2 A E Wheeler + Bassingbourn cum Kneesworth Cemetery, Cambridge

Note. It is possible that some of the above were posted to units other than
the parent OTU. However, all have been named in the unit's Operational Record
Book and for this reason they are commemorated, both here and in the Roll of
Honour. Again, it is well worth remembering that CWGC do not include details
of non-operational formations in their cemetery registers. It was, I believe,
the most serious incident involving ground staff at a Bomber Command OTU.

17 OTU		Anson I	N4997		Training

Sgt A W Dorney inj T/o Upwood for a night navigation exercise. On
Sgt R T Bartlett inj return to base, and while searching for the
Sgt P Jacobs inj flare path, the Anson ran out of petrol and
F/S L Milletts crash-landed 0110 at Shillow Hill, Wistow Wood
P/O S Philips RCAF inj between Wistow and Bury, Huntingdonshire.
Sgt W Fletcher

17 OTU		Blenheim IV	V5758		Training

Sgt G P Kerr inj T/o Upwood to practice formation flying. In
the vicinity of New Fen, an area some 4 miles
to the NNE of the airfield, an engine cut and in the ensuing forced-landing
at 1205, the Blenheim turned over and was wrecked. Despite the serious nature
of this accident, it is thought Sgt Kerr escaped serious injury.

13 Aug 1943	23 OTU	Wellington IC	X9659	—L3	Training

13 Aug 1943   **23 OTU**   **Wellington IC**   **X9659**   **—L3**   **Training**

P/O H G Pilling	inj
P/O E D Baker RCAF	
Sgt A H Harris RCAF	inj
Sgt L West	inj
Sgt G J P Kearns RCAF	
Sgt W H Bracken RCAF	
Sgt S W Griffin	inj
Sgt L C Young	inj

T/o Pershore to practice landings using wireless procedures. While approaching Abingdon airfield at around 1500, a malfunction in the flap system caused the Wellington to stall at 30 feet and crash near the runway, where it caught fire. Sgts Harris RCAF, West and Griffin were admitted to the Radcliffe Infirmary, while Sgt Young was treated in SSQ Abingdon. Within less than a year P/O Pilling and all the RCAF members of this crew had been killed on operations; P/O Pilling, Sgt Kearns RCAF and Sgt Bracken RCAF with 7 Squadron (see Bomber Command Losses, Volume 3, page 95); P/O Baker RCAF with 214 Squadron (see page 59) and Sgt Harris RCAF with 419 Squadron (see page 126). While this drama was being played out at Abingdon, Pershore was visited by The Inspector General, ACM Sir Arthur Longmore GCB, DSO, who arrived by air at 1220 and proceeded on a tour of the station.

15 Aug 1941   **20 OTU**   **Wellington IC**   **N2850**   **Training**

F/S W G B Ferguson	inj
	inj
	inj

T/o Lossiemouth. Ditched circa 1130, due to engine failure, off Wick, Scotland.

25 OTU C Flt   **Hampden I**   **AD858**   **Training**

Sgt W K Willcox	+
Sgt J Smith	+
Sgt A J G Bull	+
AC2 T Robinson	+

T/o 2150 Finningley for a night navigation sortie. At 2238, the crew were passed a first class fix, after which no signals were received. At 2255, two other crews, involved in the same exercise, reported seeing what appeared to be a fire (or a flare) burning on the surface of the sea. They also stated that a thick band of haze, above 4,000 feet, made it near impossible to determine the horizon. Sgt Willcox was the son of Captain Walter Willcox, Merchant Navy. With his crew, he is commemorated on the Runnymede Memorial.

16 Aug 1941   **25 OTU**   **Hampden I**   **X2959**   **Training**

Sgt S D Baldachin	+
Sgt T G Wood	+
Sgt D Macdonald	inj
Mstr G L Brumpton	+
Miss J Brumpton	+
Miss M Brumpton	+
Mstr A Brumpton	+
Miss L Brumpton	+
Miss S Brumpton	+

T/o Balderton for night circuits and landings but strayed slightly off course and at around 0025, while trying to locate the airfield, hit four houses in London Road, New Balderton and burst into flames. Three of the four dwellings were totally wrecked and, tragically, at No. 84, the home of Mr and Mrs W R Brumpton, six of their seven children perished, their ages ranging twixt five and 18 years. Remarkably, Mrs Brumpton was able to lower her youngest child, three year old Roy, to safety before making her exit through a bedroom window. Her husband, William, a railway worker, was on duty and had seen the flames and though realising his home was in the vicinity of the fire he had little notion of the terrible consequences that had befallen his own family. Funeral services for the children were held on 20 August (see Resumé on page 91 for further details). Sgt Baldachin of Bulawayo in Southern Rhodesia is buried in Doncaster (Rose Hill) Jewish Cemetery, while Sgt Wood lies at Woodford (Christ Church) Churchyard, Hazel Grove and Bramhall. His brother, Lance Sergeant John Mydleton Wood of 74 Field Regiment RA was killed in action on 16 October 1942, at El Alamein. He is commemorated on this famous battlefields' memorial.

17 Aug 1941   **13 OTU**   **Blenheim I**   **L1181**   **Training**

| Sgt A J Newman RAAF | |

T/o Hinton-in-the-Hedges for night solo practice. Abandoned over Northamptonshire after running out of fuel, falling at 0430, roughly a mile S of Finedon, 5 miles SSE of Kettering.

21 OTU A Flt   **Wellington IC**   **R1068**   **Training**

Sgt J F P Stuart RCAF	+
P/O G W Matthews	+
Sgt H G Mole	+
Sgt H G Hewison	+
Sgt J F Moore	+
Sgt A Jackets	+

T/o Moreton-in-Marsh. Emerged from cloud and crashed 1150 on Rhosfach near Pennal, 3 miles W of Machynlleth, Merioneth. Sgt Stuart RCAF and Sgt Moore, who came from Janesboro, Limerick, in the Irish Republic, rest in Towyn Cemetery. The others were claimed by their next of kin. A plaque to their memory has been placed in the local church.

18 Aug 1941	14 OTU	Hampden I	L4048	Training

Sgt J R Lee   +   T/o Cottesmore for a night exercise. Crashed
Sgt A D W Clay   +   at 0210 near Barrow, 4 miles NNE of Oakham.
P/O W Ellis DFM   +   Three, including P/O Ellis, a Dubliner, whose
Sgt J Webber   +   award had been Gazetted on 30 July 1940 for
Sgt F W Appleby   +   service with 49 Squadron, are buried in the
extension to Cottesmore (St. Nicholas) Church-
yard. Sgt Lee was taken to Bandon Hill Cemetery, Beddington, while Sgt Webber
rests in Hull Northern Cemetery.

	16 OTU	Hampden I	L4058	Training

Sgt E W McBarnet   +   T/o 2303 Upper Heyford for a night bombing
Sgt D E Davies   +   detail but an engine cut and the Hampden spun
Sgt L G Wright   +   in 2305, going up in flames near the airfield.
Sgt W B Sykes   +   Sgt McBarnet, who came from Bulawayo, Southern
Rhodesia, is buried in Upper Heyford Cemetery.
Sgt Davies rests in Ogmore and Garw (Pontycymmer) Cemetery; Sgt Wright lies in
Shrewsbury General Cemetery, while Sgt Sykes was interred in Saddleworth (St.
Chad) New Churchyard. Accident investigators were able to determine that in
the two minutes of flight, the pilot had retracted the port undercarriage and
partially raised the flaps.

19 Aug 1941	11 OTU	Wellington IA	N3005	Enemy action

F/S C G Andrews   inj   T/o Bassingbourn for night circuit training.
Sgt R F Guttridge   inj   Shot down by an intruder, crashing 0105 to the
Sgt R H Hazell   +   NE of Barrington, 7 miles SSW from the centre
Sgt R G P Capham   inj   of Cambridge. The first two named died from
their injuries at 0400 in Addenbrooke's
Hospital. With Sgt Hazell, who was killed outright, they rest in various
cemeteries. Sgt Capham, meanwhile, escaped relatively lightly and he was
treated in SSQ Bassingbourn for minor cuts and bruises and the after-effect
of shock.

	12 OTU	Wellington IC	T2882	Training

Sgt H H Harrington   inj   T/o Chipping Warden for a night cross-country.
Sgt McConnell   Lost power on one engine and while trying to
Sgt R Barrie   inj   land at Upper Heyford airfield, flew into a
F/S J F Bishop   inj   tree and crashed 2214, about a mile N of the
Sgt C Owen   inj   aerodrome. Typically, the crash has gone un-
Sgt N Parry   inj   reported in unit records, despite indications
Sgt W Durey   inj   that practically all on board suffered hurt
to one degree or another.

20 Aug 1941	16 OTU	Hampden I	AE138	Training

P/O T J Schofield   inj   Tasked for night flying, the crew were taxying
P/O J L Robertson   inj   at Croughton, only to be struck, violently, by
Sgt E J Thomas   +   another of the unit's aircraft. Sgt Thomas was
Sgt F Williams   +   taken home to rest in Rhondda (Trelaw) Cemetery
but his Welsh compatriot, Sgt Williams, lies in
Upper Heyford Cemetery. Both survivors received very severe burns.

	16 OTU	Hampden I	AE147	Training

Sgt T C Roux   inj   T/o Croughton for a night bombing exercise only
Sgt H Maple   inj   to smash into the Hampden, summarised above. The
Sgt Urquhart   inj   accident was attributed to a misunderstanding as
Sgt I G Stewart   inj   to which aircraft had been given permission to
proceed onto the runway from their holding point
on the flare path.

21 Aug 1941	11 OTU	Wellington IA	L7780	Training

P/O D Leatherland   T/o Steeple Morden for circuits and landings.
Wrecked 1050 after landing, inadvertently, with
the wheels still retracted.

	13 OTU	Blenheim IV	V6420	Training

Sgt S C B Abbott RAAF   T/o Bicester for a navigation exercise. Landed
heavily at 1400, lost its undercarriage and slid
into a motor transport vehicle. Sgt Abbott was killed on 9 August 1943, while
serving with 487 Squadron RNZAF. He rests in Marham Cemetery.

23 Aug   **20 OTU**   **Wellington IC**   **R1622**   **Training**
1941   Sgt T H Bagnall RNZAF   inj   T/o Lossiemouth for local night flying practice
Sgt R L Killen RAAF   +   but due to incorrect flap settings the aircraft
Sgt R F Lawrence   inj   failed to climb. Having grazed the top of a
Sgt A Thompson   +   hangar, which took away the pitot head, the
Wellington was ditched, circa 0105, roughly
four miles out in the Moray Firth. Sgt Killen RAAF rests in Kiltearn Parish
Churchyard; Sgt Thompson lies at South Shields (St. Simon, Simonside) Churchyard.
Sgt Bagnall RNZAF duly recovered from his injuries and, subsequently, proceeded
to 40 Squadron for a quite eventful first tour of duty (see Sweeping The Skies
by David Gunby, Pentland Press, 1995). Tragically, he was killed on his first
Stirling sortie with 75 Squadron (see Bomber Command Losses, Volume 3, page 279).

25 OTU B Flt   **Wellington IC**   **X9626**   **Training**
Sgt L Warren-Smith   T/o Balderton for night training. Became lost
and was given instructions, by radio, to head
for Newton. At around 0030, Sgt Warren-Smith approached a flare path, which
he assumed was Syerston's and commenced to overshoot. This procedure, however,
failed and the Wellington finished up in the station's bomb dump, which turned
out to be Newton's! Posted to 44 Squadron, Sgt Warren-Smith, a South African,
had the sad distinction of being the first Lancaster captain to be reported
missing from operations (see Bomber Command Losses, Volume 3, page 49).

24 Aug   **25 OTU**   **Hampden I**   **AE221**   **Training**
1941   Sgt D J Smith   T/o 0925 Balderton for local flying but flew
into a flock of birds which, effectively, shut
down the port engine. Unable to maintain height, the Hampden side slipped to
the ground.

25 Aug   **20 OTU**   **Wellington IC**   **R1665**   **Training**
1941   Sgt A Taylor   T/o Lossiemouth only to fly into a hillside
twixt 1 and 2 miles SW of Elgin, Moray.

27 OTU   **Wellington IC**   **X9600**   **Training**
Sgt J A Lancaster   T/o Lichfield. Overshot the base runway at
around 1020 and collided with an armoured car.

27 Aug   **11 OTU**   **Wellington IC**   **W5707**   **Training**
1941   Sgt J Price   T/o Steeple Morden for night dual practice.
F/L Max   Stalled, while trying to take overshoot action,
and came down circa 2300 amongst trees. A fire
broke out but there are no reports of injuries.

28 Aug   **13 OTU**   **Blenheim IV**   **Z6099**   **Training**
1941   P/O D J Ritchie RAAF   +   T/o Bicester for a navigation exercise. Presumed
P/O C K Bowen RCAF   +   lost over the Irish Sea at sometime after 1111.
Sgt C W Strutt   +   All are commemorated on the Runnymede Memorial.

14 OTU   **Hampden I**   **P4391**   **Training**
Sgt G H Bradley   +   T/o Cottesmore for a night flying detail.
Sgt F Grove   +   Exploded in the air 2300 approximately a mile
F/S W H Morley   +   NE from the Reserve Landing Ground at Akeman
Sgt H S Davies   +   Street, Oxfordshire. Sgt Bradley was buried
in Brackley (St. Peter) Churchyard; Sgt Grove
at Holmesfield (St. Swithin) Churchyard; F/S Morley at Littleover (St. Peter)
Churchyard, while Sgt Davies was cremated at Pontypridd Crematorium.

19 OTU   **Whitley IV**   **K9035**   **Training**
P/O Mitchiner   T/o 1545 Kinloss but engine failure resulted in
a forced-landing 1 mile E of the airfield. No
one was hurt but the Whitley was wrecked.

29 Aug   **17 OTU**   **Blenheim IV**   **R3734**   **Training**
1941   P/O J G C Grieve   T/o Upwood but the starboard engine cut and
P/O G J Rowley   being unable to maintain height, a forced-
landing was made at 1415 some 3 miles W of
Whittlesey, Cambridgeshire. Soon after this incident, P/O Grieve went to 21
Squadron and while detached to Malta was posted missing on 6 February 1942.
He is commemorated on panel 3, column 1 of the Malta Memorial.

29 Aug   **20 OTU**   **Wellington IC R1136**   **Training**
1941   P/O F C H Lewis   T/o Lossiemouth for a night exercise only to crash almost immediately. P/O Lewis had begun pilot training six months earlier at 1 EFTS Hatfield. Subsequently, he flew on operations with 149, 15, 150 and 156 Squadrons for his first tour and with the Radio Countermeasures 192 Squadron for his second. It seems he left the service during 1953.

   25 OTU   **Hampden I P4412**   **Training**
Sgt E F Grove   T/o Balderton for circuits and landings but lost
Sgt S V Beaumont   inj   control on the approach, crashing 1340 into the nearby village of Claypole. Sgt Beaumont was critically injured and he died in Newark General Hospital on 6 September 1941. Taken back to Kent, he is buried in Gravesend Cemetery. For his skipper, it was his second accident in less than a month (see page 65).

30 Aug   **25 OTU**   **Hampden I P4298**   **Training**
1941   Sgt C J H Blunt   T/o Balderton for night circuits and landings. Lost control while banking towards the runway and came down at 0115 near the village of Claypole. Although the airfield at Balderton is in Nottinghamshire, Claypole lies just over the border with Lincolnshire. It is believed Sgt Blunt escaped injury.

31 Aug   **15 OTU**   **Wellington IC X9766**   **Training**
1941   F/L R Alexander   T/o 2038 Mount Farm but almost immediately came to grief when an engine failed. The Wellington caught fire, but F/L Alexander appears not to have been hurt. He was an experienced pilot with 2,671 flying hours to his credit, 1,010 logged at the controls of Wellingtons.

   16 OTU   **Anson I N5074**   **Enemy action**
F/S P C Maries   T/o Croughton for a night cross-country. On
P/O J C Bosch   +   return to base at around 2300, the pilot was
Sgt R S J Hubbard   inj   somewhat alarmed to see tracer fire on his
Sgt E A J Hook   inj   starboard side. Almost at the same time, he
Sgt W Holland   inj   felt the impact of heavy bullets, or cannon shells, striking the Anson. P/O Bosch, who was sitting alongside him, died immediately and the three trainees, aft, were wounded. F/S Maries took evasive action and skillfully crash-landed the trainer near the airfield. P/O Bosch is buried in Upper Heyford Cemetery; he hailed from Enkeldoorn in Southern Rhodesia. Of the three wounded, Sgt Holland was posted to 106 Squadron, only to fail to return from a mine laying sortie on 22-23 January 1942 (see Bomber Command Losses, Volume 3, page 24).

   16 OTU   **Hampden I L4168**   **Training**
Sgt R N McDougall   T/o Upper Heyford for night bombing practice. Became totally lost, but eventually located Odiham airfield in Hampshire. While attempting to land here, at 0010, Sgt McDougall lost sight of the beacons and on touch down ran through a fence and into a hollow (some reports say a bomb crater) where the undercarriage gave way.

   19 OTU   **Anson I R9774**   **Training**
F/L McWatters   T/o Kinloss for a navigation exercise. Lost power and while trying to force-land, hit some telegraph wires and crashed 1545 near Tobermory (Mishnish) on the Isle of Mull.

1 Sep   **16 OTU**   **Hampden I P1285**   **Training**
1941   P/O J D Bridge   T/o Upper Heyford. On return to base, overshot
Sgt A G Harbottle   the runway and crashed 1715, hitting a lorry belonging to a contractor working on the airfield. A fire broke out, destroying both the Hampden and the vehicle. At the time of the accident, the surface wind was very light and the Hampden's flaps were only partially lowered. By the autumn of 1944, Sgt Harbottle was flying with 58 Squadron (Halifax IIs), based at Stornoway in the Hebrides. On 16 October, he was posted missing and his name is perpetuated on panel 218 of the Runnymede Memorial. It is believed his skipper (above) is the F/L J D Bridge of 141 Squadron, who died on 13 November 1943 and is buried in Oxford (Botley) Cemetery. His brother, Sgt Basil Dewdney Bridge died flying with 487 Squadron (see Bomber Command Losses, Volume 4, page 25) on 22 January 1943.

1 Sep 1941	**16 OTU** P/O W Lines	**Hampden I**	**P4320** inj	**Training**

T/o Upper Heyford. Lost power from the port engine and while banking, lost control and came down 1230 in a field adjacent to the airfield. P/O Lines injured an ankle.

16 OTU	**Hampden I**	**AD833**	**Training**
P/O C B S Fynn		+	
P/O O G S Playfair		+	
Sgt H W Butt		+	
Sgt G Morffew		inj	

T/o Upper Heyford for a night exercise. Stalled at 300 feet, in a thick ground mist, and crashed into a tree near Lancing College in Sussex. The accident happened at around 0440, while the crew were trying to land at Shoreham airfield. P/O Fynn of Umtali in Southern Rhodesia and known to his family and friends as Chum, was brought back to Upper Heyford Cemetery. P/O Playfair, whose first Christian name was Orion and who had a Bachelor of Arts (Honours) degree from London University, is buried in Caterham and Warlingham (Caterham) Burial Ground, while Sgt Butt rests in Twickenham (Hampton) Burial Ground. Sgt Morffew is described as being very seriously injured.

5 Sep 1941	**12 OTU** Sgt L H Hook	**Wellington IC**	**W5708** +	**Training**
	P/O G L Dames		+	
	Sgt W H Fagan RCAF		+	
	Sgt P M Cordy		+	

T/o Chipping Warden for night dual training. Became disorientated, while banking, and at around 0400 flew into the ground, SW of the runway. On impact the bomber burst into flames. Two lie in Brookwood Military Cemetery; Sgt Hook rests at Greenlawn Memorial Park at Chelsham, while Sgt Cordy, from Harrow in Middlesex, lies in Aston-le-Wells Roman Catholic Churchyard, Northamptonshire.

18 OTU	**Wellington IC**	**X9795**	**Training**
F/O T Lach PAF			
F/O M Sukniewicz PAF		+	
F/O C Rymkiewicz PAF			
Sgt J Grom PAF			
Sgt J Drozdzik PAF			
Sgt S Bosek PAF			

T/o Bramcote. Attempted to land at 1130 in very foggy conditions at Waddington, making a Lorenz beam approach, but overshot the runway and hit some vehicles before crashing against a hangar. F/O Sukniewicz PAF is buried in Nuneaton (Oaston Road) Cemetery. It was the unit's first serious flying accident since late April (see page 49), a quite remarkable run of good fortune.

7 Sep 1941	**10 OTU** P/O T L Weller	**Anson I**	**N9617** +	**Training**
	Sgt J E Taylor		inj	
	Sgt L Copland		inj	
	Sgt R W Keen		inj	
	Sgt F B Mitchell		inj	

T/o Abingdon for a cross-country; base-Newtown-Rhyl-Barmouth-base. Encountered thick fog and when roughly 16 miles W of Oswestry flew into the side of Moel Sych. The time of the crash is given as approximately 1040. P/O Weller is buried in Brookwood Military Cemetery.

17 OTU	**Blenheim IV**	**R3875**	**Training**
Sgt M F Fox		+	
Sgt B A Coukell RCAF		+	
Sgt E C Brearley		+	

T/o Upwood for a cross-country exercise. Spun from 2,500 feet and crashed circa 1200 into trees at Cressage, 8 miles SE of Shrewsbury and on the road leading to Bridgnorth. Two were taken to their home towns; Sgt Fox to Widnes in Lancashire and Sgt Brearley to Alfreton in Derbyshire, but Sgt Coukell RCAF of High Bridge, New Jersey, is buried in Shawbury (St. Mary) Churchyard. Eyewitnesses state the Blenheim made at least four turns before diving out of control.

27 OTU	**Anson I**	**K6190**	**Transit**
Sgt J R Turner			

T/o Sywell and set course for Lichfield. The Anson arrived at its destination at 1710, but an engine cut and the trainer crash-landed in a small field adjacent to the airfield, running into some trees before finishing up amongst some farm out-buildings.

8 Sep 1941	**13 OTU** Sgt J L Nyman	**Blenheim IV**	**V5377** +	**Training**
	Sgt J L Rodwell		+	
	Sgt C M Pratt		+	

T/o Bicester for a navigation exercise. At about 1715, the Blenheim dived, suddenly, to the ground at Mells Park, Mells, 3 miles WNW of Frome, Somerset. Two rest in Brookwood Military Cemetery; Sgt Rodwell lies in Camborne-Redruth (Redruth) Cemetery.

9 Sep   **21 OTU**   **Wellington IC**   **X9698**   **Training**
1941   P/O H J D Smiles DFM   T/o 0945 Moreton-in-Marsh for a cross-country.
    Sgt C E Catterson   +   On return to base, the weather had closed in and
                                     it was decided to head for Benson in Oxfordshire.
En route at around 1300, an aerodrome (this was very likely Moreton-in-Marsh) was
glimpsed but as the bomber descended, so the gap closed over. At this stage the
Wellington began to dive, out of control. The order to abandon was given, P/O
Smiles making good his exit at the perilously low height of 400 feet. When the
wreckage (found 200 yards S of Kitebrook House, Oxfordshire and less than two
miles SE from its home base) was examined, the body of Sgt Catterson was found
in the rear turret. He was laid to rest in Moreton-in-Marsh New Cemetery. Of
the forty-six airmen buried here, at least twenty-nine died while undergoing
training at 21 OTU. P/O Smiles had gained his DFM with 214 Squadron, details
having been published on 6 June 1941.

10 Sep   **19 OTU**   **Whitley V**   **N1415**   **Training**
1941   P/O A J Haines   T/o Kinloss for night dual circuits and landings.
    Sgt J A Eakin   +   Undershot and wrecked at 0045, after finishing up
                                     in the station bomb dump. Sgt Eakin, the second
pilot, suffered fatal injuries as a result of not being securely strapped in; he
is buried in Kinloss Abbey Burial Ground. The rest of the crew escaped unhurt.

    25 OTU B Flt   **Wellington IC**   **R1767**   **Training**
    F/O J S Willis   +   T/o Finningley for a night cross-country. Dived
    Sgt G Newman   +   to the ground, from very low altitude, onto an
    Sgt T R F J Roch   +   area described as the Horseway, about a mile NE
    Sgt F G Coster   +   of Chatteris, Cambridgeshire. Seconds prior to
    F/S R E Elms   +   crash, at 2110, a searchlight had illuminated
                                     the Wellington and it is believed the pilot was
dazzled by the brightness of the beam and became disorientated. All were taken
to their home towns for burial, the service for Sgt Coster being conducted by
the Revd R Hendy at Wooburn Cemetery, with full military honours, six days after
the tragedy. He is commemorated in the book, The Men of Wooburn War Memorial,
compiled by Barrie Thorpe, to whom I am grateful for much of the detail reported
in this summary.

    25 OTU B Flt   **Wellington IC**   **X9872**   **Training**
    F/L D J Bassett   +   T/o Finningley for night bombing training. At
    Sgt F V Martin   +   2145 flew into farm buildings near Southrey, a
    Sgt W G Kilsby   +   fenland village some 4 miles NW of Woodhall Spa
    Sgt G F Large   +   in Lincolnshire. All are buried in cemeteries
    F/S T Highton DFM   +   within the United Kingdom. F/S Highton had
    Sgt M J Byrne   +   completed a tour of operations with 83 Squadron
                                     and details of his award had appeared in the
                                     London Gazette on 18 April 1941.

10-11 Sep   **25 OTU B Flt**   **Wellington IC**   **N2805**   **Enemy action**
1941   F/L G W Walenn MID*   pow   T/o 1955 Finningley for a night bombing detail
    F/L T L Walker RAAF   pow   over the Misson ranges. Dropped two bombs, the
    W/O P A Edwards   pow   second at 2043. At 2201, Finningley responded
    W/O S C Stevens   pow   to a QDM request from this aircraft, after
    W/O W A Platt   pow   which nothing further was heard. Well over
                                     seven hours later (0531 has been quoted), the
Wellington was hit by flak, abandoned, and left to crash in Rotterdam's IJssel-
haven. F/L Walenn was amongst the Allied officers that tunnelled their way out
of Stalag-Luft III in March 1944. Recaptured (as most were) he was executed by
the Gestapo (on Hitler's orders) on, or around, 29 March. His remains are
interred in Poland at Poznan Old Garrison Cemetery. The asterisk denotes he
was twice Mentioned in Despatches.

11 Sep   **16 OTU**   **Hampden I**   **L4050**   **Training**
1941   Sgt J Ruddock   T/o Upper Heyford for night flying practice.
                                     Overshot and crashed 2200, colliding with a fuel
bowser that was stationary at the end of the flare path. A fire broke out and
both the tanker and the Hampden were destroyed. Strangely, Sgt Ruddock was taken
off Hampdens and posted to 13 OTU for Blenheim conversion. On 29 January 1942,
he was killed, along with his crew, when their aircraft crashed near Devizes in
Wiltshire, during the course of a day navigation exercise.

11 Sep 1941	**27 OTU**	**Wellington IC**	**R1460**	**Training**

Sgt H F H Taylor — T/o Lichfield for night flying practice. Held off too high and, as a result, landed heavily at 2245 and ballooned back into the air. On its second arrival, the aircraft burst a tyre, swinging off the flare path and running into a shelter. This caused the undercarriage to collapse.

12 Sep 1941	**14 OTU**	**Hampden I**	**P1301**	**Training**

Sgt A P Overall DFM + T/o Saltby for night training but collided in
Sgt V H Griffiths RNZAF + the circuit with another Hampden. Sgt Overall
Sgt D G K Smith + is buried in Black Notley (SS Peter and Paul)
Sgt E F Chamberlain + Churchyard; he had gained an immediate DFM while flying with 106 Squadron, details having being Gazetted as recently as 2 September. His crew rest in the extension to Cottesmore (St. Nicholas) Churchyard.

	14 OTU	**Hampden I**	**P4303**	**Training**

F/S D H Bartlett + T/o Saltby similarly tasked and destroyed in
Sgt J E Wall RNZAF + the manner previously described. Sgt Wall RNZAF
Sgt T I A West + is buried in the extension to Cottesmore (St.
Sgt H R Tuff + Nicholas) Churchyard, while Sgt West was taken back to the Irish Republic and laid to rest in Drumcliffe (St. Columba) Church of Ireland Churchyard, Co. Sligo. Their two companions were conveyed to their home towns.

	16 OTU	**Hampden I**	**P1323**	**Training**

Sgt S Graaff + T/o Upper Heyford for the pilot's first night
Sgt J H Bendon + solo in a Hampden. At 2115, the bomber dived into a field at Slade Farm, 3 miles S of the airfield and about a mile E of the hamlet of Northbrook. It is almost certain that the body of Sgt Graaff, who came from Bulawayo in Southern Rhodesia, was claimed by a relative as he is buried in Exeter Higher Cemetery. His brother, F/O Dewhurst Graaff, was killed on operations to St-Leu on 7-8 July 1944, while flying with 44 Squadron (see Bomber Command Losses, Volume 5, page 321). Sgt Bendon lies in Penarth Cemetery.

	19 OTU	**Whitley IV**	**K9052**	**Training**

Sgt J Reid — T/o Kinloss for night flying practice. At around 2350, the Whitley attempted to land at Dalcross in Inverness-shire but overshot the airfield and struck some trees near the perimeter. Sgt Reid, who was not hurt, had logged 200 flying hours on Whitleys.

	19 OTU	**Whitley V**	**T4333**	**Training**

Sgt A G Batchen RCAF + T/o Kinloss for a night navigation exercise.
Sgt J L Collins RCAF + It is believed the crew made landfall at 0050
F/S R F Stephens RCAF + near Fraserburgh on the NE Aberdeenshire coast
F/S R L R Younger RCAF + but, for some inexplicable reason, turned onto
Sgt M S Dawe + a reciprocal course and flew back out to sea. All are commemorated on the Runnymede Memorial.

13 Sep 1941	**13 OTU**	**Blenheim I**	**L6793**	**Training**

Sgt D A Neal RCAF + T/o Bicester for solo flying. Stalled and crashed circa 1200 in the vicinity of Juniper Hill on the border twixt Oxfordshire and Northamptonshire and a little under three miles S of Brackley. Sgt Neal RCAF rests in Caversfield (St. Laurence) Churchyard.

	16 OTU	**Hampden I**	**P1184**	**Training**

Sgt T E Barnett — T/o Croughton for night flying practice but undershot the runway and crashed 2230 into a tree. Rhodesian born Sgt Barnett had mistaken the red beam on the Glide Path Indicator for the amber.

14 Sep 1941	**11 OTU**	**Wellington IC**	**R1012**	**Training**

F/L I G O Fenton — T/o Bassingbourn. Lost oil pressure on the port engine, resulting in the propeller and reduction gear sheering off. Then the starboard motor failed and F/L Fenton forced-landed, wheels down, at Hunsdon, 4 miles E of Ware, Hertfordshire.

16 Sep 1941	**15 OTU**	**Wellington I**	L4262	**Training**

Sgt A R Patrick   inj   T/o Hampstead Norris for local night flying
Sgt A R Tacqi   inj   practice. Overshot and crashed 2235 while
Sgt W A Rowe   inj   attempting to land, coming down amongst some
                         bushes at the end of the runway. Sgt Patrick
died in the ambulance on the way to the hospital; his grave is one of the
sixty-six service plots in Harwell Cemetery.

25 OTU	**Hampden I**	P4302	**Training**

P/O D D Christie RCAF   +   T/o Balderton to practice night flying, in the
Sgt Henderson   inj   course of which the Hampden overshot the runway,
Sgt Hawkins   inj   climbed to 300 feet and while banking to the
                         left, stalled and dived into the ground. It
is suggested P/O Christie RCAF may have been distracted by the glare from his
undercarriage warning lights. Buried four days later at Newark-upon-Trent
Cemetery, his funeral was attended by F/L Betts and a party made up from airmen
of the station defence section.

17 Sep 1941	**17 OTU**	**Blenheim IV**	R3814	**Training**

Sgt D H Farley   +   T/o Upwood for a navigation exercise. Crashed
F/S W F Jeffery   +   in the North Sea. Two are commemorated on the
Sgt T F Heron RCAF   inj   Runnymede Memorial, but Sgt Heron RCAF was saved
                         and admitted to Yarmouth General Hospital.

20 OTU	**Magister I**	T9757	**Training**

F/O Lockwood   T/o Lossiemouth for local flying and authorised
                         aerobatics. Went out of control after spinning
off the top of a loop and crashed 1130 onto a bank, just to the SE of Alves and
about 5 miles W of Elgin, Moray.

19 Sep 1941	**10 OTU**	**Whitley V**	T4132	**Training**

P/O I Prentice   +   T/o 2232 Abingdon for a night flying exercise
Sgt G F Barker-Benfield   +   but, within a minute, flew into trees on Boars
Sgt H G Lintott   inj   Hill and burst into flames. All are buried in
Sgt D T Bicknell   +   cemeteries across the United Kingdom, including
                         Sgt Lintott, who died two days later from his
injuries. As a consequence of this accident, obstruction lights were placed on
the two extremities of Boars Hill ridge, these to be illuminated when aircraft
were taking off on a northerly heading.

15 OTU	**Wellington IC**	Z8864	**Training**

Sgt P J Temple   inj   T/o Mount Farm for night dual training. Wrecked
                inj   at around 2120 after landing short of the runway.

20 Sep 1941	**16 OTU**	**Hampden I**	P5314	**Enemy action**

Sgt N P van der Merwe   +   T/o Croughton for a night exercise. Caught 4
Sgt D A J Paine   +   miles NE of the airfield, while preparing to
Sgt J H Ixer   +   land, by a Ju88 intruder flown by Oblt Paul
Sgt R Leagas   +   Semrau of I./NJG2 and sent down out of control.
                         Three, including their Rhodesian born skipper,
rest in Upper Heyford Cemetery. Sgt Paine is buried in Kingsbury (St. Andrew)
Churchyard at Wembley. On 7-8 February 1945, Oblt (now Major) Paul Semrau died
with the rest of his crew when his Ju88G-6 Werke No. 620562 from Stab NJG2 was
shot down at airfield 1128.

18 OTU	**Wellington IC**	X3195	**Training**

F/S F G Neate   T/o Bramcote to practice single-engined flying
                         and while doing so, the port engine failed at
seven hundred feet. F/S Neate opened the throttles of the starboard motor but
was unable to prevent the bomber from hitting a tree and crashing circa 1620
at Burton Hastings, 3 miles ESE from the centre of Nuneaton, Warwickshire.

21 Sep 1941	**20 OTU**	**Wellington IC**	R1171	**Training**

P/O A D Morris DFM   +   T/o Lossiemouth for dual training. Overshot the
Sgt J A MacEachern RCAF   +   runway, stalled and crashed. Sgt MacEachern RCAF
Sgt G E Kelly   +   rests in Lossiemouth Burial Ground, Drainie; the
                         others were claimed by their next of kin. P/O
Morris, described as a pilot/instructor, had recently joined the unit from 40
Squadron, details of his award having been Gazetted nineteen days previous.

22 Sep
1941

12 OTU   **Wellington IC R1233**   **Training**

Sgt W Onions   T/o Chipping Warden. At 1645, in the vicinity
of the airfield, the port engine seized and
moments later the propeller came off, striking the fuselage and slicing through
hydraulic lines. This caused the bomb doors to open and with height decaying
rapidly, Sgt Onions had little option but to force -land at Redhill Farm, NE of
the aerodrome and less than a mile E of Aston le Walls village. Subsequently,
Sgt Onions went to 103 Squadron and failed to return from Köln on 30-31 May 1942
(see Bomber Command Losses, Volume 3, page 106).

24 Sep
1941

21 OTU D Flt   **Anson I K6193**   **Unknown**

Reported as being written off on this date.
Allocated to 21 OTU on 6 April 1941, the Anson had previously seen service
with 206 Squadron and 11 OTU. There are no indications as to the number of
hours flown.

25 Sep
1941

21 OTU   **Wellington IC R1237**   **Training**

Sgt R J Clarke RNZAF	inj	T/o Moreton-in-Marsh for night flying practice,
Sgt Wishart	inj	During the sortie, hydraulic failure occurred
P/O Sweeney	inj	and the starboard undercarriage jammed in the
Sgt J G Fitzgerald	+	up position. The crew circled the airfield for

about ten minutes but were unsuccessful in all
their attempts to free the unit. Subsequently, Sgt Clarke RNZAF approached the
runway, with the flaps retracted, and as a result he got down rather low and
by doing so, flew into a tree and crashed at 2330 about a mile to the NNW of
the aerodrome and in the general vicinity of Lower Lemington. Sgt Fitzgerald
is buried in Brookwood Military Cemetery in a joint grave with his brother,
Sgt Leslie Fitzgerald, who died on 31 March 1943. Sgt Clarke RNZAF recovered
from his injuries and by the spring of 1943 was in India, flying Wellingtons
with 215 Squadron, based at Jessore. On 18-19 May, his aircraft, LA988-V,
failed to return from operations over Burma. Along with the five members of
his crew, he is commemorated on the Singapore Memorial.

26 Sep
1941

12 OTU   **Wellington IA P9226**   **Training**

P/O Seammen	inj	T/o Chipping Warden for night flying practice.
	inj	Overshot and crashed at around 2015, while
		trying to land. The crew sustained superficial

injuries and their aircraft, which ran into a flare cover, was not too seriously
damaged. However, twenty-four hours later it was struck by another of the unit's
Wellingtons and in the ensuing fire, both machines were destroyed.

18 OTU   **Wellington IC T2907**   **Unknown**

Reported written off on this date with a total
of 294.20 flying hours accumulated.

18 OTU   **Wellington IC X9793**   **Unknown**

Reported written off on this date with a total
of 79.25 flying hours accumulated since allocation to the unit on 6 August 1941.

27 Sep
1941

12 OTU   **Wellington IC X9621**   **Unknown**

Reported to have crashed into Wellington IA
P9226, which had overshot the Chipping Warden the previous night (see above).

20 OTU   **Wellington IC Z8809**   **Training**

F/S F C N Kiteley	+	T/o Lossiemouth for dual training. Landed, but
Sgt D H Budden RCAF	+	smashed at high speed into a stationary aircraft
P/O R D Anderson RCAF	+	and totally destroyed. All rest in Lossiemouth
		Burial Ground, Drainie.

22 OTU   **Wellington IC X9908**   **Training**

P/O H Stiles	inj	T/o Wellesbourne Mountford for night flying
Sgt J L Bell	inj	practice but saw smoke issuing from the port
Sgt K N Carpenter	inj	engine. With the motor shut down, the crew
Sgt C J Donahue RCAF	inj	tried to regain the airfield but lost flying
Sgt K J Gill		speed and crash-landed 2304, short of the
		runway. It is not thought that their injuries

were too serious. Sgt Donahue RCAF went on to serve with 97 Squadron, gaining
a DFM (Gazetted 11 June 1943) and when killed in action with 7 Squadron (see
Bomber Command Losses, Volume 5, page 17), he had been commissioned.

27 Sep   **27 OTU**   **Wellington IA**   **P9216**   **Training**
1941   F/L L B Slade   T/o Lichfield for dual circuits and landings.
      Sgt A H Ashwood   inj   Wrecked 1515, after breaking its undercarriage
                                       on touch down and taking light. Sgt Ashwood
sustained very serious burns and was rushed to Burntwood Emergency Hospital
where he died that same evening at 2340 hours, thus becoming the unit's first
fatality since forming on 23 April 1941. His grave is in Margate Cemetery.
F/L Slade went on to gain a DSO and when posted missing from the Peenemünde
raid in August 1943, he was serving with 12 Squadron as a Flight Commander
(see Bomber Command Losses, Volume 4, page 270).

28 Sep   **16 OTU**   **Anson I**   **R9694 GA-E**   **Training**
1941   Sgt G A McKay RCAF   T/o Upper Heyford for a night cross-country.
      Sgt R B Petersen RCAF   Became lost after encountering poor visibility.
      Sgt R R Stewart RCAF   All efforts to obtain QDMs failed, due to an
      Sgt A H Gardener   unserviceable radio, and having run perilously
                                       low on petrol, the crew baled out from 6,000
feet, leaving the trainer to crash at Grove Farm, a mile N of Ivinghoe, some
seven miles ENE of Aylesbury, Buckinghamshire. Sgt Petersen RCAF and his
fellow countryman, Sgt Stewart RCAF, went to 420 Squadron and both lost their
lives in the spring and summer respectively of 1942 (see Bomber Command Losses,
Volume 3, pages 92 and 172).

      25 OTU   **Hampden I**   **P1194**   **Training**
      P/O L S Coulter   inj   T/o 0915 Balderton but the starboard engine cut
                             inj   and the Hampden came down in a field adjacent to
                                       the airfield.

29 Sep   **15 OTU**   **Wellington IC**   **L7816**   **Air Test**
1941   Sgt D J Paul   T/o Mount Farm for a pre-night flying test.
                                       While in flight, Sgt Paul experienced almost
total control failure but by displaying commendable skill, he made his way back
to base. Having lowered the undercarriage, he controlled his approach by manip-
ulating the trim tabs. Nonetheless, the Wellington crossed the threshold at
high speed (the air speed indicator was registering 120 m.p.h.) and soon after
touch down the undercarriage gave way. There are no reports of injury.

      16 OTU   **Hampden I**   **P5308**   **Training**
      Sgt E M White   +   T/o Upper Heyford to practice bombing over the
      Sgt J K Howe   +   Grendon Underwood ranges. Flew into a hillside
      Sgt K D Greenwood   +   at Corble Farm, less than a mile S of Piddington
      Sgt J Amott   +   in Oxfordshire and 11 miles WSW from Aylesbury,
                                       Buckinghamshire. Two were laid to rest in Upper
Heyford Cemetery and two were taken back to their home towns. Sgt Greenwood's
parents suffered the loss of a second son when Sgt Stanley Stuart Greenwood
failed to return from Dortmund on 22-23 May 1944, while flying as an air gunner
with 576 Squadron (see Bomber Command Losses, Volume 5, page 238).

      18 OTU   **Wellington IC**   **R3216**   **Training**
      Sgt E J H Heather   +   T/o Bramcote for an evening navigation sortie.
      Sgt S Cupryk PAF   +   On return to base, held off too high and as a
      P/O J Jozepajt PAF   +   result the Wellington stalled, crashing at 2150.
      F/O Z Stepien PAF   +   F/S Fisher and the five Polish aircrew who died
      Sgt J Ksiezyc PAF   +   are buried in Nuneaton (Oaston Road) Cemetery;
      Sgt T Astramowicz PAF   +   Sgt Heather was taken back to Reading (Caversham)
      F/S J S Fisher   +   Cemetery.
      Sgt J Zietkiewicz PAF   inj

1 Oct   **10 OTU**   **Whitley V**   **P4942**   **Training**
1941   P/O L Anderle   T/o Abingdon for a night exercise. During the
                                       sortie an engine failed and, on return to base
at 2220, it was discovered that the flaps were unserviceable. A fast landing
followed and while avoiding parked aircraft, the undercarriage collapsed. No
one was hurt but the Whitley was damaged beyond repair. Born in Czechoslovakia,
where he had joined his country's air force, P/O Anderle had accumulated in
excess of 1,000 flying hours, all prior to reaching the United Kingdom. Soon
he was to join 138 Squadron, where he served with great distinction before
losing his life over the Mediterranean on 15 December 1942 (see Bomber Command
Losses, Volume 3, page 277). He is commemorated on the Alamein Memorial.

1 Oct	**16 OTU**	**Hampden I**	**AE222**		**Training**
1941	Sgt E W Phillips		T/o 2118 Croughton for a moonlight cross-		
	Sgt D W Markall	inj	country and crashed, due to failure of the		
	Sgt R J Buckley	inj	port engine, two minutes later. Sgt Phillips		

valiantly tried to get back to the airfield but while in the circuit he ran out of height and force -landed in a field. He had been involved in a serious crash on 24 July (see page 61 for details of this and his subsequent fate).

3 Oct	**14 OTU**	**Anson I**	**R3310**		**Training**
1941	F/L B J A Rennie MC		T/o Cottesmore for a night navigation sortie.		

Abandoned 2320 in very poor weather conditions and left to crash a mile W of Sutton St. James and some 5 miles SE of Holbeach in Lincolnshire. It could well be that F/L Rennie was seriously injured as his death occurred sixteen days later. Described in the CWGC register as a pilot instructor, he is buried in the extension to Cottesmore (St. Nicholas) Church-yard. A volunteer reserve pilot, his parents lived in South Africa at Parktown, Johannesburg.

16 OTU	**Hampden I**	**P5391**		**Training**
Sgt T F Freeman		T/o Upper Heyford for a gunnery exercise. A		

little before 1700, while turning left at a relatively low speed, the Hampden entered a stabilised yaw. Believing his port engine had failed (or was about to do so), Sgt Freeman decided to land at Penhros but before doing so he saw the airfield at Towyn and landed here instead. His approach was rather fast and the Hampden ran off the runway and bounced across the local rail line before coming to a stop, completely wrecked.

4 Oct	**18 OTU**	**Anson I**	**R9708**		**Training**
1941	F/S L A Scott	+	T/o Bramcote for a navigation exercise in the		
	F/O R C Miarczynski PAF	+	company of other aircraft. Collided with the		
	F/O S Hermanowski PAF	+	tailplane of Anson R9709 (Sgt Waters) and came		
	F/S R Brown	+	down at Wolvey, 8 miles NE from the centre of		
	AC1 E C Mason	+	Coventry, Warwickshire. Both Polish officers		

and AC1 Mason are buried in Nuneaton (Oaston Road) Cemetery. F/S Scott rests in Brookwood Military Cemetery; F/S Brown was taken to South Shields (Harton) Cemetery. The other Anson landed safely.

19 OTU	**Whitley V**	**T4224**		**Training**
Sgt N Booth		T/o Forres for a navigation exercise. During		

the flight, part of the port engine's oil tank cowling came off resulting in very severe vibration. The crew aborted the sortie and returned to base but, while landing at 1945, the Whitley struck a bank and was wrecked. By the autumn of 1942, Sgt Booth was flying Mosquitoes with 105 Squadron, being reported missing from operations on 13 November (see Bomber Command Losses, Volume 3, page 260).

21 OTU	**Wellington IC**	**R1146**		**Transit**
P/O J E A H Fairfax DFM	+	T/o Edgehill in the company of other aircraft		
Sgt J F Duggan RCAF	+	from the unit, with the intention of returning		
Sgt D Winstanley	+	to Moreton-in-Marsh, from whence they had left		
Sgt O J Simmonds	+	the previous evening for night-flying training.		
Sgt V A Taylor	+	Weather conditions were poor, with a thick band		
Cpl J Laxton	+	of mist present and although the other bombers		
AC2 E C Ryall	+	reached their destination, P/O Fairfax likely		

crashed within minutes of departure (there are conflicting reports) after hitting trees near Upton House, N of the airfield. On board were members of his maintenance crew. Three, Sgt Duggan RCAF, Sgt Winstanley (whose brother, Sgt Harold Winstanley was killed while undergoing pilot training in Rhodesia on 12 March 1943 and is buried in Gwelo Cemetery) and Cpl Laxton, a pre-war member of the Auxiliary Air Force, lie in Moreton-in-Marsh Cemetery. The others were claimed by their next of kin. P/O Fairfax gained his DFM during an outstanding tour of duty with 9 Squadron (late November 1940 to mid-May 1941) during which time he flew at least thirty-three sorties as captain. His award was published in the London Gazette of 22 August 1941.

Note. Shenington would have been the more logical name for the airfield but as Eric Kaye suggests, this could have led to confusion with airfields with names similar in sound to "Shenington" and, thus, Edgehill was its chosen title.

8 Oct **15 OTU D Flt** **Wellington I** **L4323** **Training**
1941 F/O L C Boore DFM inj T/o Hampstead Norris for a navigation exercise.
Sgt B R Stevenson RCAF + At approximately 1705, one of the Wellington's
F/S J M Wilde DFM + wings brushed the ground and, out of control,
P/O W H Pinfold inj the bomber crashed at Bonam Farm, Blewbury, 9
Sgt S Davies inj miles ESE from Wantage, Berkshire. Two were
Sgt T G Holden inj taken to Brookwood Military Cemetery, while Sgt
Sgt A W Beynon + Beynon rests in Cheam (St. Dunstan) Churchyard,
Sutton and Cheam. F/O Boore had gained his wings
on 1 December 1935, while his DFM had been Gazetted on 31 May 1940. At the time
of the accident, he had amassed 1,211 flying hours. F/S Wilde's award was
published on 30 July 1940. In neither case are any squadron details shown.
It is further noted that in the CWGC register for Brookwood, Sgt Stevenson's
first Christian name is reported as Ben; in They Shall Grow Not Old, Benjamin
is indicated.

9 Oct **19 OTU** **Whitley V** **T4144** **Training**
1941 Sgt W Fleming + T/o Kinloss for night bombing practice over the
Sgt L G Masters + Tain ranges. Whilst in the training area, struck
Sgt H Hancock + by a bomb and crashed 2030, bursting into flames
Sgt A MacKenzie + at Edderton, a small village in Ross and Cromarty
overlooking Cambuscurrie Bay some 6 miles NW of
Tain. Their burials are split equally between England and Scotland.

19 OTU **Whitley V** **Z6750** **Training**
Sgt E H Brace + T/o Kinloss similarly tasked. Failed to return
Sgt P Kelly RCAF + at its scheduled time. All are commemorated on
Sgt L H Oldman + the Runnymede Memorial. Sgt Kelly RCAF was an
Sgt G W Gray + American from Cleveland, Ohio, while Sgt Oldman
hailed from Neutral Bay in New South Wales.

10 Oct **10 OTU** **Whitley V** **N1429** **Training**
1941 Sgt A J Pratley T/o Stanton Harcourt for night flying practice.
Collided with a tree and crashed 2115 while on
the approach to the runway. Prior to the crash, Sgt Pratley had made two unsuccessful attempts to land. Posted to 77 Squadron, he died when his Whitley
went into the North Sea, while returning from Emden, on 12-13 March 1942 (see
Bomber Command Losses, Volume 3, page 46).

16 OTU **Hampden I** **P4319** **Training**
Sgt C P A I Rose-Innes + T/o 2115 Upper Heyford for a night bombing
P/O B W Miller RNZAF + exercise and crashed almost immediately about
Sgt C B Van Deemter + a mile SW of the airfield, bursting into flames
Sgt P W Harris + on impact. Sgt Rose-Innes of Salisbury in
Southern Rhodesia, P/O Miller RNZAF and Sgt
Van Deemter of Kleinpoort in the Cape Province are buried in Upper Heyford
Cemetery, while Sgt Harris is the sole service burial of the Second World War
in Llandogo (St. Dochwe) Churchyard, Trelech United in Monmouthshire.

17 OTU **Blenheim I** **K7048** **Training**
Sgt P A Paquet RCAF inj T/o Upwood. Eyewitnesses say the Blenheim dived
suddenly, striking the ground at around 1600.
The accident is attributed to failure of the port engine.

25 OTU B Flt **Wellington IC** **X9928** **-R** **Training**
S/L J C Betts + T/o 1943 Balderton and crashed two minutes later
Sgt Morris inj into a field on Staple Farm, Hawton, a mile SSW
Sgt Byford inj of Newark-on-Trent, Nottinghamshire. At the time
of the crash, the Wellington's undercarriage had
been raised when, without warning, the nose of the aircraft pitched down and
before the situation could be rectified, the bomber was on the ground. A pre-war
regular officer, S/L Betts is buried in Elstree (St. Nicholas) Churchyard. His
two injured companions were admitted to Newark General Hospital.

12 Oct **17 OTU** **Blenheim IV** **V6324** **Training**
1941 Sgt M W E Paul RAAF + T/o Upwood for a navigation exercise. When about
Sgt E A Hafner + 65 miles E of Filey, Yorkshire, an engine failed
Sgt H B Morgan RAAF + and the Blenheim went into the sea. All are
commemorated on the Runnymede Memorial.

13 Oct	16 OTU	Anson I	N9668	Training

13 Oct 1941

16 OTU **Anson I** **N9668** **Training**

Sgt W H E Phillips RCAF inj T/o Upper Heyford a demonstration flight and
P/O Paxton inj had landed safely. Sgt Phillips RCAF then
taxied across the direction of the prevailing
wind and had stopped the Anson when, without warning, it was hit by one of the
unit's Hampdens. The two unnamed wireless operators escaped injury, while the
two named airmen were treated in SSQ Upper Heyford for slight head injuries and
minor cuts and bruises. Sadly, Sgt Phillips RCAF was destined to be killed in
April 1942, when his Hampden crashed at Croughton.

16 OTU **Hampden I** **P5345** **Training**

Sgt D F Allen RCAF inj T/o Upper Heyford and wrecked in the manner
described above. Sgt Allen RCAF joined the
two injured from the Anson in SSQ Upper Heyford, himself suffering from wounds
to the head.

25 OTU B Flt **Wellington IC** **N2762** **Training**

P/O D L Atkinson inj T/o Finningley for a night exercise. Undershot,
P/O A G Burt with the flaps retracted, and crashed 0050
Sgt Dann inj amongst some huts on the airfield boundary.
Sgt Titterington Hydraulic failure was the underlying cause
Sgt R Jones of the accident.
Sgt T A Evans

14 Oct 1941

16 OTU **Hampden I** **P1227** **Training**

Sgt G H A Halcro RCAF T/o Croughton for night flying practice. Landed,
Sgt H Kendall downwind by mistake, and wrecked after running
off the flare path.

22 OTU **Wellington IC** **R1654** **Training**

Sgt W L Falardeau RCAF + T/o Wellesbourne Mounford for a navigation
Sgt B I Hoese RCAF + exercise. Encountered poor weather conditions
Sgt L B Woodfield + and while flying in cloud, lost control and
Sgt R McNamara + dived into the ground at 1044, not far from
Sgt A Hildebrandt + the Gloucestershire-Oxfordshire border, about
a mile W of Cornwell, 3 miles W of Chipping
Norton. The two RCAF members of crew were buried in Little Rissington (St.
Peter) Churchyard, Sgt Hoese being an American from Worthington, Indiana. The
others were claimed by their next of kin.

14-15 Oct 1941

15 OTU **Wellington IC** **R1275** **Op: Nickel**

W/O C L Humphrys pow T/o 1910 Mount Farm tasked to fly; base-Orleans-
Sgt J C Spragge + Dreux-base and carrying 30 packages of EH(F)50/25
Sgt E A Tredenick RCAF + and 27 packages of EH(F)50/25G, plus 2 x 250lb GP
Sgt P B Tomes + delayed action bombs. Crashed in the vicinity of
Sgt T J Snell + Evreux (Eure), France, where those who died rest
Sgt E J Waldron + in the communal cemetery.

15 OTU **Wellington IC** **R1783** **Op: Nickel**

Sgt A E R Beverley + T/o 1905 Mount Farm similarly tasked and armed.
Sgt W H Box + Crashed at Barville (Eure), 18 km E of Lisieux.
Sgt D A Rutherford RCAF + All are buried in Barville Churchyard. Rather
F/S W S Barclay RCAF + unusually, no next of kin details have been
Sgt D A Cameron RCAF + appended against the RCAF members of crew.
Sgt W M McGarry +

15 Oct 1941

11 OTU **Wellington IC** **T2556** **-K** **Training**

Sgt G J McGill-Nutt RNZAF + T/o Bassingbourn for night flying practice. At
Sgt J G Nubley + approximately 2035, in poor weather, the bomber
Sgt J A Taylor + overshot the airfield, stalled and crashed, a
Sgt E P Smith inj fire breaking out immediately. Sgt McGill-Nutt
of the RNZAF rests in Bassingbourn cum Kneesworth
Cemetery, Sgt Nubley lies in Benwell (St. James) Churchyard, Newcastle-upon-Tyne
and Sgt Taylor is interred at the City of London Cemetery, Manor Park, East Ham.
It is reported that Sgt Smith escaped virtually unscathed.

18 OTU **Wellington IA** **N2866** **Training**

P/O D K M Mendela PAF T/o Bramcote for a navigation flight and force -
landed 1400 some 2 miles E of Llanbedr airfield.

16 Oct	25 OTU A Flt	Anson I	W2626	Training

16 Oct **25 OTU A Flt** **Anson I** **W2626** **Training**
1941
Sgt G S Douglas RCAF inj T/o Balderton for night circuits and landings
Sgt E H C Hardman + during which the Anson crashed 2130 in Claypole village, near the airfield. Sgt Hardman lies in Tinsley (St. Lawrence) Churchyard.

17 Oct **11 OTU** **Anson I** **R9810** **Training**
1941
Sgt H T Skett inj T/o Bassingbourn for a night exercise. Undershot
Sgt E F Bing inj the approach and wrecked 0235 after hitting a
Sgt R White inj hedge on the airfield boundary. All were taken
Sgt J E Burrell inj for treatment in SSQ Bassingbourn, Sgt Bing and
Sgt W R Miles inj Sgt Burrell having sustained very severe arm and
Sgt E S Marples inj leg injuries respectively.

15 OTU B Flt **Wellington IC** **N2808** **Training**
Sgt P J Masini + T/o Harwell. Stalled, while avoiding a tree,
Sgt L G Cockram + and crashed 1601 at Kingstoncommon Farm on the
Sgt L A H Saul + bank of the Old Canal, less than a mile NNE of
Sgt R F Whittington + Kingston Lisle, twixt 4 and 5 miles WSW from
Sgt S E Sales + Wantage, Berkshire. Five are buried in Harwell
Sgt A W Bissell + Cemetery, while Sgt Bissell rests in Heston (St. Leonard) Churchyard, Heston and Isleworth.

15 OTU B Flt **Wellington IC** **R3205** **Training**
Sgt W A C Dickinson + T/o Harwell for a 6-hour cross-country. At
Sgt H Tattersfield + 1309 the crew reported, by means of syko, their
Sgt R E Arnold + position to Silloth as being over Rhyl. At
Sgt C W Almond + 1458 Silloth transmitted a bearing, after which
Sgt C J S Buckle + nothing was heard. By this time, the weather
Sgt F W Church + over the Irish Sea was decidedly inclement with a westerly gale, accompanied by heavy rain and
a cloud base estimated at 800 feet. All are commemorated on the Runnymede Memorial. Serving with the volunteer reserve, Sgt Buckle came from Victoria in British Columbia, Canada.

16 OTU **Hampden I** **P5310** **Training**
P/O J A D Scroggie + T/o Upper Heyford for a navigation exercise in
Sgt R F A Young inj the course of which the propeller and reduction
Sgt J Bremmer inj gear sheared from the starboard engine. Unable
Sgt Hart inj to maintain height, the Hampden crashed 1500 some 3 miles SE of Aberaeron, Cardiganshire.
P/O Scroggie is buried in Cheltenham Cemetery, while Sgt Young, who died the following day from his injuries, rests at Wandsworth (Streatham) Cemetery. It is reported that Sgt Hart dislocated a shoulder and sustained rib fractures but Sgt Bremmer clambered from the wreckage with little more than shock (he may have been a member of the RCAF).

18 Oct **27 OTU** **Wellington IC** **X9821** **Training**
1941
F/S L A Hill + T/o Lichfield for dual night circuits. During
Sgt J A Gillespie RAAF + the exercise, the weather deteriorated and while
Sgt C V Irish + banking to port, about a mile N of the airfield,
Sgt P Walker + the Wellington flew into the ground. Local rescue services were hampered by the wet ground,
the bomber having skidded across several fields adjacent to a lane, aptly known as Sludgey Lane, before bursting into flames. The tragedy occurred at around 0200. Sgt Gillespie RAAF was buried in Fradley (St. Stephen) Churchyard at Alrewas, while his companions were taken to their home towns. In respect of the Australian's burial, his was the third air force interment at Fradley which would, eventually, contain thirty-three servicemen, the majority of them being casualties from 27 OTU.

20 Oct **12 OTU** **Wellington IC** **R1037** **Training**
1941
P/O K Farnes + T/o Chipping Warden for night training. Crashed
P/O C H Hayes inj at 2310 into the nearby village while trying to
Sgt C H Brumby inj go round again, bursting into flames. P/O Hayes
Sgt Ralph inj was dangerously injured and died at 5 a.m. the next day; he is buried in Malden (St. John The
Baptist) Churchyard, Malden and Coombe. P/O Farnes, a Cambridge University and England cricketer, rests in Brookwood Military Cemetery.

| 20 Oct 1941 | 15 OTU | Wellington IC | T2889 | Training |

Sgt Crump — T/o Mount Farm for night circuits and landings. Overshot the airfield at 2040 and ended up by dragging down telegraph wires bordering the airfield. No injuries reported.

| 20-21 Oct 1941 | 23 OTU | Wellington IC | Z8786 | -Q | Op: Nickel |

F/L R J Newton
F/S Cooper
Sgt F A Tait RCAF
Sgt H Smith
Sgt P N Herbert
Sgt Harrison
Sgt H F Farley
Sgt G T Ramm

T/o 1843 Pershore (6 aircraft in total) carrying 2 x 250lb, EHF 50/27 and EHF 50/27G Nickels and set course for the Paris area. During the sortie, the intercom failed and on return to base at 2317 the Wellington crashed, heavily, and the port engine caught fire. The blaze spread quickly and though the crew scrambled out through the pilot's escape hatch, several members of the fire tender crew were taken to SSQ Pershore after sustaining injuries while dealing with the fierce blaze which engulfed the bomber and set off much of the ammunition and the two bombs, that had been brought back. F/L Newton and F/S Cooper were screened personnel, while the remainder, less Sgt Harrison, were No. 4 crew on No. 18 course. Soon after this incident, they were posted to 214 Squadron and on 28-29 January 1942, their skipper, Sgt Tait RCAF, failed to return from operations (see Bomber Command Losses, Volume 3, page 26).

| 21 Oct 1941 | 19 OTU | Whitley V | P5103 | Training |

P/O L T Younie RNZAF   +
Sgt H G Roughton RNZAF   +
Sgt R T Oliver RCAF   +
Sgt J Reid   +
Sgt S Scott   inj

T/o Kinloss for a night cross-country, in the course of which the starboard engine leaked a considerable amount of glycol. Height was lost to around a 1,000 feet when, suddenly, the nose dropped and at 2359 the bomber dived into the ground at Ardestie between Arbroath and Dundee. On impact, the aircraft went up in flames. The three Commonwealth airmen rest in Kinloss Abbey Burial Ground, while Sgt Reid was taken back to Lanarkshire and interred in Rutherglen Cemetery.

| 22 Oct 1941 | 13 OTU | Blenheim IV | L9205 | Training |

Sgt D S Evans — T/o Bicester for a navigation exercise. At around 1350, the Blenheim was force-landed near the Buckinghamshire village of Marsh Gibbon, a mere 3 miles ESE from the airfield at Bicester. No one was hurt in this incident, caused by the loss of the port engine's propeller, but the bomber was consumed by fire.

| | 16 OTU | Hampden I | P5318 | Training |

Sgt E Robinson   +
Sgt R Gordon   +
Sgt S K Holland   +

T/o Upper Heyford for a night navigation sortie during which the Hampden crashed 1940 into a hillside some 300 yards S of Wiggington Church and in the direction of Paradise Farm, 6 miles SW of Banbury, Oxfordshire. Sgt Robinson rests in Shipley (Nab Wood) Cemetery, Sgt Gordon was taken home to Scotland and Leuchars Cemetery, while Sgt Holland is buried in Harpenden (Westfield) Cemetery.

| 23 Oct 1941 | 17 OTU | Blenheim I | L1305 | Training |

Sgt R S Trigg — T/o Upwood for a formation exercise but when the leader ordered the formation to break, Sgt Trigg became disorientated and at 1830 he forced-landed on the partially built airfield at Chelveston in Northamptonshire, wrecking his Blenheim in the process.

| | 18 OTU | Wellington IC | R1138 | Training |

Sgt Kozorys PAF   inj

T/o Bitteswell for night circuits and landings. Flew into a tree and crashed 2245 at Ullesthorpe some 6 miles SE of Hinckley, Leicestershire. The accident card indicates that four crew members were hurt, but they are not named in unit records.

| 24 Oct 1941 | 10 OTU | Whitley V | P5023 | Training |

F/S C E Levitt   +
Sgt W R Crowther RNZAF +
Sgt S Slater   +
Sgt G N Leadley   +

T/o 0150 Stanton Harcourt for night flying practice. Shortly before 0210, while banking SE of the airfield, the port wing struck a 60 foot tree, causing the Whitley to roll on to its back and crash near Eaton, Berkshire. The first two named were taken to Brookwood Military Cemetery; the others were claimed by their next of kin. F/S Levitt had amassed a total of 1,469 flying hours.

Note. In respect of the accident summarised at the foot of the previous page, a report from P/O Gibbs to the Chief Technical Officer (W/C W H Colder) at 10 OTU has survived the passage of time. In it he writes, "Whitley V P5023 with F/S Levitt as Captain took off from Stanton Harcourt at 0105 hours. Soon after a mist began to settle down over the aerodrome and the aircraft was given a "green" to land. Making a circuit, the aircraft lost height and was seen to go up in flames. On investigation at the scene of the crash, the aircraft struck the top of a high tree (approximately 60 foot) with the port wing. The outer portion of the wing was torn off at the points of attachment leaving the wing tip in the top of the tree. From marks on the wreckage and the tree it would appear the aircraft was banking to the left, this together with the force of impact and the loss of the wing caused the aircraft to roll over to the left and crash in an inverted position, The aircraft caught fire and was immediately burnt out. From the little that was left of the aircraft, it was possible to ascertain that the wheels had been locked down but the flaps were still up. One airscrew blade was still attached to its hub and this blade was in fine pitch. The aircraft had flown 187.03 hours. Port engine 148462 51.45, Starboard engine 148440 52.45. The aircraft was placed Category E." Attached is a note from W/C Colder who noted, "I have inspected the remains of the aircraft at the scene of the crash and concur in the above report." Bearing in mind the number of air accidents taking place, the amount of paperwork being generated must have been considerable and, thus, it is perhaps not too surprising that thousands of reports were destroyed, or considered unimportant, during the process of releasing files into the public domain.

24 Oct 1941	11 OTU	Wellington IC	T2705	Training

P/O E C Ball — T/o Steeple Morden. Bounced on landing at 1200, stalled and was wrecked in the ensuing crash, a fire breaking out soon after the impact. In his report, P/O Ball stated that upon ballooning into the air, the control column jammed.

12 OTU	Wellington IC	R1071	Training

Sgt G W Bibby	inj	T/o Chipping Warden for a night exercise. Came
Sgt T L Leighton RAAF	+	into land at around 2345, but was at a very low
Sgt Robinson	inj	altitude and while turning, steeply, towards the
Sgt Coulter	inj	flare path, flew into a hangar and burst into
Sgt McFerran	inj	flames.
Sgt Hankin	inj	
Sgt Colman	inj	Crash and Rescue:

P/O Cox
W/O Bennett
Sgt Sayer
Cpl Mitchell
AC1 Attack
AC1 Batty
AC1 Cox
AC1 Glover
AC1 Harris
AC1 Howard

Showing a total disregard for their own safety, ten members of the ground staff became involved in a desperate battle to drag the injured airmen from the blazing wreckage. Without a shadow of doubt, had it not been for their courage, the crew would have stood little chance and the death toll might well have been considerable. In the event, only Sgt Leighton RAAF perished and his funeral service was held at 1100 hours on 28 October at Aston le Walls Roman Catholic Church, followed by interment in Brookwood Military Cemetery.

16 OTU	Hampden I	P4301	Training

Sgt J C Hill	+	T/o Croughton to practice night bombing. Hit
Sgt H Weir	+	trees and came down at Charlton, 4 miles WSW
Sgt R C D Jones	+	of Brackley, Northamptonshire. Three, including
Sgt R H Brickett	+	two Rhodesians, Sgts Hill and Jones, were laid

to rest in Upper Heyford Cemetery. Sgt Weir was taken to Lewes Cemetery. It is noted that his wife had an unusual second Christian name, Louvain.

17 OTU	Blenheim IV	V6004	Training

| Sgt P D Thompson | + | T/o Upwood for formation practice. During the |
| Sgt A I W Fairbairn | + | flight, it became necessary to change over tanks |

but, tragically, the correct procedure was not followed and an engine failed. Unable to maintain height, the crew headed for Grafton Underwood airfield, Northamptonshire, where they crashed, attempting to land at 1005. The crew rest in various cemeteries.

24 Oct 1941	**20 OTU**	**Wellington IA**	**N3007**	**Training**

Sgt H M Bailey — T/o 1058 Lossiemouth but both engines cut at a thousand feet and the crew ditched in the Moray Firth. Their flight had lasted a mere two minutes.

	21 OTU B Flt	**Wellington IC**	**R1031**	**Training**

Sgt H C King + T/o 2129 Edgehill but was in trouble immediately
Sgt L H Thackwell + and four minutes later the Wellington stalled and
Sgt C H Webb + crashed at Lower Brailes, Warwickshire, a village
Sgt R W Campbell + nine miles WSW of Banbury, Oxfordshire. Locals
Sgt C K Rutt + living nearby rushed to help, amongst them a Red
Sgt S Baverstock inj Cross Auxiliary Nurse, Priscilla Righton, and it
was her timely treatment of the badly injured
rear gunner that ensured his survival. The others were not so fortunate and they now rest in various cemeteries across the United Kingdom. On 7 November 1999, Sgt Baverstock (since deceased) was reunited with his saviour and along with her son, Christopher, he was able to visit the spot where his Wellington had crashed with such terrible consequences fifty-eight years previous.

Note. Credit for much of what is reported above is issue 39 of the Bomber Command Association newsletter and Eric Kaye of Epwell, near Banbury.

25 Oct 1941	**25 OTU C Flt**	**Hampden I**	**P1234**	**Training**

P/O J W Atkin RCAF + T/o Finningley for a cross-country exercise.
Sgt L M G McDonald RNZAF + Visibility was poor and the Hampden strayed from
Sgt H Hughes + its intended course and collided with a barrage
Sgt H E Jacobs + balloon cable. Out of control, the bomber came
down at 1245, and burst into flames, near the Vickers Armstrong airfield at Weybridge, Surrey. Both Commonwealth airmen were taken to Brookwood Military Cemetery, while Sgt Hughes rests in Frodsham (St. Lawrence) Churchyard and Sgt Jacobs is buried at Newport Jewish Cemetery.

26 Oct 1941	**13 OTU**	**Blenheim IV**	**N6220**	**Training**

Sgt A G Gempton RNZAF — T/o 1029 Bicester but almost immediately an engine cut out and the Blenheim crash-landed a minute or so later in a field 2 to 3 miles SW of the airfield.

	18 OTU	**Wellington IC**	**X9807**	**Training**

P/O Z Smolik PAF + T/o Bramcote for night flying practice. While
Sgt Z Laskos PAF + banking, steeply, in order to keep the flare
Sgt J Teodorko PAF + path in sight, lost control and flew into trees
Sgt M Lydka PAF + at 2255 near Wolvey Fields, 5 miles SE from Nuneaton, Warwickshire. All were laid to rest in Nuneaton (Oaston Road) Cemetery.

	23 OTU	**Wellington IC**	**T2844 —B3**	**Air Test**

P/O H Rose + T/o Pershore. At around 1655 the dinghy broke
Sgt T N D Boyd RCAF + loose and fouled the controls. Before anyone
P/O M F Gibson RCAF + could bale out, the aircraft went into a steep
F/S W Walker + dive and both mainplanes failed, sending the
P/O R C Symes + bomber hurtling into the ground near Swindon
Sgt F H P Tolley + Farm, Stoke Orchard, 4 miles NNW of Cheltenham,
Sgt P E Lacey RCAF + Gloucestershire. The three Commonwealth airmen were taken to Gloucester Old Cemetery, while the others are buried in their home towns.

27 Oct 1941	**17 OTU**	**Blenheim IV**	**V6013**	**Training**

Sgt H W Taylor + T/o Upwood for a navigation exercise. Crashed
Sgt F R Bayliss + around 1000 at Wetmoor Farm, Gayton, 6 miles NE
Sgt J A Hedley + of Stafford. All rest in their home towns.

30 Oct 1941	**14 OTU**	**Hampden I**	**P1294**	**Training**

F/O G D Kerr + T/o Cottesmore for a cross-country flight. Seen
Sgt I M Williams + to emerge from cloud, diving almost vertically,
Sgt D Tatton + and crash at Llynclys, 3 miles SSW of Oswestry.
Sgt H Playforth + All lie in various cemeteries. Two of the crew lost brothers; LAC Stanley Rhys Williams died in South Africa on 5 March 1943, while training to be a navigator and Sgt Cyril Tatton, killed in July 1941 (see Bomber Command Losses, Volume 2, page 101).

1 Nov 1941	16 OTU	Hampden I	P5303	Training

Sgt J M Butterworth   +   T/o Upper Heyford for a navigation exercise.
Sgt A R Enderby   +   Soon after acknowledging a recall signal, dived
Sgt T G Williams RAAF   +   and crashed 1350 near Royal Leamington Spa in
Sgt R C Hollingworth RCAF   +   Warwickshire. Three were taken to Stratford-
upon-Avon Cemetery, but Sgt Enderby is buried
in Lincolnshire at Alford Cemetery. A week previous, flying with Sgt Butterworth
in Hampden I P1185, Sgt Enderby and Sgt Hollingworth RCAF had been obliged to
parachute, after which their skipper landed safely at Fairwood Common.

2 Nov 1941	17 OTU	Blenheim IV	Z5947	Training

P/O C W Bush RCAF   +   T/o Upwood. While flying in cloud, lost control
P/O A T Sims   +   and crashed at around 1715 at East Leake, some 8
Sgt E J Bush   +   miles S from the centre of Nottingham. P/O Bush
RCAF, an American from Carbondale, Illinois, was
laid to rest in Ramsey Cemetery; his crew were taken to their home towns. This
particular Blenheim had been seriously damaged on 14 April 1941, the pilot on
that occasion being Sgt Norman-Arterton, who escaped unhurt.

3 Nov 1941	15 OTU	Wellington IC	R3201	Training

P/O Nicholson   inj   T/o Hampstead Norris for dual circuits and
Sgt B L Howell   inj   landings. Stalled and crashed 1250, while
approaching the runway, finishing up amongst
trees.

5 Nov 1941	10 OTU	Whitley III	K8981	Training

Sgt G B C Miller   T/o Stanton Harcourt. Landed 1535, at base, but
ballooned back into the air and before Sgt Miller
could open the throttles to cushion its next arrival, the bomber stalled and hit
the ground with considerable force, thus becoming the last of its Mark to be
written off in Bomber Command service. For Sgt Miller, however, it was the first
of two serious accidents that would befall him during his OTU training.

6 Nov 1941	16 OTU	Hampden I	P5386	Training

Sgt R E Hatherill   +   T/o Upper Heyford to practice night bombing. At
Sgt S W Green   +   around 2000, flew into the ground at Eastmount
Sgt R Goff   +   Farm, some 2 miles E of Chalgrove airfield in
Sgt W Dott   +   Oxfordshire. Accident investigators reported
that the Hampden had struck the ground on an
even keel and in a 40 degree dive with its undercarriage retracted. All are
buried in various United Kingdom cemeteries. Sgt Hatherill lost his brother,
Cpl Charles Edwin Hatherill, while serving with the 5th Battalion, The East
Lancashire Regiment. Killed in Normandy on 29 July 1944, he rests in Bayeux
War Cemetery.

	22 OTU B Flt	Wellington IC	X9702	Training

W/O J A Rich DFM   +   T/o Stratford-upon-Avon. While in the circuit,
P/O R R Clamp   +   the port engine failed and at 1708 the aircraft
Sgt C R Whitworth   inj   landed, downwind. The throttles were opened in
Sgt D A Mitchell RCAF   inj   an attempt to go round again but after gaining
P/O J N Sanders   inj   some height, the Wellington stalled and crashed
just off the airfield at Alscot Park and caught
fire. W/O Rich had recently completed a tour of duty with 142 Squadron and
fifteen days after his tragic death, the London Gazette published his DFM. He
rests in Hutton (All Saints) Churchyard, Brentwood. P/O Clamp is buried in
Mitcham (London Road) Cemetery, Surrey. Sgt Whitworth was destined to die in
an air crash, still with 22 OTU, on 25 May 1942, while Sgt Mitchell RCAF was
posted missing in action on 28 September 1942, flying with 148 Squadron.

8 Nov 1941	17 OTU	Blenheim IV	N3626	Training

P/O J Lang   T/o Upwood for a high-level bombing exercise.
Coming down through cloud, P/O Lang lost power
from the starboard engine. Throttling back on the port motor, he lowered the
undercarriage and forced-landed 1451 on Holme Fen, Huntingdonshire.

9 Nov 1941	13 OTU	Blenheim IV	V5810	Training

P/O R H Powell   T/o Bicester. Crash-landed 1310, approximately,
at Yewtree Farm, a few hundred yards NNE of
Tathall End and between 3 and 4 miles N from Wolverton, Buckinghamshire.

9 Nov	13 OTU	Blenheim IV	Z5810		Training

9 Nov 1941

13 OTU   **Blenheim IV**   **Z5810**   **Training**

Sgt E S Bawden   inj   T/o Bicester for a navigation exercise. Lost
Sgt Griffiths   inj   oil pressure from one engine and crashed 1055
Sgt Murray   inj   while making an emergency landing, with the
                                     wheels retracted, near Blisworth, 6 miles SSW
from the centre of Northampton. The first two named were very seriously injured.
Sgt Bawden, however, returned to active duty and by the spring of 1943 he was
flying Halifaxes with 76 Squadron. Sadly, his aircraft failed to return from
Dortmund on 23-24 May (see Bomber Command Losses, Volume 4, page 156).

16 OTU   **Hampden I**   **P1225**   **Training**

Sgt W R Stipe RCAF   T/o Croughton for night bombing practice, in
                                     the course of which fog commenced to descend
over the airfield. Landed 0530, heavily, and smashed the undercarriage unit
and though the crew scrambled clear, unharmed, a fire broke out and the bomber
was destroyed.

17 OTU   **Blenheim IV**   **Z6359**   **Training**

Sgt J A C Scott   T/o Upwood but sank back, momentarily, onto the
                                     runway when the undercarriage was prematurely
retracted. On return to base at 1240, the Blenheim crash-landed and caught fire.

25 OTU   **Hampden I**   **L4176**   **Training**

Sgt H A Ogden   inj   T/o Finningley for night bombing practice. Came
Sgt McHugh   inj   down at 1912, after colliding with trees in
                                     Cantley Wood, Cantley, 4 miles E of Doncaster,
Yorkshire. Both Sgt Ogden and Sgt McHugh sustained broken knee caps. The two
unnamed members of crew escaped uninjured.

25 OTU B Flt   **Wellington IC**   **N2783**   **-Q**   **Training**

Sgt H C Howard RAAF   +   T/o Finningley for a night exercise. Crashed,
Sgt A J Coe RNZAF   inj   due to an incorrectly set altimeter, 2115 near
Sgt F M Oddy   +   Rossington, 4 miles SE of Doncaster. The two
Sgt W Holden   +   RAAF members of crew rest in the extension to
Sgt R W Durdin RAAF   +   Finningley (St. Oswald) Churchyard, while their
Sgt C W Musto RAAF   inj   two Yorkshire born wireless operators are buried
                                     in Shipley (Nab Wood) Cemetery and Bradford
(Bowling) Cemetery respectively. Sgt Coe RNZAF received burns to his hands
while Sgt Musto RAAF required treatment for facial injuries.

11 Nov 1941

13 OTU   **Blenheim IV**   **Z5800**   **Training**

Sgt C C Crozier   +   T/o 1523 Hinton-in-the-Hedges for a formation
P/O Conquer   inj   flying sortie. Two minutes later, travelling
Sgt H D Perrin   +   at high speed, the Blenheim smashed into trees
                                     at Bloxham, 3 miles SSW of Banbury, Oxfordshire.
Sgt Crozier rests in Dorchester Cemetery; Sgt Perrin lies in Welwyn Cemetery.

16 OTU   **Hampden I**   **L4035**   **Training**

Sgt A H Stack RCAF   +   T/o 1334 Croughton for circuits and landings,
Sgt J L Yeo RCAF   +   climbing steeply before stalling and crashing
Sgt S J Carberry   +   to the E of the airfield. On impact, the air-
                                     craft burst into flames. Both Canadians, they
were aged 20 and 19 respectively, lie in Upper Heyford Cemetery, while 21 year
old Sgt Carberry is buried in Glasgow (St. Kentigern's) Roman Catholic Cemetery.

12 Nov 1941

17 OTU   **Blenheim IV**   **T1793**   **Training**

P/O T B Skinner   T/o Upwood. Reported to have stalled at 20 feet
                                     while nearing the runway and in the ensuing
crash the undercarriage unit was broken, damaging the bomber beyond repair.

15 Nov 1941

11 OTU   **Wellington IC**   **R1149**   **Training**

Sgt H A Leopold RCAF   +   T/o Bassingbourn for a night exercise. Stalled
Sgt J W Early RCAF   +   while preparing to land and crashed 2233 near
Sgt G A Adkin   inj   Kneesworth, 11 miles SW of Cambridge. Visibility
Sgt A G Arnold   +   at the time of the crash was extremely poor. The
Sgt E H Jaques   +   three Commonwealth airmen rest in Bassingbourn
Sgt K H Butler RAAF   +   cum Kneesworth Cemetery; Sgt Arnold was taken
                                     to Upton-cum-Chalvey (St. Mary) Churchyard in
Slough, while Sgt Jaques is buried at Sheffield (Abbey Lane) Cemetery.

15 Nov
1941

15 OTU A Flt	Wellington IC	Z8836	-K	**Training**

P/O R M S Rutter   + T/o 2000 Mount Farm for a five-hour night
P/O E G Poole   + navigation exercise. At 2235, Linton-on-Ouse
Sgt H McG Tanner   + picked up wireless signals from this aircraft,
Sgt P C de B Summerton + at which time the bomber seemed to be about 30
Sgt G W N Dalley   + miles off the Norfolk coast. An extensive
Sgt G B D Bowden   + Air-Sea Rescue search proved fruitless and
                      all are commemorated on the Runnymede Memorial.

16 Nov
1941

17 OTU	Blenheim IV	V5421	**Training**

Sgt S E Strate RCAF   T/o Upwood for a cross-country. Encountered
                       adverse weather and at around 1330 the crew
baled out, leaving their aircraft to crash in open countryside near Sedgebrook,
4 miles WNW of Grantham, Lincolnshire.

19 OTU	Anson I	W2627	**Training**

F/S A N Bulpitt   inj T/o Kinloss for a night navigation exercise.
                   inj Iced up and ditched circa 2200 in Dornoch Firth
                   inj and roughly 2 miles WSW of Dornoch, Sutherland.
                        Shortly before entering the water, and while
descending from 8,000 feet to 2,000 feet, the wireless operator advised his
skipper that the wireless equipment had failed. Although no one was badly
hurt, the crew spent an uncomfortable nine hours in their dinghy before help
arrived. Only the pilot's name is identified.

18 Nov
1941

15 OTU	Wellington IC	R1764	**Training**

F/L R M B Field   T/o 1910 Hampstead Norris but the port tyre
                   burst, causing the Wellington to swerve off
the runway. The undercarriage then collapsed and the aircraft caught fire.
Crash and Rescue:

LAC H Jones   + LAC Jones, the duty driver of the Crash and
AC1 N Guthrie   Rescue vehicle, was struck and killed by a
                     still revolving propeller blade as he tried
to reach a member of the bomber's crew, trapped in the burning wreckage.
Meanwhile, AC1 Guthrie fought his way inside the blazing fuselage and despite
the danger from exploding ammunition and oxygen bottles, plus the distinct
possibility that the fuel tanks might explode at any moment, began to direct
a steady stream of foam towards the seat of the fire. An appreciation of his
bravery was published by the Air Officer Commanding 6 Group in group orders.
LAC Jones was taken home and buried in Whippingham (St. Mildred) Churchyard
at Cowes on the Isle of Wight.

25 OTU D Flt	Manchester I	L7248	**Training**

F/S L H Adams DFM   + T/o Finningley for a night navigation flight.
F/S R W H Baxter DFM   + Crashed 2245, following loss of power from the
P/O C Danielson   inj port engine, at Scaftworth, 7 miles NNW from
F/O D B Elleray RAAF   + Retford, Nottinghamshire. F/O Elleray RAAF is
Sgt R Rowell   inj resting in the extension to Finningley (St.
                         Oswald) Churchyard; the others who died were
taken to their home towns. F/S Adams and F/S Baxter had gained their awards
with 50 Squadron and 83 Squadron respectively, details being Gazetted on 25
April and 17 January 1941.

Note. This was the first Manchester to be written off from 25 OTU. It is
believed a total of twenty-seven L serial range examples, plus a further
seven aircraft from the R serial range, were allocated to D Flight. The
first aircraft, L7420, was issued on 7 June 1941 and the type remained in
service with the unit until disbandment in 1943. Of F/S Baxter, who had
flown with 83 Squadron, he lies in Letchworth (St. Mary) Churchyard where
the only other service burial of the Second World War concerns F/S Donald
Paul Gooby who died in the service of 83 Squadron on 12 November 1942.

21 Nov
1941

19 OTU	Whitley V	N1430	**Training**

Sgt R H Beardall RCAF inj T/o Kinloss and crashed, due to engine failure,
Sgt V E Overall   + on the N side of the airfield. Sgt Beardall RCAF
                         died on 24 November; he rests in Kinloss Abbey
burial Ground; Sgt Overall is buried in Woodgrange Park Cemetery, East Ham.

22 Nov 1941	**25 OTU A Flt** P/O T A Lumb Sgt Ashbourne RCAF P/O Chevalier Sgt W O Howell RCAF Sgt H Dracass	**Anson I**	**AW939**	**Training**

T/o Finningley for a night navigation sortie. Became lost and their situation was further exacerbated by the failure of the wireless. Abandoned, circa 2245, and left to crash at Lofthouse, 7 miles SE from the centre of Leeds.

23 Nov 1941	**13 OTU** S/L M J Tully F/L R A Henderson	**Tutor** + +	**K8171**	**Training**

T/o Bicester for local flying practice. Crashed while flying inverted, at Caversfield, on the W side of the airfield. S/L Tully, who had come to Bicester with 108 Squadron in September 1939, was taken to Scotland and Edinburgh (Morningside) Cemetery. He had been appointed Chief Ground Instructor on 19 February 1941. F/L Henderson, who was the Adjutant of the Training Wing, was cremated at Oxford Crematorium.

25 Nov 1941	**15 OTU** P/O J C Morton	**Wellington IC**	**X3197**	**Transit**

T/o 1119 Abingdon but had only climbed to about sixty feet when the port engine backfired and the power decayed. With the wheels retracted, P/O Morton crash-landed at Barton Court to the E of Abingdon and near, what in 1941, was the Great Western Railway line twixt the town and Oxford. It is indicated that P/O Morton had logged the grand total of 9,955 flying hours, 1,150 of these on Wellingtons.

26 Nov 1941	**19 OTU** Sgt H W Blackwell RCAF Sgt J Taylor	**Whitley V** + inj	**Z9279**	**Training**

T/o Kinloss for night flying. Landed at 0115 but bounced back into the air, stalled and hit the ground with such force that it burst into flames. Sgt Blackwell RCAF is buried in Kinloss Abbey Burial Ground.

27 Nov 1941	**14 OTU** Sgt R S Carson Sgt J A Tulley Sgt N J Griffiths Sgt B W Bucknell RAAF	**Hampden I** + + + +	**P1155**	**Training**

T/o Saltby for a cross-country but crashed 0835 at Buckminster, 8 miles ENE of Melton Mowbray, Leicestershire. Three lie in the extension to Cottesmore (St. Nicholas) Churchyard, while Sgt Carson was taken back to Northern Ireland and laid to rest in Omagh New Cemetery. It is noted that Sgt Griffiths had been given the name Joffre, possibly in commemoration of the French Commander-in-Chief of the First World War, General Joffre.

5 Dec 1941	**15 OTU** F/O C E Beloe Sgt T A Nesbitt Sgt H Wright Sgt M S Loader Sgt S G Parrott Sgt D J Marcus Sgt J H Mattingly Sgt A G Johnston	**Wellington IC** + + + + + + + +	**X9799**	**Training**

T/o Harwell for a night cross-country, the crew comprising of three pilots, an observer and four wireless operators. At approximately 2300, while flying between 800 and a thousand feet, collided with Tiger Moth II N6968 of 6 EFTS, which was operating from the Reserve Landing Ground at Denton. Both aircraft fell near Piddington, five miles SE of Northampton. All from the Wellington were buried in Kempston Cemetery.

	20 OTU F/S H S D Goss Sgt A R McCoy Sgt M E Kent RAAF Sgt A J Wilson RNZAF Sgt A Flint	**Wellington I** + + + + +	**L4348**	**Training**

T/o Lossiemouth for a navigation exercise. Crashed 1600 some 14 miles W of Strathy Point, Sutherland and burst into flames. The blaze was seen by the crew of another of the unit's aircraft. Three lie in Wick Cemetery and two were claimed by their next of kin.

6 Dec 1941	**13 OTU** Sgt V H Langrish P/O E L V Stanley Sgt A E Bailey F/O D H Ivens	**Blenheim IV** + + + +	**Z7962**	**Training**

T/o 1130 Bicester and crashed, due to incorrect trim tab settings, near the airfield. Two rest in Caversfield (St. Laurence) Churchyard, Sgt Langrish was cremated at Enfield Crematorium, while P/O Stanley was taken to Weston (Holy Trinity) Churchyard. F/O Ivens was being given a lift to an airfield (probably Chivenor) near his home at High Bickington, Devon. The CWGC registers show the crew as belonging to 110 Squadron but this is thought unlikely and the entry on page 189 of Bomber Command Losses, Volume 2, should be deleted.

6 Dec 1941	**17 OTU**	**Blenheim IV**	**L4894**		**Training**

P/O C H Woodworth RCAF   +   T/o Upwood. Stalled and crashed 1455, in a
F/S M Thompson   +   field near the gasworks at Ramsey, while nearing
Sgt R Barr   +   the airfield. At the time of the accident, the
wind was gusting quite strongly. Sgt Barr, who
came from Coleraine in Co. Londonderry and his Canadian skipper are buried in
Ramsey Cemetery, while F/S Thompson was taken to Liverpool (Ford) Roman Catholic
Cemetery.

7 Dec 1941	**21 OTU E Flt**	**Wellington IC**	**Z1089**		**Training**

P/O K W Watson   +   T/o Moreton-in-Marsh for a cross-country flight
Sgt J W Hubbard   +   during which the crew experienced very severe
Sgt C G Tierney   +   icing. With static blocking out all wireless
Sgt E S J T Medder   +   signals, the crew began to descend in order to
Sgt J Martin   inj   establish their position and in the process hit
Sgt R Newton   inj   some trees and crashed 1835 on Pitch Hill near
Sibford Ferris, 8 miles WSW of Banbury, Oxford-
shire. P/O Watson and Sgt Tierney were brought back to Moreton-in-Marsh New
Cemetery, Sgt Hubbard lies in Chartham Cemetery, while Sgt Medder is buried in
Whitchurch (St. Andrew) Churchyard, Tavistock. Sgt Martin owes his life to P/O
J A Bright, P/O W T G Gabriel and PC L Simons who happened to be in the area.

	21 OTU E Flt	**Wellington IC**	**Z8784**		**Training**

P/O J A Grierson RNZAF   +   T/o Moreton-in-Marsh for a dark night flying
P/O Sheppard   inj   exercise. Encountered very severe icing and
Sgt Bingley   inj   at 2000, despite the best endeavours of both
     inj   pilots, the Wellington came down in a plough
     inj   field near Benson airfield. As it slid along
     inj   the frozen ground, it collided with three trees
and burst into flames. P/O Grierson RNZAF lies
in the extension to Benson (St. Helen) Churchyard. It is reported that in the
final seconds of flight, the second pilot could be seen with both his feet on
the instrument panel, straining desperately to get the nose to rise.

	22 OTU B Flt	**Wellington IC**	**T2566**	**–C**	**Training**

P/O W J Turner DFM   +   T/o Wellesbourne Mountford. Flew into a snow
P/O J Lynas RCAF   +   storm and almost immediately lost engine power.
P/O R J Jackson RCAF   inj   Descending rapidly, the Wellington hit a tree
Sgt P R Chancellor   +   and crashed 1815 into Newbold Road, about a mile
Sgt Lane   inj   from the runway. P/O Turner, whose DFM had been
Gazetted on 24 October 1941, following duty with
405 Squadron, lies in Blackburn Cemetery; P/O Lynas RCAF is at Stratford-upon-Avon
Cemetery, while Sgt Chancellor was taken to Hastings Cemetery. Although very
badly hurt, P/O Jackson recovered and was later posted to 57 Squadron. Sadly,
he was posted missing from operations to Bremen on 29-30 July 1942 (see Bomber
Command Losses, Volume 3, page 143).

	22 OTU A Flt	**Wellington IC**	**X9625**		**Training**

Sgt J H A Cox   inj   T/o Wellesbourne Mountford. Came in to land
P/O J E Allen   inj   slightly off the centre line of the runway and
WO2 A D W Cuthbert RCAF   inj   began to overshoot. Visibility in the area was
Sgt Allen   inj   marginal with heavy snow showers and at 1825
the Wellington flew into Loxley Hill, roughly
a mile or two S of the airfield. Two died from their injuries; P/O Allen rests
in Worsley (St. Mark) Churchyard, while it seems likely that WO2 Cuthbert RCAF
had relatives in Scotland as he is buried in Glasgow (Craigton) Cemetery.

	25 OTU B Flt	**Wellington IC**	**X9612**		**Training**

F/S P Sleight   T/o Finningley for night flying practice.
Sgt H Kitto   Abandoned circa 1800 from 1,000 feet as a
result of engine failure, the Wellington coming
down in a wood between Rossington and Edlington, villages W of the airfield.

8 Dec 1941	**14 OTU**	**Hampden I**	**P2112**		**Training**

Sgt W H S Martin RAAF   T/o Saltby. By mid-afternoon the weather had
deteriorated to the extent that while in the
airfield circuit, Sgt Martin RAAF lost sight of the runway. While trying to
recognise a landmark, he allowed his speed to fall away and while banking at
fifty feet, the Hampden stalled and crashed near the aerodrome.

8 Dec   **15 OTU**   **Wellington IC** **R1391**   **Training**
1941   F/O J A Whittet   T/o Hampstead Norris. During the sortie, the
starboard engine shed its propeller. The crew
regained the airfield and landed at 1530, but were unable to prevent the bomber
from running onto rough ground, whereupon its undercarriage collapsed.

9 Dec   **14 OTU**   **Hampden I** **P1168**   **Training**
1941   P/O O K Fisher RAAF   + T/o Saltby for night circuit training. While
        Sgt K F Thornton RAAF   + turning left at 1858, some 4 miles S of the
airfield, P/O Fisher RAAF lost control, stalled
and crashed. Both are buried in the extension to Cottesmore (St. Nicholas)
Churchyard. It is noted that P/O Fisher of Leederville in Western Australia
was an Associate of the Royal Institute of British Architects.

        15 OTU   **Wellington IC** **R1769**   **Training**
        F/O A R Head   inj T/o Mount Farm for night flying practice. On
        Sgt S W Poynter   inj return to base, the Wellington came into land
        Sgt C F J Turnbull   inj with both propellers still in coarse pitch.
        Sgt R K Hanley   inj It then seemed to drift away from the flare
        Sgt K W Squirrell   + path and F/O Head initiated overshoot procedure.
        Sgt Bell   While doing so, a wing dropped and though level
flight was regained, the nose suddenly pitched
up and at 2022 the bomber stalled and crashed.

                                  Crash and Rescue:
        LAC Beasley   LAC Beasley, a nursing orderly, was one of the
first to reach the scene. Totally disregarding
the fact that the bomber, which had fallen inside a barn, was well and truly
alight, he forced his way through a broken window and managed to get inside the
fuselage. One by one, he dragged the members of the crew to safety, seemingly
oblivious of the intense heat which was setting off ammunition and threatening
to explode the fuel tanks at any moment. Sadly, Sgt Squirrell was beyond help
and he is now buried in Ipswich Cemetery. Sgt Bell, apparently, was unhurt.

        17 OTU   **Blenheim IV** **R3675**   **Training**
        Sgt S O Hill RCAF   inj T/o 1304 Upwood but while banking to the left
at 300 feet, the port engine cut. Sgt Hill RCAF
promptly throttled back the starboard motor but lost control and crashed near the
airfield. Commissioned, he lost his life on 28-29 July 1942, while serving with
18 Squadron (see Bomber Command Losses, Volume 3, page 164).

        17 OTU   **Blenheim IV** **V5373**   **Training**
        Sgt C B Wilcock   T/o Upwood. Landed 1615, downwind, swung from
the runway and finished up in the overshoot area
with its undercarriage collapsed.

10 Dec   **13 OTU**   **Blenheim IV** **L9383**   **Training**
1941   F/S G H Schrader RCAF   + T/o 1130 Bicester but the starboard engine cut
        Sgt A W Steadman   + at 50 feet and in the ensuing crash, the bomber
        Sgt W Dunn   + burst into flames. The first two named rest in
Caversfield (St. Laurence) Churchyard, while
Sgt Dunn is buried in Bishop Auckland Cemetery. On 28 October 1941, with Sgt
Knox at the controls, this Blenheim had made an emergency landing at Shawbury.
Prior to being posted to 13 OTU, F/S Schrader RCAF had been obliged to parachute
after his aircraft had flown into a barrage balloon cable.

        15 OTU   **Wellington IC** **Z9100**   **Training**
        P/O J C Cooke   + T/o Mount Farm. Lost height, due to engine
        P/O S G A Hamburger   + failure, and flew into a haystack before crashing
        Sgt T D Durrant   inj at 1530 near Littlestoke Farm, 3 miles N from
        Sgt J C R Robertson   inj Goring, Oxfordshire. Of those who died, three
        Sgt N Scott   + were claimed by their next of kin, but City of
        P/O G D Fudge   + London born P/O Hamburger is buried in Harwell
Cemetery. His mother, Elizabeth Jessie Hamburger
had been widowed on 18 October 1916, when Pte Joseph Hamburger of the Royal
Fusiliers was killed in France. P/O Fudge, who lies in Bournemouth (Wimborne
Road) Cemetery, lost his cousin, Sgt Peter Norton Fudge, when the 518 Squadron
Halifax V LK706 Y3-L in which he was flying disappeared over the Atlantic in
November 1944. Both were related to the author's wife, on her mother's side.

12 Dec
1941

15 OTU   **Wellington IC**   **T2810**   **Training**

Sgt H W Penny   T/o Hampstead Norris for a night flying exercise which ended with the crew undershooting their approach and crashing 0617 near the airfield. Interestingly, this Wellington appears on a Malta return signal dated 15 June 1941, indicating the bomber was en route to the Middle East, ex-15 OTU. However, by 22 November, it was on the unit's home strength.

13 Dec
1941

14 OTU   **Hampden I**   **X2992**   **Training**

P/O A P Webb   +   T/o Cottesmore with the intent of practising
Sgt W N Hattemore   +   single-engined flying. Lost control, stalled and crashed 1525 at Blue Point Farm , near the airfield. P/O Webb is buried in the extension to Cottesmore (St. Nicholas) Churchyard, while Sgt Hattemore was taken home to Warwickshire and interred in Beaudesert (St. Nicholas) Churchyard.

14 Dec
1941

14 OTU   **Hampden I**   **AD758**   **Training**

P/O J T Chrystal   T/o Cottesmore for practice bombing. At 1050 the crew tried to land, with a full bomb load, at Jurby airfield on the Isle of Man. On touch down, the Hampden bounced and finished up in a field, where it caught fire.

15 Dec
1941

11 OTU   **Wellington IC**   **X3170**   **Training**

Sgt A L Sanderson RNZAF   +   T/o Bassingbourn for a night cross-country.
Sgt D J Dempsey RNZAF   +   While descending at speed, in a shallow dive,
Sgt H B L Gittins RCAF   +   flew into the ground circa 2300 on Whittlesey
Sgt B L Grove-Palmer   +   Mere, some 5 miles SSE of Peterborough in
Sgt W R Myles RAAF   +   Northamptonshire. On impact, the Wellington
Sgt P N Lister   +   disintegrated. Five rest in Bassingbourn cum Kneesworth Cemetery, while Sgt Lister was taken to Arnold Cemetery.

14 OTU   **Hampden I**   **P2076**   **Training**

Sgt J C Roy RNZAF   T/o Cottesmore for a night navigation sortie.
Sgt Hugall   inj   While approaching the runway at 2235, the throttle lever controlling the port engine snapped and with the power decaying the Hampden came down in the undershoot area. Posted to 50 Squadron, Sgt Roy RNZAF was reported missing from a raid on Bremen, 25-26 June 1942 (see Bomber Command Losses, Volume 3, page 135).

15 OTU   **Wellington IC**   **R1607**   **Training**

Sgt D A G Sullivan   +   T/o Hampstead Norris for a night exercise. Reported to have crashed 2230, on return to base, on high ground. Sgt Sullivan is buried in Brookwood Military Cemetery. A contributory factor in the cause of the accident was a defective altimeter.

27 OTU   **Wellington IC**   **R1283**   **Training**

Sgt B Poupard   +   T/o Lichfield for a night navigation sortie.
Sgt T Riordan   inj   Following a spell of rough running, during which
Sgt Kitson   inj   the bomber began to lose height, the propeller
Sgt Gaffney   inj   and reduction gear came away from the starboard engine. Sgt Poupard attempted to force -land and while doing so, at 2322, he flew head-on into some trees 2 miles N of Chetwynd, a hamlet on the River Tame roughly 3 miles NE of the airfield. Sgt Poupard lies in Fradley (St. Stephen) Churchyard. Two sustained broken legs, but Sgt Gaffney escaped with slight concussion. Sgt Riordan went on to fly with 98 Squadron and was killed on 7 January 1944; he is buried in Brookwood Military Cemetery.

17 Dec
1941

20 OTU   **Anson I**   **R9585 XT–H**   **Training**

P/O V E Friesen RCAF   +   T/o Lossiemouth. Collided, over Angus, with
F/S J A Stewart RCAF   +   Master I N7931 of 8 FTS, both aircraft coming down in the vicinity of Huntley Farm and about a mile from the Reserve Landing Ground at Stracathro, from where the Master was likely operating. Both RCAF members of the Anson crew and Newfoundlander, Sgt Cook of 8 FTS, described in the CWGC register as a wireless operator and flying with the volunteer reserve, rest in Fettercairn Cemetery. There might well be other casualties, but, unfortunately, the aircraft accident record cards for both aircraft have yet to be found and the only details, so far, to hand have been obtained from 'They Shall Grow Not Old' and various Air-Britain publications.

23 Dec 1941	**12 OTU**	**Wellington IC**	**DV430**		**Training**

Sgt G H Ferguson — inj — T/o Chipping Warden for night flying practice.
Sgt C L McCallum RCAF — inj — At approximately 0415, the Wellington flew into
Sgt G E Ford RCAF — inj — the ground at Wardington, S of the airfield and
Sgt R H Badland RNZAF — inj — four miles NE of Banbury, Oxfordshire. The crew
Sgt G C Cavanagh — inj — escaped with relatively minor injuries.

	14 OTU	**Hampden I**	**L6096**		**Training**

Sgt I R Beldam — + — T/o 1524 Cottesmore with the intent to practice
Sgt F Lambert — + — overshoot procedures but crashed a mile S of the
airfield. Twickenham born Sgt Beldam was laid
to rest in the extension to Cottesmore (St. Nicholas) Churchyard; Sgt Lambert
is buried in Sheffield (Shiregreen) Cemetery. Their aircraft had come off the
productions lines as a Hereford I but had since been modified.

	16 OTU	**Hampden I**	**P1159**		**Training**

Sgt T Reynolds — T/o Upper Heyford for a high-level bombing
exercise but had become lost in the mist and
gloom of a late December day. At around 1715, the crew spotted some red lights
(which turned out to be hazard lights on buildings used by Denham Film Studios)
and coming into wind, forced-landed on Denham Golf Course in Buckinghamshire.

	21 OTU A Flt	**Wellington IC**	**DV422**		**Training**

S/L R G Williams DFC AFM — + — T/o Edgehill for general handling practice.
P/O S A Crump RNZAF — + — While demonstrating stalling and recovery,
P/O I G Grant RNZAF — + — the Wellington went into a dive and crashed,
F/S R I Peach — + — bursting into flames, at 1420 near Wild Spring
P/O A J Hopkins — + — Farm, Little Tew, 5 miles ENE of Chipping
Sgt H G Kelly — + — Norton, Oxfordshire. The first three named
lie in Moreton-in-Marsh New Cemetery. F/S
Peach rests in Sheffield (Shiregreen) Cemetery (see also Sgt Lambert of 14
OTU killed this day and reported above); P/O Peach, a South African, who had
married Barbara Dawn Hopkins of Manor Park, lies in Brookwood Military Cemetery
while Sgt Kelly was taken to Maltby Burial Ground. S/L Williams, who was the
Flight Commander of A Flight had, on 7 December, successfully force -landed a
Wellington from which the crew had baled out, as ordered. Tragically, one of
the pilots under training, Sgt D M MacAlpine, was killed. He is buried in
Glassary (Achnabreac) Burial Ground, Argyll.

26 Dec 1941	**13 OTU**	**Blenheim IV**	**P4856**		**Training**

Sgt W F Boggs RCAF — + — T/o Bicester but an engine cut and the Blenheim
Sgt F R Morris — + — spun into the ground, near the airfield. Sgt
Sgt J W Kennedy — + — Boggs RCAF, an American from New York City, was
taken to Hethe (Holy Trinity) Roman Catholic
Cemetery, while his two companions are buried in their home towns.

28 Dec 1941	**15 OTU**	**Wellington IC**	**Z9109**		**Training**

Sgt L Barker — + — T/o Mount Farm for a night flying exercise.
Sgt T S Sadler — + — Crashed 0215, while attempting to go round
Sgt C E Gilmour RAAF — + — again following a poor approach. Sgt Gilmour
Sgt H Pashley — + — RAAF was buried in Harwell Cemetery; the rest
Sgt J E Frith — + — were claimed by their next of kin. Sgt Barker
is identified on the aircraft accident record
card but his name is omitted from unit records. He rests in West Butterwick
(St. Mary) Churchyard.

	17 OTU	**Blenheim IV**	**Z5984**		**Training**

Sgt H S Thoms — inj — T/o Upwood to practice landings using wireless
Sgt G Owen — inj — procedures, followed by bombing training over
Sgt J E Wilson — inj — The Wash. Flew into the ground at 1505, while
over the North Wootton ranges, some 4 miles N
of King's Lynn, Norfolk. Eyewitnesses report that the Blenheim's starboard
engine seemed to be surging as it dived towards its intended target. Sgt Wilson
died from his injuries and he is buried at Tadcaster Cemetery in Yorkshire.

29 Dec 1941	**14 OTU**	**Oxford I**	**V3993**		**Transit**

F/O Ross DFC — inj — Attempted to t/o Abingdon but crashed without
P/O H K Spark — inj — becoming airborne due to hoar frost accumulating
P/O Coomber — inj — on the mainplanes.

29 Dec	19 OTU	Whitley IV	K9029	Training

29 Dec
1941

19 OTU   **Whitley IV**   K9029   **Training**
Sgt H Harrison RCAF   T/o Brackla. While in the circuit, the starboard
engine caught fire and the bomber was force -
landed at 1540 on, or near the airfield. No injuries reported.

21 OTU   **Wellington IC**   X9694   **Training**
P/O G V Fogarty RAAF   T/o Moreton-in-Marsh. Lost power, while in the
circuit, from the starboard engine and a crash-
landing was made at 1700, wheels up, at Jay Farm, Bledington, 4 miles SE from
Stow-on-the-Wold, Gloucestershire.

27 OTU   **Wellington IC**   T2899   **Ground**
Destroyed by fire while parked at its dispersal
on Lichfield airfield.

Resumé. At the end of the first full year of training, the bomber OTUs had
lost in the region of 400 aircraft (for a fully detailed breakdown of losses,
readers are advised to consult the appropriate appendix), of which around 345
could be attributed directly to training mishaps. Where possible, I have tried
to present as much background information as possible concerning these losses,
but the passage of time means that in a number of cases the circumstances that
brought about their demise will never be fully known. As readers will be well
aware, the reasons were legion, not least being the weather in which the crews
were expected to operate. Mechanical failure, usually engine, cut short the
lives of many embryo aircrew, but even the breakdown of wireless equipment
could have equally disastrous consequences, especially for a crew flying at
night and caught out in deteriorating weather. It will also be seen that enemy
action, principally in the form of intruders, played a not insignificant part
and had not Nachtjagdgeschwader 2 been withdrawn to the Mediterranean theatre
in the early autumn, then casualties from marauding Luftwaffe night fighters
might well have been higher.
     Unfortunately, it has to be recognised that aircrew error was the root cause
for most accidents but in stating this, I am in no way implying criticism of
the airmen concerned. In fact, given the pressing needs of the services, it
is no small wonder that there were not more accidents and a figure of around
400 reflects well the quality of aircrew training.
     Before examining the mishaps of 1942, it is worth remembering that it was
not always service personnel that lost their lives in flying accidents. The
first cases of civilian deaths, resulting from bomber OTU accidents, were reported in September 1940, when Mr and Mrs Evans and their young family died
when an 18 OTU Battle plunged onto their house in Hucknall. During 1941, there
were at least two serious incidents, by far the worst occurring in mid-August
when a 25 OTU Hampden plunged into three houses in London Road, New Balderton.
The summary explains the terrible tragedy that befell the Brumpton family but
an expansion on some of the events of that awful night are appropriate.
     At the inquest, held on the Monday following the crash, several harrowing
tales of bravery were reported to the Newark District Coroner, Mr J B Norman.
Apparently, the impact ruptured the Hampden's fuel tanks and within seconds
the Brumpton's house, which took the full force of the impact, was a mass of
flames. Mrs Brumpton, who was asleep with her youngest child in the front of
the building, immediately tried to get to her six children who were trapped in
the remains of their rooms at the back, but it was to no avail. All doorways
were already blocked by fallen masonry. Forcing open the window of her bedroom
she lowered her child to the crowd that had quickly gathered and then made
good her own escape.
     Meanwhile, at the rear of the dwelling, a Mr W H F Judson from nearby Grove
Street, clad still in his pyjamas and clutching a dustbin lid for protection
from the intense heat, had managed to climb onto the roof of an outbuilding,
from where he reached the wing of the Hampden and make his way towards the
cockpit. By this time dense volumes of smoke were issuing forth from the
bomber and though he could feel some webbing through holes in the Perspex,
Judson could not see the pilot and without a knife, or sharp instrument, he
was unable to make further progress towards freeing the airman. All the while,
the blaze was intensifying and this very brave civilian was forced to retreat
back along the wing. While doing so, the fuel tanks exploded and Mr Judson was
tossed into the road, his pyjamas alight. Although dazed and badly shaken, he
was able to beat out the flames and thus escaped serious injury.
     While this drama was being played out, the Newark Fire Brigade had arrived

at the scene, as had personnel from the local Auxiliary Fire Service. With only limited access to the rear of the properties (all three were alight), the firemen faced a daunting task and it was full two hours and more before they were able to bring the conflagration under control. However, it was not until daylight and mid-morning before the last of the bodies could be recovered from the tons of rubble that now littered the rear gardens. It was indeed a sombre scene.

As recounted in the summary (page 66), Mr Brumpton had been on duty at the nearby shunting yards and had been aware of the blaze. One can only imagine the total devastation that he must have felt upon arriving home at six in the morning to find his own house was afire and learning the awful news that six of his seven children were still trapped and that their could be little hope for their survival. Later that day, when their bodies had been removed (it was mid-morning before the last was brought out) from the ruins of what once had been a warm family home, he had the sombre duty of identifying their remains. Indeed, not only the Coroner, but all who were close to the bereaved husband and wife, spoke of their immense courage and bearing in the days that followed this tragic consequence of war.

Their immediate neighbours had remarkable escapes; from a gutted No. 84 the Richardson family emerged unharmed, while from No. 86 two spinster ladies were brought out with little more than severe shock. From the least damaged house, at No. 80 London Road, eighty-six year old Mr Joseph Atkin and his sister Miss Fanny Atkin had their tale to tell. Asleep when the bomber hit No. 84, Joseph was rudely awakened to find that one of the Hampden's propellers had scythed through the outside wall and was now lying alongside him! Although badly shocked, neither he, or his sister, suffered physical injury.

From the aerodrome at Balderton, Group Captain J C Foden AFC came to see for himself the destruction wrought and to offer his condolences to all who had suffered in this dreadful accident. Wing Commander Slocombe, the Engineering Officer supervised the removal of the wreckage (the rear fuselage and tail had been roped to a nearby apple tree in order to prevent it from slipping onto those searching through the rubble) and at the funerals for the six children, held on the Wednesday following the crash, Pilot Officer Cattell and a Guard of Honour were present.

Sadly, this would not be the last incident of its kind and, thus, it is true to say that anyone living in the immediate vicinity to airfields, operational as well as those used by the training establishments, were at risk whenever aircraft got into difficulties.

With 1942 about to dawn, the state of Bomber Command was, perhaps, at its lowest since the beginning of the war. During the high summer of 1941, the Butt Report had landed on the desk of its instigator, Lord Cherwell, Chief Scientific Advisor to the Prime Minister, Winston Churchill and, as I reported on page 129 of Bomber Command Losses, Volume 2, "his (Butt's) investigations made unpalatable reading". By the autumn, copies had been circulated amongst members of the Air Council and, eventually, through the chain of command, this disturbing analysis of the effectiveness of the bombing campaign had been read by Air Marshal Sir Richard Pierce and his senior staff at High Wycombe and by his group commanders.

An immediate improvement in the fortunes of Sir Richard's command was highly necessary but, as events were to show, he was bedevilled throughout the winter of 1941-1942 by poor bombing results, exacerbated by mounting losses. By the turn of the year, his position had become just about untenable and early in January 1942, he left High Wycombe for pastures new. His replacement was the man who forever will be associated with the history of Bomber Command, the formidable Air Chief Marshal Sir Arthur Harris. Under his direction, the bombing campaign was to go from strength to strength. The importance weighing upon those charged with discharging their training duties cannot be over emphasised. Their expertise, coupled with the dedication of their eager charges, would be crucial to the outcome of the air war over Europe in 1942 and beyond.

3 Jan   **17 OTU**   **Blenheim IV**   **P6959**   **Training**
1942

F/O M J Kingshott RAAF	+	T/o Upwood for a cross-country exercise. Dived
Sgt W Jowett	+	from the cloud base, estimated at 2,000 feet,
Sgt R M Masson	+	and failed to recover before hitting the ground
		at 1145 at Stanton upon Edgebolton, 8 miles NE

from the centre of Shrewsbury. F/O Kingshott RAAF rests in Shawbury (St. Mary) Churchyard, Sgt Jowett is buried in Bradford (Thornton) Cemetery, while Sgt Masson was taken back to Scotland and Aberdeen (Allenvale) Cemetery.

22 OTU B Flt   **Wellington IC**   **X9640**   **Training**

F/S G M Bigglestone	+	T/o Wellesbourne Mountford with a screened
Sgt C T Martin RCAF	inj	pilot, two pupil pilots and support crew for
Sgt Murphy	inj	a night exercise. During the sortie, the port
Sgt H A McLennan RCAF	+	engine failed and while approaching the airfield
Sgt Shoesmith	inj	at around 0105, the Wellington crash-landed and
		skidded, with its wheels retracted, across a

field and buried itself, head-on, into a riverbank. Nearby electricity cables were severed, plunging the aerodrome into darkness as the power supply failed. Two were killed outright and Sgt Martin RCAF succumbed to his injuries within about forty-eight hours of the accident. Funeral services for those who died took place at Stratford-upon-Avon Cemetery.

23 OTU   **Wellington IC**   **T2953**   **Training**

P/O R P Hay	+	T/o Pershore with a screened pilot, two pupil
Sgt R B Murphy RAAF	+	pilots and two wireless operators to practice
Sgt B B Connell RAAF	+	circuits and landings. During the exercise,
Sgt J H Marshall	+	the weather deteriorated and at about 0900,
Sgt H K Jones	+	while turning at very low altitude (probably
		trying to line-up with the runway) lost control

and crashed into a thickly wooded area. Both Australians were laid to rest in Pershore Cemetery; P/O Hay, the son of Professor Robert Hay and Janet Hay, was taken back to Scotland and buried in Huntly Cemetery; Sgt Jones rests in Wales at Llanidloes (Dolhafren) Cemetery, while Sgt Marshall's name is inscribed on panel 11 of the Screen Wall at Chingford Mount Cemetery.

5 Jan   **10 OTU**   **Whitley V**   **Z6979**   **Training**
1942

Sgt G B C Miller		T/o Abingdon for bombing practice. While
		nearing the exercise area, a fire developed in

the Whitley's port engine. Prompt action extinguished the blaze, but soon afterwards the fire flared up again and the bomber began to lose height. The bomb load was jettisoned and at approximately 1600 a forced-landing was carried out on Steart Flats near Lilstock, 6 miles ENE of Watchet, Somerset. It will be recalled that Sgt Miller had been involved in a nasty accident the previous November (see page 83). A little over a year later, now flying Lancasters with 49 Squadron, he failed to return from Lorient (see Bomber Command Losses, Volume 4, page 40).

6 Jan   **19 OTU**   **Whitley V**   **N1498**   **Training**
1942

Sgt D Pike	inj	T/o Kinloss for an evening navigation flight.
P/O J C Castling RNZAF	+	While descending on the last leg of the sortie,
P/O J G Irvine RNZAF	+	crashed 2030 near the summit of A'Choire Mhor
Sgt C S George	+	at Tomatin House, 15 miles SE of Inverness.
Sgt C W Green	+	Those who died rest in various cemeteries;
Sgt E F J Kane RCAF	inj	the two New Zealand born members of crew being
Sgt C M Edgehill	inj	interred in Kinloss Abbey Burial Ground. Both
		had graduated from course 12B at Blenheim. P/O

Castling RNZAF had married Patricia Bentley Castling of Church Crookham. As Jean Gardener, authoress of Aviation Landmarks, reports, a memorial to the deceased was erected in 1984, at the scene of the crash.

9 Jan   **19 OTU**   **Whitley IV**   **K9017**   **Training**
1942

F/S L Clarke	+	T/o Brackla for dual instruction under the
Sgt J M Wilson RCAF	+	command of F/S Clarke. At around 1245, the
Sgt W J Robertshaw RCAF	+	bomber smashed into trees at Cawdor, near the
Sgt R Potten	+	airfield. F/S Clarke rests in Hull Northern
Sgt R L J Edmonds	+	Cemetery, while the next three named lie in
		Kinloss Abbey Burial Ground. Sgt Edmonds was

taken south and interred in Addington (St. Mary) Churchyard, Surrey. Brackla had been in use as a satellite airfield for a mere two days.

11 Jan	**17 OTU**	**Blenheim IV**	**Z6040**	**Training**
1942	P/O C V Pereira	inj		

T/o Upwood for a cross-country but encountered very severe icing and while flying near Scolt Head the engines failed, thus necessitating an immediate emergency landing. This was effected at 1130, during which P/O Pereira, at least, sustained some form of injury.

13 Jan	**21 OTU**	**Wellington IC**	**T2911**	**Training**
1942	P/O D C Dunn			

T/o 1900 Edgehill for a night exercise. At around 1900, observers on the ground glimpsed the Wellington through breaks in the cloud cover flying extremely slowly before it crash-landed on the airfield and caught fire. It is believed the bomber hit high ground at Old Lodge Hill on the western boundary of the aerodrome. No one was badly hurt. For P/O Dunn, a screened pilot, this was the first of two accidents that he would be involved in while at Edgehill.

14 Jan	**17 OTU**	**Blenheim I**	**L1303**	**Training**
1942	F/S S S Lang RCAF	+		
	Sgt A J Sistron	+		

T/o Upwood for night flying practice. While circling the airfield at 1940, and having failed to respond to calls advising landing instructions, the Blenheim crashed at Denhills Farm. F/S Lang RCAF, who came from Cicero, Illinois, was buried in Ramsey Cemetery; Sgt Sistron rests at Lincoln (Newport) Cemetery.

	22 OTU A Flt	**Wellington IC**	**DV481**	**Training**
	F/S B D Farmbrough	+		
	Sgt G M Gee	+		
	Sgt J H O'Connor	+		
	Sgt R L Horning RCAF	+		
	Sgt G C Boudreau RCAF	+		

T/o Wellesbourne Mountford for night flying practice. While attempting to go round the circuit again, stalled and spun to the ground at 2315, N of the runway and near Charlecote being totally destroyed. Investigators reported that the aircraft's airspeed indicator and artificial horizon were unserviceable and this, coupled with adverse weather conditions, was the likely cause of the accident. F/S Farmbrough, the screened pilot and instructor, rests in Aylesbury Cemetery; Sgt Muir, who in January 1939 transferred from the army to the air force, lies in Allestree (St. Edmund) Churchyard; Sgt O'Connor was taken to Shalford Cemetery, while both RCAF members of crew were buried in the air force plot at Stratford-upon-Avon Cemetery. Their aircraft had been with the unit since Boxing Day last and had flown a mere 29.30 hours since its initial delivery to 44 MU at Edzell.

15 Jan	**12 OTU**	**Anson I**	**N5075**	**Training**
1942	F/S R P E North			

T/o Chipping Warden for a cross-country sortie. Flew into a snowstorm and iced up. With failing engines an attempt to land was made at Theale Reserve Landing Ground, Berkshire but the Anson overshot the field and in order to avoid running into trees, F/S North ground looped the trainer, damaging the airframe beyond repair.

17 Jan	**12 OTU**	**Wellington IC**	**R1340**	**Training**
1942	Sgt A R Wilson RNZAF	+		
	Sgt K S Rogers RNZAF	+		
	F/O J C Huston	+		

T/o 1115 Chipping Warden for circuit practice but the starboard engine cut and the Wellington veered violently to starboard, stalled and flew into a tree. All three airmen lie in Brookwood Military Cemetery.

	27 OTU	**Anson I**	**N5030**	**Training**
	F/S J C Addy DFM	+		
	W/O A S Patterson	inj		
	F/S H Johnston	inj		
	Sgt K H Livett RAAF	inj		
	Sgt N Dann RAAF	inj		
	F/S E C McManaman RCAF	+		
	Mr G Halford	+		

T/o Lichfield on a night navigation exercise, accompanied by an Assistant Meteorologist, Mr Glyn Halford. At 2015, flew into the cloud covered slopes of Snaefell (2,038 feet above sea level) on the Isle of Man. F/S Addy, whose DFM had been Gazetted on 24 October 1941, after service with 103 Squadron, and F/S McManaman RCAF rest in Jurby (St. Patrick) Churchyard. The injured were admitted to the Island's military hospital at Douglas. W/O Patterson was destined to lose his life during the unit's involvement with the Düsseldorf raid in late July 1942. Mr Halford's name is commemorated at Bracknell, where it appears on the Roll of Honour situated inside the main building. I am grateful to Chris Pointon, 27 OTU historian, and Ian Macregor of the Archive Section at Bracknell for this detail.

17 Jan	27 OTU	Wellington IC	X9706		Training

1942

Sgt E F Webb RAAF	+
Sgt F E Williams RAAF	+
F/S J S R Woolnough RAAF	+
Sgt J H Rogerson RAAF	+
Sgt M H Welch	+
Sgt W R Beeton	+
Sgt A W Savage	+

T/o Lichfield for night bombing practice. During the exercise, the weather deteriorated and a signal was received indicating that the Sperry compass had failed. Uncertain of their position, the crew requested a QDM. Nothing further was heard and at approximately 2105 the Wellington crashed into a wood, 2 miles S of Echilles Farm at King's Bromley, 5 miles N from Lichfield, Staffordshire. The RAAF members of crew were taken to Fradley (St. Stephen) Churchyard, while the others were claimed by their next of kin.

18 Jan	12 OTU	Wellington IC	X9931		Training

1942

Sgt B O Gates RCAF	inj
Sgt R M Lawrence RCAF	inj
P/O R B Halliday RCAF	inj
Sgt E Mason	inj
Sgt D H M Jacques RCAF	inj
Sgt S Cox	inj

T/o Chipping Warden for a night exercise. While in the circuit and NE of the runway, crashed at about 0010 in the vicinity of Redhill Wood. Not long after this incident, the entire crew were posted to 214 Squadron, failing to return from a raid against Dortmund on 14-15 April 1942 (see Bomber Command Losses, Volume 3, page 69). On that occasion, Sgt Lawrence RCAF was the captain of the aircraft.

19 Jan	20 OTU	Wellington IC	R1646		Training

1942

F/O J W Thomson DFC RNZAF	+
Sgt R J Jackson RCAF	+
F/S H J Kelley RCAF	+
Sgt J B Riley	+
Sgt B C Dickson RAAF	+
Sgt R A Milliken RAAF	+

T/o Lossiemouth for a cross-country flight and failed to return at its scheduled time. On, or around, 19 February the police relayed a message to Lossiemouth indicating that the wreckage of an aircraft had been reported in the vicinity of Clunie Water (or Clunie Glen) near Braemar in Aberdeenshire. Three days later, a service party struggled across the snow-covered countryside and confirmed that the remains were those of the Wellington. From evidence gathered at the scene it seems likely the bomber came down at around 1250 hours. All six bodies were recovered and taken for burial in Dyce Old Cemetery where four now have special memorials type "C" as their grave markers. The service numbers for the two Australians indicate they joined the RAAF on the same day and it is further noted that Sgt Milliken had married Mary Patricia Donahoe Milliken from Des Plaines, Illinois.

21 Jan	17 OTU	Blenheim IV	Z7453		Training

1942

F/O E R Parke RAAF	+
Sgt F Coakley	+
Sgt M York	+

T/o 1156 Upwood for a navigation exercise. Presumed to have crashed in the sea off Filey on the Yorkshire coast. All are commemorated on the Runnymede Memorial. In civilian life, F/O Parke RAAF had served the Melbourne City Council as a Health Inspector.

	25 OTU B Flt	Wellington IC	X9636		Training

| Sgt K W Dunlop | |

T/o Finningley for a night navigation exercise but was abandoned, due to engine failure, and left to crash 1845 at Toseland, 4 miles ENE of St. Neots, Huntingdonshire.

25 Jan	23 OTU	Wellington IC	R1803		Training

1942

Sgt I D Steward	inj
Sgt W Clayton	
Sgt P E Poulson	inj
Sgt J G Forbes RCAF	
Sgt W L F Kellow	
Sgt J H Bye RCAF	+

T/o Pershore for night bombing practice. Lost engine power and while trying to land drifted off the line of the flare path. Sgt Steward opened up in an effort to go round again but the Wellington failed to gain height and at 2108 flew into a hillside, about a mile S of the airfield. The force of the impact caused the fuselage to break in half. Sgt Bye RCAF is reported to have fallen from the aircraft (possibly in its final seconds of flight) and he is buried in Pershore Cemetery after, initially, being taken to Evesham General Hospital Mortuary. Of the survivors, four were killed on bomber operations before the year was out. Two, Sgt Forbes RCAF and Sgt Kellow, died together when their 419 Squadron Wellington failed to return from Gennevilliers (see Bomber Command Losses, Volume 3, page 99). Less than a fortnight later, Sgt Clayton, now with 12 Squadron, was killed over Germany (see page 122) and then in the December, Sgt Poulson, who had sustained slight concussion, died while raiding Duisburg with 103 Squadron (see page 282).

26 Jan
1942

| 14 OTU | | **Hampden I** | P1186 | **Training** |

P/O J M Marock RCAF   +   T/o Cottesmore for night high-level bombing.
P/O W H Lynch RAAF   +   For reasons that could not be determined, the
P/O S S White RAAF   +   Hampden dived at 0540 into the ground less than
Sgt E O'Connell RAAF   +   a mile N of Pinchbeck, 2 miles N from Spalding
in Lincolnshire. All lie in the extension to
Cottesmore (St. Nicholas) Churchyard.

| 25 OTU B Flt | **Wellington IC** | X9607 | **Training** |

S/L G H Everitt   T/o Finningley for a night navigation sortie.
Lost engine power, brought about by severe
icing, and crash-landed 1835 in a field at Draughton Crossing, Draughton,
ten miles N of Northampton. At first it was thought the bomber, which had
skidded across a ditch, could be repaired but in the event this proved not
to be feasible and the airframe was struck off charge on 22 March 1942.

28 Jan
1942

| 13 OTU | **Blenheim IV** | Z7290 | **Ground** |

Destroyed by fire at Bicester.

| 21 OTU E Flt | **Wellington IC** | Z1157 | **Training** |

Sgt A Orr   T/o Edgehill for night bombing over the Radway
Sgt C W P Rice RAAF   +   ranges. Circa 2100, collided in the air with
Sgt Fitton   inj   another of the unit's Wellingtons (R1165 of
Sgt Hollingworth   inj   C Flt, captained by Sgt H A Taylor) and is
believed to have crashed in the range area.
The other aircraft returned to Edgehill and landed safely, though Sgt Taylor
took the precaution of baling out his crew, some sustaining ankle injuries as
a consequence. Sgt Rice RAAF is buried in Moreton-in-Marsh New Cemetery. An
enquiry into the accident concluded that Sgt Taylor had been late in completing
his detail, while Sgt Orr had arrived in the range area ahead of schedule.

| 22 OTU C Flt | **Wellington IC** | X9935 | **Training** |

Sgt R H Vearncombe RCAF   +   T/o Wellesbourne Mountford for a night cross-
Sgt Haines   inj   country. Lost engine power and came down at
P/O Robson   inj   around 2220 on high ground near Compton Verney
P/O Robinson   inj   some 3 miles SE of the airfield. A fire broke
Sgt Fletcher   inj   out soon after the impact. Sgt Vearncombe RCAF
Sgt Dawe   inj   is buried in Fulham New Cemetery, Richmond. It
Sgt Edwards   inj   seems likely that his funeral was arranged by
relatives.

29 Jan
1942

| 13 OTU | **Blenheim IV** | R3907 | **Training** |

Sgt J Ruddock   +   T/o Bicester for a cross-country exercise.
Sgt R S Raines   +   Stalled and dived from the cloud base, estimated
Sgt K Riding   +   at 1,000 feet, and crashed 1310 at Fullaway Farm
near Stert, 2 miles SE of Devizes, Wiltshire. On
impact the Blenheim became a mass of flames. Two are buried in Caversfield (St.
Laurence) Churchyard, while Sgt Riding rests in Marton (St. Paul) Church Burial
Ground at Blackpool. Sgt Ruddock, it will be recalled, had previously trained
on Hampdens at 16 OTU and had been involved in a serious crash the previous
September (see page 71).

| 15 OTU | **Wellington IC** | L7801 | **Training** |

Sgt G W Roberts   T/o Hampstead Norris for a local flying sortie
Sgt D M S Bunn   but became lost, eventually encountering heavy
Sgt D McSheen   snow. At approximately 1430, the Wellington
Sgt A J F Turtill   +   hit the side of hill near Wychford and not far
distant from Chipping Norton, Oxfordshire. Sgt
Turtill is buried in Hornchurch Cemetery.

| 17 OTU | **Blenheim IV** | L8785 | **Training** |

P/O A Petty   +   T/o Warboys for a navigation exercise. At
Sgt J F Charnock   +   around 1215, having been recalled to base due
   inj   to adverse weather, the crew were seen nearing
the airfield when their aircraft stalled and
crashed to the ground. P/O Petty of Pirbright in Surrey was buried in Bury
Cemetery, while Sgt Charnock, described as a wireless operator/observer, lies
in Liverpool (West Derby) Cemetery.

30-31 Jan	18 OTU	Wellington IC	N2848	-G		Training

30-31 Jan
1942

18 OTU — **Wellington IC** — **N2848** — **-G** — **Training**

F/L C Kujawa PAF   +   T/o Bramcote for a night cross-country. While
P/O J Polczyk PAF   +   flying in cloud, the crew met conditions of snow
F/O T J Bieganski PAF   +   and quite severe icing. It is likely a decision
Sgt J Sadowski PAF   +   was made to lose height, possibly in order to
Sgt J A Tokarzewski PAF   +   try and establish their whereabouts, and while
Sgt J Fusniak PAF   inj   doing so the bomber flew into high ground near
            Buckden Pike (2,302 feet above sea level), on
Wharfedale, a mile or so NE of Buckden, in the bleak North Yorkshire moors and
some 15 miles NW of Pateley Bridge. Those who died rest in the Polish Plot at
Newark Cemetery. Despite a broken leg, Sgt Fusniak PAF crawled through the snow
to the village of Cray and raised the alarm. On 21-22 July 1942, he was shot
down during operations to Duisburg with 301 Squadron; for the second time he
was the sole survivor (see Bomber Command Losses, Volume 3, page 155). In 1972,
he returned to Buckden Pike and placed a stone in remembrance of his crew; this
is visited each year by air cadets from 246 Squadron Air Training Corps. Held
by the unit since May 1941, the Wellington had logged 194.55 flying hours.

2 Feb
1942

18 OTU — **Wellington IC** — **R1006** — **Ground**

During maintenance at Bramcote, a crane lifted
the Wellington's port engine for the purpose of flushing the oil system. While
suspended, the motor slipped and sparks set fire to a tray containing paraffin.
Before the blaze could be brought under control, the bomber was destroyed. The
time of this accident is given as 1500 hours. Allocated on 29 October 1941, no
flying totals have been appended.

4 Feb
1942

21 OTU C Flt — **Wellington IC** — **L7893** — **Training**

P/O J H Kirk   +   T/o Moreton-in-Marsh for night flying but hit
P/O H Waugh   +   a tree and crashed 2055 to the NE of the air-
Sgt W J A Brock RAAF   inj   field. Investigators probing the wreckage of
Sgt W J Howson   +   the bomber assessed that the undercarriage had
Sgt R Marshall   inj   been retracted and that the throttles were set
            for normal cruising. The first two named are
buried in Moreton-in-Marsh New Cemetery, while Sgt Howson and Sgt Marshall,
who died from his terrible injuries at 0740 on 6 February in Station Sick
Quarters Moreton-in-Marsh, were taken to their home towns. One airman, he is
not named, escaped injury. All were from No. 19 course, which passed out the
following day and were posted to Feltwell and 57 Squadron.

6 Feb
1942

13 OTU — **Blenheim I** — **L6809** — **Training**

Sgt W E Smith   +   T/o 1504 Hinton-in-the-Hedges for a solo flying
            detail but collided with a tree and crashed a
minute later, some 2 miles NE of the airfield. Sgt Smith, who likely wished to
be known as Everard-Smith (documents showing his name use this form of spelling
which links his second Christian name to his surname) is buried in Chorley (St.
Gregory) Roman Catholic Churchyard. His aircraft had initially served with 18
Squadron but had been held on unit charge since 28 November 1940. At the time
of the accident, it had amassed 593.15 flying hours.

21 OTU — **Wellington IC** — **R1047** — **Training**

F/S R K R Talbot   +   T/o Edgehill to practice bombing over the nearby
Sgt W E G Taylor RCAF   +   Radway ranges but the port propeller, along with
Sgt R F Anderson RCAF   +   the reduction gear, came off and at 1500, while
Sgt A E Jaeckels   +   circling on one engine, height was lost and the
Sgt W Gorman   +   Wellington came down at Rough Hill Farm, less
Sgt D H Tyne   inj   than a mile S of the airfield. Sgt Taylor RCAF
            is buried in Northern Ireland in Hillsborough
(St. Malachi) Church of Ireland Churchyard, having likely been claimed by his
relatives. Sgt Anderson RCAF, an American from Houston, Texas, Sgt Jaeckels and
fellow Londoner, Sgt Gorman, lie in Moreton-in-Marsh New Cemetery. Their skipper,
a screened pilot, rests in Windsor Cemetery. Sgt Tyne, despite receiving aid from
LAC D Woodward, died; he was taken to Kilnwick Percy Churchyard, Nunburnholme.

7 Feb
1942

20 OTU — **Wellington IC** — **T2720** — **Training**

Sgt C O Cairns   T/o 1804 Lossiemouth but failed to gain height,
P/O M F O Clarke   inj   stalled and crashed. A fire broke out almost
            immediately and the Wellington, which had been
on unit charge for a year and a day, was totally destroyed. It had accumulated
a total of 406.55 flying hours.

8 Feb	12 OTU	Wellington IC	X9954	Transit

Sgt W G Smith RCAF	+	T/o 0135 Waddington with the intention of
Sgt F Llewellyn RCAF	+	returning to base but crashed moments later
Sgt E G Hatch	+	while banking in the circuit, coming down
Sgt R G Holmes	+	about a mile NE of the airfield. The three
Sgt A Smith	+	Canadians were taken to Brookwood Military
F/S W R Donaldson RCAF	+	Cemetery, while their companions were claimed
Sgt T R Gamble	+	by their next of kin.

	21 OTU	Wellington IC	T2608	Training

Sgt S Appley	+
Sgt D F J Ward	+
Sgt J Pringle	+
Sgt W H Griffiths	+
Sgt J Crossley	+

T/o Moreton-in-Marsh to practice homing on
beacons with Marconi cooperation. From what
evidence is available, it seems that at some
stage in the exercise, the crew were in the
vicinity of Brize Norton airfield. It is also
reported that the Wellington, flying low, hit
an obstruction and in pulling up sharply, lost control and crashed 1510 some
2 miles N of Eastleach Turville, 10 miles ENE of Cirencester, Gloucestershire.
Those who died are buried in various cemeteries across the United Kingdom.

	22 OTU	Wellington IC	T2714 DD-C	Training

Sgt L G J Mizen	+
Sgt J G Hardie	+
P/O D J Richardson RCAF	+
F/S L J R Bechard RCAF	+
F/S E G Jenner RCAF	+
Sgt Rutherford	inj

T/o Wellesbourne Mountford for a navigation
exercise during which the wireless equipment
failed. The crew, apparently, overflew the Isle
of Man and, failing to recognise the southern
shores of Scotland, turned east and at around
1430 flew into Burn Tod Gill near Ireby, nine
miles NE of Cockermouth, Cumberland. The three
Canadians were taken to Silloth (Causewayhead) Cemetery, Sgt Mizen is buried in
Heston (St. Leonard) Churchyard and Sgt Hardie rests in Birkenhead (Landican)
Cemetery. Sgt Rutherford raised the alarm, having walked for 3 miles.

10 Feb	11 OTU	Wellington IC	X9905	Training

Sgt W Mance	+
Sgt J S Taylor	+
F/S H E Jowett RCAF	+
Sgt A C E Rogers	+
Sgt A W Ford	+
Sgt A J Foote RAAF	+

T/o 1827 Steeple Morden for a night cross-
country. By around 2035, the crew were in
extreme difficulty and while trying to plot
their position, crashed in the Harrow Green,
Leytonstone district of NE London. The bodies
were taken to Leyton Mortuary and, subsequently,
four were buried in Bassingbourn cum Kneesworth
Cemetery. Sgt Mance lies in Brookwood Military Cemetery, while Sgt Taylor rests
at Haigh (St. David) Churchyard. A typed transcript of the aircraft's wireless
log has been retained in AIR29 644 Appendix D59.

	14 OTU	Hampden I	X2989	Training
P/O W C Anderson RCAF				

T/o Saltby. Wrecked 0950 after making an
emergency landing in the airfield circuit.

	16 OTU	Hampden I	P2142	Training
Sgt E A Robinson RCAF				

T/o Upper Heyford for night training. Flying
at 2,000 feet and while circling the airfield
in preparation to land, the starboard engine cut. The order to bale out was
given and all complied, after which the bomber fell at 2045 into Tusmore Park.

	23 OTU	Wellington IC	X9805	Training
P/O D D Bonnett				

T/o Pershore for night circuits and landings.
Approaching the runway, P/O Bonnett was given
a "red", whereupon he initiated overshoot procedures. Throttles were opened
and the undercarriage and flaps were retracted but while downwind and flying
at 300 feet the starboard engine failed, necessitating a forced-landing.

	25 OTU	Manchester I	L7478	Training
P/O E R Siebold	inj			
Sgt F King	+			

T/o Finningley. Reported to have crashed at
around 1430, some 2 miles N of Bawtry airfield.
At the time, the Manchester was making ready to
land when a sudden loss of engine power caused the bomber to swing violently and
fly into the ground. Sgt King, an air gunner, was cremated in Newcastle-upon-Tyne
(West Road) Crematorium. This was the second (and last) Manchester to be
destroyed in 25 OTU service.

11 Feb
1942

10 OTU   **Whitley V N1439**   **Training**

Sgt R H Lean RCAF	+	T/o 2129 Abingdon for night circuit training
Sgt R O Colquhoun RCAF	+	only to crash a minute later, coming down in
Sgt A Robson	+	Upwood Park on the NW side of the airfield.
Sgt D E Hughes	inj	The bomber burst into flames. Both Canadians

are buried in Brookwood Military Cemetery,
while Sgt Robson was taken back to Yorkshire and Richmond Cemetery.

17 OTU   **Blenheim IV V6383**   **Unknown**

Reported to have been abandoned in the general
vicinity of Bottisham, 6 miles ENE of Cambridge, but, as yet, no supporting
documentation has been discovered.

13 Feb
1942

20 OTU   **Wellington IC T2707 JM-Z**   **Training**

Sgt C Handley   T/o Lossiemouth for a night cross-country and
set course for Tiree. Just beyond Inverness an
engine failed and the starboard propeller came off. Unable to maintain height,
the crew baled out, leaving their aircraft to crash in Glen Affric on the lower
slopes of Mullach Fraoch-Choire and about 20 miles N of Fort William. Proceeding
to the Middle East, where he joined 148 Squadron, Sgt Handley lost his life on
7 July 1942. He is buried in Egypt at Fayid War Cemetery. In respect of his
crash in Scotland, an excellent description was reported by Kevin Whittaker in
the August 1996 edition of "Wrecksearch", The Aviation Archaeology Newsletter.

21 OTU   **Wellington IC R1082 SJ-L**   **Training**

Sgt E T A Cartwright	+	T/o Edgehill. Crashed 1735 while nearing the
Sgt A E Adlam	+	airfield at Wellesbourne Mountford, coming down
Sgt J W Edwards	inj	on, or near, the Stratford road on the N side of
Sgt A W McRae	+	the aerodrome. Sgt Cartwright of Stoke Newington
Sgt M Hone	inj	was taken to Stratford-upon-Avon Cemetery, the
Sgt D B Atkinson	+	others who died rest in their home towns.

22 OTU   **Wellington IC R3229**   **Training**

P/O W A Smith	inj	T/o Stratford-upon-Avon for night training.
P/O K Mould	inj	Landed circa 2155 but due to failure of the
Sgt Mitchell	inj	flaps, the bomber ran off the end of the
Sgt G A Molozzi RCAF	inj	runway and finished up on the nearby railway.
Sgt Lane	inj	By an odd quirk of circumstance, Sgt Molozzi
Sgt Normington	inj	RCAF lost his life in similar circumstances
Sgt Murphy	inj	precisely a year later, still on the strength
F/S Swain	inj	of 22 Operational Training Unit.

14 Feb
1942

12 OTU   **Wellington IC R1027**   **Training**

P/O J R Reenberg RNZAF	+	T/o Chipping Warden for an exercise, at night,
P/O F B Richardson RNZAF	+	combining bombing, photography and navigation.
Sgt G N Duke	+	On return to base, P/O Reenberg RNZAF elected to
F/S W L Sinclair RCAF	+	overshoot but in doing so he opened the throttles
Sgt W Walsh	+	rather too quickly, causing the starboard engine
		to falter. Moments later, the Wellington clipped

a tree and crashed 2326, bursting into flames near the airfield. The three
Commonwealth airmen rest in Brookwood Military Cemetery; Sgt Duke was taken
back to Northern Ireland and laid to rest in Knocknamuckley (St. Matthias) Church
of Ireland Churchyard, while Sgt Walsh lies in Manchester (Gorton) Cemetery.

14 OTU   **Hampden I P1316**   **Ground**

While undergoing a forty-hour inspection, under
the protection of a shelter tent, at Saltby, a faulty heater lamp set fire to the
structure and the Hampden was destroyed.

16 OTU   **Hampden I P2081**   **Training**

Sgt J R Viau RCAF	+	T/o Upper Heyford for a night cross-country.
F/S W J Hodge RCAF	+	While approaching Chipping Warden airfield, the
	inj	Hampden flew into trees and crashed, heavily.
Sgt J Pegrum	inj	Sgt Viau RCAF, along with his fellow Canadian,
		was taken to Brookwood Military Cemetery. It is

believed that Pte Armand Viau of 5 General Hospital, Royal Canadian Army Medical
Corps, who died on 29 January 1942 and who also lies in Brookwood, was Sgt Viau's
elder brother. Sgt Pegrum made a good recovery and, subsequently, went on to fly
in Lancasters with 207 Squadron, teaming up with P/O John Stephens.

14 Feb   **20 OTU**   **Wellington IC**   **N2825**   **Training**
1942
P/O R E Cobb	+
P/O A S Witter	+
Sgt H Clark	+
Sgt J Bishop RAAF	+
Sgt J H Goldie RAAF	+
Sgt N A Burr	inj

T/o Lossiemouth for night flying practice. At around 2335, the Wellington crashed on a hill near Rothes, 9 miles SSE of Elgin, Moray. The cause of the tragedy was attributed to engine failure. P/O Cobb is buried in France Lynch (St. John The Baptist) Churchyard, Chalford, while the two RAAF members of crew were laid to rest in Lossiemouth Burial Ground. P/O Witter and Sgt Clark lie at City of London Cemetery and Lancaster (Scotforth) Churchyard respectively.

15 Feb   **14 OTU**   **Hampden I**   **L6020**   **Training**
1942   P/O P Chinn

T/o Cottesmore for a night exercise during which an engine caught fire. Unable to control the blaze, the crew baled out at circa 2020 and the Hampden fell near Risegate, five miles NNW of Spalding, Lincolnshire. Originally, the aircraft had come off the factory production line as a Hereford I.

17 Feb   **11 OTU**   **Wellington IC**   **T2710**   **Training**
1942
Sgt A Livingstone	+
Sgt I H Cunningham	+
Sgt P J H Hamlin RNZAF	+
Sgt H C George RNZAF	+

T/o 2010 Steeple Morden for night training but lost flying speed, stalled and crashed. A fire broke out immediately. Sgt Livingstone rests in Bathgate Cemetery; Sgt Cunningham is buried in Northern Ireland at Clonallan Church of Ireland Churchyard, while Sgt Hamlin RNZAF and Sgt George RNZAF were interred in Bassingbourn cum Kneesworth Cemetery.

19 Feb   **17 OTU**   **Blenheim I**   **L1359**   **Ground**
1942
P/O J V Hadland	
P/O S Coshall	

At 2150, while taxying at night in readiness to take off from Warboys, the Blenheim ran into Blenheim I L6808 (P/O J H Ellis RCAF) which was stationary, downwind, and with its lights switched off. Both aircraft were badly damaged, but while the latter was repaired, P/O Hadland's machine was deemed to be a write-off. P/O Coshall later joined 487 Squadron and was killed in action, flying Venturas, on 3 May 1943 (see Bomber Command Losses, Volume 4, page 131).

20 Feb   **17 OTU**   **Blenheim IV**   **Z5899**   **Training**
1942
Sgt W T Kyle RCAF	+
Sgt L S de Lisser	+
Sgt E Scott	+

T/o Upwood for a low-level (between 500 and six hundred feet) navigation exercise; base-Gillingham-Stratford-upon-Avon-Hungerford-Cottesmore-base. While flying on the second leg, the crew strayed 15 miles off track and at 1028 the starboard wingtip was sliced off by a barrage balloon cable in the Birmingham defensive area. Out of control, the Blenheim smashed into the ground. Sgt Kyle RCAF and his Jamaican observer, Sgt de Lisser of St. Andrew, rest in Sutton Coldfield Cemetery, while Sgt Scott lies in Newcastle-upon-Tyne (St. Nicholas) Cemetery.

21 Feb   **16 OTU**   **Hampden I**   **X2968**   **Training**
1942
Sgt D G Allen RCAF	+
Sgt G C Robertson	+

T/o Upper Heyford for local night flying. At around 1920, following three unsuccessful attempts to land, the Hampden crashed out of control near Wootton, a village 5 miles SW of the airfield. Sgt Allen RCAF is buried in Upper Heyford Cemetery, while Sgt Robertson was taken back to Scotland and Glasgow (Eastwood) Cemetery.

22 Feb   **12 OTU**   **Anson I**   **AW970**   **Training**
1942
P/O I G Fadden	
P/O Shapiro	
P/O King	
Sgt Innes	

T/o Chipping Warden for a night navigation exercise. Crashed, after running out of fuel and being partially abandoned, a mile E of Southrop and about 2 miles NNW of Lechlade in Gloucestershire.

         19 OTU   **Whitley V**   **P5101**   **Air Test**
P/O W D Sugrue RCAF	+
LAC J H Potts	+

T/o 1709 Forres but an engine failed and the pilot attempted to return to the airfield. Unfortunately, his turn was too tight and in the prevailing cross-wind, the bomber crashed into a tree-lined bank on the edge of the airfield. Both rest in Kinloss Abbey Burial Ground.

22 Feb   **20 OTU**   **Wellington IC** **R1449**   **Training**
1942   S/L P C Lemon   T/o 1945 Lossiemouth but an engine failed and
this resulted in the bomber stalling back to
the ground. The impact was sufficiently severe to destroy the Wellington.

23 Feb   **10 OTU**   **Whitley V** **Z6756**   **Training**
1942   P/O G W Caldwell RCAF   inj T/o Abingdon for an evening cross-country
Sgt O N Morris   exercise. At a little before 2040, an engine
Sgt A Taylor   failed and the crew attempted to land at Brize
Sgt K R Bunney   Norton airfield in Oxfordshire. In the event,
they overshot the runway, whereupon the bomber
caught fire. P/O Caldwell RCAF recovered from his injuries and is believed to
have survived the war.

        15 OTU   **Wellington IC** **DV428**   **Training**
        Sgt G W Drinkwater   inj T/o Mount Farm for a night flying detail but
                           inj when an engine failed, the Wellington crash-
                           inj landed 2310, hitting a raised shelter near the
                           inj flare path.
                           inj

24 Feb   **13 OTU**   **Blenheim I** **K7109**   **Training**
1942   Sgt R Weller   T/o Hinton-in-the-Hedges to practice single-
engined landings. At about 1615, Sgt Weller
got into difficulties and opened both throttles in an attempt to go round again.
Unfortunately, the starboard motor failed to respond and the Blenheim swung out
of control, crashed and caught fire. On 25 January 1938, this aircraft had been
allocated to Bristols for development flying, principally in opposite rotation
engine tests and general engine trials. Taken on charge by 13 OTU in September
1941, it had logged 230.40 flying hours up to the time of its demise.

25 Feb   **13 OTU**   **Blenheim IV** **V5811**   **Training**
1942   Sgt Young   T/o Bicester for low-level bombing practice.
Crashed 1200, while making an emergency landing,
at Essex Farm, 3 miles SE of the airfield, the farm being a little over a mile
NNE from the Oxfordshire village of Blackthorn.

        27 OTU   **Wellington IC** **X9682**   **Training**
        Sgt D H Dyson RAAF   + T/o Lichfield tasked for a night navigation
        Sgt C G Veal RAAF   + sortie which involved passage over the Irish
        Sgt A P R Hargrave RAAF   + Sea. At 2256 monitoring stations intercepted
        Sgt S J R Parsons RAAF   + an SOS, transmitted from this Wellington.
        Sgt R G Harkins RNZAF   + Nothing further was heard and it can only
        Sgt R C Madge RAAF   + be concluded that the crew were lost over
the sea. All are perpetuated by the Runnymede
Memorial.

26 Feb   **16 OTU**   **Hampden I** **P5319**   **Training**
1942   P/O J Maura   T/o Upper Heyford for a night navigation detail.
Sgt J G Tallentire   + Lost power from one engine and having been
Sgt J W Connell RCAF   + partially abandoned, crashed 0025 some 2 miles
Sgt K Twidale   + SE of Bourton-on-the-Water, 13 miles ESE from
Cheltenham, Gloucestershire. Sgt Connell RCAF
was brought back for burial in Upper Heyford Cemetery; Sgt Tallentire lies in
Etherley (St. Cuthbert) Churchyard, while Sgt Twidale rests at West Butterwick
(St. Mary) Churchyard. Six months later, P/O Maura, now converted to Wellingtons
and still at 16 OTU, was involved in another very serious crash.

        27 OTU   **Wellington IC** **Z8785**   **Training**
        Sgt R Longmuir RAAF   inj T/o 1440 Lichfield but twenty minutes later,
        Sgt D Jennings RAAF   inj when the port engine failed, the Wellington
        Sgt G H Mellor   crash-landed near Trent Valley Railway Station,
        Sgt T Willey   Lichfield. A fire broke out from the starboard
        Sgt W A Godfrey RAAF   inj motor, the flames spreading rapidly, consuming
the bomber. Sgt Godfrey RAAF died in hospital
from his injuries; he is buried in Fradley (St. Stephen) Churchyard. While
still at 27 OTU, Sgt Mellor survived a second nasty crash and then, having been
posted to 103 Squadron, he failed to return from Aachen on 5-6 October 1942 (see
Bomber Command Losses, Volume 3, page 234). His luck held and he evaded capture.

27 Feb   **13 OTU**   **Blenheim IV**   **Z7353**   **Air Test**
1942   P/O McMillan RAAF   T/o Bicester for a fuel consumption test. On
                                    return to base, landed 1550 but bounced back
into the air. P/O McMillan RAAF opened up to go round again, but lost control
and hit a tree. In the ensuing hard landing, the Blenheim caught fire.

28 Feb   **16 OTU**   **Hampden I**   **N9065**   **Training**
1942   Sgt J H Stilborn RCAF   T/o Croughton for a night practice bombing
                                    sortie. Landed 0030, heavily, and moments
later a fire broke out and the Hampden, which had originally been built as
a Hereford, was destroyed. Not long after this incident, Sgt Stilborn RCAF
was posted to 144 Squadron, a formation which in April 1942 transferred from
Bomber to Coastal Command. On 13 December 1942, while in action off the coast
of Norway, his Hampden was shot down into the sea. There were no survivors.

1 Mar   **16 OTU**   **Hampden I**   **P4348**   **Training**
1942   P/O R A Ray   +   T/o Upper Heyford briefed to carry out solo
                                    circuits and landings. Lost control at 1020
and spun to the ground, about a mile S of the airfield. P/O Ray is buried
in Southgate Cemetery.

         20 OTU   **Wellington IC**   **R1001**   **Ground**
                                    Damaged beyond repair at Lossiemouth airfield
when, at 1925, F/S D R Worth, also of 20 OTU, momentarily lost control of his
aircraft (Wellington IC Z8841 JM-H) and struck R1001. F/S Worth's bomber was
not too seriously damaged and, following repairs, continued in service.

4 Mar   **14 OTU**   **Hampden I**   **AD860**   **Ground**
                                    Destroyed by fire at Cottesmore airfield, a
likely cause being a fault in the aircraft's heating system.

         17 OTU   **Blenheim I**   **L6804**   **Air Test**
         Sgt G D Jessup   T/o Upwood but encountered very bad weather and
                                    while flying at 1,000 feet an engine cut. Sgt
Jessup did remarkably well to coax his crippled aircraft up to 3,200 feet before
taking to his parachute. Left to its own devices, the Blenheim crashed 1125 near
Colston Bassett, 10 miles SE of Nottingham, where it was consumed by fire.

8 Mar   **14 OTU**   **Hampden I**   **L4110**   **Training**
1942   Sgt J F MacPhail RCAF   +   T/o Saltby for night bombing practice. Came down
        Sgt A H Hanson RAAF   +   at high speed, in level flight with wheels and
                          inj   flaps extended, hitting the ground at 2204 some
                          inj   two miles NW of the airfield. On impact, the
                                    nose compartment was shattered, after which the
bomber flipped over, the engine mountings and wings being sheared off. The two
airmen who died rest in the extension to Cottesmore (St. Nicholas) Churchyard.

9 Mar   **15 OTU**   **Wellington IC**   **DV576**   **Training**
1942   Sgt D A Fleming   +   T/o Hampstead Norris for a night exercise. At
        Sgt J V Gardiner   +   approximately 2120, one of the Wellington's
        Sgt C Hirst   inj   wings clipped a tree at Aldworth, 11 miles WNW
        Sgt H Medley   +   of Reading. Those who perished are buried in
        Sgt R R Briggs   inj   various cemeteries across the United Kingdom.
        Sgt J A Saunders   inj   Sgt Saunders made a good recovery from his
                                      injuries, but while serving with 10 Squadron,
his Halifax was amongst the thirty-six aircraft that either failed to return,
or were written off following a visit to Wuppertal on 29-30 May 1943 (see
Bomber Command Losses, Volume 4, pages 168 to 173).

         21 OTU E Flt   **Wellington IC**   **R1329**   **Training**
         Sgt C E Hickman   inj   T/o Edgehill for a navigation exercise, during
         Sgt H Scott   inj   which an engine failed, followed by the loss of
         Sgt Benson   inj   its propeller. This fell at Kiln Farm, Cranby
         Sgt Caswell   inj   and soon after, at 1524, the Wellington struck
         Sgt R Hind   inj   a tree and crashed at Rookhill Farm, Offton,
         Sgt Skeel   inj   seven miles NW from the centre of Ipswich.
                                    This particular Wellington had seen service
with 12 OTU, 18 OTU and 23 OTU, before being allocated to 21 OTU on 13 January
1942. It had logged a total of 470.00 flying hours.

9 Mar **21 OTU** **Wellington IC** **Z8774** **Training**
1942 P/O R C Trench + T/o Edgehill for night circuits and landings.
  Sgt T M Fitzjohn + After receiving permission to land, the bomber
  Sgt E Millington + was seen to commence a left hand turn, but
  Sgt A L Clipson + instead of straightening out it continued to
  Sgt R Fossey + bank before hitting the ground and bursting
  into flames. Weather conditions, at the time,
were marginal. All are buried in cemeteries across the United Kingdom. The
flare path had been well marked with a double row of Glim lamps and Goose neck
flares.

10 Mar **11 OTU** **Wellington I** **L4382** **Training**
1942 Sgt D G Falconer T/o Steeple Morden to practice circuits and
  landings. At 1635 came into land, behind
another aircraft and Sgt Falconer, realising he was closing too fast on this
bomber, pulled up sharply in order to avoid a collision. In doing so, he
stalled and crashed.

11 Mar **19 OTU** **Whitley V** **Z6628** **Training**
1942 Sgt H Smith RCAF inj T/o 1928 Kinloss for a cross-country exercise
  Sgt R T Scott RCAF + but as the Whitley gained height, so an engine
  Sgt N F T Brown + cut. Sgt Smith RCAF realised he was not going
  to be able to regain the airfield and at 1630
carried out a textbook ditching in Findhorn Bay. The dinghy was released and
the injured members of crew clambered aboard. At this stage, Sgt Scott RCAF
called out to say he was going to swim ashore but, tragically, he died in the
attempt. He is buried in Kinloss Abbey Burial Ground. Sgt Brown also died and
he lies in Chingford Mount Cemetery. Later, the bomber was washed ashore.

12 Mar **11 OTU** **Wellington I** **L4351** **Training**
1942 Sgt E Eatough T/o Steeple Morden. While nearing the runway
  at around 1620, the Wellington drifted slightly
off line and was badly damaged in the heavy landing that followed. A few days
later, it was decided that repairs were possible and, subsequently, on 13 June
1942 it was declared ready for collection. However, it was decided to downgrade
the airframe as an instructional aid and with the serial 3123M applied, it was
conveyed to No. 11 School of Technical Training at Hereford.

13 Mar **13 OTU** **Blenheim IV** **R3607** **Training**
1942 Sgt P G Reddy T/o Bicester for a navigation exercise. Became
  lost in bad weather and at 1845, while trying to
make a wheels down landing, crashed at Old Hayes Farm, Ratby, 5 miles WNW from
the centre of Leicester.

  16 OTU **Hampden I** **X2906** **Training**
  P/O R A S Parker RNZAF + T/o Croughton to practice circuits and landings
  P/O G F Keele RCAF + but at 1445 was observed coming down in a flat
  spin near Mixbury, 8 miles NNE of Bicester,
Oxfordshire. Both officers are buried in Upper Heyford Cemetery.

  17 OTU **Blenheim IV** **N3538** **Training**
  Sgt W Curlet + T/o Upwood for a cross-country flight. Flew
  P/O J D L McColl + into high-tension cables and crashed 0927 about
  Sgt E Johnson + one hundred yards E of Thorp Arch church on the
  north bank of the Wharfe which separates the
hamlet of Thorp Arch from Boston Spa, 2 miles SSE of Wetherby, Yorkshire. The
Blenheim burst into flames on impact. All are buried in various cemeteries;
nearby RAF Church Fenton arranging the interment of Glasgow born P/O McColl.

  19 OTU **Whitley V** **P5099** **Training**
  Sgt E P MacEagen RAAF inj T/o Kinloss for infrared bombing practice.
  Released a flare, which lodged in the tail unit
and set fire to the fuselage. Abandoned 2055 in the Fochabers-Garmouth area,
after which the Whitley fell into nearby Spey Bay.

  22 OTU **Wellington IC** **R1719** **Training**
  S/L F S Burgis T/o Wellesbourne Mountford for a night cross-
  country. Lost power and abandoned 2010, coming
down at Magpie Farm, a mile SW of Yattendon, 10 miles W of Reading.

14 Mar
1942

18 OTU	Wellington IC	T2961		Training

P/O D M Jones   +   T/o 2045 Bramcote for a night exercise but
F/O W A Kozlowski PAF   +   within moments of becoming airborne, the bomber
F/O Z Luba PAF   inj   smashed into a small building and some trees,
Sgt T A Hipp PAF   +   roughly 200 yards beyond the airfield. The
Sgt J Stengierski PAF   +   three Polish airmen lie in Nuneaton (Oaston
Road) Cemetery, while P/O Jones was taken to
Beaufort (Carmel) Independent Chapelyard, Ebbw Vale. It is believed the pilot
either retracted the flaps too soon, or held the nose down for too long as he
built up speed.

15 Mar
1942

20 OTU	Wellington IA	N2873		Ground

Destroyed by fire at 1045 while starting up at
Elgin airfield. The blaze was caused by excessive fuel in the engine induction
system. There are no reports of anyone being hurt in this incident.

23 OTU	Wellington IC	R1342		Training

F/S A B Croskin   T/o Pershore for a night exercise. Landed at
approximately 2020 but bounced off the runway
and though F/S Croskin managed to open up the throttles to go round again, the
controls locked. With the Wellington climbing steeply, he applied left rudder
and almost immediately the port wing hit the ground. No one was hurt but the
bomber was damaged beyond repair due to the fuselage breaking in half.

16 Mar
1942

14 OTU A Flt	Hampden I	AD988		Training

S/L N S Royle DFC   +   T/o Cottesmore with OC A Flight at the controls.
Sgt D O L Dold   +   Crashed 1715 at Thistleton, 7 miles NNE from
Sgt F J Hiesler RAAF   +   Oakham. Eyewitnesses say the Hampden dived to
Sgt J A Stevenson RAAF   +   the ground from a height of 400 feet. The two
Australians and Rhodesian born Sgt Dold lie in
the extension to Cottesmore (St. Nicholas) Cemetery, while S/L Royle is buried
at Wandsworth Cemetery.

19 OTU	Lysander III	R9120		Training

Sgt T E Coogan DFM   +   T/o Kinloss for a cooperation exercise in ground
Sgt B Phillips RAAF   inj   to air firing. While in flight, the propeller
came off and though Sgt Coogan successfully put
the Lysander down on the beach at Findhorn Bay, he was unable to prevent his
aircraft from running into some anti-tank concrete blocks. Tragically, a fire
started and though Sgt Phillips RAAF either extracted himself or was dragged
from the inferno, he was so severely burnt that he died within a few hours of
the crash (the time is recorded as 1100). Along with his skipper, who gained
his DFM, Gazetted 17 January 1941, flying Whitleys with 77 Squadron, he rests
in Kinloss Abbey Burial Ground. Their aircraft was the first of its type to be
written off at a Bomber Command OTU.

17 Mar
1942

14 OTU	Hampden I	AD749		Training

Sgt H H Davis RCAF   T/o Cottesmore for a night exercise. Wrecked
at 2210 after failing to get down at Newton
airfield, Nottinghamshire, in poor visibility. Just over a month later, Sgt
Davis RCAF was killed while serving with 420 Squadron (see Bomber Command
Losses, Volume 3, page 74).

22 OTU	Wellington IC	X9946 LT-D		Training

Sgt C J Jardine   T/o Wellesbourne Mountford for night flying.
Landed at 2200 but veered off the flare path
and struck the corner of No. 9 hangar, badly damaging a crew room currently
used by A Flight. Initially assessed as repairable, the Wellington was struck
off charge on 25 March 1942.

18 Mar
1942

15 OTU	Wellington I	L4265		Training

F/S C G Wiley RCAF   +   T/o Mount Farm but began to swing from side to
Sgt R H Riedy RCAF   +   side in a quite violent manner. Attempts to
Sgt W J D Carter   inj   correct the situation were unsuccessful and
the Wellington left the runway and crashed
into a stationary Hudson I N7332 belonging to 5 Ferry Pilots Pool. Although
severely damaged, the Hudson was repaired. Those who died in the Wellington
were laid to rest in Brookwood Military Cemetery.

18 Mar **23 OTU** **Wellington IC X9627** **Weather Test**
1942 F/O D J Browne   inj   T/o 1415 Defford in practically zero wind and
Sgt J Heslop   inj   seen banking to port before a wing tip struck
     a hedge some 1 to 2 miles from the airfield.
F/O Browne received massive head injuries and he died of a cerebral haemorrhage
shortly after admittance to Worcester Royal Infirmary. He lies in Aylesbury
Cemetery. His wireless operator, Sgt Heslop, was taken to the same hospital
where he was treated for lacerations to the face, scalp and hands.

19 Mar **10 OTU** **Whitley V Z6726** **Air Test**
1942 P/O J A T Meredith   inj   T/o Abingdon. Returned to base at 1650, the
     weather being quite inclement with low cloud
and heavy rain reducing visibility. On touch-down, P/O Meredith discovered
that his brakes were ineffective and moments later the Whitley skidded into
railings surrounding the bomb dump. By the spring of 1944, now a F/L with a
Distinguished Flying Cross, he was killed while flying Lancasters with 83
Squadron (see Bomber Command Losses, Volume 5, page 216).

20 Mar **19 OTU** **Whitley IV K9044** **Training**
1942 F/O D W Mansbridge   T/o 1545 Kinloss for dual instruction but,
     due to engine failure, crashed into a field
near Rosth at the eastern end of the airfield. F/O Mansbridge rose to the
rank of S/L, gaining an Air Force Cross, before being posted missing from
operations to Ottignies. At the time, he was flying with 635 Squadron (see
Bomber Command Losses, Volume 5, page 177) on Pathfinder duties.

19 OTU **Whitley V P4998** **Training**
Sgt W Wilson   +   T/o Forres for a night exercise. At around
Sgt R J Scarff   +   0245 the Whitley was seen approaching Elgin
Sgt E W Jordan   +   airfield but it is assumed the crew realised
Sgt V Baxter   +   their mistake as the engine note suddenly
Sgt R Leyland   +   increased as the bomber commenced overshooting
Sgt R H Marsh   +   the runway. However, having climbed to about
     180 feet, the bomber banked steeply, stalled
and dived into the ground, bursting into flames on impact. All are buried in
various cemeteries across the United Kingdom.

24 Mar **19 OTU** **Whitley V N1437** **Training**
1942 F/O G G Davies DSO   inj   T/o 0125 Kinloss for night flying but an engine
Sgt C C Scott RAAF   +   failed and the Whitley smashed into trees near
P/O K Munro RAAF   inj   No. 1 site. A fire broke out and Sgt Scott RAAF
Sgt W W Harris RAAF   inj   perished before he could be dragged clear. He
     is buried in Kinloss Abbey Burial Ground.

19 OTU **Whitley V Z6933** **Training**
P/O R E Wheatley DFM   +   T/o Kinloss for a combined night dual and
Sgt D F Drake RCAF   +   wireless procedures exercise. Subsequently,
Sgt G K MacRae RCAF   +   the wreckage was discovered on Finally Hill,
P/O R R Flint   +   Angus. All were taken for burial in Montrose
Sgt F Jennings   +   (Sleepyhillock) Cemetery. P/O Wheatley, the
Sgt A Blackman   +   instructor, had served with 77 Squadron and
Sgt J Sutcliffe   +   details of his award had been published in the
     London Gazette on 24 October 1941. P/O Flint,
a Bachelor of Arts (Honours) graduate from London University, was a qualified
observer and air gunner, a quite unusual combination of trades.

25 Mar **14 OTU** **Hampden I P1298** **Training**
1942 Sgt D E Randall RAAF   T/o Cottesmore for his first solo on type.
     Came into land at 1605 but at the last moment
realised the undercarriage was not locked down. Sgt Randall RAAF advanced the
throttles but collided with a lorry, crashed and caught fire.

14 OTU **Hampden I P5398** **Training**
Sgt E J Biddulph   +   T/o Cottesmore for a night navigation sortie.
Sgt R V Daniels RAAF   +   Crashed, and burnt out, 2110 at Whittle Farm,
Sgt B Noseworthy   +   Brockhampton, 5 miles E from the centre of
Sgt A W Westgate RNZAF   +   Cheltenham, Gloucestershire. All were buried
     at Little Rissington. Sgt Biddulph came from
Southern Rhodesia while Sgt Noseworthy hailed from Newfoundland.

25 Mar **16 OTU**   **Hampden I** **P1197**   **Training**
1942   Sgt A C Hulme   T/o Upper Heyford for a high-level night bombing
                                                    sortie. During the exercise, the oil pressure
reading for the starboard engine dropped to zero and before base could be regained, the propeller sheared off. Calmly, Sgt Hulme executed a gliding turn
towards the runway and when he realised he was in danger of overshooting the
flare path, he opened up the port motor and succeeded in climbing to 800 feet.
Having flown round the circuit, he made his second approach, during which a
wingtip clipped a Nissen hut, causing the Hampden to crash out of control.
No injuries reported, despite the ensuing fire that destroyed the bomber.

18 OTU   **Wellington IC** **R1287**   **Training**
Sgt W Kazimierczak PAF   T/o 2255 Bramcote but before sufficient speed
                                        had been built up, Sgt Kazimierczak PAF selected
undercarriage up and, as a result, the Wellington skidded out of control and hit
a petrol bowser.

26 Mar **16 OTU**   **Hampden I** **P1221**   **Training**
1942   Sgt R C Dobie RCAF   +   T/o Upper Heyford for a night navigation sortie.
             Sgt N G W Boyce RCAF   +   Around 0045 the Hampden flew into the ground, at
             F/S R J O´Leary RCAF   +   high speed, roughly 4 miles S of Polebrook
             F/S D C Lindsey RCAF   +   airfield in Northamptonshire. All were laid
                                                      to rest in Old Weston (St. Swithun) Churchyard,
Huntingdonshire. F/S Lindsey RCAF was an American from Battle Creek, Michigan.

27 Mar **14 OTU**   **Anson I** **AX107 N2**   **Ground**
1942   Destroyed by fire following a refuelling
                                                          accident at Cottesmore airfield.

14 OTU   **Hampden I** **L4108**   **Training**
Sgt A R Frazer RAAF   +   T/o Saltby for a night exercise only to crash
Sgt R F King   +   near the airfield. Visibility was poor at the
                                         time. Both airmen are buried in the extension
to Cottesmore (St. Nicholas) Churchyard. Sgt King was a Newfoundlander.

21 OTU   **Wellington IC** **N2800**   **Training**
Sgt T E Dutton   +   T/o Moreton-in-Marsh for a night navigation
Sgt W Brand   +   exercise. Crashed, with an engine on fire,
Sgt A C Thomson   +   between the hamlet of Dorn and Aston Magna,
Sgt J H Young   +   about a couple of miles NW of the airfield.
Sgt H Wilson   inj   The accident occurred at around 0240 and of
                                         those who perished, Sgt Dutton was laid to
rest locally in Moreton-in-Marsh New Cemetery. His father was the Revd Canon
Fred Schofield Dutton of Heckmondwike in Yorkshire. The others were taken to
their home towns.

22 OTU   **Wellington IC** **R1472**   **Training**
Sgt W T Cormack RCAF   T/o Wellesbourne Mountford for night circuit
Sgt K Edmonds   training. At approximately 0220, the bomber
                                         overshot the runway and finished up, wrecked,
in a hedge. An investigation into the accident concluded that failure of the
airfield´s lighting system was a contributory factor. Not long after this
incident, Sgt Cormack RCAF joined 156 Squadron and lost his life during the
first 1,000 plan raid (Köln) on 30-31 May 1942 (see Bomber Command Losses,
Volume 3, page 107).

28 Mar **10 OTU**   **Whitley V** **P4953**   **Training**
1942   Sgt J A Elkington   inj   T/o 1258 Abingdon for a dual exercise but
             P/O E A Taylor RCAF   inj   lost engine power and crashed two minutes
                                                      later into trees bordering nearby Radley Road.

13 OTU   **Blenheim IV** **Z7983**   **Training**
Sgt K J Johnson   +   T/o 1125 Bicester for a navigation exercise
Sgt F A E Hollier   +   that involved the crew flying over the Irish
Sgt J Bennett   +   Sea. At 1210 a wireless transmission from
                                          the Blenheim was received, after which nothing
further was heard. All are commemorated on the Runnymede Memorial. It is
reported that heavy snow showers were prevalent in the exercise area.

29 Mar
1942

17 OTU   **Blenheim IV**   **Z5949**   **Training**

Sgt J L H Heagerty	inj	T/o Upwood for a navigation exercise during
P/O J N Jenkinson	inj	which the crew attempted to land at Sutton
Sgt E P Moakler	inj	Bridge. As the Blenheim approached the runway,

its undercarriage came into contact with a
raised bank and was torn off.

23 OTU   **Wellington IC**   **X9629**   **Training**

P/O C H Grant	inj	T/o Defford for circuits and landings with a
Sgt J K Crossing RCAF	inj	screened pilot and three pupils. While in the
Sgt J W Asseltine RCAF	inj	circuit, the port engine lost power and in the
Sgt D R Brown	inj	landing that followed, control was lost and at
Sgt R G W Swan	inj	0941 the bomber collided with the station's
Sgt W J Fry	inj	headquarters. P/O Grant, Sgt Asseltine RCAF

and the last two named were taken to Worcester
Royal Infirmary, while the less seriously hurt were treated in SSQ Defford.
Sgt Crossing RCAF reached the end of his course only to become a casualty from
the unit's participation in the Bremen raid on 25-26 June 1942.

30 Mar
1942

17 OTU   **Blenheim IV**   **R3772**   **Training**

Sgt Coleman   T/o Warboys. On return to base at 1600, the
Blenheim stalled at 30 feet, smashing the
starboard wing and undercarriage.

31 Mar
1942

13 OTU   **Blenheim IV**   **R3838**   **Training**

P/O A Burnie	+	T/o Bicester for a navigation exercise. Lost
Sgt A E Geers	+	without trace, though it is likely the aircraft
Sgt J Gray	+	came down in the North Sea. All are commemorated

on the Runnymede Memorial. Thirty-four year old
Sgt Geers was an Associate of the Chartered Institute of Secretaries.

1 Apr
1942

20 OTU E Flt   **Wellington IC**   **R1760 JM-X**   **Training**

P/O J L Bradbury RCAF	+	T/o Lossiemouth for a night bombing and cross-
P/O J D Mullins	inj	country detail. Lost its port propeller and came
Sgt W L Moots RCAF	inj	down 0004 a mile or so out from the shore of the
F/S W G Reid RCAF	+	Bay of Cruden, 9 miles SSW of Peterhead on the
Sgt J Chivers	+	Aberdeenshire coast. Of those who died, three
Sgt G H Elliott	inj	have no known graves, but Sgt Elliott, who died

from his injuries, rests in Mitford (St. Mary
Magdalene) Churchyard. F/S Reid RCAF was an American from Flint, Michigan.

2 Apr
1942

19 OTU   **Whitley V**   **Z9284**   **Training**

Sgt D M D'Eath	T/o Forres for a night cross-country flight.
Sgt I B Mann	Returned to base circa 2030 but made a rather

fast approach and as a result, overshot the
runway and crashed near the airfield. No injuries reported but, sadly, neither
pilot survived the war (though both were commissioned before they died). P/O
Mann rests in Wimbledon (Gap Road) Cemetery; the son of Major Stephen Harold
Mann and Evelyn Mary Gertrude Mann (nee Goodman), he lost his life on 27 July
1943. Less than two months later, P/O D'Easth failed to return from a visit
to Mannheim (5-6 September; see Bomber Command Losses, Volume 4, page 311)
while flying Halifaxes with 10 Squadron.

20 OTU D Flt   **Wellington IC**   **R1168 JM-G**   **Training**

F/O D H Jeffery	+	T/o Lossiemouth for a night flying exercise.
Sgt R J Coates	+	While heading for base, assisted by QDMs, the
Sgt E Hunter	+	bomber flew into a hillside at 0113 near the
Sgt G Cant	+	village of Sinsharnie, 3 miles NW of Huntly,
Sgt B A Neill RNZAF	+	Aberdeenshire. It is believed that a mis-
Sgt A S Moggach	+	understanding in respect of the QDM instructions

led to this accident. All are buried in various
cemeteries, Sgt Neill RNZAF being interred at Lossiemouth Burial Ground.

3 Apr
1942

16 OTU   **Hampden I**   **P5346**   **Training**

P/O J E Piggott RCAF	+	T/o Upper Heyford to practice low-level bombing
P/O J F Anderson RCAF	+	techniques over the Ot Moor ranges. At around
F/S R St. J Gregory RCAF	+	2130 the Hampden flew into the ground and was
Sgt W A Skinner	+	totally destroyed. All were buried in Middleton

Stoney (All Saints) Churchyard.

6 Apr	16 OTU	Hampden I	P1299		Training
1942	F/S A B McKeith RCAF	+	T/o Upper Heyford for practice bombing. Got		
	F/S W B M Wilson RCAF	+	into difficulties at 1,000 feet, the Hampden		
	Sgt F A Dann	+	finishing up in a flat spin from which it		
	Sgt H G Stalker	+	failed to recover before hitting the ground		

at 1705 near Locking airfield on the outskirts of Weston-super-Mare, Somerset. Both Canadians were buried in Weston-super-Mare Cemetery; Sgt Dann was taken to Bradford (Scholemoor) Cemetery and Sgt Stalker to Leeds (Harehills) Cemetery.

	20 OTU	Wellington IC	N2859 JM-W		Training
	P/O J R Moore RCAF	inj	T/o Lossiemouth but while climbing away from		
	Sgt D Lees	+	the runway an engine cut, causing the bomber		
	P/O R M Jenkins	inj	to swing violently and smash into trees near		
	Sgt Walton RCAF	inj	one of the dispersal sites, roughly a mile S		

of the airfield. Two were critically injured and P/O Moore RCAF died from a fractured skull within three hours of his admittance to Ermys Hospital at Elgin. Three days later, P/O Jenkins passed away; both were laid to rest in Lossiemouth Burial Ground. Sgt Lees, meanwhile, was taken to Manchester Southern Cemetery. It is believed that Sgt Walton RCAF made a good recovery and, subsequently, returned to Canada.

8 Apr	15 OTU C Flt	Wellington IC	L7818		Training
1942	W/O G E Leeke	+	T/o Harwell for a cross-country exercise during		
	Sgt W F Good	+	which a midair collision occurred between the		
	F/S S W Pook	+	Wellington and a Spitfire I R6686 from 57 OTU,		
	Sgt E Coleman	+	flown by P/O J R Lee. Out of control, both		
	Sgt F K Fairclough	+	aircraft crashed a few hundred yards apart in		
	Sgt W Wilson	+	the valley of the Broadwater stream near Cold		

Ashton, 9 miles ESE of Bristol. All rest in various United Kingdom cemeteries. P/O Lee, the Spitfire pilot, hailed from Cormanche, Texas; along with Sgt Good he is buried in Little Rissington (St. Peter) Churchyard.

Note. This tragic event is recorded in "Unsung Heroes, A Story of a Wartime Incident in the Cotswolds" by Alan White of the Severnside Aviation Society.

	22 OTU	Wellington IC	R1773		Training
	P/O J M Warnock RNZAF	+	T/o Wellesbourne Mountford for night cross-		
	Sgt V L Morris RCAF	+	country. While flying at 2,000 feet, in quite		
	F/S D S Woodley RCAF	+	turbulent air, the starboard engine failed and		
	Sgt C H Wheatley RCAF	inj	moments later, at 0120, the bomber hit a tree		
	F/S J W Scarff RCAF	+	near the church at Great Coxwell, 2 miles SW of		
	Sgt Wilmen	inj	Faringdon, Berkshire. The first three named lie		

in Black Bourton Churchyard. F/S Scarff RCAF is buried in Southport (Birkdale) Roman Catholic Cemetery. P/O Warnock RNZAF had recently completed a tour of operations with 158 Squadron, having served previously with 104 Squadron. Sgt Wheatley RCAF made a good recovery from his injuries and, eventually, went out to the Middle East for a tour of duty with 37 Squadron. On 24 November 1943, his Wellington X LN329 failed to return from Torino; along with the rest of his crew he is buried in Milano War Cemetery. It is thought that Sgt Wilmen, too, returned to active flying.

	23 OTU	Wellington IC	R1597		Training
	Sgt J M Kennedy RCAF	+	T/o Pershore for a cross-country exercise. Last		
	Sgt W McL Lomax	+	heard transmitting by wireless at 1435 and		
	Sgt W Smith	+	reported crashed 1537 at Llangammarch Wells in		
	Sgt F T Ellingham	+	the Brecon Beacons. After recovery, the bodies		
	Sgt W H Lacey	+	of the seven airmen were brought to the Lake		
	Sgt N Griffen	+	Hotel at Llangammarch, while 78 MU were tasked		
	Sgt D W Dowling	+	to clear the crash site. Four of the crew were		

brought back for interment in Pershore Cemetery and three were claimed by their next of kin. It is noted that a violent storm was raging over the Beacons and it is likely the crew fell victim to nature.

Note. Some reports suggest a Sergeant K J Matthews was included in the crew but his name does not appear in unit records and neither is there a casualty of this name in the CWGC registers for the date in question.

13 Apr
1942

15 OTU   **Wellington IC** **R1179**   **Training**
Sgt E J Twigg RNZAF   inj   T/o Harwell for a cross-country exercise. At
Sgt D A Harkness RNZAF   inj   around 1605, a mix-up in the changing of tanks
                             inj   resulted in engine failure and a crash-landing
                             inj   a mile S of Chislehampton, 7 miles SE from
                             inj   Oxford. Sgt Twigg RNZAF later served with
                             inj   166 Squadron but lost his life towards the
                                   end of February 1943 (see Bomber Command Losses,
Volume 4, page 51). Sgt Harkness RNZAF, meanwhile, proceeded to the Middle East
where he flew thirty-seven sorties with 142 Squadron, being commissioned and
gaining a DFC in the process. His death, from multiple injuries, occurred on
23 July 1944 in the most bizarre circumstances when he fell, while sleep walking,
at the New Zealand Club in Cairo. At the time he was on leave from 77 OTU at
Qastina, where he was serving as an instructor.

19 OTU   **Whitley V** **BD209**   **Training**
Sgt R H Baird RCAF   T/o Kinloss for an evening cross-country detail.
                                   Ditched 2215 in the Moray Firth some 200 yards
off Dalcross. Earlier, the Whitley's port engine had failed and the crew were
making their way back to base when the starboard motor cut, possibly due to
overheating. No one was hurt and the crew came ashore on the opposite bank of
the Firth near Fortrose.

14 Apr
1942

21 OTU E Flt   **Wellington IC** **R1085**   **Training**
Sgt J M S Millar   +   T/o Moreton-in-Marsh for a cross-country sortie
F/S L W Sheffler RCAF   +   during which a propeller came off. At 1531, while
Sgt G D Lindsay   +   banking steeply to port, the Wellington stalled
P/O R Bloor   +   and crashed at Wollerton, 1 mile SW of Tern Hill
Sgt T V Yde RNZAF   +   airfield, Shropshire. Sgt Millar is buried in
Sgt L L Bennett   +   Dumbarton Cemetery, while his crew are interred
                                   at Stoke-upon-Tern (St. Peter) Church Cemetery.

17 Apr
1942

10 OTU   **Whitley V** **AD706**   **Training**
F/O R J Finch RAAF   +   T/o Abingdon for a night navigation exercise.
Sgt D J H Mott   +   The crew returned safely to base but were obliged
Sgt C J Scattergood   +   to overshoot the runway and re-enter the circuit.
Sgt G Penman   +   While doing so, the Whitley stalled at 150 feet
Sgt T E A O'Coy   +   and before control could be regained, the bomber
                                   hit the ground with such force that it bounced
high into the air. Moments later, at 0208, it smashed back to earth and burst
into flames. All are buried in various cemeteries across the United Kingdom.

16 OTU   **Hampden I** **P1247**   **Training**
F/S W H E Phillips RCAF   +   T/o Croughton for night training. Overshot the
Sgt M A Bent RCAF   inj   runway, stalled and crashed 2305 near the air-
                                   field. P/O Phillips RCAF, who is buried in
Middleton Stoney (All Saints) Churchyard, had sustained slight injuries on 13
October 1941, following an accident involving an Anson and a Hampden from the
unit (see page 78).

18 Apr
1942

19 OTU   **Whitley IV** **K9025**   **Training**
P/O Macfarland   T/o 1524 Kinloss but after climbing to ninety
Sgt A J W R Coupar   feet lost power from the port engine and, thus,
                                   an immediate forced-landing was made with the
undercarriage only partially retracted. Before coming to a stop, the Whitley
struck a hangar and though no one was hurt, the bomber was damaged beyond repair.

19 Apr
1942

14 OTU   **Oxford I** **AS902**   **Training**
Sgt K Ball   +   T/o Cottesmore for night circuit training using
                                   the Drem lighting system as an aid to landing.
Crashed 0230 at Cold Overton, 7 miles SE of Melton Mowbray, Leicestershire and
within about 25 miles of where Sgt Ball lived at Coalville. He is buried here
in Broom Leys Cemetery.

20 Apr
1942

13 OTU   **Blenheim IV** **Z6145**   **Training**
Sgt F R Morgan RAAF   T/o 1303 Bicester for his first solo in a
                                   Blenheim IV but the port tyre burst and on
regaining the airfield, two minutes later, he crash-landed. Soon after a
fire broke out and the bomber was destroyed. Sgt Morgan RAAF was not hurt.

20 Apr	16 OTU	Hampden I	P1297		Training
1942	F/L J E Morgan RCAF		+	T/o Upper Heyford. Failed to recover from a	
	F/S D J Taynen RCAF		+	flat spin and fell circa 1630 into Fox Covert.	

Both are buried in Middleton Stoney (All Saints)
Churchyard. It is believed F/L Morgan RCAF was regular service officer.

	16 OTU	Hampden I	P5388	Training
	Sgt W J Wilkinson		T/o 1530 Upper Heyford but swung out of control	
	Sgt D S Jackson		and hit another of the unit's Hampdens. No one	
	P/O Edmunds		was hurt, despite a fire breaking out. The other	
	Sgt H A Vallis RCAF		Hampden was repaired and returned to service.	

25 Apr	11 OTU	Wellington IC	R1661		Training
1942	Sgt D M Telford		+	T/o Steeple Morden for a night cross-country.	
	Sgt D C Marsden		inj	Undershot the runway at Waddington and crashed	
	F/S C A Parke RCAF		+	0411 in the airfield's sewage works. It was	
	P/O H J Snelling		+	thought that the unfamiliar Drem lighting system	
	Sgt H W Woodward		inj	was a contributory factor in this accident. Sgt	

Telford, a pre-war regular, was laid to rest in
Longbenton (Benton) Cemetery, F/S Parke RCAF, who had married Isobel Johnstone
Parke of Earls Court, London, is buried in Waddington (St. Michael) Churchyard,
while P/O Snelling was taken to Norwich (The Rosary) Cemetery. The two injured
airmen were first treated at Bracebridge Military Hospital before admittance to
RAF Hospital Rauceby. Both were removed from all medical lists on 28 April.

27 Apr	23 OTU	Wellington IC	R1618	–D1		Training
1942	P/O L W Munro RNZAF		inj	T/o 0055 Defford for night circuits and landings	
	Sgt V Ardis RCAF		inj	and crashed almost immediately, bursting into	
	P/O T W Copson		inj	flames. Insufficient tensioning of the throttle	
	Sgt R A Hamilton RAAF		inj	friction nuts was the underlying cause of this	
	Sgt L E Bosvert RCAF		inj	accident. Five sustained injuries of such	
	Sgt C D Dixon RCAF		inj	severity that is was necessary to admit them to	
	Sgt S G Perks		inj	Worcester Royal Infirmary, while P/O Copson and	

Sgt Dixon RCAF were less seriously hurt and
were treated in SSQ Defford. P/O Munro RNZAF was destined to become a Pathfinder
captain. While flying Lancasters with 83 Squadron, he failed to return from
Berlin on 2-3 January 1944 (see Bomber Command Losses, Volume 5, page 23). Of
the others, Sgt Dixon RCAF joined 218 Squadron and died on 21 August 1942 (see
Volume 3 of the same series, page 187).

27-28 Apr	27 OTU	Wellington IC	X9635		Op: Nickel
1942	F/O L G Chick RAAF		+	T/o 2158 Lichfield briefed to scatter leaflets	
	Sgt M B Remfry RAAF		+	in the Lille region of France. All are buried	
	Sgt F J Dodd		+	in Belgium at Heverlee War Cemetery. It is	
	Sgt J R Stukins		+	noted that Sgt Remfry's cousin, Sgt B H Edye	
	Sgt A J Glaister RAAF		+	RAAF, lost his life over Belgium on 1-2 June	

1942, while raiding Essen with 26 OTU.

	27 OTU	Wellington IC	Z8901	–V		Op: Nickel
	Sgt G A Dale		+	T/o 2241 Lichfield similarly tasked. Crashed	
	Sgt W J Jewell		+	at Sautour (Namur), 3 km SSE of Philippeville,	
	Sgt A W Greer RAAF		+	Belgium. All rest in the communal cemetery at	
	Sgt W G Mutton RNZAF		+	Charleroi.	
	Sgt E C Inder RNZAF		+		

Note. As Martin Middlebrook and Chris Everitt report in "The Bomber Command
War Diaries", the night of 27-28 April 1942 was one of much diverse activity.
The city of Köln was visited by ninety-seven aircraft, mainly Wellingtons but
with a good representation from four-engined types, while a dozen Lancasters
and thirty-one Halifaxes attacked the battleship Tirpitz in Trondheim Fjord.
Other targets included the docks at Dunkerque and mines were laid in German
coastal waters. Three Lancasters and five OTU Wellingtons dropped leaflets.

28 Apr	22 OTU	Wellington IC	R3198		Training
1942	Sgt J A Schweitzer RCAF		+	T/o Wellesbourne Mountford to practice circuits	
	Sgt H C Crouch RNZAF		+	and landings. At about 0550, while turning,	
	Sgt J P Williams RCAF		+	lost control and crashed near Lowe Farm on the	

western side of the airfield. On impact, the
bomber burst into flames. All are buried in Stratford-upon-Avon Cemetery.

28 Apr **25 OTU**   **Wellington IC** **DV473**   **Training**
1942   F/L R J Hannan DFC RNZAF   T/o Finningley but while in flight a propeller
         Sgt A W Robertson   inj came off, followed soon after by an engine fire.
         Sgt J P Warren   inj The order to bale out was given and, apart from
         Sgt R J Atkin   inj the tail gunner, all complied, leaving the
         F/S R E Moore   Wellington to crash 2320, hitting some farm
         Sgt F Dyson   buildings near Rawcliffe on the NW outskirts
         Sgt W A Winthrop   + of York. Sgt Winthrop was buried in Gateshead
                                      (Saltwell) Cemetery. Of the survivors, four
were killed within six weeks of each other towards the end of the year. Sgt
Dyson (57 Squadron) was first to die and he was followed by Sgt Robertson
(115 Squadron), F/L Hannan RNZAF (207 Squadron) and, lastly, Sgt Warren with
9 Squadron. For dates and further details, please refer to Bomber Command
Losses, Volume 3, pages 258, 265 (Sgt Robertson and F/L Hannan) and 284.

29 Apr **14 OTU**   **Hampden I** **P1303**   **Training**
1942   Sgt W J Nicholls RAAF   + T/o Cottesmore to practice single-engined
         Sgt J McW Stewart   + flying. Lost control at 200 feet and dived
                                      to the ground at Gunby, 9 miles S of Grantham
in Lincolnshire. Sgt Nicholls RAAF and his Southern Rhodesian born wireless
operator were buried in the extension to Cottesmore (St. Nicholas) Churchyard.

30 Apr **19 OTU**   **Whitley V** **Z6641**   **Training**
1942   Sgt J W Einarson RCAF   T/o Kinloss but while in flight the starboard
                                         engine failed and in the ensuing forced-landing
at 0350 on the sand at Inver, 8 miles ESE of Tain, Ross and Cromarty, the bomber
was wrecked. Sgt Einarson RCAF was destined to become an outstanding Bomber
Command pilot, gaining a DFM with 44 Squadron (Gazetted 20 April 1943). On
being commissioned, he added a DFC and when killed, flying with 61 Squadron,
on the split-raid against Augsburg on 25-26 February 1944 (see Bomber Command
Losses, Volume 5, page 103) he held the rank of F/L. For his parents, his
death was a second terrible blow as his twin-brother, F/S Harold Bjorn Einarson
RCAF had failed to return from an operational sortie with 207 Squadron on 9-10
September 1942 (see the same series, Volume 3, page 208).

1- 2 May **17 OTU**   **Blenheim I** **L1313**   **Training**
1942   Sgt T E Voges   inj T/o 2357 Warboys for a night training sortie.
         Sgt Parker   inj Crashed 0005, after flying into a tree near
                                      the airfield, and caught fire.

2 May   **13 OTU**   **Blenheim IV** **L9206**   **Training**
1942   F/S J R Young RCAF   + T/o 1010 Bicester for a navigation exercise.
         Sgt H Morrison RNZAF   + Crashed 1135 some 3 miles E of Billesdon, a
         Sgt G W Boggess   + village 8 miles ESE of Leicester. Reports
                                      from eyewitnesses say the Blenheim was diving
almost vertically when it hit the ground and exploded. Two were taken to North
Luffenham (St. John The Baptist) Churchyard, while Sgt Boggess is buried in
Birkenhead (Landican) Cemetery.

         14 OTU   **Hampden I** **P1277**   **Training**
         P/O J H G Hood   T/o Saltby for night flying practice. Wrecked
                                      at 0015 after overshooting the runway. P/O Hood
had been involved in a minor flying accident on 27 April.

4 May   **15 OTU**   **Wellington IC**   **Training**
1942   P/O K S Jenner RNZAF   T/o Harwell for a cross-country exercise. Came
         P/O L D Cox   down 1630 near the Star Bog, Glenarin, in Co.
         Sgt E L Bradshaw   Antrim. This accident was attributed to the
                                        throttle controls on one engine becoming dis-
connected. Two, P/O Cox and Sgt Bradshaw, subsequently became prisoners of war.

         Note. The serial T2769 is quoted in records but no such identity was ever
         allotted to a Wellington as it comes within the 'blackout' block twixt the
         production batches T2701-T2750 and T2801-T2850.

         17 OTU   **Blenheim I** **L8373**   **Training**
         F/S J G Bruce   T/o 1500 Warboys for dual instruction and
         Sgt H Hardman   came immediately to grief when a tyre burst.
                                      Later converted as a training aid (3354M).

4 May
1942

23 OTU	**Wellington IC T2881**		**Ground**

By 2000, at Defford, this Wellington had been bombed up in readiness for a night training exercise. At 2240, the crew arrived and commenced their pre-flight inspection but, unbeknown to anyone in authority, someone had entered the aircraft and moved the jettison bar to "jettison". Consequently, when the captain, Sgt R F Butler, tested the bomb doors opening mechanism, one of the practice bombs fell out and immediately ignited. The crew scrambled out and were unhurt but they were not able to save the bomber from going up in flames. Not long after this incident, Sgt Butler was posted to 115 Squadron and was reported as a prisoner of war (see Bomber Command Losses, Volume 3, page 154).

5 May
1942

14 OTU	**Hampden I**	**P1351**	**Training**
Sgt J S Peters RAAF	inj	T/o 2319 Saltby for night flying practice and	

inj climbed, normally, to 500 feet. However, on inj raising the flaps, the Hampden yawed and lost height, coming down within a minute about two miles SW of the airfield. On 25-26 June 1942, now flying with 50 Squadron, Sgt Peters RAAF failed to return from Bremen (see Bomber Command Losses, Volume 3, page 135).

14 OTU	**Hampden I**	**AE186**	**Training**
Sgt J Page		T/o 1350 Cottesmore but swung out of control, coming to a stop with a smashed undercarriage.	

22 OTU	**Wellington IC**	**Z1086 DG-Q**	**Training**
Sgt A H Craven	+	T/o Wellesbourne Mountford for night flying	
Sgt L H Blake RCAF	+	practice. While going round again, possibly	
F/S D A Blue RCAF	inj	after overshooting, stalled at 100 feet and	
P/O M M Osten RCAF	+	crashed 2359, bursting into flames.	
Sgt C W Milton RCAF	inj		
		Crash and Rescue:	
S/L F G Mogg		S/L Frank George Mogg, a Medical Officer, was amongst the first to reach the blazing bomber.	

Despite the intense heat, he managed to locate F/S Blue RCAF, who was trapped by debris across his left leg. For at least ten agonising minutes, S/L Mogg worked at cutting away the tangle of wire and struts and succeeded in getting the critically injured airman out of the wreckage. Sadly, his efforts (for which he was awarded the George Medal) were to no avail and F/S Blue RCAF died soon after reaching Stratford Hospital. Along with his fellow countrymen, he is buried in Stratford-upon-Avon Cemetery. Sgt Craven was taken to Hornchurch Cemetery. By one of those cruel ironies of fate, Sgt Milton RCAF recovered from his injuries and rejoined the training programme but on 8 November 1942 he was tasked to accompany P/O T D Withington DFM RCAF on a solo flying detail and both died when their Wellington crashed near Harbury, Warwickshire.

6 May
1942

13 OTU	**Blenheim IV**	**L8755**	**Training**
Sgt T A Crawford RCAF	+	T/o 1105 Bicester in the company of eleven other	
Sgt D J McKenzie RNZAF	+	aircraft for a navigation exercise. Presumed to	
F/S W N Ward	+	have crashed in the North Sea. On 21 July 1942,	
		Sgt Crawford's body was washed onto Ameland in	

the Dutch Frisian Islands; he is buried in Nes General Cemetery. His crew are commemorated on the Runnymede Memorial.

16 OTU	**Hampden I**	**AD826**	**Training**
F/S A G Maxwell RCAF	+	T/o Upper Heyford for a night cross-country.	
F/S J P Hancock RCAF	+	Crashed 0257 and burnt out at Bourne End Farm,	
F/S D K O'Brien RCAF	+	Wootton, 4 miles SW of Bedford. All rest in	
Sgt T L Brown RCAF	+	Kempston Cemetery.	

7 May
1942

21 OTU	**Wellington IC**	**T2824**	**Training**
Sgt J A Johnson	+	T/o Edgehill for night circuits and landings.	
Sgt H E Perry	+	At 0118 an SOS was transmitted and two minutes	
Sgt L W Cowell	+	later the bomber came down on the Stratford Road	
Sgt R H Walker	+	just above the village of Balscote, 4 miles WNW	
Sgt H Marillier	+	from the centre of Banbury, Oxfordshire. Sgt	
		Cowell and Sgt Marillier, the latter hailing	

from Ermelo in the Transvaal, are buried in Moreton-in-Marsh New Cemetery; the the others were claimed by their next of kin.

7 May	23 OTU D Flt	Wellington IC	Z1053	Training

7 May
1942

23 OTU D Flt   Wellington IC Z1053   Training

P/O P J A H Palin	+	T/o Pershore for night bombing, armed with
F/S G L M Mesheau RCAF	+	6 x 250lb practice bombs, sand filled. At
Sgt J M L Charbonneau RCAF	+	approximately 0340, the Wellington stalled
Sgt L F Fisher	+	and dived, almost vertically, to crash at Lower
F/S J M Sadler RCAF	+	Moor between the airfields of Pershore and
Sgt V S Henderson RAAF	+	Defford in Worcestershire. All are buried
		in Pershore Cemetery. Thirty-six year old

Sgt Fisher came from East London in South Africa, where he had enlisted. The
cause of the crash was attributed to the propeller and reduction gear shearing
from one of the engines.

8 May
1942

21 OTU   Wellington IC Z1161   Training

Sgt R I Hart	inj	T/o Moreton-in-Marsh for a night cross-country.
Sgt P W S Brooke	inj	Partially abandoned before crashing 0250, due
Sgt H H J Rohrlach RAAF	+	to a fire in the port engine, into a tree near
Sgt W L Williams RAAF	+	Beckingham, 11 miles NNW of Grantham, Lincoln-
Sgt I McN Fergusson	+	shire. Both Australians are buried in Thurlby
Sgt T J Tighe RCAF		(St. Germain) Churchyard. Sgt Fergusson rests
		in Leicester (Gilroes) Cemetery. Two, Sgt Hart

and Sgt Tighe RCAF, were destined to be killed on bomber operations before the
year was out, the former with 106 Squadron on 1-2 June and the latter while
flying with 149 Squadron on 30 September-1 October (see Bomber Command Losses,
Volume 3, pages 112 and 229).

22 OTU   Wellington IC Z8861   Training

Sgt J G Wood	+	T/o Wellesbourne Mountford for a night cross-
F/S D F Glinz RCAF	+	country. Last heard on wireless at 0217, the
F/S W R Howard RCAF	+	message indicating a forced-landing was imminent.
F/S H R Williams RCAF	+	All are commemorated on the Runnymede Memorial.
Sgt V G Carter	+	Sgt Wood's parents lived in Brazil at Sao Paulo.

8- 9 May
1942

10 OTU   Whitley V   P5057   Training

Sgt R W Morin RCAF	+	T/o 2355 Abingdon for a night navigation flight.
Sgt A J B Kemp	+	Flew into high ground 0415 at Waen Carno in
Sgt D N Sellars	+	Montgomery. Both RCAF airmen and Sgt Sellars
Sgt D H Jones	+	rest in Brookwood Military Cemetery, while their
Sgt S T Paterson RCAF	+	two companions were claimed by relatives. It is
		noted that Sgt Kemp was a Scoutmaster.

13 May
1942

17 OTU   Blenheim IV   V5384   Training

P/O H G Zavadowsky RCAF	+	T/o 1545 Upwood for a practice bombing detail.
P/O R E Corr	+	Successfully released part, if not all the bombs
Sgt J White	+	carried but three minutes later, at 1630, dived
		from 1,000 feet and crashed at Butchers Farm,

Thorney, 6 miles NE from the centre of Peterborough, Northamptonshire. All were
brought back to Upwood; P/O Zavadowsky RCAF and P/O Orr, the latter from Terenure
on the southern outskirts of Dublin and a holder of an Art Teacher's Diploma, are
buried in Ramsey Cemetery, while Sgt White was interred in Bury Cemetery.

15 May
1942

14 OTU   Oxford I AT479   Training

| Sgt J S Thompson RCAF | | Landed 1905 at Cottesmore but while taxying was |
| | | struck by one of the unit's Hampdens, P1185, |

captained by Sgt R E Taylor RCAF who, unwittingly, had landed too close to the
Oxford. No one was hurt and, subsequently, Sgt Taylor RCAF, an American from
Boonville, Indiana, went on to serve with 420 Squadron, gaining an immediate
DFM which was Gazetted on 23 March 1943. Sadly, on 27-28 May 1943, now serving
with 432 Squadron, he lost his life during operations to Essen (see Bomber
Command Losses, Volume 4, page 167).

19 OTU   Whitley V   AD692   Training

Sgt A J Mulligan RCAF	inj	T/o Kinloss for a night navigation exercise.
Sgt Woods	inj	At 0111, the starboard engine failed and the
	inj	crew turned about, setting a course which would
	inj	take them in the direction of Loch Shin in
	inj	Sutherland. En route, and at 0140, the port
		motor lost power and in the ensuing forced-

landing, the Whitley smashed through a stone built sheep pen and was wrecked.

16 May
1942

	16 OTU	Hampden I	P2120		Training

P/O W H Parr   +   T/o Upwood for a night navigation sortie. Lost
F/S D C Macnab RCAF   +   control at 10,000 feet and spun in, 2359, near
F/S K G McKee RCAF   +   Saxilby, 6 miles NW from the centre of Lincoln.
One member of the crew, said to have been the
air gunner, managed to parachute. His less fortunate colleagues are buried in
Scampton (St. John The Baptist) Churchyard. Their Hampden was the last to be
written off by 16 OTU, soon to convert to Wellingtons.

17 May
1942

	18 OTU	Wellington IC	N2806	-T	Training

Sgt W Kubera PAF   +   T/o Bramcote for a night cross-country, which
F/O A B Switalski PAF   +   was to be the crew's final exercise prior to
P/O E Baczkiewicz PAF   +   completion of their course and posting to an
Sgt J Bogusiak PAF   +   operational squadron. Shortly before 0125, a
Sgt E L Kaliciecki PAF   +   Royal Observer Observation Post caught sight
of the Wellington, on fire, and moments later
it crashed at Chollerford, 3 miles NNW of Hexham, Northumberland. All lie in
the Polish Plot at Newark-upon-Trent Cemetery.

17-18 May
1942

	19 OTU	Whitley V	P5043	-B	Training

P/O B C Cosham   inj   T/o 2330 Kinloss for a night exercise. Crashed
Sgt A Baylis   inj   at around 0025 after flying into rising ground
Sgt C H Pratt RCAF   inj   on the approach to Lossiemouth airfield, the
Sgt A S McLaren   inj   crew having signalled their intention to land
due to engine trouble. Both P/O Cosham and
Sgt Baylis succumbed to their dreadful injuries on 22 May and were laid to rest
in Birmingham (Lodge Hill) Cemetery and Alcester Burial Ground respectively.
Cruelly, as often was the case, their two companions recovered but were killed
on bombing operations later in the war. Sgt McLaren, posted to 49 Squadron, was
first to die when his Lancaster was brought down over Germany on 29-30 March
1943 (see Bomber Command Losses, Volume 4, page 83), while Sgt Pratt RCAF, who
went to the Middle East theatre of operations and joined 142 Squadron, was
killed on 7 July 1943, when his Wellington X HE760 was shot down near Palermo.
Sgt Baylis had transferred from the army to the air force in January 1939.

18 May
1942

	18 OTU	Wellington IC	DV783		Transit

P/O J Klimczyk PAF   +   T/o 0015 Thurleigh but dived into ground, near
F/O A Wisniewski PAF   +   the airfield and burst into flames. All rest
Sgt W J Kempski PAF   +   in the Polish Plot at Newark-upon-Trent. After
P/O A K Skora PAF   +   a relatively accident free run lasting the best
Sgt Z Kozlowski PAF   +   part of two months, the unit had suffered two
fatal crashes on consecutive days.

	20 OTU	Wellington IA	P2516	XL-C	Training

F/L J D Royal   +   T/o 1030 Lossiemouth with the intention of
F/S E R Hamilton RCAF   +   demonstrating blind flying techniques. As
Sgt G W Thornton   +   the bomber gathered speed, so it swung off
the runway and smashed into an excavator,
Mr W Duncan   +   working near No. 7 Gun Post. The impact was
of such force that an explosion blew apart the
Wellington and mortally injured the driver of the excavator. The first two
named are buried in Lossiemouth Burial Ground, while Sgt Thornton was taken
to Newcastle-upon-Tyne (Byker and Heaton) Cemetery. It will be recalled that
F/L Royal, a staff pilot, had survived two previous accidents (see pages 62
and 63).

19-20 May
1942

	18 OTU	Wellington IC	N2813		Training

Sgt P Bakalarski PAF   T/o 2340 Bramcote for a night cross-country.
Encountered very severe icing and when both
engines cut, the crew baled out leaving their aircraft to crash circa 0250 some
three miles W of Rhayader, Radnorshire.

20 May
1942

	21 OTU	Anson I	AX430		Ground

Damaged beyond repair at 0310 after being struck
by Wellington IC DV811, of the same unit, landing at Moreton-in-Marsh with a crew
of three; Sgt E D B Rae, Sgt G H Rappon and F/O M R Griffiths. No one was hurt
and the Wellington was soon repaired. Sgt Rae, meanwhile, left soon after this
incident on posting to 70 Squadron in the Middle East. On 5 September 1942, his
aircraft was reported missing and he now lies in Tobruk War Cemetery.

21 May 1942	21 OTU	Anson I	N5259	Training

	F/S E V Shaw	+	T/o Moreton-in-Marsh authorised to fly a low-
	Sgt E Brocklebank	+	level cross-country. At about 1730, the Anson
	Sgt W H Watkins RAAF	inj	flew into a line of high-tension cables a mile
	F/S Townsend	inj	or so E of Kingham, 4 miles SW from Chipping
	Sgt F Dodd	inj	Norton, Oxfordshire. F/S Shaw rests in Belfast

(Dundonald) Cemetery, while Sgt Brocklebank is buried in Moreton-in-Marsh New Cemetery.

	21 OTU	Wellington IC	R1142	Training

	F/S G H Wilsher	+	T/o Edgehill for dual instruction in overshoot
	Sgt J Anderson	+	procedures. Landed, heavily, at 2350 and the
	Sgt H Swales	+	throttles were advanced in order to go round
	Sgt T A Worley RAAF	+	again. It seems likely, however, that damage
	Sgt A R Murray	inj	had occurred as the bomber stalled and crashed

two miles E of the airfield. Of the four who perished, Sgt Worley RAAF was interred in Moreton-in-Marsh New Cemetery, while the rest were taken to their home towns. Sgt Murray, a Rhodesian, made a good recovery but was killed on the night of 11-12 August 1943, while flying in Wellington X HZ544 BL-Z of 40 Squadron (see page 371 of 'Sweeping The Skies' by David Gunby (The Pentland Press, 1995)). The five members of his crew have no known graves and all are commemorated on the El Alamein Memorial.

	25 OTU	Wellington IC	DV841	Training

	Sgt R D Roberts RAAF	+	T/o Finningley for a navigation exercise.
	F/S W N Reeves RCAF	+	Crashed 1755 at Emma Pits Pond on West Paddy
	Sgt R Groom RAAF	+	Moor, a mile NW of Crook in Co. Durham. Eye-
	F/S R M Boates RCAF	+	witnesses state the Wellington seemed to be
	F/S A F Roberts RCAF	+	flying normally at around 8,000 feet when,

without warning, it spun to the ground with smoke pouring from one of its engines. All are buried in Darlington West Cemetery.

22 May 1942	27 OTU	Wellington IC	R1158	Ground

While being refuelled at Lichfield, a union joint on the bowser worked loose, allowing petrol to spill and spread along the ground. Before anyone realised what was happening, the fuel came into contact with a Hurricane lamp and seconds later the Wellington was a mass of flames. A time has not been indicated, but mention of a Hurricane lamp suggests the accident occurred during the hours of darkness.

24 May 1942	13 OTU	Blenheim IV	R3599	Training

	Sgt C D Typer		T/o 0905 Bicester for a navigation exercise.
	Sgt W D Heap	+	While over Wiltshire, ran into a very severe
	Sgt K J Allwood	+	rain storm and though Sgt Typer attempted to

climb above the storm, he was unsuccessful and at 1,500 feet the Blenheim went out of control. It is thought that all baled out but only the pilot landed safely, the bomber, meanwhile, plunging into the ground at Green Farm near Trowbridge. Sgt Heap lies in Twickenham Parochial Cemetery, while Sgt Allwood, who came from Erdington in the NW suburbs of Birmingham, is buried in Wiltshire at Melksham Church Cemetery.

25 May 1942	15 OTU	Wellington IC	X3216	Air Test

	W/C H J Walker		T/o 2030 Harwell following re-rigging but

as the bomber lifted from the runway, W/C Walker immediately perceived that it was unsafe to continue the test and, throttling back, he touched down on the runway. However, he was not able to bring the Wellington to a stop before racing into the overshoot area, where a large pile of subsoil had been deposited by contractors.

	22 OTU	Wellington IC	AD625	Ground

	F/O J J Gale	inj	While waiting for clearance to take off from
	P/O Morris	inj	Stratford-upon-Avon, the Wellington was struck
	Sgt J S Williams RNZAF	+	at 0240 by another of the unit's aircraft and
	Sgt D Callaghan RNZAF	+	totally destroyed. Both survivors were taken
	Sgt M Wilkinson RNZAF	+	to Stratford Hospital, very seriously injured.
	Sgt J E Hough	+	Of those who died, Sgt Hough was taken to
	Sgt V R Pascoe RAAF	+	Macclesfield Cemetery, while the others were

laid to rest in Stratford-upon-Avon Cemetery.

25 May	22 OTU	Wellington IC	DV480		Training

25 May 1942 · 22 OTU · Wellington IC · DV480 · Training

Sgt C R Whitworth	+
Sgt Noyes	inj
F/S J L Gibby	+
F/S R D Cook RCAF	+
Sgt R E Herbert RNZAF	+

T/o Stratford-upon-Avon for a night navigation exercise and destroyed in the manner described at the foot of the previous page. A particularly strong cross-wind was deemed to have been a contributory factor in this tragic accident. Sgt Whitworth is buried in Shepshed Cemetery; both Commonwealth airmen rest in Stratford-upon-Avon Cemetery, while F/S Gibby, a member of the pre-war Auxiliary Air Force, lies in Tunbridge Wells Cemetery.

25 OTU · Wellington IC · R1151 -L · Training

F/O S le V Wood DFC	+
F/S R A Coles	+
Sgt Livingstone	inj
LAC G L Emms	+

T/o 1441 Bircotes for dual instruction. Landed ten minutes later, but by mistake downwind, and while trying to go round failed to gain height. Banking in a strong gusting wind, control was lost and the bomber crashed into a belt of trees, bursting into flames. F/O Wood rests in Woodchurch (Holy Cross) Churchyard at Birkenhead, F/S Coles lies at Stivichall (St. James) Churchyard and LAC Emms is buried in King's Lynn Cemetery.

26 May 1942 · 19 OTU · Whitley V · P5092 ZV-A · Training

P/O G K Chadwick	+
Sgt E G Kinsey	+
Sgt J Green	+
Sgt P Crane	+
F/S C D A Whitehead	+

T/o 2229 Kinloss for a night bombing exercise over the Innes Links range, the crew being from No. 36 Course. At around 2359, eyewitnesses saw debris falling from the sky, over the range area, 3 miles ESE of Lossiemouth airfield. At daybreak, the bulk of the wreckage was found near Innes House, the Whitley having broken into two sections in the wake of the photoflash exploding. P/O Chadwick rests in Kinloss Abbey Burial Ground, while his crew are lying in cemeteries in their home towns. It is likely Sgt Kinsey and Sgt Crane joined the air force within days of each other and may have known each other in civilian life as both lie in Moston (St. Joseph's) Roman Catholic Cemetery.

21 OTU · Wellington IC · X9934 · Ground

Destroyed 2332 at Moreton-in-Marsh after being hit by 1446 Flt Wellington IC DV657. In the blaze that followed the collision bombs from one of the aircraft exploded. The cause of the accident was a tyre bursting on the 1446 Flt aircraft, as it took off. At least two members from its crew, P/O J Clark RAAF and F/S L C Laver RAAF, were injured.

28 May 1942 · 20 OTU · Wellington IC · R1377 · Training

Sgt D Downing RAAF	
Sgt M J A Wyllie RAAF	
Sgt W J Taylor RAAF	
Sgt D A Radke RAAF	
Sgt W G Reed RAAF	inj

T/o Lossiemouth for a night cross-country. On return to base at 0150, the crew were confronted with very poor visibility and, as a result, misjudged their first attempt to land. However, the Wellington's port wing seemed to drop and Sgt Downing RAAF decided not to overshoot and thus he crash-landed on the airfield. Sgt Reed RAAF was admitted to SSQ Lossiemouth with a dislocated shoulder. However, his injury was not too serious and within a couple of weeks the entire crew were on the strength of 460 Squadron. On 2-3 July 1942, they joined Sgt A M Johnston RAAF for a visit to Bremen (see Bomber Command Losses, Volume 3, page 146) but failed to return. Three survived to become prisoners of war, but on 22 April 1943, while attempting to escape from Lamsdorf, Sgt Wyllie RAAF was shot and killed. He is buried in Cracow Military Cemetery. His entry in the Cracow cemetery register indicates he was Mentioned in Despatches.

20 OTU · Wellington IC · Z8852 -L · Training

Sgt B W McClennan RCAF	+
Sgt Braithwaite RAAF	inj
Sgt Browes RAAF	inj
Sgt Crompton	inj
Sgt Brin RCAF	inj

T/o 0005 Elgin for a night exercise and, similar to the crew summarised above, returned to base at 0220 to discover the weather was absolutely appalling with sleet reducing visibility to a minimum. Not surprisingly, the crew overshot the flare path and while going round again, flew into some trees near Fodda Bridge, a mile to the E of the airfield. The pilot, Sgt McClennan RCAF is buried in Lossiemouth Burial Ground, his crew subsequently recovered from their injuries.

Chapter Three

A Summer of Operations

30-31 May to 16-17 September 1942

During the night of 28-29 March 1942, Bomber Command raided the Baltic Sea port of Lübeck and in near perfect weather conditions left this ancient town a mass of flames. Palm Sunday 1942, thus heralded the beginning of the terrible retribution that would befall every major German industrial centre before the cessation of hostilities three years hence. It had taken Bomber Command's new chief a little over a month to stamp his authority on a campaign that had wavered so badly in the winter of 1941-1942.

In retrospect, Lübeck had been lightly defended but Harris had demonstrated that, with careful planning, a concentrated force of bombers was capable of bringing untold misery to the citizens of the Third Reich.

A month later, Rostock was the focal point for four attacks, at the end of which the Germans, for the first time, coined the term "Terrorangriff" ("terror raid") to describe the suffering caused.

However, despite these obvious successes, Harris knew that it was going to take a lot more than a couple of good results against relatively secondary targets in the Baltic to persuade the doubters in the War Cabinet. The public imagination had to be caught, not only with the name of a German city that was well known, but this city had to be hit by a force unsurpassed by anything that had been reported thus far in the air war. The seeds of inspiration for what would come to be known as the "Thousand Plan" raids had been sown.

It is not necessary to explain, in detail, the planning process, suffice to say that by including the bomber Operational Training Units the magical figure of 1,000 aircraft could be attained. As history tells us, the first choice was Hamburg but a spell of poor weather in late May led to Hamburg being abandoned in favour of the Rhineland city of Köln.

As a measure of the contribution made by the training establishments, of the 1,047 aircraft mustered, three-hundred and sixty-five were drawn from just thirteen units (No. 13 OTU and No. 17 OTU, equipped with Blenheims did not participate, though the former was tasked to provide aircraft for any search and rescue details that might be forthcoming, after the raid). The bulk of the force was Wellingtons, two-hundred and ninety-nine to be precise, while No. 10 OTU fielded twenty-one Whitleys and Hampdens were provided by Nos. 14 and 25 OTUs, No. 16 OTU having converted to Wellingtons as the the final touches were being added to the Operational Plan. It was, without any shadow of doubt, a quite magnificent effort.

Much consideration was given to the choice of crews for much was going to be asked of these eager young men, not yet fully trained. It was intended to provide each trainee crew with an experienced captain but in the event, close on fifty aircraft took off without the luxury of a seasoned pair of hands at the controls.

This was a tremendous gamble on the part of High Wycombe for it was an accepted practice that pilots from the training units would, on posting to their operational squadrons, fly at least one, possible two, sorties with an experienced crew before being entrusted to take their own crew into the hostile skies above Germany. Now, and in the weeks ahead, it was going to be a case of sink or swim for many of those involved in these historic air attacks.

Generally, all acquitted themselves well and, in percentage terms, losses from the training units engaged over Köln were lower than their operational counterparts. This would not always be the case but the outcome of this first 1,000 bomber raid had exceeded all expectations.

Anxious not to lose the momentum created by this successful foray into the enemy heart-land, Harris turned his attention to the key industrial centre of Essen. Lying towards the western fringes of the Ruhr, an area synonymous with German war production, Essen was of particular importance with its sprawling mass of factories, dominated by those of Krupps, churning out a myriad of munitions essential to maintain the effectiveness of all three services. Not surprisingly, the German High Command had not been niggardly in providing the Ruhr with adequate protection from the attention of Bomber Command. Well before the spring of 1942, a defensive screen of search-light and anti-aircraft (flak) batteries were in place. So robust were these measures that a healthy respect was firmly entrenched in the minds of aircrews charged with attacking Germany's industrial base. Indeed, Essen had long been regarded as on a par with Berlin as having the toughest defensive system in the whole of Nazi Germany.

But, it was not only the searchlights and flak (plus the increasing effectiveness of the Luftwaffe's night-fighter arm) that gave Essen its protective shield. As war output increased, so an almost permanent industrial haze settled over the Ruhr making it almost nigh impossible to distinguish the towns and cities that lay beneath.

One of the many innovations that had been tested of late was a navigational aid known as Gee. Early in March 1942, the Command had launched three Gee-guided raids on the Ruhr, Essen being the primary target on each occasion but, in the main, the results had been disappointing (it is interesting to note that the first success of Gee came in the middle of March when Köln was bombed by a medium force of just over one-hundred and thirty aircraft).

Since these early operational trials, when relatively few bombers had sets fitted (and, consequently, few navigators trained in its usage), steps had been taken to ensure that an adequate supply of sets were available to the bomber force and it was now hoped that Gee would enable a telling blow to fall on Essen. In addition, the first wave (mainly Wellingtons drawn from 3 Group squadrons) would release flares in an attempt to concentrate the bombing into as tight an area as possible.

But it was to no avail. Crews reported the presence of haze stretching as far as the eye could see and, not for the first time, Essen was little damaged, though with the presence of so many bombers over the Ruhr, a number of centres were hit and some useful damage was inflicted.

From Köln, thirteen OTU aircraft had been lost to enemy action; one had ditched off the East Anglia coast, two were destroyed in crashes while trying to land and a fourth, a Hampden from No. 14 OTU, collided over Cambridgeshire with a 78 Squadron Halifax. In the wake of Essen, thirteen more bombers needed replacing in the training system.

The third raid in the series was launched during the night of 25-26 June and though it fell short of the standards set by the first it was, nonetheless, a vast improvement over the Essen debacle at the beginning of the month (the diarist at No. 26 OTU did not agree with this official assessment, noting, rather tersely that Bremen had been a, "Very disappointing operation".

Certainly, the casualty rate amongst the OTUs involved rose sharply with twenty-eight aircraft written off. As the summaries will show, of the active units only three would file safe returns for their aircraft.

From a training viewpoint, utilising the OTUs in this way had a disrupting influence on the entire training programme and for the screened personnel, the past few weeks must have been more akin to the operational units that they had recently departed, rather than the settled existence of a training station.

Furthermore, as the summer wore on, so the OTUs would be called upon to participate in five major operations (though involvement would not be on the scale of that asked for the "Thousand Plan" raids). On each occasion casualties were inflicted, Düsseldorf being particularly bad for No. 16 OTU, which lost five from thirteen Wellingtons sent on 10-11 September.

Fittingly, the last attack in which the OTUs were ordered to take part was directed against Essen and though the overall force numbered less than four hundred aircraft, it was reckoned to be the most damaging yet on this key target. At least fifteen high explosive bombs smashed into the Krupps complex and, at the height of the raid, a bomber went down, laden with incendiaries, to crash into the same area.

A few statistics are appropriate. Forty-one aircraft were lost, including two that crashed within the United Kingdom and their demise can be attributed to enemy action.

Of the two aircraft reported destroyed over friendly territory, one was a Wellington from No. 27 OTU, while from the remainder, seventeen belonged to the training units.

Before continuing with the summaries, a few lines concerning the activities of No. 10 OTU based at Abingdon.

Early in August 1942, this Whitley-equipped unit was instructed to detach aircraft and crews to St. Eval in Cornwall where, under the auspices of Coastal Command, they would join in the task of anti-submarine patrols over the Bay of Biscay and in the Western Approaches. As is well known, the scourge of the U-boat was having a near crippling effect on the Allied war effort; losses amongst the merchant shipping convoys crossing from North America and Canada being alarmingly high.

Unit records show that twenty-six aircraft were fitted with auxiliary fuel tanks and as the month progressed, so these bombers joined the hard-pressed regular squadrons, a welcome boost to the unceasing Battle of the Atlantic seas.

The first anti-submarine sweeps were flown on 12 August and from an input of five sweeps the next day, Sgt Boyd and his crew were reported missing. On this occasion, the outcome was a happy one for all were picked up and by 16 August were en route for home via the Isles of Scilly.

Flying anti-submarine patrols was a lonely and often very dangerous occupation. Even if assisted by radar, crews sighted a U-boat, the outcome of any depth charge was no foregone conclusion. U-boats were certainly not adverse to fighting it out on the surface and more than one anti-submarine crew paid the ultimate price for pressing on with an attack in the face of withering return fire.

In the period covered by this chapter, No. 10 OTU lost six aircraft on such sorties, but only one resulted in the deaths of all six crew members (another crew were sampling the dubious delights of internment in Spain after being forced to ditch one-hundred and eighty miles south-west of the Bishops Rock).

The remaining four losses are traced to three successful ditchings (the first being mentioned above) and a landing accident at St. Eval on 5 September, from which five crew members required medical attention.

This detachment continued well beyond the period of "Operation Torch" (the North Africa landings) and did not end until the high summer of 1943, by which time the Wehrmacht

had been chased out of North Africa and the far as the inspirations of Adolf Hitler were
writing was well and truly on the wall, as concerned.

30-31 May   **11 OTU Y Sqn**   **Wellington IC**   R1065 KJ-Z   **Op: Köln**
1942
W/O J H Bulford   pow   T/o 2240 Steeple Morden using call sign 5QXZ and
W/O D Dunkley   pow   armed with 2 x 500lb GP bombs, 4 SBC each with
W/O R Higham   pow   sixty x 4lb incendiaries, IFF and two flame
W/O T A Guthrie RNZAF   pow   floats.
W/O A S Day   pow

12 OTU   **Wellington IC**   X9874   **Op: Köln**
P/O R L W Ferrer   +   T/o 2320 Chipping Warden. Came down in the sea,
P/O A Lucki RCAF   +   while returning to base, off the port of Harwich
Sgt K H Buck RCAF   +   in Essex. The three survivors were picked up by
F/S R Grundy   inj   a motor vessel and taken to RN Hospital Shotley
F/S J D McKenzie RCAF   inj   (HMS Ganges) where F/S McKenzie RCAF died from
his injuries. He is buried in Ipswich Cemetery.
The others who died are commemorated on the Runnymede Memorial. Sgt Buck RCAF
lost his life while operating against Dortmund in May 1943, flying Halifaxes with
102 Squadron (see Bomber Command Losses, Volume 4, page 136).

14 OTU   **Hampden I**   L4173 GL-T2   **Op: Köln**
F/L W L Cameron RCAF   +   T/o 2310 Cottesmore. Severely damaged by enemy
Sgt J E Sheridan RAAF   +   action and the entire return flight was made on
F/S M F Porter   inj   one engine. Permission to land at Horsham St.
Sgt E H East   inj   Faith was sought (and given) but F/L Cameron's
approach was too fast and he elected to go round
again. However, at 500 feet, the Hampden's remaining motor cut and at 0530 the
bomber plunged into Overbury Road, Hellesdon in the western suburbs of Norwich.
Those who died rest in Norwich Cemetery. On 30 May 1996, a memorial plaque with
their names inscribed was unveiled during a service of dedication at the Ilford
Plant Hire premises in Boundary Road, Mr Chris Howard of Dereham, Norfolk, being
the driving force behind this ceremony. He is also the author of the booklet,
"Fate Has No Reason", which delves into the loss of a 9 Squadron Lancaster in
late January 1943 (see Bomber Command Losses, Volume 4, page 29).

14 OTU   **Hampden I**   P2116 GL-L2   **Op: Köln**
F/L T E P Ramsay   pow   T/o 2257 Cottesmore. Shot down by Lt Manfred
P/O W H Gorton   +   Meurer, III./NJG1, crashing 0205 near Diepenveen
P/O V E Woolnough DFM   +   (Overijssel), 4 km NNW of Deventer, Holland.
Sgt F H Falk   +   Those who died are buried in Diepenveen General
Cemetery. P/O Woolnough's award was published
in the London Gazette on 21 November 1941. He had served with 144 Squadron.
Sgt Falk had enlisted in Newfoundland during August 1940; he was the son of
Capt Enoch Falk and Fanny E Falk of St. John's.

14 OTU   **Hampden I**   P5321 GL-P3   **Op: Köln**
S/L D B Falconer DFC   T/o 2306 Cottesmore. Homebound, collided with a
W/O C Holmes   +   Halifax from 78 Squadron, flown by P/O G C Foers
P/O J H Knowling   +   (see Bomber Command Losses, Volume 3, page 105)
P/O H S Little   +   and crashed 0405 near March, Cambridgeshire. In
his report, S/L Falconer stated he emerged from
a rain cloud and was confronted by another aircraft, with its navigation lights
on, and was unable to take avoiding action. Of his crew, two are buried in Bury
Cemetery, while P/O Little rests in Wetheral Cemetery. Less than a year previous,
while serving on 49 Squadron, S/L Falconer had survived a very serious Hampden
crash (see Volume 2, page 74). Sadly, he was killed while commanding 156 Squadron
and by one of those ironies of fate, the target at the time was Köln (see Volume
5, page 525).

15 OTU   **Wellington IC**   R1791   **Op: Köln**
W/O D J Paul DFM   pow   T/o 2314 Harwell. Believed shot down at 0246 by
W/O S M Green   +   Lt Niklas, 6./NJG1, crashing at Marchienne
F/S T L Lyons   +   (Hainaut), in the SW outskirts of Charleroi,
F/S B Evans DFM   evd   Belgium. Those who perished rest in the local
Sgt J McCormack   +   communal cemetery. Both DFM recipients had, until
recently, served in the Middle East (37 Squadron
and 108 Squadron), their awards being Gazetted on 9 April 1941 and 7 April 1942.

30-31 May   **15 OTU**   **Wellington II**   **W5586**   **-U**   **Op: Köln**
1942

W/O J E Hatton	pow	T/o 2340 Harwell. Believed shot down at 0215 by
F/L J B Harper	pow	Oblt Reinhold Knacke, 3./NJG1. By 7 July 1942,
W/O R Hill	pow	Mrs Hatton had received a postcard from her
Sgt R J Collins RAAF	evd	husband advising that he was a prisoner of war,
W/O F R Hindle	pow	and undergoing treatment for a broken ankle.

Sgt Collins RAAF returned to the United Kingdom
on, or by, 21 July 1942. It is much suspected that their aircraft had been used
to train crews destined for service in the Middle East.

22 OTU   **Wellington IC**   **R1235**   **-O**   **Op: Köln**

F/S C J Matthews	+	T/o 2255 Elsham Wolds. Shot down by a night-
F/S P G Barclay RCAF	+	fighter and crashed at Kalenberg, 4 km NE from
P/O W F Caldwell DFM	+	Kall. All are buried in Rheinberg War Cemetery.
Sgt D H Edwards RNZAF	+	P/O Caldwell and P/O Tallis had served previously
P/O D A R Tallis DFM	+	with 9 Squadron and 102 Squadron respectively and

their awards were published on 27 July 1943 and
9 May 1941. Four days later, Sgt Edwards's brother, F/L Norman John Edwards,
serving with the Royal Air Force, failed to return from Bremen while flying
with 101 Squadron (see Bomber Command Losses, Volume 3, page 116).

22 OTU   **Wellington IC**   **R1714**   **Op: Köln**

F/L A C Hamman DFC & Bar	+	T/o Elsham Wolds. Those who perished are buried
W/O E Neesom MID	+	in Rheinberg War Cemetery. F/L Hamman, a regular
W/O K P E Monk	pow	officer, came from Cape Town. It is believed his
F/S R R Harrison RCAF	+	tail gunner, F/S Hawkins, joined the Volunteer
F/S W S Hawkins	+	Reserve circa 1937 as a trainee pilot.

22 OTU   **Wellington IC**   **DV701**   **-P**   **Op: Köln**

F/O H R Blake DFC RNZAF	+	T/o 2248 Elsham Wolds. Shot down at Zons on the
F/S D S MacLean RCAF	+	south bank of the Rhine, 12 km S from the centre
F/S R N A Creswell RCAF	+	of Düsseldorf. At least three bodies were
F/S J R Wanbon DFM	+	recovered, since when their graves have remained
F/S N Grattan RCAF	+	untraced. Thus, all are commemorated on the

Runnymede Memorial. F/S Wanbon had gained his
award, Gazetted 22 August 1941, while serving with 51 Squadron. F/O MacLean
had gained a Bachelor of Science degree at New Brunswick.

22 OTU   **Wellington IC**   **DV843**   **-Q**   **Op: Köln**

P/O W A Fullerton DFM	+	T/o 2244 Elsham Wolds. Outbound, shot down circa
F/O L J Tait	+	2340 by Oblt Wilhelm Beier, I./NJG1, at Dinte-
F/S J K Napier DFM	+	loord (Noord Brabant), 6 km NNE of Steenbergen
Sgt R A Armstrong RCAF	+	in Holland. All rest in Bergen op Zoom War
F/S R M Sanders	+	Cemetery (Sgt Armstrong RCAF is buried in the

Canadian section). P/O Fullerton had previously
served with 104 Squadron and F/S Napier with 51 Squadron, their DFMs being
promulgated on 23 September 1941 and 30 January 1942 respectively. It is also
noted that the former was a Licentiate of the Royal Academy of Music.

23 OTU   **Wellington IC**   **N2851**   **-F3**   **Op: Köln**

F/S W R C Johnson RCAF	+	T/o 2312 Stradishall. Crashed 0010 near Graven-
Sgt J Donn-Patterson RAAF	+	deel (Zuid Holland), 7 km SW of Dordrecht. The
Sgt M L Glenton-Wright RAAF	+	pilot and tail gunner are buried in Crooswijk
Sgt G F Bolton RAAF	+	General Cemetery; the others are commemorated
Sgt R A Broodbank RAAF	+	on the Runnymede Memorial. Sgt Donn-Patterson

of Coff's Harbour, New South Wales, was an
Instructor in the Surf Life Saving Association of Australia. Sgt Glenton-
Wright's parents lived at, or in time came to Dulverton in Somerset.

25 OTU   **Wellington IC**   **L7802**   **-P**   **Op: Köln**

F/L C G Hughes	pow	T/o 2246 Finningley. Hit by flak while flying
W/O B C Whittle	pow	at 13,050 feet over the target area. F/L Hughes
F/S R Baker	pow	managed to draw clear of Köln but the fire in
W/O R V C Oliver	pow	the Wellington's starboard engine could not be
F/S F G Greensides	pow	extinguished and with the flames threatening to
W/O L R Read	pow	explode the petrol tanks, the order to abandon

was given. All did so and the bomber plunged
at 0146 onto the Julianastraat at Elsloo (Limburg), 5 km SW of Geleen, Holland.

30-31 May	26 OTU	Wellington IC	W5704	-S		Op: Köln
1942	F/O W R H Whiting		+		T/o 2345 Graveley. Shot down circa 0130 by,	

| | 26 OTU | Wellington IC | W5704 | -S | | Op: Köln |

30-31 May 1942

26 OTU — Wellington IC — W5704 — -S — Op: Köln

- F/O W R H Whiting — +
- Sgt J H G Garrick — +
- Sgt J M Hall RNZAF — +
- Sgt R C Williams — +
- Sgt A N Young RNZAF — +

T/o 2345 Graveley. Shot down circa 0130 by, it is thought, Hptm Werner Streib, I./NJG1 and crashed at Middelberg (Noord Brabant), 16 km W of Eindhoven, Holland, where all are buried in Woensel General Cemetery. Both RNZAF members of crew had been attached from 27 OTU.

26 OTU — Wellington IC — DV707 — -D — Op: Köln

- F/S E J Ford DFM — +
- P/O D C August — +
- W/O D W Caswell — pow
- F/S F F Barker DFM — +
- F/S J Thompson — +

T/o 2315 Graveley. Thought to have fallen victim to Lt Niklas, 6./NJG1, crashing in the vicinity of Venlo (Limburg) Holland, where those who died were first laid to rest. Since the cessation of hostilities, their remains have been interred at Jonkerbos War Cemetery. F/S Ford and F/S Barker gained their DFMs, Gazetted respectively on 24 October and 2 September 1941, while serving with 9 Squadron in the case of the former and 103 Squadron for the latter. W/O Caswell was taken into captivity with quite severe burns and wounds caused by cannon shell splinters.

26 OTU — Wellington IC — DV709 — -F — Op: Köln

- Sgt J J Dixon — +
- Sgt Scroggie RCAF — inj
- Sgt Green — inj
- Sgt Broadhurst — inj
- Sgt B B Camlin — +

T/o 0019 Graveley. Crashed 0435 while making an emergency landing in a field near Soham Flour Mill, some 13 miles NE of Cambridge. Sgt Dixon and Sgt Camlin, the tail gunner hailing from Belfast, were buried in Beck Row (St. John) Churchyard at Mildenhall, while those who were extracted, alive, from the overturned bomber were taken to RAF Hospital Ely. Prior to the flight, they had been warned of an imminent posting to 57 Squadron.

26 OTU — Wellington IC — DV740 EU-O — Op: Köln

- W/O F G Hillyer — pow
- Sgt D H Fletcher — +
- P/O A C White — +
- Sgt D S B Vincent — +
- Sgt H L Smith — +

T/o 2305 Graveley. May have fallen to the guns of Oblt Patuschka, 4./NJG2, crashing at Alem in the Province of Gelderland, 14 km WNW of Oss (Noord Brabant), Holland. Those who died are buried in Uden War Cemetery. P/O White's father was the Venerable Arthur White MA of Orrell in Lancashire.

Note. Formed on 15 January 1942 at Wing in Buckinghamshire, 26 OTU had enjoyed a remarkably good run of fortune until this particular night. Akin to all the training establishments, 26 OTU had fielded a mixture of screened and all pupil crews, mustering twenty in total.

31 May 1942

25 OTU — Wellington IC — Z1151 — Unknown

Reported crashed at Bircotes and burnt out.

1- 2 Jun 1942

10 OTU D Flt — Whitley V — Z6581 — -P — Op: Essen

- S/L D B G Tomlinson DFC — +
- P/O R R H Rowe — +
- P/O J O Little DFM — +
- F/S J E McDonald RCAF — +
- Sgt J D O'Sullivan — +

T/o 2340 Abingdon. Shot down by Hptm Alfred Haesler, III./NJG1 and crashed 0148 in open countryside, the tail section breaking away and falling across a wire fence near Breedenbroek (Gelderland), 39 km ESE of Arnhem. All rest in Gendringen Roman Catholic Cemetery. P/O Little gained his DFM while serving with 405 Squadron, details being Gazetted on 21 November 1941. P/O Rowe was a Bachelor of Science graduate from London University; Sgt O'Sullivan was a qualified Scout Master, while their skipper, S/L Tomlinson had been Officer Commanding D Flight for exactly a year.

11 OTU — Wellington IC — DV767 OP-J — Op: Essen

- P/O J F Stanley — +
- W/O K Railton — +
- Sgt W E James — +
- F/S T L Kennedy — +
- W/O G B Spenceley — pow

T/o 2322 Steeple Morden using call sign 3AQJ and armed with 2 x 500lb GP, 4 SBC each container holding 60 x 4lb incendiaries. IFF was also fitted. Those who died rest in the Reichswald Forest War Cemetery, having being exhumed from graves located at Krefeld. W/O Spenceley was seriously wounded.

1– 2 Jun 1942	**12 OTU**	**Wellington IC**	**T2904**	**Op: Essen**

F/L D P Fox
W/O Paveley
Sgt Berry
F/S Whaley
Sgt Marks   inj

T/o 2300 Chipping Warden. Returned to base at around 0355 with the starboard engine stopped. Crashed while attempting to land. Sgt Marks was not seriously injured.

	12 OTU	**Wellington IC**	**X3203**	**Op: Essen**

F/L M N Aicken RNZAF   pow
F/S A W Dormand   +
F/S H Crossland RCAF   +
WO2 H J Elliott RCAF   pow
WO2 H J Lafortune RCAF   pow

T/o Chipping Warden. Caught at 14,000 feet over Essen in the flak barrage. The two airmen who died are buried in the Reichswald Forest War Cemetery. F/L Aicken RNZAF and WO2 Elliott RCAF are reported as being wounded.

	15 OTU	**Wellington IC**	**X3209**	**Op: Essen**

F/O R R Head
P/O G Watson
F/S R Stoodly
Sgt A R G Hart RAAF
F/S H S Nicholson

T/o 2335 Harwell but a tyre burst as the bomber gathered speed and in the ensuing crash, the Wellington was wrecked. Sgt Hart RAAF proceeded soon afterwards to the Middle East, where he lost his life on 29 October 1942. With no known grave, he is commemorated on column 265 of the Alamein Memorial.

	16 OTU	**Wellington IC**	**DV763 XG-H2**	**Op: Essen**

P/O R J Robinson DFC   +
F/O C O´Brien   +
WO2 E T Beal RCAF   pow
W/O J M Forster   pow
Sgt H E De Mone RCAF   evd

T/o 2312 Upper Heyford. Crashed 0234 at Perk in the Province of Brabant, 17 km NNE from Brussels. It is believed the crew fell victim to Hptm Walter Ehle, II./NJG1. Both officers were buried in Perk Churchyard, since when their bodies have been exhumed and taken to Adegem Canadian War Cemetery. W/O Forster required medical attention for his wounds. This was the unit´s first loss since converting to Wellingtons from Hampdens.

	18 OTU	**Wellington IC**	**HF891 –N**	**Op: Essen**

F/L W L Tweedie   +
W/O J A Nutt   +
P/O M Eustachiewicz PAF   +
Sgt R A Brown   +
Sgt S W Straigis PAF   +

T/o 2243 Hemswell. Crashed in the general vicinity of Mönchengladbach where all were first buried. Since 1945, their remains have been transferred to Rheinberg War Cemetery. Very tragically, the death of W/O Nutt marked the third of three sons lost by Stephen Charles Nutt and his wife, Mary Louise Nutt. Sgt Peter Norman Nutt, aged nineteen had been the first, posted missing from operations with 97 Squadron on 15 May 1941 (see Bomber Command Losses, Volume 2, page 58). Then, on 6 February 1942, Sgt Kenneth Charles Nutt, also aged 19, failed to return to Castle Archdale from a 201 Squadron Sunderland patrol. Both are perpetuated by the Runnymede Memorial. All three had joined the air force, prior to the outbreak of war.

	20 OTU	**Wellington IC**	**X9975 JM-P**	**Op: Essen**

P/O S S Martin DFC RCAF   +
F/S B J Daley RNZAF   +
Sgt T W Belton   +
Sgt T I McKenzie   +
F/S A Marvell DFM   +
Sgt G C Falconer   +

T/o 2253 Stanton Harcourt. Presumed to have crashed in the North Sea. Five are commemorated on the Runnymede Memorial, while F/S Marvell, whose award had been published as recently as 26 May, following service with 103 Squadron, is buried in Bergen General Cemetery.

	21 OTU	**Wellington IC**	**W5618 –W**	**Op: Essen**

F/S F B Albright RCAF   +
F/S J H Forsyth RCAF   evd
Sgt E V Stephens RAAF   +
Sgt R T Burt RAAF   +
W/O D A G Watkins RAAF   pow
P/O W M Richards RCAF   +

T/o 2307 Moreton-in-Marsh. Last heard making a wireless transmission at 0416 and was advised to steer a course of 282 degrees. Nothing further was heard. Those who died in the crash rest in Charleroi Communal Cemetery, while as early as 6 June, F/S Forsyth RCAF was hit and killed by an express train at, or near, Chalon-sur-Saone station in Saone-et-Loire, having made considerable progress through France on his attempted evasion. He now lies in Choloy War Cemetery. W/O Watkins RAAF, meanwhile, saw out the rest of the war in various prisoner of war camps and was almost certainly involved in the long trek westwards, early in 1945, ahead of the advancing Russian armies.

1- 2 Jun	23 OTU	Wellington IC	R1266	-G2	Op: Essen

1942

```
1- 2 Jun   23 OTU          Wellington IC  R1266   -G2              Op: Essen
1942       F/O W J Mawdesley RAAF      +   T/o 2305 Stradishall.  Crashed near the Terwindt
           F/S F J B Scrimes RCAF      +   Brickyard at Kerkdriel (Gelderland) on the W bank
           F/S T L J Norrie RCAF       +   of the Maas, some 13 km WNW of Oss in the neigh-
           Sgt K N Killby              +   bouring Province of Noord Brabant.  All are buried
           P/O G W Murray RCAF         +   in Uden War Cemetery.  F/S Norrie RCAF was an
                                           American from Baltimore in Maryland.


           23 OTU          Wellington IC  Z8867   -L               Op: Essen
           F/L W J Ewart MID           +   T/o 2255 Stradishall. Crashed at Heer (Limburg)
           P/O R A Minchin             +   Holland.  All were first buried at Venlo, since
           F/S D R Stuart              +   when their remains have been exhumed and taken to
           P/O G Gascoyne DFM          +   Jonkerbos War Cemetery.  P/O Gascoyne won his DFM
           P/O R Scriven               +   while serving with 75 Squadron, details appearing
                                           in the London Gazette on 18 July 1941.  His
    brother, F/S John Patrick Gascoyne, died on 21 February 1945 while flying with
    49 Squadron (see Bomber Command Losses, Volume 6, page 86).  His grave is not far
    distant from that of his brother, being in the Reichswald Forest War Cemetery.


           25 OTU          Wellington IC  DV434   -F2              Op: Essen
           F/L R F Jessop            pow   T/o 2259 Finningley.  Shot down by Oblt Beese
           WO2 J A Nugent RCAF       pow   of I./NJG1 and crashed 0200 at Horst (Limburg),
           F/O W J Clough RCAF       pow   twelve km NW of Venlo, Holland.  Sgt Reid now
           W/O R A Booth             pow   rests in Jonkerbos War Cemetery, having been
           F/S R J A Johnstone       pow   brought here from Venlo.  His service number
           Sgt G T Reid               +   shows he enlisted in Rhodesia circa June 1940.


           26 OTU          Wellington IC  HX375   -X               Op: Essen
           Sgt K Edmonds               +   T/o 2259 Graveley carrying 600 gallons of fuel
           F/S K B Utman RCAF          +   and armed with a 500lb GP bomb, 6 SBC, each
           Sgt B H Edye RAAF           +   holding 90 x 4lb incendiaries.  Crashed circa
           Sgt G Horner                +   0130 near Antwerpen, where all are now buried
           F/S R I Derry RCAF          +   in Schoonselhof Cemetery.  Sgt Edye's cousin,
                                           Sgt Maurice Ben Remfry RAAF of 27 OTU had been
    killed during operations to Lille on 27-28 April 1942 (see page 110).  He, too,
    is buried in Belgian soil at Heverlee War Cemetery.


  3 Jun    10 OTU          Whitley V      T4173                    Training
1942       Sgt K W Jone                    T/o 1030 Abingdon for a navigation exercise.
                                           Two hours and thirty minutes into the sortie,
    an engine caught fire and the Whitley was damaged beyond repair in a forced-
    landing 2 miles W of Marloes, 7 miles WNW of Milford Haven, Pembrokeshire.


           13 OTU          Blenheim IV    T2397                    Training
           Sgt C Nicholson           inj   T/o 1030 Bicester but both engines cut as the
           Sgt A Wheeler              +   aircraft climbed and a minute later it crash-
                                           landed near the Oxfordshire village of Bucknell
    some 2 miles WNW of the airfield.  Sgt Wheeler rests in Huddersfield (Edgerton)
    Cemetery.  It is reported that Sgt Nicholson's injuries were not serious.


           14 OTU          Oxford I       AS904                    Air Test
           S/L D J Bell DFC            +   T/o Cottesmore. While flying straight and level
           LAC R D Price              +   the trainer went into a slow flat spin from
           AC1 F A Hill               +   which it failed to recover before hitting the
                                      +   ground near Greetham, 5 miles NE of Oakham.
                                           Three are buried in the extension to Cottesmore
    (St. Nicholas) Cemetery; as yet, the fourth airman has not been identified.


           17 OTU          Blenheim IV    V6238                    Training
           Sgt A H Rew                     T/o Warboys.  Landed heavily on one wheel at
                                           nearby Wyton but on opening up to go round
    again, the port engine cut and the Blenheim crash-landed 2000 and was damaged
    beyond economical repair.


  4 Jun    12 OTU          Wellington IC  Z8964                    Training
1942       Sgt D D Dunlop              +   T/o 0930 Chipping Warden.  Forty minutes later,
           Sgt C F Lock               +   the Wellington flew into trees bordering the
           AC2 L S Honeker            +   Fair Mile near Henley-on-Thames, Oxfordshire.
                                           All lie in cemeteries within the United Kingdom.
```

4 Jun **17 OTU** **Blenheim IV** **V5566** **Training**
1942 P/O G Nadaraja + T/o Upwood for a navigation exercise. Presumed
P/O F J Barker + lost over the North Sea, possibly in the area of
Sgt R E Doman + 5343N 0056E. P/O Nadaraja, who came from Ceylon,
and Sgt Doman are commemorated on the Runnymede
Memorial, while P/O Barker is buried in Stamford Cemetery, his body having been
washed ashore eight days after being posted missing.

4- 5 Jun **27 OTU** **Wellington IC** **X9699** **Training**
1942 Sgt V Turner inj T/o 2249 Lichfield for a night cross-country.
Sgt J M Panos RAAF inj During the sortie, an engine caught fire and
Sgt R Ziser RAAF inj course was set for Bassingbourn. On arrival,
Sgt W A Faulkner RAAF inj the crew overshot their first attempt to land
Sgt Woodhouse RAAF inj and after going round again, crashed 0021 off
the end of the runway. Four were treated in
SSQ Bassingbourn but Sgt Woodhouse RAAF was taken to RAF Hospital Ely, having
lost the phalanx of his right big toe and fractured his right tibia and fibula.
Sadly, Sgt Ziser RAAF never returned to Australia. Posted to 150 Squadron, he
died when his Wellington crashed on the approach to Elsham Wolds (see Bomber
Command Losses, Volume 3, page 237) on 10 October 1942.

5 Jun **15 OTU** **Wellington IC** **Z8894** **Training**
1942 W/O J Herriot T/o 0130 Harwell for a night cross-country.
F/L R A Craigie Late on in the flight, the starboard engine
failed and though various speed ranges were
set, ranging between 100 and 120 miles per hour, height could not be maintained
and at around 0500 a forced-landing was carried out, on a hillside, at Tackley,
seven miles WSW of Bicester, Oxfordshire.

6 Jun **14 OTU** **Hampden I** **L4133** **Training**
1942 P/O R H Broadley + T/o Saltby for flying practice, during which
Sgt H G Thurgar + flying speed was lost and, at around 1345, the
Sgt R L Norris + Hampden spun into the ground some 2 miles E of
Sgt J D Henning RAAF + the airfield at a location given as Mere Bam,
South Stoke, practically on the Leicestershire
border with Lincolnshire. Sgt Henning RAAF lies in the extension to Cottesmore
(St. Nicholas) Churchyard, while the others were taken to their home towns.

20 OTU D Flt **Wellington IC** **DV713 ZT-W** **Training**
F/S H J Palmer RCAF + T/o Lossiemouth for a navigation exercise.
F/S A C C Peircey RCAF + While over the sea, the crew encountered a
Sgt F H Mitchell + severe electrical storm and while trying to
P/O J R Walker + get beneath the cloud base, had the misfortune
Sgt J Sinden + to fly straight into the sea some 8 miles ESE
of Peterhead on the Aberdeenshire coast. All
are commemorated on the Runnymede Memorial.

26 OTU **Wellington IC** **DV835** **Ground**
Destroyed by fire at 1300 while parked, facing
towards the south, at Wing airfield. The day was abnormally hot with a shade
temperature of 86 degrees. Thus, it is believed, ammunition in the bomber's
front turret self ignited.

8 Jun **10 OTU** **Whitley V** **BD378** **Training**
1942 Sgt G Ryan + T/o Abingdon for a cross-country flight. At
P/O J Hayward + around 1700, the bomber was seen approaching
F/S G O Doten RCAF + the runway when, for no apparent reason, it
Sgt F K Heaton + swung away, the engine note rising as power was
inj applied. Moments later, without gaining any
height, the Whitley smashed into the ground
and caught fire. Those who died are buried in various cemeteries, or, as in
the case of Sgt Ryan, commemorated in a garden of remembrance.

11 Jun **18 OTU** **Wellington IC** **T2898** **Training**
1942 Sgt J Laudan PAF T/o 1528 Hemswell for a navigation sortie. Lost
power, and being unable to maintain height, came
down just beyond the airfield. A technical inspection suggested the Wellington
could be repaired but there is no evidence to show this was done. Sgt Laudan
subsequently became a prisoner of war, while still serving at 18 OTU.

11 Jun 1942	25 OTU	Wellington IC	R1073	—01	Training

Sgt B E Rooke + T/o 1300 Finningley and headed for the airfield
Sgt B E F Jones + at Lindholme with the intention of carrying out
circuits and landings. At 1315, the Wellington
went out of control and dived into the ground, just to the E of Canberra Cottage
Farm, a mere 300 yards or so from Lindholme's runway. Both airmen are buried in
the extension to Finningley (St. Oswald) Churchyard.

	25 OTU	Wellington IC	R1454	—N2	Training

Sgt H Hutchinson T/o 1330 Finningley for local flying practice.
Approaching the runway, the bomber's starboard
wing dipped and before corrective action could be taken, the main wheels touched
the runway. Out of control, the Wellington skidded into some trees and was
destroyed in the ensuing fire.

12 Jun 1942	12 OTU	Wellington IC	Z1177		Training

P/O W P Bolton + T/o Chipping Warden for a night exercise. Iced
P/O B J S Vavasour + up, stalled and spun in at 0200, crashing near
P/O A J Majury + Confuit Farm, Churchill, 3 miles SW of Chipping
Sgt J E Counihan + Norton, Oxfordshire. P/O Bolton, an American
Sgt Mannering inj from Chicago, Illinois and Sgt Counihan were
buried in Brookwood Military Cemetery, while
the others who perished were taken to their home towns.

11–12 Jun 1942	25 OTU	Wellington IC	R1375	—N	Training

Sgt W B Barrett RCAF T/o 2240 Bircotes for a night navigation sortie.
Returned to base but, at 0235, undershot the
runway, careered through a hedge and collided with a large pile of stones and
cinders. The impact wrenched off the undercarriage and, soon afterwards, the
Wellington caught fire.

13–14 Jun 1942	12 OTU	Anson I	DJ103		Training

F/S A McA Sargeant inj T/o 2200 Chipping Warden for a night cross-
country, during which the crew became totally
lost. Four baled out, after which F/S Sargeant forced-landed 0230 not far from
Stevenage in Hertfordshire. He made a good recovery from his injuries; went to
an operational squadron and was later reported to be a prisoner of war.

14 Jun 1942	26 OTU	Wellington IC	DV710		Training

Sgt S Glover T/o Cheddington for circuits and landings.
Two hours into the exercise, Sgt Glover took
off for yet another circuit, only to find the Wellington was reluctant to climb.
Landing alongside the flare path, the undercarriage gave way and not long after
a fire broke out.

14–15 Jun 1942	19 OTU	Whitley V	P5005		Training

F/S E J Nelms RCAF + T/o 2355 Kinloss for a night navigation flight.
Sgt R T Aspinall inj On return to base, the crew made a controlled
Sgt E L Williams + descent through the overcast but for reasons
Sgt J J Taylor inj that could not be explained, the pilot turned
Sgt A H Lawrence inj right to enter the circuit instead of left.
Consequently, at 0217 the bomber struck high
ground near the hamlet of Califer, 4 miles SSE of the airfield. F/S Nelms RCAF
is buried in Kinloss Abbey Burial Ground, while P/O Williams was taken back to
Wales and interred at Pembroke Dock (Llanion) Cemetery. Until now, their aircraft had led a charmed existence for this was the Whitley flown by the late
Group Captain Leonard Cheshire VC OM on his well publicised operation to Köln
on 12-13 November 1940. Coded DY-N of 102 Squadron, Cheshire brought P5005
back to Linton-on-Ouse with a massive rent in the fuselage having taken a direct
hit from an anti-aircraft shell. For his outstanding actions on this operation
(and others), Cheshire received an immediate DSO, being the first junior officer
in Bomber Command to be so honoured. Repairs to the Whitley were carried out but
according to Richard Morris's fine autobiography of Leonard Cheshire (Viking,
2000), it was very severely damaged, while parked at Topcliffe, on 21 December
1940 (see page 67 of the biography for a first-hand account).

16 Jun 1942	14 OTU	Hampden I	AD787 GL—M1		Training

Sgt R L Featherstone RAAF T/o Saltby for local flying. Touched down 1930
but swung out of control and crashed.

16 Jun
1942

22 OTU   **Wellington IC**   **Ground**

While parked at its dispersal on Stratford-upon-Avon airfield, smoke and flames were seen issuing from the port wing. Despite the prompt arrival of the station's fire services, the Wellington was burnt out. Its identity is in doubt; one source quotes X9279 which comes within a batch of 250 Albacore aircraft produced for the Royal Navy, while unit records describe the bomber as DD5 (probably a misprint for DD-S).

17 Jun
1942

13 OTU   **Blenheim I** L6774   **Training**

P/O H T Bichard   inj T/o Hinton-in-the-Hedges for solo practice.

While flying at 300 feet, the port engine burst into flames, the fire spreading rapidly to the fuselage. Keeping a cool head, P/O Bichard succeeded in landing, at 1610, on the airfield, by which time the cockpit was alight. His aircraft had been well used, having served with three operational units and four training establishments.

17 OTU   **Blenheim IV** L4838   **Ground**

Sgt D A S Tomkins   At 2015, Sgt Tomkins was running up his engines prior to taking off from Upwood for a night exercise when the Blenheim burst into flames. It is strongly suspected that he was later commissioned, only to lose his life on 8-9 April 1943, while flying with 218 Squadron (see Bomber Command Losses, Volume 4, page 98 (where his rank is shown as Sgt)).

17 OTU   **Blenheim IV** R3611   **Training**

Sgt P C Thompson   inj T/o 0940 Alconbury but having climbed to a mere
P/O R T O'Neill   + fifty feet, the starboard engine cut causing the
Sgt Williams   inj the Blenheim to dive into the ground 500 yards S
of the airfield. Sgt Thompson was lifted from the wreckage with fractures to both the tibia and fibula of one of his legs, Sgt Williams was grievously hurt with a fractured spine, while P/O O'Neill was beyond all medical aid. He is buried in Bradford (Thornton) Cemetery. By some strange co-incidence, an AC2 William O'Neill lost his life this very same day while serving in Iraq. From Manchester, he rests in Basra War Cemetery.

24 OTU   **Whitley V** BD358   **Training**

F/S W T Rushton   + T/o 1525 Honeybourne for a navigation exercise
P/O L Rowlinson   + involving the crew, which was made up of a
Sgt G E Hibben   + screened pilot and wireless operator, four
Sgt E M Taylor   + trainees and two passengers, in overwater
Sgt A F Alcock RCAF   + flying. At 1955, the bomber returned to base
Sgt Harris   inj and was seen, while on the cross-wind leg, to
LAC H G Foot   + lower the flaps. As it did so, so the nose
AC2 J Murray   + appeared to rise quite sharply. Immediately, the flaps were retracted and the Whitley continued with its approach but as it turned finals, and the flaps were once again lowered, the nose pitched up and the aircraft stalled, plunging to the ground on the boundary of the airfield, where it burst into flames. Those who died rest in various cemeteries across the United Kingdom. This was the first major accident involving an aircraft from the unit since its formation in mid-March 1942.

18 Jun
1942

14 OTU   **Hampden I** AT223   **Training**

P/O R H G Boosey RCAF inj T/o Cottesmore for a night exercise. While
                  inj nearing the airfield, at around 0015, the port
                  inj engine failed and the Hampden crashed some 200
                  inj yards E of the aerodrome.

19 OTU   **Anson I** N9621   **Training**

Sgt P C Cato   T/o 0015 Kinloss for a night cross-country.

In deteriorating weather, the crew became uncertain of their position and their plight was further exacerbated when the wireless equipment failed. Subsequently, out of fuel, the Anson was abandoned and left to crash circa 0435 on Melcum Hill near Tarland, some nine miles ENE of Ballater, Aberdeenshire. Not long after this incident, Sgt Cato left on posting to 102 Squadron, only to lose his life on 1-2 October 1942, while raiding Flensburg (see Bomber Command Losses, Volume 3, page 231). He is buried in Kiel War Cemetery.

21 Jun **11 OTU** **Wellington IC** R1336 **Training**
1942 Sgt A S Forbes RNZAF T/o 1235 Steeple Morden for solo flying but the
port tyre burst and moments later the port
undercarriage collapsed. No one was hurt but the Wellington was destroyed
by the fire that broke out soon afterwards. Sgt Forbes RNZAF was destined
to see most of the war out in captivity at Lamsdorf.

21-22 Jun **12 OTU** **Wellington IC** T2548 **Training**
1942 Sgt W Connelly + T/o 2137 Chipping Warden for a night cross-
Sgt H A Dickinson inj country. On return to base at 0152, the bomber
Sgt E L Taylor + crashed on Redhill, NNE of the airfield, and
Sgt F J Tranter + burst into flames. Sgt Connelly is buried in
Sgt E Wilde inj Abbey Cemetery, Thorn; Sgt Taylor rests at
Woodston Cemetery, while Sgt Tranter lies
at Stoke-on-Trent (Burslem) Cemetery.

22 Jun **12 OTU** **Wellington IC** T2835 **Training**
1942 Sgt W S O Randle inj T/o Chipping Warden for a night flying exercise
inj during which one of the engines shed its
inj propeller, causing a fire to break out. In the
ensuing emergency landing, the Wellington hit a
tree and crashed 0158 near Caxton, 10 miles NW of Cambridge. No one was too
badly hurt and not long afterwards, Sgt Randle went to 150 Squadron. On 16-17
September 1942, his aircraft was shot down over Belgium (see Bomber Command
Losses, Volume 3, page 221), but along with four other members of his crew,
he evaded capture. Later commissioned and rising to the rank of G/C he has,
since his retirement from the air force, been instrumental in raising funds
for the Royal Air Force Museum at Hendon.

23 OTU **Wellington IC** X9748 **Ground**
At 0930, while undergoing a major inspection in
its hangar at Pershore, a fire broke out in the region of the astrodome and the
bomber was completely destroyed. It is much suspected that petrol was being
used as a cleaning agent.

23 Jun **23 OTU** **Wellington IC** X3172 **Training**
1942 P/O W L Farquharson T/o 0435 Pershore for a dawn cross-country.
Sgt H Mills While in flight, a propeller came off and the
P/O F L Todd RCAF pilot tried, without success, to raise Pershore
Sgt W A Williams using his TR9 radio transmitter. Meanwhile, he
Sgt E A Periman lost sight of the airfield due to haze and while
Sgt W G Teague circling the beacon, lost height and crash-
landed, the fuselage being severely fractured
forward of the cockpit. Later, P/O Todd RCAF became a casualty of war while
raiding Aachen with 419 Squadron on 5-6 October 1942 (see Bomber Command Losses,
Volume 3, page 235).

25 Jun **23 OTU B Flt** **Wellington IC** L7891 **Training**
1942 F/S C G McDonald RCAF + T/o 1655 Pershore for a cross-country. Dived
P/O C D Chant + from 3,000 feet and crashed 1835 as a consequence
P/O A W Smith + of the dinghy breaking from its stowage and
P/O L G Morrison RCAF + fouling the controls. Wreckage was spread over a
Sgt F W Sims + wide area to the W of Tiddington, 8 miles ESE of
Oxford. The two Canadians were buried just across
the border with Buckinghamshire at Haddenham (St. Mary) Churchyard, while the
others were taken to their home towns. P/O Chant had attained a Master of
Science degree from London University.

25-26 Jun **10 OTU** **Whitley V** P4944 **-A** **Op: Bremen**
1942 Sgt E D Williams RAAF + T/o 2252 Abingdon. Both Commonwealth members
Sgt G M Murphy + of crew lie in Hamburg Cemetery, Ohlsdorf; the
Sgt L N Reynolds + rest are commemorated on the Runnymede Memorial.
WO2 G L Wilkinson RCAF + F/S House's service number indicates he joined
F/S F C House + the service at Uxbridge, shortly after the outbreak of hostilities in September 1939. For
this, the third raid in the series of 1,000 bomber attacks, 10 OTU contributed
twenty aircraft, comprising of the usual mixture of seasoned and novice crews.
From this number, fifteen claim to have made successful attacks, while one crew
was obliged to make an early return after their compass failed.

25–26 Jun   **10 OTU**   **Whitley V**   **P5004**   **—G**   **Op: Bremen**
1942   P/O W W Colledge RCAF   T/o 2259 Abingdon. Ditched in the North Sea
      Sgt J V Karleff   from where all were picked up by an Air-Sea
      Sgt A J Ennals   Rescue launch. For his actions during the
      Sgt E A Taylor   course of this operation, P/O Colledge RCAF
      Sgt W E McCarthy   was awarded the DFC. On 1 July 1943, now
serving at 3 Flying Instructors School at
Castle Combe, his Oxford I X6858 crashed a mile S of Wickwar, 14 miles SSW
of Stroud, Gloucestershire, killing both members of crew. He is buried in
Bath (Haycombe) Cemetery, Englishcombe.

10 OTU   **Whitley V**   **AD689**   **—W**   **Op: Bremen**
F/S N M Oulster RCAF   +   T/o 2306 Abingdon. Crashed on the W bank of
Sgt G A Hunt   +   the Ems at Dalum, 10 km NW of Lingen (Ems),
Sgt D I Parry   +   where the crew were first buried. Their graves
Sgt S J Webster   +   are now in the Reichswald Forest War Cemetery.
Sgt H Cooke   +   Sgt Cooke of Bulawayo in Southern Rhodesia
joined the Royal Air Force along with his
twin brother, Grimwood Choke Cooke, who, before his death in action on 21–22
December 1942 (see Bomber Command Losses, Volume 3, page 284) was the holder
of the DFC and DFM.

10 OTU   **Whitley V**   **BD201**   **—L**   **Op: Bremen**
W/O N R Parsons   pow   T/o 2254 Abingdon. Shot down by Hptm Helmut
W/O J G Moriarty   pow   Lent, II./NJG1 and crashed 0256 onto land owned
Sgt G Ewen   +   by Mr Beemsterboer near Wervershoof (Noord
F/L R Van Toen   pow   Holland), 6 km SSE of Medemblik. Sgt Ewen
W/O G McB Harris   pow   is buried in Bergen General Cemetery.

11 OTU Y Sqn   **Wellington IC**   **R1078 TX–Q**   **Op: Bremen**
F/O S G King RCAF   pow   T/o 2316 Steeple Morden using call sign HU1Q and
WO2 F C Main RCAF   +   armed with 2 x 500lb GP bombs, 3 x SBC each with
Sgt F G Barber RNZAF   +   90 x 4lb incendiaries and fitted with IFF. Said
Sgt I H Reeves RNZAF   +   to have been shot down by a Bf 110, crashing near
W/O W N Hollands RNZAF   pow   Schale, 21 km NE of Rheine. Those who died were
buried at Rheine, since when their remains have
been exhumed and taken to the Reichswald Forest War Cemetery. WO2 Main RCAF was
an American from Eureka, California.

11 OTU Y Sqn   **Wellington IC**   **X3213 KJ–L**   **Op: Bremen**
F/S R Holden   +   T/o 2312 Steeple Morden using call sign 6MTL and
F/S R N Urquhart RCAF   +   similarly armed and equipped. Hit by flak and
F/S C T R Matthewman   +   crashed on the E side of the Zwischenahneer Meer
Sgt L A Mitchell RNZAF   +   and 3 km NE from the centre of Bad Zwischenahn.
Sgt V A B Falk RNZAF   +   All were buried in the Neufriedhof at Oldenburg
on 1 July, since when their bodies have been
interred in Sage War Cemetery.

11 OTU Y Sqn   **Wellington IC**   **DV778 KJ–A**   **Op: Bremen**
Sgt J C Cubitt   +   T/o 2314 Steeple Morden using call sign 6MTA and
Sgt W H Flower RNZAF   +   similarly armed and equipped. Crashed in the
Sgt R J Parish RNZAF   +   general area covered by the Heligoland Bight.
Sgt S L Wilton RNZAF   +   Three bodies were later recovered from the sea
F/S F W Mutton   +   and now lie in various German cemeteries, while
panels 81 and 117 respectively perpetuate the
names of Sgt Cubitt and Sgt Flower RNZAF.

Note. Although Y Sqn has been annotated against these three Wellingtons, it is
noted that the former carried a code combination suggesting it belonged to a
flight different from the other two, though all appear to have been based at
the Steeple Morden satellite. In each case, AM Form 78 has been annotated with
the hours flown; R1078 with 179.00, X3213 with 458.55 and DV778 with 203.50.

12 OTU   **Wellington IC**   **R1349**   **Op: Bremen**
F/S A C R Wilson   +   T/o Chipping Warden. Presumed crashed in the
F/L D P Drussel   +   sea off the Dutch coast. F/S Golightly has no
P/O R G Addis   +   known grave and as such is commemorated on the
F/S D W Taylor   +   Runnymede Memorial, panel 74, while his four
F/S F J Golightly   +   companions rest in Bergen op Zoom War Cemetery.

25-26 Jun   **12 OTU**   **Wellington IC**   **R1410 KX-M**   **Op: Bremen**
1942

Sgt J T Shapcott	+	T/o Chipping Warden. Crashed in the North Sea,
P/O P Morris	+	it is thought off the Dutch Frisian Islands
Sgt R H Smith	+	chain. P/O Morris and Sgt Smith are buried on
Sgt F R West RNZAF	+	Texel and Ameland respectively (the former having
Sgt L R Elvin	+	been washed up S of Texel on 12 July), while the
		others are perpetuated by the Runnymede Memorial.

When lost, it is strongly believed this Wellington was still carrying the code
combination applied during its 311 Squadron days.

12 OTU   **Wellington IC**   **Z8800**   **Op: Bremen**

Sgt W J Bagley	T/o 2240 Chipping Warden. Hit by flak, which
Sgt Keane	damaged the fuel tanks. At approximately 0540,
P/O Morrison	when some 25 miles off Cromer, Norfolk, the
Sgt Gowan	crew were obliged to ditch. All were picked
Sgt Dinsdale	up, unharmed, by a minesweeper.

12 OTU   **Wellington IC**   **DV951**   **Op: Bremen**

F/O E J Cooper	pow	T/o Chipping Warden. Believed shot down by Oblt
W/O C H Homer	pow	Herbert Lütje, III./NJG1 at 0058, shortly after
F/S L W Chatterton	pow	bombing, near Wietmarschen. Sgt Read sustained
Sgt A P Read	inj	wounds to his stomach, lungs and head and these
W/O H J Camden	pow	proved fatal (though he was admitted to the
		Krankenhaus at Lingen (Ems)). He is buried

in the Reichswald Forest War Cemetery. W/O Homer and F/S Chatterton were also
wounded, though F/S Chatterton's injuries are described as "slight".

14 OTU   **Hampden I**   **P5312 GL-J3**   **Op: Bremen**

F/L Count T E Salazar DFC	+	T/o 2252 Cottesmore. Crashed in the vicinity
Sgt T S Gaffney RAAF	+	of Borkum, where those who died in the crash
F/S R J Horlock	+	were laid to rest. Sgt Cusden was dreadfully
Sgt H S Cusden	pow	burnt and he died from his injuries on 18
		September. All now lie in Sage War Cemetery,

F/L Count Salazar was the son of the Count and Countess Demetria Salazar of
Malvern in Worcestershire.

15 OTU   **Wellington IC**   **DV737**   **Op: Bremen**

P/O D C Evans	+	T/o 2241 Harwell. All are buried in Becklingen
Sgt R I Coffin	+	War Cemetery. Their Wellington had been taken
Sgt T P Morgan	+	on charge, ex-18 MU Dumfries on 16 April 1942,
Sgt A G Leyland	+	and in its brief existence had logged a total
Sgt M Sweeney	+	of 275.45 flying hours.
Sgt J McK Kennedy	+	

15 OTU   **Wellington IC**   **DV935**   **Op: Bremen**

Sgt J S Leather	+	T/o 2244 Harwell. Presumed lost off the coast
Sgt H Bloor	+	of Holland. Five bodies were eventually given
Sgt J McK D Oliver	+	up by the sea and are now at rest in various
Sgt R T Fage	+	Dutch cemeteries. Sgt Lake is commemorated on
Sgt D T Stanners	+	panel 87 of the Runnymede Memorial. Sgt Bloor
Sgt G Lake	+	was a Bachelor of Science graduate from
		Birmingham University.

16 OTU   **Wellington IC**   **X9982 XG-A2**   **Op: Bremen**

P/O W C Samuel DFM	+	T/o 2255 Upper Heyford. Lost without trace.
P/O V P De Wallens	+	All are commemorated on the Runnymede Memorial.
Sgt J Hatch	+	P/O Samuel had previously flown Hampdens with
WO2 W Tait RCAF	+	49 Squadron and details of his award had been
F/S F G Fry	+	Gazetted on 23 December 1941.
Sgt D J White	+	

18 OTU   **Wellington IC**   **T2612**   **-H**   **Op: Bremen**

P/O M Niemczyk PAF	+	T/o 2250 Bramcote. Last heard, en route, on
F/O Z Wieczorek PAF	+	wireless advising they were under attack from
Sgt S Wolski PAF	+	a night-fighter. Subsequently, crashed near
Sgt A Rozdzynski PAF	+	Andijk (Noord Holland), 15 km NE of Hoorn. It
Sgt W J Mikos PAF	+	is believed they had fallen victim to Hptm
		Helmut Lent, II./NJG2. All are buried in
		Bergen General Cemetery.

| 25-26 Jun 1942 | 18 OTU | Wellington IC | T2717 | —C | Op: Bremen |

18 OTU   **Wellington IC**   **T2717**   **—C**   **Op: Bremen**

25-26 Jun 1942

P/O R Balicki PAF   +   T/o 2254 Bramcote. Lost without trace. All
F/O F Kusek PAF   +   are commemorated on the Northolt Memorial.
Sgt J B H Lech-
   Pierozynski PAF   +
Sgt K Cacko PAF   +
Sgt J E F Jaskiewicz PAF   +

18 OTU   **Wellington IC**   **DV765**   **—N**   **Op: Bremen**

F/S J Laudan PAF   pow   T/o 2255 Bramcote. Sgt Rajpold PAF died in
F/L K Boratynski PAF   pow   captivity on 26 August 1943; he is buried in
W/O A Pozorski PAF   pow   the 1939-1945 Berlin War Cemetery. W/O Pozorski
Sgt C Rajpold PAF   pow   was an American citizen, who had volunteered
W/O W Kowalik PAF   pow   his service for the Polish Air Force. Their
                                         skipper had been involved in a serious crash
                                         earlier in the month (see page 124).

20 OTU   **Wellington IC**   **T2723 ZT-N**   **Op: Bremen**

WO2 N W Levasseur RCAF   pow   T/o 2241 Snaith. Hit by flak and crashed 0418
Sgt R G A Brathwaite RAAF   +   in the sea, W of Terschelling. The three who
Sgt W A Carruthers   +   died are buried in Westerschelling General
F/S R C Marchant RCAF   +   Cemetery. Sgt Brathwaite RAAF of Killara in
WO2 G C Thomson RCAF   pow   New South Wales was a qualified Barrister.
                                         Their aircraft had been on charge since 11
March 1941 and, when reported missing, it had logged 487.25 flying hours.

21 OTU   **Wellington IC**   **X3179 SJ-U**   **Op: Bremen**

F/S I F McManus RAAF   +   T/o 2229 Edgehill. Lost without trace. All
W/O J G Simpkin   +   are commemorated on the Runnymede Memorial.
F/S F Cross   +   Sgt O'Quinn was a Newfoundlander from Loudres,
Sgt A O'Quinn   +   serving with the Royal Air Force.
Sgt N F Poulton   +

22 OTU   **Wellington IC**   **X9701 LT-D**   **Op: Bremen**

Sgt R W Davison   T/o 2228 Wellesbourne Mountford. Ditched some
Sgt R Dempsay RCAF   sixty miles off Great Yarmouth, Norfolk, while
Sgt G D Murray RCAF   on the return flight. All were picked up by
Sgt G F J Phalempin RCAF   an Air-Sea Rescue launch, on 30 June. Their
Sgt J G Cameron RCAF   Wellington had been damaged over Essen on 1-2
                                         June, and had been returned to service just
hours before the Bremen operation got under way. It had been a reasonably well
used aircraft, having been allotted ex-12 MU Kirkbride on 29 June 1941. When
lost, it had recorded 329.45 flying hours. Soon after this incident, all were
posted to 214 Squadron and on 13-14 October 1942, they were reported missing
(see Bomber Command Losses, Volume 3, page 239). It was later signalled that
Sgt Cameron RCAF was a prisoner of war.

22 OTU   **Wellington IC**   **X9980**   **—K**   **Op: Bremen**

WO2 D R Torkelson RCAF   +   T/o 2229 Wellesbourne Mountford. Lost without
F/S W H Gardner RCAF   +   trace. All are commemorated on the Runnymede
F/S A Yankoski RCAF   +   Memorial.
F/S D A Millard RCAF   +
F/S J C Hadley RCAF   +

23 OTU   **Wellington IC**   **X9875**   **—D3**   **Op: Bremen**

F/S D F Lord RCAF   +   T/o 2245 Pershore. Presumed lost off the coast
Sgt T W Joy   +   of Holland. Two, Sgt Joy and Sgt Sudbury, are
Sgt R T Sudbury   +   buried in cemeteries at Harlingen and Amsterdam
Sgt C G Cockayne   +   respectively, while the others are commemorated
Sgt J Rooney   +   on the Runnymede Memorial.

23 OTU   **Wellington IC**   **DV475 BY-G**   **Op: Bremen**

F/S J K Crossing RCAF   +   T/o 2233 Pershore. Shot down by Oblt Werner
Sgt R A Chapman   +   Rowlin of III./NJG1 and crashed 0256 at Azelo
Sgt T H Inch   +   in the Province of Overijssel some 5 km N of
Sgt J R Jones   +   Delden, Holland. All are buried in Ambt-Delden
Sgt J Swales   +   General Cemetery. Sgt Chapman, who came from
                                         Croydon, was a Bachelor of Laws.

25-26 Jun	24 OTU	Whitley V	Z9441		Op: Bremen

1942
P/O J A Preston RCAF	+	T/o 2306 Honeybourne armed with 1 x 500lb HE GP,
P/O E L Bedford	+	24 x 30lb and 360 x 41b incendiaries and carrying
P/O W G W Lapham	+	705 gallons of petrol. Described as an all pupil
F/S C R Robinson RCAF	+	crew, they crashed at Geversdorf, 4 km NNE from
Sgt A E Owen	+	Cadenberge. All lie in Becklingen War Cemetery.

24 OTU	Whitley V	BD266		Op: Bremen

F/S F M Cole RCAF	+	T/o 2236 Honeybourne armed as above and carrying
P/O S A Cheeseman	+	a similar petrol load. Presumed down in the sea
P/O H W Blackford	+	off the coast of Holland. Sgt Rixon's body was
F/S P C Omilianouski RCAF	+	recovered from the sea and buried in Huisduinen
Sgt W P Rixon	+	Military Cemetery on 23 July 1942, since when
		his remains have been exhumed and reinterred

in Bergen op Zoom War Cemetery. His four companions are perpetuated by the
Runnymede Memorial. They are described as a pupil crew.

24 OTU	Whitley V	BD379		Op: Bremen

F/O J B Monro RNZAF	+	T/O 2220 Honeybourne armed with 2 x 500lb HE GP,
F/O G R Lind RAAF	+	24 x 30lb and 360 x 41b incendiaries and carrying
F/S J Storey	+	705 gallons of petrol. The crew are described as
P/O I P Clark	+	"screened". At 0411, the direction finding
Sgt H H Hudson	+	station at Sealand intercepted an SOS signal,
		originating from this Whitley, and responded,

"MBAN 4942 2nd cl - 0411". Nothing further was heard and it is presumed the
bomber came down in the sea off the Frisian Islands. In view of the distance
and the proximity to the enemy coast, it was decided not to mount an Air-Sea
Rescue operation. Four now rest in Westerschelling General Cemetery on the
Island of Terschelling, while F/O Lind RAAF has no known grave.

26 OTU	Wellington IC	DV721	-N		Op: Bremen

W/O C J Stirling DFM RNZAF	+	T/o 2240 Wing armed with 1 x 500lb GP and 6 SBC
F/S H H Jordan	+	each containing 90 x 41b incendiaries. All lie
F/S A R Watkins	+	in Kiel War Cemetery. Details of the DFM held
F/O A Sharples	+	by W/O Stirling RNZAF, who had served previously
F/S D H Baddeley	+	with 150 Squadron, were published in the London
		Gazette on the day he died, 26 June. His tail

gunner, F/S D H Baddeley had participated in the Battle of Britain, having been
a member of 25 Squadron, equipped with Blenheim IFs.

27 OTU	Wellington IC	R1162	-R		Op: Bremen

P/O T F Lamb RCAF	+	T/o 2247 Lichfield. Lost without trace. All
Sgt J B Mathers RAAF	+	are commemorated on the Runnymede Memorial.
Sgt N H Cox RAAF	+	
Sgt K H Poynting RAAF	+	
Sgt J M Synnott RAAF	+	

28 Jun	11 OTU	Wellington IC	R1445 KJ-Y		Air Test

1942
P/O J E Casey DFC RNZAF	+	T/o 1730 Steeple Morden for a night flying test
LAC R L Wilson	+	but lost power on one engine. Attempting to go
		round the circuit, the bomber stalled off a

tight turn and crashed into a house at Ashwell in Hertfordshire, a mere 2 miles
SW of the airfield. F/O Casey RNZAF, an experienced pilot with around 450 hours
on Wellingtons, was laid to rest in Bassingbourn cum Kneesworth Cemetery. His
ground staff companion, LAC Wilson, was taken home to Northern Ireland and
buried in Bangor Cemetery.

29 Jun	11 OTU	Wellington IC	X3173		Training

1942
Sgt J Elliott	+	T/o Steeple Morden to practice night circuits
Sgt S Armory RNZAF	+	and landings. In the half-light of dawn, the
Sgt K A Hendry RNZAF	+	port propeller and reduction sheared away.
P/O D P Wadey RNZAF	inj	Eyewitnesses say that the crew flew at least
Sgt Cole RNZAF	inj	two circuits, desperately trying to pump the
		undercarriage down, but at 0410 the Wellington

stalled and crashed near the village of Ashwell, scene of the previous day's
accident. P/O Wadey RNZAF was taken to RAF Hospital Ely with serious chest
injuries; Sgt Cole RNZAF was treated in SSQ Steeple Morden for abrasions and
shock. Of those who died, two rest locally and Sgt Elliott lies in Edmonton
Cemetery.

29 Jun **1942**	**13 OTU**	**Blenheim IV**	**R3848**	**Training**

P/O R D Robinson — inj — T/o 1050 Bicester for a cross-country exercise. Lost engine power and crashed 1430 at Brook Farm near Moorhouse, 9 miles SSE of Retford, Nottinghamshire. P/O Robinson was taken to SSQ Ossington.

14 OTU	**Hampden I**	**AD848 GL-G**	**Training**

Sgt T A Krome RAAF + T/o Cottesmore for a night cross-country. Dived
P/O F F A Wood RCAF + almost vertically and crashed 2343 between
Sgt R O'Keefe + Moorends and Thorne, 11 miles or so NE from
Sgt W A Robson RAAF + Doncaster, Yorkshire. All are buried in Hatfield
(Woodhouse) Cemetery. Sgt O'Keefe came from
Stephenville in Newfoundland, while nineteen year old Sgt Robson RAAF had
recently married Frances Marion Robson of Winnipeg, Manitoba.

20 OTU	**Wellington IC**	**Z8978**	**Training**

Sgt P S Hammond — T/o 1420 Lossiemouth tasked for a dual exercise
Sgt W R Caldwell — but as their aircraft gathered speed, the port
tyre burst, leading to an immediate collapse of
the undercarriage. As the bomber skidded to a halt, a fire broke out. Neither
pilot was hurt though, sadly, they would not survive the war. Selected for
Pathfinder duties with 156 Squadron, Sgt Hammond failed to return from Bremen,
while flying as a second pilot, on 13-14 September 1942 (see Bomber Command
Losses, Volume 3, page 215), while on 12-13 July 1943, while raiding Torino
with 100 Squadron, Sgt Caldwell's Lancaster crashed in France (see Volume 4
of the same series, page 228).

22 OTU	**Wellington IC**	**R1036**	**Training**

Sgt H Jones + T/o Stratford-upon-Avon for a night exercise.
Sgt M W Fedirchyk RCAF + Overshot 0300 from a fast approach and crashed
F/S J G J Fedigan RCAF + amongst trees, less than a mile from the air-
P/O C D H Archer RCAF + field. Of the four who perished, Sgt Jones was
Sgt Blott — inj — taken to Bebington (St. Andrew) Churchyard,
while the others rest in Stratford-upon-Avon
Cemetery. It is noted that F/S Fedirchyk RCAF was an American from Chicago,
Illinois. He was the second airman from this city to die in less than a month
while flying at a bomber OTU (see page 125).

30 Jun **1942**	**14 OTU**	**Hampden I**	**AD802 GL-V1**	**Training**

Sgt R T Pierson + T/o Saltby for a night navigation exercise.
Sgt J L Allison RAAF + Spun and crashed 0230 near Shelford, 6 miles
Sgt E F Hunt RAAF + ENE from the centre of Nottingham. The three
Sgt A H Stephens RAAF + Australians are buried in the extension to
Shelford (SS Peter and Paul) Churchyard, while
Sgt Pierson lies in Carlton (St. Mary) Roman Catholic Churchyard. Sgt Stephens
of Mosman in New South Wales held a Diploma in Agriculture (Hawkesbury).

22 OTU	**Wellington IC**	**R1782**	**Training**

P/O B Dallenger RNZAF — T/o 1610 Stratford-upon-Avon airfield but sank
back to the ground and was destroyed in the
ensuing fire. P/O Dallenger RNZAF progressed to Stirlings and was posted
missing from Pathfinder duties with 7 Squadron on 16-17 September 1942 (see
Bomber Command Losses, Volume 3, page 217). Buried in Holland, he had flown
at least ten operational sorties.

1 Jul **1942**	**21 OTU D Flt**	**Wellington IC**	**X9637 SJ-V**	**Training**

P/O R E C Elsworth + T/o Moreton-in-Marsh for a navigation sortie.
Sgt F D Schmeltz RCAF + Crashed 1630 in the sea off Fowey on the S
Sgt J F Clark + coast of Cornwall. Two bodies were recovered
Sgt R E Thompson + and taken for burial; Sgt Schmeltz RCAF, an
Sgt G R Waters + American from Reading, Pennsylvania, rests
Sgt R Cunningham + in Illogan (St. Illogan) Churchyard, Camborne-
Sgt G B Amery + Redruth, while Sgt Clark is interred at Plymouth
(Efford) Cemetery. The others are commemorated
on the Runnymede Memorial. It is noted that Sgt Waters hailed from Portreath
and perhaps caught a brief glimpse of his home on Cornwall's north coast, away
to the WSW from where his aircraft went into the water.

1 Jul   **22 OTU**   **Wellington IC** **P9279**   **Unknown**
1942   Reported as missing on this date, but no
evidence as to what happened has, as yet, been unearthed. Taken on unit
charge in early May 1941, AM Form 78 has been annotated with 573.55 flying
hours. Prior to its arrival on 22 OTU, the Wellington had seen operational
service with 99 Squadron.

1– 2 Jul **23 OTU**   **Wellington IC** **R1284**   **Training**
1942   Sgt K H Cartland   inj T/o 2335 Pershore for night circuit training.
        Sgt R McH Hall RCAF   inj At 0110, took off for yet another circuit, the
        Sgt R C Webb RCAF   inj flap setting reported as between fifteen and
                                  twenty degrees. Eased off with the air speed
indicator registering 85 miles per hour and the undercarriage was retracted.
With both hands on the controls, the pilot noticed the speed building up to
one-hundred and ten miles per hour and with the engines running normally, the
Wellington hit the ground and caught fire. It was assumed that, inadvertently,
backward pressure on the control column was relaxed before sufficient height
had been attained.

3 Jul   **10 OTU**   **Whitley V** **N1360**   **Ground**
1942   Destroyed by fire at 1320, at Abingdon, while
                           undergoing maintenance and cleaning.

        19 OTU   **Whitley V** **BD255**   **Training**
        W/O W E Wilson   inj T/o 1545 Kinloss for an air firing exercise.
        P/O R E Williams   Roughly forty-five minutes later, white smoke
                           was seen issuing from the starboard engine and
with the same, the oil temperature rose to 105 degrees while the pressure fell
to around 30lb per square inch. W/O Wilson, later to serve with distinction
as a Mosquito pilot, ditched twixt 4 and 5 miles off Portknockie from where
all were picked up forty-five minutes later by a fishing boat and transferred
to an Air-Sea Rescue launch. P/O Williams went to 102 Squadron and was lost
over Belgium on 5 October 1942 (see Bomber Command Losses, Volume 3, page 234).

5 Jul   **13 OTU**   **Blenheim IV** **R3912**   **Training**
1942   Sgt J F Anderson   + T/o 0950 Bicester for a cross-country. Shortly
        Sgt A Hogg   + before 1220, eyewitnesses saw the Blenheim in a
        Sgt G I McBoyle   + near vertical dive, entering a large area of
                           whitish cloud which was estimated to have its
base at 3,000 to 5,000 feet. On emerging from the cloud, the bomber appeared
to straighten out but then dived again and crashed at Pawlett Hams on the E bank
of the River Parrett, 4 miles N of Bridgwater, Somerset. Sgt McBoyle of Fratton
in Portsmouth was laid to rest in Bridgwater (Quantock Road) Cemetery, his two
companions were taken back to Scotland.

        14 OTU   **Hampden I** **AD766**   **Training**
        Sgt C M Ross RAAF   T/o 1712 Saltby and climbed normally to 600
                           feet. However, as the engines were throttled
back, so the Hampden yawed to port. Sgt Ross RAAF tried to take corrective
action but was unable to prevent his aircraft from coming down, at 1715, some
two miles W of Skillington, 6 miles SSW of Grantham, Lincolnshire.

        29 OTU   **Tiger Moth** **T6307**   **Air Test**
        P/O A C Shilleto   inj T/o North Luffenham. While flying inverted,
        P/O W A W Strachan   inj the nose dropped and the trainer crashed at
                           around 1520. This was the first accident
reported from the unit since its formation on 21 April 1942. P/O Shilleto
made a good recovery from his injuries but was killed in similar circumstances
when air testing a 14 OTU Wellington X on 13 July 1944.

6 Jul   **22 OTU**   **Wellington IC** **R1465 LT-Y**   **Training**
1942   F/S J B Kemp RCAF   + T/o Wellesbourne Mountford for a night cross-
        F/S E E Mittell RCAF   + country. Crashed 0030 on Waen Rhydd in the
        Sgt K F Yuill RCAF   + Brecon Beacons, 4 miles S of Talybont. All
        F/S H C Beatty RCAF   + are buried in Hereford Cemetery. A plaque and
        Sgt J P Hayes RCAF   + cairn now mark the crash site. On 17 August
                           1944, F/L Kenneth Donovan Kemp RCAF, brother
to F/S Kemp RCAF, was killed in action while flying with 405 Squadron (see
Bomber Command Losses, Volume 5, page 386).

7 Jul **15 OTU**　　　　**Wellington IC R1141**　　　　　　　**Training**
1942　W/O W H Kellaway　　　　　　　　　T/o 1150 Harwell for a dual exercise in circuits
　　　　　　　　　　　　　　　　　　　and landings. Ten minutes later, while coming
into land without the aid of flaps, the Wellington began to sink and when the
throttles were advanced, the starboard engine failed to respond thus resulting
in the bomber hitting the ground close to the airfield boundary.

　　　　20 OTU　　　　**Wellington IC R1467**　　　　　　　　**Ground**
　　　　　　　　　　　　　　　　　　　Destroyed 1645 by fire while starting engines
　　　　　　　　　　　　　　　　　　　on Elgin airfield, Moray.

　　　　21 OTU　　　　**Wellington IC T2962**　　　　　　　**Training**
　　　　Sgt F H S Bush　　　　　　　　+　T/o Moreton-in-Marsh for a cross-country flight.
　　　　Sgt T G Baycroft RCAF　　　inj　Crashed 1700 and caught fire while making an
　　　　Sgt R J McKean　　　　　　　+　emergency landing near Llangrove, 4 miles NNW of
　　　　Sgt L C Baker　　　　　　　inj　Monmouth. Of those who died, Sgt Bush was taken
　　　　Sgt A Hill　　　　　　　　inj　for cremation at the South London Crematorium,
　　　　Sgt H A Hill　　　　　　　inj　while Sgt McKean rests in Cathcart Cemetery.

7- 8 Jul **19 OTU**　　　　**Whitley V AD707 UO-M**　　　　**Training**
1942　W/O E O Johnson RNZAF　　　+　T/o 2315 Kinloss for a night navigation sortie
　　　　P/O J Lorkin　　　　　　　+　to Port Douglas on the Isle of Man and return.
　　　　Sgt J J S Corderoy　　　　+　At circa 0340, the crew of another aircraft saw
　　　　Sgt J S Wardle　　　　　　+　what is firmly believed to be this Whitley going
　　　　　　　　　　　　　　　　　+　down in flames to crash in the Sound of Jura. It
　　　　　　　　　　　　　　　　　　　is reported that at least one body was recovered
(this being as late as 4 December 1942), but the majority are commemorated on
the Runnymede Memorial. For the recent raid on Bremen, this Whitley had been
captained by Sgt F McL Macdonald RCAF, who was killed a few months later while
serving with 161 Squadron (see Bomber Command Losses, Volume 3, page 224).

8 Jul **17 OTU**　　　　**Blenheim I L1197**　　　　　　　**Training**
1942　Sgt R M Overns RCAF　　　　　　T/o Upwood. Landed here at 1050 and while doing
　　　　　　　　　　　　　　　　　　　so collided with Blenheim IV L9328, captained by
Sgt L J Hopkins. The latter, which was seen too late approaching from the port
side, was repaired, only to be written off at Upwood on 1 October 1942.

　　　　17 OTU　　　　**Blenheim IV R3669**　　　　　　　**Training**
　　　　F/S D I Grant RNZAF　　　　　　T/o Upwood but lost engine power and crashed
　　　　　　　　　　　　　　　　　　　at 1740 near Wellingore airfield, Lincolnshire.
Subsequently, F/S Grant RNZAF re-mustered to air bomber and by the summer of
1944, he was flying with 619 Squadron. He failed to return from Revigny-sur-
Ornain (see Bomber Command Losses, Volume 5, page 338) and is buried in France.

9 Jul **15 OTU B Flt**　　**Wellington IC DV932**　　　　　　**Training**
1942　P/O H E J Giles　　　　　　+　T/o Harwell. Landed at around 1630, touching
　　　　Sgt J S D S Haley　　　　　+　down about two thirds of the way along the
　　　　Sgt D Bradshaw　　　　　　+　runway. Those watching on the ground heard
　　　　Sgt N Wade　　　　　　　　inj　the engine note increase but soon after lift
　　　　Cpl D Vail RCAF　　　　　　+　off they saw the Wellington bank steeply, to
　　　　LAC G S Miller RCAF　　　　+　avoid some trees, and while doing so it went
　　　　　　　　　　　　　　　　　　　out of control and crashed into a field adjacent
to the WSW side of the airfield. The two RCAF groundcrew and Sgt Bradshaw were
taken to Brookwood Military Cemetery, while P/O Giles and Sgt Haley were claimed
by their next of kin. It is suspected that Sgt Haley's third and fourth Christian
names, Da Silva, perpetuated a family name on his mother's side.

11 Jul **18 OTU**　　　　**Wellington IC Z1072**　　　　　　**Training**
1942　Sgt A Kosturkiewicz PAF　　+　T/o Bramcote and crashed almost immediately.
　　　　P/O H Franczak PAF　　　　inj　The two airmen who died rest in the Polish Plot
　　　　F/S K Ziolkowski PAF　　　inj　at Newark-upon-Trent Cemetery.
　　　　F/O W Peski PAF　　　　　　inj
　　　　P/O M Wodzinski PAF　　　　inj
　　　　F/S J Adamczyk PAF　　　　inj
　　　　P/O M Mazurkiewicz PAF　　+
　　　　Cpl F Jaruszewski PAF　　　inj
　　　　Cpl J Szpek PAF　　　　　　inj

11–12 Jul   **10 OTU**   **Whitley V**   **P4956**   **Training**
1942   Sgt S H J White   T/o 2000 Abingdon for a night cross-country.
Towards the end of the sortie, the starboard
engine failed and, as the bomber began to lose height, the port engine seized.
With commendable skill, Sgt White put the Whitley down at 0230 on Kidlington
airfield, Oxfordshire, but was unable to prevent the bomber from finishing up,
wrecked, in the overshoot area. Towards the end of the month, he and his crew
would be involved in another close shave, this time while on operations.

22 OTU E Flt   **Wellington IC**   **AD631 LT–V**   **Training**
Sgt H J Murray RCAF   inj   T/o 2300 Wellesbourne Mountford for a night
navigation exercise, which terminated, by
mistake, at 0210 on Long Marston airfield, Gloucestershire. Fatigue and an
unserviceable flap indicator led to the Wellington over-running the landing
area and smashing through some perimeter fencing.

12 Jul   **13 OTU**   **Blenheim IV**   **N3625**   **Training**
1942   F/O J W Welford   T/o Bicester. Forced-landed 1245, due to
Sgt Hanrahan   inj   failure of the port engine, near the hamlet
of Lenborough, just over a mile SSE from the
centre of Buckingham. A fire broke out and the bomber was destroyed.

14 OTU   **Hampden I**   **X2974**   **Training**
P/O L G Lyons RAAF   T/o Saltby for a night exercise, during which
P/O M G Lees   +   a midair collision occurred at 2337 with a 25
F/S G E Pickel RCAF   +   OTU Wellington IC Z8837 (F/L E I J Bell).
Partially abandoned, the Hampden crashed some
four miles SW of Newark, Nottinghamshire. P/O Lees is buried in Bracebridge
(All Saints) Churchyard, while F/S Pickel RCAF rests in Newark-upon-Trent
Cemetery. F/L Bell, meanwhile, landed his aircraft and following repairs
the Wellington continued in service. By coincidence, it was issued to 14 OTU
on 7 September 1942, remaining on charge until written off on 19 May 1943.

15 OTU A Flt   **Wellington IC**   **DV739**   **Training**
F/O A J Leslie RAAF   +   T/o 1825 Harwell and crashed almost immediately
F/S E Hannath   +   when the port engine cut. F/O Leslie RAAF was
AC1 W Morgan   inj   buried in Harwell Cemetery, while F/S Hannath,
a pre-war regular airman, was taken home and
interred in Cleethorpes Cemetery.

23 OTU   **Wellington IC**   **R1414**   **Training**
Sgt R R Foltz RCAF   T/o 1605 Pershore for local flying. Wrecked
Sgt J L Lymburner RCAF   at 1745 when Sgt Foltz RCAF inadvertently
Sgt R N V Burke RCAF   landed with the wheels still retracted. Sgt
Sgt J P Duval RCAF   inj   Duval RCAF sustained mine burns to his hands
and face and was admitted to Evesham Hospital.
Along with his skipper, who hailed from Mansfield, Ohio, he was posted to
425 Squadron and both became casualties during operations to Hamburg on
9 November 1942 (see Bomber Command Losses, Volume 3, page 259).

12–13 Jul   **10 OTU**   **Whitley V**   **BD194**   **Training**
1942   P/O A S Pearson   inj   T/o 2227 Stanton Harcourt for night dual.
Sgt W G Snelling   inj   Initially, all went well but while flying
P/O G R Guest   inj   at 6,000 feet the engines lost power and the
P/O Robinson   Whitley was wrecked 0032, at base, in the
Sgt Thompson   ensuing forced-landing and fire that followed.
Lt H R F Tyrer   inj   No one was badly hurt, Lt Tyrer of 82 Search-
light Regiment sustaining a badly sprained
ankle. He had accompanied the crew in order to gain air experience.

13 Jul   **20 OTU**   **Wellington IC**   **N2821 ZT–M**   **Training**
1942   Sgt H R W Whittle   inj   T/o Lossiemouth for a night navigation sortie.
Crashed at approximately 0400, following loss
of power, at Maggieknockater some 8 miles WSW of Keith, Banff. By the early
winter of 1943, Sgt Whittle (now commissioned and converted to Halifaxes) was
serving with 76 Squadron. On 26 November he failed to return from operations
to Stuttgart (see Bomber Command Losses, Volume 4, page 402). It is believed
he was engaged on his twenty-second sortie as captain.

13 Jul	23 OTU	Wellington IC	R1062		Training

13 Jul 1942 — **23 OTU** — **Wellington IC R1062** — **Training**

Sgt J Law
Sgt G Moorhouse
Sgt R R Stover RCAF
Sgt G W Miller RCAF — inj
Sgt G J Folks RCAF
Sgt R E Hawken RCAF — inj

T/o 0005 Pershore for night flying. At around 0150, the Wellington landed but bounced rather alarmingly and the throttles were opened in order to go round again. Unfortunately, this circuit was never completed as the bomber came down in a field and was totally wrecked (the accident investigation report speaks of the fuselage being broken, both mainplanes fractured and the port engine torn from its mountings). The two injured airmen were admitted to SSQ Pershore, though neither were too seriously hurt. Sgt Moorhouse, it is noted, had been involved in a minor accident three days previous when Wellington IC R1446 crash-landed on the airfield. He, along with Sgt Folks RCAF, is thought to have survived the war, but Sgt Law was killed on 4 September 1942, while serving with 75 Squadron (see Bomber Command Losses, Volume 3, page 203), Sgt Miller RCAF and Sgt Stover RCAF both died in separate incidents while flying with 149 Squadron (see Volume 4 of the same series, pages 76 and 107 respectively), while Sgt Hawken went to the Middle East and lost his life when his 148 Squadron special duties Liberator crashed into a hillside in Yugoslavia on 3 November 1943. He is buried in Belgrade.

14 Jul 1942 — **21 OTU** — **Wellington IC X9617 SJ-E** — **Training**

F/O D C Dunn
Sgt A N Lancaster
Sgt C M Leach

T/o 1512 Edgehill but the port engine failed and two minutes later, while trying to regain the airfield, the Wellington crash-landed. An investigation revealed that, following recent maintenance, the securing nuts on No. 2 cylinder not been sufficiently tightened. It will be recalled that F/O Dunn, a screened pilot, had crashed earlier in the year (see page 94). Sgt Lancaster went to the Far East and by the spring of 1943, he was flying Blenheims with 113 Squadron. On 25 May 1943, he was posted missing and his name is perpetuated by the Singapore Memorial.

14-15 Jul 1942 — **23 OTU** — **Wellington IC DV700** — **Training**

Sgt R F Shirley — +
Sgt C L Morton RCAF — inj
Sgt J R Martin RCAF — inj
Sgt C S Coburn RCAF — inj
F/S C W Auld RCAF — +

T/o 2305 Pershore for night flying practice. Obliged to forced-land 0145, after the starboard engine lost power, a mile N of Old, 8 miles NNE from Northampton. The two deceased were taken, initially, to the Royal Oak Inn at Walgrave, while the injured were treated at RAF Chelveston. Sgt Shirley now lies in Eastbrookend (Dagenham) Cemetery, while F/S Auld RCAF is buried at Chelveston (St. John The Baptist) Churchyard, Chelveston-cum-Caldecott. He was an American from Chicago, Illinois.

16 Jul 1942 — **27 OTU** — **Wellington IC P9285** — **Enemy Action**

Sgt B W Richards RAAF — +
Sgt W B Barr — +
Sgt D S Large — +
Sgt R Brooke — +
Sgt J A Alcorn RAAF — +

T/o 1043 Lichfield with 15 eleven-and-a-half pound practice bombs, setting course for the North Sea. At about 1230, while signalling, the radio direction finding plot failed and nothing further was heard. Overdue action was taken when the crew failed to return by their estimated arrival time of 1600. All are commemorated on the Runnymede Memorial, enemy action being suggested as the most likely cause of their demise.

17 Jul 1942 — **10 OTU** — **Whitley V BD223** — **Training**

WO2 D H Thompson RCAF

T/o 0115 Stanton Harcourt for general night flying. Wrecked 0245 in a landing accident. WO2 Thompson RCAF went to 428 Squadron and was posted missing following the 27-28 May 1943 raid on Essen (see Bomber Command Losses, Volume 4, page 167).

27 OTU — **Wellington IC Z8980** — **Training**

Sgt T F Thompson — inj
P/O J W Moore — inj
Sgt J H Levett — inj
Sgt K J H Harris RAAF — inj
Sgt J H Roden RAAF — inj

T/o Lichfield for a night cross-country. Came down at 0050 on Burbage Moor, 8 miles SW of Sheffield, Yorkshire and caught fire. All sustained quite serious injuries and Sgt Levett was admitted to the Royal Hospital at Sheffield suffering from burns and a compound fracture to one of his legs. Both Sgt Roden RAAF and Sgt Harris RAAF were destined to lose their lives; the former with 150 Squadron and the latter with 460 Squadron (see Bomber Command Losses, Volumes 3 and 4, pages 224 and 15 respectively).

17-18 Jul   **10 OTU**   **Whitley V**   **BD395**   **Training**
1942   Sgt L H Matthews   +   T/o 2305 Stanton Harcourt for local night
     Sgt H A Baxter   +   flying. At approximately 0025, the Whitley
     Sgt W Stephen   +   was heard, flying extremely low, and was thought
     Sgt R W W Basham   +   to be in difficulties. To assist the crew, the
     Sgt K A R Evans   +   airfield lights were switched on but it was to
                                no avail and in poor visibility the bomber flew
into the ground, less than a mile from the runway. All lie in various cemeteries.
F/S Andrew Stephen, brother to Sgt Stephen, was killed while serving in the Far
East with 215 Squadron. He is buried in Maynamati War Cemetery, Bangladesh.
Sgt Evans came from Salisbury in Southern Rhodesia.

19 Jul   **22 OTU B Flt**   **Wellington IC**   **DV934 LT-C**   **Training**
1942   P/O J W M Harley RCAF   +   T/o Wellesbourne Mountford for night flying.
     Sgt C P Ralph RCAF   +   At around 0210, the Wellington, flying at 400
     Sgt Caddell   inj   feet, was observed to head down the flare path
                                when, without warning, it dived to the ground
and finished up, on fire, in the nearby River Dene. Crash and Rescue:

S/L F G Mogg GM   The Senior Medical Officer was one of the
                                first to arrive at the scene and he recovered
the body of the pilot, P/O Harley RCAF. Along with Sgt Ralph RCAF, he was
buried in Stratford-upon-Avon Cemetery. Sgt Caddell, meanwhile, was admitted
to the local EMS Hospital with multiple leg injuries and burns to his face and
scalp.

27 OTU   **Wellington IC**   **N2749**   **Training**
     Sgt K H C Steinbach RAAF   +   T/o Lichfield for a night navigation sortie.
     Sgt E D R Jennings RAAF   +   Crashed 0308 into houses near the fish dock at
     Sgt W H Condon RAAF   +   Milford Haven, Pembrokeshire. Five were laid
     Sgt K J Bradley RAAF   +   to rest locally in Pembroke Dock Military
     Sgt G E Warburton RAAF   +   Cemetery, while Sgt Cooke was taken back to
     Sgt M Cooke   +   Buckinghamshire and buried in Wolverton (New
                                Bradwell) Cemetery. Police eyewitnesses say
the Wellington was firing off red Verey cartridges and appeared to be flying
on one engine.

27 OTU   **Wellington IC**   **DV800**   **Training**
     Sgt E H Longbottom RAAF   +   T/o Lichfield for a day cross-country. While
     Sgt L D Traylen   +   over North Wales, the crew strayed 10 miles N
     Sgt R I Bowen   +   of their intended track. At around 1230, now
     Sgt S J Wilson   +   flying above cloud (base 2,000 feet), it is
     Sgt R T Bannister RAAF   +   assumed the pilot decided to let down through
                                the overcast in order to establish their position
and while doing so had the terrible misfortune to smash into the Black Ladder
mountains near Carnedd Dafydd in Snowdonia. The two Australians were taken to
Caernarvon Cemetery, the others were claimed by their next of kin.

20 Jul   **20 OTU**   **Wellington IC**   **HF867 JM-X**   **Training**
1942   Sgt J L Powell   inj   T/o Elgin for local night flying. At 0404,
     Sgt Harrington   inj   having returned to base with engine trouble,
                     inj   Sgt Powell came in without the aid of flaps
                     inj   and touched down two thirds of the way across
                     inj   the airfield and at least 200 feet left of the
                                flare path. Moments later, the Wellington ran
into an office building and caught fire. Crash and rescue:

F/L E B R Lockwood   This officer braved the intense heat from the
                                burning bomber and dragged Sgt Harrington clear
of the flames, undoubtedly saving his life. Sgt Powell sustained massive head
injuries and died later in the day. He is buried in Southgate Cemetery.

24 Jul   **13 OTU**   **Blenheim I**   **L6646**   **Training**
1942   Sgt M E Tuttle   +   T/o Bicester for a solo exercise in single-
                                engined flying, approaches without the aid of
flaps and glide approaches. At 1505, spun and crashed, bursting into flames,
a mile NW of Brackley airfield, Northamptonshire. Sgt Tuttle is buried in
Hethe (Holy Trinity) Roman Catholic Cemetery; he came from Birr, Co. Offaly
in the Irish Republic.

24 Jul
1942

25 OTU		**Wellington IC**	**T2707**	**-L**	**Training**

W/O J L Smith   +   T/o 0330 Finningley for night circuits and
W/O C E Lutwyche   +   landings. Twenty minutes into the detail, and
Sgt A E Barrows   +   under local ground control, overshot the runway
Sgt W McDonald   +   and climbed to between 800 and 1,000 feet. Then,
                                           having reached a position roughly a mile NW of
the airfield, collided with another of the unit's Wellingtons, both machines
bursting into flames. Three are buried in the extension to Finningley (St.
Oswald) Churchyard, while Sgt Barrows was taken to Kensington (Gunnersbury)
Cemetery, Brentford and Chiswick.

25 OTU		**Wellington IC**	**DV476**	**Training**

P/O R C S Beck DFM RNZAF +   T/o 0320 Finningley with the intention of
P/O J V Robinson   +   carrying out a night exercise. However, it is
Sgt H C Jellyman   +   thought a technical fault caused the crew to
P/O W C Waterson   +   make an early return and while doing so came
Sgt N B Hyde   +   into contact with the aircraft described above,
Sgt S J Plume   +   with disastrous consequences. P/O Beck RNZAF
F/S F C Ethell   +   had gained his DFM, Gazetted on 13 March 1942,
                                           while serving with 408 Squadron. He is buried
in the extension to Finningley (St. Oswald) Churchyard. The others were taken
to their home towns. F/S Ethell was the son of the Revd Thomas Frederick Ethell
and Bertha Annie Ethell of Whalley Range, Manchester.

26 Jul
1942

12 OTU		**Wellington III**	**Z1750**	**Training**

F/S T J Pugh   T/o 1105 Chipping Warden to practice feathering
W/O M P Murray   procedures. Soon after commencing the exercise
                                         the starboard engine was shut down but when it
came to re-starting the motor, no response was forthcoming. Losing height, the
bomber crash-landed 1120 at Charwelton, 14 miles WSW of Northampton. Neither
pilot was hurt but their Wellington was destroyed by fire. It was the first
of its Mark to be written off at a Bomber Command Operational Training Unit.

19 OTU		**Whitley V**	**BD349**	**Training**

P/O R T Meek   +   T/o Kinloss for an evening cross-country. At
Sgt C E Hayes   +   around 1900 a wireless signal was intercepted,
Sgt J E Millar   +   "Starboard engine unserviceable, height 11,300
Sgt G G Scott   +   feet". Then, at 1927, possibly while trying to
Sgt T B McGee RCAF   +   gain the airfield at Tain, the bomber plunged
                                         into the Dornach Firth. Eyewitnesses say the
Whitley's starboard wing was on fire. The body of Sgt McGee RCAF was recovered
and taken to Kinloss Abbey Burial Ground, but the others are commemorated on the
Runnymede Memorial. Sgt Scott came from Ocean Falls, British Columbia.

27 Jul
1942

11 OTU		**Wellington IC**	**DV813**	**Ground**

Sgt K H Doherty RNZAF   inj   Taxied into two of the unit's Wellingtons,
Sgt T J Sherborne RNZAF inj   parked on Bassingbourn airfield. The impact
Sgt F J Wade   inj   was sufficiently severe to render Sgt Doherty
                                         very seriously injured and he was taken to RAF
Hospital Ely with compound fractures to the left tibia and fibula. His two
companions were less seriously hurt and both soon returned to duty.

28 Jul
1942

21 OTU D Flt		**Anson I**	**N5022**	**Enemy Action**

                                         Destroyed at Moreton-in-Marsh during the course
of an enemy air attack. Less seriously damaged and, subsequently, returned to
service were: N4945, N5369, N9734, AX294 and AX295 UH-S.

28-29 Jul
1942

10 OTU		**Whitley V**	**BD353**	**-V**	**Op: Hamburg**

Sgt S H J White   T/o 2203 Abingdon. Ditched 0534 some 10 miles
P/O R G Woods   south-east of Tynemouth on the Northumberland
Sgt K C Hammond   coast. It will be recalled that earlier in the
Sgt A F Hawkins   month, Sgt White had put up an extremely good
Sgt R G Snook   show in force -landing his crippled Whitley
                                         at Kidlington (see page 135). By September,
the first three named had been posted to 158 Squadron (equipped with Halifaxes)
and were about midway through their first tour of operations when they were
posted missing from operations to Lorient at the end of January 1943 (see
Bomber Command Losses, Volume 4, page 29).

28-29 Jul   **16 OTU**   **Wellington IC**   **L7894**   **-U2**   **Op: Hamburg**
1942   F/S R E Stageman RCAF   +   T/o 2157 Upper Heyford. All were initially laid
      WO2 C C D Hinks RCAF   +   to rest in Hamburg Cemetery, Ohlsdorf, since
      Sgt J G Watson   +   when F/S Stageman RCAF has been exhumed and
      F/S P B Andrew RCAF   +   taken first to Neuville-en-Condroz US Military
      F/S R E Fahey RCAF   +   Cemetery in Belgium and thence to his home city
                                         of Chicago, Illinois.

      16 OTU   **Wellington IC**   **R1450**   **-Y1**   **Op: Hamburg**
      F/L F Lowe   pow   T/o2214 Upper Heyford. Passing over Schleswig
      F/L P W Langford MID RCAF   pow   at 11,500 feet, intercepted and shot down by a
      P/O A F Litzow   +   night-fighter. Those who died in the crash lie
      Sgt W J Atchison   +   in Kiel War Cemetery, while F/L Langford RCAF
      Sgt T H Cray RNZAF   +   rests in Poznan Old Garrison Cemetery, Poland,
      W/O W White   pow   having been shot by the Gestapo on, or around,
                                         31 March 1944. On 17 April 1944, during
operations over the South Pacific, P/O Geoffrey Haughton Cray MID RNZAF lost
his life while flying in SBD-5 Dauntless NZ5050 of 25 Squadron RNZAF (see
page 212 of For Your Tomorrow by Errol W Martyn).

      22 OTU   **Wellington IC**   **X3201**   **-O Bar**   **Op: Hamburg**
      F/S P C Noel RCAF   +   T/o 2200 Wellesbourne Mountford. Postwar, the
      F/L E W Bell RCAF   pow   two airmen who died were laid to rest in Hamburg
      WO2 W C Warren RCAF   pow   Cemetery, Ohlsdorf, since when the parents of
      F/S R T Gammon RCAF   +   F/S Noel RCAF requested his remains be exhumed
      WO2 J Pierce RCAF   pow   and returned to Memphis, Texas.

      22 OTU   **Wellington IC**   **X9696**   **-Z**   **Op: Hamburg**
      F/S R B Ayers RCAF   +   T/o 2204 Wellesbourne Mountford. All are buried
      F/S J E Evans RCAF   +   in Kiel War Cemetery. Immediately after this
      F/S F E Johnson RCAF   +   aircraft had departed, the Battle Order was
      F/S E G White RCAF   +   cancelled. Unfortunately, all attempts to
      F/S E L Wagner RCAF   +   recall the two Wellingtons failed.

29 Jul   **24 OTU**   **Whitley V**   **BD205**   **Transit**
1942   Sgt A C Combe   T/o 0905 Horsham St. Faith loaded with bombs
      Sgt Demone RCAF   inj   and a near maximum fuel load with the intention
      Sgt Williams   inj   of returning to base. Due to poor trim settings
                                         the Whitley failed to become airborne and having
crossed Fifers Lane and through the back garden of the Firs Public House, the
bomber finished up on, or near, a garage forecourt, demolishing three petrol
pumps. Amazingly, there was no fire and no one was too seriously hurt, though
Sgt Demone RCAF did require medical attention for a broken nose. Some twelve
hours previous, the crew had taken off from Horsham St. Faith with the intention
of bombing Hamburg but due to adverse weather, they had been recalled.

30 Jul   **14 OTU**   **Hampden I**   **P5397**   **Training**
1942   Sgt A R Gruber RCAF   T/o Cottesmore for a night flying exercise
                                         during which a midair collision occurred with
another of the unit's Hampdens, AE192 flown by P/O C E McIntosh RCAF. Some
reports suggest this collision took place over Windsor Castle park but after
being abandoned, Sgt Gruber's aircraft came down circa 0315 about a mile NW
of Market Deeping, 10 miles SSW of Spalding, Lincolnshire. P/O McIntosh RCAF,
meanwhile, landed safely and later he received a commendation for his handling
of a very difficult situation.

31 Jul-   **14 OTU**   **Hampden I**   **L4117 GL-N**   **Op: Düsseldorf**
1 Aug 1942 P/O D J Curtin   T/o 0008 Cottesmore. This turned out to be a
      P/O S J Walker   inj   very eventful sortie, during which the Hampden
      Sgt R Hawkes   inj   survived two attacks from fighters and was hit
      F/O H G Clarke RAAF   inj   by flak in the bargain. Somewhat disorientated
                                         by these events, the crew strayed from their
course and, subsequently, crash-landed in a field at Loddiswell, 16 miles SW
from Torquay, Devon. F/O Clarke RAAF died from his injuries and he is buried
in Exeter Higher Cemetery.

Note. It will be observed that the crew were flying a veteran Hampden which
had seen operational service with 61 Squadron. It had been on unit charge
since early July 1941.

31 Jul–	14 OTU	Hampden I	N9062 GL–W3	Op: Düsseldorf

```
31 Jul-    14 OTU              Hampden I  N9062 GL-W3              Op: Düsseldorf
1 Aug 1942 W/O E F Collins RAAF     pow  T/o 2353 Cottesmore.  Shot down by Oblt Heinrich
           Sgt L Lobb                +  Alexander Prinz zu Sayn-Wittgenstein-Sayn, of
           W/O G B Russell RNZAF    pow  I./NJG1, crashing 0330 between Oisterwijk and
           W/O M S Whiting RAAF     pow  Moergestel (Noord Brabant), two small towns
                                         some 6 km ENE and E respectively of Tilburg,
           Holland.  Sgt Lobb, a schoolmaster from St. Austell in Cornwall, is buried in
           Tilburg (Gilzerbaan) General Cemetery.  Their adversary was to become one of
           the Luftwaffe's outstanding fighter aces, eventually being killed in action
           during the night of 21 January 1944, by which time he had taken his tally of
           victories to eighty-four.

           14 OTU              Hampden I  P1185 GL-B2              Op: Düsseldorf
           WO2 N E McGowan RCAF     pow  T/o 0003 Cottesmore.  Believed to have fallen
           P/O D G McLean RCAF       +  victim to a night-fighter, crashing at Leffinge
           Sgt S A Shailer RAAF      +  (West Vlaanderen), a village on the S side of
           F/S G T Bloomer RCAF      +  Oostende Airport, Belgium.  Those who died now
                                         lie in Adegem Canadian War Cemetery.

           14 OTU              Hampden I  P5322 GL-U3              Op: Düsseldorf
           F/O R E Guthrie RAAF      +  T/o 0001 Cottesmore.  Two are buried in Rheinberg
           Sgt C A B McMullin        +  War Cemetery, while Sgt McMullin is commemorated
           F/S E T Hunking RCAF      +  on panel 89 of the Runnymede Memorial.  F/O
           WO2 J H Morrison RCAF    pow  Guthrie RAAF held a Bachelor of Arts degree.

           16 OTU          Wellington IC  DV736  -F2               Op: Düsseldorf
           F/S E H Vickers RAAF      +  T/o 2339 Upper Heyford.  Crashed 0215 at Dilsen
           F/S R D Gibson RCAF       +  (Limburg), 18 km NE of Genk, Belgium.  All are
           F/S T J Armstrong RCAF    +  buried in Heverlee War Cemetery.  F/S Vickers
           Sgt N A Long              +  was a screened pilot whose initial OTU training
           Sgt F P G Moore RNZAF     +  had been conducted at Lichfield with 27 OTU.
           Sgt G Redhead             +

           16 OTU          Wellington IC  HF852  -C2               Op: Düsseldorf
           F/S E G Robertson RCAF    +  T/o 2355 Upper Heyford.  Crashed 0225 near
           F/S L G Harvie RCAF       +  Elsendorp (Noord Brabant), 20 km NNE of Helmond
           Sgt D H Kurtz RCAF        +  in Holland.  Four rest in Eindhoven (Woensel)
           Sgt H L Cox               +  General Cemetery, while F/S Hueston RCAF has
           F/S E F Hueston RCAF      +  been taken to Groesbeek Canadian War Cemetery.
                                         F/S Robertson RCAF, an American, came from
                                         Richmond, California.

           21 OTU          Wellington IC  X9983 SJ-D               Op: Düsseldorf
           Sgt B R Anstee            +  T/o 2348 Edgehill.  Believed shot down by flak
           Sgt I D Singer            +  (though Air Ministry records suggest a night-
           Sgt D G Brimfield         +  fighter), falling 0220 twixt Bemelen and Berg
           W/O D Riley              pow  Terblijt (Limburg), 5 km ENE from the centre of
           Sgt R Howells             +  Maastricht, Holland.  Those who perished now lie
           Sgt R H Callaghan         +  in Jonkerbos War Cemetery, having been brought
                                         here from a cemetery at Venlo (this amends some
           of the data published in Bomber Command Losses, Volume 3, page 170).

           23 OTU          Wellington IC  X9917  -N                Op: Düsseldorf
           F/O J L Dowdeswell       pow  T/o 2322 Pershore, the crew comprising entirely
           F/L A G Allen            pow  of screened personnel.
           W/O G C Maddams          pow
           W/O E E Brocklehurst     pow
           F/L M T C Shields        pow

           24 OTU              Whitley V  Z9512                    Op: Düsseldorf
           F/L A W Thompson        pow  T/o 2320 Honeybourne armed with 1 x 500lb HE GP,
           P/O C L Szumlinski RCAF   +  64 x 30lb incendiaries and carrying 705 gallons
           F/S W V Donahue RCAF      +  of petrol.  Those who died in the crash rest in
           F/S E L Styles            +  the Reichswald Forest War Cemetery.  On 5 July
           Sgt E J Jones RCAF        +  1944, F/L Thompson was shot and killed; his
                                         grave is in Poland at Malbork Commonwealth War
           Cemetery.  At 42, F/S Styles was well above the average age of airmen employed
           on aircrew duties.  His service number identifies him as being a Civilian
           Wireless Reservist called up in August 1939.  All are described as unscreened.
```

31 Jul–   **24 OTU**   **Whitley V**   **BD347**   **Op: Düsseldorf**
1 Aug 1942 P/O G Silva RAAF   evd   T/o 2340 Honeybourne armed with 1 x 500lb HE GP,
         Sgt J B R Black   evd   540 x 4lb incendiaries and carrying 705 gallons
         Sgt A J Whicher   evd   of petrol. Set on fire as a result of at least
         Sgt W T Whiting   +   two night-fighter attacks and crashed circa 0400
                                                near Fleurus (Hainaut), 12 km NE of Charleroi,
Belgium. Sgt Whiting is buried in Gosselies Communal Cemetery. Apart from Sgt
Black, they are described as screened. P/O Silva RAAF had previously served
with 77 Squadron and following his successful evasion he transferred to Coastal
Command. Tragically, he was posted missing on 13 June 1943, while flying
Catalina flying boats with 210 Squadron. He is commemorated on panel 189
of the Runnymede Memorial.

25 OTU   **Wellington IC**   **T2909**   **–E**   **Op: Düsseldorf**
F/S P Prime RCAF   +   T/o 2336 Finningley. Presumed lost off the
Sgt H Buchan   +   coast of Holland. F/S Prime RCAF, an American
P/O E B Willoughby RCAF   +   from Oconomowoc, Winsconsin, was washed onto a
F/S J Tait RCAF   +   beach near Zandvoort on 19 August and he now
Sgt E C Cohen   +   rests in Amsterdam's New Eastern Cemetery.
                                                His crew are commemorated on the Runnymede
Memorial. Sgt Cohen had joined the pre-war Auxiliary Air Force. Although
shown here as E, their aircraft had been E2 for the three 1,000 bomber raids.
AM Form 78 shows a total of 346.10 flying hours.

25 OTU   **Wellington IC**   **DV439**   **–H**   **Op: Düsseldorf**
F/L P P L E Welch   pow   T/o 2341 Finningley. Attacked at 13,000 feet
F/L J Hamilton   pow   over Tilburg (Noord Brabant), Holland by a
WO2 S Valensky RCAF   pow   night-fighter. F/S Penney RCAF is buried in
WO2 D J Veasey RCAF   pow   Bergen op Zoom War Cemetery. It is reported
F/S W F Penney RCAF   +   that F/L Hamilton was seriously wounded. Along
                                                with F/L W McD Morison of 103 Squadron, who had
been the victim of a midair collision on 5-6 June 1942 (see Bomber Command
Losses, Volume 3, page 119), F/L Welch made a valiant attempt to escape from
captivity. Both officers finished up in Colditz, where they became involved
in the design and production of the famous Colditz glider. For this information,
I am, indeed, grateful to David Chamberlin. For the recent attacks on Köln and
Bremen, this aircraft had been coded D1. Its total flying hours came to 280.00.

25 OTU   **Wellington IC**   **DV560**   **–K**   **Op: Düsseldorf**
Sgt V L Simonson RCAF   +   T/o 2345 Finningley. Hit by flak and crashed at
Sgt V S Mason   +   approximately 0245 into the Wilhelminastraat at
F/S W H Treadwell RCAF   +   Wemeldinge (Zeeland), Holland. All are buried
Sgt J B Campbell RCAF   +   in Vlissingen Northern Cemetery. As Y1, this
Sgt W H Day   +   Wellington had taken part in the three "Thousand
                                                Plan" attacks. Taken on charge on 13 April 1942,
                                                the bomber had flown 199.40 hours.

25 OTU   **Wellington IC**   **DV829**   **–L**   **Op: Düsseldorf**
P/O C J Frith   pow   T/o 2349 Finningley. Coned at 9,500 feet by
Sgt C H Moody   +   searchlights and, soon after, hit by flak.
Sgt G C Padkin   +   While trying to escape from the beams, the
Sgt O L Sharpe RAAF   +   bomber lost height and while partially out
Sgt J R Campbell   +   of control, flew into a pylon and crashed.
                                                Those who died now rest in Rheinberg War
Cemetery. A participant in all three 1,000 bomber raids, operating then as F3,
the Wellington had amassed 111.15 flying hours in three months of usage.

27 OTU   **Wellington IC**   **R1526**   **Op: Düsseldorf**
F/L E Walker   +   T/o 2327 Lichfield. All are buried in Rheinberg
W/O A S Patterson   +   War Cemetery. The first two named were regular
F/S J K Stone   +   service airmen, while F/L Court's service number
F/L A W Court   +   indicates he joined the air force under the
F/S N K Judd RAAF   +   commissioned air gunners' scheme. It seems
                                                likely that all were screened. W/O Patterson
had been very seriously injured when one of the unit's Ansons crashed on the
Isle of Man in the January (see page 94). Rather unusually, this Wellington
had arrived in Bomber Command via a Beam Approach Training Flight and a Coastal
Command Operational Training Unit.

31 Jul–	**27 OTU**	**Wellington IC**	DV552	**—N**	**Op: Düsseldorf**

31 Jul–
1 Aug 1942
27 OTU   **Wellington IC**   DV552   **—N**   **Op: Düsseldorf**

F/O M G McNeil RNZAF   +   T/o 2341 Lichfield. Crashed 0330 at Huldenberg
F/O A F R Nash RAAF   +   in the Province of Brabant, 23 km SE of Brussels.
Sgt O Morgan RAAF   +   All are buried in Huldenberg Churchyard. Between
Sgt J D O´Halloran RAAF   +   February and June 1941, F/O McNeil RNZAF had
Sgt C H R McKee RAAF   +   served with 218 Squadron, taking part in at least
Sgt C D Luedeke RAAF   +   sixteen operational sorties. In civilian life,
Sgt O´Halloran RAAF was a solicitor and had
served as Proctor and Attorney of the Supreme Court in New South Wales.

1 Aug
1942
10 OTU   **Whitley V**   Z6562   **Transit**

Sgt F J H Heathfield   inj   T/o 1130 Abingdon probably bound for St. Eval
Sgt J P Roberts   inj   but the starboard wing hit a totem pole and the
Sgt P A Taylor   inj   bomber landed just off the airfield, swerved
Sgt D A Goodman   inj   sharply to port and lost its undercarriage.
Sgt E Bradley RCAF   inj   Moments later a fire broke out. It was noted
F/L J Tunstall   inj   that for 45 minutes prior to the accident, the
Whitley had been running its engines while
awaiting clearance to take off. Sgt Heathfield later joined 51 Squadron and
became a prisoner of war in 1943.

14 OTU   **Hampden I**   P2129   **Training**

Sgt E A Coates RAAF   inj   T/o Cottesmore for high-level bombing, at
Sgt C W Webb RCAF   inj   night. Crashed 2330 about a mile SE of the
Sgt J A Ramsey RCAF   inj   airfield after a flare ignited, setting light
Sgt D L Paul RAAF   inj   to the bomb bay.

2 Aug
1942
15 OTU   **Wellington IC**   DV445   **Training**

Sgt D V Goocock   T/o 2328 Harwell for a night exercise with full
Sgt P H Griffiths   inj   flap selected. The aircraft failed to climb and
  inj   while trying to force -land in a ploughed field
  inj   crashed into a line of trees. Sgt Griffiths went
to the Far East, joining 99 Squadron. He lost
his life on 14 February 1944, and is buried in Rangoon War Cemetery.

4 Aug
1942
20 OTU E Flt   **Wellington IC**   R1272 JM-W   **Training**

Sgt D C Jackson   inj   T/o 0020 Lossiemouth for a night navigation
Sgt G H Wynne   +   exercise. Became lost, though the pilot thought
Sgt G H Churchley   inj   his aircraft was over the sea and shortly before
Sgt G Navey RCAF   +   0330 began to descend. In doing so, he flew
Sgt H S Dunbar   +   into The Buck, a 2,366 foot high mountain in
The Grampians, 3 miles SE of Cabrach, Banff.
Local villagers carried the dead and injured on stretchers for two miles in
order to get them to waiting ambulances, the two survivors being rushed to Dr.
Gray´s Hospital at Elgin. Sadly, Sgt Churchley, who had sustained a fractured
skull and a compound fracture to his left leg, did not survive; he is buried in
Northfield (St. Laurence) Churchyard extension. Those who died in the crash lie
in Lossiemouth Burial Ground. Thirty year old Sgt Wynne, a solicitor, was a
member of the pre-war Auxiliary Air Force.

4- 5 Aug
1942
10 OTU   **Whitley V**   Z9432   **Training**

Sgt G A Cooke   +   T/o 2255 Abingdon for a night cross-country.
Sgt K A Gleadall   +   Crashed at around 0200, on high ground, near
Sgt W F Jacobs   +   Home Farm, Hazleton, 9 miles ESE Cheltenham,
Sgt W A Lansley   +   Gloucestershire. Those who died lie in various
Sgt V B R Burtt   inj   cemeteries. LAC John George Jacobs, brother to
Sgt Jacobs, went down with HMS Courageous on 17
September 1939; he is commemorated on panel 2 of the Runnymede Memorial.

21 OTU   **Anson I**   N5257   **Training**

P/O E T Baker   T/o 2210 Moreton-in-Marsh for night navigation
training. At around 0055, the Anson force -
landed in a field, SW of the airfield, after losing power from the starboard
engine. By the winter of 1943, P/O Baker (now a F/L) was flying Halifaxes on
Pathfinder duties with 35 Squadron. Sadly, on 18-19 November 1943, his aircraft failed to return from Mannheim (see Bomber Command Losses, Volume 4,
page 383). A little over two months later, on 29 January 1944, his brother,
F/S George Arthur Baker, lost his life while on active service. He is buried
in Brookwood Military Cemetery.

4– 5 Aug   **20 OTU D Flt**   **Wellington IC**   **T2966**   **—C**   **Training**
1942

Sgt J F Heyman	inj
Sgt W D Crawford	inj
Sgt S E Monger-Godfrey	inj
Sgt N Wood RCAF	inj
F/S B D Crane RCAF	inj

T/o 2315 Elgin for a night exercise. Overshot the airfield circa 0230 and came down at Quarry Wood on the western edge of the town of Elgin. Failure of the port engine was a contributory factor. All were taken to Dr. Gray's Hospital, where Sgt Heyman died from his burns. He is buried in Kent at Ashford (Bybrook) Cemetery. For F/S Crane RCAF, this proved but a brief respite for having returned to duty he was killed on 29 September 1942, shortly before completing his training.

5 Aug   **26 OTU**   **Wellington IC**   **X9675**   **Training**
1942

P/O G F Pentony	inj
Sgt G R Phipps RCAF	+

T/o 2045 Wing for a night navigation sortie. During the flight, a conrod broke up inside the starboard engine, damaging the pistons of Nos. 5, 6 and 7 cylinders. Almost immediately, the motor burst into flames and at around 2330 the order to abandon was given, leaving the bomber to crash at Burton Coggles, 7 miles SSE of Grantham, Lincolnshire. Sgt Phipps RCAF, an air gunner, is buried in Grantham Cemetery.

6 Aug   **20 OTU B Flt**   **Wellington IC**   **R1097 JM–R**   **Training**
1942

Sgt Churchill RCAF	inj
	inj
	inj

T/o 1113 Lossiemouth. Returned to base and landed at 1428, but Sgt Churchill RCAF thought he was going to overshoot the runway. Opening the throttles to go round again, the Wellington began to gather speed but as it did so, the starboard engine burst into flames and, out of control, it crashed just beyond a hangar on the NW side of the airfield. All were taken to Dr. Gray's Hospital where, it is believed, one airman died, though, as yet, he remains unidentified.

20 OTU   **Wellington IC**   **R1448 XL–Y**   **Training**

F/S M L Donohoe	+
Sgt J Woods	inj
Sgt J M Thompson	+

T/o Elgin for circuits and landings. During the exercise the crew became aware of excessive vibration from the port engine and before the unit could be shut down, the fuel pump sheared and escaping petrol set light to the motor. An emergency landing was called for but the flames spread with remarkable speed into the mainplanes and as the bomber descended through 400 feet, the port wing came off and the Wellington crashed just to the NE of D Flight's dispersal area. F/S Donohoe, a pre-war regular airman, is buried in Saffron Waldon Cemetery, while Sgt Thompson lies in Acomb (St. Stephen) Churchyard, York.

6– 7 Aug   **16 OTU**   **Wellington IC**   **R1075**   **Training**
1942

P/O J Maura	
P/O P L Moxey	+
Sgt N G Crabtree	+
LAC R L Smith	+

T/o 2207 Upper Heyford for a night navigation flight. Strayed from track and, unwittingly, entered the Birmingham barrage balloon defences. At 0132, the bomber clipped a tethering cable and crashed at Erdington on the E side of the city. P/O Maura and two others managed to bale out, but the others were not so fortunate. P/O Moxey, a Welsh International Rugby Trialist for three years, 1935 to 1937, and a representative in the RAF Rugby Football Teams for the past three seasons, is buried in Great Yarmouth (Gorleston) Cemetery. Sgt Crabtree rests in Birmingham (Witton) Cemetery, while LAC Smith was brought back to Upper Heyford and interred in Middleton Stoney (All Saints) Churchyard. It will be recalled that P/O Maura had abandoned a Hampden in the February (see page 101), in which three members of his crew lost their lives.

7 Aug   **22 OTU**   **Anson I**   **AX258**   **—O**   **Ground**
1942

At 0730, while pumping petrol at Wellesbourne Mountford, it is believed a static electricity discharge occurred, setting the Anson on fire. A Court of Inquiry found that the principal cause lay in the absence of bonding between the Zwicky nozzle and the aircraft's fuel tanks.

9 Aug   **19 OTU**   **Whitley IV**   **K9021**   **Training**
1942

Sgt W M Wood	
Sgt G C Wright	

T/o Kinloss for dual instruction. Landed 1000 but swung, deliberately, in order to avoid an obstruction. Damaged beyond repair when its undercarriage collapsed. Posted to 76 Squadron, Sgt Wright was killed on the Plzen raid in April 1943 (see Bomber Command Losses, Volume 4, page 112).

9 Aug
1942

20 OTU D Flt   **Wellington IC**   **L7845 ZT-Z**   **Training**

F/S A G W Keene RCAF	+	T/o 1200 Elgin for a cross-country. Crashed
Sgt A Kirby RCAF	+	an hour later and burnt out some 3 miles SW
Sgt J Weatherson	+	of Loch Lee, Angus. The cause of the accident
Sgt O K L Jensen RCAF	+	was attributed to the cowling detaching from
Sgt T W Holman	inj	the port engine and striking the propeller.

The three RCAF members of crew are buried in
Fettercairn Cemetery, Kincardine, while Sgt Weatherson was taken to Hebburn
Cemetery. Sgt Holman was treated at Forfar Infirmary.

20 OTU   **Wellington IC**   **DV712**   **Training**

P/O H J Patteson RCAF		T/o 2200 Elgin for night flying but an engine
Sgt F P D Quinn RCAF		cut and the bomber was forced-landed, straight

ahead. Sgt Quinn RCAF was killed in the course
of a minelaying operation on 8-9 December 1942, having converted to Lancasters
and joined 101 Squadron (see Bomber Command Losses, Volume 3, page 273).

10 Aug
1942

22 OTU   **Wellington IC**   **R1505**   **Training**

Sgt J P Jolley RCAF		T/o Wellesbourne Mountford for a night cross-
F/S C Toronczuk RCAF	+	country. Shortly before 0500, the bomber lost

its starboard propeller and the crew headed for
Waddington. Unfortunately, they were unable to pick up the flare path lights,
or make contact by radio. Then, the port engine began to play up and the crew,
with the exception of F/S Toronczuk RCAF, baled out NE of Cranwell airfield,
Lincolnshire. F/S Toronczuk's body was recovered from the wreckage and laid
to rest in Cranwell (St. Andrew) Churchyard. Not long after this incident,
Sgt Jolley RCAF went to 419 Squadron but failed to return from Köln on 15-16
October 1942 (see Bomber Command Losses, Volume 3, page 242).

11 Aug
1942

14 OTU   **Hampden I**   **AE155 GL-S**   **Training**

F/S R P Davis RCAF	+	T/o Saltby for low-level bombing practice, at
F/S J H O'Connor RCAF	+	night. Crashed 0330 at Edenham, 2 miles NW of
Sgt D H Barton RAAF	+	Bourne, Lincolnshire. Two lie in the extension

to Cottesmore (St. Nicholas) Churchyard, while
F/S Davies RCAF was taken to Sheffield (Tinsley Park) Cemetery, his funeral
being most likely arranged by relatives.

12 Aug
1942

23 OTU   **Wellington IC**   **Z1159**   **Training**

F/S A M Hornseth RCAF	+	T/o 0120 Pershore for night training. Landed
P/O J G Stewart RCAF	+	at around 0250 but, it is said, rather awkwardly
Sgt V A G Valiquette RCAF	inj	and while trying to go round again climbed too

steeply and stalled into the ground 600 yards
off the end of the runway. Both Canadians are buried in Pershore Cemetery.
Sgt Valiquette's injuries are described as mild abrasions and shock.

24 OTU   **Whitley V**   **Z9470**   **Training**

Sgt J A McIntosh RNZAF	inj	T/o Honeybourne for night navigation exercise,
Sgt Wagner	inj	No. 5. During the sortie, the port engine lost
Sgt W P James RCAF	+	power. A flare path was sighted (this turned
Sgt Maughan	inj	out to be a dummy at Bugthorpe) and it was only
Sgt Perry	inj	at the last moment that the crew realised the

deception. Applying full power to the starboard
motor, Sgt McIntosh RNZAF tried to climb away but flew into rising ground, known
locally as Meadale, near Kirby Underdale, 14 miles ENE from the centre of York,
where the injured were taken. Sgt James RCAF, a graduate from the University of
Manitoba, is buried in Barmby-on-the-Moor (St. Catherine) Churchyard. It was
over a year before Sgt McIntosh RNZAF was able to resume active flying and,
sadly, while well into a tour of duty with 75 Squadron his Lancaster failed
to return from Osterfeld on 30 November 1944 (see Bomber Command Losses,
Volume 5, page 497).

26 OTU   **Wellington IC**   **DV868**   **Training**

Sgt R J Carson	T/o 0135 Cheddington for night flying. Crashed
Sgt C A Smith	circa 0320 while attempting to go round again.
Sgt F Sayles	In his report, Sgt Carson said he realised he
P/O J C Cogill	was to one side of the flare path and though he
Sgt R J Booth	retracted the undercarriage in readiness to go

round again, he lost all flying speed.

13 Aug 1942	**10 OTU Det** Sgt F Boyd Sgt W G Wishart Sgt T Parker Sgt R F Crouch Sgt A J Hendry	**Whitley V Z9300**	**Op: AS Patrol**

T/o St. Eval for a seven-and-a-half hour patrol one of five crews so tasked. Ditched 1610, due to loss of power from the port engine. All were able to get into the dinghy and three days later they were picked up by a RN destroyer. This was the first Whitley to be lost from the detachment at St. Eval.

12-13 Aug 1942	**14 OTU** Sgt R J Hudson RAAF	**Anson I R9608 -Z**	**Training**

T/o 2130 Cottesmore for low-level bombing practice, at night. Landed 0135, but ran off the end of the runway and finished up, wrecked, in a hedge. Having converted to Lancasters, Sgt Hudson RAAF was posted for Pathfinder duties with 156 Squadron and was reported missing on 24 June 1943 (see Bomber Command Losses, Volume 4, page 205).

14 Aug 1942	**17 OTU** Sgt S J Roche	**Blenheim IV V5699**	**Training**

T/o 1415 Upwood but failed to become airborne and though the throttles were closed, Sgt Roche was unable to prevent his aircraft from smashing into the hedge bordering the airfield. Proceeding to 226 Squadron, he lost his life in a flying accident on 3 February 1943 (see Bomber Command Losses, Volume 4, page 34).

	19 OTU F/O G H Sawley RAAF P/O T W Osborn Sgt U J Banham Sgt J S Graham Sgt D M McCutcheon	**Whitley V N1486** + + + + +	**Training**

T/o 0148 Kinloss for a combined night cross-country and bombing exercise. Dived almost vertically into the sea at 0214, roughly 2 miles N of Findhorn, Moray. The Runnymede Memorial perpetuates the memory of this crew.

15 Aug 1942	**20 OTU** Sgt O K L Jackson	**Anson I R9579 -F**	**Training**

T/o Lossiemouth but due to engine failure was obliged to ditch 0144 in the Moray Firth some ten miles NE of the airfield. A high-speed launch from Buckie picked up the six crew and after being given hot baths and drinks, none were the worse for their unscheduled adventure.

16 Aug 1942	**14 OTU** Sgt J M Churchill F/S M Henry RCAF Sgt R O Lungair RCAF Sgt T B Phillips RCAF	**Hampden I P4318 GL-O** inj inj inj inj	**Training**

T/o Cottesmore for a night navigation sortie. Crashed 0230 into high ground on Arkengarthdale Moor in the vicinity of Healaugh and Reeth, two villages some 11 miles SSW of Barnard Castle, Yorkshire. F/S Henry RCAF and Sgt Phillips RCAF, both of Vancouver in British Columbia, died from their injuries and they now lie in Catterick Cemetery.

	17 OTU AC1 R A Munro	**Blenheim IV V6399** inj	**Ground**

While servicing electrical equipment on the Blenheim at Upwood, a fire broke out, 1110, in the starboard engine nacelle, destroying the bomber.

17 Aug 1942	**11 OTU** P/O J G Neilson RNZAF	**Wellington IC R1407 KJ-N**	**Training**

T/o Steeple Morden for night circuits and landings. This was a frustrating exercise for on no less than three occasions, P/O Neilson RNZAF was obliged to overshoot after being given "reds" from the flare path controller. Then, on his fourth approach he inadvertently failed to lower his undercarriage and at 0145 hit the runway with the wheels retracted. Posted to 218 Squadron, he gained a Distinguished Flying Cross, but while serving as an instructor with 1657 HCU, he died when his Stirling I W7571 crashed taking off from Stradishall.

18 Aug 1942	**20 OTU** F/S H I Smith RCAF P/O W A Miller RCAF P/O A E Macgregor RCAF F/S A J Linden	**Anson I DJ178 -J** inj + + + inj	**Training**

T/o Lossiemouth for a navigation exercise. Flew into high ground near Barnedale, probably between Wick and Lybster, Caithness. Those who died rest in Wick Cemetery. Initially treated at Bignold Hospital, F/S Smith RCAF was later taken to RAF Hospital Halton.

18–19 Aug	**21 OTU**	**Wellington IC**	**R1345**	**Training**
1942	Sgt M R Derrick RCAF	+	T/o 2120 Moreton-in-Marsh for a night cross-	
	Sgt H E Drake	+	country. Lost without trace. Their names	
	Sgt A Pogrel	+	are perpetuated on the panels of the Runnymede	
	Sgt C A Williams RAAF	+	Memorial. Delivered to the unit a mere four	
	P/O R A Castell	+	days previous, the Wellington's total flying	
			hours amounted to 277.30.	

19 Aug	**18 OTU**	**Wellington IC**	**T2903**	**Training**
1942	F/S S Dusza PAF	+	T/o 1000 Bramcote for a navigation exercise.	
	Sgt S Fatyga PAF	+	Four hours after departure, and while flying	
	P/O S K Kepinski PAF	+	in poor visibility, the bomber smashed into a	
	Sgt E Tuliszka PAF	+	hillside near Chipping Campden, 5 miles NW of	
	Sgt R S Czopik PAF	+	Moreton-in-Marsh, Gloucestershire. All rest	
	Sgt S Lis PAF	+	in the Polish plot at Newark-upon-Trent Cemetery.	

18–19 Aug	**29 OTU**	**Wellington IC**	**DV881**	**Training**
1942	Sgt J D Gray		T/o 2222 Woolfox Lodge to practice night bombing.	

Returned to base at 0022 but made a bad approach and touched down at an angle to the flare path. Crossing to the left hand side of the runway the Wellington ran at fairly high speed towards the perimeter and it was here that the port brake was applied. This slewed the aircraft round, whereupon the undercarriage collapsed.

20 Aug	**19 OTU**	**Whitley V**	**BD291**	**Training**
1942	Sgt K A Peters RCAF		T/o Kinloss for an air firing detail. While	

flying at a 1,000 feet, the engines lost power and the bomber alighted in Spey Bay, 1505, between Lossiemouth and Portknockie. No one was hurt and a fishing vessel soon had the crew aboard and heading into Lossiemouth harbour. Not long after, Sgt Peters RCAF went to 76 Squadron only to be posted missing from his first operation as captain (see Bomber Command Losses, Volume 3, page 233), the target being Aachen on 5-6 October 1942.

	25 OTU	**Wellington IC**	**T2715 –E**	**Training**
	Sgt B G Crew RCAF		T/o 2130 Finningley for a night navigation	

exercise. Within an hour, the crew became uncertain of their position and Sgt Crew RCAF decided to let down through the cloud cover in order to establish a visual check. At 4,000 feet, the bomber entered cloud and moments later it impacted on high ground on the western side of The Pennines, 14 miles S of Alston, Cumberland. Assuming the distance given to be accurate, this would place the crash in the region of Dufton Fell and possibly E of the Knock-Dufton-Murton road in neighbouring Westmoreland.

21 Aug	**15 OTU**	**Wellington IC**	**T2557**	**Training**
1942	P/O A W Stilwell	+	T/o Harwell for a night cross-country. At	
	P/O A M Henderson	+	around 0505, the Wellington collided with	
	Sgt P O'Brien	+	Oxford II T1339 of 6 FTS (Sgt S E Downs)	
	Sgt N F Boxwell	+	and crashed at Colts Farm, Over Norton, about	
	Sgt M S Haynes	+	a mile NNE of Chipping Norton, Oxfordshire.	
	Sgt F Gillard	+	The wreckage of the Oxford is reported to	
			have been recovered from Jewdell House, Church	

Street, Chipping Norton. All are buried in cemeteries in the United Kingdom and the Irish Republic. It is noted that P/O Henderson was the son of Major Ian Macdonald Henderson and Kathleen Mary Henderson of Woking and that Sgt O'Brien held a Master of Arts degree with honours. As a rider to the Court of Inquiry, it was emphasised that crews should be especially vigilant at night with the skies being so crowded.

	19 OTU	**Anson I**	**DJ106**	**Training**
	Sgt J Llewellyn	+	T/o Kinloss for a navigation exercise. This	
	F/S G Fillingham	+	ended in tragedy when the Anson flew into Ben	
	P/O W Gilmour RCAF	+	Macdui (4,296 feet above sea level) in the	
	F/S K E Carruthers	+	Cairngorms some 10 miles or so SE of Aviemore.	
	Sgt J B Robertson	+	Three rest in Kinloss Abbey Burial Ground, Sgt	
			Llewellyn is buried in Wales at Garnant (Old	

Bethel) Welsh Congregational Chapelyard, Llandilofawr, while F/S Carruthers lies in Windemere (St. Mary's) Cemetery. The wreckage of their aircraft was found on 24 August and reported to Kinloss by the Royal Observer Corps, but it was nearly midnight on 27 August before all bodies had been brought back to base.

22 Aug	10 OTU Det		Whitley V	Z6645 JL-V		Op: AS Patrol
1942	Sgt E D W Davis	int	T/o St. Eval. Ditched 1630 some 180 miles SW			
	Sgt D A Jones Ford	int	of Bishop Rock off the Isles of Scilly. Their			
	Sgt D P P Hurst	int	dinghy was eventually sighted by the Spanish			
	Sgt J Vaughan	int	fishing trawler "Mardomingo" and later that			
	Sgt T A Berwick	int	same day (22 August) they were landed at La			
	Sgt D S Aird	int	Coruna. In due course, the crew came back to			

England aboard a RN destroyer with the very
Iberian sounding name of HMS Bachaquero.

	10 OTU Det		Whitley V	Z9294		Op: AS Patrol
	P/O C Neve	+	T/o St. Eval similarly tasked. Lost without			
	P/O J H Burgess	+	trace. All are commemorated on the Runnymede			
	P/O A R Cook	+	Memorial. Two, P/O Cook and Sgt Dodds, came			
	Sgt R H Lucas	+	from Co. Durham.			
	F/S F B Croke RCAF	+				
	Sgt C Dodds	+				

25 Aug	15 OTU		Wellington IC	DV595		Training
1942	P/O N Falkinder	+	T/o 0001 Harwell for night bombing practice			
	Sgt D Greet	+	over the Odstone bombing ranges. At 0100, while			
	P/O A S Walmsley	+	over the range, collided with Wellington IC			
	Sgt F T G Cannon	+	N2755/T (Sgt R S Baker and Sgt J H Rank) and			
	Sgt R J Coombs	+	crashed 2 miles SE of Uffington, 6 miles WNW			
	F/S F H Rathjen RAAF	+	of Wantage, Berkshire. All are buried in			

Harwell Cemetery. Sgt Greet was the son of
F/L Clifford Greet, serving with the Volunteer Reserve, while Sgt Coombs came
from a naval background, his father being Chief Petty Officer John Coombs RN.
Subsequently, the Air Officer Commanding No. 92 Group issued a Commendation
to Sgt R S Baker for his skillful airmanship in landing N2755 safely. On
12 December 1944, while parked at 18 MU Dumfries, N2755 was wrecked after
being hit by Hurricane IV KZ220.

	22 OTU		Wellington IC	X9929		Training
	P/O E F J Stoll RCAF	+	T/o Wellesbourne Mountford for night flying			
	Sgt E T Spears RCAF	+	training. For no apparent reason, the bomber			
	F/S A Leether RCAF	+	dived from 500 feet and hit the banks of the			
	P/O G L Shaw RCAF	+	River Avon near Wasperton, 5 miles NE from			
	Sgt R H Harper RCAF	+	Stratford-upon-Avon, where all are buried in			

the local cemetery. On 11 July 1944, the
younger brother of P/O Shaw RCAF, P/O Ernest Anson Shaw, was killed when his
408 Squadron Lancaster crashed in Leicestershire (see Bomber Command Losses,
Volume 5, page 326). Both were thirty years of age when they died.

26 Aug	21 OTU		Wellington IC	Z1160		Transit
1942	Sgt D B White		T/o 1144 Honeybourne but shortly afterwards,			
	P/O M Holub RCAF		having reached 500 feet, experienced engine			

trouble. Sgt White tried to regain the air-
field but before he could lower the undercarriage, his aircraft hit the ground.
1146, downwind and crashed through a hedge. P/O Holub RCAF was involved in
a similar incident when, on 4 September, he was obliged to crash-land his
aircraft (Wellington IC X9933) at Gaydon. On this occasion the damage was
slight and the bomber was soon returned to service. Ten days later, on 13-14
September 1942, he failed to return from Bremen.

27 Aug	10 OTU Det		Whitley V	N1443		Op: AS Patrol
1942	Sgt R A Hodgson		T/o St. Eval. Lost power and being unable to			
			maintain height, ditched at 1215. All were			
			picked up later in the day.			

28 Aug	12 OTU		Wellington III	BJ726		Training
1942	Sgt I S McLennan RAAF	inj	T/o 1205 Chipping Warden for flying practice.			
	Sgt Akehurst	inj	Flying between 400 and 500 feet, the starboard			
	Sgt Palmer	inj	engine failed and a forced-landing was made at			
	Sgt Conville		around 1215 near Braunston, 3 miles NW of			
	Sgt Wright	inj	Daventry, Northamptonshire, a fire breaking			
			out soon after. Sgt Palmer and Sgt Wright,			

the latter suffering from a broken nose, were admitted to Rugby St. Cross
Hospital. It is not thought that any had sustained life threatening injuries.

28 Aug 1942	13 OTU	Blenheim IV	N6169		Training
	Sgt E A Hooker		+		T/o 0925 Bicester for a navigation exercise.
	Sgt F L James		+		At 1058, a wireless message was received from
	Sgt C W Free		+		this aircraft, after which nothing further

was heard. However, it was established that a head-on collision occurred with another of the unit's Blenheims, both aircraft plunging into the North Sea some 26 miles NE of Flamborough Head. All are commemorated on the Runnymede Memorial.

	13 OTU	Blenheim IV	V6197		Training
	Sgt S C Moss RAAF				T/o 0905 Bicester, similarly tasked and making
	Sgt F A W Nice		+		for the same area. A routine wireless message
	Sgt F H Edwards		+		was transmitted at 1009. Then, at some time

after 1058, the Blenheim collided with the aircraft summarised above. Miraculously, Sgt Moss RAAF was thrown clear and he was picked up three days later, his dinghy having drifted to within about twenty miles of the coast. In his statement, he said that at the time of the collision, the weather was extremely hazy. Not long after this alarming incident, he was posted to fly Venturas with 464 Squadron and became a prisoner of war following the Squadron's first operational sorties on 6 December 1942 (see Bomber Command Losses, Volume 3, page 270).

	14 OTU	Hampden I	AE312 GL-H		Training
	F/S N A Clare RCAF		+		T/o Cottesmore for a night exercise. Stalled
	F/S G A Gray RCAF		+		and crashed 0020, bursting into flames on
	F/S D E Brownlee RCAF		+		impact, at Thistleton, 7 miles NNE of Oakham.
	Sgt J J E G R Patry RCAF		+		It is very likely that F/S Clare RCAF was

claimed by his Scottish relatives as he is buried in Aberdeen (Springbank) Cemetery, Peterculter, while his fellow countrymen rest in the extension to Cottesmore (St. Nicholas) Churchyard.

	24 OTU	Whitley V	BD380		Training
	Sgt A C Combe		inj		T/o Honeybourne for a Command Bullseye over
	Sgt Millar RCAF				Aintree Racecourse. Abandoned circa 0200
	P/O Graham				when the camshaft bearing caps failed on the
	Sgt Lancashire				starboard engine, resulting in the propeller
	Sgt Curtis				windmilling out of control. Prior to baling
	Sgt Fear				out, the crew attempted to secure ground

assistance by putting out Darkie and Mayday calls, but to no avail. Sgt Combe sustained a very serious eye injury and he was taken to Mostyn Hall Hospital, Ledsham, possibly not far from where the Whitley crashed, described as 500 yards NW of Ledsham Hill, Little Sutton in Cheshire.

	29 OTU	Wellington IC	DV834		Training
	Sgt G H Dodd		inj		T/o 1415 North Luffenham but swung quite badly
	F/S L L Jones RCAF		+		and though several attempts were made to correct
	Sgt R G Walters RCAF		inj		the situation, the Wellington left the ground in
	Sgt G W Hall		inj		an unusual attitude. It then banked steeply to

starboard before stalling and hitting the ground, whereupon it burst into flames. Sgt Walters RCAF died the next day from his injuries and he was laid to rest in North Luffenham (St. John The Baptist) Churchyard. Toronto born F/S Jones RCAF was claimed by his Cornish relatives and buried in St. Just Methodist's Chapelyard. It was considered that the pilot's slender build was a contributory factor.

29 Aug 1942	15 OTU	Wellington IC	N2816		Ground
	LAC Mundell				Parked at Hampstead Norris, this Wellington
					was undergoing ground-running by maintenance

staff when at 1315 a fire broke out behind the bulkhead of the starboard engine nacelle, quickly spreading out of control.

	18 OTU	Wellington IC	X9642		Training
	Sgt T Kuzminski PAF		inj		T/o 0205 Bramcote for a night bombing exercise.
			inj		Lost power from the starboard engine and crash-
			inj		landed 0245 some 15 miles NW of Gainsborough,
			inj		Lincolnshire. In March 1943, Sgt Kuzminski PAF,
					now with 300 Squadron, failed to return from a

mining sortie off St. Nazaire (see Bomber Command Losses, Volume 4, page 77).

29 Aug
1942

22 OTU   **Wellington I L4310**   **Ground**
While being drained of fuel, at Wellesbourne
Mountford, a fire broke out and the bomber was totally destroyed. The Court
of Inquiry concluded that the accident, which occurred at 1600, was most likely
caused by petrol vapour igniting due to either an electrical short circuit or
earthing failure.

30 Aug
1942

26 OTU   **Wellington IC DV825   -U**   **Training**
Sgt R V McDougall RCAF   inj T/o 1500 Cheddington for circuit training.
Sgt A P Hendriksen   inj Landed at 1545 but bounced back into the air
                                 and stalled. A fire broke out on impact.
Sgt Hendriksen was critically injured and he was taken to the Princess Mary's
Hospital at Halton, where he died on 5 September. His grave is in Malden (St.
John The Baptist) Churchyard, Malden and Coombe. Later commissioned, his
skipper was killed during operations to Düsseldorf on 22-23 April 1944 (see
Bomber Command Losses, Volume 5, page 180). At the time, he was flying with
166 Squadron.

31 Aug
1942

13 OTU   **Blenheim IV Z7302**   **Ground**
Wrecked while dispersed at Catfoss airfield
in Yorkshire, having been hit by Halifax II BB196 of 76 Squadron (see Bomber
Command Losses, Volume 3, page 200) flown by Sgt A I T Moir.

14 OTU   **Hampden I P1205   -D1**   **Training**
Sgt K R Fisher RCAF   T/o Cottesmore for a low-level bombing sortie
P/O D F Foy RCAF   inj over the Grimsthorpe ranges. Crashed 1545 in
                                 the range area (some 4 miles W of Bourne,
Lincolnshire) having been unable to recover from a stabilised yaw at low
altitude. P/O Foy RCAF was very badly burned and he died the next day.
His grave is in the extension to Cottesmore (St. Nicholas) Churchyard. Aged
nineteen, he was the son of Captain G H Foy of Britannia, Ontario.

17 OTU   **Blenheim IV Z6352**   **Training**
Sgt T Mair   T/o 1615 Upwood for a cross-country. Wrecked
                            inj at 1900 in a crash-landing, with the under-
                            inj carriage down, at Ramsey St. Mary's, 3 miles
                                 to the NW of Ramsey, Huntingdonshire. On 10
December 1943, and now flying Mosquitoes with 487 Squadron RNZAF, Sgt Mair was
brought down over Holland. Along with his navigator, W/O K L O Blow DFC, he
is buried in Den Ham General Cemetery.

21 OTU   **Wellington IC R1232**   **Training**
F/S B A Smith   +   T/o Moreton-in-Marsh for night flying. While
P/O M Dunn   +   attempting to overshoot the runway at 2110,
Sgt A Perrett   +   went out of control and hit a tree. Of those
Sgt J F Boyer RCAF   inj who died, all were taken to their home towns
                                 for burial.

24 OTU   **Whitley V P5100**   **Training**
Sgt G W West   +   T/o 2140 Honeybourne for local night flying.
F/S W H Terwilliger RCAF   +   At 2212, overshot the flare path and removed
Sgt Bowman   inj part of a wing against some trees at Bowers
                                 Hill Farm, Badsey, 2 miles ESE from Evesham,
Worcestershire. Detroit born F/S Terwilliger RCAF rests in Evesham Cemetery
while Sgt West was taken to West Wickham (St. John The Baptist) Churchyard
at Beckenham. Sgt Bowman escaped with relatively minor injuries.

1 Sep
1942

22 OTU   **Wellington IC W5625**   **Training**
Sgt R A Nickless   inj T/o Stratford-upon-Avon for the pilot's first
Sgt J M Broughton RCAF   inj night solo on type. At 2106 landed heavily,
                                 bounced twice and crashed on the airfield.
At the time of the crash, light rain was falling which might have impeded Sgt
Nickless's vision.

24 OTU   **Whitley V BD375**   **Training**
Sgt S W Templar   T/o 1945 Honeybourne for a night cross-country.
Sgt L S C Tait   +   Crashed 2355, due to engine failure, near the
                                 goods yards at Honeybourne Station. Sgt Tait,
the adopted nephew of Dorothy Dunn, rests in Corfe Mullen Cemetery, Dorset.

2 Sep
1942

10 OTU   **Whitley V**   **N1391**   **Training**

Sgt P Gammon RCAF	inj	T/o Abingdon for a night navigation sortie.
F/O H J Walters	inj	Crashed 2335, while making an emergency landing,

hitting some trees near Cow Lees, Bedworth, some six miles NNE of Coventry, Warwickshire. Five members of the crew baled out, as instructed and were not hurt.

14 OTU   **Hampden I**   **L4162**   **-O**   **Training**

Sgt D Wilson	+	T/o Cottesmore for night flying practice. Came
Sgt J K Johnston RCAF	+	down at 2205 near Thistleton, 7 miles NNE of
F/S J J P Wardrop RCAF	+	Oakham. The three Canadians are buried in the
Sgt P V Norris RCAF	+	extension to Cottesmore (St. Nicholas) Church-

yard, while Sgt Wilson was taken to Dalton (Holy Trinity) New Churchyard. The wife of Sgt Norris RCAF had a most unusual first Christian name, Verdun, possibly being named as such to commemorate the thousands of French soldiers who died in the First World War defending the fortress city of the same name.

15 OTU   **Wellington IC**   **X3192**   **Training**

Sgt J H Thomas	+	T/o 2144 Harwell for a night exercise which
Sgt B J Foster	+	ended 30 minutes later when the Wellington
P/O D Dove	+	stalled while approaching the runway and
Sgt G S Catto	+	ended up a mass of flames amongst trees,
Sgt J E Wilkinson	+	just inside the airfield perimeter. Two,
Sgt J Linacre	inj	Sgt Foster and Sgt Wilkinson, were buried

in Harwell Cemetery, while the others who died were taken to their home towns.

3 Sep
1942

11 OTU   **Wellington IC**   **Z8808 KJ-E**   **Training**

F/L P R Coney RNZAF	inj	T/o Bassingbourn for a night cross-country.
Sgt J Wilding RNZAF	inj	Ran into extremely adverse weather and came
Sgt M B Grainger RNZAF	inj	down circa 0030 some 4 miles W of Southwaite
Sgt J H F Kemp	inj	House Farm, Ramsgill, 4 miles NE of Pately
F/S J E Burrel	inj	Bridge, Yorkshire. All were admitted to
Sgt G W Wilford	inj	Harrogate Hospital.
Sgt W G Reader	inj	

11 OTU   **Wellington IC**   **DV718 OP-H**   **Training**

Sgt G F Ridgway RNZAF	+	T/o Bassingbourn similarly tasked. Strayed W
P/O D H Lyne	inj	of track and crashed between 2 and 3 miles SW
Sgt W Allinson	+	of Angram Bridge, near Pately Bridge, Yorkshire.
Sgt H W Spencer	+	P/O Lyne was taken to Harrogate Hospital, while
Sgt P McLarnon	+	his less fortunate companions were recovered by

a rescue party from RAF Topcliffe. Later, Sgt Ridgway RNZAF was interred in Windhill Methodist Cemetery, Shipley while the others were claimed by their next of kin.

19 OTU   **Whitley V**   **Z6760 ZV-S**   **Training**

F/S R J Pollock RCAF	+	T/o 0146 Forres for a night exercise, though
P/O L I Alter	+	watchers on the ground were concerned by the
Sgt A F Rooke	+	length of the aircraft's take off run. Then,
Sgt T V Robinson	+	having lifted off and climbed to about forty
Sgt J D Frost	+	feet, an engine cut. Gradually, the bomber

began to bank to the left before hitting a raised bank and bursting into flames. F/S Pollock RCAF and Sgt Rooke were taken to Kinloss Abbey Burial Ground, the others to their home towns. P/O Alter was a Member of the Pharmaceutical Society.

21 OTU   **Wellington IC**   **X9606**   **Training**

P/O E W Catley	inj	T/o Edgehill for a night exercise. Wrecked
Sgt J D Muir	inj	at around 0315 after flying into trees about
P/O R Davis	inj	a mile N of the airfield. At the time of the
Sgt J A W Williams	inj	accident, the crew were making ready to land.
Sgt F Pettitt	+	Sgt Pettitt rests in Birmingham (Brandwood)
Sgt H L McGill	inj	Cemetery. Sgt Muir later joined 162 Squadron,

radio countermeasures unit based at Benina in Libya. On 18 May 1943, his aircraft failed to return from operations and he is commemorated on panel 7, column 2, of the Malta Memorial.

4 Sep 1942	25 OTU W/C E E Collins	Anson I	R9699	Training

T/o 2330 Finningley but swung out of control and ran into Wellington IC DV494, belonging to the same unit. The Anson was wrecked but the Wellington was less badly damaged and following repairs, continued in service. In the aftermath of this accident, an instruction was issued that goose neck flares be used to augment the Drem flare path lighting as the contours of the airfield interfered with flare path continuity, when viewed from the cockpit of smaller aircraft.

25 OTU		Wellington IC	DV600	—L3	Training
F/S W B Sage RCAF	+	T/o 2100 Finningley for a night cross-country.
F/S G E Derbyshire RCAF	+	Crashed 2230 on High Scaw Fell near Rosthwaite
Sgt J L Brovender RCAF	+	in Borrowdale, 6 miles SSW of Keswick, Cumber-
F/S J Anderson RCAF	+	land. Sgt Brovender RCAF was taken to Blackpool
Sgt H B Burnett	+	Cemetery, while his three fellow Canadians were

laid to rest at Silloth (Causewayhead) Cemetery. Sgt Burnett is buried in Scotland at Culter Parish Churchyard, his being the sole service grave from the Second World War.

25 OTU		Wellington III	X3940	—N Bar	Training
F/S D A Green	+	T/o 2050 Finningley for a night exercise.
F/S F E Meers RCAF	+	During the sortie, an engine caught fire and
Sgt K M Perkins RCAF		the bomber was partially abandoned before
Sgt W P Suter RCAF		crashing 2145 at Grimston Park, S of Tadcaster,
Sgt E Perran		Yorkshire. The two airmen who died, F/S Green

of Rondebosch in the Cape Province where his father, the Revd Harry Norman Green had a living, and F/S Meers RCAF rest in the extension to Kirby Wharfe (St. John The Baptist) Churchyard. Nearly six months later, on 7-8 February 1943, Sgt Perkins RCAF lost his life when his 44 Squadron Lancaster failed to return from Lorient (see Bomber Command Losses, Volume 4, page 38). Sgt Perran had enlisted in Newfoundland, circa August 1940.

5 Sep 1942	10 OTU Det	Whitley V	Z6481	Op: AS Patrol
P/O D F S Bertera	inj	T/o 0935 St. Eval. Returned to base at 2225
F/O N S Grant	inj	but undershot the runway and crashed at Higher
Sgt B A Stoker	inj	Denzell Farm. P/O Bertera recovered from his
Sgt W G Fewell	inj	injuries and by the spring of 1943, was flying
Sgt L H H Stipt	inj	Halifaxes with 158 Squadron. Shot down during

operations to Mannheim on 16-17 April 1943 (see Bomber Command Losses, Volume 4, page 114), he successfully evaded capture.

24 OTU		Whitley V	AD666	Training
Sgt D W Weiner		T/o 2219 Honeybourne for a night exercise but
Sgt J H E Howe		swung badly, eventually coming to a stop with

the fuselage broken and irreparably damaged.

6 Sep 1942	16 OTU	Wellington IC	DV937	Training
Sgt K J Johnson RNZAF		T/o 1100 Upper Heyford for a cross-country.

Wrecked 1210 in an emergency landing on Perdiswell Hall airfield in Worcestershire. The Wellington ended up with its undercarriage retracted, just beyond the boundary hedge. Before the month was out, Sgt Johnson RNZAF would survive a ditching while operating to Düsseldorf.

20 OTU E Flt		Wellington IC	N2822 JM–F	Training
F/S J W Biggs RCAF	+	T/o Lossiemouth for night flying. Crashed into
P/O F F Ross	+	the Moray Firth, 2200, 6 miles N of the airfield.
Sgt R W Sherwin	+	All are commemorated on the Runnymede Memorial.
F/S F H R Wright RCAF	+	Sgt Sherwin was an Associate of the Royal
F/S E T O'Neil RCAF	+	Institute of British Architects.

21 OTU		Wellington IC	X9942	Training
Sgt C A O'Halloran RNZAF	+	T/o 2115 Moreton-in-Marsh but while banking
Sgt E D Sale RNZAF	+	at 200 feet, lost control and at 2117 smashed
F/S D McM Gilmour RCAF	+	into trees near Sezincote, a Gloucestershire
Sgt W F Carey	+	village some 2 miles WSW of the airfield.
Sgt G H Bennett	+	Four were laid to rest in Moreton-in-Marsh

New Cemetery, while the tail gunner was taken back to his home town. Eight days later, the O'Halloran's lost another son when Sgt William Peter O'Halloran RNZAF died while flying with 1651 HCU.

6 Sep   **26 OTU**   **Wellington IC**   **Z1073**   **Training**
1942   Sgt J H Bond   inj   T/o Little Horwood for night dual. Crashed
         Sgt E W Cox   inj   circa 0440 after overshooting the airfield.
                                   inj   This was the unit's first accident since a
                                   inj   detachment arrived at Little Horwood three
                                         days previous. Sgt Cox later converted to
Halifaxes and was killed on 17 April 1943 while serving with 51 Squadron (see
Bomber Command Losses, Volume 4, page 110).

6– 7 Sep   **10 OTU**   **Whitley V**   **AD669**   **Training**
1942   P/O W E Hinchcliffe RCAF   inj   T/o 2045 Abingdon for a night navigation sortie
                                       which took the crew northwards to Scotland. At
around 0300, having lost engine power, the crew attempted to land at Charterhall
airfield but undershot the approach, wrecking the Whitley in the process. On
23-24 August 1943, P/O Hinchcliffe RCAF, now an Avro Lancaster pilot and serving
with 426 Squadron, was posted missing from operations over Berlin (see Bomber
Command Losses, Volume 4, page 287).

7 Sep   **22 OTU**   **Wellington IC**   **HF865**   **Training**
1942   F/S P N Templeton RCAF   +   T/o Stratford-upon-Avon for a night cross-
         F/S G B Robb RCAF   +   country. Crashed 2320 after losing power and
         Sgt A J Temple RCAF   +   appearing to stall in a right hand bank, a mile
         Sgt F H Downland RCAF   +   to the E of Stratton Audley, 3 miles NNE from
         Sgt R A Jackson RCAF   +   Bicester, Oxfordshire. All were laid to rest
                                         in Bicester Cemetery. Their American born
skipper was the nineteen year-old son of Judge R H Templeton of Wellington,
Texas. His near namesake, Sgt Temple RCAF, was a Bachelor of Science.

7– 8 Sep   **20 OTU**   **Wellington IC**   **T2913 ZT–B**   **Training**
1942   Sgt C Moulds   inj   T/o 1955 Lossiemouth for a combined night
         F/L T V G Blanks   inj   navigation and bombing exercise. Ran low
         Sgt R H Mason   inj   on fuel, leading to loss of power from the
         F/S H Paul   inj   starboard engine. Crashed 0345 at Longmore
         Sgt G J MacMillan RCAF   inj   some 5 miles SW of Elgin, Moray. All were
         Sgt A Clark   inj   taken to Dr. Gray's Hospital, where, it is
         P/O J Gwyther   inj   reported, surgeons amputated the air bomber's
                                         right leg. F/S Paul, who sustained massive
head injuries, died within twenty-four hours; he is buried in Dundee Western
Necropolis (or Balgay Cemetery).

8 Sep   **16 OTU**   **Wellington IC**   **DV830**   **Training**
1942   P/O H A Larkin   inj   T/o 1100 Upper Heyford for a combined bombing
                                     inj   and navigation exercise. During the flight, the
                                     inj   port engine caught fire and in the ensuing
                                         forced-landing at 1450, the Wellington hit
         Sgt J H Hall   +   a tree and crashed near Rednal airfield, some
                                         five miles ESE of Oswestry, Shropshire. Reports
indicate that the starboard wing had lost some of its covering, prior to the
crash. Sgt Hall of Motherwell in Lanarkshire lies in Oswestry General Cemetery.
Many thousands of miles away, a P/O E L Hall, an observer with 209 Squadron,
died this same day; he rests on Madagascar in Diego Suarez War Cemetery.

9 Sep   **10 OTU Det**   **Whitley V**   **Z6638**   **Op: AS Patrol**
1942   F/S R O O Warren RCAF   T/o St. Eval. Shortly before 1640, the starboard
                                       motor caught fire and the crew were obliged to
ditch in the Bristol Channel, towards the Welsh coast. A cracked oil cooler is
thought to have been the cause of the blaze. Tragically, F/S Warren RCAF was
destined to be lost, with his crew, from a similar sortie later in the month.

         25 OTU   **Wellington IC**   **DV433**   **–M1**   **Training**
         Sgt R V Turpitt   +   T/o 2325 Finningley for night circuit training.
         P/O P W Dormon   +   Landed five minutes later, but rather heavily,
         Sgt L H Davies   +   and Sgt Turpitt attempted to go round again.
         Sgt D C A P R Denville   +   At the time, the wind was rather light and
                                         though the Wellington lifted from the runway,
it flew into trees nearby having failed to gain altitude. All are buried in
cemeteries scattered across England and Wales. Although the outcome was fatal,
the Court of Inquiry concluded that the pilot made the correct decision in
electing to overshoot.

10 Sep
1942

21 OTU　　　　　**Wellington IC**　**X9952**　　　　　**Ground**
While being started up at 2210 in readiness
for night flying from Edgehill, a fire broke out in one of the carburettors
and when the engine backfired, the bomber burst into flames. Held by the unit
for six days less than a full year, it had amassed 370.00 flying hours.

24 OTU　　　　　**Whitley V**　**BD279**　　　　　**Training**
Sgt D V Childers RCAF　　　　　　　　T/o 2010 Honeybourne for a night navigation
Sgt Adams　　　　　　　　　　inj　sortie. About two hours or so into the flight,
　　　　　　　　　　　　　　　　　　the starboard engine emitted a shower of sparks
and sheets of flame quickly followed. An SOS was transmitted and Hemswell
responded, sending at least three QDMs which, although helpful in giving the
crew a course to steer, were nullified by the flare path remaining unlit.
Unable to pick out the airfield, the crew baled out leaving their aircraft
to crash twixt 2 and 3 miles SW of Hemswell, Lincolnshire. Sgt Adams sprained
his ankle and also needed treatment for mild concussion.

10-11 Sep
1942

10 OTU　　　　　**Whitley V**　**BD193**　**-Q**　　　　　**Op: Düsseldorf**
Sgt A J Adams　　　　　　　　　　+　T/o 2022 Stanton Harcourt. Crashed 0200 on its
Sgt J Sweeney　　　　　　　　　　+　return to base. Sgt Adams rests in Brookwood
Sgt I L Wethered　　　　　　　　+　Military Cemetery, the others who perished were
Sgt T J Willcocks　　　　　　　+　taken to their home towns, Sgt Sweeney being
Sgt F B B Bayly　　　　　　　　　+　cremated at Manchester Crematorium.

11 OTU　　　　　**Wellington IC**　**DV890 OP-G**　　　　　**Op: Düsseldorf**
Sgt N J Rowe RNZAF　　　　　　　+　T/o 2036 Bassingbourn using call sign 6UNG. Shot
Sgt J Inskip RNZAF　　　　　　　+　down at Gelsenkirchen-Bismarck, where all were
Sgt W A O'Malley RNZAF　　　　+　first buried on 14 September. Since 1945, their
Sgt T P Hurley RNZAF　　　　　+　remains have been taken to the Reichswald Forest
Sgt M D Gorton　　　　　　　　　+　War Cemetery. For the raid on Köln, at the end
　　　　　　　　　　　　　　　　　　of May 1942, this aircraft had been coded TX-E.

11 OTU　　　　　**Wellington IC**　**DV930 TX-O Bar**　　　　　**Op: Düsseldorf**
Sgt T F Munro RNZAF　　　　　　+　T/o 2105 Steeple Morden using call sign GC80 Bar.
Sgt J F Stanley RNZAF　　　　+　Turned back and crashed 2345 in the stack yard at
Sgt K H Vigers　　　　　　　　　+　Herne Hill Farm, Chediston, 2 miles NW from
Sgt A S Renwick　　　　　　　inj　Halesworth, Suffolk. Sgt Renwick sustained
Sgt R W Freeman　　　　　　　　+　massive injuries and died within a few hours of
　　　　　　　　　　　　　　　　　　the tragedy. The two RNZAF airmen (both hailed
from Christchurch, Canterbury) are buried in Ipswich Cemetery, the others rest
in their home towns. It is likely that the funeral service for Sgt Vigers was
conducted by his father, the Revd Edgar Hall Vigers MA, whose home was at Abbots
Ripton, a mere stone's throw from where his son lies at Little Stukely.

14 OTU　　　　　**Hampden I**　**L4131 PL-A**　　　　　**Op: Düsseldorf**
F/S J C Kerr RCAF　　　　　　　+　T/o 2020 Cottesmore. Crashed at Marl, where all
Sgt D H Chapman RCAF　　　　　+　were initially laid to rest. Their graves are
F/S W O Anderson RCAF　　　　+　now located in the Reichswald Forest War Cemetery.
Sgt W D Deatherage RCAF　　　+

16 OTU　　　　　**Wellington IC**　**R1297 JS-R**　　　　　**Op: Düsseldorf**
W/O W S Harrison RAAF　　　pow　T/o 2100 Upper Heyford. Hit by flak while flying
F/L E J Seaman　　　　　　　pow　at 10,000 feet in the vicinity of the target.
W/O E Lockwood　　　　　　　pow
F/S P N Faber　　　　　　　　pow
W/O F A A Browne　　　　　　pow

16 OTU　　　　　**Wellington IC**　**R1346 JS-F**　　　　　**Op: Düsseldorf**
Sgt K J Johnson RNZAF　　　　　　T/o 2027 Upper Heyford. Turned back early, due
Sgt I F Leng　　　　　　　　　　to engine trouble and was obliged to ditch at
Sgt A Boswell　　　　　　　　　　approximately 2330, some 500 yards from the
Sgt B A Rogers RCAF　　　　　+　sluice gates at Holland-on-Sea, Essex. Of the
Sgt A E Sedin　　　　　　　　　+　two who died, Sgt Rogers RCAF lies in Ipswich
Cemetery, having been brought here from Clacton
Mortuary, while panel 93 of the Runnymede Memorial perpetuates the name of Sgt
Sedin. It will be recalled that Sgt Johnson RNZAF had been involved in a crash
on 6 September (see page 151). Converted to Lancasters, he was nearing the end
of his first tour of operations (with 44 Squadron) when he failed to return from
Berlin (see Bomber Command Losses, Volume 4, page 83).

10-11 Sep
1942

16 OTU   **Wellington IC**   **T2606 JS-Y**   **Op: Düsseldorf**

W/O D G Oxenham RAAF	pow
W/O B Bing	pow
W/O F Dean	pow
F/S L Waterson	pow
F/S P Martin	pow

T/o 2117 Upper Heyford. Believed to have been shot down by Ofw Heinz Strüning, falling into the Bleiswijksepolder N of Rotterdam.

16 OTU   **Wellington IC**   **DV775 KG-O**   **Op: Düsseldorf**

WO2 K C Bonter RCAF	pow
P/O A H Childs	+
W/O R J Harvey	pow
F/S D R Smith RCAF	+
F/S R C Daoust RCAF	+

T/o 2037 Upper Heyford. Ditched in the North Sea. On 16 September, the two survivors were found in their dinghy and taken into captivity. Two bodies were later washed ashore; P/O Childs is buried in Bergen General Cemetery, Holland, F/S Smith RCAF rests in Germany at Kiel War Cemetery, while F/S Daoust RCAF is commemorated on the Runnymede Memorial.

16 OTU   **Wellington IC**   **HX365 XG-N**   **Op: Düsseldorf**

F/S J F Irvine RCAF	+
Sgt W D Carrick	+
Sgt J F Deaton	+
Sgt H Wright	+
Sgt G R Harboard	+

T/o 2051 Upper Heyford. Lost without trace. All are commemorated on the Runnymede Memorial.

20 OTU   **Wellington IC**   **T2561**   **Op: Düsseldorf**

Sgt C A Sherman RCAF	+
Sgt E Hilton	+
Sgt A Nicholas	+
Sgt E T Briggs	+
F/S F W Gennett RCAF	+

T/o Elsham Wolds. Crashed near Elsendorp (Noord Brabant), 20 km NNE of Helmond, Holland. All were buried in Eindhoven (Woensel) General Cemetery, since when the bodies of the two RCAF members of crew have been transferred to the Canadian War Cemetery at Groesbeek. It is noted that F/S Gennett RCAF was an American from Bedford, Indiana.

22 OTU   **Wellington IC**   **R1616**   **Op: Düsseldorf**

F/S J D Williams RCAF	+
P/O W T B McBratney RCAF	+
Sgt W T Cranna RCAF	+
Sgt C H L Bell RCAF	+
F/S R W Hughes RCAF	+

T/o 2005 Stratford-upon-Avon. Shot down by a night-fighter and crashed at around 2345 near Biervliet (Zeeland), Holland. All are buried in Vlissingen Northern Cemetery. This particular Wellington had amassed 533.45 flying hours since its acceptance at 46 MU Lossiemouth on 6 March 1941. The total is remarkable in that R1616 was badly damaged on operations in late July 1941 (while on the strength of 304 Squadron), spending the best part of the next four months undergoing repairs. Issued to 22 OTU on 18 November 1941, the Wellington was again out of commission for a month in the spring, following a flying accident.

22 OTU   **Wellington IC**   **X9932**   **Op: Düsseldorf**

F/S D L Pablo RCAF	+
Sgt C E Pollard RCAF	+
P/O C R Sullivan RCAF	+
F/S W H Johnson RCAF	+
Sgt E S McCasky RCAF	+

T/o 2030 Stratford-upon-Avon. All are buried in the Reichswald Forest War Cemetery. F/S Pablo, serving with the RCAF, was an American from Emo in Montana.

25 OTU   **Wellington III**   **Z1725 -M**   **Op: Düsseldorf**

F/S M K Matson RCAF	+
F/S J H Charron RCAF	+
Sgt S T Southgate	+
F/S F R Molton	+
Sgt H W Hancock	+

T/o 2024 Finningley. Crashed 2255 at Dortmund-Ellinghausen. All were buried on 15 September in the Hauptfriedhof (Am Gottesacker), but since the cessation of hostilities their remains have been taken to the Reichswald Forest War Cemetery.

25 OTU   **Wellington III**   **BJ987 -L**   **Op: Düsseldorf**

F/S R E Bertram RCAF	+
F/S C J Eggleton RCAF	+
F/S F J Gallagher RCAF	+
F/S R M George RCAF	+
P/O J R Agar	+

T/o 2022 Finningley. Presumed down in the sea off Belgium. F/S Bertram RCAF is buried in the Canadian War Cemetery at Adegem, at Oostduinkerke Communal Cemetery are the graves of F/S Eggleton RCAF and P/O Agar, the former being commemorated by a special memorial Type C, while two are perpetuated on panel 104 of the Runnymede Memorial.

10-11 Sep   **26 OTU**   **Wellington IC**   **DV703**   **—C**   **Op: Düsseldorf**
1942   Sgt C C Ogilvie RAAF   +   T/o 2056 Wing armed with 4 x 500lb GP bombs.
       W/O L Hedley   pow   Attacked from below by a night-fighter whose
       P/O J M'Ilveen   +   cannon shells severed petrol and oil pipes and
       Sgt J W Gardner   +   set light to the fuselage. Communication between
       F/S J B Higginson RCAF   +   the crew was impossible as the blaze immediately
                                         destroyed the intercom system. W/O Hedley managed
to speak to his skipper, who told him to bale out. He did so, though lost
consciousness in the process. Out of control, the Wellington hit the ground at
around 0015, some 500 metres NW of Overhetfeld, on the NW side of Niederkrüchten.
Those who died are now buried in Rheinberg War Cemetery. Eventually taken to
Stalag VIIIB, W/O Hedley gave a statement on 30 April 1943, to RSM S Sherriff,
the Camp Leader, outlining his recollections of the last moments of this sortie.

Note. I am greatly indebted to Brian Ogilvie of Australia, whose late uncle
was the gallant skipper of this aircraft, for much of the information set out
in the above summary.

       26 OTU   **Wellington IC**   **DV867**   **—E**   **Op: Düsseldorf**
       Sgt A I L Downs RAAF   +   T/o 2100 Wing similarly armed. Shot down at 0032
       Sgt J J Kearns   +   by Uffz Fritz Schellwatt, NJG1, crashing between
       Sgt R H Kirkpatrick   +   Stramproy and Hunsel (Limburg), two small
       Sgt J W Rowling   +   villages 8 km SSE and 10 km SE respectively of
       Sgt T P Allenby RCAF   +   Weert, Holland. All were laid to rest at Venlo,
                                         since when their remains have been reinterred at
Jonkerbos War Cemetery. Sgt Allenby RCAF was an American from Saratoga Springs
in New York State. Sgt Kearns had previously served in the army.

11 Sep   **15 OTU**   **Wellington IC**   **HE102**   **Training**
1942   P/O A C Peet   inj   T/o 2005 Hampstead Norris for night circuits
       Sgt E F Hicks   inj   and landings. At 2330, the bomber took off in
                           inj   a stalled attitude, whereupon the undercarriage
                           inj   and flaps were raised. Hitting the ground, the
                           inj   Wellington caught fire.

       17 OTU   **Blenheim IV**   **L4891**   **Air Sea Rescue**
       Sgt B M Harvey RCAF   T/o 1640 Upwood but swung out of control, veered
                                  off the runway and collided with a tractor. Soon
after this incident, Sgt Harvey RCAF (an American from Waltham, Massachusetts)
was posted to fly Venturas with 464 Squadron. On 6 December 1942, his aircraft
was one of the sixteen Bomber Command losses from the daylight strike on the
Phillips works at Eindhoven (see Bomber Command Losses, Volume 3, pages 269-270).

       17 OTU   **Blenheim IV**   **R3591**   **Training**
       W/C C C Hodder AFC   inj   T/o 1330 Upwood but the starboard engine cut and
                           inj   the Blenheim was forced-landed, virtually in line
                           inj   with the runway and a mile W of the airfield, in
                                  the approved manner. Having made a good recovery
from his injuries, W/C Hodder was posted to command 180 Squadron at Foulsham, but
lost his life on 22 January 1943, when his Mitchell was shot down off the Belgian
coast (see Bomber Command Losses, Volume 4, page 25).

       18 OTU   **Wellington IC**   **R3280**   **Training**
       Sgt C Swiatkowski PAF   +   T/o Bramcote for a night navigation exercise.
       F/O W Szumbarski PAF   +   Last heard sending, by wireless, an SOS at 2347,
       Sgt K Paszkot PAF   +   the signal bearing suggesting the crew were over
       Sgt J Abraham PAF   +   the Irish Sea and in the vicinity of the Isle of
       Sgt K Oles PAF   +   Man. Despite a search, nothing was found and
                                  all are commemorated on the Northolt Memorial.

11-12 Sep   **24 OTU**   **Whitley V**   **BD391**   **Training**
1942   P/O Oakes   T/o 1945 Honeybourne for a night cross-country.
                                  Although the crew returned to base on completion
of the exercise, they were unable to land due to the weather conditions. Low on
petrol, the Whitley was force-landed at 0220 on the Relief Landing Ground at
Windrush, 16 miles ESE of Cheltenham, Gloucestershire. Earlier, Abingdon had
tried to give assistance, but had not been successful.

13 Sep   **28 OTU**   **DH94 Moth Minor AW151 (G-AFMZ)**   **Unknown**
1942

T/o Wymeswold but on return to base, and landing, its undercarriage collapsed. Impressed from the Civil Register on 26 June 1940, this aircraft had passed through a number of units prior to its arrival at Wymeswold on 6 September 1942. Following the accident, here described, it was sent to a de Havilland repair facility but was struck off charge on 5 March 1943. It held the dubious distinction of being the first aircraft to be written off by the unit since its formation on 16 May, four months previous.

13-14 Sep   **10 OTU**   **Whitley V BD275 -Y**   **Op: Bremen**
1942

W/O C B P Nind RAAF	pow	T/o 2348 Abingdon. Twenty year old Sgt Gosden
W/O S Jolly	pow	from Hythe in Kent is buried in Rheinberg War
Sgt D C Gosden	+	Cemetery. In captivity, W/O Nind RAAF exchanged
F/S J Tweddle	pow	identities with a P Garner, described as being a
F/S F J R Eminson	pow	member of the Australian Imperial Force.

11 OTU   **Wellington IC X3169 KJ-X**   **Op: Bremen**

F/L M E S Dickenson	pow	T/o 2341 Steeple Morden using call sign 3ZOX.
W/O G H Dow RNZAF	pow	
W/O H C M Jarvis	pow	
W/O J Akehurst	pow	
W/O R S Davey	pow	

11 OTU   **Wellington IC X9744 KJ-S**   **Op: Bremen**

S/L R A Nicholson	pow	T/o 0002 Steeple Morden using call sign 3ZOS.
F/L G T Hunt	pow	Abandoned in the vicinity of Papenburg, Germany,
Sgt O M Jameson	pow	after being by hit by flak.
W/O R O Riddle	pow	
W/O M W E Wild	pow	

14 OTU   **Hampden I L4109 GL-S**   **Op: Bremen**

F/S R Grabek RCAF	+	T/o 2354 Cottesmore. Crashed near Stadskanaal
Sgt G E C Coldron RCAF	+	in the Province of Groningen, 26 km E of Assen,
WO2 R Carlson RCAF	pow	Holland. The two airmen who died are buried in
WO2 T F Needham RCAF	pow	Onstwedde (Stadskanaal) General Cemetery.

14 OTU   **Hampden I AD845 GL-B Bar**   **Op: Bremen**

Sgt H D Beames		T/o 0002 Cottesmore. Crashed 0625, on return
Sgt D McKay		to base, coming down in a field SSW of the
Sgt M B Anderson		airfield having run out of fuel. This was
Sgt W R Jordan		the last Hampden to be written off from Bomber
		Command under operational circumstances.

Note. I very much suspect that the captain of the above crew, Sgt H D Beames was a Canadian. If this is the case, then he was subsequently commissioned and by the winter of 1943-1944, was flying Halifaxes with 434 Squadron. On 19-20 February 1944, he participated in the infamous Leipzig raid and was shot down, outbound, by a night-fighter (see Bomber Command Losses, Volume 5, page 91). He is buried in Hannover War Cemetery.

16 OTU   **Wellington IC X9660**   **Op: Bremen**

P/O P S Duff DFC RNZAF	+	T/o Upper Heyford. Last heard, transmitting
P/O D M Wilson	+	by wireless, at 0500 and, presumably, on the
Sgt R G Nicholls	+	return flight. All are commemorated on the
Sgt R A Salchenberger RCAF	+	Runnymede Memorial. P/O Duff RNZAF had flown
Sgt T H Freestone	+	an operational tour with 106 Squadron, his
		navigator, P/O Wilson, hailed from Rakeny,
		Co. Dublin in the Republic of Ireland.

19 OTU   **Whitley V BD256**   **Training**

Sgt E I Johnston RCAF		T/o 2150 Kinloss for a night cross-country.

During the sortie, the wireless equipment failed and the crew became hopelessly lost. At 0530, by which time their aircraft was low on petrol, they took to their parachutes, the Whitley coming down at Powblack Farm, Kippen, 9 miles W of Stirling. Sgt Johnston RCAF did not, as may have been expected, proceed to a 4 Group squadron but converted to Lancasters and died in the service of 49 Squadron on 20-21 December 1942 (see Bomber Command Losses, Volume 3, page 281).

13–14 Sep   **21 OTU**   **Wellington IC**   **HE116 SJ-B**   **Op: Bremen**
1942

P/O M Holub RCAF	+
Sgt B L Hancock	+
F/S W Pedersen RCAF	+
Sgt S Davies	+
Sgt R S C Plowright	+
Sgt R F Stay	+

T/o 2340 Edgehill. Presumed lost over the North Sea. Three bodies were later washed ashore and taken for burial in cemeteries both in Holland and Denmark. Their three companions are commemorated on the Runnymede Memorial. P/O Holub RCAF had survived at least two incidents while undergoing training as page 147 testifies.

22 OTU   **Wellington IC**   **R1588**   **Op: Bremen**

P/O F H de Nevers RCAF	+
P/O R G Hill RCAF	+
F/S P Sutherland RCAF	+
Sgt H F MacArthur RCAF	+
F/S R H Galipeau RCAF	+

T/o 2327 Stratford-upon-Avon. Presumed lost over the North Sea. The body of F/S Galipeau RCAF, an American from Coleraine, Minnesota, was found on Romo Island where he was buried, that same day, 20 October 1942, in Kirkeby Cemetery. His fellow countryman, Sgt MacArthur of Braintree, Massachusetts, is commemorated with the rest of the crew on the Runnymede Memorial.

22 OTU   **Wellington IC**   **R1658**   **Op: Bremen**

Sgt J H Davies	+
Sgt G L Dixon RCAF	+
F/S J T Reid RCAF	+
Sgt R E Brown RCAF	+
F/S G I Fee RCAF	+

T/o 2336 Gaydon. Lost without trace. All are commemorated on the Runnymede Memorial.

22 OTU   **Wellington IC**   **HD991**   **Op: Bremen**

Sgt G S Bickerton RCAF	+
P/O D C King RCAF	+
F/L W J Shaver RCAF	pow
Sgt J H Dew	pow
F/S D Murray RCAF	+

T/o Stratford-upon-Avon. Claimed by Lt Lothar Link, II./NJG2 at 0255 near Ramspol (Overijssel) and to the NW of Kampen, Holland. Those who lost their lives are buried in Amersfoort (Oud Leusden) General Cemetery.

26 OTU   **Wellington IC**   **X9786**   **-F**   **Op: Bremen**

P/O R L Hage	+
Sgt K D Jones	+
Sgt A K Smith	+
Sgt D Fisher	+
WO2 J A Gartland RCAF	pow

T/o 2353 Wing carrying 4 x 500lb GP bombs. Shot down at 0548 by Hptm Wilhelm Dorman, III./NJG1, plunging into the IJsselmeer, some 2 km W of Elburg. Those who died are buried in the New Eastern Cemetery at Amsterdam. P/O Hage was an American, serving with the Volunteer Reserve, from Missoula in western Montana.

27 OTU   **Wellington IC**   **L7815**   **Op: Bremen**

Sgt W J P Fletcher RAAF	+
Sgt J A Turnbull RAAF	+
Sgt F W Lewis	+
Sgt J G Milne RAAF	+
Sgt F Thompson	+

T/o 2331 Lichfield carrying 4 x 500lb GP bombs. Within minutes of lifting off, the port engine began to falter and the crew made an immediate return to base. Tragically, while turning finals, the Wellington spun out of control and crashed. A mere nine minutes had elapsed from the time of their departure. On impact, the aircraft became a mass of flames. The three Australians are buried in Fradley (St. Stephens) Churchyard, while the others were taken back to their home towns. In the aftermath of this accident, a party of ground staff were detailed to mount guard on the wreckage. At 0320, there was a tremendous explosion and when rescuers reached the scene they found the following casualties:

Cpl R M S Zucker	+	Buried Hazelrigg Jewish Cemetery.
LAC K Ward	+	Buried Fradley (St. Stephens) Churchyard.
AC1 C Aveyard	+	Buried Ossett (Holy Trinity) Churchyard.
AC1 A Marten	+	Buried Prestayn (Christ Church) Churchyard.

29 OTU   **Wellington IC**   **R1459**   **Op: Bremen**

P/O J L Munro RNZAF	
P/O F G Rumbles	
Sgt K W Knight	
Sgt P E Pigeon RCAF	
Sgt E S Speight	

T/o 2347 North Luffenham only to crash three minutes later at Empingham, 6 miles E of Oakham when the engines failed. Remarkably, no one was hurt. P/O Munro RNZAF later flew Lancasters with 97 Squadron and 617 Squadron.

14 Sep **19 OTU** **Whitley V** **BD267 UO–K** **Training**
1942 Sgt R A Lockhart RCAF + T/o Kinloss for a navigation exercise. Reported
Sgt R E McRitchie RCAF + to have flown into the sea, circa 1425, some 4
P/O A G Grant + miles off Aberdeen. It is thought the crew were
Sgt J E Holmes + trying to get beneath the cloud base, though it
Sgt R Clarke RCAF + is conceivable that the pilot had lost control
in the thick overcast. Several vessels searched
for survivors, but found no trace. However, three days later, the body of Sgt
Clarke RCAF was recovered by a trawler off Girdle Ness and, it was reported,
his parachute was in the ready position. Along with Sgt Holmes (details of
where he was found have not been entered in unit records), he is buried in
Kinloss Abbey Burial Ground. The others have no known graves.

15 Sep **14 OTU** **Hampden I** **AD740 GL–E** **Training**
1942 F/S A D Cooper RCAF + T/o Cottesmore for night flying practice. During
F/S J A M St. Pierre RCAF + one approach to the runway, the Hampden clipped
Sgt P C Neuls RCAF + a hedge and while trying to go round again the
Sgt Rushford inj bomber stalled and crashed 2336, narrowly missing
a hangar. Those who perished lie in the extension
to Cottesmore (St. Nicholas) Churchyard alongside the crew of a 419 Squadron, aircraft that had crashed nearby earlier in the day (see Bomber Command Losses,
Volume 3, page 216).

16 Sep **11 OTU** **Wellington IC** **DV878** **Training**
1942 Sgt W C Carney T/o Bassingbourn for night flying. While
flying at 2,000 feet, the No. 6 piston in
the port engine broke up and moments later the crew were aware of flames fanning
back from the damaged motor. Attempts to extinguish the blaze by operating the
extinguisher failed and Sgt Carney announced he was having great difficulty in
seeing, due to the now intense glare. However, aided by a running commentary
from his tail gunner (unnamed in the records), he was able to maintain control
and at 0154 he pulled off an excellent forced-landing, in a field, quite close
to the base airfield. Subsequently, both airmen were praised for showing great
initiative in the face of very difficult circumstances.

12 OTU **Wellington III** **BJ728** **Training**
Sgt R G McCarthy RNZAF + T/o Chipping Warden for a night navigation
Sgt W J Ferguson + exercise. At around 0610, while over the town
Sgt D G W Arnold + of Conway in Caernarvonshire, the starboard
Sgt J F S Ritchie + engine failed. A course for base was set but
Sgt A Lyon RCAF inj just over an hour later, the pilot announced
he was going to make a precautionary landing
at Little Rissington in Gloucestershire. However, soon after entering the
circuit, the port engine faltered and at 0710 the Wellington came down at
Lower Farm, Milton-under-Wychwood and burst into flames. Crash and Rescue:

Mr Roberts A civilian clerk, working near the scene of
the crash, ran to the spot and found the
tail gunner, Sgt Lyons RCAF, lying amidst the wreckage of the rear fuselage
and pulled him clear. Apparently, he (Sgt Lyon) had been trying to find his
colleagues trapped in the shattered aeroplane. Suffering from second degree
burns, the young Canadian was taken to SSQ Little Rissington and thence by
air ambulance to Princess Mary's Hospital, Halton. Sgt McCarthy RNZAF and
Sgt Ferguson rest in Little Rissington (St. Peter) Churchyard, while Sgt
Arnold (he was a schoolmaster) and Sgt Ritchie were taken to their home towns.

22 OTU **Wellington IC** **X9671** **Air Test**
P/O A J Fawcett RCAF + T/o 1519 Stratford-upon-Avon for a night flying
WO1 J W O'Brien RCAF + test ahead of the night's scheduled operation
F/S F A C Macauley RCAF + to Essen. Climbed normally to around 800 feet
P/O H Casimiri RCAF + but while banking to the left, suddenly began to
F/S D H Halstead RCAF + dive and while being recovered the port wing and
AC1 L Holloway + tail section broke off. Totally out of control,
AC2 D McMillan + the bomber smashed onto the Dorsington road near
Pebworth, a village just inside the border with
Worcestershire and about 6 miles SW of the airfield. Five lie in Evesham Cemetery
but F/S Macauley RCAF of Nassau in the Bahamas was taken to Bexhill Cemetery (in
They Shall Grow Not Old he is shown as hailing from Newstead Paget on Bermuda).
AC2 McMillan is buried in Airdrie (St. Joseph's) Roman Catholic Cemetery.

16–17 Sep	10 OTU	**Whitley V**	P4931	—J		**Op: Essen**

16–17 Sep
1942

10 OTU   **Whitley V** P4931   —J   **Op: Essen**

W/O L A Death RNZAF	pow
F/L W L Merryfield	pow
F/S C C Simonson RCAF	pow
WO2 A Restivo RCAF	pow
F/L W L Kell RCAF	pow

T/o 2013 Abingdon. Heard on wireless at 0128 transmitting an SOS signal. Came down, soon afterwards, in the North Sea some 20 km off Domburg (Zeeland), Holland. This was the last Whitley to be reported missing from a bombing operation over Germany, though 10 OTU were to lose a considerable number of their aircraft and crews during anti-submarine patrols over the Bay of Biscay and in the Western Approaches.

11 OTU   **Wellington IC** Z1108 TX–K   **Op: Essen**

P/O W A Hoskins RNZAF	+
P/O G C R Goodwin RNZAF	+
Sgt J L M Illingworth	+
Sgt R W Michelin	+
Sgt G E Charlesworth	+

T/o 2029 Steeple Morden using call sign 5Q9K. Crashed at Dinslaken on the E bank of the Rhine some 15 km NNW of Duisburg. All were buried in the Nordfriedhof at Düsseldorf, though their graves are now in the Reichswald Forest War Cemetery.

11 OTU   **Wellington IC** DV480 OP–N Bar   **Op: Essen**

P/O I A Grant RNZAF	+
P/O J L Speedy RNZAF	+
P/O R H Groom	+
Sgt S Swain	+
Sgt W Buckley	+

T/o 2030 Bassingbourn using call sign 5CUN Bar. Crashed in the North Sea. Four are buried in Dutch cemeteries, while Sgt Buckley rests at Heverlee War Cemetery, Belgium, thus suggesting he left the aircraft well before the crash.

11 OTU   **Wellington IC** DV612 OP–L   **Op: Essen**

F/O V D Benefield RNZAF	+
W/O N F James	pow
W/O J Longden	pow
Sgt E J Outen RNZAF	+
W/O F T Hooper	pow

T/o 2012 Bassingbourn using call sign 5CUL. Coned by searchlights while flying at 10,000 feet. Hit by flak, the Wellington fell near Duisburg. The two airmen who died are buried in the Reichswald Forest War Cemetery.

12 OTU   **Wellington III** BJ650   **Op: Essen**

F/L M B Mallet	+
Sgt J H Evans	+
Sgt S C Wedgwood	+
Sgt V F Vinnicombe	+
Sgt J L La Bossiere RCAF	+

T/o 2024 Chipping Warden. Intercepted by a night-fighter and sent down to crash in a swimming pool at Veldhoven (Noord Brabant), six km SW of Eindhoven, Holland. Three are buried in Woensel General Cemetery, while the last two named rest in the Canadian War Cemetery at Groesbeek. Their eta at Essen had been scheduled for 2220.

12 OTU   **Wellington III** BJ730   **Op: Essen**

WO2 C W Hall RCAF	+
Sgt D C Marsh	+
P/O F J Adams	+
Sgt N Whitfield	+
Sgt G M Caldwell RCAF	+

T/o 2026 Chipping Warden scheduled to reach the target by 2222. All rest in Rheinberg War Cemetery. Eighteen year old Sgt Marsh was the stepson of Wilfred Charles Girdler of Ashtead in Surrey.

15 OTU   **Wellington IC** N2778   **Op: Essen**

F/S S B Robson RCAF	+
Sgt J A J D Hatton	+
P/O J S Shaw	+
Sgt G E Jones	+
F/S H D Van Norman RCAF	+
Sgt T A Drew RCAF	+

T/o 2014 Harwell. All now lie in the Reichswald Forest War Cemetery. P/O Shaw had gained a Bachelor of Science degree.

15 OTU   **Wellington IC** X9920   **Op: Essen**

Sgt W J Nobbs	+
Sgt T J Fraser	+
Sgt J H Stirk	+
F/S D Miller RNZAF	+
Sgt F K A Seals	+
Sgt R G Ware	+

T/o 2002 Harwell. Shot down by Lt Eberhard Gardiewski, II./NJG2, crashing 0012 onto land owned by Mr Ligthart twixt Heiloo and Alkmaar in Noord Holland. All rest in Bergen General Cemetery. It is noted that Sgt Seals had belonged to the pre-war Auxiliary Air Force.

Note. To the best of the author's knowledge, these were the last Wellingtons reported missing from operations by 15 OTU. In a little under two-and-a-half years of service, the unit had lost one aircraft on a Nickel sortie over France and seven in the course of the recent spate of bombing operations (one of these being destroyed in a take-off accident).

16–17 Sep 1942	21 OTU	Wellington IC	HE110 SJ–Q	Op: Essen

P/O S W Dodge + T/o 1953 Edgehill. Shot down 0123 by Oblt Walter
Sgt H C Roake + Barte, 4./NJG1, crashing at Spalbeek (Limburg),
P/O C C Hendley-Cross + eight km WSW of Hasselt, Belgium. All rest in
Sgt K D Downing + Heverlee War Cemetery. P/O Dodge was an American
Sgt A E Confait + from Redwood City, California, while Sgt Confait
Sgt K J Smith + came from the Seychelles.

22 OTU	Wellington IC	Z1084	Op: Essen

F/L J Dawson DFC + T/o 1955 Stratford-upon-Avon. Shot down near
WO1 P S O Brichta DFM RCAF + Ahaus, 21 km NW of Coesfeld. All are buried
F/S W K Hughes + in the Reichswald Forest War Cemetery. WO1
WO1 L J Lemoine RCAF + Brichta RCAF had recently completed a tour of
P/O G C Goold RCAF + operations with 49 Squadron and details of his
award were Gazetted on 22 September, a little
under a week since he had been posted missing. His father, Lt Geoffrey J O
Brichta of the 2nd Canadian Mounted Rifles (British Columbia Regiment) had lost
his life in France on 16 March 1917, whilst attached to 16 Squadron RFC. He is
buried in the extension to Barlin Communal Cemetery. Designed by the celebrated
British architect, Sir Edwin Lutyens, this extension is the resting place for
one-thousand-and-ninety-four Commonwealth servicemen from the First World War.

23 OTU	Wellington III	X3799 –E	Op: Essen

F/S W C McBean RCAF + T/o 2018 Pershore. Those who lost their lives
F/S T Baillie RCAF + are buried in Rheinberg War Cemetery.
WO2 M O Edwards RCAF pow
WO2 A E Parr RCAF pow
F/S J C Carswell RCAF +

23 OTU	Wellington III	Z1730 –J	Op: Essen

F/S K B Tanner RCAF + T/o 2022 Pershore. Crashed at Baerl near Repelen
F/S J Donaldson RCAF + Lohmansheide near Krefeld, where the crew were
F/S J Needler RCAF + interred in the Hauptfriedhof. Since 1945, their
Sgt J A C Smith RCAF + remains have been taken to the Reichswald Forest
F/S J L Nibblett RCAF + War Cemetery. Sgt Tanner RCAF and F/S Nibblett
RCAF were Americans; the former, a Bachelor of
Arts graduate from the University of Texas, came from Eastland, Texas, while his
tail gunner hailed from Salisbury, Maryland.

23 OTU	Wellington III	BJ720 –U	Op: Essen

F/L T F Tyrrell + T/o 2012 Pershore. All are buried in Rheinberg
F/S D R Philp RCAF + War Cemetery. Serving with the RCAF, F/S Philp
Sgt A Skinner + was an American from Rochester in New York State.
F/O T W Sutton +
F/S P Stewart +

25 OTU	Wellington III	BJ969 –B	Op: Essen

F/S A F Rees RAAF pow T/o 2026 Finningley. Shot down by a night-
Sgt E A Hall + fighter and crashed near Rheine, where those
Sgt H W Crock + who perished were buried on 22 September. In
Sgt R H Fuller + the years following the peace, their bodies
Sgt J F Oakley + have been exhumed and reinterred in the
Reichswald Forest War Cemetery. Sgt Oakley
came from St. Johns in Newfoundland.

26 OTU	Wellington IC	DV723 –H	Op: Essen

Sgt P L Looney RAAF + T/o 2019 Wing. Lost without trace. All are
Sgt J Clayton + commemorated on the Runnymede Memorial.
Sgt J T Pate +
Sgt A E W Butler +
Sgt C G Calcutt +

26 OTU	Wellington IC	DV941 –G	Op: Essen

Sgt L W Streeter RNZAF + T/o 2029 Wing. Crashed off the coast of Holland.
Sgt W G Archer + Sgt Streeter RNZAF is buried in Noordijk General
Sgt A M Bartlett + Cemetery, while F/S Johnson RCAF lies in the New
F/S D A White RCAF + Eastern Cemetery at Amsterdam. The rest of the
F/S H E Johnson RCAF + crew are commemorated on the Runnymede Memorial.

16–17 Sep   **27 OTU**   **Wellington IC**   **N2782**   **–A**   **Op: Essen**
1942   P/O F Lupton   +   T/o 1949 Lichfield. All are buried in Rheinberg
      W/O M L Pierpoint   +   War Cemetery. Prior to joining the air force,
      P/O A Easton   +   P/O Easton was a police officer serving with the
      P/O E J C Wheble   +   Criminal Investigations Department at Liverpool.
      F/L P G Felce   +

      27 OTU   **Wellington IC**   **X9876**   **–B**   **Op: Essen**
      P/O R A Curle   T/o 1948 Lichfield. While over the target, a
      P/O E C Crapp RAAF   burst of flak destroyed the aircraft's port
      P/O R H Chapman RAAF   aileron. Displaying commendable airmanship,
      P/O H Riding RAAF   P/O Curle regained the south coast, by which
      Sgt G W Durdin RAAF   time the Wellington was almost impossible to
                                           control. Thus, at 0320, the order to bale out
was given, leaving the bomber to crash at Collingbourne Ducis, 3 miles N of
Tidworth, Wiltshire. Like so many crews that had survived a close brush with
death, their demise came within a few months. P/O Chapman RAAF went to 460
Squadron and, on 25 October 1942, while on leave in Torquay, died when an
enemy bomb hit the hotel in which he was staying. His four companions survived
a little longer, but all were killed on 4–5 March 1943 while flying with 100
Squadron (see Bomber Command Losses, Volume 4, page 60).

Note. The raid on Essen marked the end of the training units involvement in
Main Force operations, but before moving on to the next chapter, it is worth
presenting a table showing the losses sustained by these establishments in
the eight major attacks. Excluding the two Blenheim units, of the eighteen
that participated, only 28 OTU at Wymeswold emerged with a clean sheet.

Unit	Köln	Essen	Bremen	Hamburg	Düsseldorf	Düsseldorf	Bremen	Essen		
10 OTU		1	4	1		1	1	1	:	9
11 OTU	1	1	3			2	2	3	:	12
12 OTU	1	2	4					2	:	9
14 OTU	3	1			4	1	2		:	11
15 OTU	2	1	2					2	:	7
16 OTU		1	1	2	2	5	1		:	12
18 OTU		1	3						:	4
19 OTU			1						:	1
20 OTU		1	1			1			:	3
21 OTU		1	1		1		1	1	:	5
22 OTU	4		2	2		2	3	1	:	14
23 OTU	1	2	2		1			3	:	9
24 OTU			3		2				:	5
25 OTU	1	1			4	2		1	:	9
26 OTU	4	1	1			2	1	2	:	11
27 OTU			1		2		1	2	:	6
29 OTU							1		:	1
Total	17	13	30	5	16	16	13	18	:	128

Addendum. During the preparation of this chapter, the loss of a 19 OTU Whitley from the
first attack on Bremen was, inadvertently, omitted. The relevant details are:

25–26 Jun   **19 OTU**   **Whitley V**   **Z6730 UO–Z**   **Op: Bremen**
1942   WO2 J J Makarewicz RCAF   pow   T/o 2243 Abingdon. Crashed at Hedwigenkoog,
      W/O L L Brown   pow   five km NNW of Büsum. W/O Hale was amongst a
      W/O R A Hale   pow   batch of airmen that arrived in Liverpool on
      Sgt P Bell   pow   2 February 1945, aboard the Letitia.
      W/O W Henderson   pow

Chapter Four

Training for Victory

17 September 1942 to 5-6 June 1944

The period between mid-September 1942, and the eve of D-Day, witnessed the emergence of a bombing fleet capable of striking at all but the most distance targets in Europe.

Along the way Bomber Command had had its fair share of triumphs and disappointments. In respect of the latter, the mind numbing Battle of Berlin in the winter of 1943-1944 stands out as a particularly hard cross to bear and its culmination in the ill-fated raid on the distant city of Nürnberg was the nadir in Bomber Command's history.

Although Berlin had cost Bomber Command savage losses in both men and material, it had not blunted its ability to any significant degree. Throughout the spring of 1944, under the direction of Supreme Headquarters Allied Expeditionary Forces, Bomber Command struck at every major rail centre in the occupied countries, causing such disruption to services that the Wehrmacht was hindered at practically every turn in their efforts to maintain supplies to their armies defending the strategic areas of Normandy and the Pas de Calais.

The previous year, too, had seen several notable successes, particularly in respect of a series of damaging attacks on industry in the Ruhr, while in the high summer of that same year, Hamburg had been bombed with a ferocity hitherto unseen in the annals of modern aerial warfare.

In no small measure, none of this would have been possible but for the Trojan work carried out by the training establishments, both at home and abroad. By the late summer of 1942, airmen were emerging from the many stages of ab initio and intermediate flying to gather at the Operational Training Units in ever increasing numbers. As it will be remembered, the bomber training units, in 1940, had numbered but eleven; now as autumn 1942 unfurled its rustic colours, this figure had doubled.

Further encouraging signs was the gradual increase in more modern types arriving on stream. During the summer of 1942, several units commenced equipping with Wellington Mk. IIIs (the stalwart Mk. ICs would remain in use until the early months of 1944) and from 1943 onwards, Mk. Xs began to appear as Main Force squadrons became predominantly four-engined formations.

Returning to the autumn of 1942, the long serving Hampdens were withdrawn and when, in the summer of 1943, No. 2 Group left Bomber Command for pastures new, the reason for retaining the Blenheim as a bomber trainer was no longer a requirement. Yet another 1930s'

type was consigned to the history books. For a while yet, the Mk. V Whitley continued to give service and the last examples would not be withdrawn until well after D-Day. It had proven to be an excellent bomber trainer.

In the main, however, the Wellington was the dominant trainer and by the end of the period concerning the chapter, nineteen such units existed (during 1943, three more OTUs had been established, each receiving the Wellington as its principal type).

Additionally, a myriad of other types were introduced to fill specialist training roles and by mid-1943 Martinets were being used in some numbers as gunnery trainers. Hurricanes came on the scene in 1944, to provide crews with a reasonably fast fighter affiliation trainer, while the faithful Anson was still a common sight, plying its trade as a navigation trainer. However, as the months rolled by, their numbers on the bomber units gradually decreased.

Oxfords, too, were held at most units but, as the summaries will show, only No. 14 OTU, at Cottesmore, had the misfortune to lose more than a few.

With the shifting emphasis on training requirements, two of the bomber OTUs extant in September 1942 were disbanded prior to June 1944. First to go was the Yorkshire based No. 25 OTU at Finningley, training ceasing here as early as February 1943. Then, just over a year later, on 15 March 1944, No. 23 OTU at Pershore was closed down. In between these events, No. 81 OTU, a Whitley unit at Whitchurch Heath in Shropshire, was given up to No. 38 Group for airborne forces training in readiness for D-Day.

In addition to the normal run of training, No. 10 OTU, it will be recalled, had in the summer of 1942, detached a sizeable force of Whitleys and crews to St. Eval on the north Cornish coast from whence they had commenced anti-submarine operations over the Bay of Biscay and in the Western Approaches.

In the run-up to Operation Torch (the Allied landings in French North Africa in November 1942), the work of this detachment had provided a tremendous fillip to the far stretched resources of Coastal Command.

However, in the aftermath of the landings, instead of returning to Abingdon, the force was retained until the summer of 1943 and, as a measure of the gruelling business of anti-submarine warfare, the detachment lost no fewer than forty-seven Whitleys in the months covered by this chapter. On their return, many messages of appreciation were signalled to their Abingdon headquarters.

And so, in the wake of a hot summer of bombing operations, the OTUs now reverted to the general run-of-the-mill training programme.

Despite the importance of the past four months in boosting Main Force operations, it had, nonetheless, caused a considerable disruption to the training syllabus. Furthermore, a number of screened personnel, so vital to the needs of the OTUs, had become casualties and their replacement was no easy matter. However, an influx of new personnel arrived to fill the gaps and as autumn gave way to the dark shades of winter, life on these establishments soon resumed the norm.

18 Sep 1942	10 OTU Det	Whitley V	Z6974		Air Test

	Sgt D G Murray RCAF		inj	T/o 1230 St. Eval and crashed almost immediately
	F/S W W Evans RCAF		+	in a welter of flame. F/S Evans RCAF rests in
	AC1 R E L Stevens		+	St. Columb Major Cemetery; AC1 Stevens is buried
	AC2 G P Hunter		+	in Yeovil Cemetery, while AC2 Hunter was taken

home to Scotland for burial at Edinburgh (Newington or Echo Bank) Cemetery. Although very seriously injured, Sgt Murray RCAF recovered and is believed to have survived the war.

	25 OTU	Wellington III	BJ976	-G	Training

	Sgt G Nicol	+	T/o 0040 Bircotes for night bombing practice.
	Sgt W Bakes	+	At around 0130, reportedly having just taken
	Sgt J C Dalton	+	off from Bircotes and climbed to between 200
	Sgt P B E Woodham	+	and 300 feet, flew over the small spur of North
			Nottinghamshire and crashed just inside the

county of Yorkshire at Tickhill. Sgt Woodham of Deal, Kent, was buried in the extension to Finningley (St. Oswald) Churchyard; the others were taken to their home towns.

21 Sep 1942	10 OTU Det	Whitley V	Z6795	JL-W	Op: AS Patrol

	F/L N J Mundell RNZAF	pow	T/o St. Eval. Ran out of fuel and was obliged
	F/S K G D'Arcy	pow	to alight in the sea. All were picked up and
	W/O J F Grier	pow	taken into captivity. Subsequently, the Whitley
	W/O I G Keiller	pow	was recovered, virtually intact, and pictorial
	WO2 E G P Hart RCAF	pow	proof of this is shown in 'RAF Coastal Command
	WO2 E J Christian RCAF	pow	1936-1969' by Chris Ashworth, the original
			photograph having been secured by H Nowarra

and submitted via A S Thomas (another photograph of the Whitley appears on page eleven of The Whitley File by R N Roberts, Air-Britain (Historians) 1986, this illustration being sent via T E Willis). It is suggested that Brest was the most likely recovery point. Of the crew listed above, F/S D'Arcy and WO2 Christian RCAF are not shown in the Allied air forces prisoner of war file (AIR20/2336); it is possible both were repatriated ahead of the final editing of this file in March 1945.

	10 OTU Det	Whitley V	Z9472		Op: AS Patrol

	WO2 R O O Warren RCAF	+	T/o St. Eval. Believed to have been lost in
	P/O B B Cooper	+	the same area as the aircraft summarised above
	Sgt J R Stott	+	but without the same fortuitous outcome for its
	Sgt I J Sims	+	crew. A dramatic change in weather conditions
	Sgt J H Southwell	+	is believed to have caused both crews great
			difficulties and resulted in their aircraft

running out of fuel. All are commemorated on the Runnymede Memorial. It will be recalled that WO2 Warren RCAF, an American from Kansas City, Missouri, had ditched earlier in the month (see page 152). He had recently married Kathleen M Warren of Gorham, Maine.

22 Sep 1942	19 OTU	Whitley V	N1393		Training

	F/O J S M Helme	+	T/o 1058 Forres but the starboard engine cut.
	Sgt L Bacon	+	The crew attempted to go round the circuit but
	Sgt M W Mazier RCAF	+	crashed, downwind, smashing into a Nissen hut
	Sgt G W Catling	+	near C Flight's dispersal, bursting into flames.
	F/S J Simpson DFM	+	Three rest in Kinloss Abbey Burial Ground and
	Sgt W Brown	+	three were claimed by their next of kin. F/S
	Sgt C J Usher	inj	Simpson had flown with 58 Squadron, details of
			his DFM having been Gazetted on 22 August 1941.

24 Sep 1942	18 OTU	Wellington IC	DV708		Training

| | P/O L Krempa PAF | | T/o 2013 Bramcote. Hydraulics failed and crash- |
| | | | landed off the end of the short runway at 2218. |

24 Sep 1942	20 OTU	Wellington I	L4296		Training

F/S H Jackson · T/o Lossiemouth for dual circuits and landings.
Sgt E J Roberts · Landed 1025, awkwardly on one wheel, and in the ensuing crash the bomber was wrecked.

	22 OTU	Wellington IC	DV653		Training

Sgt J W Dunford · T/o Stratford-upon-Avon for a night exercise.
Sgt M R Foran RCAF · + Returned to base and landed, aided by flood lights, at 2336 only to crash into the Watch Office. Sgt Foran RCAF is buried in Stratford-upon-Avon Cemetery.

25 Sep 1942	10 OTU Det	Whitley V	Z6485	—A	Op: AS Patrol

P/O D G Marshall · T/o St. Eval. Shot down over the Bay of Biscay
Sgt J H Bakewell · by, it is likely, a Ju 88. The crew were picked
Sgt E E Chipperfield · up the following day, two being slightly hurt.
Sgt J B Dover
P/O Duffill
Sgt Shirley

	10 OTU	Whitley V	AD667		Training

Sgt P E Cunningham · + · T/o 2052 Abingdon and crashed within moments
Sgt E D Morgan · + · of lifting from the runway. It is thought Sgt
Sgt A T Clemson · + · Cunningham pulled back on the throttles in
Sgt E E Chambers · inj · mistake for the exactor controls. He is buried
AC1 Pippard · inj · in Folkestone New Cemetery; Sgt Morgan was cremated at Enfield Crematorium, while Sgt Clements was laid to rest in Hammersmith New Cemetery.

26 Sep 1942	12 OTU	Wellington III	BJ697	—G	Training

F/S K S H Bird · inj · T/o Chipping Warden for a night cross-country.
Sgt W D Barr · inj · Reported to have flown into high ground at 0030
Sgt W A Fairweather · inj · in the Black Mountains approximately 4 miles N
Sgt J Head · inj · of Abercraf, Brecon. F/S Bird succumbed to his injuries on 29 September; he is buried in Cliddesden (St. Leonard) Churchyard.

	19 OTU	Whitley V	P5075		Training

Sgt B D Mathers · inj · T/o 1205 Kinloss for a navigation exercise. While changing tanks, an engine failed and the crew were obliged to ditch 1435 in Loch Ryan, near Wigtown. Taken to RAF Stranraer, none were too badly hurt.

	24 OTU	Whitley V	BD232		Training

Sgt C A Stuart RNZAF · + · T/o 1918 Honeybourne for a navigation sortie
Sgt V R Smith · + · which involved the crew overflying the Irish
Sgt W R Hughes · + · Sea. At 1934, an acknowledgement was received
Sgt J P Hookey · + · for two QDY signals, but the Whitley failed to
Sgt J Hassall · + · return to base at its briefed estimated time of arrival. Two days later, the wreckage of the bomber was sighted on Foel Fras Mountain, some 4 miles W of Dolgarrog in Caernarvonshire. The crew had been approximately 12 miles W of track. Sgt Stuart RNZAF, whose brother Sergeant William Douglas Stuart RNZAF had been killed on 24 October 1941, while staging to Malta with 40 Squadron (see page 359 of 'Sweeping The Skies' by David Gunby, The Pentland Press, 1995) and Newfoundland born Sgt Hookey are buried in Caernarvon Cemetery. The others were taken to their home towns.

	26 OTU	Wellington IC	DV821		Training

Sgt L F Bertrand RCAF · inj · T/o 0938 Wing for a cross-country exercise.
Sgt S Langley · inj · Crash-landed 1153 at Greenhow Hill, roughly
Sgt H Beazley RCAF · inj · three miles WSW of Pateley Bridge, Yorkshire,
Sgt J C Keightley · + · after the starboard propeller and reduction
Sgt S Hitchen · inj · gear came off. As the propeller detached, so it struck the side of the Wellington, killing Sgt Keightley (he is buried in Harrow (Wealdstone) Cemetery). Police Constable Fred Graham and some locally based soldiers soon reached the scene of the crash and they were instrumental in pulling the badly injured members of crew clear of the wreckage, which had caught fire. Subsequently, three soldiers and PC Graham received commendations in recognition of their brave actions.

27 Sep **10 OTU Det** **Whitley V** **AD708** **Op: AS Patrol**
1942   WO2 D H Thompson RCAF   inj   T/o St. Eval. Landed 0745 on the short runway
       Sgt C N Ellis   and swung out of control, the undercarriage
       Sgt A T Wall   giving way in the process. As the crew scrambled
       P/O H S Smith   clear, a fire developed. For WO2 Thompson RCAF,
       Sgt D Thomas   this was his second serious accident (see page
       Sgt E Campell   136 for details and a note on his subsequent
                                    fate). Sgt Ellis was destined to fail to return
       from a similar patrol, early in October; later, he was reported as a prisoner.

26-27 Sep **10 OTU** **Whitley V** **BD376** **Training**
1942   Sgt N G Clark   +   T/o 2135 Stanton Harcourt for a night exercise.
       P/O D R C Bartlett   +   Crashed 0045, while trying to go round again,
       P/O B R Steel   +   bursting into flames on impact. All are buried
       Sgt F B Mitchell BEM   +   in various cemeteries, Sgt Minney of Glasgow
       Sgt A R Minney   +   being taken to Kettering (London Road) Cemetery.

27 Sep **23 OTU** **Wellington III** **BJ719** **Training**
1942   Sgt J G A Patry RCAF   T/o 1536 Pershore but it is thought the throttle
                                    friction nuts had not been sufficiently tightened
       and as the aircraft began to climb, the power decayed and the Wellington crash-
       landed, sliding through a hedge before coming to a stop. On 21-22 June 1943,
       Sgt Patry RCAF (now commissioned) failed to return from Krefeld while flying with
       408 Squadron (see Bomber Command Losses, Volume 4, page 196). He is buried in the
       Reichswald Forest War Cemetery.

29 OTU **Wellington III** **X3705** **Training**
       F/S H Hyde   T/o 1925 Woolfox Lodge for night flying. During
       Sgt W E McCrae RCAF   inj the sortie, the pilot shut down the port engine,
                                    believing it to be on fire and having regained
       the airfield, crash-landed at 2215. An investigation into the fire revealed a
       faulty spark plug which had allowed a mixture of petrol and air to escape into
       the slipstream and ignite.

28 Sep **13 OTU** **Blenheim IV** **R3761** **Training**
1942   Sgt A W Anderson   +   T/o 1545 Bicester but the port engine stalled
       Sgt T D R Pullin   inj causing the Blenheim to hit the ground and
       Sgt T Pollock   inj catch fire. Sgt Anderson of Elderslie in
                                    Renfrewshire was buried in Bicester Cemetery.

20 OTU C Flt **Wellington IC** **Z8981 XL-T** **Training**
       P/O J P Mahoney   T/o 2117 Lossiemouth but collided with trees
                                    bordering the airfield and crashed near Drainie
       School. Of the crew of eight, three were slightly hurt and one was admitted to
       Dr. Gray's Hospital for attention to a knee injury. P/O Mahoney eventually
       proceeded to 101 Squadron and was reported missing from Berlin in August 1943
       (see Bomber Command Losses, Volume 4, page 284). He has no known grave.

29 Sep **20 OTU D Flt** **Wellington IC** **N2758 ZT-J** **Training**
1942   F/L W R I Walmsley   +   T/o Lossiemouth for a night exercise. At
       Sgt W D Crawford   +   around 0015, the bomber ploughed into the
       Sgt S E Monger-Godfrey   +   side of Moorhead Hill (480 feet above sea
       F/S B D Crane RCAF   +   level and obscured by cloud), 3 miles E of
       Sgt W G Banham   inj Macduff, Aberdeenshire. F/L Walmsley and
                                    his Canadian wireless operator rest alongside
       each other in Lossiemouth Burial Ground. The others who died were taken to
       their home towns. Sgt Banham was very seriously injured and following initial
       treatment at Banff Hospital was transferred to Aberdeen Royal Infirmary. It
       will be recalled that three members of the crew had been badly hurt in a crash
       on 5 August (see page 143 for details).

30 Sep **14 OTU** **Wellington IC** **T2747** **Training**
1942   P/O E P Howarth RCAF   +   T/o Cottesmore and while flying in low cloud,
       Sgt W H Ellwood   +   hit the ground in the vicinity of Market Overton
       F/S W H Backs RCAF   +   some 5 miles NNE of Oakham. Both Canadians were
                                    buried in the extension to Cottesmore (St.
       Nicholas) Churchyard, while Sgt Ellwood was taken to Harrow (Harrow Weald)
       Cemetery. This was the first Wellington written off by the unit.

30 Sep– **23 OTU** **Wellington III** **X3751** **Training**
1 Oct 1942 F/S R J Woodruff RCAF + T/o 2022 Pershore for a night navigation sortie
Sgt R Sandham RCAF + base-Conway-Douglas-Fishguard-base and carrying
F/S M J Bracey RCAF + six by 250lb sand filled practice bombs, an F24
Sgt L W Robert + 8-inch camera and IFF. At 2018, Sgt Roberts,
F/S W E Scott RCAF + the aircraft's wireless operator made a test
call with base, after which nothing further was
heard. Having failed to return by its scheduled time, overdue action was taken
at 0230 with No. 15 Group co-ordinating the Air-Sea Rescue operation. Despite an
extensive search (aircraft from bases in Northern Ireland were also involved),
no trace of the Wellington or its crew were found and their names are now
perpetuated on the panels of the Runnymede Memorial.

1 Oct **12 OTU** **Wellington III** **BJ692** **Training**
1942 Sgt R A Williams T/o Chipping Warden for night flying. Shortly
before 0005, the port engine began to vibrate,
quite alarmingly, and when an explosion occurred in the exhaust system, the
motor cut completely. An emergency landing was made on Wheaton Aston Relief
Landing Ground but before coming to a stop, the Wellington ran into Oxford I
EB720 belonging to 11 (Pilots) Advanced Flying Unit, wrecking both aircraft.

14 OTU **Wellington IC** **R1401** **Training**
F/S J O McCabe RNZAF inj T/o 1945 Cottesmore for night flying. Landed
inj at 2025 but ballooned back into the air and
inj before corrective action could be taken, the
bomber stalled and crashed.

17 OTU **Blenheim IV** **L9328** **Training**
Sgt F Armit T/o 1555 Upwood but crash-landed, wheels up,
in a field 300 yards beyond the runway and on
the NE side of the aerodrome. This particular Blenheim had been damaged at
Upwood on 8 July 1942 (see page 134).

17 OTU **Blenheim IV** **V6315** **Training**
Sgt G Darbyshire + T/o 1420 Upwood but after climbing to around
P/O F L Austin + 350 feet, the port engine cut. An initial
Sgt F A Reeve + swing to port was corrected and the aircraft
momentarily straightened out before diving
to the ground, a mile W of the airfield. Sgt Reeve was buried locally in
Bury Cemetery but his two companions were taken to their home towns.

2 Oct **18 OTU** **Wellington IC** **DV802** **Training**
1942 Sgt M Hesse PAF + T/o 2133 Bramcote but as the aircraft gained
Sgt J Stangryciuk PAF inj height, flames were seen streaming back from
Sgt E S Mistecki PAF + the port engine. Banking steeply to port,
the bomber crashed out of control at Ryton
near Nuneaton, Warwickshire. The two airmen who died rest in the Polish Plot
at Newark-upon-Trent Cemetery.

5– 6 Oct **19 OTU** **Whitley V** **BD213** **Training**
1942 Sgt J A Williamson + T/o 2030 Kinloss for a night navigation flight.
F/S M Charton RCAF + The last wireless signal, in response to a QDM,
P/O J M Sinclair + from this aircraft was made at 0053, the
Sgt G C Roper + operating making, "I will call you back later".
Sgt E S W Hatch + Five minutes after this transmission, the bomber
smashed into the ground 2 miles E of Castletown
and 5 miles E of Thurso, Caithness and burst into flames. Two, F/S Charton RCAF
and P/O Sinclair, lie in Kinloss Abbey Burial Ground, the others were claimed
by their next of kin. At the time of the tragedy, the crew were on the last
leg of their exercise and proceeding on track.

6 Oct **15 OTU** **Wellington IC** **HD942** **Training**
1942 P/O I F Mackenzie inj T/o 1950 Harwell for night flying. Crashed
P/O C G R Greenhill inj circa 2250 onto rising ground near Letcombe
inj Bassett, 2 miles SSW of Wantage, Berkshire.
inj After completing his course, P/O Mackenzie
inj converted to Stirlings and was posted to 90
inj Squadron. He died on operations in April 1943
(see Bomber Command Losses, Volume 4, page 123).

7 Oct	28 OTU	Wellington IC	R1801		Training

1942

W/O D A Gee	+	T/o Wymeswold for dual and right-hand seat
Sgt A V Barker	+	flying experience. Shortly before 1608, the
F/S L Jones	+	Wellington was seen jettisoning fuel; it then
		crashed at Woodhouse Eaves, 3 miles S from

Loughborough, Leicestershire. All rest in various cemeteries. At the Court of Inquiry, a rigger suggested that there may have been extensive stripping of fabric from a vital area of the starboard wing. Whatever the reason, it was the first aircraft written off from the unit since its formation in the May, a quite remarkable run of good fortune.

8- 9 Oct	10 OTU Det	Whitley V	AD671		Op: AS Patrol

1942

W/O C N Ellis	pow	T/o St. Eval. Reportedly shot down by a Ju 88
WO2 W A Gammon RCAF	pow	flown by Lt Dieter Meister. F/O Cochran was
W/O L H Dean	pow	amongst the Allied officers that broke out from
W/O F D Garrett	pow	Stalag Luft III on 25 March 1944. Captured and
F/O D H Cochran	pow	handed over to the Gestapo, he was shot on, or
WO2 W C Roach RCAF	pow	around 31 March and his body was cremated soon
		after at Natzweiler. His ashes are now interred

in Poznan Old Garrison Cemetery, Poland. W/O Ellis had already experienced one close shave while serving with the detachment (see page 165 for details).

9 Oct	15 OTU	Wellington IC	DV776		Unknown

1942 Reported to have been wrecked in a landing accident at Holbeach Marsh, 3 miles NNE of Holbeach, Lincolnshire. An accident card was raised but never completed, thus the name of the pilot, duty and cause are not known. And, as was all too frequently the case, the unit makes no mention of the incident whatsoever in its records.

16 OTU	Wellington IC	R1389		Unknown

Reported as lost without trace but there is no evidence to support this, either by way of an aircraft accident card or an entry in unit records.

10 Oct	16 OTU	Wellington III	BK257		Training

1942

Sgt J Ferguson	+	T/o Upper Heyford for a night cross-country.
Sgt R G Macdonald	+	It is thought the crew were searching for a
Sgt J A Fox	+	landmark when the Wellington hit a tree and
F/S D R Robertson RCAF	+	crashed 2315 into a plantation at North Cotes
Sgt B H Sparrow RCAF	+	in Yorkshire. Three, both Canadians and Sgt
		Macdonald are buried in Filey (St. Oswald)

Churchyard, while their two companions were taken to their home towns.

21 OTU	Wellington IC	X9695		Training

Sgt A H Wood	inj	T/o Moreton-in-Marsh but at around 1630, the
P/O H G Pugh	inj	crew were obliged to force'-land between two
Sgt Baker		Oxfordshire villages, namely Balscote and
Sgt R A Shelton	inj	Shutford, 4 miles W of Banbury. This mishap
Sgt W Lear	inj	was attributed to double engine failure.

11 Oct	17 OTU	Blenheim IV	T1931		Training

1942

Sgt L Partridge	+	T/o 1245 Upwood but an engine cut and within
Sgt W R Hopcroft	+	moments the Blenheim was engulfed in flames
Sgt F Mac-C Poole	+	after hitting trees bordering the airfield.
		Two were laid to rest locally in Bury Cemetery

but Sgt Poole was taken home to be buried in Camberwell New Cemetery.

25 OTU	Wellington III	BK188		Training

P/O S J Lupton		T/o 1150 Finningley but swung out of control in
		the strong cross-wind and the undercarriage
		collapsed.

13 Oct	10 OTU Det	Whitley V	BD290		Op: AS Patrol

1942

Sgt J W McL Merry	+	T/o St. Eval. Probably came down in the sea off
WO2 P F B Creech RCAF	pow	the Biscay coast as Sgt Merry of Hamilton in
W/O J T Johnston	pow	Lanarkshire is buried in la Rochelle (St. Eloi)
WO2 J D Carmichal RCAF	pow	Communal Cemetery. Two of the crew went into
WO2 M H Treanor RCAF	pow	captivity in a wounded state.

13 Oct **22 OTU**   **Wellington IC**   **DV490**   **Training**
1942   F/S W R C Sinclair RCAF   +   T/o 1944 Stratford-upon-Avon but two minutes
            P/O R S Elsom DFM   +   later, having lost power from an engine, came
            Sgt E P Hunt RCAF   +   down at Preston on Stour on the SSW side of the
            Sgt D O Broughton RCAF   inj   airfield. The two Canadians (both hailed from
                                           British Columbia) rest in Stratford-upon-Avon
Cemetery, while P/O Elsom, who has served with 218 Squadron, is buried in
Loughborough (Leicester Road) Cemetery. His award would not be published
until 29 December 1942. Sgt Broughton RCAF recovered from his injuries and
by the spring of 1943, he was flying with 429 Squadron. On 12-13 May 1943,
his Wellington crashed in Holland while raiding Duisburg (see Bomber Command
Losses, Volume 4, page 144).

27 OTU   **Wellington IA**   **N2985**   **Training**
Sgt A A Harlem RAAF   T/o Lichfield armed with practice bombs and
                                  fitted with IFF for a night exercise. Crash-
landed 2200, having suffered starboard engine failure, on High Ercall airfield
in Shropshire and caught fire. The crew, five in number, had managed to lower
the undercarriage but the unit would not lock. On 30-31 August 1943, now with
199 Squadron and flying Stirlings, Sgt Harlem RAAF did not return from a raid
on Mönchengladbach (see Bomber Command Losses, Volume 4, page 298).

27 OTU   **Wellington IC**   **Z8854**   **Training**
F/L F Fanta   +   T/o Church Broughton for a night navigation
Sgt J Hrala   +   exercise. Shortly before 2305, the Wellington
P/O M Mucha   +   was observed, flying at about 1,000 feet, with
F/O V Obsil   +   its navigation lights on. Banking, it flew up
Sgt R Jelinek   +   the line of the flare path before commencing a
Sgt E Turkl   +   gentle turn to port, slowly losing height, but
                       instead of levelling out the bomber flew into
the ground at Watery Lane, Scropton, 11 miles SW of Derby and burst into flames.
From Czechoslovakia, all are buried in Scropton (St. Paul) Churchyard extension.
It is noted that fifteen of the sixteen service graves in this extension are for
airmen who died while serving at 27 OTU.

15 Oct **10 OTU Det**   **Whitley V**   **Z9435**   **Op: AS Patrol**
1942   P/O G R Tart   +   T/o St. Eval. Lost without trace but suspected
            F/S S Nicolson   +   to have fallen victim to enemy fighter attack.
            F/S G H Thornley   +   All are commemorated on the Runnymede Memorial.
            Sgt J McDonald   +   Sgt McDonald was aged 41, well over the age
            Sgt N A Revitt   +   associated with operational flying.
            Sgt B L Rogers   +

11 OTU   **Wellington IC**   **DV717**   **Training**
Sgt V X Kirby RNZAF   +   T/o Westcott for a combined night bombing sortie
Sgt R J Fuller RNZAF   +   and navigation exercise. Emerged from cloud and
Sgt J L Lloyd RNZAF   +   crashed 2055 at Breck's Farm, Maplebeck, 7 miles
Sgt E A McCord RNZAF   +   to the NW of Newark-upon-Trent, Nottinghamshire.
Sgt I R Styles RNZAF   +   Four were buried in Ollerton Cemetery, but Sgt
                            McCord RNZAF was taken back to Eire, from where
he had emigrated to New Zealand four years previous, and laid to rest in Ardagh
Cemetery, Co. Longford. At the time of the Köln raid in May 1942, this air-
craft had carried the combination OP-A.

18 OTU   **Wellington IV**   **Z1482**   **Enemy Action**
Sgt H Nowakowski PAF   +   T/o Bramcote tasked for a night exercise. Came
P/O J Rysztok PAF   +   down near Campigny (Eure), 18 km NW of Brionne,
Sgt H Zachel PAF   +   France. All rest at Campigny. The Court of
Sgt F Kornafel PAF   +   Inquiry reported, "presumed crew decided to drop
Sgt J Karny PAF   +   their "live" bomb in German occupied territory".

21 OTU   **Wellington IC**   **R1667**   **Training**
Sgt G S Calder   +   T/o 2145 Moreton-in-Marsh for a night cross-
P/O J Herrington   +   country. Crashed 2305 some 200 yards from Park
F/O R Franks   +   Drain Station, York, and burst into flames. The
Sgt A M Foster RCAF +   two RCAF airmen (P/O Shadle was an American from
P/O C C Shadle RCAF +   Melrose, New Mexico) rest in the extension to
                         Finningley (St. Oswald) Cemetery; their three
                         companions were taken to their home towns.

16 Oct   **19 OTU**   **Whitley V**   **BD212**   **Training**
1942   F/S M H Hargreaves RCAF   +   T/o Kinloss on "Lookie III", a searchlight
        Sgt J R MacKinnon RCAF   +   cooperation exercise in the area of Tyneside.
        P/O J L G Campbell   +   Although officially lost without trace, it is
        Sgt D A A Saunders   +   very much suspected that the Whitley fell
        Sgt T G Sinnett   +   victim to an Allied night-fighter which, later,
                                      claimed to have shot down an enemy aircraft in
the vicinity where it was known the bomber was operating. All are commemorated
on the Runnymede Memorial. P/O Campbell held a Bachelor of Arts degree.

17 Oct   **23 OTU**   **Wellington III**   **BJ911**   **Training**
1942   Sgt J N Wright   inj   T/o 0250 Pershore for night circuit practice.
        Sgt F K Brown   inj   At circa 0330, Sgt Wright realised he was in
        Sgt J E Desjardins RCAF   +   danger of under-shooting the runway. However,
                                      when he opened the throttles, the starboard
motor failed to respond and the Wellington crashed, heavily, breaking into two
pieces. Sgt Desjardins RCAF was buried in Pershore Cemetery. Sgt Wright made
a good recovery and during his tour of operations with 432 Squadron, he gained
a well deserved Distinguished Flying Medal (Gazetted 14 September 1943).

20-21 Oct   **21 OTU**   **Wellington IC**   **HD984**   **Training**
1942   P/O T Proctor   +   T/o 2250 Moreton-in-Marsh for a night cross-
        P/O E J Dando   +   country. Lost without trace. The entire crew
        Sgt C S George   +   are perpetuated on the Runnymede Memorial. It
        F/S E W Chessor RCAF   +   was unusual for a Wellington to operate with a
                                      four-man crew but, to date, these are the only
                                      names traced.

25 Oct   **10 OTU**   **Whitley V**   **EB357**   **Training**
1942   Sgt D J Howlett   T/o 1146 Stanton Harcourt for a navigation
                                      exercise. While away from base, the weather
deteriorated to such a degree that on returning to Stanton Harcourt at 1806,
the crew totally misread the landing signals and, thus, came in downwind.
Moments later, to their surprise, they were beyond the runway and in a local
quarry. No one was badly hurt, but the Whitley was wrecked. Posted to the
Middle East, Sgt Howlett was killed on 1 December 1943 while flying Halifaxes
on Special Duties with 624 Squadron. He is buried in Greece at Phaleron War
Cemetery.

        29 OTU   **Wellington III**   **BJ896**   **Training**
        Sgt T Bromley   T/o 1535 North Luffenham but failed to gain
                                      height, smashing through a barbed wire fence
and crashing into a gun post. No injuries reported, but the bomber was deemed
to be beyond economical repair.

26 Oct   **20 OTU B Flt**   **Wellington IC**   **R3230 JM-S**   **Training**
1942   Sgt R J Beldin   T/o 2052 Lossiemouth but the air speed indicator
                                      failed to register and Sgt Beldin aborted the
take off. However, the Wellington was, by this time, travelling at quite a pace
and in order to stop within the confines of the airfield, he raised the undercarriage. Seconds later, the aircraft skidded into an air raid shelter. From
the five members of crew, two required medical attention.

        21 OTU   **Wellington IC**   **Z8967**   **Training**
        Sgt H B R Venning   inj   T/o Moreton-in-Marsh for a cross-country flight
        P/O Churchouse   inj   during which both engines failed. At 1130, the
        Sgt Hargreaves   inj   Wellington crash-landed on Overton Heath air-
        Sgt Hearwood   inj   field, a satellite landing ground for No. 7
        Sgt K L Jeffries   inj   Flying Instructors School.

        22 OTU   **Wellington IC**   **DV785**   **Training**
        Sgt A H Whitted   inj   T/o Stratford-upon-Avon for night circuits
        Sgt W A H Hamilton   inj   and landings. Shortly before 0640, Sgt Whitted
                                inj   realised that his approach to the runway was
                                inj   off the line of the flare path and he opened
                                    up in order to go round again. As was so often
the case, the engines failed to pick up and the Wellington came down in a field
near Salford Priors, 8 miles WSW from Stratford-upon-Avon. Sgt Whitted had
enlisted in the Royal Air Force, while domicile in Canada.

27 Oct
1942

10 OTU Det	**Whitley V**	Z6959	**Op: AS Patrol**
Sgt A V Howarth	+		
Sgt G Bagshaw			

T/o 1720 St. Eval. During the patrol, the crew became most concerned at the excessive rate of oil consumption and, rightly, the aircraft was turned about. Soon after doing so, a fire broke out (possibly brought about by glycol leaking) and though the blaze was extinguished, their problems were further exacerbated when a bearing failed, causing one of the connecting rods to break through the side of the crankcase. Valiantly, Sgt Howarth kept the ailing bomber in the air and on gaining the coast, ordered his crew to bale out. Having ascertained all were safely away, he tried to force ¯-land but crashed 1920 out of control a mile E of St. Erme, 3 miles NNE of Truro, Cornwall. He is buried in Birmingham (Witton) Cemetery. Very sadly, Sgt Bagshaw, having survived this close call, failed to return from a similar operation towards the end of November 1942.

22 OTU	**Wellington IC**	X9943	**Training**
P/O P Geldart			

T/o Stratford-upon-Avon for night solo circuits and landings. Landed 0125 but ran into another of the unit's aircraft (Wellington III HF628) which was stationary at the end of the flare path and awaiting clearance to taxi onto the runway. Amazingly, no one was hurt (Sgt K E L Coats and Sgt T H Maxwell RCAF were aboard the second aircraft) and HF628 was repaired and returned to service. On 25-26 August 1943, it failed to return from a Nickel operation.

28 Oct
1942

10 OTU Det	**Whitley V**	Z6580	**Op: AS Patrol**
F/S J H Austin	+		
Sgt B J Bradsell	+		
Sgt L S Bridges	+		
Sgt R V Howes	+		
Sgt E T W Lampitt	+		
Sgt N C Reinelt	+		

T/o St. Eval. Lost without trace. All are commemorated on the Runnymede Memorial.

29 Oct
1942

10 OTU Det	**Whitley V**	Z6579	**Op: AS Patrol**
F/O M G Grant	+		
P/O W F Raffan	+		
Sgt E Cheetham	+		
Sgt E Marsden	+		
F/S J D Maxwell RCAF	+		
Sgt G C J Heywood	+		

T/o St. Eval. Believed to have crashed near Taule (Finistere), 6 km NW of Morlaix, France. All are buried in Taule Communal Cemetery.

10 OTU Det	**Whitley V**	Z9217	**Op: AS Patrol**

Reported in unit records to have departed from St. Eval on an anti-submarine patrol from whence it failed to return. However, no further information has been appended.

19 OTU	**Whitley V**	AD710	**Training**
F/S J E Williams DFM	+		
F/O W I Charteris RNZAF	+		
Sgt G W Day	+		
Sgt E O Oddy	+		
Sgt J H Barnett	+		

T/o Kinloss for a night navigation exercise. Flew into a violent electrical storm and, it is believed, a lightning strike set light to the starboard engine. As the bomber plunged out of control, two members of the crew managed to bale out before it smashed into the ground at around 0055, near Dalcross, Inverness-shire. F/O Charteris RNZAF is buried in Kinloss Abbey Burial Ground; the others were taken to their home towns. F/S Williams gained an immediate DFM while raiding Bremen with 115 Squadron, the citation being published in the London Gazette on 24 July 1942.

19 OTU	**Whitley V**	BD254	**Training**
Sgt A J W R Coupar			

T/o Kinloss for a night cross-country and crashed in circumstances similar to those described above, though not until 0140 at Cont na Craig Farm, Potarch, 6 miles WNW of Banchory, Aberdeenshire. It will be recalled that Sgt Coupar had been involved in a serious crash on 18 April 1942 (see page 109).

Note. Unit records indicate that the electrical storm broke over Kinloss at 0020 and lasted until practically first light. Four aircraft were airborne and an immediate recall message was broadcast. Of the two that got down safely, Sgt Isaacs was at Wick, while Sgt Hooper telephoned in from Edzell where he had managed to scrape in, practically out of petrol.

30 Oct	10 OTU Det	Whitley V	BD293		Op: AS Patrol
1942	Sgt G C Wright			T/o St. Eval. Ditched 1456 in the Atlantic from
	Sgt A J N Edwards		+	where the three survivors were rescued three days
	F/S R J L Fournier RCAF		+	later. Panels 83 and 103 respectively perpetuate
	F/S W Wright			the names of their less fortunate colleagues.
	Sgt H Macewen RCAF			

31 Oct	10 OTU Det	Whitley V	Z6879		Op: AS Patrol
1942	S/L G R Coates RNZAF		inj	T/o 0800 St. Eval. Ditched 1415, following
	Sgt S E Cockerill		inj	engine failure and an inability to maintain
			inj	height. After thirty-one hours adrift, the
			inj	crew were picked up by an RN destroyer, which
			inj	had been alerted to their plight by one of the
				search aircraft (S/L G P Towsey DFC RNZAF).

Note. On 4 July 1948, S/L Coates was the captain of the Avro York MW248 of 99 Squadron which had the awful misfortune to collide with a Scandinavian Airlines DC-6 SE-BDA Agnar Viking, both aircraft crashing between Ruislip and Harefield. There were no survivors from either machine and so died a gallant New Zealander who had transferred after the war from the RNZAF to the Royal Air Force. During the Second World War, in which he gained a Distinguished Flying Cross, he is known to have served with 51 Squadron, 296 Squadron and 156 Squadron. For this data, I am indebted to Errol Martyn, author of 'For Your Tomorrow', and Colin Hanson, compiler of 'By Such Deeds - Honours and Awards in the Royal New Zealand Air Force 1923-1998'.

	25 OTU	Wellington III	BK234		Training
	Sgt T M G Gray		+	T/o 1850 Finningley for a Bullseye exercise
	F/O D R Harding		+	which culminated over North Wales in a midair
	Sgt S E Blackman		+	collision between the Wellington and a 256
	Sgt J D Forsyth		+	Squadron Beaufighter IF X7845 JT-G operating
	Sgt S G Cook		+	from Woodvale airfield, Lancashire. Both
				machines fell some 2 miles from Bangor in

Caernarvonshire. All are buried in cemeteries scattered across the United Kingdom. Interestingly, CWGC initially published the OTU crew as belonging to 256 Squadron, but in recent years the registers have been corrected to show 25 OTU (an unusual occurrence as training unit details are rarely mentioned in these publications). Furthermore, it would seem that F/O Harding has been exhumed from Westminster City Cemetery and reinterred at Hanwell Cemetery, Middlesex. The two officers killed in the Beaufighter were S/L R De-W K Winlaw, an Honours graduate from Cambridge and the son of the Revd George Preston Kelsall Winlaw. Prior to the war, thirty year-old S/L Winlaw had been on the teaching staff of Harrow School. S/L C T Ashton, eleven years his senior, had also passed through Cambridge and was an exceptional sportsman, excelling at cricket, football and hockey, attaining Blues in all three sports. In civilian life he had been a chartered accountant.

	30 OTU	Wellington IC	Z1083		Training
	W/O W L Primrose		+	T/o 1920 Hixon for practice bombing at night.
	Sgt D M Belgrove		+	Overshot from its first landing approach and
	P/O D S Hegan		+	while going round again stalled at 500 feet,
	Sgt R H Woolliams RCAF		+	crashing 2050 at Grange Farm, Amerton adjacent
	Sgt A P Cunningham		+	to the northern boundary of the airfield. The
	Sgt D C Hawk RCAF		+	two RCAF airmen rest in Hixton (St. Peter)
				Churchyard, Stowe, the others being taken to

their home towns. It is noted that Sgt Hawk RCAF was an American from Portland, Indiana. P/O Hegan was the third university graduate to lose his life this day (see the above summary). He had passed through Oxford, gaining a Bachelor of Arts degree. Formed at Hixon on 28 June 1942, this was the unit's first fatal air accident.

1 Nov	20 OTU C Flt	Wellington IC	X9668 XL-K		Training
1942	Sgt V G Bryant			T/o Lossiemouth for an exercise during which
				the starboard engine failed. Consequently, at

approximately 1400, the crew forced-landed their aircraft, just to the W of Portknockie, Banff. From the seven members of crew, two are reported to have been slightly hurt. Although at first sight the damage appeared insignificant, a further technical examination ruled out repairs and the airframe was broken down for spares during December 1942.

2 Nov
1942

13 OTU   **Blenheim IV** **R3902**   **Training**

Sgt T Wilson   T/o 1430 Bicester but as the Blenheim gathered
Sgt E A Colburn   speed, the starboard engine failed. Sgt Wilson
managed to turn into a dispersal lane, only to
be confronted by another aircraft, taxying towards him. Swerving towards a
nearby hedge, his aircraft came to rest on a mound of earth, where it caught
fire. Both members of crew (they were unhurt) and Sgt Bryant of 20 OTU (see
the previous summary) had transferred from the army to the air force sometime
after January 1939.

6 Nov
1942

13 OTU   **Blenheim IV** **R3874**   **Training**

Sgt A S E Blackshire   inj   T/o 1515 Bicester but having gained a mere
P/O D Newell   inj   one hundred feet, the starboard motor cut.
Sgt W Donald   inj   Immediately, the Blenheim banked to starboard
Sgt C L Harrison   inj   and dived into trees at Stoke Little Wood,
twixt 2 and 3 miles NW of the airfield. All
were rushed to the Radcliffe Infirmary, where Sgt Blackshire died that same
evening. He is buried in Bicester Cemetery.

26 OTU   **Wellington IC** **DV885**   **Training**

P/O H D Murray   +   T/o Little Horwood. Reported as crashed near
Sgt J W Wilde   +   the airfield. P/O Murray, a Canadian from
Sgt J M Lennox   +   Vancouver serving with the Volunteer Reserve,
F/S W C Ferguson DFM   +   was taken to Yorkshire and buried in Kirk
Sgt H Bailey   +   Sandall (St. Oswald) Churchyard, Barnby Dun-
Sgt Clarke   inj   with-Kirk Sandall. The others rest in their
home towns. Late in 1941, F/S Ferguson was
serving with 101 Squadron and while raiding Essen, his aircraft came under
attack from a Ju 88. Operating his guns to good effect, he drove the enemy
aircraft off and later, shortly after crossing the coast on the return leg,
he despatched a second attacker, which was last seen diving towards the sea
wreathed in flames. His immediate award of the DFM was published in the
London Gazette on 6 January 1942.

7 Nov
1942

10 OTU   **Whitley V** **AD714**   **Training**

Sgt A W Taney   +   T/o 0001 Stanton Harcourt for night circuit
Sgt L F K Spratt   +   training. Five minutes later, the bomber was
Sgt R J Nicholas   inj   seen making what appeared to be a normal
Sgt N R Pickett   inj   approach to land when, for some inexplicable
Sgt D Gordon-Kay RCAF   +   reason, Sgt Taney elected to overshoot. The
nose of the Whitley rose as it cleared the air-
field but as it turned, downwind, so it dived out of control and crashed at
Ferryman's Farm, Northmoor. Sgt Gordon-Kay RCAF rests in Brookwood Military
Cemetery, while the others who died were taken to their home towns.

26 OTU   **Wellington IC** **Z1158**   **Training**

F/S G B Leddy   T/o 1900 Wing for night circuit practice.
Wrecked 1917 following a heavy landing.

7- 8 Nov
1942

14 OTU   **Hampden I** **L4100**   **Training**

Sgt M G K East RCAF   inj   T/o 1915 Cottesmore for a high-level night
Sgt H A Webb RCAF   inj   cross-country, flying for most of the sortie
Sgt J L Warren RCAF   inj   above 10,000 feet. On return to base, at
Sgt G C Gale RCAF   inj   around 0015, undershot the runway and crashed
roughly a mile E of the airfield. This was
the last Hampden to be written off in Bomber Command service. Sgt East RCAF,
who sustained a rather painful back injury, subsequently converted to Short
Stirlings and lost his life while on operations with 90 Squadron on 26 May
1943 (see Bomber Command Losses, Volume 4, page 161). On 20 November 1944,
his brother, F/O John Douglas East RCAF, died when his Halifax II W7875 of
1656 HCU crashed near Doncaster. Sgt Gale RCAF, meanwhile, had died raiding
Duisburg with 7 Squadron in April 1943 (see the same volume, page 96).

Note. This particular Hampden had been held on unit charge since 12 July
1941, and including its service with 44 Squadron and 106 Squadron, it had
amassed a total of 876.35 flying hours. Until the accident, summarised
above, it seems to have enjoyed trouble free service. Unfortunately, the
names of those in addition to the pilot have not been recorded in unit
records.

8 Nov	**13 OTU**	**Blenheim IV**	**T1991**	**Training**
1942	Sgt J P Hannah RNZAF	inj	T/o 1740 Bicester for night flying practice	
	Sgt E T Owen	inj	during which the port engine failed and the	

crew returned early to base. Approaching the runway, at around 1830, the Blenheim hit a hedge 300 yards short of the threshold, badly damaging the undercarriage. Sgt Hannah RNZAF managed to keep some semblance of control but could not prevent the bomber from hitting the ground, hard, some 50 yards short of the Chance lights. Before coming to a stop, the port engine was torn from its frame and the port mainspar buckled. Sgt Hannah RNZAF sustained a fractured right tibia and fibula while Sgt Owen broke his left femur and ankle. Both were admitted to the Princess Mary's Hospital at Halton. Unit records indicate Sgt Hannah's service number as 412682, while Errol Martyn shows in his first volume of 'For Your Tomorrow' a F/S Wilfred James Hannah RNZAF 412683 as failing to return, twenty-four hours previous to the accident here described, from a minelaying operation off the Gironde Estuary while flying Stirlings with 15 Squadron (see also Bomber Command Losses, Volume 3, page 254).

	18 OTU	**Wellington IV**	**Z1325**	**Training**
	Sgt E Brill PAF	+	T/o Bramcote for night flying practice. At	
	P/O J Bozalek PAF	inj	circa 2150 the Wellington stalled, while low	
	P/O S Tomicki PAF	inj	flying, crashing near Hinckley, Leicestershire.	
	Sgt S Madejski PAF	inj	Sgt Brill PAF is buried in Newark-upon-Trent	
	Sgt W Hanczakowski PAF	inj	Cemetery. P/O Tomicki PAF lost his life while	
	Sgt E Kasperowicz PAF		on operations to Duisburg in April 1943 (see	

Bomber Command Losses, Volume 4, page 98).

	20 OTU A Flt	**Wellington IC**	**DV726**	**Training**
	F/S I D MacLean DFM	+	T/o Lossiemouth for a night exercise carrying	
	Sgt J Holderness	+	2 x flash bombs and 2 x photoflash flares.	
	Sgt A E Davies	+	Shortly before 2300, the port engine failed	
	Sgt J R Rogers	inj	and the Wellington crashed, bursting into	
	Sgt G Jones	+	flames, on Covesea Golf Links on the northern	
	F/S B H Batten Wilkins	+	fringes of the airfield. Of the deceased,	
	Sgt McWhirter	inj	three are buried in Lossiemouth Burial Ground	
	Sgt A W F Welfare	inj	while the others were taken to their home towns.	

Two of the survivors were treated at Dr. Gray's Hospital at Elgin, while Sgt McWhirter, whose left femur had been fractured, was admitted to Inverness Hospital. Their skipper had served with 99 Squadron and details of his award had appeared in the London Gazette on 14 April 1942.

	21 OTU	**Wellington IC**	**R1777**	**Training**
	P/O J S Ambler		T/o Moreton-in-Marsh for a cross-country,	
			with instructions to land before dusk, even	

if this meant curtailing the exercise. However, it seems likely the crew became uncertain of their position as it was around 1900 that they tried to land at Chipping Norton airfield, Oxfordshire. On touch down, the Wellington swung and ran into an obstruction.

	22 OTU	**Wellington III**	**DF742**	**Training**
	P/O T D Withington DFM RCAF	+	T/o Gaydon for solo practice. Stalled at low	
	Sgt C W Milton RCAF	+	altitude and crashed 1607 near the station at	
			Harbury, a largish village on the Banbury to	

Royal Leamington Spa railway and some 4 miles NNW of Gaydon airfield. Both airmen are buried in Stratford-upon-Avon Cemetery. Prior to his arrival at the unit, P/O Withington RCAF had served in the Middle East with 108 Squadron and notification of his award would be Gazetted on 22 January 1943.

	23 OTU	**Wellington III**	**BJ818**	**Training**
	Sgt R H Batchelor		T/o 1515 Pershore for circuits and landings.	
			Wrecked thirty minutes later in a crash 1 mile	
			to the W of the airfield.	

9 Nov	**10 OTU Det**	**Whitley V**	**Z9439 -K**	**Op: AS Patrol**
1942	Sgt I M Morgan		T/o 0508 St. Eval but almost immediately the	
			crew had to turn back when the oil temperature	

on the starboard engine rose alarmingly. Experiencing great difficulty in lining up with the runway, Sgt Morgan crashed (off his third approach) approximately one hundred yards short of the flare path.

9 Nov 1942	12 OTU	Wellington III	Z1731		Training

F/S W J Lovejoy +
Sgt W J Brown +
Sgt F J Frayne +
Sgt W A Smith +
Sgt R Walker +

T/o Chipping Warden for a night navigation exercise. Last heard on wireless at 0128. All are commemorated on the Runnymede Memorial.

	14 OTU	Wellington IC	X3163		Training

Sgt J W C Spencer   inj
Sgt Stewart   inj

T/o Cottesmore for night flying. Overshot the airfield and crashed 0248 near Barrow, 4 miles NNE of Oakham and caught fire. Moments earlier the Wellington had bounced into the air, having shattered its port propeller.

	20 OTU D Flt	Wellington IC	DV882 ZT-G		Training

F/S W J Pope RCAF +
Sgt R MacF Don +
Sgt H Dale +
F/S D C Ferguson RCAF +
Sgt A R Morgan +
Sgt M M Stewart +

T/o Lossiemouth for a night navigation sortie armed with 8 flash bombs, 2 photoflashes and two reconnaissance flares. Lost without trace. All are commemorated on the Runnymede Memorial.

	22 OTU	Wellington III	HF648 LT-L		Training

F/O D B Clements RCAF +
F/S C S Boomer RCAF +
P/O A A Hebert RCAF +
P/O J L Doray RCAF +
F/S G W Wilken RCAF +

T/o 1914 Gaydon but the starboard engine failed and within sixty seconds the aircraft was down near the village of Lighthorne on the northern side of the airfield. All rest in Stratford-upon-Avon Cemetery.

13 Nov 1942	10 OTU Det	Whitley V	Z6725		Op: AS Patrol

P/O A L Homes
Sgt K M W Pond
F/S R E Dorman
P/O S R Jeffrey
Sgt G Tombe
Sgt J G Ramshaw

T/o 0825 St. Eval having been briefed for a ten hour mission. Ditched 1050, following loss of power. There are no reports of anyone being hurt.

	16 OTU	Wellington III	X3984		Training

Sgt H T Forrest   inj
P/O Cornish   inj

T/o 1559 Upper Heyford for the pilot's first solo on type but a swing developed and the Wellington ended up, wrecked, near the bomb dump. Both members of crew were admitted to hospital. It was recommended that on return to duty, Sgt Forrest be given a three day break, after which he should be dual checked.

16 Nov 1942	19 OTU	Whitley V	P5105		Training

P/O D L C Thomas   inj
Sgt R Stone   +
Sgt R L Pett   +
Sgt H S Fraser RCAF   inj
Sgt Williams

T/o Kinloss for a night cross-country. Both engines failed and while attempting to alight in the River Dee, 2 miles W of the Aberdeenshire town of Ballater, the Whitley smashed into a suspension bridge and crashed at 2225. Those who died were claimed by their next of kin.

	29 OTU	Wellington III	X4001		Training

Sgt J H Black RAAF   inj
P/O E Lambert   inj
P/O F W Bartlett   inj
Sgt R G Moore   inj
Sgt P G Rothera   inj
Sgt Napier

T/o 2115 North Luffenham for night flying but ran into a fuel bowser, whose driver had misunderstood a signal and had, inadvertently, commenced crossing the runway in the path of the Wellington.

16-17 Nov 1942	25 OTU	Wellington III	BK193 -A		Training

Sgt F C Allcroft RCAF
F/S E R Newson   +

T/o 1745 Finningley for a Bullseye sortie. After 6.20 hours flying, the pilot ordered the nacelle tanks to be changed but due to an error in the procedures, both engines cut. In the moments before the crash 2 miles NW of Maltby, Yorkshire, some of the crew baled out but F/S Newson did not survive. He lies in Streatham Park Cemetery, Mitcham. Sgt Allcroft RCAF (now commissioned and wearing the Distinguished Flying Cross) perished whilst on Pathfinder duties with 83 Squadron on 3 January 1944 (see Bomber Command Losses, Volume 5, page 23).

17 Nov
1942

11 OTU	Wellington IC X9614		**Training**
F/O F S Haden RNZAF	+	T/o 1130 Westcott but an engine burst into
Sgt R J Walker	+	flames and F/O Hayden RNZAF tried to forced-
P/O W R Taylor	+	land, straight ahead. Unfortunately, some
Sgt I P Bygrave	+	trees lay in his path and while trying to
P/O D S Williams	inj	lift the Wellington's nose to clear these
		obstructions, he lost control and crashed.

Those who perished rest in various cemeteries. P/O Williams was admitted to Princess Mary's Hospital, Halton. This particular Wellington had been coded TX-J at the time of the Köln raid in May 1942, while earlier, on 10 April 1942, it had been damaged in a wheels-up landing at Steeple Morden, Sgt Croall being the pilot on that occasion.

18 Nov
1942

10 OTU B Flt	Anson I N5004	**Training**
Sgt P L Lockhart		T/o 0130 Abingdon for a night navigation sortie.

Deep into the exercise, the crew became totally lost as all land features were blotted out by the total cloud cover. All, as ordered, baled out after which Sgt Lockhart forced-landed 0630 in an orchard at Hawkin's Farm near the hamlet of Pitstone, twixt 7 and 8 miles ENE of Aylesbury in Buckinghamshire. Not long after this incident, Sgt Lockhart was posted to Honeybourne as a staff pilot with 24 OTU. In January 1943, he was injured in a landing accident at Chipping Norton.

10 OTU	Whitley V EB360		**Training**
Sgt A F Adams	inj	T/o 1157 Stanton Harcourt for a navigation
Sgt G W F Abrams	inj	exercise. At 1218, the crew transmitted a
P/O J Monaghan	inj	routine wireless message, after which nothing
Sgt T F Hadley	inj	was heard. In transpired that the engines lost
Sgt A F Turl	inj	power and their plight could not be signalled
		as the W/T equipment had failed. All were

rescued, suffering from exposure, having ditched in the North Sea approximately sixty miles E of Mablethorpe on the Lincolnshire coast.

21 OTU	Wellington IC T2574		**Op: Nickel**
Sgt R L Jones RNZAF	+	T/o 1743 Moreton-in-Marsh and set course for
Sgt A W Mason	+	the Nantes region of France. While flying at
P/O K M Holroyde	+	11,000 feet, over the English Channel, an engine
Sgt S Rushworth	+	caught fire and it can only be assumed, that
Sgt T C Beddowes	inj	having turned back, the pilot decided to carry
		out a premeditated descent through cloud. While

doing so, he flew into the ground between Liss and Longmoor, 4 miles WSW from Liphook, Hampshire. Of those who died, Sgt Jones RNZAF is buried in Brookwood Military Cemetery, while the rest were taken to their home towns.

20 Nov
1942

11 OTU	Wellington IC R1163		**Training**
Sgt R L D Phair RAAF	+	T/o 1102 Westcott for a navigation sortie;
P/O C W Clare RNZAF	+	base-Market Rasen-Mablethorpe-5320N 0035E and
P/O A Booth	+	return. Fifteen minutes after departing base,
Sgt T Connor	+	the crew made a routine wireless call, after
Sgt P J Flynn	+	which nothing was heard. All are commemorated
		on the Runnymede Memorial. P/O Booth was a

Member, either of the Pharmaceutical Society, or of the Philological Society.

15 OTU	Wellington IC T2886		**Training**
Sgt P A Best	inj	T/o 1730 Harwell for a night exercise. Shortly
		before 2345, the induction manifold washers

failed on No. 3 cylinder, thus allowing air to enter the unit, and this caused a fire to break out. Skillfully, Sgt Best forced-landed some 2 miles NE of East Ilsey, 7 miles SE from Wantage, Berkshire. This particular Wellington had served with the unit for a mere two months and, including its previous service with 300 Squadron and 18 OTU, had chalked up 458 flying hours.

18 OTU	Wellington IC DV770	**Training**
P/O J Sckelowski PAF		T/o 2013 Bramcote for night circuits and
Sgt Z Weyna PAF		landings. Landed 2036, probably further
		along the runway than he would have wished,

and on the wet airfield surface the brakes proved to be ineffective. Still running at high speed, the Wellington left the landing area and finished up in a ditch and across one of the hedges bordering the perimeter.

20 Nov   **27 OTU**   **Wellington III**   **Z1744**   **Training**
1942

Sgt J R Barlow RAAF	+	T/o 0803 Lichfield for a combined bombing and
F/O J Love RAAF	+	photograph exercise. Early in the flight, the
F/O K Pettiford RAAF	+	Wellington was approached by two Spitfires,
Sgt W J Baker RAAF	+	reportedly from an American unit, one passing
F/S H J Buckley	+	so close that it took away the trailing aerial
F/S S Cheek RAAF	inj	and rendered the W/T equipment unserviceable.

At approximately 1410, eyewitnesses on the
ground saw the aircraft flying low over some factory buildings near Leek in
Staffordshire and then, to their horror, it smashed into high ground at a
place known locally as Hen Cloud. F/S Cheek RAAF was found unconscious near
the wreckage and he was taken to Leek Cottage Hospital before being transferred
to Cosford Military Hospital. His four fellow Australians now rest in Fradley
(St. Stephen) Churchyard; F/S Buckley lies in Pontypridd (Glyntaff) Cemetery.
F/O Pettiford RAAF was a Bachelor of Arts graduate from Sydney University.

21 Nov   **21 OTU**   **Wellington IC**   **R1211**   **Training**
1942

Sgt T B McAneney RCAF	inj	T/o Edgehill for night flying practice. While
Sgt D Jackson	inj	so engaged, the sky clouded over and at 0115 a
P/O L W Gill	inj	QFE signal intended for another aircraft was
Sgt A L Eastwick	inj	intercepted and, erroneously believing the
Sgt A Johnson	inj	information was intended for his Wellington,

Sgt McAneney RCAF reset his altimeter and by
doing so he now thought he was 400 feet higher than he actually was. Consequently, while descending in readiness to land he flew into trees about a
mile N of the airfield. Lying in Budapest War Cemetery is an officer of this
same name and initials, having failed to return to Amendola on 26 June 1944,
while flying with 150 Squadron against an oil refinery near the city.

22 Nov   **10 OTU Det**   **Whitley V**   **Z6751**   **Op: AS Patrol**
1942

Sgt B A Tidman	+	T/o 0800 St. Eval. During the ten-hour sortie
F/O D McHarrie	inj	the wireless equipment failed and having made
Sgt D L Crossey RCAF	inj	landfall, the crew were uncertain of their
Sgt D M Shyba RCAF	inj	position. In the gloom of a late November
Sgt J Wilson RCAF	inj	evening, they tried to land, 1830, at Carew
Sgt M D Woods RCAF	inj	Cheriton airfield, Pembrokeshire, but hit the

tops of some trees. On impact, the Whitley
caught fire. Sgt Tidman lies in Great Burstead (St. Mary Magdalene) Churchyard.

     12 OTU   **Wellington III**   **BK261**   **Training**

Sgt R H Church	+	T/o 2310 Chipping Warden for night bombing.
Sgt H W S Bristow	+	While flying at 5,000 feet, the photoflash
Sgt F P Nettleton	+	exploded in the flare 'chute, the effect of
Sgt T W Haver	+	the blast being sufficient to cause structural
Sgt B Hillberg	+	failure and at 2330 debris fell at Shotteswell

a Warwickshire village close to the border with
Oxfordshire and about 4 miles NNW from the centre of Banbury. All are buried in
various United Kingdom cemeteries.

     23 OTU   **Wellington III**   **X3567**   **Unknown**

Reported as being wrecked, this day, in a
landing accident at Pershore, the bomber running off the end of the runway.

     27 OTU   **Wellington III**   **BK247**   **Training**

Sgt Britton RAAF	inj	T/o 1730 Lichfield armed with 11 practice
Sgt J A B Cooper RAAF	inj	bombs for a night bombing exercise. At 1901
Sgt Hickson	inj	the Wellington crashed, heavily, into Elmhurst
Sgt Morris	inj	Park, Elmhurst, a mile NE of Lichfield. A fire
Sgt Tuxford RAAF	inj	broke out but the badly injured crew made good

their escape. Two were detained at RAF Hospital
Cosford, Sgt Morris having sustained an upper fracture to one of his arms. By
the summer of 1943, Sgt Cooper RAAF was flying with 103 Squadron but on 25-26
July, while raiding Essen, his Lancaster failed to return (see Bomber Command
Losses, Volume 4, page 242).

25 Nov   **27 OTU**   **Wellington IC**   **R1403**   **Unknown**
1942   Reported crashed and burned out near the
small town of Eaglescliffe in Co. Durham, 9 miles E of Darlington.

27 Nov | **20 OTU B Flt** | **Wellington IC** | **T2722 JM-K** | **Training**
1942 | F/S J C Binge | + | T/o Lossiemouth for a night exercise and,
| Sgt P S Sutton | + | reportedly, ditched due to engine failure
| Sgt B Lowery | + | circa 0200 in Spey Bay, E of the airfield.
| P/O J Bluck | + | In the weeks that followed, five bodies were
| Sgt L E Harrison | + | recovered, that of Sgt Sutton being found off
| Sgt T F Blythe | + | the Dutch Frisian Islands (he now rests in
| Sgt H C Ballinger RCAF | + | Vlieland General Cemetery). Three are buried
| | | in Lossiemouth Burial Ground, F/S Binge was

taken to Blidworth (St. Mary of The Purification and St. Lawrence) Churchyard, while the last two named are commemorated on the Runnymede Memorial.

28 Nov | **17 OTU** | **Blenheim IV** | **V5882** | **Training**
1942 | F/O F W Wilson | | T/o Upwood. Touched down 1245 near the sodium
| | | flare path (in order to avoid another aircraft

that had encroached onto the runway) and ran into some flare holders.

28 OTU B Flt | **Wellington IC** | **R1786** | **Training**
W/O R J Fryer | | T/o Wymeswold for circuit practice. Landed
Sgt F R Smith RAAF | | at 1500 but as the bomber gathered speed to
| | go round again, the engines cut. W/O Fryer

immediately closed the throttles and raised the undercarriage and a few seconds later the Wellington came to a stop, wrecked, just beyond the runway. He died just under a year later in another very serious crash at Wymeswold.

28 OTU A Flt | **Wellington IC** | **X9941** | **Training**
Sgt L A Peers RCAF | inj | T/o 1929 Wymeswold for a night exercise but
Sgt D Potter | inj | clipped a tree and crashed at Hoton, 3 miles
F/S J B Jamieson RCAF | + | NE of Loughborough, Leicestershire. Buried
| | nearby at Burton-on-the-Wolds Church Cemetery

is F/S Jamieson RCAF, the son of Dr. D A Jamieson and Eva B Jamieson of Ottawa while Sgt Potter succumbed to his injuries on 30 November and he was taken to Middlesbrough (Acklam) Cemetery. Eventually, Sgt Peers RCAF found himself in the Middle East, serving with 624 Squadron at Blida in Algeria. On 14 July 1944, his Halifax failed to return from a Special Duties flight over France. He has no known grave and is commemorated on the Runnymede Memorial.

30 OTU | **Wellington IC** | **X9801** | **Training**
Sgt C R Kroemer RAAF | inj | T/o 2049 Hixon and crashed almost immediately
| | after, having climbed to around 400 feet, the

starboard engine cut, causing the Wellington to sink back into some trees just beyond the flare path.

29 Nov | **10 OTU Det** | **Whitley V** | **EB362** | **Air Test**
1942 | F/O G A Osborn | | T/o 1545 St. Eval. Crash-landed 1600 and
| | | caught fire at Lanhearne Barton, close to

St. Mawgan airfield, Cornwall. Displaying great gallantry, F/O Osborn was instrumental in saving the life of his observer, who had been trapped in the wreckage. On 14 March 1943, now serving with 161 Squadron, F/O Osborn's Halifax crashed near Fawley (see Bomber Command Losses, Volume 4, page 78) and for a second time this brave officer had no hesitation in remaining in the blazing bomber, helping to free his crew. In recognition of these acts of courage, he was awarded the George Medal and a First Bar, the citations being published in the London Gazette on the same day, 13 July 1943.

15 OTU | **Wellington IC** | **R1466** | **Training**
Sgt R J Christian | + | T/o Harwell for a night exercise during which
Sgt G A Brown | + | it seems that the pilot, quite unknowingly,
Sgt F R Haines | + | lost height and at 2010 flew into Moss Hill,
Sgt M E J Grace | + | Berkshire. All rest in various cemeteries
Sgt L R Johnston | + | across the United Kingdom.

30 Nov | **10 OTU Det** | **Whitley V** | **AD691** | **Op: AS Patrol**
1942 | Sgt G Bagshaw | + | T/o St. Eval. Lost without trace. All are
| Sgt E O P Bell | + | commemorated on the Runnymede Memorial. It
| P/O D V Smith | + | will be recalled that Sgt Bagshaw had saved
| Sgt B Briscoe | + | his life by parachute as recently as the end
| F/S W H Mackintosh MID | + | of October, while returning to St. Eval (see
| Sgt W M Knowles | + | page 170).

30 Nov	18 OTU	Wellington IV	Z1414		Training
1942	P/O H Kolacz PAF		inj		
	Sgt L Krukowski PAF		+		
	P/O L Orchol PAF				
	P/O T Jencka PAF				
	Sgt W Marczuk PAF				
	Sgt J Kmiecikiewicz PAF				

T/o 1445 Bramcote for bombing practice. While away from base, the weather worsened considerably and a recall message was transmitted (and acknowledged) by wireless. But, shortly before 1830, the crew were obliged to take to their parachutes and the Wellington crashed at Newnham Lodge Farm, Monks Kirby, 5 miles NNW of Rugby, Warwickshire. Sgt Krukowski PAF is buried in Newark-upon-Trent Cemetery. Of his five colleagues, Sgt Marczuk PAF went to 300 Squadron and was killed on operations to Duisburg in April 1943 (see Bomber Command Losses, Volume 4, page ninety-eight); P/O Kolacz PAF died when his 305 Squadron Mosquito VI NS901 flew into trees near Lasham airfield, Hampshire, on 25 May 1944 (he was returning to base from Bonn and he, too, lies in Newark-upon-Trent Cemetery) and P/O Jencka lost his life on 17 August 1944, when his 1586 Flight Liberator VI EW275 based at Brindisi in Italy crashed during the course of a special duties operation.

	22 OTU	Wellington III	HF633		Training
	P/O E I R Davidson RCAF		+		
	F/S V Meanwell RCAF		+		
	F/O R F Mallett RCAF		+		
	Sgt A Watson		+		
	Sgt W C Seed		+		
	Sgt S E Strydom		+		

T/o Gaydon for a night navigation exercise. Returned to base in conditions of low cloud and failing visibility and, at 0240, the bomber flew into trees while circling the airfield. Three rest in Stratford-upon-Avon Cemetery; F/S Meanwell RCAF lies in Horncastle Cemetery (his funeral may have been arranged by friends or relatives in the United Kingdom), while Sgt Watson and Sgt Seed were taken to their home towns.

	81 OTU	Whitley V	EB339		Training
	Sgt T J T Evans		+		
	Sgt L C Lawson		+		
	Sgt J Overend		+		
	Sgt Whitebeard		inj		

T/o 0055 Whitchurch Heath for a night exercise which ended eight minutes later when the bomber approaching the runway, smashed into trees 450 yards short of the flare path. On impact, the Whitley burst into flames. Sgt Evans of Finsbury Park is buried locally in Ash (Christchurch) Churchyard, Whitchurch Rural, but the others who perished were claimed by their next of kin. This was the first major accident reported from 81 OTU since its formation on 10 July 1942.

1 Dec	12 OTU	Wellington III	BK250		Training
1942	Sgt B F McMurchy RCAF				
	Sgt H Walters		inj		
	Sgt E T J O´Donoghue		inj		
	F/S D J Phillips RCAF		inj		
	Sgt G A Hutchinson		inj		

T/o 1200 Chipping Warden in a strong cross-wind and within moments the Wellington had swung out of control and was heading towards the fire tender bay. Somehow, Sgt McMurchy RCAF managed to avoid a group of civilian workers, but he was unable to prevent his aircraft from hurtling, at speed, into the control tower. With its momentum barely diminished, the bomber ran over a civilian owned car before finishing up against one of the hangars, where it began to burn with some intensity. Crash and Rescue:

F/O Gaudin

An assistant Medical Officer, was quickly on the scene, preceded by the Station Medical Officer (unnamed), and along with the Dental Officer and nursing staff, commenced giving first aid to the more severely injured. The crew were dragged to safety, though two sustained very severe burns. Subsequently, following local treatment, they were taken by ambulance to Horton General Hospital, along with two other members of crew who were not quite so badly injured. A WAAF (unnamed), who had been on duty in the Control Tower, was also admitted to the same hospital, having suffered burns to her face, hands and legs. Not surprisingly, she was also in a state of deep shock. Later, a civilian worker was also taken to Horton General Hospital with an incised facial injury. Very sadly, two of the aircrew died the next day; Sgt Walters and Sgt O´Donoghue. The former was taken to Middlesbrough (Acklam) Cemetery, the latter to nearby Banbury Cemetery. It is further indicated that two civilians perished, struck down near the hanger before they could make good their escape. It is thought that around twenty-four persons were hurt.

2 Dec	14 OTU	Wellington IC	L7850 VB-Y		Training
1942	Sgt B Brown RAAF				

T/o 1440 Cottesmore and forced landed at 1540 at Exton Park, 3 miles SE of the airfield. Accident investigators reported that the cylinder head nuts had not been tightened.

2- 3 Dec	27 OTU	Wellington III	X3944		Training

2- 3 Dec
1942

27 OTU   Wellington III X3944   Training

Sgt R E Mitchell RAAF   +   T/o 1718 Lichfield tasked for a Bullseye sortie.
Sgt A Brindle   +   In conditions of lowering visibility, the bomber
Sgt K H Park   +   crashed 0008 in the River Tame, 500 yards from
Sgt R H Sankey RAAF   +   Chetwynd (or Sater's Bridge), a hamlet to the
Sgt J B Muir RAAF   +   ESE of Alrewas and within a stone's throw from
the NE side of the airfield. The three RAAF
members of crew were buried in Fradley (St. Stephen) Churchyard, while their
two companions were taken to their home towns.

4 Dec
1942

14 OTU   Wellington IC DV929   Training

F/O W F Reilly   +   T/o 2213 Cottesmore for a night exercise but
Sgt G Groves   +   climbed far too steeply and crashed within two
Sgt J W Hyde   +   minutes of departure, coming down near the local
Sgt M Knapton   +   village. F/O Reilly rests in the American
Sgt D R Gladish RCAF   inj   section of Brookwood Military Cemetery; the
others who died were taken to their home towns.

19 OTU B Flt   Whitley V EB387   Training

Sgt J D Bradley   +   T/o 1730 Kinloss for a cross-country exercise.
Sgt F J Fowler   +   During the evening, the local weather worsened
Sgt H Bell   +   and a general recall message was broadcast.
Sgt T Collingwood   +   At 2223 flames were seen directly S of the
Sgt B D Gregory RCAF   +   airfield and it was soon confirmed that the
Whitley, which had received a "green" from the
airfield controller, had flown into trees at Woodhead Farm, literally within
sight of the runway. Sgt Gregory RCAF rests in Kinloss Abbey Burial Ground,
while the others were claimed by their next of kin.

5 Dec
1942

15 OTU   Wellington IC DV724   Training

Sgt B G Hawkes   +   T/o Harwell for a night exercise but within a
Sgt G A Griffiths   +   few minutes the starboard engine cut and before
Sgt R Craven   +   the crew could return to base, the Wellington
Sgt L H Harper   +   stalled and crashed 2112 amongst trees near
Sgt R E Edgson   inj   Ardington, 2 miles ENE of Wantage, Berkshire.
Sgt Hawkes and Sgt Edgson, the latter dying
from his injuries within 24 hours of the tragedy, were taken to their home
towns while their three colleagues were laid to rest in Harwell Cemetery.

21 OTU   Wellington IC DV563   Training

P/O B W Taylor   T/o Edgehill for night flying practice. At
approximately 0015, the Wellington was caught
in a severe downdraft as it approached the airfield from the direction of Old
Lodge Hill (on the NW side of the aerodrome) and coupled with a gusting wind,
the pilot lost control, crashed and bounced onto the airfield and caught fire.

6 Dec
1942

12 OTU   Wellington III BJ614   Training

F/L D A Shead   T/o Chipping Warden for a night exercise.
Sgt J R Longstaff   +   During the sortie, the gyros failed and at
    inj   around 0245 the Wellington came into land at
    inj   Harwell. Unfortunately, the approach was made
downwind and the bomber was wrecked when it
ran beyond the runway and into the overshoot area. Sgt Longstaff was cremated
at Leicester City (Gilroes) Crematorium. Not long after this incident, F/L
Shead was posted to 427 Squadron but failed to return from a gardening duty
on 21-22 January 1943 (see Bomber Command Losses, Volume 4, page 24). Along
with his crew, he is commemorated on the Runnymede Memorial.

14 OTU   Wellington IC R1522 -Q   Training

Sgt W J Collins RNZAF   +   T/o 0008 Cottesmore tasked for a night training
Sgt L R Arps RCAF   +   exercise but crashed almost immediately near
Sgt C W Furlong   +   Barrow, 4 miles NNE of Oakham, the wreckage
Sgt B C Beard   +   being spread along the Cottesmore to Market
    inj   Overton road. Of those who died, three were
laid to rest in the extension to Cottesmore
(St. Nicholas) Churchyard, while Sgt Furlong was taken to Theydon Bois (St.
Mary) Churchyard. The Court of Inquiry concluded that the flaps were raised
in mistake for the undercarriage and at low altitude the aircraft was back
on the ground before the pilot realised his error.

6 Dec	28 OTU	Wellington IC	R1223	Training

1942

F/S R M Williams	inj	T/o 1630 Wymeswold for night flying practice.
Sgt F R Page	inj	At 1940, the bomber was seen on approach to
Sgt D R Loyd	inj	the runway but before reaching the threshold
Sgt N K Millard	+	it veered off the centre line and the throttles

were advanced in order to go round again. While doing so, the Wellington crashed into trees just to the SW of Hoton, a village some 3 miles NE of Loughborough, Leicestershire. Twenty-four hours after the crash, Sgt Loyd died from his terrible injuries. Along with Sgt Millard, he is buried in Burton-on-the-Wolds Church Cemetery.

7 Dec	10 OTU	Whitley V	Z9478	Training

1942

| Sgt B G Cameron | T/o 1820 Abingdon for a night cross-country. |
| Sgt A E Arter | Returned to base circa 2250 but was wrecked |

after landing short of the runway and ending up in an armaments compound. A fire broke out, but the crew scrambled clear with little more a few scratches. Sgt Arter eventually became a Pathfinder captain, flying Halifaxes with 35 Squadron. On 23-24 August 1943, he was briefed to operate as a backer up over Berlin (his sixth operation in this role) but failed to return (see Bomber Command Losses, Volume 4, page 280).

8 Dec	21 OTU	Wellington IC	DV425	Training

1942

Sgt V T Drew	+	T/o Moreton-in-Marsh for night circuits and
Sgt L A McGuire RAAF	+	landings. While so engaged, it began to rain
Sgt C E Raggett	+	(quite heavily) and the crew were advised to

hold off until the storm had passed through. Unfortunately, control was lost and the bomber came down 4 miles downwind of the flare path at 0005, hitting the ground at High Furze, a mile to the W of Burmington and about 2 miles SSW from Shipston-on-Stour, Warwickshire. Two were taken to their home towns, while Sgt McGuire RAAF was laid to rest in Moreton-in-Marsh New Cemetery.

9 Dec	10 OTU	Whitley V	P5040	Training

1942

| Sgt G W Ward RAAF | T/o 1100 Stanton Harcourt for a cross-country |
| | exercise. Shortly before 1545, a serious glycol |

leakage resulted in engine failure. Selecting a suitable field for his forced-landing, Sgt Ward RAAF commenced his approach and all was proceeding to plan until a line of high-tension cables loomed into view. Pulling hard back on the control column, he managed to avoid the wires but could not prevent his Whitley from stalling into a field at Tar Farm, 3 miles SE of Witney, Oxfordshire. On 10 August 1943, Sgt Ward RAAF was killed over Germany while flying Halifaxes with 102 Squadron (see Bomber Command Losses, Volume 4, page 264).

10 OTU Det		Whitley V	Z6658	–S	Op: AS Patrol

Sgt D G Harvey	inj	T/o 1400 St. Eval. Ditched 1515, after the port
Sgt M W Borne	inj	engine caught fire. P/O Franklin, for reasons
Sgt J T Broughton	inj	that are not explained, failed to get into the
Sgt D Yates	inj	dinghy and his body was washed onto a beach in
P/O F Franklin	inj	South Wales two days later. He is buried in
Sgt D Barker	inj	Lancashire at Crompton Cemetery.

11 OTU		Wellington IC	AD592	Training

F/L F Chambers RNZAF	+	T/o Westcott for bombing practice over the Ot
F/O J F Emeney	+	Moor ranges in Oxfordshire. Believed to have
F/O C H E Jay RNZAF	+	encountered very severe turbulence as witnesses
Sgt D S Colley	+	state that the Wellington rolled suddenly and
Sgt P Dennerly	+	dived into the ground at 1845, in the area of
		the ranges. All are buried in cemeteries in

the United Kingdom; apparently, although serving with the RNZAF, F/L Chambers and F/O Jay were English born. Their loss was the start of a quite miserable month for 11 OTU for by New Year's Eve, another six Wellingtons had been lost in crashes that claimed at least another ten lives.

19 OTU		Whitley V	N1412	Training

| Sgt G Hibbs | T/o Kinloss and forced-landed 1104, wheels up, |
| | on a rifle range near the head of Findhorn Bay. |

In his statement, Sgt Hibbs said his controls had jammed, but a technical inspection could find no fault and it was concluded that the Whitley had been caught in a very severe downdraft.

9 Dec	21 OTU	Wellington IC	DV810		Training

9 Dec 1942 — 21 OTU — Wellington IC — DV810 — Training

P/O S Baker

Sgt A St. C Turner RAAF — inj

Sgt D N Dawson RAAF — inj

Sgt R D Weeks RAAF — inj

Sgt W S Sinclair RAAF

Sgt A G Allwright — inj

T/o Moreton-in-Marsh for a night cross-country. Flew into high ground at 2340 on Broomhead Moor near Stocksbridge, 7 miles SW of Barnsley, Yorkshire. Four, Sgts Turner RAAF, Dawson RAAF, Sinclair RAAF and Allwright, were destined to die on 19 April 1943, with 40 Squadron (see page 369 of 'Sweeping The Skies' by David Gunby).

9 Dec 1942 — 26 OTU — Wellington IC — DV880 — Training

P/O R Waugh

T/o 1025 Wing but came to grief when a tyre burst, causing the bomber to leave the runway and crash at fairly high speed. A fire developed in the region of the starboard engine, but the crew were able to scramble to safety, without injury.

9-10 Dec 1942 — 10 OTU — Whitley V — AD699 — Training

F/O A P C Dunlop — +

Sgt T R Beattie — +

Sgt T R Attridge — +

P/O E H Jones — +

Sgt E W Smith — +

T/o 1905 Abingdon for a night cross-country. Crashed 0110 and caught fire at Church Farm, Little Wittenham, 9 miles SSE of Oxford. The son of William Wallace Cathcart Dunlop and Adele Marie Francoise Dunlop of St. Johns, Barbados and stepson of John Cecil Wippell of Cross Roads, Jamaica, F/O Dunlop is buried in Brookwood Military Cemetery. His crew were taken to their home towns.

9-10 Dec 1942 — 24 OTU — Whitley V — EB388 — Op: Nickel

F/O F P Saunders — +

P/O J P Cranstoun — +

P/O N F Sibley — +

Sgt B K Trubshaw — +

Sgt J H Carter — +

T/o 1824 Honeybourne in the company of four other Whitleys, each carrying a quantity of F155 and F157 packages, course being set for the Orleans region of France. Came down at Senonches (Eure-et-Loir), 36 km WNW from Chartres. All rest in Senonches Communal Cemetery. Three, P/O Cranstoun, P/O Sibley and Sgt Carter were not yet twenty.

9-10 Dec 1942 — 25 OTU — Wellington III — BK259 -A — Op: Nickel

Sgt K A G Miller RCAF — inj

Sgt R H Pennells — inj

Sgt J H S Harsley

Sgt M H King

Sgt W Foster

T/o 2055 Finningley and set course for Lille. Released Nickels at 2315 from 18,000 feet in the target area. Weather conditions in the area were quite cloudy and light flak was also experienced. While returning to base and upon crossing the coast at Berch-sur-Mer (sic), observed at least sixteen flak ships. However, engine trouble manifested itself and at 0220 the bomber forced-landed at Arram, a hamlet practically on the NE perimeter of Leconfield airfield, Yorkshire.

10 Dec 1942 — 11 OTU — Wellington IC — DV777 — Training

Sgt F G James — inj

Sgt F Hall — inj

Sgt E S Kirkpatrick RNZAF — +

Sgt E A Horsley — inj

Sgt G C Spurden — inj

T/o Oakley for practice bombing, at night, possibly over the Radway ranges. Encountered adverse weather and when the crash came at 0212 near Byfield, 15 miles WSW of Northampton, the Wellington had strayed from its intended course. Sgt Kirkpatrick RNZAF was taken to Banbury Cemetery. Sgt James was admitted to Horton General Hospital with head injuries, while the others who survived were treated in SSQ Chipping Warden. Subsequently, Sgt Horsley, a Freeman of Coventry, was killed on 14 March 1943; he is buried in Cambridge City Cemetery, while Sgt Spurden lost his life on 22-23 March 1944, while on operations with 44 Squadron (see Bomber Command Losses, Volume 5, page 123).

10 Dec 1942 — 11 OTU — Wellington IC — DV916 — Training

Sgt F E Darch — +

Sgt J T Swift — +

Sgt L A Arbutt — +

Sgt R Weston — +

Sgt T D Kent — +

T/o Westcott for a night navigation flight. While trying to find the aerodrome, with the cloud base reported to be as low as 500 feet, the Wellington crashed 0240 at East Claydon, six miles SSE of Buckingham. They were about six miles from their base. Sgt Kent lies in Westcott (St. Mary) Churchyard; Sgt Darch rests at Wandsworth (Putney Vale) Cemetery; Sgt Swift is in Castleford (Whitwood) Cemetery; Sgt Arbutt was taken to Chingford Mount Cemetery and Sgt Weston to Rolvenden (St. Mary) Churchyard.

10 Dec	20 OTU B Flt	Wellington IC	L7867 JM-J		Training
1942	F/O J W Heck RAAF		+		
	Sgt J Towers		+		
	Sgt W E Riley		+		
	Sgt M Hutt		+		
	Sgt J Hemmings		+		
	Sgt P E Underwood		inj		

T/o Lossiemouth armed with 8 practice bombs, two smoke floats and 2 sea markers. Reported to have crashed 1500, descending through the cloud cover, onto Ben Alder near Fort William in Argyllshire. F/O Heck RAAF and his Liverpool born navigator, Sgt Riley, rest in Lossiemouth Burial Ground while the others who died were claimed by their relatives. Sgt Underwood was admitted to Fort William Hospital.

	22 OTU	Wellington III	DF736 DD-L		Training
	WO1 D M Smardon RCAF		+		
	Sgt F J Baker		+		
	Sgt A E Nash RCAF		+		
	Sgt W E Halliday		+		
	F/S W Suttill RCAF		+		

T/o Gaydon for a night cross-country. On return to base, crashed, inverted, 0008 at Little Hill Farm on the N side of Wellesbourne Mountford airfield. At the time of the crash, there was total cloud cover and it is thought the pilot lost control as he banked in the strong gusting wind. The three RCAF members of crew are buried in Stratford-upon-Avon Cemetery while Sgt Baker and Sgt Halliday rest in Ramsgate and St. Lawrence Cemetery and Belfast (Dundonal) Cemetery respectively.

11 Dec	10 OTU Det	Whitley V	Z9437 -O		Op: AS Patrol
1942	P/O F L Perrers		int		
	Sgt W Walpole		int		
	Sgt J Clapperton		int		
	Sgt R B Newton		int		
	Sgt J F White		int		
	Sgt F J Crowe		int		

T/o St. Eval. Forced-landed on the beach at Salinas (Asturias), Spain, after encountering problems with the engines.

	12 OTU	Wellington III	BK243		Training
	Sgt R B Lapsley RNZAF		inj		
	F/S D H Fryer		inj		
	Sgt M H Pierson		inj		
	Sgt P H Sharpe		inj		
	Sgt G A Furste RCAF		inj		
	Sgt J R Nash		inj		

T/o Turweston for a night exercise. Crashed while flying a low circuit, having broken out of cloud, described as having a base between a thousand and 200 feet. Sgt Furste was an American serving with the RCAF; he was very seriously injured. Crash and Rescue:

LAC Chapman
LAC Hansford
LAC B V Icke
LAC D L Jenkins

These four airmen were soon on the scene and equipped with crowbars and metal cutting shears they set about freeing the trapped crew. Two, the pilot and F/S Fryer, were in a critical state and F/S Fryer (it is believed) died at the scene. He is buried in High Wycombe Cemetery, though it is noted that his parents address is given as Freshwater on the Isle of Wight. Sgt Lapsley RNZAF was taken to Northampton General Hospital where he succumbed to his injuries the next day; he rests in Banbury Cemetery. Later, the Station Commander at Turweston complimented the four airmen, principally involved in the rescue, for their prompt action.

	15 OTU	Wellington IC	Z1093		Training
	F/S G Hall				

T/o 1913 Harwell with the intention of carrying out a night training flight but, due to incorrect flap settings, the Wellington failed to become airborne. With insufficient runway left in which to bring the aircraft to a stop, F/S Hall retracted the undercarriage and moments later the bomber skidded, at high speed, into the overshoot area where the starboard engine commenced to burn.

	25 OTU	Wellington III	BK211 -X		Training
	Sgt H H Barker		+		
	Sgt D M Heycock		+		
	Sgt D Holmes		+		
	Sgt E Clarke		+		
	Sgt A Bateman		+		

T/o 1908 Finningley for a Bullseye sortie but, tragically, became hopelessly lost. In the last few minutes of their flight, the crew put out an SOS call. On its receipt, it was assessed that the bomber was over the English Channel and at around 2220 the Wellington was ditched, N of Cherburg. All are commemorated on the Runnymede Memorial. This particular aircraft had been involved in a Nickel raid over Rouen on 5 December, when its captain had been Sgt G W Armstrong.

11 Dec　　**26 OTU**　　　　**Wellington IC**　**X9622**　　　　　　　**Training**
1942　　Sgt E C Jones　　　　　　+　T/o 1815 Little Horwood for a night cross-
　　　　Sgt S R Appi　　　　　　+　country. At approximately 2215, the bomber was
　　　　Sgt W B Barclay　　　　+　seen in the circuit but as it turned towards the
　　　　Sgt Lennox　　　　　　+　runway, it stalled and dived into the ground. On
　　　　Sgt D Bell　　　　　　+　impact a column of smoke and flame shot into the
　　　　F/S D J Clark RCAF　　inj　night sky. The Court of Inquiry suggested that
　　　　　　　　　　　　　　　　a film of rain across the windscreen may have
distorted the pilot's vision. F/S Clark RCAF, an American from Seattle in the
State of Washington, was taken to Princess Mary's Hospital, Halton, where he
lingered for nearly a day. He is buried in Halton (St. Michael) Churchyard.
His skipper rests in Aylesbury Cemetery, while the rest of the crew were taken
to their home towns.

　　　　27 OTU　　　　**Wellington III**　**X3961**　　　　　　　**Training**
　　　　F/S G R Cook　　　　　inj　T/o 1942 Lichfield for a night exercise, only to
　　　　F/S F T J Bryant　　　+　crash fourteen minutes later at Stychbrook Farm
　　　　F/S C R Shade RAAF　　inj　near the airfield. The accident was attributed
　　　　Sgt W T Chandler　　　+　to failure to remove the pitot tube cover prior
　　　　P/O W Harrison　　　　inj　to departure, thus rendering the air speed
　　　　F/S D E H Smith　　　　+　indicator inoperative. Three died in the crash
　　　　Sgt H P Wishart RAAF　inj　and within twenty-four hours two others (F/S
　　　　Sgt I O Maxwell　　　inj　Cook and P/O Harrison) had passed away. Sgt
　　　　　　　　　　　　　　　　Wishart RAAF lost his battle for life on 22
December. Along with F/S Bryant, he rests in Fradley (St. Stephen) Churchyard.
The others were claimed by their next of kin. P/O Harrison was the son of Sir
William Ernest Harrison and Lady Harrison of Gatley, Cheadle. F/S Shade RAAF
made a full recovery and, subsequently, he was commissioned. By the spring of
1945, he was flying Beauforts with 8 Squadron RAAF, operating from Tadji. On
21 April, he failed to return from an anti-submarine patrol; he is commemorated
on the Lae War Memorial at Papua, New Guinea.

11-12 Dec　**25 OTU**　　　　**Wellington III**　**BJ620**　**-T**　　　　**Training**
1942　　S/L C Anextein　　　　inj　T/o 2014 Finningley briefed to participate in a
　　　　P/O A Booth　　　　　　inj　Command Bullseye exercise. Due to deteriorating
　　　　Sgt A Tanswell　　　　+　weather, the crew were diverted to Wymeswold
　　　　Sgt J B Reay　　　　　　　airfield, Leicestershire. Arriving here at
　　　　Sgt H Ellis　　　　　　　around 0120, the bomber flew into trees near
　　　　Sgt W Hardaker　　　　inj　the perimeter and crashed on the airfield
　　　　Sgt A L Payne　　　　　　boundary. Sgt Tanswell is buried in Cheetham
　　　　　　　　　　　　　　　　Hill (St. Luke) Churchyard, Manchester. The
survivors were, eventually, posted to various squadrons and during 1943, three
were killed on operations. Sgt Reay, now of 12 Squadron, died over the United
Kingdom while returning from Lorient in mid-February; in mid-June, Sgt Payne's
100 Squadron Lancaster crashed in Germany and then, on Christmas Eve, while
raiding Berlin, Sgt Hardaker's 115 Squadron Lancaster failed to return (see
Bomber Command Losses, Volume 4, pages 40, 183 and 438 respectively). This
was the last major incident involving a 25 OTU aircraft ahead of the unit's
disbandment on 1 February 1943.

12 Dec　　**11 OTU**　　　　**Wellington IC**　**R3214**　　　　　　　**Training**
1942　　P/O G C Crew　　　　　　　T/o Westcott for a night exercise. Landed
　　　　　　　　　　　　　　　　at 1950, in a strong cross-wind, whereupon
the undercarriage gave way. Although not seriously damaged, the airframe was
downgraded with effect from 25 December for instructional purposes with 3473M
applied.

　　　　20 OTU A Flt　　**Wellington IC**　**DV551**　　　　　　　**Training**
　　　　Sgt P Turner-Jones　　inj　T/o 1900 Lossiemouth carrying 8 flash bombs,
　　　　Sgt P Colgan　　　　　　inj　two smoke floats, 2 flame floats and 2 sea
　　　　Sgt D R Tarbuck　　　　inj　markers. During the exercise, the port engine
　　　　P/O G W Cox　　　　　　+　failed and on reaching base, at circa 2115, the
　　　　Sgt H O McNeice　　　　inj　starboard motor cut as the crew made ready to
　　　　Sgt F A Ingram RCAF　　　land. The injured were taken to Dr Gray's
　　　　　　　　　　　　　　　　Hospital, where in the mid-afternoon of the
thirteenth, Sgt Tarbuck died; he is buried in Heswall (St. Peter) Churchyard.
P/O Cox rests in Penarth Cemetery. Sgt Ingram RCAF, described as an American,
escaped unharmed.

12 Dec 1942	28 OTU	Wellington IC	T2896	Training

P/O E C Loughead RCAF   +   T/o 2040 Wymeswold for night circuits and
Sgt C G Foster RNZAF   inj   landings. Reported that the crew lost sight
Sgt Godfrey   inj   of the flare path and at 2300 crashed into
F/S Crickmore   inj   trees not far distant from Loughborough,
Leicestershire. P/O Loughead RCAF rests
in Burton-on-the-Wolds Church Cemetery. Sgt Foster's injuries were so severe
that it was nine months before he was passed fit to resume pilot training. In
due course, he flew Lancasters out of North Killingholme with 550 Squadron and
was midway through his tour when he failed to return from the costly Nürnberg
raid in March 1944 (see Bomber Command Losses, Volume 5, page 157). Errol
Martyn also reports that Sgt Foster's brother, P/O Athol Foster RNZAF died
along with his pupil while instructing on Tiger Moths at 4 EFTS Whenuapai,
New Zealand, on 30 July 1941.

13 Dec 1942	19 OTU	Whitley V	BD294	Training

Sgt G P Godwin RAAF   T/o 1130 Kinloss for a cross-country. Five
hours later, and due to failure of one or both
engines, the Whitley was put down in the Moray Firth, off the hamlet of Covesea
which lies on the north side of Lossiemouth airfield.

14 Dec 1942	10 OTU Det	Whitley V	AD687	Op: AS Patrol

Sgt F S Higginbottom   +   T/o St. Eval. Presumed lost over the sea. Two
P/O G T Thomson   +   bodies were recovered, those of P/O Thomson and
Sgt J E Watson   +   Sgt Watson. The former is buried in Edinburgh
Sgt D W J Hanson   +   (Morningside) Cemetery, while Sgt Watson was
Sgt J Patton   +   taken to Lytham St. Anne's (Park) Cemetery.
The others are commemorated on the Runnymede
Memorial.

	22 OTU	Wellington III	HF632	Training

F/S R F James RCAF   +   T/o Wellesbourne Mountford for a navigation
P/O E L Lasby RCAF   +   detail. While returning to base, spun out of
P/O R H Miller   +   control and crashed 1659 into Kissing Tree Lane
Sgt S E Swallow   +   at Alveston, 2 miles NE of Stratford-upon-Avon
Sgt R G Causier RCAF   +   and within sight of the airfield. Funerals for
the three Canadian members of crew were held at
Stratford-upon-Avon Cemetery; eighteen year old P/O Miller rests in Sheffield
(Crookes) Cemetery, while Sgt Swallow was taken back to Kent and buried in
Canterbury Cemetery. At least one of the five (though he is not named) lived
for a few hours before dying in Stratford EMS Hospital.

16 Dec 1942	15 OTU	Wellington IC	T2902	Training

Sgt A Clouting   +   T/o 1923 Harwell for a night exercise but
Sgt W Stewart   +   while circling the airfield, ten minutes after
F/O G W Stone   +   departing, came down a mile S of Blewbury,
Sgt S E A Carter   +   some 3 miles SSE of Didcot, Berkshire. All
Sgt J S T Baxter   +   were taken to their home towns for burial,
two in Scotland and three in England.

16-17 Dec 1942	14 OTU	Wellington IC	R1603	Training

Sgt G H Weeden RCAF   T/o 2310 Cottesmore for night flying. While
in flight, one or more of the cylinder bracing
struts fractured and at 0100 the Wellington forced-landed on the boundary of
Harlaxton airfield, Lincolnshire. It is strongly suspected that Sgt Weeden
was commissioned and, if this is the case, died when his 617 Squadron Lancaster
crashed in France while carrying out Special Operations Executive duties on 10
December 1943 (see Bomber Command Losses, Volume 4, page 419).

	23 OTU	Wellington III	X3336	Training

F/S R V W Bellew   +   T/o 1838 Pershore carrying 8 x eleven-and-a-half
Sgt A J Dubben   +   pound practice bombs and equipped with Gee and
P/O A Higgins RCAF   +   IFF. Strayed from track and crashed on Carlside
P/O R S Goodwin   +   Fell near Bassenthwaite, 7 miles ENE from
Sgt G W Hicks   +   Cockermouth, Cumberland. P/O Higgins RCAF of
Sgt R W Lawton RCAF   +   Toronto is buried in East Wickham (St. Michael)
Churchyard, Bexley, his parents living nearby at
Welling. Sgt Lawton RCAF rests in Silloth (Causewayhead) Cemetery, as does his
skipper, F/S Bellew. The others were taken to their home towns.

17 Dec
1942

10 OTU Det   **Whitley V** **EB363** **–Q**   **Op: AS Patrol**
Sgt M T Denham RNZAF   + T/o 0725 St. Eval armed with 4 x 250lb depth
P/O P A Davies   + charges and headed out over the Atlantic. At
Sgt R Rawcliffe   + approximately 1240 the Whitley was operating
P/O V J Wotton   + off the coast of north-west France when it was
F/S T H Miller   + intercepted by a fighter and shot down into the
P/O R Sword   + sea. Sgt Denham RNZAF is buried in Concarneau
                            Communal Cemetery; P/O Davies, who had gained
a University of Oxford Secondary Teachers' Art Certificate, was washed ashore
on 11 March 1943 and laid to rest that same day in St. Brieuc Western Cemetery,
while P/O Wotton's grave can be found in the English Cemetery at Dinard. The
others are commemorated on the Runnymede Memorial.

13 OTU   **Blenheim IV** **Z7422**   **Training**
F/O F H Tan   T/o 2350 Finmere for night flying but the
Sgt M Leyden   starboard engine cut and F/O Tan immediately
Sgt S J Bate   closed the throttles and applied the brakes.
                          Realising he was not going to stop within the
confines of the airfield, he raised the undercarriage and, eventually, his
Blenheim came to a halt 150 yards beyond the flare path, wrecked.

18 Dec
1942

10 OTU Det   **Whitley V** **AD684** **–H**   **Op: AS Patrol**
Sgt K B Dowding   T/o 0800 St. Eval but within forty-five minutes
                          the crew were back at base, their aircraft
having lost power from its starboard engine. Landing cross-wind, on a wet
surface, the brakes proved ineffective and the Whitley finished up against
a bank on the edge of the airfield. The final impact was quite severe and
two members of crew required medical attention.

20 OTU   **Wellington IC** **X9911 JM–B**   **Training**
Sgt H C Dixon RCAF   T/o 1230 Lossiemouth for a cross-country sortie.
                          Returned to base circa 1600 but having overshot
the runway and while trying to go round again, failed to maintain height and
crashed, heavily, breaking the Wellington's back. Ten months later, and now
commissioned, Sgt Dixon RCAF was flying Spitfires at 8 OTU Dyce when he failed
to return from a training sortie in Spitfire V AB124. He is commemorated on
panel 175 of the Runnymede Memorial.

20 Dec
1942

12 OTU   **Wellington III** **Z1617**   **Training**
Sgt G Campain   inj T/o 0523 Chipping Warden for practice bombing
                          (probably on the Radway ranges). Returned to
base but while approaching the runway, stalled and crashed 0623. The Court of
Inquiry found that fatigue was the most likely cause, having discovered that
it was Sgt Campain's second sortie of the night. Less than a month later,
and not long after returning to flying duties, he was dead, killed while flying
under tutelage from S/L Foreman DFC.

21 OTU   **Wellington IC** **R1344**   **Training**
Sgt J D Muir   T/o Edgehill for night practice bombing over
Sgt R G Percival   + the Radway ranges. The first photoflash was
                          successfully released but the second jammed in
the flare chute and exploded. With flames streaming from the fuselage, Sgt Muir
ordered everyone to bale out but receiving no acknowledgement from his wireless
operator and, thus, believing he may have been incapacitated by the explosion,
Sgt Muir decided to forced-land. This he did, at 0215, most skillfully, in a
field at Compton Wynyates on the W side of Lady Elizabeth's Hill and nearly
five miles ENE of Shipston-on-Stour, Warwickshire. Sadly, his suspicions
proved correct and Sgt Percival was buried in Moreton-in-Marsh New Cemetery.
It will be recalled that Sgt Muir, whose log book was endorsed "highly commended"
for his actions this night, had crash-landed on 3 September (see page 150 for
this and details of his subsequent fate).

21 OTU   **Wellington IC** **R1534**   **Training**
P/O E F Elliott RAAF   T/o Moreton-in-Marsh for a cross-country.
                          Abandoned 1315, following total failure of
the starboard engine, in the vicinity of Upper Talwedd, Radnorshire. The
accident investigation team reported that it seems likely No. 2 cylinder head
on the starboard engine exploded.

21 Dec	13 OTU		Blenheim IV	Z7361		Training
1942	W/O D Lyth			inj	T/o 0955 Bicester but failed to gain flying	

speed and crashed into a parked Albemarle.
It transpired that the Blenheim had run its engines for approximately forty
minutes prior to its attempted departure.

	13 OTU		Albemarle	P1459		Ground

Wrecked in the manner described above. This
was the first and only Albemarle to be written off at a Bomber Command
Operational Training Unit.

	14 OTU		Wellington IC	T2887		Training
	Sgt G S Boyle			inj	T/o 0740 Cottesmore for a navigation exercise.	
	Sgt Tomlinson			inj	Crash-landed 1030, following a fire in the	
	Sgt Brown			inj	starboard engine of such intensity that the	
	Sgt Gay			inj	unit burnt through its mountings and fell from	
	Sgt Woods			inj	the aircraft, at Millhill Farm near Bingham,	

nine miles E of Nottingham.

22 Dec	26 OTU		Wellington IC	Z8950		Training
1942	Sgt C G Randolph			+	T/o 1924 Wing in the company of other aircraft	
	Sgt J Patterson			+	for a night bombing exercise, the crews being	
	Sgt W K Charlton			+	made up of pupils from No. 11 Course and their	
	Sgt D S Waltho			+	instructors. At approximately 2030, this air-	

craft was involved in a midair collision with
another of the Wellingtons, both machines smashing into the ground near the
village of Hoggeston, 7 miles NNW of Aylesbury, Buckinghamshire.

	26 OTU		Wellington IC	DV915		Training
	P/O E G Wagstaff RNZAF			+	T/o 1924 Wing similarly tasked and lost in the	
	Sgt E C King			+	manner described previously. P/O Wagstaff RNZAF	
	Sgt W Precey			+	and two others from his crew rest in Aylesbury	
	Sgt G Gardner			+	Cemetery, while the others (and those from Sgt	
	Sgt J D Osborne			+	Randolph's crew) lie in cemeteries across the	
	Sgt J Feord			+	United Kingdom. Sgt Charlton (see above) was the	

son of Capt Rudolph Charlton, Royal Artillery.

23 Dec	27 OTU		Wellington III	BJ834		Training
1942	Sgt W F Mizon RAAF			inj	T/o 1842 Church Broughton for night flying	
	Sgt C R Morgan RAAF			inj	practice. Crash-landed 1922, wheels up after	
	Sgt C J Hoggett			inj	the port engine caught fire, on the airfield.	
	Sgt A J Barnett			inj	Sgt Barnett was killed on the Augsburg raid on	

25-26 February 1944 (see Bomber Command Losses,
Volume 5, page 105) while flying with 467 Squadron.

24 Dec	10 OTU Det		Whitley V	AD711	—R	Op: AS Patrol
1942	Sgt F P O'Malley			inj	T/o 0920 St. Eval. On return to base, at 1830,	
	Sgt R E Pigney			inj	the weather conditions were appalling and the	
	Sgt H T Brown			inj	Whitley crashed at Sea View Farm, near the air-	
	Sgt H E Williams RCAF			inj	field. In his statement Sgt O'Malley said he	
	Sgt D McMillan RCAF			inj	saw three white lights as he made his approach	
	LAC S Hughes			inj	through the mist and he took these to be the	

flare path indicators. On realising this was
not the case, he increased power to go round again but as he pulled back on the
control column there was a grinding noise as the bomber ploughed into the ground.

	10 OTU Det		Whitley V	BD261		Op: AS Patrol
	Sgt R A Brant			+	T/o St. Eval similarly tasked. Ditched 1000, due	
	Sgt J B Woods				to engine failure, off Pedn-men-du Point near	
	Sgt A B P Rumsey			+	Sennen, a village near Land's End and 4 miles	
	Sgt J F Bootle			+	SSW of St. Just. Sgt Rumsey is commemorated on	
	Sgt R J Simmons RCAF				panel 92 of the Runnymede Memorial, while Sgt	

Brant and Sgt Bootle are buried in Boston (Holy
Trinity) Churchyard and Southport (Duke Street) Cemetery respectively.

Note. By the winter of 1942-1943, the St. Eval detachment were keeping a
reasonable set of records and for most entries the aircraft's individual
letter is shown. As an indication of the strength of the detachment, it
is believed that the only letters not taken up were I, L, N, W and X.

28 Dec　　**10 OTU Det**　　　　　**Whitley V**　**Z6669**　**–F**　　　　　　　**Op: AS Patrol**
1942　　Sgt F Charlton　　　　　　　+　T/o 0553 St. Eval. On return to base, in the
　　　　　P/O Clutterbuck　　　　　　　　gloom of evening, the weather was so poor that
　　　　　Sgt Glencross　　　　　　　　　the crew were advised to divert to Exeter.
　　　　　Sgt Llewellyn　　　　　　　　　However, the Whitley was very low on fuel and
　　　　　Sgt J R Worthington　　　　　　Sgt Charlton decided that his best course of
　　　　　Sgt Le Marchant　　　　　　　　action was to gain altitude and bale his crew
　　　　　　　　　　　　　　　　　　　　out. This he did, after which he tried to save
his aircraft by forced-landing. Thus, at 1720, he began his approach to a field
at Coobes Head Farm, Lewannick, 4 miles WSW of Launceston, Cornwall but in the
last few seconds before touch down he lost control and crashed. On impact, his
aircraft burst into flames and so died a very gallant pilot who undoubtedly
took the ultimate risk with his own life in order to save those of his crew.
Taken back to Durham, he is buried in Ferryhill Cemetery.

　　　　　23 OTU　　　　**Wellington III**　　**BK517**　　　　　　　　　**Air Test**
　　　　　F/O J G Bryne　　　　　　　　　+　T/o 1120 Pershore but encountered very poor
　　　　　F/S J T McDonald RCAF　　　　　+　weather conditions and twenty-five minutes into
　　　　　F/S W McMillan　　　　　　　　　+　the test, the bomber hit a tree and crashed near
　　　　　LAC L H Nicholson　　　　　　　+　Bodicote, 2 miles SSE of Banbury, Oxfordshire.
　　　　　AC2 J E G Beaumont　　　　　　　+　F/S McDonald RCAF was taken to Middleton Stoney
　　　　　AC2 G Broadhurst　　　　　　　　+　(All Saints) Churchyard; the others were claimed
　　　　　　　　　　　　　　　　　　　　by their next of kin.

29 Dec　　**11 OTU**　　　　　**Wellington IC**　　**R1174**　　　　　　　　　**Training**
1942　　Sgt F R W Henderson　　　　　+　T/o Westcott for a combined navigation and
　　　　　Sgt Wright　　　　　　　　　inj　bombing exercise. Emerged from cloud, in a
　　　　　Sgt F W R Cumpstey RNZAF　　　+　dive, and crashed 1915 on Morvil Mountain near
　　　　　Sgt F H Sherriff　　　　　　　+　Fishguard, Pembrokeshire. Most, possibly all,
　　　　　Sgt Gillies　　　　　　　　　inj　managed to bale out before the final impact.
　　　　　　　　　　　　　　　　　　　　Sgt Henderson is buried in Tunbridge Wells
Cemetery and Sgt Sherriff rests at Heswall (St. Peter) Churchyard, Wirral.
Sgt Wright was admitted to Haverford West County Hospital, concussed, with
compound fractures and burns. The other survivors were treated at the East
Lancashire Battalion Sick Quarters in Fishguard. Sgt Cumpstey RNZAF went on
to fly with 75 Squadron and was half way through his tour of operations when
he was killed at the end of July 1943 (see Bomber Command Losses, Volume 4,
page 252).

　　　　　15 OTU　　　　　　**Defiant I**　**N1704**　　　　　　　　　　　**Training**
　　　　　W/C R S Ryan　　　　　　　　　　　T/o 1450 Harwell for cine camera gun training.
　　　　　　　　　　　　　　　　　　　　Forced-landed at 1520 after a severe glycol
leakage caused the engine to overheat, starting a fire behind the bulkhead.
W/C Ryan was unhurt but the Defiant, believed to have been the first of its
type written off at a bomber OTU, lay wrecked in a field 1 mile to the W of
Pangbourne, 5 miles WNW from the centre of Reading.

30 Dec　　**11 OTU**　　　　　**Wellington IC**　　**X9681**　　　　　　　　　**Training**
1942　　P/O J W G Palmer-Lettington　+　T/o Westcott for a night exercise. Crash-
　　　　　　DFM　　　　　　　　　　　　landed with total engine failure, colliding
　　　　　P/O I S Gow　　　　　　　　　inj　with a tree, at Ashendon on the S side of the
　　　　　F/O J S Hutton　　　　　　　　+　airfield. P/O Palmer-Lettington, whose award
　　　　　F/O D P Wadey RNZAF　　　　　inj　was gained in the service of 108 Squadron and
　　　　　Sgt A E Parker　　　　　　　inj　Gazetted on 22 January 1943, is buried in
　　　　　　　　　　　　　　　　　　　　Wandsworth (Streatham) Cemetery, while F/O
Hutton, whose parents lived in Buenos Aires, Argentina, lies in Westcott (St.
Mary) Cemetery. P/O Gow and F/O Wadey RNZAF were very seriously injured and
both were taken to Princess Mary's Hospital, Halton suffering from multiple
bone fractures. Sgt Parker escaped with minor cuts and abrasions, and shock.

31 Dec　　**11 OTU**　　　　　**Wellington IC**　　**DV764**　　　　　　　　　**Training**
1942　　Sgt A J Thomas　　　　　　　inj　T/o Westcott for a night exercise. Lost power
　　　　　Sgt H A Stewart　　　　　　　inj　from one engine and while trying to reach Wing
　　　　　Sgt L P Dennis　　　　　　　inj　airfield, crashed 2330 at Burcott Farm, Burcott,
　　　　　Sgt R Boxall　　　　　　　　inj　a hamlet on the N side of Wing village. Three,
　　　　　Sgt L H Farquhar　　　　　　inj　Sgts Thomas, Dennis and Farquhar were taken to
　　　　　　　　　　　　　　　　　　　　Halton to join their colleagues injured in the
crash, described above. Sgt Stewart subsequently became a prisoner of war. It
is noted that at the end of May 1942, their Wellington had been coded OP-E.

31 Dec	16 OTU	Wellington III	Z1665	Training

1942

F/L V E Sutherland RNZAF	+	T/o 1815 Upper Heyford for an evening bombing
P/O J A Foulkes	+	detail but crashed a few minutes later, into a
P/O R Cowin	+	wood, near Barton Abbey, 4 miles WSW from the
P/O D F S Clarke	+	airfield. The first two named rest in Middleton
Sgt K A Brooks	+	Stoney (All Saints) Churchyard, while the others
Sgt J R Simpson	+	who died were taken to their home towns. Prior
Sgt I E Lambert	inj	to his appointment as a staff pilot at 16 OTU,
		F/L Sutherland RNZAF had flown with 405 Squadron.

	19 OTU	Whitley V	N1371	Training

W/O C M Browning	+	T/o Kinloss for a night bombing exercise only
Sgt M J F Teasdale	+	to crash into Findhorn Bay, roughly a mile E of
Sgt W S Peacock	+	Burghead and almost in line with the flare path.

Eyewitnesses stated that the bomber's engines seemed to be running normally but having climbed to around 300 feet, the Whitley banked and dived into the sea. W/O Browning is commemorated on panel 72 of the Runnymede Memorial, his service number indicating he had joined the air force in the early 1930s. Sgt Teasdale is buried in Wick Cemetery, while Sgt Peacock was interred at Winlanton (St. Paul) Roman Catholic Cemetery. An attachment of the Royal Air Force Regiment located the wreckage during the mid-afternoon of New Years Day and an Air-Sea Rescue launch was summoned to the scene. However, rough seas prevented the launch from closing on the wreckage and it was decided that any future salvage work would be conducted from the shore.

Resumé. So ended a most eventful year for the Bomber Command training units. During the twelve months past, six new formations had come into being, four being equipped with Wellingtons, while Whitleys filled the establishments for No. 24 OTU at Honeybourne and No. 81 OTU at Whitchurch Heath and, basically, these would be the dominant types throughout 1943 and well into 1944. As has been mentioned in the summaries, Nos. 14 and 16 OTUs gave up their Hampdens in favour of Wellingtons, while the two Blenheims units (Nos. 13 and 17 OTUs) were deemed sufficient to service the needs of No. 2 Group. Not surprisingly, this expansion had witnessed an increase in accidents, while the operational role that the training units were tasked for in the summer of 1942 had robbed the Command of many experienced staff. The disruption caused to the training programmes was duly noted by several units, though it must be said that the trainees had responded quite magnificently to the challenge and, certainly, without the input from these establishments, the '1,000 plan' raids on Köln, Essen and Bremen would not have been possible.

But of paramount importance was the overall state of Bomber Command. At the beginning of the year the Command was in the doldrums; its then Commander-in-Chief, Sir Richard Peirse no longer had the confidence of the Air Staff and was in the process of making way for his successor, while the conclusions of the recently released Butt Report were still being digested in the corridors of power. The future of Bomber Command looked bleak indeed.

Now, a year later, a total transformation had taken place. At High Wycombe a new air of confidence prevailed and this had spread to the bomber groups and the squadrons operating under their authority. The reasons for this new wave of optimism stemmed directly from Sir Richard's replacement, namely Air Marshal Sir Arthur Harris. Students of air force history are well versed in the knowledge as to how Sir Arthur, ably supported by his deputy Air Vice-Marshal Robert Saundby, set about revitalising the fortunes of his command. Between them, they laid the foundations for the future conduct of the bombing campaign which, by the end of 1942, was beginning to show the first signs of a successful outcome to the now near nightly battle over Occupied Europe and Germany itself.

1 Jan
1943

11 OTU   **Wellington IC DV926**   **Ground**
At 0600, while being refuelled at Oakley from a nine-hundred gallon fuel bowser, the earthing connector came off. Seconds later a static discharge ignited petrol vapour and in the ensuing blaze the Wellington was destroyed.

2 Jan
1943

13 OTU   **Blenheim IV V6147**   **Training**
Sgt W Stokes   T/o 0950 Bicester for a navigation exercise.
Sgt D H Redmond   inj While returning to base, at around noon, the
Sgt F J M White   crew noticed smoke billowing from the starboard
                                     engine and soon after a severe vibration was
felt. Closing down the engine, course was set for Watchfield airfield, but at 1235, while turning towards the runway, the port motor cut and the Blenheim crash-landed near Shrivenham, Berkshire.

18 OTU   **Wellington I L4379**   **Training**
P/O A Ratajczak PAF   T/o 1015 Bramcote for a cross-country flight,
P/O C Czekalski PAF   during which icing affected the carburettors.
Sgt A E Korzeniowski PAF + Crashed 1245 (possibly after being abandoned)
Sgt J Drapala PAF   near Nottingham. Sgt Korzeniowski PAF rests
Sgt R Baszowski PAF   in Newark-upon-Trent Cemetery. On 27 July
Sgt M Nogacki PAF   1945, P/O Ratajczak was killed when his 301
                                     Squadron Warwick III HG226 encountered bad
weather over France and spun into the ground 32 km S of Lyon. Along with three fellow countrymen, he is buried in the extension to Mazargues Cemeter, Marseille.

2- 3 Jan
1943

24 OTU   **Whitley V EB389**   **Training**
Sgt A Little   + T/o 2329 Honeybourne for a high-level bombing
P/O R P Mason   + sortie, at night. It is believed the photoflash
Sgt K J Fielding   + exploded prematurely, leading to a catastrophic
Sgt D Bell   + crash at 0005 into Weston Park, Cherington, 3
Sgt J Davidson   + miles SSE of Shipston-on-Stour, Warwickshire.
                                     Sgt Little, who had gained a Bachelor of Science
degree in agriculture at Edinburgh University, is buried in Clunie Churchyard; his London born navigator, P/O Mason, was taken to Evesham Cemetery; Sgt Bell lies in Rossington (St. Michael) Churchyard; Sgt Fielding rests at Barking (Rippleside) Cemetery, while Sgt Davidson is interred at Croy Parish Churchyard.

3 Jan
1943

19 OTU C Flt   **Whitley V N1469   -Z**   **Training**
Sgt J H Whiting RAAF   T/o Kinloss for a night cross-country. Came
Sgt Bell   down at circa 0030 on Mannoch Hill, some 3 miles
Sgt Simpson   NW of Archiestown, 12 miles S from Elgin, Moray.
Sgt Thompson   The weather at the time was extremely poor with
Sgt Fowler   sleet showers reducing visibility almost to nil.
                                     By early evening, the entire crew were back on
station, two being admitted to SSQ suffering from severe bruising. A remarkably concise record of events has been preserved in the unit's Operational Records Book and a precis of these reports can be found in the appendices.

3- 4 Jan
1943

22 OTU   **Wellington X HF751**   **Training**
F/O E C Badcoe   T/o Gaydon for a night navigation exercise.
P/O M H J Hammill   While nearing the airfield, the port propeller
                                     went into fully fine and the crew were further
inconvenienced by the undercarriage failing to lock in the down position. Thus, at 0001 the bomber crash-landed, wheels retracted, and with the port engine stopped. No one was hurt, but the first Mk. X Wellington to be involved in a major accident at a bomber training establishment was deemed to be beyond economical repair. Before the year was out, P/O Hammill (who had joined 408 Squadron) was a prisoner of war (see Bomber Command Losses, Volume 4, page 149).

4 Jan
1943

21 OTU   **Wellington IC W5613**   **Training**
Sgt R Clark RNZAF   + T/o Moreton-in-Marsh for a night navigation
Sgt Wilson   detail. Crashed 0025 at Orchardleigh Park, some
Sgt Osborne   two miles NW from Frome, Somerset, following an
Sgt A J Cook   + uncontrollable fire in the starboard engine.
Sgt W Perkins   + Sgt Clark RNZAF was taken to the city of his
                                     birth and interred in Glasgow (Riddrie Park)
Cemetery, Sgt Cook rests in Frinton-on-Sea (St. Mary) Churchyard, while Sgt Perkins of Sale in Cheshire is buried in Bath (Haycombe) Cemetery, Englishcombe.

4 Jan
1943

22 OTU   **Wellington III**   **HF685**   **Training**
Sgt V W Richards   T/o 0253 Gaydon for a night exercise but stalled
                              at 300 feet and crashed on the left hand side of
the runway. From the evidence available, it seems he (Sgt Richards) survived
the war.

5 Jan
1943

20 OTU   **Wellington IC**   **R3232 ZT-H**   **Training**
S/L D E W Adamson   +   T/o Lossiemouth for an evening navigation
Sgt R G A Styles   +   sortie. Reported by the Royal Observer Corps to
P/O R I Bernstein   +   have crashed near Auchtermuchty, Fife. All rest
P/O L A Tramson   +   in cemeteries across Scotland and England. P/O
P/O W Singer   +   Singer had attended Edinburgh College of Art,
Sgt W S Hogg   +   gaining a Diploma. An investigation into the
                              cause of the crash concluded that it was most
likely an engine had failed and that the pilot put the live engine into fine
and opened the throttle, but owing to his inexperience he failed to correct the
resultant swing and finished up in a spiral dive. It then seems he closed the
throttle to the live engine and attempted to straighten out. Failing to arrest
his descent, he switched on his landing lights for a forced-landing but crashed
in the attempt.

6 Jan
1943

10 OTU Det   **Whitley V**   **BD272 -M**   **Op: AS Patrol**
F/O T Franks   +   T/o St. Eval armed with 6 x 250lb depth charges
Sgt R S Williams   +   and carrying two F24 cameras. Lost without
F/O H J Godfrey   +   trace. All are commemorated on the Runnymede
F/S R Johnson   +   Memorial.
F/S H Watts   +

8 Jan
1943

17 OTU   **Blenheim IV**   **L4895**   **Training**
F/L R H Moore   T/o 1625 Upwood only to crash, in the circuit,
                              five minutes later. F/L Moore reported that
the starboard engine lost power as he climbed away. His aircraft had been on
the strength of 17 OTU since 22 April 1940, and had amassed a very respectable
1,262 flying hours.

17 OTU   **Blenheim IV**   **V6393**   **Training**
P/O G P R Weil   T/o 1400 for a navigation exercise. While over
                              the Kent countryside, encountered heavy rain
and, later, icing. Force-landed 1745, without injury, having suffered total
communications failure.

8- 9 Jan
1943

19 OTU   **Whitley V**   **P4969 UO-O**   **Training**
Sgt J M Parsons RAAF   T/o 2300 Kinloss for a night cross-country,
                              combined with bombing. Towards the end of the
sortie, the starboard engine caught fire and the Whitley force-landed, 0445,
on or near Lossiemouth airfield. Not long after this incident, Sgt Parsons
made the conversion to Lancasters and was posted to 467 Squadron. On 25-26
May 1943, while operating against Düsseldorf, his aircraft was shot down by
flak over Belgium (see Bomber Command Losses, Volume 4, page 164).

9 Jan
1943

14 OTU   **Wellington IC**   **W5629**   **Training**
Sgt J F H Mahony   +   T/o 1031 Cottesmore only to crash at 1036 about
P/O J P Butler   +   a mile from Ashwell station, 3 miles N from
Sgt J H Dillman RCAF   inj   Oakham, bursting into flames. The three who
Sgt R C Havelock   +   died were taken to their home towns. It is
Sgt J Hill   inj   noted that P/O Butler came from a titled family
P/O H D Link RCAF   inj   and was an ex-Cambridge University graduate.

9-10 Jan
1943

11 OTU   **Wellington IC**   **X9953**   **Training**
Sgt C Hoy   +   T/o Westcott for a night navigation exercise.
Sgt V J Sharp RNZAF   inj   Iced up; abandoned and crashed 0001 near Burbage
P/O E J Mansell   inj   on the S side of Hinckley, Leicestershire. Sgt
Sgt J E Hoey   inj   Hoy is buried in a joint grave at Hull Eastern
Sgt I Tvrdeich RNZAF   inj   Cemetery with his brother, F/O Stanley Hoy, who
                              lost his life on 12 February 1943. Of the four
survivors, two were destined to lose their lives; Sgt Hoey, who was posted to
75 Squadron was killed on 23-24 September 1943, while four nights later his
colleague, Sgt Sharp RNZAF, serving with 90 Squadron, died in a crash near
Cambridge (see Bomber Command Losses, Volume 4, pages 330 and 336 respectively).

10 Jan
1943

10 OTU Det   **Whitley V** **Z6464**   **—G**   **Op: AS Patrol**

Sgt J R Terry	+	T/o 0900 St. Eval but swung to port and, out of
Sgt A I Davies	+	control, collided with a B.24 Liberator 239230
Sgt A R Knowles	inj	belonging to the 1st AS Squadron USAAF, which
Sgt K Sanderson	inj	had been parked 100 yards off the runway. In
Sgt L W West	inj	seconds both aircraft were ablaze and before
Sgt Amos		either crew could make good their escape, the

depth charges exploded. Sgt Terry is buried at
West Ham in Manor Park Cemetery, while his co-pilot was taken back to Wales and
laid to rest in Rhondda (Ferndale) Cemetery. Of the others aboard the Whitley,
only Sgt Amos got out, unscathed. From the ten airmen aboard the Liberator, two
were killed outright and two died from their wounds (see Addendum for details).

20 OTU   **Wellington IC** **T2713**   **Training**

P/O P C Anscombe	inj	T/o 1751 Lossiemouth for a night navigation
P/O R J Frost	+	detail. When a little over an hour into the

exercise, an engine began to overheat and the
oil pressure fell to zero. The unit was throttled back but when power was re-
applied, the motor cut completely. The order to bale out was given and the
Wellington crashed 1915 at Cunnighie Farm, near Ladybank, Fife. One of the
injured was admitted to a Military Hospital at Larbert after sustaining a
fracture to his lower spine. Sadly, P/O Frost failed to leave the aircraft
and on impact he was tossed from his rear turret. He is buried in Eastbourne
(Ocklynge) Cemetery, while resting nearby in Eastbourne (Langney) Cemetery is
Sgt Reginald Arthur Frost who died in the service of 612 Squadron on 6 May
1943. Both airmen shared a common first Christian name, Reginald, though it
is not known if they were related. The Wellington, here summarised, had been
held on unit charge since mid-December 1941, and had accumulated 731.20 flying
hours (including usage with 57, 149 and 115 Squadrons).

11 Jan
1943

14 OTU   **Wellington IC** **DV449**   **Training**

Sgt C P Bradshaw   T/o 1555 Cottesmore for circuits and landings.
                          Touched down at 1600, heavily, and bounced back
into the air. Before Sgt Bradshaw could catch the bomber on the throttles, it
stalled at a mere thirty feet and crashed into a motor transport vehicle, with
fatal consequences for its civilian driver.

16 OTU   **Wellington III** **Z1669**   **Training**

P/O Manuel   T/o Upper Heyford for a night navigation flight.
Sgt Nunez   Became lost and crashed 2205 into high ground,
                          obscured by cloud, near All Stretton, 12 miles
south-south-west of Shrewsbury. There are no reports of anyone being hurt,
despite the manner in which the aircraft came to grief.

22 OTU   **Wellington III** **HZ104**   **Training**

P/O E E Fisher RCAF   inj T/o Wellesbourne Mountford for a night exercise.
                          Due to adverse weather (the wind was gusting very
strongly), the crew were advised to land at Cosford airfield in Staffordshire. At
2304, while approaching the runway, the Wellington hit a telegraph pole and came
down near the perimeter. Eighteen year old P/O Fisher RCAF was admitted to RAF
Hospital Cosford, where he died three days later. He is buried in Donnington (St.
Cuthbert) Churchyard.

27 OTU   **Wellington III** **BK405**   **Training**

F/O R H Tye RNZAF	+	T/o 1535 Church Broughton with the intention of
Sgt W R Wearne RAAF	+	carrying out circuits and landings, combined with
Sgt I R McDonald RAAF	+	single-engined flying. At around 1550 the pupil
Sgt J Kerr	+	pilot went through the drills in readiness to
Sgt J S Eccles RAAF	+	shut down the port engine but, tragically, he

feathered the starboard propeller. Immediately,
the bomber spun and crashed at Boylestone, 7 miles S of Ashbourne, Derbyshire.
F/O Tye RNZAF, an experienced Wellington captain and veteran of an operational
tour with 75 Squadron, along with two of the Australians, lies in the extension
to Scropton (St. Paul) Churchyard, Foston and Scropton. Sgt Eccles is believed
to have been an Englishman, serving with the RAAF; he is buried in his parents
home town of Salford, Lancashire. Sgt Kerr was taken to St. Albans Cemetery.
Their aircraft was relatively new having been held in storage at 23 MU Aldergrove
from 19 October 1942 until its acceptance by the unit in mid-December. Its total
flying came to 25.40 hours.

11 Jan 1943	81 OTU	Whitley V	LA766		Training

WO1 D R Roberts RCAF   +   T/o 1607 Whitchurch Heath for an evening cross-

Sgt C E Aaron   +   country with a screened pilot, navigator, wire-

P/O R J Binham   +   less operator and five pupils. Crashed 2050,

Sgt A T Strachan   +   having acknowledged four QDMs, some 23 miles

Sgt D B Lister   +   from base and in the county of Denbigh. Four

F/S R Smeaton   +   were interred in Wrexham Cemetery, while the

Sgt M J Buckle   +   rest were taken for burial or cremation (as in

F/S W H Stewart RCAF   +   the case of Sgt Strachan) in their home towns.

---

13 Jan 1943   **12 OTU**   **Wellington III**   **X3338 JP-P**   **Training**

S/L D M Foreman DFC   +   T/o 1735 Chipping Warden for high-level bombing

Sgt G Campain   +   practice. At 1830, while flying at 900 feet,

P/O D W C Jepp   +   the port engine failed and five minutes later

Sgt B Sober   +   the starboard motor cut. Immediately, the

Sgt W H J Nott   +   aircraft spun out of control and crashed some

Sgt J G Arnold   inj   two miles NE of Woodford, 6 miles ESE from

Kettering, Northamptonshire. Those who died rest in various cemeteries. P/O Jepp was the son of Major John William Jepp and Emily Mary Jepp of Farnham in Surrey. Sgt Arnold was found, unconscious, in the rear turret. Sgt Campain, it will be recalled, had been injured in a serious accident a little over three weeks previous (see page 185) and had only just being deemed fit to resume flying duties.

---

26 OTU   **Wellington IC**   **T2619**   **Training**

Sgt C D Belcher   T/o Wing for a navigation exercise. While

Sgt J C Paynter   over the West Country, the port propeller came off followed by partial failure of the starboard engine. Crash-landed 1441, wheels up, while trying to reach Davidstow Moor airfield in Cornwall, 12 miles WNW of Launceston and on the N side of Bodmin Moor. Three weeks later, Sgt Belcher and his crew were obliged to bale out during the course of a night cross-country.

14-15 Jan 1943   **29 OTU**   **Wellington X**   **DF614**   **Op: Nickel**

Sgt E A Kelly   +   T/o North Luffenham and set course for Nancy.

Sgt G W Brothwell   +   Believed shot down between Baromesnil and

Sgt D C Nelson   +   St-Remy-Boscrocourt, two villages in Seine-

Sgt A S Grove   +   Maritime and some 6 km to 10 km S of the small

Sgt S Cookson   +   coastal town of le Treport. Sgt Grove lies in the former, while Sgt Cookson is buried at the latter, their three companions having been interred at Dieppe Canadian War Cemetery. It is noted that Sgt Nelson's parents lived at St. Saviour on the Channel Island of Guernsey. Ordered as a Wellington Mk.III, the bomber was converted to Mk.X standards prior to being issued to 29 OTU.

---

15 Jan 1943   **16 OTU**   **Wellington III**   **BJ763**   **Training**

P/O J C Boodrie   +   T/o 2015 Barford St. John for night circuits

Sgt R E Keene   +   and landings. At approximately 2155 an engine cut and this led to a crash, on rising ground, about 4 miles E of the airfield and less than a mile NNE of Aynho, a village in Northamptonshire, some 5 miles SSE of Banbury, Oxfordshire. P/O Boodrie rests in St. Albans Cemetery, while Sgt Keene of Hayes, Middlesex, was taken to Middleton Stoney (All Saints) Churchyard.

---

23 OTU   **Wellington III**   **X3964**   **Training**

F/S W J A Duplin RCAF   +   T/o 2317 Pershore for night circuit training.

Sgt J H Robson   +   All went well until 2342 when the centre cam-

Sgt W E Barr RCAF   +   shaft roller bearing disintegrated in the port engine. With only 200 feet in hand and with full flap selected, the pilot stood no chance whatsoever and the bomber smashed into the ground, just beyond the runway. All are buried in Pershore Cemetery.

---

23 OTU   **Wellington III**   **BK512**   **Training**

F/O A M H Gain RCAF   +   T/o 1800 Pershore for a Bullseye armed with

Sgt E A Antrobus   practice bombs. Crashed one hour later, after

Sgt V M White RCAF   the starboard engine siezed, at Orton-on-the-

Sgt V M Caplin   Hill, Leicestershire, 4 miles E from Tamworth,

Sgt D J Burge   Staffordshire. F/O Gain RCAF was laid to rest in Pershore Cemetery.

16 Jan	10 OTU D Flt	Whitley V	BD234	-P	Training

16 Jan 1943 — **10 OTU D Flt** — **Whitley V** — **BD234** — **-P** — **Training**

Sgt D Brown — inj
Sgt W Rose — inj
Sgt R A Wakeling — inj
Sgt W F Martin — inj
Sgt T B Rowan — inj

T/o 0001 Stanton Harcourt for a night exercise. Crashed 0120, due to port engine failure brought about by glycol leakage, at Twelve Acre Farm on the W side of Eynsham and roughly 2 miles N from Stanton Harcourt village. Two of the injured had to be admitted to the Radcliffe Infirmary.

19 Jan 1943 — **20 OTU C Flt** — **Wellington IC** — **HD985** — **XL-R** — **Training**

Sgt R F Wilkins RCAF — +
Sgt C B Morris — +
P/O R V Say — +
Sgt A R Eastbury — +
Sgt A G Walters — +
Sgt T M Slattery — +

T/o 1411 Lossiemouth armed with 8 practice bombs, flame floats, smoke floats and signal cartridges, but as the Wellington lifted from the runway an engine stalled (due to failure of the reduction gear) and the aircraft crashed on the nearby beach. Sgt Wilkins RCAF was laid to rest in Lossiemouth Burial Ground, while the others were claimed by their next of kin.

22 Jan 1943 — **10 OTU Det** — **Whitley V** — **Z6753** — **-S** — **Op: AS Patrol**

Sgt B W E Wedderburn
Sgt B J Clinging
Sgt F O Ross RCAF
P/O P Sandal
Sgt F C Fidgeon
Sgt S H C Brown

T/o 0605 St. Eval. At 1410, sighted a Ju88. After engaging the enemy aircraft, the Whitley escaped into a fortuitous bank of cloud. On completing their mission, the crew returned to base only to encounter such atrocious weather that Flying Control ordered them to make for Cleave airfield on the north Cornish coast near Bude. This relatively small, pre-war aerodrome, was used by anti-aircraft co-operation flights and at 1640 the Whitley overshot its runway and ended up hard against an earth bank. Apart from P/O Sandal, all were posted to 76 Squadron and were killed during operations to Plzen on 16-17 April 1943 (see Bomber Command Losses, Volume 4, page 111).

11 OTU — **Wellington IC** — **X9641** — **Transit**

Sgt W G Shillinglaw RAAF

T/o 1239 Bassingbourn with the intention of returning to Oakley. Climbed to 1,500 feet at which point the starboard engine cut. Sgt Shillinglaw RAAF put the nose down and had just commenced a right hand turn at 1,200 feet when the motor caught fire. However, the flames were extinguished and four minutes after its departure, the Wellington crash-landed back on the airfield. Subsequently commissioned, Sgt Shillinglaw was posted to 218 Squadron only to be lost over Belgium on 21-22 June 1943 (see Bomber Command Losses, Volume 4, page 195).

19 OTU C Flt — **Whitley V** — **AD686** — **-V** — **Training**

Sgt F B Solomon RCAF

T/o 2015 Kinloss for a night cross-country. At 2055, a wireless message was received indicating that the starboard engine had cut out at 10,000 feet and the bomber was losing height. This loss of altitude was arrested at 9,000 feet and course was set for Perth, but when the port engine began to overheat the captain, wisely, decided to bale out his crew. Thus, at 2200, or thereabouts, the Whitley crashed between the Blairgowrie to Kirkmichael Road and the Blairgowrie to Dunkeld Road, some 18 miles NNW of Perth. All were taken to the Bridge of Earn Hospital for a check up before being returned to Kinloss.

29 OTU — **Wellington III** — **X3307** — **Training**

F/O J P Farrow DFM RNZAF — inj
F/L G H Pemberton — inj
LAC E Wakefield — inj
AC1 C Downend — inj

T/o 1410 Bruntingthorpe for circuit training. Fifty minutes later, the starboard engine burst into flames and the bomber came down 2 miles SW of the airfield. F/O Farrow, who had gained his DFM flying Hampdens with 408 Squadron (Gazetted on 10 February 1942), went on to become an outstanding Mosquito pilot, flying Pathfinder missions with 692 Squadron. On 26-27 June 1944, his aircraft was hit by flak NW of Aachen during operations to mark some railway workshops at Göttingen (see Bomber Command Losses, Volume 5, page 304). Having managed to bale out, F/O Farrow RNZAF was made a prisoner of war. F/L Pemberton lost his life in a Stirling crash on 23 November 1945 (possibly Mk.V PJ904 which came to grief at Lyneham). Serving at the time with 46 Squadron, he is buried in Lyneham (St. Michael) Churchyard, Wiltshire.

23 Jan 1943	**11 OTU**	**Wellington IC**	**X9616**		**Training**

Sgt C C P Logan RAAF   inj   T/o 1845 Oakley for a night cross-country but
Sgt A J Robinson RNZAF   inj   due to a defective No. 2 cylinder on one of the
Sgt N T Lawrence   inj   engines, a trailing exhaust valve stuck wide
Sgt W H Garvin   open. In turn, this lead to a situation where
Sgt B L Cooksley RNZAF   inj   the crew thought the entire engine was ablaze.
While trying to regain the airfield, the air-
craft hit some trees and crashed short of the runway. No one was too badly
hurt but the Wellington was consumed by fire. Sadly, two from the crew never
saw the dawn of 1944; Sgt Garvin was posted missing from operations on 25 July
and Sgt Logan RAAF failed to return on 24 September. Both had been serving
with 75 Squadron and their fates are described in Bomber Command Losses,
Volume 4, pages 238 and 329 respectively.

	14 OTU	**Wellington IC**	**DV842**		**Training**

F/S F N Crouch RAAF   inj   T/o 0918 Saltby for circuits and landings.
P/O J N Jotcham   inj   Circa 0940, following a normal take off, the
                        inj   starboard engine cut and the bomber crash-
                        inj   landed a mile S of Harlaxton airfield in
Lincolnshire.

	15 OTU	**Wellington IC**	**R1799**		**Training**

Sgt A G H Nichols   +   T/o Harwell for an evening navigation sortie.
P/O G W Lean   +   At 1905, while making a fourth attempt to go
Sgt D W Miles   +   round again, the starboard engine faltered and
Sgt P De V McMahon   +   with only 20 feet or so in hand, Sgt Nichols
Sgt P R Leigh-Morgan   inj   was unable to prevent his aircraft from crashing
                               into the stream bordering the airfield and near
the village of Limington, on the ESE side of Ilchester, Somerset. P/O Lean, who
hailed from St. Leonards-on-Sea, rests in Bridgwater (Quantock Road) Cemetery,
Sgt McMahon was taken back to the Irish Republic and interred in Glasnevin (Or
Prospect) Cemetery, Co. Dublin, while their companions lie in their home towns.

24 Jan 1943	**17 OTU**	**Blenheim IV**	**L9333**		**Training**

Sgt R M Leeming   T/o 1204 Upwood for a navigation detail. On
                               return, fog had encroached upon the local area
and while trying to land at nearby Warboys, the Blenheim crashed 1659, flipping
on to its back. Sgt Leeming and his crew, apparently , escaped serious injury.
His aircraft had had a reasonably unusual history in that it was first issued
to a Coastal Command Operational Training Unit (No. 1), before being passed to
No. 2(Coastal) OTU but was then switched to one of Fighter Command's training
establishments, namely 54 OTU. Its involvement with Bomber Command commenced
on 30 July 1942, when it was accepted at Upwood. When written off, it had
chalked up a useful 830 flying hours, in total.

	20 OTU	**Wellington IC**	**N2769 JM-E**		**Training**

F/L R H B Field   +   T/o Lossiemouth for a night navigation exercise.
Sgt R Webb   +   Last heard on wireless at 2128, when a QDH was
Sgt R C Evans   +   obtained on the leg between St. Abb's Head and
Sgt H A S Fraser   +   5800N 0030W. Despite an exhaustive search by
F/S O W Stone RCAF   +   two Ansons and 7 Wellingtons, no trace of this
                               aircraft, or its crew, were found. All are
commemorated on the Runnymede Memorial. F/S Stone RCAF was an American from
Silver Grove, Kentucky.

	24 OTU	**Anson I**	**AX432**		**Training**

Sgt P L Lockhart   inj   T/o 1830 Honeybourne for a night cross-country.
                        inj   Landed 2135 at Chipping Norton airfield but ran
                               beyond the landing area and crashed into a hut.
On 9 January, this Anson (with S/L White at the controls) had force -landed at
Gatwick with engine trouble, returning to Honeybourne two days later. It may
be recalled that Sgt Lockhart had served as a staff pilot on B Flight 10 OTU and
on 18 November 1942 had been involved in a crash-landing (see page 175).

25 Jan 1943	**22 OTU**	**Wellington X**	**HF735**		**Training**

Sgt J A Mason   T/o Wellesbourne Mountford. Landed 1238, but
                               touched down at least two thirds of the way
along the runway. Consequently, the Wellington finished up in the overshoot
area, damaged beyond repair.

25–26 Jan 1943	15 OTU	Wellington IC	R1491	Training

Sgt G G Ottley + T/o 2146 Harwell for a navigation exercise, by
Sgt L C Muston + night. At around 0140, six minutes before its
Sgt J S Todd + final impact, Royal Observer Corps lookouts saw
Sgt C Edwards + the Wellington on fire and it is believed it may
Sgt B H Parker + have hit Coed Coclior, 1,180 feet above sea
level, fracturing fuel lines or tanks before
Mr E William + being catapulted back into the air and impacting
Mrs A J William + on Bwlchy Lilw farmhouse near Llansilin, 20 miles
Mstr T D William inj south-south-east of Ruthin, Denbigh. Three of the
Miss A William inj crew are commemorated on the Runnymede Memorial,
but Sgt Muston of Fulham and Sgt Todd of Epsom
are interred in Oswestry General Cemetery. It is further reported that a land
girl, employed at the farm, escaped unharmed and, possibly, one other daughter
of the William's family.

26 Jan 1943	23 OTU	Wellington III	Z1695	Training

Sgt J S Cornfield RCAF + T/o Pershore tasked for a Bullesye sortie. At
P/O R P Love + circa 2130, the bomber caught fire in flight and
Sgt T A J Whalley + the wings, along with the tail unit, broke away.
Sgt B P Enright + Moments later, the fuselage thudded into Runham
F/O D R A MacDougall RCAF + Marshes near Halvergate, 5 miles WNW of Great
Sgt J J Snyder RCAF + Yarmouth, Norfolk. In the last few minutes
prior to this tragedy, the Wellington had been
illuminated by searchlights. Sgt Cornfield RCAF was taken to the Jewish section
of Norwich Cemetery, four were buried at Scottow Cemetery, while Sgt Whalley
rests in Oxford (Rose Hill) Cemetery. Sgt Enright hailed from Limerick in the
Irish Republic, while Sgt Snyder RCAF was an American from Kansas City, Missouri.
Three days previous, Sgt Cornfield RCAF had crash-landed Wellington III X3956
(repaired) at Shawbury, in which Sgt N Montgomery had dislocated his shoulder.

	29 OTU	Wellington III	BJ779	Training

F/L J H Clark + T/o North Luffenham similarly tasked. While
Sgt J Amost + flying at 12,000 feet became coned in search-
Sgt J H Renshaw + lights and dived, 2215, inverted into the ground
P/O S J Powell + a mile E of Wyton airfield, Huntingdonshire.
Sgt D A Pauling + Eyewitnesses state that in the seconds prior
to its terminal dive, Verey distress flares
were fired from the Wellington. Sgt Renshaw and New Zealand-born Sgt Pauling
lie in Houghton and Wyton Burial Ground, the others being taken to their home
towns. Errol Martyn reports in his magnificent tribute to New Zealand airmen
who died in both wars that Sgt Pauling had originally enlisted in the Fleet Air
Arm but transferred to the air force in January 1942, training as an air gunner.

26–27 Jan 1943	21 OTU	Wellington IC	X9667	Enemy Action

Sgt G G Ellis + T/o 1830 Moreton-in-Marsh briefed for a Bullseye
F/O F H Mitchell RAAF + sortie which involved the crew in flying out over
Sgt E H Tucker + the North Sea to a position at least fifty miles
P/O D Llewelyn + off the coast. Shot down by Lt Wolfgang Kűthe,
Sgt R E Elvin + IV./NJG1 and fell 0025 into the Waddenzee, E of
W/O J N Morgan pow Wieringen (Noord Holland). Those who perished
Sgt N G Smith RAAF + rest in cemeteries along the coast of Holland.

27 Jan 1943	10 OTU Det	Whitley V	Z6875 —P	Op: AS Patrol

Sgt W T Mercy T/o 0800 St. Eval attached to 59 Squadron. While
Sgt P C Cummings returning to base, the crew became aware of dense
F/O F G Gibbs white smoke pouring from the starboard engine.
Sgt F W Dudgeon Diverting to the Scilly Island of St. Mary's, the
Sgt H B Collidge Whitley hit a belt of trees while trying to land
Sgt R M Noye on the island's airfield and at 1659 finished up
in Lambstone Quarry. It would appear that Sgt
Mercy eventually flew as an air gunner, losing his life in the service of 207
Squadron on 12 September 1944 (see Bomber Command Losses, Volume 5, page 421).

Note. It is possible the crew have not been reported in their correct order
of trades. However, Sgt Mercy is shown on Form AM 1180 as the captain of the
Whitley and the service number reported on this form matches that recorded in
the Dűrnbach War Cemetery register, published by CWGC.

27 Jan
1943

| 21 OTU B Flt | Wellington IC P9240 | Training |

Sgt C Clarke + T/o Moreton-in-Marsh for an evening cross-
Sgt H E Hole + country. It is thought likely that Sgt Clarke
Sgt N S Devereux-Mack + descended through the cloud cover in order to
Sgt G B Tarran + establish his position. In doing so, he flew
Sgt A V McD Buckingham RCAF + into the ground a mile S of Brigg, a small
Lincolnshire town in the north of the county,
seven miles ESE of Scunthorpe. RAF Kirton-in-Lindsey arranged the funeral
services for Sgt Devereux-Mack and Sgt Buckingham RCAF, while their companions
were claimed by their next of kin.

28 Jan
1943

| 14 OTU | Wellington IC Z8896 | Training |

F/S D J Farrell RCAF + T/o 0945 Cottesmore for a navigation flight.
Sgt F J Emberson + While attempting to land at Waddington airfield
Sgt R Badcock + in Lincolnshire, spun in off a left-hand turn
Sgt M McMillan + and crashed 1230 near the runway. It is thought
Sgt G G Nielsen + the crew, who are buried in various cemeteries
across the land, were experiencing problems
with the port engine. In its early service days, their Wellington had served
as a test vehicle both at the Aeroplane & Armament Experimental Establishment
at Boscombe Down and at the Royal Aircraft Establishment Farnborough where it
had tested special wireless equipment. In total, it had flown 122.00 hours.

| 20 OTU B Flt | Wellington IC HF858 | Training |

P/O P D O'Carey + T/o Lossiemouth for a night cross-country
P/O J D Birch + carrying 8 flash bombs and 2 each of flame
Sgt J Collingridge + floats, photo flashes, reconnaissance flares,
Sgt R H Credland + sea markers and smoke floats. Believed to
Sgt E S Bala + have ditched circa 2145 in the Moray Firth.
Subsequently, an empty dinghy was found; all
are commemorated on the Runnymede Memorial. P/O Birch hailed from Renvyle,
Co. Galway in the Republic of Ireland.

29 Jan
1943

| 17 OTU | Blenheim I L8718 | Training |

F/S A A Mitchell RCAF + T/o 2226 Upwood for a night exercise only
Sgt W R Deacon + to crash 2231 and burst into flames at Abingdon
Pigotts, 14 miles SW of Cambridge and within
sight of Bassingbourn airfield. F/S Mitchell RCAF rests in Bury Cemetery (his
parents were further grieved when they were informed that another son, F/O
Thomas Ridley Mitchell RCAF, was presumed killed on 13 March 1944 when his
Hurricane 5663 dived into the sea off Labrador). Sgt Deacon, meanwhile, was
taken home to Monmouth and interred at Abertillery (Aberbeeg) Cemetery.

| 22 OTU | Wellington X HF650 | Training |

F/S J L McConnell RCAF + T/o Wellesbourne Mountford for a night sortie.
P/O E McL Tew RCAF + Stalled at 1,000 feet and crashed 2355 in the
F/S G L Hall RCAF + circuit of Edgehill airfield, coming down near
F/S W E Douglass RCAF + Epwell, 6 miles W of Banbury, Oxfordshire.
F/S W A Boundy RCAF + All are buried in Moreton-in-Marsh New Cemetery.

| 23 OTU | Wellington III X3586 | Training |

F/S J A Wilson RCAF + T/o 1138 Stratford-upon-Avon for a navigation
P/O R J Archer RCAF + exercise. While flying through a scattering
F/S K H Mount RCAF + of cloud collided, at 2,000 feet, with a bomber
Sgt W Adams + from the same unit, both aircraft disintegrating
Sgt W Argo RCAF + and crashing 1215 on, or near, Honington airfield
in Suffolk. The four RCAF members of this crew,
along with their four fellow Canadians from the second aircraft, are buried in
Honington (All Saints) Churchyard. Sgt Adams was taken to Bradford (Scholemoor)
Cemetery in Yorkshire.

| 23 OTU | Wellington III Z1685 | Training |

F/S W R Harron RCAF + T/o 1120 Stratford-upon-Avon similarly tasked
Sgt M J Kelly RCAF + and lost in the manner described in the previous
F/S R E Oswald RCAF + summary. Sgt Yarker is buried in Over Silton
Sgt P Yarker + (St. Mary) Churchyard, his grave being the sole
Sgt R C Alderson RCAF + service plot from the two World wars. Like Sgt
Adams from the other Wellington, he hailed from
Yorkshire. F/S Oswald RCAF was an American from Hillside, New Jersey.

29 Jan   **23 OTU**   **Wellington III**   **BK503**   **Training**
1943

P/O M A Clancey	inj	T/o Pershore for flying practice. Lost power
P/O W C Coleman RCAF	inj	from both engines and while attempting to
P/O G G Weston RCAF	+	force-land hit some trees near Earl's Croombe
Sgt C W Wyer	inj	some 9 miles SSE of Worcester and crashed 1117,
Sgt J A R T Auclair RCAF	+	heavily. Both Canadians are buried in Pershore

Cemetery. P/O Coleman RCAF recovered from his injuries, only to be taken prisoner later in the year while serving with 419 Squadron (see Bomber Command Losses, Volume 4, page 369).

29-30 Jan   **16 OTU**   **Wellington III**   **X3890**   **Training**
1943

F/S G L Hosford GM	+	T/o 1555 Upper Heyford for an evening cross-
Sgt Tait	inj	country. This detail was successfully completed
F/O Boucher	inj	and the crew returned to base, but while still
Sgt K Lawson	+	airborne they were ordered to fly a second
P/O F L Farla	+	sortie, though of shorter duration and it was
F/S G Wartnaby	+	during the course of this additional duty that
Sgt Adair	inj	the Wellington crashed 0005 into the side of
Sgt D B E Skinner RCAF	+	Brown Clee Hill near Kidderminster, Worcester-
		shire. P/O Farla and Sgt Skinner RCAF were

taken to Bridgnorth Cemetery, while the others who died rest in cemeteries scattered across the United Kingdom. F/S Hosford, whose parents address is given as Tottenham, Middlesex, is buried in Northern Ireland at Dundonald (St. Elizabeth) Church of Ireland Churchyard, Co. Down.

21 OTU   **Wellington IC**   **W5705**   **-E**   **Op: Nickel**

F/S J W McCausland RCAF	+	T/o 1756 Moreton-in-Marsh and headed for France
Sgt P E Farren	+	and, subsequently, released its cargo of leaflets
Sgt F C W Palmer	+	in the vicinity of Nantes. Damaged by enemy
Sgt G W Ayres	+	action and while trying to reach base, crashed
Sgt F A Morgan	+	near Stroud in Gloucestershire. F/S McCausland
		RCAF is buried in Cirencester Cemetery, as is

Sgt Farren. The others were taken to their home towns. Sgt Morgan's elder brother, Rifleman Colin Frederick Morgan of the 2nd Battalion, Rifle Brigade, was killed in action of 23 November 1941. He is commemorated on the Alamein Memorial. As recently as 26 January, F/S McCausland RCAF had displayed great presence of mind when the port engine of Wellington IC R1649 exploded at 4,000 feet while descending towards base. Turning onto finals, he was baulked by another aircraft, which was on the flare path. Calmly, he retracted the undercarriage and force-landed alongside the other aircraft, causing minimal damage to his Wellington.

27 OTU   **Wellington III**   **X3941**   **Training**

Sgt W A Catron RAAF	+	T/o Church Broughton for a Bullseye exercise.
Sgt K B Killeen RAAF	+	During the sortie, the weather around Church
	inj	Broughton began to close in and at 0059 a
	inj	recall message was transmitted by wireless.
	inj	This was not acknowledged. QDMs were also
		signalled, before and after 0123. At circa

0200 reports came in to say a Wellington had crashed on a hillside in Darley Dale about 4 miles from Matlock, Derbyshire. The two airmen who died rest in the extension to Scropton (St. Paul) Churchyard.

28 OTU   **Wellington IC**   **R1011**   **-M**   **Training**

F/L A W Lane	+	T/o 1924 Wymeswold similarly tasked. Crashed
P/O C D Brown	+	circa 0145 into a 1,700 foot high hill in the
Sgt R G Rouse	+	Low Moors area of Derbyshire. F/L Lane was
	inj	cremated at Cheltenham Crematorium, P/O Brown
	inj	is buried in Edinburgh (Liberton) Cemetery,
		while Sgt Rouse rests in Manchester Southern

Cemetery. The two survivors were admitted to Ashton Hospital.

28 OTU   **Wellington IC**   **R1538**   **Training**

Sgt C A Reynolds	inj	T/o 1900 Wymeswold similarly tasked. Crashed
F/S F W Bull	inj	at around 0215 at Cellarhead, 5 miles ENE from
Sgt T Butterley	+	the centre of Stoke-on-Trent, Staffordshire.
F/S R R Clarke		Sgt Butterley is buried in Portsmouth (Kingston)
Sgt A Priest	+	Cemetery; Sgt Priest lies in Stoke-on-Trent (St.
		Peter) Church Cemetery.

30 Jan   **16 OTU**   **Wellington III**   **X3889**   **Training**
1943   Sgt C P Newton   T/o 1520 Upper Heyford with both propellers set
in fixed pitch. This caused excessive over
speeding which, in turn, led to overheating. Eventually, the starboard airscrew
was feathered and a precautionary landing was made, 1645, at Silverstone. On
touch down, the Wellington began to drift and Sgt Newton realised he was heading
for some huts. In order to avoid what might prove to be a very serious accident,
he deliberately raised the undercarriage. At the subsequent Court of Inquiry,
his inexperience and the fact that he had landed on an unfamiliar aerodrome were
duly taken into account.

31 Jan   **15 OTU**   **Wellington IC**   **Z8871**   **Training**
1943   Sgt F C Swain   T/o Harwell for a night navigation exercise.
Attempted to land at Hemswell but levelled off
too high and arrived 0556 with some force on the runway. Both oleos collapsed
and having slid to a stop, the Wellington caught fire. Sgt Swain eventually
went to 196 Squadron and failed to return 28-29 April 1943 from a minelaying
sortie to the "Forgetmenots" region (see Bomber Command Losses, Volume 4,
page 127). He is buried, along with his crew, in Abenra Cemetery.

16 OTU   **Wellington III**   **X3990**   **Training**
Sgt E J Guth   +   T/o 0409 Upper Heyford for bombing practice.
Sgt G F Priest   +   Dived and crashed six minutes later at Heath-
Sgt J F Eden   +   field House, Bletchingdon, 8 miles NNW from
Sgt J H Beasley   +   the centre of Oxford. All were buried, or
Sgt E Fowell   +   cremated, at various locations throughout
Sgt S U Trowbridge RCAF   +   the United Kingdom.

19 OTU A Flt   **Whitley V**   **LA837**   **-F**   **Training**
Sgt P W Barrett   +   T/o 1035 Kinloss for a cross-country flight.
P/O S J Stenning   +   Late in the afternoon, while receiving homing
Sgt J R C Rugeroni-Hope   inj   advice from direction finding stations, all
Sgt J Douglas   +   contact ceased at around 1700. Subsequently
Sgt A P Watson   inj   it was established that the bomber had flown
into high ground 2,000 feet above sea level
in the Hills of Cromdale, 6 miles ENE from Grantown-on-Spey, Moray. Of those
who died, three were claimed by their next of kin, while P/O Stenning of North
Kensington was buried locally in Kinloss Abbey Burial Ground. It is noted that
Sgt Rugeroni-Hope died from his injuries on 2 February 1943.

1 Feb   **11 OTU D Flt**   **Wellington IC**   **X9798**   **-N**   **Training**
1943   P/O A Cameron DFM   +   T/o Westcott for a night exercise. Overshot
Sgt D Ryan   +   the runway, lost control and crashed 0013 at
Sgt G H Brookes RNZAF   +   Ashendon, 7 miles W from Aylesbury, Bucking-
Sgt W E Hopkins   +   hamshire. Weather conditions were dreadful;
F/S W C Gilpin DFM   +   low cloud and rain severely reducing visibility.
Sgt T G Knope   +   Those who died rest in various United Kingdom
Sgt D R Taylor   inj   cemeteries. Although serving with the RNZAF,
Sgt Brookes was English born and his grave is
in Burton-upon-Trent Cemetery. P/O Cameron's DFM, awarded for his outstanding
service with 12 Squadron, had been Gazetted on 30 January 1942. F/S Gilpin,
whose parents address is given as Kitscoty, Alberta, gained his award with
115 Squadron, details being published on 23 December 1941. Sgt Taylor was
taken to the Princess Mary's Hospital at Halton where surgeons attended to
his fractured tibia and fibia.

22 OTU   **Wellington X**   **HF646**   **Training**
Sgt R E Todd RCAF   T/o Wellesbourne Mountford for night circuits
and landings. At 1908, he landed without the
aid of flaps and by doing so finished up in the overshoot area, where the bomber
caught fire. In his post accident statement, Sgt Todd RCAF indicated his entire
concentration had been taken up with problems with the throttles, though he had
believed flapless landings were part of his exercise. However, this had not been
sanctioned in the authorisation book. Due to the confusion on this point and
bearing in mind his relative inexperience, no further action was taken. Posted
to 426 Squadron, he failed to return from operations to Bochum in late March
1943 (see Bomber Command Losses, Volume 4, page 87). It is noted that he was
an American from Colorado Springs, Colorado.

1 Feb **26 OTU** **Wellington IC** **X9755** **Training**
1943 Sgt D A J McDonald + T/o Little Horwood for an evening exercise.
F/S C D Donald RCAF + During the flight, the starboard engine caught
Sgt G E McGeown + fire and all efforts to extinguish the flames
Sgt T H E Henwood inj were unsuccessful. While attempting to force -
Sgt C D Hore inj land, at 1850, the aircraft hit some trees and
crashed near Beachampton Rectory, Beachampton,
four miles ENE of Buckingham. Sgt McDonald, who had married Frances Nellie
Gamble McDonald of Bessemer, Alabama, is buried in Aylesbury Cemetery. F/S
Donald RCAF was taken to Brookwood Military Cemetery, while the others who
died (including Sgt Henwood who succumbed to his injuries while being treated
at Halton) rest in various cemeteries.

2 Feb **81 OTU** **Whitley V** **Z6496** **Training**
1943 Sgt A C Best inj T/o 1820 Whitchurch Heath for a night cross-
country. On return to base at 2200, a glycol
leakage from the starboard engine caused the motor to fail. Sgt Best lowered
the undercarriage, at 900 feet, but the Whitley sank rapidly and crashed,
short of the runway. A fire broke out and it is thought every member of
crew sustained injuries of one sort or the other.

3 Feb **27 OTU** **Wellington III** **BK241** **Training**
1943 Sgt F G Bell RAAF + T/o 1812 Church Broughton for a night cross-
Sgt A W Reid + country. Returned to base, circa 2300, and
Sgt K V Howes RAAF + commenced to circle in readiness to land. At
Sgt F J Keown + 2302, however, the Wellington went into a flat
Sgt R K Hodson RAAF + spin and crashed 4 miles to the NE of the air-
field. Sgt Keown was taken back to Northern
Ireland and buried in Belfast (Dundonald) Cemetery, while the others were laid
to rest in the extension to Sproston (St. Paul) Churchyard, their funerals
being the last for air force personnel in this graveyard.

30 OTU **Wellington III** **BK184** **Training**
Sgt J King T/o 1120 Hixon for a navigation exercise, during
Sgt Payne inj which, and following a spell of rough running,
the starboard engine caught fire. Sgt King was
able to feather the propeller but was not able to maintain height. Having made
a successful descent through the cloud cover, he force -landed, flaps retracted,
at 1430 in a field near Skerry Hall Farm, possibly between Fylingthorpe and Robin
Hood's Bay, 5 miles SE of Whitby, Yorkshire.

5 Feb **26 OTU** **Wellington IC** **DV725** **Training**
1943 Sgt C D Belcher T/o Wing for a night exercise. Abandoned, due to
engine failure and no success in finding an air-
field in order to force -land, from 7,000 feet, leaving the bomber to crash at
approximately 0010 in the vicinity of Bottisham, some 6 miles ENE from the centre
of Cambridge. This was Sgt Belcher's second close shave (see page 192).

6 Feb **14 OTU** **Wellington IC** **W5667** **Training**
1943 W/O H Murray + T/o 0925 Saltby for dual instruction. Forty
Sgt J Evans + minutes after the exercise had begun, the bomber
Sgt S F Peachey + was stalled at 2,000 feet with the undercarriage
Sgt J Sykes + and flaps lowered. Before being fully recovered,
Sgt H Sharp + the Wellington hit the ground and burst into
flames, some 8 miles NE of Boston, Lincolnshire.
Nineteen year old Sgt Peachey of Chislehurst in Kent was buried in the extension
to Cottesmore (St. Nicholas) Churchyard, his four companions being taken to their
home towns. It was recommended that exercises of this nature, involving heavy
aircraft, should not be attempted below 3,000 feet.

6- 7 Feb **11 OTU C Flt** **Wellington IC** **N2761** **-C** **Training**
1943 Sgt T Lindley RNZAF + T/o Westcott for a night cross-country carrying
Sgt P Butterworth eight flash bombs, a photoflash, camera and IFF.
Sgt L F Croker RNZAF + At 10,000 feet the port motor burst into flames
Sgt E N Common + and the Wellington was partially abandoned at
Sgt E M Noble RNZAF 5,000 feet before crashing 0050 at Fletcher Field
near Ashley, 5 miles WNW of Corby, Northampton-
shire. Those who died rest in cemeteries at North Luffenham and Lancaster. It
is reported that Sgt Noble RNZAF subsequently became a prisoner of war.

7 Feb **26 OTU**   **Wellington IC** **HF908**   **Training**
1943   P/O M M Johnstone RCAF   T/o 2248 Little Horwood for night dual but at
       P/O W E Handy   three hundred feet, the starboard engine caught
       Sgt Barnes   inj fire. The instructor immediately took over the
                                       controls and managed to coax the Wellington up
to 600 feet before the crippled motor cut completely. By this time, he had
commenced a circuit with the intention of landing back on the airfield, but
reduced to a single-engine he was obliged to crash-land, 2250, in a field at
Weston Lane, Winslow, 6 miles SE of Buckingham. For displaying coolness and
commendable skill, P/O Johnstone's flying log received a "green" endorsement.
Similar to Sgt Noble RNZAF, identified at the bottom of the previous page, he
later became a prisoner of war.

       30 OTU   **Wellington III** **BK434**   **Training**
       Sgt R D Lewis RAAF   +   T/o Hixton for a night cross-country. Returned
       Sgt K H Austin   +   to base at 0115 and made what appeared to be a
       Sgt J McGinnes   +   perfectly good landing. However, Sgt Lewis RAAF
       Sgt J J Kenny   +   opened up and took off for a second circuit but
       Sgt D C Rowse RNZAF   +   climbed too steeply, stalled at around 1,000 feet
                                        and before he could recover the situation, his
aircraft hit a tree and crashed at The Rectory at Ingestre Park, near Weston and
less than a mile off the S side of the airfield. Both Commonwealth airmen rest
in Hixon (St. Peter) Churchyard, while the others were claimed by their next of
kin, Sgt Kenny being taken back to the Irish Republic and interred in Glasnevin
(or Prospect) Cemetery, Co. Dublin.

8 Feb **10 OTU**   **Whitley V** **LA784**   **Training**
1943   F/S F E Gullison RCAF   +   T/o 0056 Abingdon for a night exercise, during
       Sgt S W Marshall   +   which the crew attempted to land at Harwell.
       Sgt P G Cust   +   On touch down, the Whitley bounced badly and
       Sgt O O Openshaw   +   while going round again crashed 0116 a mile or
                                  inj   so to the SSW of the airfield. Three rest in
                                        Brookwood Military Cemetery, while Sgt Openshaw
was taken to Llanfechain (or Llanfechan) (St. Garmon) Churchyard. It is noted
in 'They Shall Grow Not Old' that F/S Gullison RCAF had narrowly escaped serious
injury or death when two Fleet Finch trainers (4753 and 4783) belonging to No.
17 EFTS Stanley, Nova Scotia, collided in the air above the airfield.

9 Feb **13 OTU**   **Blenheim IV** **T1862**   **Training**
1943   Sgt R W Henderson   T/o 1450 Finmere but an engine cut and the
       F/S C C Ferguson   Blenheim crashed back to the runway, ran on
       Sgt L S Dorgie   to soft ground and flipped onto its back.

       19 OTU D Flt   **Whitley V** **Z9156** **-I**   **Training**
       Sgt A R Kelner   inj T/o 1827 Kinloss for a night navigation sortie.
       Sgt Armitage   At 2316, wireless messages were exchanged with
       Sgt Tonkin   Renfrew and roughly half-an-hour later, while
       Sgt Archibald   flying at 8,000 feet, the port engine failed.
       Sgt Bellis   All baled out, the first four named eventually
                                       being taken to the RN Auxiliary Hospital at
Kingseat where Sgt Kelner was treated for a broken ankle. Late in the afternoon
of 10 February, the Whitley was discovered about a mile NNW of Edinglassie and,
apparently, apart from a smashed undercarriage, did not appear to be too badly
damaged. It was, however, written off charge.

9-10 Feb **81 OTU**   **Whitley V** **LA769**   **Training**
1943   W/O K W Dunlop   inj T/o 2132 Whitchurch Heath for a night cross-
       P/O D P R Wild   +   country, incorporating practice bombing and
                                  inj infrared photography. Shortly before 0227,
                                       when it was abandoned, a con-rod failed causing
the starboard engine to seize. Tragically, P/O Wild's parachute opened inside
the aircraft and he returned to the controls in a desperate attempt to force -
land. Although succeeding in reaching the airfield, he crashed, out of control,
alongside the runway. A Bachelor of Arts graduate from Oxford, he is buried in
Northwood Cemetery.

10 Feb **13 OTU**   **Blenheim IV** **T2162**   **Training**
1943   Sgt E A Fitzsimmons RAAF   T/o 0922 Bichester but crashed 1217 at Park Farm
                                        Bylaugh, 3 miles NE of East Dereham, Norfolk.

10 Feb
1943

23 OTU   **Wellington III** **BK256**   **Training**
F/S G McI Johnston RCAF   inj T/o 2140 Pershore for a night navigation flight
Sgt J S Armstrong RCAF   which had to be aborted due to the port engine
Sgt R J Stone   inj losing power. F/S Johnston RCAF succeeded in
Sgt J G A McPherson   regaining the Pershore circuit but as he turned
Sgt J R Archambault RCAF   inj towards the funnels at 2230, so the starboard
                                  motor cut, causing the bomber to crash heavily
between Fladbury and Lower Moor. The impact was severe and F/S Johnston RCAF
sustained some very painful facial injuries that included a compound fracture
to his nose. Sadly, having made a complete recovery and joining 434 Squadron,
he became one of the many casualties from the Peenemünde raid (see Bomber
Command Losses, Volume 4, pages 270-276). Two months earlier, on 21-22 June
1943, Sgt Archambault RCAF had been killed while raiding Krefeld with 408
Squadron (see the same volume, page 196).

11 Feb
1943

17 OTU   **Blenheim IV** **Z7349**   **Training**
Sgt F L Stark   T/o 0855 Upwood for a training sortie. Came
                                  down at 1020 in a field NE of St. Ives in
Huntingdonshire, having lost the use of both engines.

22 OTU   **Wellington III** **HZ109**   **Ground**
                                  At 1645, while undergoing inspection in a
hangar at Wellesbourne Mountford, a headband torch slipped from its wearer
and fell into a drip tray. Moments later the Wellington was on fire and it
was later concluded that either a spark or a short circuit had ignited the
residue of petrol vapour in the tray.

12 Feb
1943

23 OTU   **Wellington III** **X3608**   **Training**
Sgt A N E White   +   T/o 2000 Pershore for a night sortie equipped
Sgt J T Backsimchuk RCAF   inj with IFF and an F24 camera, a photoflash and
Sgt G L Sinclair RCAF   a single flame float. Abandoned 2203, due to
Sgt F G Leahy   icing, crashing near Llanrhaedr-ym-Mochnant,
Sgt D M J Labelle RCAF   practically on the Denbigh/Montgomery border,
                                  eleven miles WSW from Oswestry where Sgt White
rests in the town's general cemetery (he had fatally delayed his departure
from the stricken aircraft). Subsequently, from the survivors, Sgt Labelle
became a prisoner of war in the wake of the Peenemünde raid (see Bomber Command
Losses, Volume 4, page 276).

13 Feb
1943

10 OTU   **Whitley V** **Z6467**   **Training**
F/S R Fisher   inj T/o 1836 Abingdon for a cross-country exercise
Sgt G W H Smith   inj with a screened pilot instructor. While flying
Sgt A Johnson   inj at 6,000 feet, the port engine shed its coolant
P/O A A Japp   +   and seconds later the unit burst into flames.
F/S C W Charlton   inj Crash-landed 2240 near White Waltham airfield
Sgt N Clemence   inj in Berkshire. P/O Japp is buried in Brookwood
                                  Military Cemetery.

22 OTU   **Wellington X** **HF759**   **Training**
WO1 L S Carpenter RCAF   +   T/o Wellesbourne Mountford for a navigation
F/S L M Fleming   +   exercise which went well until the crew returned
P/O S H Amys RCAF   +   to base at 1237. Then, while on finals, a flap
P/O M S Jacobs RCAF   +   pin snapped. The pilot at the controls made an
Sgt R C H Boulton RCAF   +   heroic effort to overshoot and gain height but
Sgt J G Campbell RCAF   +   with his aircraft at an unusual angle of attack
WO2 G A Molozzi RCAF   +   he lost control at between 100 and 150 feet.
Sgt R Kennedy RCAF   +   The seven RCAF members of crew were interred
                                  in Stratford-upon-Avon Cemetery (P/O Amys was
the son of Dr. Charles H Amys and Mary E Amys), while F/S Fleming was taken
to Buckfastleigh (Holy Trinity) Churchyard. A year previous to the day, WO2
Molozzi RCAF had been injured, at the unit, in a landing accident (see page 99).

30 OTU   **Wellington X** **HE466**   **Training**
Sgt E G Frezell RCAF   +   T/o Hixon for a night cross-country. Flew into
P/O F K Thorogood   +   the eastern slopes of Foel Grach, Snowdonia, a
Sgt C G Bennett   +   tragic error in navigation being the most likely
Sgt G N Rafferty   +   cause. Sgt Frezell RCAF rests in Caernarvon
Sgt E Towler   +   Cemetery; his crew went to their home towns.

14 Feb
1943

24 OTU   **Whitley V** BD285   **Transit**
F/S H A Peterson RNZAF   inj T/o Greenham Common with the intention of
Sgt J J Roxburgh RCAF   inj returning to base (either Honeybourne or Long
                          inj Marston) but engine failure thwarted their
                               intentions and while trying to force -land
came down at 1718 near Longborough, Gloucestershire. It seems most likely
the crew were attempting to reach Moreton-in-the-Marsh, 3 miles distant to
the north-north-east. A fire broke out on impact.

15 Feb
1943

22 OTU   **Wellington III** HF613 DD–R   **Training**
Sgt J D Kester RCAF   +   T/o Wellesbourne Mountford for a cross-country.
Sgt R F Cairns RCAF   +   It is possible icing forced the crew to descend
Sgt B E Wilkinson RCAF   +   and in doing so they became enveloped in a snow
Sgt W A Marwood   +   storm. Out of control, the bomber crashed 1311
Sgt W J Hackett RCAF   +   at Hope, 7 miles ENE of Chapel-en-le-Frith,
                              Derbyshire and on the SE side of the High Peak
district between Manchester and Sheffield. Three of the Canadians were taken to
Buxton Cemetery, but it is likely the funeral for Sgt Wilkinson RCAF was arranged
by relatives as he is buried in Warrington Cemetery. Sgt Marwood is interred at
Nottingham General Cemetery.

28 OTU D Flt   **Wellington IC** N2809   –H   **Training**
Sgt J Andrew   +   T/o 1130 Castle Donington for a cross-country.
Sgt E Brook   +   Returning to base at around 1630, encountered a
Sgt A D Scott   +   heavy snowstorm and crashed at Hermitage Farm,
Sgt F W Gurney   +   Whitwick, 2 miles NE of Coalville, Leicestershire.
Sgt D Marsden   +   Sgt Andrew is buried in the extension to Dunholme
                              (St. Chad) Churchyard, Sgt Brook and Sgt Scott lie
in Bradfield (Oughtibridge) Cemetery and Hull Western Cemetery respectively, Sgt
Gurney rests at Old Fletton Cemetery, while Sgt Marsden is at Elland Cemetery.

16 Feb
1943

13 OTU   **Blenheim IV** V6317   **Training**
Sgt R J Sparke   T/o 1535 Bicester but an engine failed and in
P/O R B Foster   order to avoid over running the airfield, the
Sgt T L Buttery   undercarriage was retracted. Skidding onto a
                              mound of earth, the Blenheim caught fire. On
completing his training, Sgt Sparke converted to Bostons and was posted to
Tunisia where he joined 114 Squadron. Killed on 18 July 1943, his grave is
in Enfidaville War Cemetery.

17 Feb
1943

14 OTU   **Wellington IC** T2558   –G   **Training**
Sgt J M Cousin   +   T/o 0420 Saltby for night flying. Crashed 0650
Sgt S W C Cannel   +   about a mile NW of Sproxton, 8 miles ENE from
Sgt T J Anderson   +   Melton Mowbray, Leicestershire. A fire broke
Sgt T Walker   +   out and the bomber was totally destroyed. Eye-
Sgt Woods   inj witnesses state that the Wellington appeared to
                              bank steeply after overshooting and then stalled
from a height estimated at around 800 feet. Those who died rest in cemeteries
in England and Scotland. Sgt Woods survived, albeit with severe leg injuries.

18-19 Feb
1943

12 OTU   **Wellington III** BK160   –S   **Op: Nickel**
Sgt J E Parkes RAAF   +   T/o 1907 Chipping Warden, course being set for
P/O A R Shepherd   +   the Orleans area of France. Lost without trace.
Sgt A R York   +   All are commemorated on the Runnymede Memorial.
Sgt K W Keen   +   P/O Shepherd and nineteen year old Sgt York
Sgt A H Martin RAAF   +   shared the same Christian names, Alfred Raymond.

19 Feb
1943

10 OTU   **Whitley V** BD374   **Training**
Sgt A Fletcher   inj T/o 1111 Stanton Harcourt but within four
                               minutes the Whitley was on the ground at Yew
Tree Farm, Standlake, 8 miles WSW from the centre of Oxford. Badly shaken,
the crew reported that the starboard engine had failed at around 100 feet, it
is believed due to a coolant leakage. Sgt Fletcher made a good recovery and
on completion of his course proceeded to a Halifax HCU before being posted to
Snaith, where he joined 51 Squadron. In late July 1943, he failed to return
from operations against Hamburg (see Bomber Command Losses, Volume 4, page 248).
From his crew, six, including Sgt Fletcher, are commemorated on the Runnymede
Memorial, while the seventh member is buried in Hamburg Cemetery, Ohlsdorf.

20–21 Feb   **19 OTU D Flt**   **Whitley V**   **LA780**   **–R**   **Training**
1943   Sgt A J Pearce   T/o 1835 Forres for a night navigation exercise.
                                        On return to base at 0019, the starboard engine
cut at 500 feet over the Whiterow site on the SW side of the airfield and the
Whitley came down a mile S of Balnageith, hitting some trees in the process.
No one was hurt and the crew walked to the airfield and reported their presence
to the Watch Office. Sgt Pearce went on to fly Lancasters with 619 Squadron and
was killed in action during the Peenemünde raid in August 1943 (see Bomber
Command Losses, Volume 4, page 276).

21 Feb   **10 OTU Det**   **Whitley V**   **Z6812**   **–T**   **Op: AS Patrol**
1943   Sgt V H Hatchard   T/o 0757 St. Eval. At around 1300 the crew were
         P/O G H Vanderstraeten   obliged to ditch in position 4615N 1225W, having
         P/O F A James   lost power due to a suspected glycol leakage.
         Sgt J Leedham   Prior to alighting in the sea, all depth charges
         Sgt S Brown   were jettisoned. Roughly four hours later, a
         Sgt J S W Fowles   naval corvette picked up the crew. Not long after
                                         this incident, the crew (less P/O Vanderstraeten)
were posted to 102 Squadron. On 13-14 May 1943, their Halifax failed to return
from Bochum (see Bomber Command Losses, Volume 4, page 147), only P/O James
surviving as a prisoner of war.

24 Feb   **22 OTU**   **Wellington III**   **DF564 DD–V**   **Training**
1943   Sgt A E Hatch RCAF   T/o Gaydon for night circuits and landings.
                                         During one of the circuits, Sgt Hatch RCAF
noticed the reading from the port rev counter was decreasing. Presuming the
motor was failing he crash-landed at 2216 to the left of the flare path, his
undercarriage folding up on impact. A technical inspection found no fault with
the port engine but an examination of the instruments revealed a broken rev
counter drive. On 12-13 May 1943, now flying with 428 Squadron, Sgt Hatch RCAF
failed to return from Duisburg (see Bomber Command Losses, Volume 4, page 144).

25 Feb   **19 OTU D Flt**   **Whitley V**   **LA826**   **–B**   **Training**
1943   Sgt A W Rowell   +   T/o 2224 Forres but two minutes later flew into
         P/O M F Old   +   high ground 5 miles SW of the airfield. Sgt
         Sgt J A Millar   +   Millar of Perth lies in Kinloss Abbey Burial
         Sgt W Scott   +   Ground, while the others were taken to their
         Sgt R W Stokes   +   home towns. Accident investigators were able to
                                         determine that the bomber was in level flight
at the moment of impact and that its airspeed was considerable.

27 Feb   **16 OTU**   **Wellington III**   **X3985**   **Training**
1943   F/O G Brayshaw   +   T/o 1200 Upper Heyford for a cross-country. A
         P/O C H Nichols   +   little under three hours later, the Wellington
         P/O D O Moss   +   developed engine trouble and the crew attempted
         Sgt B C Burton   +   to land at Colerne airfield in Wiltshire. The
         Sgt C E Vyse RCAF   +   approach, however, was not to the satisfaction
                                         of F/O Brayshaw and he attempted to go round
again but while S of the aerodrome he lost control and crashed at Hazelbury
House Farm, Box, 6 miles SW from Chippenham. On impact the bomber burst into
flames. Described as a pilot under training, F/O Brayshaw (a holder of a City
and Guilds of London Certificate) is the sole service burial in Stainland
Methodist Chapelyard, Elland. His crew lie in churchyards in Devon, Yorkshire
and London.

         29 OTU   **Wellington III**   **BJ760**   **Training**
         Sgt J Pickett RNZAF   T/o 1034 North Luffenham but the port tyre
                                         burst and seconds later, having swung from
the runway, the undercarriage collapsed. After converting to Lancasters,
Sgt Pickett RNZAF joined 57 Squadron at Scampton but failed to return from
the Torino raid on 12-13 July 1943 (see Bomber Command Losses, Volume 4,
page 228). Errol Martyn believes he was on his nineteenth sortie.

28 Feb   **20 OTU D Flt**   **Wellington IC**   **N2823**   **Training**
1943   Sgt W P Corrie   +   T/o 2130 Elgin for a night exercise but failed
         Sgt J Tyldesley   +   to climb. Banking at a mere 30 feet, trying to
         Sgt R A W Cockram   +   avoid trees, the bomber went out of control and
         Sgt G E Woolley   inj   crashed. Those who died were taken to their home
                                         towns; Sgt Woolley went to Dr. Gray's Hospital.

28 Feb–	29 OTU	Wellington III	Z1666	Op: Nickel

1 Mar 1943 Sgt J E Ford + T/o 1652 North Luffenham and is assumed to have
Sgt A W Gillespie + carried out a successful duty. However, while
Sgt W A Champion + returning to base it is strongly believed that
Sgt V P Thompson + an electrical fault occurred, leaving the crew
Sgt J McD McKinnie + without communications. Flying above cloud, the
captain was left with two options; abandon the
Wellington, or descend through the cloud cover in an attempt to establish their
position. Sgt Ford chose the latter and at around 0200 the Wellington smashed
into the side of a hill at Widdington Farm, Rushall, near Upavon airfield in
Wiltshire and disintegrated. All rest in various cemeteries within the United
Kingdom.

1 Mar   10 OTU   Whitley V   AD694   Training
1943   Sgt P D Dennehy   +   T/o 2307 Abingdon for a bombing exercise but the
Sgt S G Mills   inj port engine cut. The crew tried to return to
P/O A Sidey   +   base but the Whitley stalled, at around 1,000
Sgt E Sweetapple   inj feet, and crashed 2315 on high ground a mile S
of Chorley brickworks in Oxfordshire. Those who
perished were claimed by their next of kin.

12 OTU   Wellington III BK467   –C   Training
Sgt P A Thompson RAAF inj T/o Turweston for bombing practice. On return
Sgt A J Abrahams   inj to base, the Wellington came in off-line of the
Sgt G O John   +   flare path and while going round again, an
Sgt R Crebbin   +   engine failed. Unable to bring the bomber
Sgt Crompton   inj under control, Sgt Thompson RAAF crashed 2106
in the airfield circuit, a fierce blaze breaking
out on impact. Sgt John is buried in the SE corner of the Chancel at St. Fagan
Churchyard, Aberdare, while Sgt Crebbin lies in Liverpool (Allerton) Cemetery.

15 OTU   Wellington IC   X3171   Training
Sgt D L Barley   +   T/o 1100 Harwell for a cross-country. Lost
Sgt W S Gibson   +   control, while flying in cloud, and dived almost
P/O J Donnelly   +   vertically to crash 1515 at Blackburn Fell
P/O T Winstanley   +   (possibly in or near the Harwood Forest area
Sgt D R Bending   +   and perhaps close to the village of Elsdon,
Sgt G Marshall   +   some 3 miles ESE of Otterburn, Northumberland).
If this was the case, then Sgt Gibson died a
mere sixteen miles or so NNW of where he is buried in Stamfordham (St. Mary)
Churchyard (his parents address is given as Newcastle-upon-Tyne), while Sgt
Marshall, too, was not far distant, his grave being in Co. Durham at Trimdon
Grange Cemetery. The rest of the crew are interred in burial grounds both
in England and Scotland.

22 OTU   Wellington III HF674 LT-F   Training
Sgt P L J Logan RCAF   inj T/o Gaydon for a combination of night circuits
Sgt J J March RCAF   inj and overshoot procedures but at 300 feet both
Sgt R L Swindle   inj motors cut and the bomber came down 2040 near
Sgt A W Klauer RCAF   inj Bromson Hill House, Ashorne, 2 miles NNW of the
airfield. In the post-accident enquiry, it was
noted that Sgt Logan RCAF, despite having very little altitude in hand, managed
to feather the port airscrew and then held the aircraft in a straight line up
to the moment of impact. His predicament had been brought about by plug failure.

23 OTU   Wellington X   HE484   Training
P/O W Harrison RCAF   T/o 2100 Pershore for a night exercise. Soon
after setting out the port engine failed, and
this was followed by hydraulic failure. At circa 2145, the crew baled out,
leaving their aircraft to crash near Priors Marston, 12 miles ESE from Royal
Leamington Spa, Warwickshire.

3 Mar   12 OTU   Wellington III BK400   Training
1943   F/L E D Spratt   +   T/o 1040 Chipping Warden for a cross-country.
P/O S W Shepherd   +   Lost control, in cloud, and crashed 1255 just
Sgt A R Burgess   +   under 2 miles SW of Little Tew and about three
Sgt J A Willis   +   miles ESE of Chipping Norton, Oxfordshire. All
Sgt A F Ash   +   rest in various churchyards in England and
Sgt V S Allen   +   Scotland.

3 Mar 1943	**13 OTU**	**Blenheim IV**	**T1798**	**Training**
	P/O G W M Francis	inj	T/o 1025 Bicester but an engine failed and	
	Sgt J E H Gregory	inj	while trying to return to the airfield, the	
	Sgt G K McMillan	inj	Blenheim stalled and crashed 1030 near the	
			village of Launton on the eastern outskirts	

of Bicester town. All three members of crew were severely injured; two, the pilot and his observer, were rushed to the Radcliffe Infirmary with fractured spines (Sgt Gregory also sustained a broken right ankle), while Sgt McMillan was admitted to St. Hugh's Military Hospital with very serious head injuries that included a skull fracture.

	15 OTU	**Wellington IC**	**HF906**	**Training**
	Sgt R H Millar	+	T/o 2005 Hampstead Norris for a night navigation	
	Sgt L N Abercrombie RNZAF	+	sortie which was scheduled to last for 4 hours.	
	Sgt G A Hovell	+	Not long after departure, the wireless equipment	
	Sgt B C Lock	+	failed and the exercise was aborted. At around	
	Sgt S E Harmes	+	2030, the Wellington was reported on approach to	
			land but this was abandoned in favour of another	
	Mrs E A Chiverton	+	circuit. While so engaged, the bomber stalled	
	Miss A Playle	+	from 100 feet and smashed into The Bungalow,	
			Common Barn farmhouse on the N side of Hermitage,	

five miles NNE of Newbury, Berkshire. Three, Sgt Millar, Sgt Abercrombie RNZAF and Sgt Lock rest in Harwell Cemetery, Sgt Hovell lies in Hammersmith New Cemetery while Sgt Harmes is buried in Guildford (Stoke) New Cemetery. Miss Playle was a nurse companion to Mrs Chiverton. They were aged 60 and 68 respectively.

4- 5 Mar 1943	**28 OTU**	**Wellington IC**	**Z1109 —T**	**Op: Nickel**
	F/S C C Atkin RAAF	+	T/o Wymeswold. Hit by marine flak and partially	
	F/S C E Gunning	pow	abandoned before crashing 0126 onto land owned	
	F/S G S Loveday	pow	by Mr Van Hootegem at Nieuwe Sluis (Zeeland) in	
	F/S R H Roskell	pow	Holland. F/S Atkin RAAF rests in the Northern	
	Sgt J A Molloy	+	Cemetery at Vlissingen, while nineteen year old	
			Sgt Molloy is commemorated on panel 159 of the	
			Runnymede Memorial.	

5 Mar 1943	**11 OTU**	**Wellington IC**	**DV923**	**Training**
	Sgt D Black	+	T/o Westcott for a night navigation exercise.	
	Sgt A B Dixon RNZAF	inj	Returned to base circa 0155 but overshot its	
	Sgt A G Pearson	inj	approach and crashed at Long Crendon, 9 miles	
	Sgt H Terry	+	WSW of Aylesbury, Buckinghamshire. Sgt Black	
	Sgt L W E Banks	inj	is buried in Tollcross (Central) Churchyard,	
	Sgt L C Davenport	inj	Glasgow, while Sgt Terry rests in Middleham	
			(SS Alkelda and Mary) Churchyard. The injuries	

ranged from relatively slight (Sgt Banks got away with a badly sprained ankle) to the severe, both Sgt Dixon RNZAF and Sgt Davenport being admitted to the Princess Mary's Hospital at Halton with various bone fractures and burns.

	12 OTU	**Wellington III**	**BK433**	**Training**
	Sgt R V N Moss	+	T/o Chipping Warden tasked for a night sortie.	
	Sgt A Witton	+	At around 0220, dived into the ground near the	
	Sgt D W Alexander	+	airfield's No. 8 site. Those who perished lie	
	Sgt G J Gates	+	in various cemeteries. Sgt Napier was rescued,	
	Sgt Napier	inj	relatively unscathed, but was classified as	
			suffering from acute shock.	

	19 OTU B Flt	**Whitley V**	**Z9319 —F**	**Training**
	Sgt S G Matheson RCAF		T/o 0955 Kinloss for a cross-country. Shortly	
			before 1300, while flying at 10,000 feet, the	

crew observed white smoke gushing from the starboard engine and almost straight away the lick of flame was also seen. Fortunately, the extinguishers quelled the blaze but course for base was set. Gradually, the bomber lost height and it was decided to land at Middleton St. George airfield in Co. Durham but while doing so, Sgt Matheson RCAF misjudged his height and hit a tree, just short of the runway. It is not thought that anyone was seriously hurt.

	21 OTU	**Wellington IC**	**R1601**	**Training**
	Sgt B Job		T/o Moreton-in-Marsh for a night cross-country.	
			Crash-landed 0125, the undercarriage collapsing,	

at Honiley airfield in Warwickshire. No injuries reported.

5 Mar	**29 OTU**	**Wellington III**	BK390	**Training**
1943	Sgt K H Long		+	T/o 0159 North Luffenham for a combined high
	Sgt T F J Glover		+	and low-level bombing exercise. Crashed 0209
	Sgt D C Fisher		+	after flying into houses at Coates, a village
	Sgt B F Mullett		+	twixt 2 and three miles ENE of Whittlesey in
	Sgt F McDougall		inj	Cambridgeshire. Of those who died, two, Sgt

Long of Southampton and Sgt Mullett of Killiney
in Co. Dublin (his father was Capt H A Mullett, formerly of the Royal Dublin
Fusiliers) are buried in North Luffenham (St. John The Baptist) Churchyard,
while two were taken to their home towns. It is suggested Sgt Long may have
descended in order to establish his precise position.

8 Mar	**21 OTU**	**Wellington IC**	X3219	**Training**
1943	Sgt A McDougall		+	T/o Moreton-in-Marsh for an evening cross-
	Sgt J S Horton		+	country. Crashed 2125 at Barton St. David,
	Sgt B J Caine		+	five miles SE of Street, Somerset and burst
	Sgt F M Brum		+	into flames. All are buried in churchyards
	Sgt A B Cowie		+	in England and Scotland. An examination of

the wreckage led the investigators to think
that both engines failed in succession, while within the debris of what had
been the starboard unit, fifty yards of wire was discovered.

10 Mar	**10 OTU Det**	**Whitley V**	BD202 —G	**Op: AS Patrol**
1943	Sgt J P Ingram		+	T/o 0600 St. Eval armed with 6 x 250lb depth
	Sgt J E L Woollam		+	charges. An SOS was intercepted, indicating
	Sgt W S Young		+	the presence of enemy aircraft. Nothing further
	Sgt J Mitchell		+	was heard. All are perpetuated by the memorial
	F/O R Marriott		+	at Runnymede. Sgt Woollam was the son of Col
	Sgt W Mills		+	Samuel Edward Woollam, Justice of the Peace.

	12 OTU	**Lysander III**	P1668	**Training**
	F/S S R Grant		inj	T/o 0955 Chipping Warden for drogue towing and
	LAC Devine		inj	air firing. The exercise was completed and at

approximately 1140, F/S Grant overflew the air-
field at 200 feet and released the drogue ahead of landing. Moments later, the
Lysander's engine spluttered. The throttle was immediately advanced but the
motor failed to pick up and with very little height to play with, a forced-
landing was carried out, in a field, adjacent to the aerodrome. However, the
ground was rather soft and the aircraft tipped onto its nose. An examination
of the engine revealed a defective port magneto and plug of No. 5 cylinder. A
little over a month later, F/S Grant was involved in a similar accident, though
on this occasion his aircraft was a Martinet.

	14 OTU	**Wellington IC**	DV864 —M	**Training**
	Sgt H Henderson		+	T/o North Luffenham for a night cross-country.
	Sgt J McLean		+	On return it is thought that Sgt Henderson was
	Sgt T W Agnew		+	confused between the similarity of the base
	Sgt Martin		inj	beacon and that sited near the local Q site.
	Sgt Hoyle		inj	Thus, at 0350, he crashed near Walk Farm, close

to the decoy site. Sgt McLean is buried in the
extension to Cottesmore (St. Nicholas) Churchyard. Sgt Henderson was taken to
Archaracle Cemetery, Ardnamurchan, while his fellow Scot lies in Greenock
Cemetery.

	23 OTU	**Wellington III**	X3349	**Training**
	WO1 J W H Heard RCAF		+	T/o 1900 Pershore for a night cross-country,
	P/O R G Moorby RCAF		+	the crew comprising of three navigators and two
	Sgt J V Ellis RCAF		+	air bombers. At 2115, the bomber flew into the
	Sgt J A Dixon		+	ground near Little Horwood airfield. The five
	Sgt N Kulyk RCAF		+	RCAF members of crew were taken to Brookwood
	Sgt W B Wallace RCAF		+	Military Cemetery, while Sgt Dixon is buried

in Colton (Holy Trinity) Churchyard.

	29 OTU	**Wellington III**	BK543	**Training**
	Sgt J A Brock RAAF			T/o 1945 Woolfox Lodge for an evening exercise.

Lost power at 2,300 feet and in the ensuing
landing at 2010 a tyre burst, wrecking the bomber. Sgt Brock RAAF died in the
service of 50 Squadron (see Bomber Command Losses, Volume 4, page 204), the
occasion being the raid on Wuppertal on 24-25 June 1943.

11 Mar	15 OTU	Wellington III	X3874		Training

11 Mar
1943

15 OTU   **Wellington III** **X3874**   **Training**

F/L P S Marriott DFM   +   T/o 1030 Harwell for dual and familiarisation
Sgt C A Chipman   +   on type, plus single-engined flying procedures.
Sgt J Gannon   +   Lost power from the port engine, dived and came
Sgt J E Siddell   +   down 1115 just to the E of Didcot, Berkshire in
Sgt J Carver   +   an area known as Fleet Meadow. Sgt Chipman lies
                                in Harwell Cemetery, the others were taken to
their home towns. F/L Marriott, a pre-war Volunteer Reserve pilot, won his DFM
in the service of 115 Squadron, details being published on 7 March 1941. This
was the first Mk. III Wellington written off by the unit. Taken on charge ex-
48 MU Hawarden in mid-January 1943, it had flown a total of 90.05 hours.

27 OTU   **Wellington III** **BJ835**   **Training**

P/O S Norris   T/o 1935 Lichfield for a night exercise. At
                                approximately 2050 the starboard engine failed
and a forced-landing was carried out at Gnosall, some 7 miles WSW from the
centre of Stafford. A fire broke out almost immediately.

11-12 Mar   **14 OTU**   **Wellington IC** **Z1154**   **-P**   **Training**
1943

Sgt N C Powell   T/o 1930 Cottesmore for a night navigation
                                flight during which, while operating at 11,000
feet, an engine failed. Crashed 0115 at Holwell, 3 miles NNW of Hitchin in
Hertfordshire, while trying to land on the short flare path at Panshangar, an
airfield then being used by No. 1 Elementary Flying Training School.

12 Mar   **20 OTU C Flt**   **Wellington IC** **DV919 XL-A**   **Training**
1943

Sgt G E Morris   +   T/o Lossiemouth armed with 8 practice bombs and
Sgt P J Fitzgerald RAAF   +   set out on a course base-Mull of Kintyre-Scarra
Sgt S R Wright RAAF   +   and return to base, a distance of around 455
Sgt J H W McDonagh RAAF   +   miles in total. At approximately 1145, the crew
Sgt T Robinson   +   of another aircraft reported seeing a Wellington,
Sgt H S Stockbridge RAAF   +   believed to be this aircraft, descending from
                                10,000 to 1,000 feet before suddenly diving
steeply towards the sea. Despite an extensive search, no trace could be found
and all are commemorated on the Runnymede Memorial.

12-13 Mar   **23 OTU**   **Wellington III** **BK346**   **Training**
1943

Sgt C W Jackson RCAF   T/o 1920 Stratford-upon-Avon for a night cross-
Sgt H B Klhorn RCAF   country. Overshot 0225 and crashed near the
Sgt J T Kidd   inj   airfield. Sgt Kidd needed treatment for cuts
                               to his left eye and right side of the forehead.

13 Mar   **11 OTU**   **Wellington IC** **R1025**   **Training**
1943

Sgt C Smith   inj T/o Westcott for a night navigation exercise.
Sgt L V F Etwell RNZAF   inj Experienced handling problems and despite
P/O N J Fletcher   inj trimming the starboard wing had a marked tendency
Sgt J S J McPhail RNZAF   inj to drop. Thus, in order to keep the bomber on a
Sgt W G Bates   inj level attitude, left-hand bank was necessary. On
                               regaining Westcott at 0115, Sgt Smith managed to
make a reasonable approach down to 150 feet (his air speed at this time being 95
miles per hour) at which point the starboard wing dropped to such an alarming
degree that before the situation could be recovered, the aircraft was on the
ground and totally wrecked. All were taken to Station Sick Quarters suffering
from shock and minor cuts and bruises. The two New Zealanders ended the war in
captivity, while Sgt Smith and P/O Fletcher were killed on 19 September 1943,
while flying with 37 Squadron (based at Kairouan in Tunisia). Both are buried
in Bolsena War Cemetery, on the eastern side of Lake Bolsena, Italy.

13-14 Mar   **27 OTU**   **Wellington III** **Z1681**   **Training**
1943

P/O G A McReath RAAF   inj T/o 1850 Lichfield for a night navigation
F/O A R Heins RAAF   + exercise. Returned to base circa 0040 and
Sgt Woodhouse   inj made an extremely low approach. In doing so,
P/O W W Alexander RAAF   + the Wellington hit a tree, the force being
Sgt J Denyer   + sufficient to roll the bomber over. Those who
P/O W J Vincent   inj died rest in Fradley (St. Stephen) Churchyard.
                               Delivered ex-works to 38 MU Llandow on 25 April
1942, the bomber had been held in storage until 29 December, when it was issued
to the unit. In total, its airframe and engines had accumulated 128.15 hours
of flying.

15 Mar 1943	11 OTU C Flt	Wellington IC	X9792 KJ-Q	Training

Sgt J H Lawson RNZAF + T/o Westcott for a day cross-country. On return
Sgt J Brims RNZAF + to base, the Wellington landed somewhat askew and
Sgt D R Trigg + the throttles were opened in order to go round
Sgt E S Evans + again. The climb seemed normal but after reaching
Sgt A J H Williams + an estimated height of 120 feet, the nose pitched
up, steeply, and the aircraft stalled back to the
ground at 1654, just off the NE end of the south-west/north-east runway. Both
the New Zealanders and Sgt Trigg, whose brother Sgt Edgar John Alexander Trigg
died while flying Beaufighters with 248 Squadron on 7 September 1943, are buried
in Westcott (St. Mary) Churchyard, Sgt Evans rests in Gravesend Cemetery, while
Sgt Williams (his father was the Revd Arthur Anderson Williams MA) was interred
at Conway (St. Agnes) Churchyard.

	22 OTU	Wellington III	DF567 LT-K	Training

Sgt J S McLeod RCAF T/o Gaydon for night flying practice. Stalled
at 50 feet and wrecked 2030 in the resultant
crash, the bomber catching fire on the ground.

16 Mar 1943	24 OTU	Whitley V	AD676	Training

Sgt A F Evans T/o 1228 Long Marston but swung to port, the
undercarriage breaking under the strain. Sgt
Evans proceeded to 158 Squadron, via a Halifax conversion, and failed to return
from his ninth sortie (Cannes, on 11-12 November 1943) as captain (see Bomber
Command Losses, Volume 4, page 378).

	26 OTU	Wellington IC	AD590	Training

F/O J Taplin T/o Wing for night circuits and landings but
as the Wellington was about to lift from the
runway, the starboard tyre burst. F/O Taplin managed to get into the air and
fly round the circuit, touching down at 2350. However, as the speed dropped
the bomber swung and the undercarriage collapsed.

18 Mar 1943	11 OTU	Wellington IC	DV814	Training

F/O P Reynolds T/o Westcott for an evening exercise. At 2105,
in rather poor visibility, undershot the runway.

20 Mar 1943	27 OTU	Wellington III	X3547	Training

F/S L D Watson RAAF + T/o Lichfield for a cine camera gun exercise,
Sgt D Williams + the last three in the crew list being identified
F/S W D K Forbes RAAF + as air gunners. Crashed 1520, after flying into
Sgt J E Rouse + a barrage balloon cable, at Barrows Green in the
Sgt F R Conway + NE outskirts of Crewe, Cheshire. It is much
F/S L G Coppins + suspected that the crash site was attended by
Sgt H T Holley + RAF Cranage as the two Australians were taken
Sgt L F Hills + for burial at Byley (St. John) Churchyard. The
other members of crew lie in cemeteries both in
England and Wales.

22 Mar 1943	30 OTU	Wellington III	Z1683	Training

F/L R Edwards T/o 1520 Seighford for fighter affiliation work
but the starboard undercarriage collapsed and
having skidded to a halt, the Wellington caught light and was destroyed.

23-24 Mar 1943	16 OTU	Wellington III	X3991	Op: Nickel

P/O V N Ballard RAAF + T/o Upper Heyford to leaflet the Orleans region.
P/O P W Masters + Crashed at Pontgouin (Eure-et-Loir), some 25 kms
P/O A R Dicker + west-north-west of Chartres, France. All lie in
Sgt J E Jones + Pontgouin Communal Cemetery, their funerals
Sgt H R Kinder + being held on 25 March.
P/O G B Gibson +

26-27 Mar 1943	10 OTU	Whitley V	LA844	Training

Sgt D Jackson + T/o 1947 Stanton Harcourt for a cross-country.
Sgt F S Hilt + On return to base at 0254, ran off the runway
P/O J Auld + at very high speed, crashing into a local quarry
P/O W K McF Weir + where it burst into flames. All were taken to
Sgt R J Roberts + their home towns. Sgt Jackson had transferred
from the army to the air force.

29 Mar **18 OTU** **Wellington IC** **DV804** **Training**
1943 Sgt M Zarebowicz PAF + T/o 2145 Finningley for the pilot's first solo
Sgt S Grabarczyk PAF + landings, at night, on type. At 2200 permission
to land was granted but, tragically, while doing
so Sgt Zarebowicz PAF lost control and crashed with some force. Along with his
wireless operator, Sgt Grabarczyk PAF, he rests in Newark-upon-Trent Cemetery.

31 Mar **10 OTU Det** **Whitley V** **BD412** **-V** **AS Patrol**
1943 Sgt S S Morrow + T/o 0701 St. Eval armed with 6 x 250lb depth
Sgt J C Walton + charges and with orders to search south-west
Sgt J Travis + of the Bishop's Rock for a motor vessel. Failed
Sgt J E Elwell + to acknowledge a wireless signal, transmitted at
F/S S J G Rutherford MID + 1705 and, therefore, is assumed lost over the
P/O H B Currall + sea. Five are commemorated on the Runnymede
Memorial, but in Camelford (Chapel Street)
Methodist Chapelyard is the grave of Sgt Travis of Middleton, Manchester.
F/S Rutherford's third Christian name was Gascoyne, thus preserving his
father's family name of Gascoyne Rutherford.

13 OTU **Blenheim IV** **V6099** **Training**
F/O E A Perry RNZAF + T/o 0935 Bicester for a navigation exercise but
P/O G I Gunter + failed to return at its due time back at base.
Sgt H Applegarth + Twelve days later the smashed remain of the
Blenheim were found on the 3,030 feet high Elidr
Fawr, some 3 miles NE of Llanberis, Caernarvonshire. Two rest in Caernarvon
Cemetery, while Sgt Applegarth was taken to Sutton and Cheam (Sutton) Cemetery.
P/O Gunter is believed to have been a Member, either of the Pharmaceutical
Society or the Philological Society.

14 OTU **Wellington IC** **X9944** **Ground**
At 1730, while parked at Cottesmore, struck
by another of the unit's Wellingtons and destroyed in the fire that followed.

14 OTU **Wellington IC** **AD628** **Training**
F/S R W Humphrey RAAF inj T/o Cottesmore and wrecked in the manner outlined
P/O M A Crombie RAAF inj above, the bomber hitting a hangar as well. Sgt
Sgt W T Cuthbertson RAAF + Cuthbertson RAAF is buried in the extension to
Sgt E A Robinson + Cottesmore (St. Nicholas) Churchyard, while Sgt
Sgt T McDaniel RAAF inj Robinson rests in Runwell (St. Mary) Churchyard.

2 Apr **16 OTU** **Wellington III** **BK246** **Training**
1943 F/S A L Robinson RNZAF + T/o 2035 Upper Heyford for a high-level bombing
Sgt J Kendrick + exercise. Before completing the duty, contacted
Sgt H W Holden + base indicating the airspeed indicator was un-
Sgt P L Carey + serviceable. At 2150, the Wellington crashed
Sgt J R Nesbit + at Vicarage Farm, Kirtlington, 9 miles NNW from
Sgt A Woodhouse + the centre of Oxford. Three of the crew,
P/O J G Lyon + including F/S Robinson RNZAF, a veteran of
forty-eight operational sorties in the Middle
East with 70 Squadron, are buried in Middleton Stoney (All Saints) Churchyard.
Lying near him is P/O Lyon, a staff pilot at No. 3 (Pilots) Advanced Flying Unit,
who had joined the crew as a passenger; he held a Bachelor of Arts degree. In
'They Shall Grow Not Old', Sgt Kendrick is reported to have hailed from Winnipeg
in Manitoba, but his CWGC entry indicates his parents were of Elsworth, the
Cambridgeshire village where he is buried in Holy Trinity Churchyard.

19 OTU D Flt **Whitley V** **LA830** **-L** **Training**
Sgt J Terence inj T/o 1430 Kinloss for a cross-country flight.
Sgt H L Shead inj The first hint of trouble came at 1641 when the
Inverness Direction Finding Station intercepted
a wireless message from the Whitley, "landing on sea - glycol leak". At 1717 an
Air-Sea Rescue Anson was scrambled, along with Spitfires from 165 Squadron based
at Petershead. It seems, however, that the Whitley had remained in the air and a
fix taken at 1732 indicated the bomber was nearing the coast. Then, at 1745,
No. 14 Group at Raigmore signalled a report indicating the Whitley was down at
QK4083 (2 miles S of Rosehearty). Rescue services were sent and the survivors
taken to Fraserburgh Hospital. Sgt Shead, who died at the scene, is buried in
Southall Cemetery, his five companions were not badly hurt.

3 Apr
1943

15 OTU	Wellington IC	T2809	**Training**

F/S C E Fothergill — T/o Hampstead Norris for gunnery training. Following the failure, at 2,000 feet, of the port engine, the bomber was forced-landed 1515 at Radley Farm, NE of Hungerford in Berkshire.

15 OTU	Wellington IC	DV833	**Training**

Sgt L E Ayres + T/o 2030 Hampstead Norris for a night cross-
Sgt W A Clark + country. Returned to base early and overshot
P/O D N A Griffin + twice. Then both engines cut, simultaneously.
Sgt D R Williams + While gliding in a straight and level attitude
Sgt W Harvey + the port engine suddenly burst into life and this resulted in the Wellington spinning into the ground, at 2300, one hundred yards NW of the chalk runway. Sgt Ayres was buried in Harwell Cemetery, his crew were dispersed to their home towns. Sgt Williams was the son of the Revd David Williams and Mabel Williams of Llanfair Dyffryn Clwyd.

26 OTU	Wellington III	BK553	**Training**

Sgt G P Slade inj T/o 1345 Little Horwood for solo circuits and landings but when a tyre burst, at high speed, the undercarriage promptly collapsed. This was the unit's first serious accident since receiving Mk. III Wellingtons.

4 Apr
1943

16 OTU	Wellington III	X3471	**Training**

F/S D G Nicoll RCAF + T/o Upper Heyford for low-level bombing, at
Sgt F G Bower + night, over the Ot Moor ranges. Lost control
Sgt G Hardy + at 1,500 feet and crashed 0003 in the range
Sgt C F Ball + area. Three rest in Middleton Stoney (All
Sgt M Shibko + Saints) Churchyard, Sgt Bower is buried in Hucknall Cemetery and Sgt Hardy was taken to Leeds (Harehills) Cemetery. Sgt Ball was known to his friends as Doogie.

20 OTU B Flt	Wellington IC	R1779	**Training**

Sgt F A W Hood + T/o Lossiemouth armed with 6 flash practice
Sgt W Rusby inj bombs, 1 by 4-inch training flare and two each
Sgt F L Myatt inj of flame floats, sea markers and smoke floats.
Sgt A F Davidson + Crashed 0200 while attempting to force-land on
Sgt S H Mortensen inj Binn Hill, some 2 to 3 miles E of the airfield
Sgt L R Laird inj and two miles WNW from Garmouth, Moray. Of those who died, Sgt Davidson was buried in Lossiemouth Burial Ground, while his skipper was taken to Ayr Cemetery. It is noted that his service number denotes he was a transferee from the army in 1939. Those who were injured escaped relatively lightly, considering the severity of the crash; all were taken to Dr. Gray's Hospital at Elgin.

27 OTU	Wellington III	BK508	**Air Test**

Sgt Law — T/o Church Broughton for a night flying test.
Sgt P A White + Coming into land, and while at 900 feet on the crosswind leg, an articulated rod in the starboard engine failed. Unable to maintain height, the bomber force-landed 1736 but hit a tree while doing so and caught fire. Sgt White was cremated at Harrogate Crematorium.

6 Apr
1943

16 OTU	Wellington III	BJ979	**Op: A-S Rescue**

F/S J J Britton + T/o Upper Heyford and set course for the search
Sgt H Mottershead + area E of Wick. Lost without trace. All are
P/O J F King + commemorated on the Runnymede Memorial. Sgt
Sgt E G Ufton DFM + Ufton, whose initial OTU instruction had been
F/S J T Houghton + with 27 OTU Lichfield, had recently served a tour with 106 Squadron, his award having been Gazetted as recently as 22 January 1943.

27 OTU	Wellington X	HE210	**Training**

W/O A G Cross RAAF — T/o 1559 Lichfield for an air firing exercise but swung out of control in the strong crosswind and lost its undercarriage. It was the first Wellington of its Mk. to be written off by the unit. Taken on charge in mid-December 1942, it had flown relatively few hours, a mere 35.15 being appended.

8 Apr   **14 OTU**   **Oxford II** **AB665**   **Training**
1943   Sgt A A Moors RCAF   + T/o Cottesmore for a training exercise which
        Sgt J A Lemmerick RCAF   + ended in a tragic midair collision with a
                                        Lancaster I L7545 from 1654 HCU, both machines
plummeting to the ground at Burton Lazars, 2 miles SE of Melton Mowbray in
Leicestershire. The two Canadians are buried in the extension to Cottesmore
(St. Nicholas) Churchyard. Sgt Lemmerick's brother, F/O George Earl Lemmerick,
lost his life on 29 January 1944, during operations to Berlin with 419 Squadron
(see Bomber Command Losses, Volume 5, page 61).

9 Apr   **26 OTU**   **Wellington IC** **R1628**   **Training**
1943   F/O N R S Humphreys RNZAF inj T/o 2128 Little Horwood but an engine caught
                                    fire and the Wellington came down two minutes
later at White House, midway between the village of Thornborough and Buckingham.
After recovering from his injuries, and converting to Stirlings, F/O Humphreys
joined 623 Squadron and was well into his tour of operations when he was killed
on 5–6 September 1943 (see Bomber Command Losses, Volume 4, page 316). Errol
Martyn adds that he had been aboard the Waiwera, torpedoed in mid-Atlantic
while en route to England on 29 June 1942. Until its allotment to the unit
on 7 April 1942, the Wellington here summarised had served as a test vehicle
both at Boscombe Down and at Farnborough. No flying hours are appended.

10 Apr   **11 OTU**   **Wellington IC** **X9615**   **Training**
1943   W/O T W Burke RNZAF   inj T/o 0225 Oakley for night circuit training but
        Sgt H W Allen   + hit a Drem light pole and crashed, almost in a
        Sgt F W Bourne RCAF   inj straight line with the runway. Sgt Allen of
                                      Dagenham in Essex was buried locally in Westcott
(St. Mary) Churchyard. W/O Burke RNZAF sustained a compound fracture of his left
tibia and fibia, a fractured left ankle and right metacarpal, plus cuts to his
head and left knee. He was admitted to the Radcliffe Infirmary at Oxford, as
was Sgt Bourne RCAF, though he was less seriously hurt. It is noted that of
the ten air force burials at Westcott, nine concern 11 OTU personnel. The
tenth grave is that for W/O Arthur Figg MSM who died, aged 46, on 26 May 1941.

        30 OTU   **Wellington III** **BK179**   **Training**
        F/O R Haynes   + T/o 0510 Seighford for infrared bombing but
        Sgt T E Jervis   + crashed five minutes later in Ranton Woods,
        Sgt L R Bray   + Ranton, in the airfield circuit and about five
        Sgt R F Knight   + miles W of Stafford. All lie in various burial
        Sgt F Yates   + grounds across the United Kingdom.

        30 OTU   **Wellington III** **DF611** **–W**   **Training**
        F/S R A Jones   + T/o 0450 Seighford similarly tasked. Lost
        F/S J F Spencer   + engine power and forced-landed 0530 on a fairly
        F/S G K Parsons   + straight road near Hartington, 10 miles NNW of
        F/S R J Perrin   inj Ashbourne, Derbyshire. As the bomber slid to
        F/S J Douglas   inj a stop, so it slewed to one side and hit a very
                                      solid stone wall, the impact splitting open one
of the aircraft's fuel tanks. Immediately, the Wellington became engulfed in
flames. Those who perished were taken to their home towns.

        81 OTU   **Whitley V** **LA771** **–P**   **Training**
        Sgt W Berry   + T/o 1022 Whitchurch Heath but climbed too
        Sgt L H Garnham   inj steeply, stalled and hit the ground sixty
        Sgt G B Whalley   inj seconds later and burst into flames. Sgt
        Sgt B H Stedman RCAF   inj Berry rests in Bolton (Heaton) Cemetery, while
                                    Sgt Garnham, who died from his injuries two days
later lies in Romford Cemetery. Sgt Stedman RCAF was an American from Woodstock
Illinois; he survived the war.

11 Apr   **26 OTU**   **Wellington III** **BJ879**   **Training**
1943   P/O D E J Bint DFM   + T/o Little Horwood for night dual circuits and
        Sgt F B McHugh   + landings. At 0015, flew into the station's
        Sgt C J Fox   + water storage tower, crashing about 500 yards
        Sgt J L L Belanger RCAF   + short of the threshold. P/O Bint, who gained
                                    his award with 150 Squadron (Gazetted 11 August
1942) was cremated at Oxford Crematorium, Stanton St. John; Sgt Belanger RCAF
is buried in Brookwood Military Cemetery; Sgt McHugh was taken to Oscott College
Cemetery in Warwickshire, while Sgt Fox lies at Boultham (St. Helen) Churchyard.

11 Apr 1943	81 OTU	Whitley V	EB342	Training

Sgt A C Browning — inj — T/o Whitchurch Heath for a night cross-country
Sgt J F Hallett — inj — flight. Wrecked 0330, while making an emergency
Sgt G E Davies — + — landing, at Moxhall Farm, Acton, a mile or so NW
Sgt J Smith — inj — of Nantwich, Cheshire. Sgt Davies of Netherfield
Sgt Bragg — in Nottinghamshire rests in Ash (Christchurch)
Churchyard (this burial ground being used by the
unit, though only sporadically). Sgt Browning recovered from his injuries and
following conversion to Lancasters, he was posted to 57 Squadron. On 2-3 August
1943, he failed to return from Hamburg (see Bomber Command Losses, Volume 4,
page 255).

11-12 Apr 1943	23 OTU	Wellington III	BJ786	Training

F/S F E Rogers RCAF — + — T/o 2115 Pershore for a night navigation sortie.
F/S J O T A A G Toupin RCAF — + — A report from the Royal Observer Corps indicates
F/S A N MacLellan RCAF — + — the Wellington was flying normally when, without
Sgt R A Killham RCAF — + — any hint of trouble, it dived to the ground at
Sgt D H Smith RCAF — + — 0130 at Foley Cote Hill, a little less than two
F/S A A Dorzek RCAF — + — miles SE of Sawley village, 4 miles SW of Ripon
in Yorkshire. Five of the crew were taken to
Dishforth Cemetery, but Sgt Smith RCAF, who hailed from Elfros in Saskatchewan,
is buried in Warwick Cemetery (likely having been claimed by relatives). Of his
five companions, it is noted that F/S Rogers RCAF was a mere seventeen years of
age. Two years earlier, he had been declared the Senior Athletic Champion at
Port Colborne High School, Ontario. Less than four months after his death, his
twenty-one year old brother, F/O Frederick Lennox Rogers RCAF, also a pilot and
serving with 428 Squadron, failed to return from operations against Hamburg (see
Bomber Command Losses, Volume 4, page 259).

13 Apr 1943	12 OTU	Martinet I	HP373	Training

F/S S R Grant — inj — T/o 1400 Chipping Warden for cine camera gun.
Lost power and crashed 1520, flipping onto
its back, about a mile W of Upper Heyford. This was the first Martinet to
be written off at a Bomber Command Operational Training Unit; it will also
be recalled that F/S Grant had been involved in a Lysander accident on 10 March
(see page 206). From this second serious incident, he was fortunate to escape
with only minor cuts to his face.

13 OTU	Blenheim I	L8379	-B	Training

F/O D G Mossman — T/o 1943 Finmere for a demonstration flight
P/O E R Semple RCAF — but an engine cut and the instructor retracted
the undercarriage in order to remain within the
confines of the airfield. According to unit records, part of the demonstration
was to show the effects of taking off in coarse pitch.

13 OTU	Blenheim IV	V6510		Transit

Sgt A E Fotherby — T/o 1305 Snaith and set course for Bicester
Sgt A Wallwork — on what should have been the final chapter in
Sgt E H Price — a very protracted exercise that had been
interrupted two days previous when the crew
made an emergency landing at Doncaster. Departing the same day, the port
engine lost power and the Blenheim was force -landed at Snaith. For most
of the twelfth, the engines underwent plug cleaning and ground running tests.
Then, as indicated above, it left Snaith only for the oil pressure to drop,
thus necessitating the port propeller to be feathered. At the time, the crew
were in the vicinity of Hucknall and it was here that a wheels up landing was
duly accomplished. The crew escaped injury, but their aircraft was deemed to
be beyond worthwhile repair.

81 OTU	Whitley V	EB346	-G	Training

F/O L H Page — + — T/o 2139 Whitchurch Heath for a night navigation
Sgt H B Harrison — + — detail. When some two hours or so into the
Sgt E G Sibbery — + — exercise, the port engine failed and the airscrew
Sgt A W Frapwell — + — was feathered. However, at 2344, control was lost
Sgt A E Martin — + — and the Whitley crashed less than a mile NE of
Sgt D B McCartney — + — Fridaythorpe, 9 miles WNW of Great Driffield,
Sgt S Levitus — + — Yorkshire. All were taken for burial in their
home towns and villages.

13–14 Apr **30 OTU** **Wellington III** **DF610** **Op: Nickel**
1943   Sgt H E Bull RAAF   inj T/o 2114 Hixon in the company of six other
          Sgt F C Sherratt   inj aircraft. While heading towards the Kent
          Sgt P C Willars   inj coast, homebound, the crew were obliged to
          Sgt H Kershaw   inj ditch at 0010 in the Strait of Dover off
          Sgt A W G Meech   inj Dungeness. All were picked up by an Air-
          Sgt R M Anderson   inj Sea Rescue launch. Six weeks later all,
                                         apart from Sgt Kershaw, were killed while
          raiding Wuppertal with 460 Squadron (see Bomber Command Losses, Volume 4,
          page 172).

14 Apr **15 OTU** **Wellington III** **BK345** **Training**
1943   F/S C C Povey   inj T/o 0005 Harwell for night circuit training,
          F/O J S Messent   +   the screened pilot (F/S Povey) demonstrating
          P/O J Loughram   inj single-engined procedures. Ten minutes later,
          Sgt B S Burch   inj with F/O Messent at the controls, the bomber
          Sgt R T Chinn   inj side-slipped, while banking, and crashed at
          Sgt O J Davies   inj Churn Hill on the SSW side of Blewbury, some
                                         five miles SW of Wallingford, Berkshire. F/O
          Messent was cremated at West Norwood Crematorium, Lambeth. After recovering
          from their injuries, the last four named eventually arrived at Tempsford, in
          Bedfordshire, joining 138 Squadron. On 19-20 September 1943, they were part
          of a Halifax crew tasked for a Special Operations Executive mission (Parsnip 7
          Lettuce 12) over Holland. Sadly, they failed to return (see Bomber Command
          Losses, Volume 4, page 323), though in course of time P/O Loughram and Sgt
          Davies were reported as prisoners of war.

15 Apr **21 OTU** **Wellington IC** **Z1142** **Training**
1943   Sgt C A Good   +   T/o 2253 Enstone but swung, possibly due to a
          Sgt F C Townsend   +   tyre bursting, and crashed into the windsock,
          F/O G H D Druce   +   bursting into flames. Sgt Good was taken to
          Sgt C Rhodes RAAF   inj his home of the Isle of Man and interred in
                                         Douglas Cemetery; F/O Druce rests at Reading
          (Henley Road) Cemetery, Eye and Dunsden, while Sgt Townsend is buried at
          Streatham Park Cemetery, Mitcham. Sgt Rhodes RAAF was dreadfully injured
          and he was admitted to Banbury Hospital. Although repatriated to Australia,
          he never fully recovered and his death was announced on 21 May 1946. Buried
          in Sydney War Cemetery, his unit is still shown as 21 OTU. On 10 January 1942,
          while on the strength of 103 Squadron, this Wellington was hit in the bomb bay
          and set on fire. The crew were ordered to bale out and F/L G E McGill RCAF
          complied. Soon after his departure, the flames were extinguished and the
          bomber made a safe return. Meanwhile, F/L McGill RCAF was captured, ending
          up in Stalag Luft III. In March 1944, he was amongst the large group of
          Allied air force officers that succeeded in breaking out from the camp. Like
          so many of the escapees, he was recaptured and was summarily executed by the
          Gestapo on, or around, 25 March. His remains lie in Poland at Poznan Old
          Garrison cemetery.

16 Apr **12 OTU** **Martinet I** **HP372** **Training**
1943   W/O D Fairclough-Smith   inj T/o 1605 Chipping Warden for cine camera gun.
                                         While changing fuel cocks the engine faltered
          and moments later the Martinet had stalled and crashed, 1740, onto the Brackley
          Road. W/O Fairclough-Smith was taken to the Radcliffe Infirmary at Oxford for
          attention to a fractured left humerus.

17 Apr **10 OTU Det** **Whitley V** **BD226** **–X** **Op: AS Patrol**
1943   Sgt L G Smith   +   T/o St. Eval armed with 6 x 250lb depth charges
          F/O C Thwaites   +   and fitted with two F24 cameras. Called on the
          Sgt W Davis   +   wireless, indicating the presence of enemy air-
          P/O H W Barnett   +   craft, but nothing further was heard. All are
          Sgt K Ray   +   commemorated on the Runnymede Memorial.
          Sgt J H Reynolds   +

          81 OTU **Whitley V** **LA768** **Training**
          Sgt R C S Findley   +   T/o 2136 Whitchurch Heath for a night cross-
          F/S Whitley   inj country, Crashed 2331 at Aylesbeare, 6 miles
          Sgt H Derbyshire   +   ESE of Exeter. Sgt Findley lies in Stockton
          Sgt Hill   inj Heath (St. Thomas) Churchyard; Sgt Derbyshire
          Sgt Randall   inj is buried at Lowton St. Mary's Churchyard.

19 Apr   **14 OTU**   **Wellington II**   **W5352**   **−D**   **Training**
1943   Sgt B Jones RAAF   T/o 0200 Cottesmore for a night cross-country.
         Sgt Ryan   inj   Abandoned from circa 10,000 feet, after the port
                                         propeller detached, crashing 0230 at Langtoft,
ten miles SW of Spalding, Lincolnshire. Sgt Ryan sustained a broken ankle.
Built as the first Wellington in a batch of 200 Mk. II aircraft, delivered
between October 1940 and July 1941, this particular example had been intended
as a Mk. IC with the serial T2545. However, another airframe was constructed
and numbered T2545, though over the years this has led to some confusion when
reporting on such matters.

22 OTU   **Wellington III**   **DF743 LT−L**   **Training**
F/S J O Munro RCAF   +   T/o 1034 Gaydon for a cross-country, the two
F/O H B Elliott RCAF   +   Belgian soldiers reportedly joining the crew
Sgt W C Scott RCAF   +   for air testing. At 1044, the Wellington emerged
Sgt A A Chambers   +   from cloud and crashed, exploding on impact, at
WO2 A E Lightheart RCAF   +   Staple Farm, Withington, 7 miles SE of Cheltenham
Pte E Battaille   +   in Gloucestershire. The four RCAF members of
Pte F De Pauw   +   crew were buried in Cirencester Cemetery, Sgt
                                       Chambers lies in Northampton (Towcester Road)
Cemetery, while the two Belgian Special Air Service paratroopers were taken to
Kensal Green Cemetery, London. Since 1945, their remains have been exhumed and
returned to Belgium; Pte Battaille to Wevelgem and Pte De Pauw to Charleroi-Nord.
On 19 April 1998, a memorial plaque was dedicated at Withington Church with Major
R Brinton of the Parachute Regiment and various service associations, including a
party from the Belgian Special Air Service, in attendance. I am, indeed, most
grateful to Yves Brasseur for supplying details of this crew.

19−20 Apr   **10 OTU**   **Whitley V**   **P4989**   **Training**
1943   F/O A O G Richards RAAF   +   T/o 2120 Abingdon for a night cross-country.
                                       It is believed the pitot tube became partially
iced over giving rise to erratic air speed readings. Stalled and crashed 0130
at Horton, 3 miles NE of Chipping Sodbury, Gloucestershire. F/O Richards RAAF
is interred at Brookwood Military Cemetery.

11 OTU   **Wellington IC**   **T2883**   **Training**
Sgt J R Richmond   T/o 2120 Westcott for a night exercise, during
                                       which a propeller came off. Force -landed 0115
without injury to the crew, though, sadly, Sgt Richmond was destined to be
killed two weeks later during another night training sortie.

21 Apr   **15 OTU**   **Wellington IC**   **DV936**   **Training**
1943   F/S D E Hamlyn   +   T/o Harwell for a navigation exercise. Shortly
         Sgt H M Holmes   +   before 1115, a cylinder head barrel, between Nos.
         Sgt A G Page   +   fourteen and fifteen fins, fractured leading to a
         P/O N G Woodward   +   catastrophic engine fire followed by structural
         Sgt L F J Short   +   failure of the starboard wing. Totally out of
         Sgt W P Hoare   +   control, the bomber smashed into the ground at
         F/S G E Boyes RAAF   +   Wychbold, 8 miles NNE of Worcester. F/S Boyes
                                         of Hobart, Tasmania, is buried in Pershore
Cemetery, while the bodies of his six companions were taken to their home towns.

17 OTU D Flt   **Blenheim IV**   **V6525**   **Training**
Sgt J H Simpson   T/o 1400 Steeple Morden but ran over some flints
                                       on the runway, bursting a tyre in the process.
Out of control, the bomber swerved violently and having come to a stop, caught
fire. Four days previous, the headquarters of 17 OTU had moved from Upwood to
Silverstone to prepare for the conversion from Blenheims to Wellingtons and the
incident summarised here was the last to involve the now obsolete Bristol-built
aircraft (in 17 Operational Training Unit service).

22 Apr   **10 OTU**   **Whitley V**   **N1374**   **Training**
1943   F/O R V Moore   +   T/o 2348 Abingdon for a night exercise. Reported
         F/O S Hetherington   +   to have stalled at 500 feet, crashing 2350 about
         P/O R W H Stock   +   a mile NW of Longworth, 8 miles NNW of Wantage,
         F/S L N Ingram RAAF   +   Berkshire. All were claimed by their next of kin.
         Sgt W L White   +   Since its acceptance, initially with 19 OTU, this
                                         veteran bomber had flown a total of 1127.00 hours.

22 Apr **13 OTU** **Blenheim IV R3745** **Training**
1943 Sgt S E Skudder T/o Bicester. Written off, in poor weather
Sgt A G Reay conditions, 1155 in a failed attempt to over-
Sgt A Berry shoot the runway. As recently as 3 April, this
Blenheim had been involved in a taxying accident.

23 Apr **30 OTU** **Lysander II N1308** **Ground**
1943 Wrecked 0316 at Hixon after being struck by
Wellington X HE390 (F/L A E Spurr RCAF) which was taxying towards its dispersal
pan. Damage to the bomber was slight and following repairs it was returned to
service. On 11 August 1943, however, it was destroyed in a midair collision
with a Miles Master trainer. F/L Spurr RCAF, meanwhile, went on to fly with
103 Squadron and was killed during operations to Mülheim in June 1943 (see
Bomber Command Losses, Volume 4, page 200).

24 Apr **23 OTU** **Wellington X HE206** **Training**
1943 F/O R C Henderson inj T/o 1430 Stratford-upon-Avon for a combined
F/S A L Olsson RCAF inj exercise involving the crew in navigation and
W/O C H Balfort RAAF inj circuit procedures. Wrecked 1840, during the
Sgt J O Koivu RCAF second phase of the detail, when the starboard
Sgt J Doyle inj wing hit the ground following a particularly
Sgt J A Williams heavy landing which sent the Wellington through
Sgt E J Weston inj 180 degrees. On coming to a stop, the starboard
Sgt K M Pulham RCAF engine caught fire and soon the bomber was well
and truly alight. F/S Olsson RCAF and Sgt Koivu
(both commissioned) were killed in action with 426 Squadron on 26-27 March 1944
(see Bomber Command Losses, Volume 5, page 143). F/O Henderson and Sgt Williams
eventually went to the Middle East and, by coincidence, joined 70 Squadron. On
25 November 1943, the former was lost over Italy, while operating from Djedeida
in Tunisia; he is buried in Catania War Cemetery. Then, on 26 June 1944, Sgt
Williams (almost certainly on his second tour as he is described in 23 OTU
records as a screened wireless operator) failed to return to the squadron's
base at Cerignola, Italy; he rests in Budapest War Cemetery, Hungary.

25 Apr **29 OTU** **Wellington III X3816** **Training**
1943 F/O D R McLean RCAF + T/o 2145 Woolfox Lodge for a night cross-
Sgt V A Rice + country. Crashed fifteen minutes later in
Sgt G Dunn + the vicinity of Stocking Farm near Belgrave
Sgt J G P Adams + in the NNE suburbs of Leicester, bursting into
Sgt J Riley + flames. F/O McLean RCAF is buried in Burton-
on-the-Wolds Church Cemetery, his crew were
taken to their home towns in England and Northern Ireland.

27 Apr **13 OTU** **Blenheim IV L8850** **Training**
1943 F/S A H Swanson RAAF + T/o 0100 Bicester (attached from 26 OTU) for a
Sgt H O Foster + night cross-country. When near Stewkley, 10 miles
Sgt E S Frostwick + ESE of Buckingham, at 0315, the Blenheim exploded.
F/S Swanson RAAF was taken to Halton (St. Michael)
Churchyard, while his two compatriots were taken to their home towns.

27-28 Apr **19 OTU C Flt** **Whitley V LA841 ZV-E** **Training**
1943 Sgt E Mitchell + T/o 2200 Kinloss for a night cross-country.
F/S E S Blake RCAF + Dived at high speed and crashed 0200 into the
Sgt J S Grocock + Moray Firth, 2 miles off Nairn. In the morning
Sgt D B Griffiths RAAF + the wreck of the Whitley was located, lying on
Sgt D McLachlan + its back, the lowered undercarriage protruding
Sgt A G Debenham + clear of the water. An inflated dinghy was
floating nearby. Three, the two commonwealth
airmen and Sgt Grocock lie in Kinloss Abbey Burial Ground while the others were
claimed by their next of kin.

29 OTU **Wellington III X3882** **Op: Nickel**
Sgt R Steer T/o 2231 North Luffenham and set course for
France. While returning to base, strayed from
track and at 0620 the crew attempted to land at Seething airfield in Norfolk,
which was still under construction. On touch down, the Wellington crashed into
some heavy plant, parked in front of Thwaite Cottage. In due course of time,
Seething would be known as Station 146, base for the B-24 Liberators of the
448th Bomb Group United States Army Air Force.

28 Apr
1943

81 OTU		**Whitley V**	**EB341**	**–D**	**Training**

F/O D C Bradshaw
P/O W T Shannon

T/o 2212 Whitchurch Heath for a night cross-country. Not long into the detail, both engines began to leak glycol and at 2342, while trying to reach Twinwood Farm airfield, Bedfordshire, the bomber crashed just to the east of their hoped for salvation. A month or so later, having been posted to Elsham Wolds and 103 Squadron, the two officers were lost while raiding Köln on 3-4 July 1943 (see Bomber Command Losses, Volume 4, page 220).

29 Apr
1943

21 OTU **Anson I** **N5005** **Training**

F/S B Pickin

T/o Moreton-in-Marsh for a night exercise. While circling the aerodrome at 0105, with the undercarriage down and the altimeter reading 800 feet, the starboard engine cut due to lack of fuel. F/S Pickin told his navigator (unnamed) to change tanks but it would seem that in his haste to do so, a mistake was made and having lost height to 400 feet, the port engine stopped. Putting the Anson into a straight glide, the pilot tried to reach the runway but the port wing clipped a tree and the flight ended in a field twixt the airfield and the nearby town of Stow-on-the-Wold, Gloucestershire.

1 May
1943

13 OTU **Blenheim IV** **Z6100** **Training**

Sgt P J Heamolle
Sgt H L James
Sgt J Richardson

T/o 1440 Bicester but a motor transport vehicle suddenly appeared in front of the Blenheim and in order to avoid a collision, Sgt Heamolle swung his aircraft into a nearby hedge. Before the year was out, Sgt James and Sgt Richardson were flying with 114 Squadron in Italy. On 4 January 1944, their Boston failed to return to Celone and both now rest near San Donato in the Canadian War Cemetery at Moro River.

21 OTU **Wellington IC** **N2847** **Training**

P/O P J Temple
Sgt R E Hayward

T/o Enstone for a night exercise during which the hydraulics failed. Landed 0230, without the assistance of flaps, bounced and crashed with sufficient force to cause a fire to break out, destroying the bomber.

2 May
1943

11 OTU **Wellington IC** **Z8806** **Training**

Sgt J R Richmond +
Sgt L R Crouch +
Sgt H J Cox +
Sgt E D Scott +
Sgt T N Harker +
Sgt J A Cheetham +

T/o 0144 Westcott and set course for the ranges at Warpsgrove, NE of Chalgrove in Oxfordshire. Lost control and crashed 0245 at Stadhampton, seven miles SE of Oxford. It is thought the pilot, who had been involved in an accident a fortnight previous (see page 214) may have been flying with only the aid of his instruments. All are buried in cemeteries scattered across the counties of England.

13 OTU **Blenheim I** **L1204** **Training**

P/O W Boyd inj
Sgt S H Dodds inj

T/o Bicester for low flying instruction. While near Waddesdon, 5 miles NW of Aylesbury in Buckinghamshire, the two pilots were distracted by a flock of birds and, therefore, neither saw the line of telegraph wires that lay in their path. At 1500, with cable wrapped around the port propeller, and the splintered remains of a telegraph pole behind them, the aircraft crash-landed, wheels up, in a field. This was the unit's last major accident prior to leaving Bomber Command on 1 June 1943, for life with No. 70 Group. It was also the last Blenheim to be written off from an OTU controlled by Bomber Command. Briefly, it has served with 110 Squadron (twice), 101 Squadron (twice), 82 and 107 Squadrons, 8 Beam Approach Training Flight, 1442 Flight and thence to 13 OTU on 6 March 1942. In total, it had logged 1201.05 flying hours.

24 OTU **Whitley V** **Z9362** **Training**

F/O J C N Lewis +
Sgt E J Beer +
Sgt D E Watts +

T/o Honeybourne using call sign 3WZ-U for a night navigation exercise, setting a northerly course towards the Scottish border. At 0217, was obliged to alight in the sea, due to engine failure, about a mile S of Ardrossan Harbour on the Ayrshire coast. Of those who lost their lives, F/O Lewis rests in Brampton (St. Martin) Old Churchyard in Cumberland, Sgt Beer was brought to Brookwood Military Cemetery, while Sgt Watts is commemorated on panel 169 of the Runnymede Memorial.

2- 3 May   **10 OTU**   **Whitley V**   **Z9318**   **Training**
1943   F/O M G Harrison   inj   T/o 2155 Abingdon for a night cross-country.
       P/O Rees   While off the Pembrokeshire coast, flying at
       Sgt Smith   7000 feet, the starboard engine shed its coolant
       Sgt Cleaver   and with power decaying rapidly, along with
       F/S Pryde   altitude, the Whitley was ditched 0025 in the
region of St. Ann´s Head, 6 miles WSW from
Milford Haven. For the next seven-and-a-half hours, the crew drifted in their
dinghy before being rescued by HMS Fury. F/O Harrison required medical attention
for a foot injury.

81 OTU   **Whitley V**   **EB405**   **-A**   **Training**
       Sgt H J Spiers   +   T/o 2235 Sleap for a night navigation sortie.
       Sgt H Leather   +   Crashed into trees at 0420, following two failed
       Sgt J J Brown   +   attempts to land, and burst into flames near
       Sgt J W Scott   +   Loppington, 3 miles W of Wem, Shropshire. Sgt
       Sgt W A Cadel   +   Spiers of Teddington, Middlesex, was buried in
                                  Ash (Christchurch) Churchyard, his being the
last of three unit interments in this burial ground, while his crew were taken
to their home towns in England, Wales and Scotland.

3 May   **22 OTU**   **Wellington III**   **HF810**   **Training**
1943   Sgt S R W Laine RCAF   T/o Wellesbourne Mountford for a night cross-
                                  country. Wrecked 0300 while trying to make an
emergency landing, on one engine, at Husbands Bosworth airfield, Leicestershire.
Subsequently commissioned, Sgt Laine RCAF went on to gain a Distinguished Flying
Cross before being killed on operations to Berlin with 408 Squadron on 27-28
January 1944 (see Bomber Command Losses, Volume 5, page 54).

24 OTU   **Whitley V**   **BD219**   **Training**
       Sgt M Harker   +   T/o 1709 Long Marston for circuits and landings.
                     inj   Stalled and crashed 1712, clipping a tree in the
                     inj   process, some 300 yards from Marston Railway
                                    Station. Sgt Harker rests in Thirsk Cemetery.
His two injured companions (unnamed) were taken to Stratford-upon-Avon Hospital.

4 May   **22 OTU**   **Wellington X**   **HE217**   **Training**
1943   F/S J W Freeman RCAF   +   T/o Wellesbourne Mountford for a night cross-
       F/S K C G Bourne RCAF   +   country. While banking in the circuit at 0255,
       Sgt E H Park RCAF   +   stalled and crashed near the runway. All were
       Sgt C R S Blenkhorn RCAF   +   laid to rest in Stratford-upon-Avon Cemetery.
       Sgt K Hodgson RCAF   +   Sgt Park RCAF hailed from Lewisburg, Tennessee,
       F/S A W Klauer RCAF   +   a town east of route 65 running twixt Nashville
                                      and Birmingham, Alabama.

4- 5 May   **29 OTU**   **Wellington III**   **BK210**   **Training**
1943   Sgt W J Drew   inj   T/o 2210 North Luffenham for a night navigation
       Sgt S I Rudkin   inj   detail. One hour into the sortie, the port
       Sgt R Welch   inj   engine began to misfire and it was not long
       Sgt W Sparks   inj   before the temperature began to rise. With
       Sgt T H R James   inj   the oil pressure dropping, the exercise was
       Sgt H Bassett   inj   aborted and the crew headed for base. Their
       Sgt J T Jopling   first attempt to land was thwarted by scuds of
                                    low cloud, and while going round again the
troublesome motor failed completely and the bomber force -landed amongst trees
some 1,500 yards NNE of the airfield. A technical inspection revealed that the
plugs on Nos. 2 and 6 cylinders had worked loose. Eventually, Sgt Drew qualified on Lancasters but on 17-18 August 1943, he, along with the above (less
Sgt Welch), failed to return from Peenemünde (see Bomber Command Losses,
Volume 4, page 271). At the time they were serving with 44 Squadron.

5 May   **21 OTU**   **Anson I**   **DG985**   **Training**
1943   F/S S A Payne   +   T/o Moreton-in-Marsh tasked for a navigation
       P/O A R Fox   +   exercise, at night. Encountered low cloud and
       F/O W T McCormack RAAF   +   at 0220 the Anson flew into the side of a hill
       Sgt W J Shirley   +   near Blockley, Gloucestershire, some 3 miles
       F/S S R Mosey   +   WNW of the airfield. F/O McCormack RAAF was
       Sgt L F Evans   +   buried in Moreton-in-Marsh New Cemetery, while
                                     the others were claimed by their next of kin.

5 May　　**21 OTU**　　　　**Wellington IC**　**R1242**　　　　　　　　**Training**
1943　　F/S R J Miller RAAF　　　　+　T/o Moreton-in-Marsh for a night flying detail.
　　　　　　　　　　　　　　　　inj　Reported to have overshot the runway and crashed
　　　　　　　　　　　　　　　　inj　at around 0215, some 3 miles WNW of the airfield
　　　　　　　　　　　　　　　　inj　(possibly in the vicinity of the Anson accident
　　　　　　　　　　　　　　　　　　described at the foot of the previous page).
　　　　The funeral for F/S Miller RAAF took place at Moreton-in-Marsh New Cemetery.
　　　　Taken on unit charge on 9 March 1941, this Wellington had suffered its first
　　　　flying accident six weeks later (26 April) when F/O L H Folkhard forced-landed,
　　　　wheels up, at Moreton-in-Marsh.

22 OTU　　　　**Wellington X**　**HF630**　　　　　　　　**Training**
F/S A A F Hall RCAF　　　　+　T/o Wellesbourne Mountford for a cross-country
F/O J Cherkinsky RCAF　　　+　flight. At 1259, the starboard engine cut and
Sgt J E L Burgess RCAF　　　+　the bomber dived into the ground near Hidcote
WO1 F R Santo RCAF　　　　+　Manor, Hidcote Bartrim, a mile ESE of Mickleton,
Sgt G E Foster RCAF　　　inj　a north Gloucestershire village 8 miles NNW from
　　　　　　　　　　　　　　　　Moreton-in-Marsh. Those who died were taken to
Evesham Cemetery. WO1 Santos's twin brother, P/O John Alexander Santo RCAF, a
navigator serving with 429 Squadron, was killed during the night of 31 July -
1 August 1944 (see Bomber Command Losses, Volume 5, page 366).

6 May　　**14 OTU**　　　　**Wellington IC**　**Z1068**　　　　　　　　**Training**
1943　　Sgt E G Kerrigan RAAF　　　　T/o 0115 Cottesmore tasked for a night bombing
　　　　　　　　　　　　　　　　　detail. Recalled, due to adverse weather, but
　　　　was unable to locate the airfield. While flying low, stalled and crashed 0345
　　　　near North Witham, 9 miles SSE of Grantham, Lincolnshire. No one was seriously
　　　　hurt though the navigator is thought to have sustained cuts and abrasions to
　　　　his right ankle.

19 OTU D Flt　　**Whitley V**　**BD381**　**-V**　　　　　**Training**
Sgt L R Thomas　　　　　+　T/o 1320 Kinloss for a cross-country. Abandoned
　　　　　　　　　　　　　　　(apart from the pilot) following failure of the
port engine, crashing circa 1630 some 300 yards E of Dewshill Colliery, West
Lothian. It is reported that three days elapsed before the body of Sgt Thomas
was found; he is buried in Malden (St. John The Baptist) Churchyard, his service
number indicating he had transferred to the air force from the army during the
early part of 1939.

6- 7 May　　**29 OTU**　　　　**Wellington III**　**BK441**　　　　　　　**Training**
1943　　Sgt W Mason　　　　　　+　T/o 2058 North Luffenham for a night cross-
　　　　F/S A Darby RCAF　　　+　country, during which the crew encountered
　　　　Sgt R A Page　　　　　+　low cloud. Thus, possibly while trying to
　　　　P/O M J Meatyard　　　+　establish their position, the Wellington flew
　　　　Sgt W G Hutchinson　　+　into Greenlaws Hush between Thatch Mires and
　　　　Sgt S M Marfleet　　　+　High Wood Meadows, SE of St. John's Chapel, 16
　　　　Sgt R E Stephens　　　+　miles SW of Consett, Durham. All are scattered
　　　　　　　　　　　　　　　　in cemeteries across the United Kingdom. At the
　　　　Remembrance Day service in 1994, Sgt Ian Slater of North Luffenham laid a wreath
　　　　at St. John's Chapel Memorial; aptly, his wife Caroline was once a resident of
　　　　the village. For this information, I am indebted to David Thompson and various
　　　　reports published in 'The North Echo' during October and November 1994.

8 May　　**20 OTU**　　　　**Wellington IC**　**DV949**　　　　　　　**Training**
1943　　Sgt J H Watson　　　　　　T/o 0034 Lossiemouth for a night navigation
　　　　　　　　　　　　　　　　　exercise. Nearly two hours into the detail,
　　　　the starboard engine gave so much trouble that Sgt Watson, fearing for the
　　　　safety of his crew, ordered everyone to bale out. He then force -landed the
　　　　ailing bomber at 0229 on an unlit airfield on Benbecula, where it caught fire.

11 May　　**15 OTU**　　　　**Martinet I**　**HP425**　　　　　　　**Training**
1943　　F/O J S Moore　　　　　+　T/o Harwell briefed to carry out a fighter
　　　　F/O L C Martin　　　　+　affiliation exercise with a Wellington. It
　　　　　　　　　　　　　　　　is not clear if the affiliation part of the
　　　　flight was carried out, but at around 1510, while attempting a second aero-
　　　　batic roll, the pilot lost control and spun into the ground less than a mile
　　　　south-west of West Hagbourne and about 2 miles SSW from Didcot, Berkshire.
　　　　F/O Moore rests in the City of London Cemetery at Manor Park, East Ham, while
　　　　his air gunner passenger, F/O Martin, lies in Adwell (St. Mary) Churchyard.

11 May 1943	24 OTU	Whitley V	EB353		Training

Sgt L P Patterson — inj — T/o 0055 Long Marston for a night exercise.
Sgt F Harrold — + — When the starboard engine lost power a forced-
P/O T B Curry — + — landing became necessary. While doing so, at approximately 0130, the Whitley struck a tree and crashed at Ilmington, 3 miles NW of Shipston-on-Stour, Warwickshire. Sgt Harrold was taken to Dudley (St. John) Churchyard, while P/O Curry is buried at Chingford Mount Cemetery. Miraculously, Sgt Patterson was thrown clear and he was subsequently admitted to Stratford-upon-Avon Hospital.

12 May 1943	18 OTU	Wellington III	BK353		Training

S/L E P Zakrzewski PAF — + — T/o 1425 Finningley to practice single-engined
F/O T M Opulski PAF — + — flying, during the course of which control was
Sgt M J Frankiewicz PAF — + — lost at 2,000 feet and at 1530 the Wellington
Sgt R Drapala PAF — + — dived into the ground near Belton, 2 miles NNE
Sgt T Pasternak PAF — + — of Grantham, Lincolnshire. All were interred in Newark-upon-Trent Cemetery. Amongst the recommendations that emerged from the Court of Inquiry into this tragedy was that future exercises of this nature should not take place below 4,000 feet.

	20 OTU B Flt	Wellington IC	R1153	–D	Training

F/O T Booth — + — T/o Lossiemouth for a low-level bombing detail.
P/O P C S Bird — + — Caught fire in the air and crashed 1847 into
P/O A Smith — + — the sea. An Air-Sea Rescue search found some
Sgt J A Scott — + — wreckage in position 5751N 0240W, approximately
Sgt R E Allen — + — eight miles from Portsoy on the Banff coast. All are commemorated on the Runnymede Memorial.

	22 OTU	Wellington X	HE218		Training

WO1 M J S Kerby RCAF — + — T/o Wellesbourne Mountford for a night cross-
WO2 D E Elliot RCAF — + — country. On return to base at around 0100, an
Sgt J Piket RCAF — + — engine cut and the aircraft dived to the ground
Sgt J H Collett RCAF — + — at Compton Verney Lake, 3 miles ESE of the air-field, bursting into flames on impact. All are buried in Stratford-upon-Avon Cemetery.

	29 OTU	Wellington III	BK123		Training

Sgt F T Allen — + — T/o 1215 North Luffenham for local circuit
Sgt J S Harris — + — training but strayed from the airfield and
Sgt J A Douglas RAAF — + — crashed 1240 at Scottlethorpe, 5 miles SSW of Scunthorpe, Lincolnshire. Sgt Allen is buried in Feltham Cemetery, Sgt Harris was taken to Smethwick (Uplands) Cemetery and, as expected, Sgt Douglas RAAF of Thirroul in New South Wales was interred in North Luffenham (St. John The Baptist) Churchyard, his being the last of eighteen air force funerals held at this church in World War 2.

13 May 1943	24 OTU	Whitley V	Z9510		Training

Sgt E E Russell — + — T/o 1105 Long Marston for a cross-country.
Sgt A H Burn — + — While in flight, the port engine suddenly
Sgt G F Broadbent — + — burst into flames, resulting in the bomber
Sgt E G Cooper — + — crashing to the ground, 1340, at Castle Eaton,
Sgt H Millward — + — some 7 miles NNW from Swindon, Wiltshire. All were claimed by their next of kin.

	28 OTU	Wellington IC	DV714		Training

F/O W R Bean — inj — T/o 1251 Wymeswold for circuit training. On
F/O J F Wright — inj — landing at 1315, the bomber bounced back into
Sgt W R Coleman — inj — the air, causing the control locking bar to jam.
P/O D R Cooper — + — Moments later, it hit the ground, hard, and caught fire. P/O Cooper rests in Manchester Cemetery.

	81 OTU	Whitley V	EB338		Training

F/O E J Bull — inj — T/o 1805 Whitchurch Heath for an evening cross-
Sgt N J Prime RNZAF — inj — country. Twice lost the use of the port engine
Sgt T Kennedy — inj — and crashed 1835 at Alsop en le Dale, 18 miles
Sgt G Belec RCAF — + — north-west of Derby. Sgt Belec RCAF rests in
Sgt S Otty — inj — Ashbourne Cemetery. Nearly a year later, F/O
Sgt E F Harris — inj — Bull was killed while serving with 30 OTU.

14 May   **11 OTU**   **Wellington IC DV826**   **Training**
1943   Sgt E F Baptiste   T/o 1510 Westcott for a bombing detail, armed
with 6 x 250lb sand filled bombs. As the
Wellington lifted from the runway, the port engine failed. Two minutes later,
having skillfully retained control and coaxed the ailing Wellington around the
circuit, Sgt Baptiste overshot his landing. For this relatively inexperienced
pilot, it was his third very serious accident in twelve days. On 3 May he had
been obliged to forced-land at Mount Farm airfield in Oxfordshire, while two
days later he came close to wrecking another Wellington, this time at Westcott.

21 OTU   **Wellington IC T2562**   **Training**
F/S K P Rogers RNZAF   T/o Moreton-in-Marsh for a night exercise.
At around 0100, the Wellington caught fire
in the air as a result of a photoflash flare becoming jammed in the flare
chute. Displaying remarkably good airmanship, F/S Rogers RNZAF forced-landed
his crippled machine near Banbury, Oxfordshire. Subsequently, his flying log
book was endorsed "highly commended".

14-15 May **27 OTU**   **Wellington III X3785**   **Training**
1943   F/O J W Robb   +   T/o 2241 Lichfield for a night cross-country,
F/O T A Ley RAAF   +   combined with a Bullseye operation. At 0234,
P/O G H Cone   +   Sgt Lee sent a brief standby for message signal
Sgt A W Sayers   +   but before this could be transmitted, the air-
Sgt G S Lee   +   craft dived, near vertically, into the ground
Sgt E L Clark   +   (narrowly missing an isolated farmhouse) 1 mile
north of Lake Vyrnwy in Montgomeryshire. All
are buried in various cemeteries across the United Kingdom. F/O Robb's father,
Chief Engineering Officer John William Robb DSC Merchant Navy, lost his life at
sea on 29 November 1943. A second family, too, suffered a double tragedy for
Sgt Albert Laurie Sayers, brother to Sgt Sayers, died when his 207 Squadron
Lancaster crashed during the course of the St-Leu raid on 7-8 July 1944 (see
Bomber Command Losses, Volume 5, page 324). In remembrance of the Wellington
crew, a memorial picture drawn by Rob Evans was unveiled at The Tavern Inn
(part of the Vyrnwy Hotel complex) on 18 August 2001.

15 May   **21 OTU**   **Wellington IC DV598**   **Transit**
1943   F/S G W Roberts   inj   T/o 1612 Doncaster but after climbing to a mere
P/O C J Clayton RCAF   inj   one hundred-and-fifty feet, both engines began
                           inj   to overheat. With the power failing, rapidly,
                           inj   the Wellington was forced-landed, more or less
straight ahead, into a wood near Edlington. Just
three minutes had elapsed since the bomber had commenced its take off roll.

30 OTU   **Wellington III BK139**   **Training**
P/O A D Roscoe   inj   T/o Hixon for a night navigation sortie. While
Sgt T E Smith   inj   over Wales, the port engine began to emit smoke
Sgt C Jackson   inj   and sparks. The screened pilot assumed control
Sgt W A Carr   inj   and headed for the Caernarvonshire airfield of
Sgt E Stabler   inj   Llandwrog, then a satellite station for No. 9
F/S K A Birrell RAAF   inj   (Observers) Flying Unit at Penrhos. On arrival
Sgt A Edgar   +   at 0234, he flew a rather tight circuit and
crashed on, or near the landing ground. Sgt
Edgar is buried in Brookwood Military Cemetery. A technical inspection of the
port engine revealed pieces of broken piston ring and white metal in the sump
filter and it is suspected that a sleeve and piston assembly failed.

30 OTU   **Wellington X HE468**   **Training**
F/O J H G Watson   +   T/o Hixon similarly tasked. Returned to base
Sgt G A Cure   +   only to dive and crash 0357 out of control at
P/O E G Farrow   +   Mountford Farm, Salt Heath. F/O Watson rests
Sgt T J Campbell   +   in Kimblesworth (SS Philip and James) Churchyard,
F/S D P Boyle RAAF   +   Sgt Cure was taken to Birmingham (Hansworth)
Sgt J Hedge   +   Cemetery, P/O George rests at Foulsham (Holy
Lt P A Roberts   +   Innocents) Churchyard, Sgt Campbell is buried
in Kensal Green (St. Mary's) Roman Catholic
Cemetery, Hammersmith, F/S Boyle's funeral was likely arranged by relatives as
his grave is in St. Helens Cemetery, Sgt Hedge lies in Edingthorpe (All Saints)
Churchyard, Bacton, while their army passenger, Lt Roberts of 80 Searchlight
Regiment, Royal Artillery, is interred at Pensax (St. James) Churchyard.

16 May
1943

16 OTU	**Wellington III**	**BK154**	**Training.**

Sgt E Mearis
T/o 1645 Barford St. John for circuits and landings. Touched down normally and the throttles were opened up for another circuit. Seconds later, amidst a cloud of dust, the Wellington lay wrecked just beyond the runway. It is supposed the undercarriage had been retracted prematurely. A month later, Sgt Mearis had another close shave, this time having to take to his parachute.

16–17 May
1943

19 OTU	**Whitley V**	**BD295 UO-N**	**Training**

F/L R W P Macfarland	inj
Sgt K J Sampson	+
F/O A C Barrie	+
Sgt R Hartley	+
F/S A T Hawkins	+
Sgt R A Hartwell	inj
Sgt Padley	inj

T/o 2027 Kinloss for a combined night cross-country and bombing detail over the Clunas ranges, SSW of Nairn. At 0157, while trying to pinpoint their position, the crew flew into high ground that had been shielded from their sight by cloud. Sgt Hartley rests in Kinloss Abbey Burial Ground; the others who died, including Sgt Hartwell, lie in their home towns.

17 May
1943

10 OTU Det	**Whitley V**	**Z9438 –J**	**Op: AS Patrol**

Sgt J H Casstles	+
Sgt R K Tewfik	+
Sgt G D Evans	+
Sgt J L Hamilton	+
Sgt R E L Johnson	+
Sgt D Seigal	+

T/o 1148 St. Eval and headed for the Bay of Biscay. After failing to return by its estimated time of 2200, overdue action was initiated. Sadly, no trace of the Whitley, or its crew, were found and their names are perpetuated on the Runnymede Memorial. Sgt Hamilton was a solicitor from Browns Town, Jamaica.

10 OTU Det	**Whitley V**	**BD260 –P**	**Op: AS Patrol**

Sgt S J Barnett	int
Sgt J H Pike	int
Sgt G O Sharpe	int
Sgt L Whitworth	int
P/O R Price	int
Sgt H A Weber	int

T/o 0935 St. Eval similarly tasked. During the morning, a wireless message was intercepted and its content indicated the Whitley was under attack from a pair of Ju88s (likely from KG/40). Subsequently, it came to light that the crew had ditched at around midday some 130 km NW of Cape Finisterre. Rescued by a fishing boat and landed at Vigo in Spain, all underwent a spell of internment before being deported to Gibraltar and thence to England.

24 OTU	**Whitley V**	**BD204**	**Training**

Sgt J W Clark	inj
Sgt J A Inverarity RCAF	inj

T/o 1555 Honeybourne for a navigation detail. Force -landed 1745, after fluctuating radiator temperatures led to the port engine being shut down, on mudflats near the Flintshire resort of Rhyl, Sgt Clark sustaining a fractured skull. By the summer of 1944, Sgt Inverarity RCAF was flying with 408 Squadron. On 8 June, his Lancaster failed to return from an attack on a rail junction at Acheres (see Bomber Command Losses, Volume 5, page 262).

19 May
1943

14 OTU	**Wellington IC**	**Z8837**	**Training**

F/S F Morris RAAF	inj
Sgt J E Sanderson	+

T/o 2225 Cottesmore for a night detail but as the bomber approached lift off, the starboard engine cut. Out of control, the Wellington careered through a hedge and commenced to burn. Sgt Sanderson of Hampstead is buried in the extension to Cottesmore (St. Nicholas) Churchyard. On 12 July 1942, this aircraft, then on the strength of 25 Operational Training Unit, had been involved in a midair collision with a 14 Operational Training Unit Hampden (see page 135 for details).

20 May
1943

10 OTU	**Whitley V**	**Z9207**	**Training**

F/L E O C Tandy
Sgt C M Hall

T/o 0330 Stanton Harcourt for dual circuits and landings. Twenty minutes later, with Sgt Hall at the controls, the Whitley came into land but F/L Tandy judged his pupil was too high and instructed him to overshoot, which he did. Approaching the threshold for a second time, F/L Tandy checked the controls and (as he stated later) considered them to be particularly sluggish. Assuming command, he completed the landing but touched down rather fast. In order to avoid running off the airfield, he attempted to swing the bomber on to the perimeter track but the strain on the undercarriage proved too much and the unit promptly gave way.

21-22 May 1943	**24 OTU** Sgt S W Rabbitts	**Whitley V** inj	**BD373**	**Training**

T/o 2230 Honeybourne tasked for a Command Bullseye. Became lost and after calling for assistance, the wireless operator began to pick up emissions from balloon squeakers. Abandoned circa 0250 and crashed near Rocester, 16 miles ESE of Stoke-on-Trent, Staffordshire.

	26 OTU Sgt G P Slade Sgt D A Knight RCAF	**Wellington III** inj inj inj inj inj inj	**BJ669**	**Training**

T/o 2135 Wing similarly tasked. Lost power from the starboard engine and Sgt Slade, at 0145, attempted to land at Church Broughton airfield in Derbyshire (then in use as a satellite for 27 OTU), but overshot the runway and crashed, heavily.

22 May 1943	**18 OTU** Sgt J Nenko PAF F/L A Klosinski PAF Sgt F Kunka PAF Sgt J Bielawski PAF Sgt S Borkowski PAF	**Wellington III** + + + + +	**BJ656**	**Training**

T/o 1201 Finningley for a cross-country. Broke up in flight and crashed 1416 at Swanbourne, two miles ESE of Winslow, Buckinghamshire. All were taken for burial in Halton (St. Michael) Churchyard. Of the eighty-nine service plots in this churchyard, twelve belong to Polish Air Force personnel.

	28 OTU Cpl E L Bond	**Wellington IC**	**R1216**	**Ground**

While undergoing engine running at Wymeswold, a technical fault developed and at 1620 the Wellington caught fire and was soon a mass of flames.

23-24 May 1943	**27 OTU** Sgt C W Astle Sgt C F S Wells Sgt C A Warnes Sgt W Antcliffe Sgt A Drury	**Wellington III** + + + + +	**BK489**	**Op: Nickel**

T/o Lichfield and set course for the Paris area. Lost without trace. All are commemorated on the Runnymede Memorial.

25 May 1943	**11 OTU** F/O J V Newton RAAF	**Wellington IC**	**P9280**	**Training**

T/o Oakley to practice circuits and landings. Landed at 1125 but having reached the end of the runway, the crew noticed flames coming from the port engine. F/O Newton ordered an immediate evacuation of the aircraft. Although the fire tender crew quickly reached the scene and quelled the blaze, the Wellington was damaged beyond economical repair. F/O Newton RAAF progressed to Pathfinders and by the early part of 1944, was serving with 7 Squadron. Sadly, his aircraft was one of the forty-one losses incurred during the raid on Braunschweig in the middle of January (see Bomber Command Losses, Volume 5, pages 30 to 35). As remarked in the footnote, his second Christian name was Verdun.

	11 OTU Sgt R D Stirling RAAF	**Wellington IC**	**R1729**	**Training**

T/o 1505 Oakley similarly tasked but swung and crashed, breaking the fuselage at the astro hatch with a further serious fracture ten feet further aft. The port mainplane was badly damaged and both undercarriage units were torn from their mountings.

26 May 1943	**24 OTU** Sgt W A D McConnell	**Whitley V** + inj	**LA845**	**Training**

T/o 1029 Honeybourne but an engine failed and the bomber crashed two minutes later at Great Collin Farm, Willersey, 8 miles NW from Moreton-in-Marsh, Gloucestershire. Sgt McConnell is buried in Ilford (Barkingside) Cemetery. It is believed his entire crew were injured.

27 May 1943	**10 OTU Det** P/O W P Hugh F/O T M Hilton Sgt W R K Boles Sgt D G Rodwell Sgt W G Hutchinson Sgt A C Brizell	**Whitley V**	**BD282**	**-P**	**Op: AS Patrol**

T/o 1146 St. Eval and headed for the Bay of Biscay. At 1433, M of 58 Squadron received and rebroadcast a message that originated from Whitley P, "SOS am down in posn" (not given), the call from P/O Hugh's aircraft having ceased abruptly. Subsequently, they were picked up by a navy destroyer.

27 May	14 OTU	Anson I	N9829		Air Test

27 May
1943

14 OTU   **Anson I**   **N9829**   **Air Test**

F/L A McM Gillies   +   T/o 1920 Cottesmore but ten minutes later, while
Cpl T J Norris   +   attempting a manoeuvre near the airfield, a wing
LAC S Philip   +   detached and the trainer dived into the ground.
F/L Gillies was an experienced pilot with 1,193
flying hours to his credit; of these, 399 had been logged on Ansons. He rests
in New Kilpatrick (or Hillfoot) Cemetery. Cpl Norris, whose service number
suggests he joined the pre-war Volunteer Reserve for pilot training, lies in
Fulham Old Cemetery, while LAC Philip is buried in the extension to Cottesmore
(St. Nicholas) Churchyard. His funeral was the last to be held at this burial
ground for airmen serving at 14 OTU (at least sixty-nine members of the unit
have been identified in the register for St. Nicholas).

29 May
1943

10 OTU Det   **Whitley V**   **BD278**   **-C**   **Op: AS Patrol**

Sgt K G McAlpine   T/o 0925 St. Eval and set course for the Bay of
P/O A W Appelby   Biscay. At 1930, the aircraft failed to respond
Sgt G W Taylor   to wireless messages, requesting an estimated
Sgt A J Meyers   time of arrival at base. Subsequently, it was
Sgt L Chant   discovered that after twelve hours or more in
Sgt D A Baverstock   the air, and now running low on petrol and devoid
of radio aids, the crew ditched alongside a
British coaster, their position now being approximately 5216N 0533W.

23 OTU   **Wellington III**   **X3704**   **Flypast**

F/O G S Hynam DFC RCAF   +   T/o 1825 Stratford-upon-Avon to participate in
Sgt P E Zoeller   +   a "Wings for Victory" flypast over Pershore
Cpl H Allan   +   where Air Chief Marshal Sir Edgar Ludlow-Hewitt
AC2 G R Band   +   (he had been Air Officer Commanding-in-Chief at
AC2 W A Gravell   +   Bomber Command between September 1937 and April
1940) was taking the salute at a march past led
Mrs O M Berry   inj   by bands of the Royal Canadian Air Force and the
Worcestershire Regiment. Lost a wing and crashed
at 1910 behind the Star Hotel in Pershore (a propeller blade from the Wellington
is displayed at the rear of the hotel), killing its crew and injuring Mrs Berry,
who was admitted to Pershore Hospital. F/L Hynam RCAF, an American from Akron,
Ohio, who had gained his DFC while flying with 420 Squadron, and Sgt Zoeller are
buried in Pershore Cemetery, the others were taken to their home towns.

30 May
1943

10 OTU Det   **Whitley V**   **Z9440**   **-N**   **Op: AS Patrol**

Sgt L O Slade   int   T/o 0800 St. Eval armed with 6 x 250lb depth
Sgt W J Wood RCAF   int   charges and equipped with two F24 cameras,
Sgt W F Wicks   int   course being established for their patrol area
Sgt G F Dimmock   int   over the Bay of Biscay. At approximately 1220,
P/O B A Russell RCAF   int   a U-boat was sighted in position 4530N 1030W
Sgt G W Vines   int   and the crew commenced their first attack.
The return fire from the surfaced submarine
was intense and as the Whitley passed over its target, Sgt Vines attempted to
engage the enemy gunners. Unfortunately, after firing two short bursts, his
guns jammed. Furthermore, it was apparent that only two of the depth charges
had released but, undeterred, Sgt Slade made a second low-level run and while
doing so his aircraft was hit a number of times. With one engine out of action,
a ditching became inevitable and after signalling base with an SOS and putting
some distance between themselves and the U-boat, the crew ditched circa 1255 at
4625N 1010W, from where they were rescued by the Evaristo Perez, a Spanish
fishing trawler. Subsequently, having returned to the United Kingdom, Sgt
Wicks became a prisoner of war, while Sgt Slade flew a tour of operations with
76 Squadron, most of his trips being in Halifax III MZ516 Vera the Virgin.

31 May
1943

19 OTU A Flt   **Whitley V**   **Z9216**   **-H**   **Training**

Sgt R A Knight   T/o 0015 Kinloss for a night exercise but when
the starboard engine failed, was obliged to
ditch 0125 in Loch Fyne, N of the Island of Arran. It is much suspected that
the crew alighted towards the W side of the Loch, as all were brought to
Campbeltown on Kintyre, where they were looked after by the navy at HMS Seahawk.
Sgt Knight, who had transferred to the air force from the army, converted to
Lancasters and eventually joined 9 Squadron. On 5-6 September 1943, his aircraft
was lost raiding Mannheim (see Bomber Command Losses, Volume 4, page 311). He was
on his sixth sortie as captain.

31 May
1943

26 OTU   **Wellington III** **BJ977**   **Ground**
P/O J Metgales
Sgt G M Claydon

Caught fire 1400, while starting engines, at
No. 13 dispersal pan, Little Horwood.

28 OTU   **Wellington IC** **R1282**   **Transit**
P/O J W O'Hara RCAF

T/o 1600 Harwell and crashed almost immediately.
The Court of Inquiry uncovered a range of faults
that attributed to the accident, a faulty flap gauge reading being just one. P/O
O'Hara RCAF progressed to Pathfinders and was posted to 7 Squadron. While flying
as second pilot, he failed to return from Milano on 14-15 August 1943 (see Bomber
Command Losses, Volume 4, page 267).

2 Jun
1943

11 OTU   **Wellington IC** **DV732**   **Training**
Sgt R H Trangmar RNZAF

T/o Westcott for a navigation exercise, at night.
Crashed 0230 on a hillside near Eyam (a village
made famous for the actions of its rector, the Revd William Mompesson, his wife,
Catherine and the preacher at the local chapel, William Stanley, when during the
terrible plague years of the mid-1660s, they sealed the village against the outside world and thus prevented the disease from spreading to other parts of rural
Derbyshire), 10 miles WNW of Chesterfield.

20 OTU A Flt   **Wellington IC** **R1701** **—U**   **Training**
F/O A T L Rossignol   +
F/O E E Adlard   +
Sgt E Morgan   +
P/O J Fallon   +
Sgt D E Faulkner   +
Sgt J R J Clarke   +

T/o Lossiemouth for a cross-country. Crashed
at around 1130 at Pigdoni Farm near Morpeth,
Northumberland. Eyewitnesses tell of the bomber
exploding in the air, possibly as a result of
being struck by lightning. All rest in various
cemeteries. F/O Rossignol was an American from
Washington, DC, serving with the Volunteer
Reserve.

24 OTU   **Whitley V** **Z6639**   **Training**
F/S H G Hagen RCAF   +
Sgt R S Phillips   +
F/S D H Kelly RCAF   +
Sgt D A Marriott   +
Sgt G E Ekins   inj

T/o 1115 Honeybourne for a cross-country. While
flying in cloud, flew into the side of a hill,
some 200 yards from Broadway Tower, 6 miles SE
of Evesham, Worcestershire. On impact (at 1415)
the bomber burst into flames. Both RCAF members
of crew rest in Evesham Cemetery, F/S Hagen RCAF
it is noted being a graduate from Arcadia University, Wolfville, Nova Scotia.
The others, including Sgt Ekins who died from his injuries, were claimed by
their next of kin.

Note. At the time of this tragedy, Broadway Tower was being used as a Royal
Observer Corps post and first on the scene were two corps members, Albert Lowe
and Ernest Hollington. Braving the flames, the two men pulled all five airmen
clear and though four were dead, a fifth man was still alive. Taken to the
shelter of the nearby tower, he died soon afterwards. In June 1998, a special
commemorative event, marking the 55th anniversary of the crash, took place at
Broadway Tower, during which a plaque and a specially commissioned painting by
the artist Michael Barnard was unveiled in the tower's restaurant. I am indebted to Zebra Club News, Volume 16, Issue 4, December 1998, for much of the
detail given in this footnote.

3 Jun
1943

10 OTU Det   **Whitley V** **BD414** **—J**   **Op: AS Patrol**
F/S D F Bavin RAAF   +
P/O H D Pepper RCAF   +
F/O D T Dorward RCAF   +
Sgt C A Richardson   +
P/O C A Nicholls   +
F/S E H Neilson RCAF   +

T/o 1045 St. Eval carrying 6 x 250lb depth
charges, course being set for the Bay of Biscay.
Having failed to return by 2045, overdue action
was taken but no trace of the aircraft, or its
crew were found. All are commemorated on the
Runnymede Memorial.

21 OTU   **Wellington IC** **T2569**   **Training**
Sgt S N Heyes   inj
                          inj
                          inj
                          inj

T/o 1215 Moreton-in-Marsh but almost immediately
came to grief. A technical inspection of the
starboard engine revealed that a valve in No. 1
cylinder had jammed, thus causing the unit to
fail. In order to remain within the confines
of the airfield, Sgt Heyes retracted the undercarriage. Subsequently, a salvage
team from Weybridge declared the Wellington as being beyond worthwhile repair.

3 Jun   **26 OTU**   **Wellington III**   **BJ766**   **Training**
1943   P/O H P Vanrenen RAAF   T/o 1857 Wing, possibly for local flying. Came
     Sgt E Crossland   inj   down at 1942, due to engine failure, at College
     Sgt A G Mason   inj   Farm on the S side of the hamlet of Hillesden,
                                        some 3 miles SSW of Buckingham. The Wellington
caught fire, both of the injured being taken to Buckingham Hospital.

3– 4 Jun   **26 OTU**   **Wellington X**   **HE746**   **Training**
1943   Sgt L A Southam   +   T/o 2340 Wing for a night navigation detail.
     Sgt H J Newel RCAF   inj   Burnt out at 0405, after crashing 2 miles N of,
     Sgt H Parker   +   and while approaching, Dumfries airfield. Not
     Sgt G W Mullis   +   long before, the crew had put out a call advising
     Sgt J C Kent RCAF   +   that their starboard engine had failed. Sgt Kent
                                          was buried in Dumfries (St. Andrew's) Roman
Catholic Cemetery, while the others who perished were taken to their home towns.
Sgt Newel RCAF was very seriously injured, being admitted to the local hospital
with a ruptured liver. In recent years, the daughter of Sgt Mullis has presented
a commemorative plaque to the Dumfries and Galloway Aviation Museum where, on
the lower floor of the old watch tower, a propeller blade from the Wellington
is displayed.

3– 4 Jun   **28 OTU**   **Wellington IC**   **DV613**   **Op: Nickel**
1943   Sgt J W Shearek   T/o 2329 Castle Donington. While returning to
     Sgt Broomfield   inj   base an engine failed and at 0304 the bomber
                                          was ditched 35 miles SSE of St. Catherine's
Point on the Isle of Wight. Sgt Broomfield, it is reported, sustained a broken
leg. The survivors were adrift for eight hours before being picked up.

4 Jun   **26 OTU**   **Wellington III**   **BJ647**   **Training**
1943   Sgt L A Butler   inj   T/o 1120 Little Horwood for local flying. At
     Sgt G A Tilley   inj   around 1250, the Wellington was approaching the
     Sgt N E Ellacott   +   runway when another aircraft crossed its flight
                                          path. Sgt Butler increased power in order to go
round again but, inadvertently, raised the flaps instead of the undercarriage.
With very little height in hand he was unable to rectify the situation before
the bomber thudded into the ground, near the airfield. Crash and Rescue:

     Sgt G W L Mathews   accompanied by three colleagues ran to where
                                          the aircraft lay burning and displaying great
courage, pulled the crew clear. Sgt Butler was in considerable distress and
he was rushed to the Princess Mary's Hospital at Halton, where it was found
his spine was fractured. Sgt Tilley, too, was admitted to Halton, though his
injuries proved less severe. Sadly, Sgt Ellacott was beyond all medical aid
and he now lies in Camberwell New Cemetery.

6 Jun   **30 OTU**   **Wellington III**   **BJ801**   **Training**
1943   F/S E R Swindells RCAF   +   T/o 1100 Hixon on a navigation exercise, the
     F/S E S Smith   +   course of which took the crew over the North
     Sgt R E Gill   +   Sea where gunnery was to be practised. Lost
     Sgt J E Plummer   +   without trace, having failed to return at its
     Sgt R E P West   +   due time of 1800. All are perpetuated on the
     Sgt L B Hewer RCAF   +   panels of the Runnymede Memorial.

8 Jun   **16 OTU**   **Wellington III**   **BJ981**   **Training**
1943   F/O F A Barber   +   T/o 1359 Upper Heyford for a cross-country.
     F/O S T Daniels   +   Suffered catastrophic structural failure and
     Sgt F J M Tremble   +   spiralled 1700 into the ground some 3 miles
     Sgt L H Lyle   +   north of Towcester, Northamptonshire. All
     Sgt G A Robbins   +   are buried in various cemeteries, F/O Barber
                                          being described as a flying instructor, while
F/O Daniels was known to his family and friends as Peter.

          26 OTU   **Wellington III**   **BJ833**   **Training**
     F/S J F Calvesbert RAAF   +   T/o 1653 Little Horwood for local flying.
     Sgt G Fall   +   Dived and crashed 1758 at Sionhill Farm on
     Sgt E H Palava RCAF   +   the eastern side of East Claydon, 6 miles
                                          south-south-east of Buckingham. The two
Commonwealth airmen were taken to Brookwood Military Cemetery, while Sgt
Fall is buried in Harrogate (Stonefall) Cemetery.

9 Jun	18 OTU	Wellington III	BK331	Training

1943   Sgt I G Gulden   T/o 1335 Finningley for a cross-country, during which the port engine gave trouble. Attempted to land at Cranage airfield in Cheshire, but overshot the runway and crashed circa 1520 at Yatehouse Farm, just over a mile SW of Byley and twixt 1 and 2 miles NNW from the centre of Middlewich.

	29 OTU	Lysander TT	V9901	Training

F/L A R Dunn   T/o 0945 Bruntingthorpe for drogue towing.
P/O C G Key   inj   At 1030, overshot the landing ground at Holbeach and struck a bank. Although he was a very experienced pilot with 1,022 flying hours to his credit (though only two of these had been logged on Lysanders), faced with an unfamiliar airfield, F/L Dunn is judged to have come in too fast, touching down on the narrowest part of the landing area. Just over a year later, and now promoted to S/L, he was killed over Germany while flying with 83 Squadron (see Bomber Command Losses, Volume 5, page 293). P/O Kay was taken to SSQ Holbeach, but was not detained.

10 Jun	16 OTU	Wellington III	BJ985	Training

1943   Sgt J O Bonnett   T/o Upper Heyford for a night cross-country.
Sgt Bartlett   Returned to base at around 0540, low on fuel and faced with rather inclement weather. As he prepared to land, Sgt Bonnett ordered his air bomber to open balance cock B and standby to operate the nacelle tank toggles. Unfortunately, the main cocks were turned off and with both engines misfiring, an unscheduled arrival was made at Park Farm, Fritwell, 6 miles NW of Bicester, Oxfordshire.

10–11 Jun	24 OTU	Whitley V	BD442	Op: Nickel

1943   Sgt L F Cook   +   T/o Honeybourne and set course for Nantes. At
Sgt D L Williams   +   2246 a position signal was transmitted to the
Sgt J Montieth   +   crew, but this was not acknowledged. Presumed
Sgt J Dawson   pow   crashed in the target area. Those who died lie
Sgt W H Cox   +   in the town's Pont-du-Cens Communal Cemetery.
Sgt W T Seaman RCAF   +   Sgt Williams was a Member of the Pharmaceutical Society.

11 Jun	14 OTU	Wellington IC	DV678	Training

1943   F/O L B Patkin RAAF   T/o 0920 Cottesmore briefed for training raid No. 3. While operating at 6,700 feet, both engines commenced misfiring, the port engine being most troublesome. Coming down through a break in the clouds, the Wellington was crash-landed 1050 at Chatsworth Park, the ancestral home of the Duke and Duchess of Devonshire, in Derbyshire. Proceeding, eventually, to 467 Squadron, F/L Patkin RAAF was shot down during operations to Berlin on 1-2 January 1944 (see Bomber Command Losses, Volume 5, page 21). He is buried in Hannover War Cemetery.

	22 OTU	Wellington III	HF813	Training

F/O E J K Le Claire RCAF   +   T/o Wellesbourne to practice circuits and
Sgt J T Anderton   +   landings, at night. Crashed 0415, as a result of an engine cutting, at Staple Hill Farm, W of the village of Moreton Paddox and some 2 miles E of the town of Wellesbourne Mountford. F/O Le Claire RCAF is buried in Stratford-upon-Avon Cemetery, Sgt Anderton was taken to Prestwich (St. Mary) Churchyard.

11–12 Jun	30 OTU	Wellington III	BK559	Op: Nickel

1943   F/S T G Dellar RAAF   +   T/o 2300 Hixon and set course for Nantes.
F/S D M Davis RCAF   +   Became hopelessly lost and, very uncertain of
F/S J G Perfect   pow   their position, the Nickels were deposited at
Sgt B C Reeves   evd   around 0330. The crew then attempted to set a
F/S H J D G Adams   pow   course for home, though the Wellington was by this time very low on petrol. Eventually, the order to bale out was given, three complying at 5,000 feet. However, the pilot did not have his parachute and Sgt Davis RCAF decided to remain with the aircraft which, it is believed, crash-landed at Guyancourt (Seine-et-Oise), 7 km SW of Versailles. F/S Dellar RAAF rests in the local communal cemetery, but Sgt Davis RCAF is buried in the South of France in the extension to Mazargues Cemetery, Marseilles. Although their dates of death match, I believe it is likely Sgt Davis RCAF survived the crash and, subsequently, died while making an attempt to evade capture.

12 Jun	28 OTU	Wellington IC	R1324		Op: A-S Rescue
1943	F/O D E Paul		+	T/o Wymeswold and headed for the North Sea and
	P/O J E Norris		+	the briefed search area. Presumed lost in the
	F/S D G Bird RCAF		+	area of operations. On 17 July, the body of
	Sgt W A Drew		+	Sgt Drew was discovered on Vlieland and he was
	Sgt G Swan		+	buried in the island's general cemetery. The
	Sgt J D Halvorsen RCAF		+	others are commemorated on the panels of the

Runnymede Memorial. Sgt Halvorsen RCAF was an American from Chicago, Illinois.

12-13 Jun	26 OTU	Wellington X	HE240		Training
1943	Sgt E A Askew		inj	T/o 2300 Wing for night flying. At around 0125,
			inj	a sleeve bearing failed in one of the engines

and within a few seconds the unit had seized. Unable to maintain altitude, Sgt Askew forced-landed near Stewkley Road in Wing village. For his handling of a very difficult situation, his flying log was annotated with a "green" endorsement.

14 Jun	10 OTU Det	Whitley V	BD220	—G	Op: AS Patrol
1943	W/O A J Benson DFM RAAF		pow	T/o 0949 St. Eval armed with 6 x 250lb depth
	W/O R L Rennick RAAF		pow	charges, course being set for a patrol area over
	F/L T J J Lee		pow	the Bay of Biscay. Seriously damaged while
	F/S G T Graves		pow	attacking U-564 (Oblt Fiedler) and later put
	F/L A Kingsley RCAF		pow	down in the sea approximately 80 miles SW of

the Scillies. Three days later, their dinghy was sighted by the crew of a French fishing boat, reportedly the Jazz Band, skippered by a Capitaine Francois, and landed in France. W/O Benson's DFM was published in the London Gazette on 24 August 1943. For a fuller account of the action, briefly summarised here, readers should consult 'Conflict Over The Bay' by Norman Franks and published by William Kimber, 1986.

	27 OTU	Wellington III	BJ672		Training
	F/S W D Weir RAAF		+	T/o Lichfield for a navigation exercise. Lost
	F/S V C McQuade RAAF		+	without trace. All are commemorated on the
	F/S G H Gray RAAFAAF		+	Runnymede Memorial.
	F/S R McL Grieve RAAF		+	
	Sgt J S Lee RAAF		+	

	27 OTU	Wellington III	BJ843		Training
	F/S E G Holden RAAF		+	T/o Lichfield similarly tasked. Lost without
	F/S R A Hatfield RAAF		+	trace. All are commemorated on the Runnymede
	F/S T A Belot RAAF		+	Memorial.
	F/S L H Macdonald RAAF		+	
	Sgt P L Cashion RAAF		+	

Note. Apart from the names of the two pilots, unit records are totally devoid of any information pertaining to the crews. However, in respect of F/S Weir's crew, I have been able to verify their names and crew order, and by consulting the excellent Australian War Museum's Roll of Honour database, those listed as F/S Holden's crew are confirmed as belonging to 27 Operational Training Unit.

16 Jun	11 OTU	Wellington IC	DV443		Training
1943	F/L J A Hegman DFC RNZAF		inj	T/o 1046 Oakley to demonstrate single-engined
	P/O C R Bennett RAAF		inj	landings but lost power on climb out. While
			inj	trying to regain the airfield, the Wellington
			inj	crash-landed 1050, a fire breaking out almost
			inj	immediately. A veteran of fifty-three sorties

flown with 162 Squadron in the Middle East, F/L Hegman RNZAF went on to become a Pathfinder captain with 7 Squadron. On 15-16 February 1944 (flying his 73rd sortie, in total), he failed to return from Berlin (see Bomber Command Losses, Volume 5, page 74).

	12 OTU	Wellington III	Z1721	—W	Training
	F/S H P Griffith RAAF		+	T/o 0323 Chipping Warden only to explode 15
	P/O T W Adam RCAF		+	minutes later at Broomhill Farm, near Edgehill
	F/O G B Booth RCAF		+	airfield. Four lie in Banbury Cemetery, while
	Sgt F J Welsby		+	Sgt Welsby rests in Marton (St. Paul) Church
	Sgt K E Troake		+	Burial Ground, Blackpool. F/O Booth RCAF was

an American from Van Buren, Ohio.

16 Jun　**16 OTU**　　**Wellington III**　**BK244**　　　　　　　**Training**
1943　Sgt E Mearis　　　　　　　T/o Barford St. John for a night exercise.
　　　　　　　　　　　　　　　　　Lost power from the starboard engine and at
around 0050 the crew took to their parachutes, roughly a mile NW of Wyton
airfield in Huntingdonshire. A month earlier, to the day, Sgt Mearis had
crash-landed at base (see the first entry on page 221).

17 Jun　**27 OTU**　　**Wellington III**　**BJ845**　　　　　　　**Training**
1943　F/S M B Fettell RAAF　　　　+　T/o Lichfield for a night cross-country. While
　　　　Sgt R W E Bennett RAAF　　　　over Gloucestershire, was involved in a midair
　　　　Sgt R M Hilliard RAAF　　　　collision with a Lancaster. Partially abandoned
　　　　Sgt R Morrison　　　　　　　before crashing 0150 near Bibury, 7 miles NE of
　　　　Sgt Watt　　　　　　　　　　Cirencester, where F/S Fettell RAAF is buried.
　　　　Sgt N Shapley　　　　　　　The survivors, including Sgt Shapley who had
　　　　　　　　　　　　　　　　　joined the crew in order to gain air experience
flying, were taken to South Cerney airfield from where they were driven back to
Lichfield. Sgt Hilliard RAAF, to whom I am indebted for much of the information
given in this summary, went on to gain a commission and the Distinguished Flying
Cross during service with 466 Squadron and 35 Squadron.

19 Jun　**11 OTU E Flt**　　**Martinet I**　**HP464**　　　　　　**Training**
1943　P/O N G Cromie RNZAF　　　　+　T/o Oakley for an air firing detail off the
　　　　W/O F W Reed　　　　　　　+　Norfolk coast, involving Wellingtons from the
　　　　　　　　　　　　　　　　　same unit. At around 1640, and approaching
the completion of the exercise, the Martinet lost height and ditched off Burnham.
Eyewitnesses say that both crew members managed to get clear of the fast sinking
aircraft but, tragically, before help reached them, they had drowned. Later, the
body of the pilot was recovered and he lies in Cranworth (St. Mary) Churchyard,
an unconfirmed report suggesting this was the village of his fiancée. Prior to
joining 11 OTU, P/O Cromie RNZAF had flown Stirlings with 218 Squadron. His
drogue operator is buried in Kent at Tunbridge Wells Cemetery.

　　　　16 OTU　　**Wellington III**　**X3884**　　　　　　　**Training**
　　　　F/S W L Hill　　　　　　　　T/o 1735 Upper Heyford for an evening exercise.
　　　　　　　　　　　　　　　　　Crash-landed 1840, wheels up, in a field near
Beckley, an Oxfordshire village on the south side of Ot Moor. Almost a year
later, on 14 June 1944, F/S Hill was presumed to have lost his life; his name
is now commemorated on panel 218 of the Runnymede Memorial.

　　　　30 OTU　　**Wellington III**　**BK142**　　　　　　　**Training**
　　　　Sgt F T Powell　　　　　　　T/o 1215 Seighford for local flying. Twenty-five
　　　　　　　　　　　　　　　　　minutes later, a piston failed and the Wellington
crashed 2 miles W of the airfield and caught fire. Subsequently, the Court of
Inquiry commended the crew for their actions in ensuring everyone got clear of
the blazing bomber, two of their number having been hurt in the crash-landing.

20 Jun　**10 OTU Det**　　**Whitley V**　**LA814**　**-L**　　　　**Op: AS Patrol**
1943　F/S H Martin　　　　　　　+　T/o 1145 St. Eval and set a course that would
　　　　F/O C M Bingham RCAF　　　　+　take them to the Bay of Biscay. Here they came
　　　　Sgt W I Ettle　　　　　　　+　upon a U-boat and in the engagement that ensued
　　　　Sgt R W Warhurst　　　　　+　the Whitley was shot down, in flames. All are
　　　　F/O A B C Durnell RCAF　　　+　commemorated on the Runnymede Memorial. It is
　　　　P/O F W E Tomlins　　　　　+　indicated that they were able to send a brief
　　　　　　　　　　　　　　　　　wireless transmission, at 1640, 'GXBF 2829'.

　　　　24 OTU　　**Whitley V**　**EB349**　　　　　　　**Training**
　　　　Sgt A J Loman　　　　　　inj　T/o Long Marston, Crashed 1630 at the rear
　　　　　　　　　　　　　　　　inj　of the local police station and caught fire.
　　　　P/O J M Brown RCAF　　　　+　P/O Brown RCAF rests in Stratford-upon-Avon
　　　　　　　　　　　　　　　　　Cemetery. It is thought a jammed elevator
trim tab was the primary cause of this accident.

　　　　26 OTU　　**Wellington X**　**HE753**　　　　　　　**Training**
　　　　W/O R F D Huband　　　　　　T/o 2315 Wing to practice feathering, at night.
　　　　P/O C D Woodley RCAF　　　　At 2350 an engine cut and the bomber was written
　　　　　　　　　　　　　　　　　off in the forced-landing that followed. Just
under a year later, P/O Woodley was killed over France while flying Lancasters
with 15 Squadron (see Bomber Command Losses, Volume 5, page 265). The next day
(9 June), W/O Huband, still serving as an instructor, died in a crash at Wing.

21 Jun   **81 OTU**   **Whitley V**   **EB402**   **Training**
1943   Sgt E T Jones RCAF   T/o 1430 Tilstock for a cross-country flight.
     Sgt Smith   At around 1900, the supercharger on the port
     P/O E N Hooke RCAF   inj   engine broke up, causing a drastic reduction
     Sgt Lofts   in power. The order to abandon was given and
     Sgt Johnson   most complied, though Sgt Hanson had the awful
     Sgt R H Hanson   +   misfortune to fall into the River Dee and drown.

He rests in Mytholmroyd (Scout Road) Methodist Chapelyard, Hebdon Road, his grave being the sole service burial from either of the two World wars. Meanwhile, Sgt Jones RCAF headed for Hawarden airfield, Cheshire, where he landed, way down the runway, at 1910. Realising he would not be able to stop within the airfield perimeter, he raised the undercarriage, thereby wrecking the Whitley.

22 Jun   **10 OTU Det**   **Whitley V**   **EB334**   **-F**   **Op: AS Patrol**
1943   F/O P A Shelton RCAF   T/o St. Eval to patrol an area of the Bay of
     Sgt F Healey   Biscay. On return to base, the weather over
     Sgt M D Tymchuk RCAF   most of Cornwall was awful and this led to the
     Sgt J McG Hughes   aircraft being crash-landed 2322, wheels up, at
     Sgt J Sneddon   Chapman's Well, near Launceston. Apart from
     Sgt E C Eccleston RCAF   Sgt Healey, all were posted to 77 Squadron, only

to disappear without trace while raiding Hannover on 27-28 September 1943 (see Bomber Command Losses, Volume 4, page 335).

     16 OTU   **Wellington III**   **BK262**   **Training**
     Sgt H Wallis   T/o 0243 Upper Heyford with the intention of

carrying out a night exercise. However, the port engine caught fire and the airscrew came off. As the crew tackled this problem, so the starboard motor began to overheat. With little option but to land as quickly as possible, they headed for Warboys in Huntingdonshire. Although this airfield was reached, the landing was, to say the least, heavy and the Wellington was later declared beyond economical repair.

22-23 Jun   **30 OTU**   **Wellington X**   **HE527**   **Op: Nickel**
1943   F/S J Hennessy RAAF   +   T/o Hixon and set course for Paris. Hit by
     F/O G T Freemante   pow   flak over Cherbourg (Manche), where those who
     Sgt J Anderson   +   died now rest in the Old Communal Cemetery.
     F/S R J Franklin   pow   F/S Hennessy's parents, Patrick and Mary
     Sgt R J P Chandler   +   Hennessy, lived in the Irish Republic at Dun
     F/S W Gilroy   pow   Laoghaire, Co. Dublin.

24 Jun   **10 OTU**   **Whitley V**   **BD281**   **Ex: Tucker**
1943   F/S P L Denman   +   T/o Abingdon to participate in Exercise Tucker,
     F/S B P Horrobin RNZAF   +   an army cooperation exercise involving No. 685
     P/O H D Belsher   +   Amphibious Warfare Company, Royal Engineers.
     Sgt B T Scammell   +   Dived to near ground level in a mock attack on
     Sgt D Lingard   +   a bridge, but while climbing away the port wing
     W/O W J Stevens   +   struck a tall tree. Out of control, the bomber
     Sgt E H Elgar   inj   crashed 1110 at Tythrop House on the NW side of

Kingsey and a little over 6 miles SW from Aylesbury, Buckinghamshire. Of those who died, three were taken to North Hinksey for burial in Oxford (Botley) Cemetery. F/S Denman, who had joined the air force on a direct transfer from the army, was cremated at Nottingham Crematorium West Bridgford. The others, too, were claimed by their next of kin. Sgt Scammell, a schoolmaster in civilian life, had joined the Volunteer Reserve at Gander Bay in Newfoundland.

25 Jun   **12 OTU**   **Wellington III**   **X3658**   **-F**   **Training**
1943   F/S T H German   T/o 1755 Chipping Warden and crashed a couple

of minutes later in a field at Lower Boddington on the north Oxfordshire border with Northamptonshire and 8 miles NNE of Banbury. Dirty breaker points were discovered in the engine that had failed. Initially assessed as repairable, the bomber was written off charge five days later.

26 Jun   **29 OTU**   **Wellington X**   **HE372**   **-X**   **Training**
1943   Sgt C G Piper   inj   T/o Bruntingthorpe for a night detail but one

of the propellers jammed in fine pitch. Unable to maintain altitude, Sgt Piper forced-landed 0145, in a field, a mile to the north-west of Gilmorton, 11 miles WNW from Market Harborough, Leicestershire.

26–27 Jun **12 OTU**   **Wellington III** **BJ965** **─J**   **Training**
1943   F/O F S Taylor RCAF   +   T/o 2325 Chipping Warden for a night cross-
            P/O G M Roberts   inj   country. Crashed 0115, after the port engine
                                             failed, at Deer Gallow Rocks, 2 miles N of
            Embsay, a village 2 miles NE of Skipton, Yorkshire. F/O Taylor RCAF rests
            in Harrogate (Stonefall) Cemetery.

27 Jun   **27 OTU**   **Wellington III** **BK453**   **Training**
1943   P/O D W Laufer RAAF   T/o Church Broughton for a night exercise.
                                             Approaching the airfield, the starboard engine
            cut and the bomber lost height, quite rapidly, and clipped a line of high-
            tension cables. Soon after the impact, at 0439, the Wellington caught fire.
            The Court of Inquiry remarked favourably on P/O Laufer's handling of the
            situation that he was faced with.

28 Jun   **15 OTU**   **Wellington IC** **DV879**   **Training**
1943   Sgt G M Burcher RAAF   T/o 1015 Hampstead Norris but an engine cut,
                                             sending the aircraft crashing out of control.
            Subsequently, the airframe became a training aid with the serial 3948M applied.

            18 OTU   **Wellington III** **DF671**   **Training**
            Sgt H W Heron   T/o 1435 Finningley for a navigation detail.
                                             On return to base at 1715, the flaps partially
            failed, causing the starboard wing to drop and the nose of the bomber to yaw
            away from the centre line. Sgt Heron promptly raised the undercarriage and
            forced-landed. Posted to 166 Squadron, he failed to return from operations
            at the end of August 1943 (see Bomber Command Losses, Volume 4, page 297).

            22 OTU   **Wellington III** **HF643** **DD–L**   **Training**
            F/S F E Gladwin RCAF   +   T/o Gaydon for a navigation exercise. Lost
            F/O P D Lidster RCAF   +   power and in the emergency landing that ensued,
            F/S W G Mitchell RCAF   +   downwind, at Long Marston airfield the bomber
            Sgt L Hirst   inj   went out of control and smashed into two
            Sgt W R Barclay RCAF   +   Whitleys belonging to the resident 24 OTU. Those
                                               who died rest in Oxford (Botley) Cemetery.

            24 OTU   **Whitley V** **EB350**   **Ground**
                                             Wrecked in the manner described above.

            24 OTU   **Whitley V** **EB352**   **Ground**
                                             Wrecked in the manner described above.

28–29 Jun **23 OTU**   **Wellington III** **BK408**   **Training**
1943   Sgt W P Loring RCAF   T/o 2300 Pershore for a Bullseye exercise.
            Sgt D H D Grover RCAF   Abandoned 0220 after the port engine failed,
            Sgt G Svearson RCAF   crashing at Llanwerne Court, Hereford. From
            Sgt R A Harris   information reported in'They Shall Grow Not
            Sgt J E J Page RCAF   Old', Sgt Grover RCAF was killed when his 425
            Lt D G Scoular   Squadron Halifax crashed near Bradford on Avon
                                            on 26 March 1944 (see Bomber Command Losses,
            Volume 5, page 141; the summary, their reported, indicates Bidford-on-Avon and
            omits the name of Sgt Grover RCAF).

29 Jun   **11 OTU**   **Wellington IC** **R1780**   **Ground**
1943   At 1330, the Wellington was undergoing engine
            running at Westcott when, without warning, the trailing edge of the wing began
            to burn. The flames spread quickly and the bomber was destroyed. The Court of
            Inquiry concluded that petrol had leaked from a joint on a test rig, mounted
            near the motor being run, and on coming into contact with the exhaust promptly
            ignited. Thus, as fuel continued to spill, so it was blown by the slipstream
            onto the surfaces of the mainplanes.

            22 OTU   **Wellington III** **X3888**   **Training**
            Sgt J H Cartlidge   inj   T/o Wellesbourne Mountford for an air to sea
                                        inj   firing exercise. While banking low over the
            F/O R F Ready RCAF   +   Bristol Channel, a wing dug into the water.
                                        inj   Ditched 1142 a mile to the W of Flat Holm.
                                        inj   F/O Ready RCAF is buried in Weston-super-Mare
                                               Cemetery.

29 Jun   **29 OTU**   **Wellington III** **Z1668**   **Training**
1943   Sgt A G G Johnson   T/o 0319 Bitteswell for night circuits and
                                       landings. While these were in progress, the
        starboard engine failed and a forced-landing followed at 0349 near Glebe Farm,
        Lutterworth, close to the airfield.

1 Jul   **81 OTU**   **Whitley V** **BD411**   **Training**
1943   Sgt L W Bugg   T/o 2335 Tilstock but the port engine shed its
        F/S Homer   propeller and the Whitley crashed out of control.
                                       Sadly, having survived this quite nasty incident,
        Sgt Bugg died, along with his crew, in mid-July in a crash near Whitchurch.

1- 2 Jul   **30 OTU**   **Wellington III** **BK255** **-C**   **Op: Nickel**
1943   Sgt L W Fisher   + T/o Seighford in the company of seven other
        Sgt M Bloomfield   + aircraft. Crashed, while returning to base,
        Sgt K R Burrows   + in Deep Meadow, Spain Farm, S of Exeter air-
        Sgt S E Pegg   + field. Sgt Fisher rests in Hendon Cemetery,
        Sgt B S Sheldon   inj Sgt Bloomfield lies at Leeds (Geldard Road)
                                       English Hebrew Cemetery, Sgt Pegg is interred
        in St. Marylebone Cemetery, while Sgt Burrows was cremated at Stockport.

2 Jul   **18 OTU**   **Wellington III** **BK505**   **Training**
1943   Sgt J Cegta PAF   inj T/o 1710 Finningley for local circuit training.
                                       Wrecked at 1725 when, following a very heavy
        landing, a tyre burst followed by total collapse of the main undercarriage.

        23 OTU   **Wellington III** **X3366**   **Training**
        F/O J H Emmerson   T/o 2315 Stratford-upon-Avon for a night dual
        P/O J G White RCAF   check, but a tyre burst and the bomber crashed
                                       out of control. Subsequently, P/O White RCAF
                                       became a prisoner of war.

        29 OTU   **Wellington III** **X3801**   **Training**
        Sgt W R Willard RCAF   + T/o Bruntingthorpe for a night cross-country
        F/S J H G Kirby   + during which the crew were instructed to divert
        F/O D Lister   + to Wellesbourne Mountford airfield, as weather
        Sgt C F A Rivers   + conditions were deteriorating. Unfortunately,
                                 inj visibility around the diversion airfield was
                                       poor and the aircraft crashed circa 0245 into
        high ground some 3 miles SSW of Mountford Farm, Warwickshire and caught fire.
        Sgt Willard RCAF lies in Stratford-upon-Avon Cemetery, F/S Kirby is buried in
        Watford North Cemetery, F/O Lister (described as an air bomber/pupil pilot) was
        cremated at Hull Crematorium, while Sgt Rivers was taken to Crookham (Christ
        Church) Churchyard, Fleet.

        29 OTU   **Wellington III** **BK437**   **Training**
        P/O N Harland   inj T/o Bruntingthorpe similarly tasked and lost in
        Sgt A C Croft   inj the circumstances described above, except for
        Sgt J H Elliott RCAF   inj the distance which is reported as 2 miles S of
        Sgt E P Shorten RAAF   inj Mountford Farm. The entire crew were taken to
        Sgt F C Butler   inj the EMS Hospital at Stratford-upon-Avon. P/O
                                       Harland recovered from his injuries, though he
        was destined to finish the war as a prisoner. Sgt Croft and Sgt Butler went on
        to serve with Lancaster squadrons, the former with 106 Squadron and the latter
        with 57 Squadron. Both were killed over France, the circumstances being given
        in Bomber Command Losses, Volume 5, pages 305 and 97 respectively. It is also
        observed that S/L Cope DFC DFM and F/L Bolton were appointed to head the Court
        of Inquiry (the former is thought to be ex-Sgt John Cope who gained a DFM with
        104 Squadron, Gazetted 23 September 1941).

3 Jul   **19 OTU D Flt**   **Whitley V** **LA877** **-W**   **Training**
1943   Sgt D C Hunt   + T/o Kinloss for bombing practice. As reported
        Sgt E A Deacon   + from the Royal Observer Corps, the Whitley came
        F/S D J Gillies RCAF   + down at 0005 on Meallan Odhar, 7 miles SW from
        Sgt R N Cowie   + Dalwhinnie, Inverness. Sgt Deacon and the two
        Sgt K P Gemmel RCAF   + RCAF members of crew were brought back to rest
                                       in Kinloss Abbey Burial Ground (Sgt Gemmel's
        father was S/L Kenneth Shaw Gemmel), while their companions were interred in
        their home towns.

| 3- 4 Jul 1943 | 29 OTU | Wellington III | X3871 | | Training |

Sgt B C Smith — T/o 2320 Bruntingthorpe for local night flying practice. At 0135 a heavy arrival on the runway terminated the detail and, later, the bomber was declared beyond economical repair. Sgt Smith, meanwhile, converted to Lancasters and was killed during the München raid on 2-3 October 1943 (see Bomber Command Losses, Volume 4, page 343). At the time, he was serving with 44 Squadron.

| 4 Jul 1943 | 26 OTU | Wellington X | HE337 | | Training |

Sgt R J Donald — inj — T/o 0010 Wing for a night flying exercise.
Sgt J Gibson RCAF — inj — Overshot the base runway at 0135 and having
Sgt J E Maddox — inj — come to a halt, caught fire.
Sgt H Bennis RCAF — inj

| 5 Jul 1943 | 10 OTU Det | Whitley V | —X | | Op: AS Patrol |

F/S K R Clarke RAAF — + — T/o 0856 St. Eval for operations over the Bay
F/O J F Newman — + — of Biscay. Scheduled to return to base at 1740,
Sgt N Allen — + — nothing further was heard, though it is now known
Sgt H J J Neve — + — that five rest in the Department of Finistere at
Sgt E W White — + — Plouguerneau Communal Cemetery, while panel 169
Sgt L G Stewart RCAF — + — of the Runnymede Memorial perpetuates the memory of Sgt White. Situated 24 km north of Brest, Plouguerneau Communal Cemetery contains fifteen service graves from both World wars. The aircraft's serial remains a mystery; BD359 is often quoted but this Whitley survived until 19 July 1943.

| | 16 OTU | Wellington III | BK249 | | Training |

W/O McGuilay — inj — T/o 1530 Upper Heyford for a cross-country. After a mere thirty minutes of flying, the engines failed through lack of petrol and a forced-landing ensued at Kempsford, three miles WSW of Lechlade, Gloucestershire and practically on the border with Wiltshire. It is believed that errors occurred in the checking of fuel tanks.

| 6 Jul 1943 | 16 OTU | Wellington III | BJ984 | | Air Test |

W/O H E Fryer — T/o 1650 Upper Heyford but fifteen minutes later
Cpl C F Hand — + — the outer section of the port wing came off. Out of control, the bomber crashed near the airfield. As it plunged earthwards, W/O Fryer managed to bale out but forty-two year old Cpl Hand, a married man, was not so fortunate. He now rests in Stone Cemetery, his service number indicating that he joined the Volunteer Reserve (probably at Padgate, but possibly via Cardington) soon after the outbreak of war.

| | 22 OTU | Wellington III | HF629 | | Training |

Sgt J L Sills RCAF — T/o 2310 Gaydon but due to failure of the automatic mixture controls, an engine cut. In order to avoid running off the airfield, Sgt Sills RCAF raised the undercarriage. Not long after this incident, he was posted to the Middle East where, at Kairouan, he joined 424 Squadron. On 6-7 September 1943, as captain of Wellington X HE492, he failed to return from Battipaglia. He is buried in Italy at Salerno War Cemetery.

| | 26 OTU | Wellington III | Z1684 | | Training |

Sgt E M Clark — inj — T/o 0928 Little Horwood for local flying. Some
Sgt R C Cheeseman — inj — thirty minutes later, the Wellington landed but
Sgt B J Peters — inj — due to its very heavy arrival the undercarriage
Sgt R Mitchell — inj — collapsed, severely injuring all on board. Sgt Mitchell was taken to Halton where he died in the Princess Mary's Hospital; he is buried in Glasgow (Eastwood) Cemetery. Sgt Clark resumed his training and by the latter stages of the war he was in Burma with 357 Squadron, a Special Duties unit equipped principally with Dakotas and Liberators. On 30 July 1945, he was posted missing and his name is commemorated on column 449 of the Singapore Memorial.

| | 27 OTU | Wellington III | BJ713 | | Training |

F/L L J Simpson RAAF — inj — T/o 2246 Church Brought for a night dual cross-
P/O W N T Russell RAAF — inj — country but as the bomber lifted from the runway
P/O C E Heath — inj — the starboard engine cut and the aircraft came down just beyond the airfield. F/L Simpson RAAF went to 460 Squadron and was made a prisoner of war during 1944.

6 Jul 1943	27 OTU	Wellington X	HE698	Training
	F/S J Leary RAAF			

T/o Lichfield for a cross-country but when No. 6 cylinder failed on one of the engines, the crew were obliged to force -land, 1640, on Cannock Chase in Staffordshire.

6- 7 Jul 1943	29 OTU	Wellington III	BK197	Training
	Sgt F J Austen			

T/o 2238 Bruntingthorpe for a night navigation exercise. While descending from 2,900 feet, both engines lost power and the bomber was crash-landed at 0405 near Dunchurch, some 3 miles SSW of Rugby, Warwickshire. After converting to Lancasters, Sgt Austen joined 57 Squadron at East Kirkby from whence he failed to return from Mannheim in late September 1943 (see Bomber Command Losses, Volume 4, page 329).

	30 OTU	Wellington X	HE238 -U	Training
F/O A Beare	+			
Sgt G D Barker	+			
Sgt J I Middleton	+			
Sgt J E Ratcliffe	+			
Sgt V C Cummins RCAF	+			
2Lt T E Fenwick RA	+			

T/o 2340 Hixon tasked for a Bullseye. Emerged from cloud, in a steep dive, and failed to pull out before hitting the ground, 0344, at Hanging Wicket, some 1 to 2 miles E of the airfield and in the area of Abbots Bromley, Staffordshire. Three, the pilot, Sgt Middleton (whose parents address is given as Calcutta, Bengal) and 2Lt Fenwick of 154 Heavy Anti-Aircraft Regiment, Royal Artillery, attached, were buried in Stafford Cemetery, while Sgt Cummins RCAF rests in Chester (Blacon) Cemetery. The others were claimed by their next of kin.

7 Jul 1943	15 OTU	Wellington IC	X3160	Training
W/O C W Brooks RAAF	+			
F/L R K Kitney DFM	+			
F/O R V Paul	+			
Sgt R G Bates	+			
Sgt R A J Farahar	+			
F/S J R Tonkin RAAF	+			
F/S J F Hansen RAAF	+			
Sgt L H H Dearing RAAF	+			

T/o 1105 Harwell for a cross-country. Caught fire following the failure of the holding down studs to No. 6 cylinder in the port engine and at 1310 the bomber broke up in the air, the main debris falling over White Horse Hill, some two miles N of Odstone, a hamlet 1 mile NE from Ashbury, 5 miles NW of Lambourn, Berkshire. The four Australians lie in Oxford (Botley) Cemetery, while the others were taken to their home towns. F/L Kitney had flown Wellingtons with 103 Squadron, his DFM having been published in the London Gazette on 14 April 1942.

	21 OTU	Wellington IC	DV698	Training
F/S R H Collis RAAF	+			
Sgt L W Bacon	+			
Sgt F C Grievson	+			
Sgt A E D Ross	+			
Sgt F G Howard	+			

T/o 0940 Moreton-in-Marsh for a cross-country. At approximately 1030, the Wellington broke out of cloud over Oxfordshire, near Chipping Norton airfield, and collided with Oxford I LW783 from the locally based No. 6 (Pilots) Advanced Flying Unit. Both machines fell close to each other and burst into flames. F/S Collis RAAF was taken to Oxford (Botley) Cemetery, while Sgt Ross was laid to rest in Moreton-in-Marsh New Cemetery. The others were claimed by their next of kin. It is believed F/L G E Ferguson was the captain of the Oxford and that, though injured, he survived.

	26 OTU	Wellington III	X3955	Training
Sgt R L Wynniatt	inj			
Sgt G F Parkinson	inj			
Sgt R J Hardwick	inj			
Sgt R C Selth	+			
Sgt A C Horley	+			
Sgt H J Callon	inj			
Sgt A G A Keenor	inj			

T/o 1632 Wing but swung very badly. Still travelling at high speed, Sgt Wynniatt managed to get the Wellington into the air but at an abnormal angle of attack. Thus, with the starboard wing partially stalled, the bomber went out of control and crashed. Critically injured, Sgt Wynniatt was admitted to Halton where he died soon after arrival. He is buried in Bournemouth (Wimborne) Road Cemetery, while eastwards along the coast lies Sgt Horley in Hove New Cemetery. Sgt Selth rests in Streatham Park Cemetery.

8 Jul 1943	17 OTU	Wellington III	X3934	Training
F/O G Chambers	+			
Sgt F E Harrison	+			
P/O J A Jackson	+			
Sgt I G Jones	+			

T/o 1547 Turweston but stalled three minutes later and crashed at Priesthaywood Farm, a mile north-north-east of Syersham and 6 miles SW of Towcester, Northamptonshire. All lie in various burials grounds. This was the unit's first major accident since giving up its Blenheims in favour of Wellingtons.

12 Jul	10 OTU Det	Whitley V	BD681	—N	Op: AS Patrol

12 Jul
1943

10 OTU Det **Whitley V** **BD681** **—N** **Op: AS Patrol**

F/S C T Rudman + T/o 1047 St. Eval and set a course that would
Sgt M J R Ryan + take them to the Bay of Biscay. At 1550, distress
Sgt R V Turner + calls were received indicating they were being
Sgt W A Speller + attacked by enemy fighters. Thirteen minutes
Lt J D Williams USAAF + later, Chivenor picked up an SOS but the signal
Sgt R R Riddell RCAF + strength was very weak. Lt Williams USAAF is
commemorated at the US Military Cemetery at
Cambridge, the others are perpetuated on the panels of the Runnymede Memorial.

13 Jul
1943

16 OTU **Wellington III** **Z1743** **Training**

F/O D F McLaughlin RAAF T/o 0105 Upper Heyford for a night navigation
F/O R J Martin + detail. Crashed at approximately 0500, while
inj trying to forced-land with the starboard engine
inj out of action, at Shropshire Farm, Alveley, six
miles SSE of Bridgnorth, Shropshire. F/O Martin
is buried in the northern part of Henbury (St. Mary) Church Cemetery, Bristol.

13-14 Jul
1943

12 OTU **Wellington III** **BJ702** **Op: Nickel**

W/C N A Bray DFC inj T/o 2350 Chipping Warden and set course for the
P/O G Wilde Rennes area. Outbound, a pinpoint was obtained
F/O G Parkinson inj on the south coast over Portland and the French
P/O R Stokes coast was crossed a mile or so off track. Course
Sgt Perkins was then altered for the target area. When SW of
F/S Fitchett the Orne and in the Mortain-Domfront region,
flying straight and level at 16,500 feet, hit
below the port engine by predicted flak (0120). The engine and port mainplane
being badly damaged. At no time did anyone see searchlights. W/C Bray tried to
continue but was forced to turn back as he was unable to maintain altitude.
While recrossing the coast at 0135, there was much searchlight activity and
light flak and though no hits were scored, the bomber lost 2,000 feet in taking
evasive action. Over the sea, Nickels were jettisoned and these carried away
the trailing aerial. An SOS was transmitted by wireless and the IFF equipment
was switched on. By this time, the Wellington was almost impossible to control
and at 0210 a ditching was made. After thirty-four hours in their dinghy, an
Air-Sea Rescue launch located the crew. No one was too badly hurt, though their
skipper had sustained a broken nose.

81 OTU **Whitley V** **LA831** **Training**

Sgt L W Bugg + T/o 2250 Tilstock for a night cross-country.
Sgt S V Stephens + At 0415, for reasons that could not be explained,
F/O F Bird + the Whitley dived into the ground at Quina Brook,
F/O A D Kelly RCAF + Prees, 5 miles SSE of Whitchurch, Shropshire. F/O
Sgt D Waite + Kelly RCAF and Sgt Munt were buried in Chester
Sgt D Munt + (Blacon) Cemetery, the others were taken to their
home towns. It will be recalled that Sgt Bugg
had been involved in a serious crash at the beginning of the month (see page 231).
His grave in White Notley Churchyard is the sole service burial from either of the
two World wars. For some years, an engine from this aircraft was kept at Cosford
Aerospace Museum but has since been donated to the Shropshire Wartime Aircraft
Recovery Group. The CWGC register shows F/O Kelly's first Christian name as
Alan, while 'They Shall Grow Not Old' gives Allen.

15 Jul
1943

22 OTU **Wellington III** **HF812** **Training**

WO1 W S Pullar RCAF T/o Gaydon for local flying. Crash-landed
Sgt A B Wilson RCAF circa 1030 at Blythefield Farm, Southam, some
seven miles ESE of Royal Leamington Spa in
Warwickshire. It is suggested the accident was caused by the starboard engine
spark plugs overheating, or possibly by the starboard pitch control lever being
inadvertently moved as the pilots were changing seats.

23 OTU **Wellington III** **X3453** **Training**

P/O A J C Van Rassel RCAF T/o 2255 Pershore for a night bombing detail.
Sgt G W Howard RCAF While carrying out a practice overshoot at 2330,
the port engine cut at 300 feet and in the
aftermath of the forced-landing that resulted, the bomber caught fire. It was
not long after this incident that Sgt Howard RCAF proceeded to 429 Squadron, via
a Halifax conversion course, and on 22-23 October 1943, he was shot down over
Belgium while raiding Kassel (see Bomber Command Losses, Volume 4, page 370).

16 Jul   **10 OTU Det**   **Whitley V**   **BD276**   **—S**   **Op: AS Patrol**
1943   F/S T E N Redway RAAF   +   T/o 0551 St. Eval for operations over the Bay
       Sgt J Kirby   +   of Biscay. At 1310, signalled "MTB1 early 60
       F/S J S Ogilvy RCAF   +   minutes". At 1408, the Whitley touched down,
       Sgt G C Wilkinson   +   but ballooned back into the air and before the
       Sgt C E Munday   inj   situation could be remedied the bomber crashed
       Sgt P Stemkoski   inj   into a parked Hampden I P1204 belonging to
                                      No. 1404 Meteorological Flight. In the explosion
       AC2 L W M James   +   that followed, another of the Flight's Hampdens,
                                      AD757 was destroyed. The two Commonwealth airmen
were taken to Bath (Haycombe) Cemetery, the others being claimed by their next
of kin. It is strongly suspected, though no mention is made in unit records,
that AC2 James died in this accident. He is buried in St. Columb Major Cemetery,
a burial ground that was used from time to time by St. Eval.

11 OTU   **Wellington IC**   **DV720**   **Training**
       F/O E A Holdaway RNZAF   T/o 2240 Westcott but the port engine cut.
       P/O A E Mason RAAF   F/O Holdaway RNZAF immediately chopped the
                                      throttles and raised the undercarriage. Moments
later, still travelling at high speed, the bomber skidded off the airfield and
finished up in a railway cutting, where it caught fire. It is believed that
both officers survived the war.

17 OTU   **Wellington III**   **BJ797**   **Training**
       F/O D G McAlpine   T/o 1505 Silverstone but swung violently and
       Sgt R E Heap RAAF   inj   crashed into trees, injuring the tail gunner.
                                      Late in December 1943, flying Lancasters with
50 Squadron, F/O McAlpine's aircraft came down in the North Sea (see Bomber
Command Losses, Volume 4, page 440). By a quirk of coincidence, his tail
gunner (and sole survivor) was an Australian.

17 Jul   **26 OTU**   **Defiant I**   **N3509**   **Transit**
1943   S/L R P Todd   T/o 1030 Wing and headed for Desford. Arriving
                                      at his destination at 1115, S/L Todd was faced
with very marginal weather conditions and while trying to land, he overshot the
runway and clipped Tiger Moth I N6741 of the resident No. 7 Elementary Flying
Training School. The Defiant was wrecked, but the Tiger Moth was repaired and
returned to service.

18 Jul   **10 OTU Det**   **Whitley V**   **LA880**   **—R**   **Op: AS Patrol**
1943   F/O G C Hamilton   +   T/o 0603 St. Eval for a Bay of Biscay patrol.
       F/O J D S Goldring   +   Lost without trace. All are commemorated on
       F/O G W F Button   +   the Runnymede Memorial.
       Sgt F Mills   +
       F/O S Lees   +
       Sgt J A J Jarman   +

19 Jul   **10 OTU Det**   **Whitley V**   **BD359**   **—X**   **Op: AS Patrol**
1943   Sgt R H Breffitt   T/o 1024 St. Eval and set course for the Bay
       Sgt C J Chaplin   of Biscay. At 1905, the crew were instructed,
       Sgt S L Williams   by wireless, to divert to Chivenor in North
       Sgt C H R Slade   Devon as the weather conditions around St. Eval
       Sgt W R Heale   were inclement. At 2040, having acknowledged
                                      the diversion message, the crew estimated their
position as Plympton, indicating they were low on fuel. It seems that course
for Chivenor was maintained though in the latter stages the Whitley flew over
the Bristol Channel. Then, with the North Devon coast in view, they ditched
at 2102 off Barnstaple. This was the last Whitley to be reported written off
from the St. Eval detachment, which was withdrawn just four days later.

22 OTU   **Wellington X**   **HE480**   **Training**
       F/O C Grose RCAF   +   T/o 1102 Wellesbourne Mountford but crashed a
       Sgt K L Richmond RCAF   +   minute later on the banks of the Avon at Hampton
       Sgt D M Wilkinson   +   Lucy on the NNW side of the airfield. Both
                                      Canadians are buried in Stratford-upon-Avon
Cemetery, while Sgt Wilkinson was taken to Greatham Church Cemetery. F/O Grose
was attempting his first solo on type and the most likely cause of the accident
seems to be engine failure.

19 Jul   **28 OTU D Flt**   **Wellington IC** **DV455**   **Training**
1943   Sgt F Chase RCAF   T/o 1140 Castle Donington for a navigation
                                      detail. At 1420, or thereabout, the Wellington
crashed near Llandigach, some 1 to 2 miles NE of Bodedern on Anglesey, the crew
having taken to their parachutes. The cause of the accident was traced to total
failure of the port engine, followed by an uncontrollable fire.

19-20 Jul **24 OTU**   **Anson I** **DJ242 TY-U**   **Training**
1943   P/O K F Smith   inj T/o 2217 Honeybourne for a night exercise. While
                                    flying at 1,000 feet, the starboard engine cut,
necessitating an emergency landing at 0052 on the road leading to Evesham and
quite close to the base airfield. Having recovered from his injuries, P/O Smith
converted to Halifaxes. Posted to 161 Squadron, he was killed in a midair
collision on 23 January 1944 (see Bomber Command Losses, Volume 5, page 52).

22 Jul   **27 OTU**   **Wellington III** **BJ963**   **Training**
1943   F/S T J Clayton   + T/o Lichfield for a navigation exercise which
      F/S N R Linton RAAF   + involved the crew flying over the sea. It is
      Sgt A J H Bock RAAF   + reported that the weather along the flight path
      F/S A C Mack   + was perfect and wireless signals received from
      Sgt H J Richardson RAAF + the aircraft gave no hint of trouble. However,
                                    they failed to return by their appointed time
and, subsequently, all are commemorated on the Runnymede Memorial.

           17 OTU   **Lysander TT** **R9075**   **Unknown**
                                     Reported to have ditched.

23 Jul   **24 OTU**   **Whitley V** **Z9167 FB-O**   **Training**
1943   F/O A M Shalless RAAF   + T/o 0001 Honeybourne for high-level bombing
      Sgt S H Carter   + practice over the Idlicote range. At 0150,
      P/O G H I Smith   + flew into high ground (described in some reports
      Sgt B Lillyman   + as a cliff) between Hampton Lucy and Wasperton,
      Sgt W C Bull   + four miles NE of Stratford-upon-Avon. Three,
                                    F/O Shalless RAAF, P/O Smith and Sgt Bull were
conveyed to Oxford (Botley) Cemetery, while Sgt Carter was taken to Sunderland
(Mere Knolls) Cemetery and Sgt Lillyman to Potters Bar (St. Mary) Church Cemetery.

23-24 Jul **18 OTU**   **Wellington X** **HE730**   **Training**
1943   Sgt G E Palmer   + T/o Finningley for a night navigation sortie.
      Sgt N C Cleaver   + Believed to have crashed in the Bristol Channel
      Sgt D E H Stroud   + after calling for help, by wireless. Four have
      Sgt W J Thorne   + no known graves, while Sgt Edwards is buried in
      Sgt K Edwards   + Coalville (Hugglescote) Cemetery.

25 Jul   **19 OTU A Flt**   **Whitley V** **LA878 ZV-A**   **Training**
1943   P/O J W Einarson DFM RCAF   T/o 0835 Kinloss for a cross-country. Ditched
      Sgt J M Smith   circa 1100 some 10 miles E of Largo Bay in the
                                    Firth of Forth while trying to make the airfield
at Drem with only one serviceable engine. The crew of seven took to their dinghy
and at 1218 they were picked up by a trawler. Transferred to a naval vessel,
they were taken into Methil. P/O Einarson RCAF had recently completed a tour
of operations with 44 Squadron, his DFM being published in the London Gazette
on 20 April 1943. Following his spell of instructing, he went to 61 Squadron
and was killed during the split-raid on Augsburg in February 1944 (see Bomber
Command Losses, Volume 5, page 103). His twin brother and fellow pilot, F/S
Harold Bjorn Einarson RCAF had been posted missing on 10 September 1942, while
serving with 207 Squadron (see the same series, Volume 3, page 208). Sadly,
Sgt Smith, too, died when his 102 Squadron Halifax plunged into the sea off
Flamborough Head in January 1944 (see the same series, Volume 5, page 46).
At the time of his death, he was engaged in a raid on Magdeburg.

27 Jul   **20 OTU**   **Wellington X** **HE684**   **Training**
1943   Sgt P Hicken   inj T/o 1343 Lossiemouth but a tyre burst followed
      Sgt B R Kidson   inj by total collapse of the undercarriage. All were
      P/O R T Thornton RCAF inj admitted to Dr. Gray's Hospital. On 24-25 May
      Sgt G Trotter   inj 1944, while flying Bomber Support operations
      P/O R J Vincent   inj with 192 Squadron, Sgt Hicken's Halifax was
                                    shot down over Belgium (see Bomber Command
                                    Losses, Volume 5, page 243).

27–28 Jul **12 OTU** **Wellington III** **BK342** **Training**
1943   Sgt W D Brickwood   T/o 2250 Chipping Warden for a night cross-
country. Lost power and at 0210 was extensively
damaged having failed to reach the airfield at Shobdon in Herefordshire. After
a close technical inspection, the Wellington was struck off charge on 4 August
1943. Accepted by the unit, direct from 48 Maintenance Unit at Hawarden, on
29 December 1942, the Wellington had accumulated 455.50 flying hours.

30 Jul **15 OTU** **Wellington IC** **DV877** **Training**
1943   Sgt J M Hart   inj T/o 1017 Harwell for a cine camera gun exercise
   W/O A Proctor   inj and crashed almost immediately, due to engine
   Sgt A E T Lewin   inj failure, near The Monument. Thirty-seven year
   Sgt A A J Wilson   inj old Sgt Webb is buried in Harrow (Eastcote Lane)
   Sgt J Snoddon   inj Cemetery, while Sgt Roberts was taken back to
   Sgt R W Chadwick   inj Wales and interred at Penmaenmawr (Dwygyfylchi)
   Sgt H G O Webb   + Cemetery.
   Sgt W S Roberts   +

   21 OTU **Wellington IC** **DV888** **Training**
   Sgt N F Westhoff RAAF   T/o 0155 Moreton-in-Marsh but the port engine
failed and Sgt Westhoff RAAF very skillfully
force-landed, straight ahead, in the direction of Stow-on-the-Wold. Following
the Court of Inquiry, his flying log book was endorsed "commended". Sadly, not
long after his arrival in India he died while serving with No. 22 Ferry Control
RAF at Allahabad (26 January 1944). His grave is in Delhi War Cemetery.

31 Jul **23 OTU** **Wellington III** **X3997** **Ground**
1943   Burnt out 2218 at Pershore. This particular
Wellington had been allocated to the unit on 6 August 1942, ex-44 MU Edzell.
Its movement card has been annotated to show 570.55 flying hours.

   23 OTU **Wellington III** **BJ581** **Air Test**
   F/O J T Gilbert   + T/o Pershore with a screened pilot and two
   Mr H G Maxton   + civilian employees of Vickers Armstrong.
   Miss G R Lloyd   + Crashed 1815 in the vicinity of Honiley
airfield, Warwickshire. F/O Gilbert is
buried in Weymouth Cemetery.

31 Jul– **24 OTU** **Whitley V** **N1390** **Training**
1 Aug 1943 P/O K O Law RNZAF   inj T/o 2251 Long Marston for a night exercise.
   Sgt S Smith RCAF   Crashed 0001 roughly 100 yards SW of the airfield boundary after a propeller hit the run-
way and shattered. Sgt Smith RCAF, after converting to Halifaxes, lost his
life while raiding Mannheim in mid-November 1943 (see Bomber Command Losses,
Volume 4, page 385). At the time he was serving with 429 Squadron.

1 Aug **10 OTU** **Whitley V** **LA916** **Training**
1943   W/O G G Webb RAAF   T/o 1518 Stanton Harcourt to demonstrate
feathering procedures. Crash-landed 2209,
in a cornfield some 400 yards NE of the airfield after the starboard engine
failed to restart.

   30 OTU **Wellington X** **HE917** **Training**
   F/S P J Clifton   inj T/o Hixon for a night exercise. Having lost
   Sgt C M Carr RCAF   inj the use of the hydraulics, the crew had to
   Sgt A E Dimock RCAF inj land without flap assistance. Consequently,
   Sgt A L Rookes   inj their arrival on the runway at 0335 was at
   Sgt J A Johnstone   inj high speed and while being deliberately swung
to avoid a hedge, the bomber crashed onto the
nearby rail line and caught fire. After converting to Stirlings, Sgt Carr RCAF
was posted to 623 Squadron. On 3–4 October 1943, his aircraft failed to return
from Kassel (see Bomber Command Losses, Volume 4, page 348).

2 Aug **18 OTU C Flt** **Wellington III** **X3800** **Training**
1943   Sgt L A Charlton   + T/o 1510 Finningley to practice single-engined
   Sgt R H Smith   + flying. Dived and crashed 1530 at Wroot, near
   F/S E H Sherman RAAF + the airfield. F/S Sherman RAAF and Sgt Perry lie
   Sgt J W Perry   + in Finningley (St. Oswald) Churchyard; Sgt Smith
and Sgt Charlton were taken to their home towns.

2 Aug	23 OTU	Wellington III	BK504	Training

1943
P/O J D C Craton RCAF   inj   T/o 1620 Pershore for circuit training. At 1705
F/L G R Dixon   inj   the Wellington approached the runway with F/L
F/O W B Coucill RCAF   inj   Dixon, a Central Flying School instructor (on
Cdt R N Carter   inj   a liaison visit) at the controls. However, the
       screened pilot, P/O Craton RCAF, considered they
were too high and travelling too fast to complete a safe landing and he assumed
command, announcing he would overshoot. As the bomber began to climb, the
starboard engine failed and moments later they were down, in a wood, near the
airfield. A fire broke out and Cdt Carter was mortally injured. Aged sixteen,
he is buried in the western extension to Sedgley (All Saints) Churchyard.

	28 OTU	Wellington IC	Z1107	Training

Sgt J H Borland   +   T/o 1603 Castle Donington for a cross-country
Sgt G H Clarkson   +   but the starboard engine burst into flames and
Sgt J D Hayes   +   while trying to extinguish the blaze, the bomber
Sgt S P Pithara   +   stalled and plunged to the ground near Breedon-
Sgt R McK Stapley   +   on-the-Hill, six miles NNW of Coalville in
       Leicestershire. Sgt Pithara of Cyprus rests in
Burton-on-the-Wolds Cemetery; the others were claimed by their next of kin.

2- 3 Aug	18 OTU	Wellington X	HE526	Op: Nickel

1943
Sgt N Walker   inj   T/o 2350 Finningley but an engine failed and
P/O L T Bowers   inj   a crash-landing quickly followed at Partridge
P/O H C Atkinson RCAF   inj   Hall Farm, about 2 miles downwind of the flare
Sgt J R Taylor   inj   path.
Sgt S Edwards   inj
F/L Hill

3 Aug	12 OTU	Wellington III	X3876	Training

1943
Sgt M G Scollick   inj   T/o 2240 Chipping Warden for a night exercise
Sgt I A Macphee RCAF   inj   but some twenty minutes later, the port engine
Sgt W P Crosby   inj   failed and the bomber was abandoned. Reported
Sgt S D Oakes RCAF   inj   crashed between Little Alne and Henley-in-Arden,
Sgt W N Gould RCAF   inj   five and 7 miles respectively NW of Stratford-
Sgt Burtonshaw   inj   upon-Avon, Warwickshire. Sadly, Sgt Gould RCAF
       lost his life, while still being trained, in a
       flying accident on 21-22 September 1943.

	14 OTU	Wellington IC	DV823	Training

Sgt L Curatolo RCAF   T/o 0137 Oakley for a night detail. Crash-
       landed 0146 near Langar airfield, Nottingham-
shire after an exhaust stub on the starboard engine burnt through, thus giving
the impression that the motor was on fire. Sgt Curatolo RCAF later converted
to Lancasters but was lost in action during January 1944, while operating to
Braunschweig with 44 Squadron (see Bomber Command Losses, Volume 5, page 30).

3- 4 Aug	16 OTU	Wellington III	BJ585	Training

1943
Sgt G Wilson   +   T/o 2206 Upper Heyford for a night navigation
Sgt P J Charlier   +   exercise. Shortly before 0100, the starboard
P/O R W Papineau   +   engine lost its oil and the crew requested an
Sgt L Phillips   inj   immediate priority landing. While trying to
Sgt S J Angus   inj   do so, control was lost and the Wellington came
       down at 0106 near the airfield at Ramsbury in
Wiltshire. Sgt Wilson of Burnside in Lanarkshire and P/O Papineau, who hailed
from Hampton, Middlesex, rest in Andover Cemetery, while Sgt Charlier was taken
to Kensal Green (St. Mary's) Roman Catholic Cemetery. At the time, Ramsbury was
being used as a relief landing ground for No. 15(Pilots) Advanced Flying Unit.

4 Aug	16 OTU	Wellington III	BK205	Training

1943
F/S D L Redfern RCAF   +   T/o Upper Heyford and crashed soon afterwards
F/O J McKenna   +   at Lower Heyford Mill, roughly 2 miles SW from
P/O T Johnstone RCAF   +   the airfield. Both Canadians rest in Oxford
Sgt S A Schofield   +   (Botley) Cemetery. F/O McKenna and Sgt Nicol
Sgt W L Nicol   +   were both taken back to Lanarkshire, the former
       to New Stevenston (St. Patrick's) Roman Catholic
Cemetery, Bothwell and the latter to Lanark (St. Catherine's) Cemetery. Sgt
Schofield lies in Chadderton (St. Matthew) Churchyard. Their aircraft had been
allotted to the unit, from 38 MU Llandow, on 26 September 1942.

4 Aug
1943

| 27 OTU | | Wellington X | HE703 | **Training** |

F/S F J Matthews RAAF   +   T/o Lichfield for a night navigation exercise.
F/S E S Newell RAAF   inj   At approximately 2350, while flying at 13,000
F/S E C Thompson RAAF   +   feet, the front oil retainer on the port engine
P/O C P Luther RAAF   inj   ran dry and the unit failed. Soon afterwards,
F/S K Forbes   inj   the starboard motor lost power and the bomber
Sgt J E McCarthy   inj   crashed into Walton Road, Sale, Cheshire and
caught fire. Those who lost their lives were
taken to Chester (Blacon) Cemetery, the first from 27 OTU to be laid to rest
in this regional cemetery. Very sadly, having survived this awful accident,
three of the four injured were killed by the spring of 1944. P/O Luther RAAF
died with 7 Squadron, while Sgt McCarthy and F/S Newell RAAF lost their lives
in the service of 460 Squadron and 466 Squadron (see Bomber Command Losses,
Volumes 4 and 5, pages 420, 96 and 121 respectively).

6 Aug
1943

| 23 OTU | | Wellington III | BK430 | **Training** |

F/S J P R Labbe RCAF   +   T/o 2240 Pershore for a Bullseye sortie, armed
F/O N Solomka RCAF   +   with practice bombs. When the oil supply to the
F/S W McK Arril RCAF   +   big end bearing on the starboard engine ran dry,
F/S J P G M De Bellefeuille   +   the unit failed and at 2340 the Wellington came
   RCAF   down at Bronington, a little over 3 miles WSW of
WO2 F C J-L Therien RCAF   +   Whitchurch, Shropshire. Five rest in Chester
Sgt R Searston   +   (Blacon) Cemetery, while Sgt Searston is buried
in Alfreton Cemetery, Derbyshire.

7 Aug
1943

| 10 OTU | | Whitley V | LA843 | **Training** |

Sgt H Jackson   T/o 1520 Abingdon for circuit training and
wrecked ten minutes later as a consequence of
landing with such force that the undercarriage was smashed completely.

| 21 OTU | | Wellington IC | R1508 | **Training** |

Sgt R V Carson RAAF   T/o Moreton-in-Marsh with the intention of
taking part in a Bullseye exercise. During
the sortie, the starboard engine failed and all efforts to obtain help, via
wireless, failed due to intense static. Thus, when the motor caught fire, the
captain ordered everyone to bale out and soon after giving this instruction,
his aircraft crashed at 0245 near Beaconsfield, Buckinghamshire.

| 22 OTU | | Wellington III | HF612 | **Training** |

W/O T S Heyes DFM   +   T/o Wellesbourne Mountford for a night detail.
Sgt W G Hill RCAF   +   Eyewitnesses state the Wellington was gliding
F/O P M Hetherington RCAF   +   in, under control, with one engine stopped when
Sgt B Bradshaw   +   the nose was raised in order to clear a high
Sgt D M Martin RCAF   +   hedge, It then stalled at 40 feet, plunging
into a field of wheat stubble at Stapleton Hill
Farm, less than a mile from the runway. On impact the bomber burst into flames.
The three Canadians and Sgt Bradshaw rest in Stratford-upon-Avon Cemetery, while
W/O Heyes was taken to Manchester (Philips Park) Cemetery. He had won his award
serving with 429 Squadron, details being Gazetted on 10 September 1943. The time
of this terrible tragedy is reported as either 2305 or 2310.

| 26 OTU | | Wellington III | X3790 | **Training** |

Sgt W Davies   +   T/o Little Horwood for a night flying detail.
Sgt J Harrington   inj   At circa 0255, the Wellington approached the
Sgt J Y Sowter   +   runway but was obliged to overshoot. While
Sgt J P V McKeon   +   doing so, Sgt Davies lost control and moments
Sgt C H C Fietz RAAF   +   later his aircraft smashed into the high street
at Winslow, 6 miles SE of Buckingham, totally
demolishing the Chandos Arms and nearby dwellings. The carnage was dreadful,
for in addition to the four airmen killed, no less than thirteen civilians died
(their details are recorded on the next page). Of the aircrew who perished, Sgt
Davies was buried in Pontnewydd (Holy Trinity) Churchyard, Cwmbran, Sgt Sowter
was cremated at Oxford Crematorium while two were laid to rest in Oxford (Botley)
Cemetery. Sgt Harrington was dreadfully injured, as was the crews' mascot,
"Wimpy" the cat (which was found in Sgt Harrington's battle dress blouse). Like
so many airmen, he had falsified his age in order to enter the service and was a
mere sixteen year old when accepted in May 1941. Sgt McKeon had recently joined
the crew as a replacement for Sgt Samuel Smith, killed on 30 July when he walked
into the arc of a still revolving propeller.

7 Aug	Mr T Cox	+	Licensee of the Chandos Arms, aged 54.
1943	Mr W Hawkins	+	4 Rose Cottages, aged 67.
	Mrs N Hawkins	+	4 Rose Cottages, aged 67.
	Mr I Goldberg	+	6 Rose Cottages, aged 67.
	Mrs A Goldberg	+	6 Rose Cottages, aged 66.
	Mrs L Hoberman	+	6 Rose Cottages, aged 41.
	Mstr V Hoberman	+	6 Rose Cottages, aged 7.
	Mr S Mullis	+	8 Rose Cottages, aged 35.
	Mrs D Mullis	+	8 Rose Cottages, aged 39.
	Mstr T Mullis	+	8 Rose Cottages, aged 10.
	Miss K Mullis	+	8 Rose Cottages, aged five months.
	Mr T Paintin	+	82 High Street, aged 55.
	Mr D Paintin	+	82 High Street, aged 18. Mrs Cox, of the Chandos

Arms, survived, as did two young girls from the Mullis family. A commemorative plaque was unveiled precisely fifty years after this terrible tragedy at a special service held in the Winslow Parish Church of St. Laurence.

28 OTU	**Wellington IC**	**X9638**		**Training**
F/S R W Bagley		+	T/o 0137 Castle Donington for a night detail	
Sgt R A Owens		+	during which the No. 2 cylinder barrel on the	
Sgt G A Long RCAF		+	port engine fractured. This led to the unit	
Sgt D W B Pimm		+	catching fire and sending the Wellington down	
Sgt J J Davidge		+	to crash 0203 near the airfield. Sgt Long RCAF	

rests in Oxford (Botley) Cemetery; Sgt Davidge lies in Burton-on-the-Wolds Cemetery; the others were claimed by relatives.

8 Aug	**26 OTU**	**Wellington III**	**BJ892**		**Training**
1943	Sgt R A Young		+	T/o 1021 Wing for a cross-country. It is thought	
	Sgt S J Morton		+	the crew were attempting to descend below the	
	Sgt W A Chamberlain		+	cloud base, with the engines throttled back in	
	Sgt A P L Walker		+	order to prevent over speeding, when control was	
	Sgt K McKenzie		+	lost and the bomber crashed 1346 at Hiswell Farm	
	Sgt R W J Reeve		+	Icknield Way, Tring, Hertfordshire. All rest in	
	Sgt C S Newton		+	Halton (St. Michael) Churchyard.	

9 Aug	**82 OTU**	**Wellington X**	**MS471**	**—G**	**Training**
1943	P/O W W Adams		+	T/o Ossington for a cross-country. On return to	
	F/O F Graham Bell		+	Ossington, and while in low-level flight, the	
	P/O H Ibbott RCAF		+	starboard engine failed and the Wellington came	
	Sgt R W Ballauff		+	down on the main road leading to Newark-on-Trent	
	Sgt P Baldwin		+	between Wellow and Ompton, 10 miles SSW from	

Retford in Nottinghamshire. Two were laid to rest in Ollerton Cemetery, two, P/O Adams and F/O Graham Bell were cremated, while P/O Ibbott RCAF is likely to have been claimed by relatives as he lies in Bedford Cemetery. This was the first total write off since the formation of the unit on 1 June 1943.

11 Aug	**27 OTU**	**Wellington X**	**HE178**		**Training**
1943	Sgt R W Jarvis			T/o Lichfield for a local training detail.	
	Sgt R Tattersall		+	Shortly before 1540, the starboard engine's	

front oil retainer failed and this led to a total seizure of the reduction gear, which in turn caused the propeller to break away. With the airfield in sight, Sgt Jarvis forced-landed, but hit some trees some 3 miles NNE of Tamworth, Staffordshire. Sgt Tattersall is buried in Oswaldtwistle (Immanuel) Churchyard.

30 OTU	**Wellington X**	**HE390**	**—R**		**Training**
F/L L W Metcalfe DFC		+	T/o Seighford for circuits and landings. At	
Sgt S G Cochrane		+	approximately 0940, Master II W9073 from No.	
Sgt E W C Bryant		+	5(Pilots) Advanced Flying Unit at Ternhill	
Sgt C Yates		+	emerged from the cloud base, estimated at 800	
Sgt F Powis		+	feet, and collided with the Wellington. Both	

aircraft fell in the vicinity of Derrington Farm and Vicarage Farm near the airfield. Sgt Cochrane and Sgt Powis were taken to Stafford Cemetery, while the others who died were claimed by their next of kin. The Master was crewed by F/S C A Simmons and Sgt J W Mudie RAAF, both of whom lost their lives. On 23 April 1943, the Wellington had struck, and wrecked, Lysander II N1308 at Hixon (see page 215).

11-12 Aug	28 OTU	Wellington IC	DV731	Op: Nickel

1943

F/S R R Keeler RCAF	+	T/o Castle Donington and set course for France.
Sgt J P Soltau	inj	Reported to have been hit by flak, which led to
F/S C Green RCAF	+	the Wellington coming down at 0637 in the sea
Sgt G J Broughton	+	off Shoreham, Sussex. Three are commemorated
Sgt D A Cardy	+	on the Runnymede Memorial, Sgt Broughton was
Sgt A Kahn	inj	cremated at Bradford and two were picked up
		by an Air-Sea Rescue launch.

14 Aug	19 OTU	Anson I	N9671 XF-P	Training

1943

W/O A K Farlam RAAF	+	T/o 1435 Kinloss for a navigation training
F/O H H Kirby DFC	+	detail. At approximately 1505, the Anson was
Sgt E S A Gray	+	seen diving, with both engines running at full
Sgt F J Pellatt	+	power, from 4,000 feet and failing to recover
Sgt R Brown	+	before hitting the ground roughly a mile E of
Sgt K Ashmore	+	Arbroath airfield, Angus. An examination of

the wreckage revealed that most of the fabric had peeled away from the starboard wing. All rest in cemeteries scattered across the United Kingdom and it seems likely that the funeral for W/O Farlam of Neutral Bay in New South Wales was arranged by relatives as he is buried in Surrey at Cheam (St. Dunstan) Churchyard, Sutton and Cheam.

	21 OTU	Wellington IC	X9618	Training

F/O A J White RAAF	+	T/o Enstone for a training exercise. While
F/O H M Beyer RAAF	+	nearing the airfield at 1705, their appears
Sgt F I Hardaker RAAF	+	to have been a misunderstanding in the orders
F/S L G Sellen RAAF	+	to manipulate the fuel cocks as an engine cut
		and the Wellington dived to the ground less

than a mile from the runway and caught fire. The four Australians were taken to Oxford (Botley) Cemetery. It is reported that the tail gunner (he is not named) escaped serious injury.

	82 OTU	Martinet I	JN639	Training

F/S W E Jenkins		T/o 1544 Ossington for a fighter affiliation
		detail but force -landed a minute later, due

to engine failure, careering through a hedge to finish up on a nearby road.

14-15 Aug	29 OTU	Wellington III	X3786	Training

1943

F/O C B Owen	T/o 2235 Bruntingthorpe for a night navigation
	sortie. When well into the exercise, the crew

suspected that the aircraft's hydraulic system was showing signs of failure and after advising base of their suspicions, they were ordered to head for Wittering airfield in Northamptonshire. As they approached the runway at 0415, however, both engines cut through lack of petrol and in the ensuing forced-landing the Wellington was damaged beyond economical repair.

15-16 Aug	21 OTU	Wellington IC	R1152	Op: Nickel

1943

F/S F M Gilkeson RAAF	+	T/o Moreton-in-Marsh and set course for France.
Sgt Macgovern		On return, intercepted by a Mosquito and, in a
Sgt Malingran		tragic case of mistaken identity, was shot down
F/S Rollasin		at 0052 into the Deer Park at Wimborne St. Giles,
Sgt E Causer	+	ten miles NE of Blandford Forum, Dorset. Three
		managed to bale out and, it is reported, their

skipper made a valiant effort to try and save his aircraft. He is buried in Brookwood Military Cemetery, while Sgt Causer rests at Whitehaven (Hensingham) Cemetery in Cumberland.

16 Aug	18 OTU	Wellington III	BJ671	Ground

1943

F/O L Rebinski PAF	Caught fire at 0135 while starting engines at
F/S Ozmaxiarz PAF	Finningley. Almost a year later to the day,
	14 August to be precise, F/O Rebinski PAF lost

his life while on operations with 300 Squadron (see Bomber Command Losses, Volume 5, page 384).

	27 OTU	Wellington X	MS475	Training

Sgt D O Glendening RAAF	inj	T/o Lichfield for night flying practice. At
		0124 the Wellington overshot the airfield and

crashed heavily, Sgt Glendening RAAF sustaining a broken leg. The accident was attributed to failure of the port engine's crankshaft main roller bearing.

16 Aug **29 OTU** **Wellington III BK550** **Training**
1943 Sgt N P Holmes T/o 1030 Bitteswell for a cross-country flight.
While away from base, the wind direction changed
and having failed to notice this, Sgt Holmes landed 1030 downwind and crashed
off the end of the runway.

17 Aug **16 OTU** **Wellington III Z1678** **Ground**
1943 While undergoing a restart, at Barford St. John,
the port engine burst into flames which quickly enveloped the rest of the aircraft. At the Court of Inquiry into its loss, which occurred at 1610, it was
stated that the engine had been turned over three times before the magneto
switches were placed "on" contact, resulting in a flood of rich mixture fuel
into the exhaust manifold and on "contact" this ignited.

23 OTU **Wellington III Z1694** **Training**
F/S F D Johnson RCAF + T/o 2052 Pershore on a special night exercise
F/O A T Duke RCAF + carrying 4 x 500lb GP bombs, IFF, Gee and
F/S G W Holditch RCAF + camera. While in the vicinity of Wymeswold
F/S J Taylor RCAF + (and an estimated 22 miles off track) the
Sgt J A Vanlint + Wellington dived and crashed 2302 about two
Sgt R H Chisnell RCAF + miles NW of the airfield. The five RCAF airmen
were taken to Oxford (Botley) Cemetery, while
Sgt Vanlint was buried in Chingford Mount Cemetery. Two were Americans; F/O
Duke RCAF and F/S Taylor RCAF, the former hailing from Newark, New Jersey and
the latter from Worcester, Massachusetts. Nineteen year old Sgt Chisnell's
father was a serving officer, F/L W G H Chisnell.

28 OTU **Wellington IC X9883** **Ground**
F/S P Sleight Shortly after landing 1125 at Castle Donington
from an air test, the Wellington caught fire
and was destroyed. At the Court of Inquiry it was stated that excessive flaming
from the port exhaust had been observed during the glide approach and it was
deduced that the undersurfaces of the wing had ignited.

17-18 Aug **23 OTU** **Wellington III X3424** **Training**
1943 P/O F M Potter T/o 2355 Pershore for night training. Landed
P/O H D Paddison RCAF circa 0135 and the throttles were advanced to
go round again. However, the power decayed and
the instructor cut the throttles. However, he was unable to prevent the bomber
from running off the runway and into a tree. Extensive damage was done to the
port wing and the back of the aircraft was fractured. P/O Paddison RCAF went
on to fly Halifaxes and lost his life on operations to Berlin in January 1944
(see Bomber Command Losses, Volume 5, page 41).

18 Aug **11 OTU** **Wellington IC R1337 —M** **Training**
1943 F/S H Harries RNZAF + T/o 2104 Westcott tasked for a Bullseye detail
F/O B James + and in addition to the five airmen aboard, two
F/O F Saunders + soldiers joined the crew. Lost without trace.
Sgt S P Hawkes + The air force personnel are commemorated on the
Sgt F Meaker + Runnymede Memorial; the names of the soldiers
Sgt J S Webb + are not known. F/S Harries RNZAF came from
  + East Perth in Western Australia.
  +

18 OTU **Wellington X HE279** **Training**
F/L W J Stevens T/o 0305 Finningley to practice night circuits
P/O Bowen-Bravery and landings but a tyre burst sending the
Wellington swinging out of control, the main
undercarriage unit giving way under the strain.

27 OTU **Wellington X LN432** **Training**
S/L C E Payne RAAF T/o 2157 Lichfield for a night exercise but
it seems the propellers became stuck in the
fixed pitch position and the Wellington crashed out of control, a fire breaking
out soon after it came to a stop. Three members of the crew (they are not named)
are reported to have been slightly hurt. Taken on charge the previous month, no
flying hours total has been appended to AM Form 78.

18–19 Aug	12 OTU	Wellington III	BJ587		Training
1943	F/S A M Lovelle-Draper RAAF		+	T/o Chipping Warden for a Bullseye exercise.
	Sgt S W Wood		+	Presumed to have been lost over the sea. Two
	F/S A J Hogan RAAF		+	bodies were recovered; F/S Hogan RAAF, listed
	Sgt F E Worden RAAF		+	as the second navigator, is buried in Scotland
	F/S D Russell RAAF		+	at Newton Stewart Cemetery, while F/S Russell,
	Sgt W D McDonald		+	a fellow countryman, rests in Chester (Blacon)

Cemetery. Their four companions are commemorated on the Runnymede Memorial.

21 Aug	21 OTU	Wellington IC	T2475		Training
1943	Sgt F M Jude RAAF			T/o Moreton-in-Marsh for a night navigation exercise. Shortly before 2310, the port engine

failed and the Wellington crash-landed at Neston on the E bank of the River Dee some dozen miles or so NNW of Chester. At the Court of Inquiry, Sgt Jude RAAF was praised for his excellent handling of a very difficult situation.

	82 OTU	Wellington X	HE332	–J	Training
	F/S H O Shaw RAAF		inj	T/o 2132 Ossington for a night flying detail.
	F/O F G Ingham		+	Crashed 2337 after colliding with trees on the
	Sgt R W Hughes		+	approach to the base runway. F/O Ingham rests
	F/S E A McCasker RCAF		inj	in Brighouse Cemetery, while Sgt Hughes was
	Sgt Jennings			taken to Portsmouth (Milton) Cemetery. Both
	Sgt Dye			are described as air bombers.

23 Aug	17 OTU	Wellington III	BJ990		Training
1943	Sgt A L Hinton RAAF			T/o 2145 Turweston but the starboard engine cut causing the Wellington to veer out of control

and crash into the Standard Beam Approach hut, just beyond the runway.

24 Aug	82 OTU	Wellington III	BK399	–W	Ground
1943	F/O O L Macfarlane RNZAF			At 1100, while stationary at Ossington, the
	Sgt L W C Wheeler			Verey pistol was accidentally discharged, inside the fuselage, setting light to the aircraft. Sgt

Wheeler lost his life in March 1944, while participating in the last Main Force raid on Berlin (see Bomber Command Losses, Volume 5, page 129). At the time he was serving with 15 Squadron.

25 Aug	17 OTU	Wellington X	HE555		Training
1943	P/O J A C Munro			T/o Turweston tasked for a training exercise. After the starboard engine's crankshaft bearing

inner track failed, the Wellington came down at 1100 in a field twixt Blisworth and Roade, 5 miles SSW and 6 miles S respectively from Northampton.

25–26 Aug	22 OTU	Wellington III	HF628		Op: Nickel
1943	F/S F T Cooper RCAF		+	T/o Wellesbourne Mountford in the company of
	F/O W H Mitchell RCAF		pow	three other aircraft (three crews from the unit's
	F/S C F Pick RCAF		+	satellite at Gaydon were also tasked). Shot down
	F/S G R Simmons		pow	from 10,000 feet over the French coast by the
	Sgt N C Brown RCAF		+	combined efforts of flak and a night-fighter.

Two have no known graves, but Sgt Brown RCAF is buried in the Canadian War Cemetery at Calais, having been brought here from Le Touquet. This Wellington had been badly damaged at Stratford-upon-Avon on 27 October 1942, during which Wellington IC X9943 was written off (see page 170).

	81 OTU	Whitley V	LA937		Training
	F/O K N Laing RCAF		+	T/o 2050 Sleap for a night navigation exercise.
	Sgt T W Fair RCAF		inj	On return to base, both engines faltered with
	Sgt T R Armstrong RCAF		+	the bomber about to touch down. Thus, in the
	Sgt R G Henderson		inj	ensuing forced-landing at 0310, F/O Laing RCAF
	Sgt R Guile		inj	crashed into the airfield's watch office. In
				addition to those aboard the Whitley, who were
	W/C D S Robertson		inj	injured, at least three members of the watch
	AC1 Ferguson		inj	office were admitted to hospital and around
	ACW2 J M Viney WAAF		inj	fifteen others were treated locally for minor

cuts and abrasions. F/O Laing RCAF and his fellow Canadian, Sgt Armstrong, are buried in Chester (Blacon) Cemetery.

26 Aug 1943	20 OTU A Flt	Wellington X	HE802	—S		Training

F/S F E Adams RCAF   + T/o Lossiemouth on a cross-country flight. It
F/S B E Clark RCAF   + is believed the Wellington was struck by an
Sgt B G Donbavand   + object of some sort, which may have damaged
F/S E H Weeks RCAF   + the propellers (injuries to the pilot suggest
Sgt A P King   + he may have been killed, or incapacitated, by
Sgt K G Soutar RCAF   + a fragment of propeller blade entering the
cockpit), before it crashed on Corry Down in
Aberdeenshire. The non-RCAF members of crew were claimed by their relatives
while funeral services for the four Canadians were held at Lossiemouth Burial
Ground, Draine.

	30 OTU	Wellington III	BK359	—F		Transit

P/O H A Vernon RCAF   T/o Seighford with the intention of returning
to Hixon but as the Wellington accelerated, a
swing developed and upon leaving the runway a wing clipped a motor transport
vehicle. The bomber now headed for a group of civilians and P/O Vernon RCAF
tried desperately to get his aircraft into the air, but to no avail and it
finished up, wrecked, in the middle of No. 5 runway. Miraculously, no one
seems to have been badly hurt, though one of the civilians was admitted to
hospital with a badly lacerated leg.

27 Aug 1943	24 OTU	Whitley V	BD207 FB—P		Training

Sgt R M McKay RCAF   T/o 1228 Honeybourne for a flying detail which
ended in a forced-landing at 1243, following
engine failure.

27–28 Aug 1943	19 OTU A Flt	Whitley V	Z9469	—L		Training

S/L J M Kirkpatrick   T/o 2335 Kinloss for night dual instruction.
Sgt A Whittle   Crashed 0049 on high ground some 4 miles SW
Sgt T W Hanrahan   of the airfield and caught fire. It seems no
Sgt P Harper   one was badly hurt; subsequently, Sgt Whittle
became a prisoner of war.

28 Aug 1943	10 OTU	Whitley V	EB358		Training

Sgt H M Male   + T/o Abingdon for a night cross-country. It is
Sgt H Coupe   + strongly suspected that the Whitley exploded at
F/S J C Tucker RAAF   + approximately 0045, scattering debris over a
Sgt R F Higgs   + wide area some 2 miles S of Great Wilbraham,
Sgt E W Fitch   + five miles E from the centre of Cambridge. All
rest in various United Kingdom cemeteries.

29 Aug 1943	29 OTU	Wellington III	BK431	—J		Training

F/O J H Heath RNZAF   + T/o 1125 Bruntingthorpe for an air firing detail
W/O W J P Gibbons   + with a staff captain and screened wireless oper-
Sgt S Godson DFM   + ator, a gunnery instructor, an Air Training Corps
Sgt J A Fairhurst   + cadet passenger and three trainee air gunners.
Sgt V Graham   + Tragically, fifteen minutes after leaving base
Sgt L C Salmon   + the bolts securing the lower port wing spar
Cdt J D Woodward ATC   + failed (due to metal fatigue) and the Wellington
hurtled into the ground near Oakham. F/O Heath,
whose parents had originated from Lincolnshire, was taken to his birthplace and
laid to rest in Cleethorpes Cemetery. His crew were claimed by their relatives
and it is noted that the sixteen year old air cadet belonged to 1434 Squadron.
Sgt Godson, the gunnery instructor, had recently arrived from 50 Squadron and
details of his award had been Gazetted as recently as 17 August. It is further
noted that F/O Heath RNZAF, who had flown a tour of operations in the Middle East
with 37 Squadron, had been involved in a serious accident on 22 July 1943, after
which his Wellington X HZ412 needed extensive repairs. W/O Gibbons, too, had
been involved in a previous training accident (see page 52).

30 Aug 1943	82 OTU	Wellington X	HE632		Training

Sgt A N Stockdale DFM   T/o 0030 Bircotes with a screened pilot and
Sgt Fisher   pupil with the intention of carrying out a night
check dual. As the bomber gathered speed, a
swing developed and before this could be corrected the Wellington came off the
runway and crashed. Sgt Stockdale had not long since returned from the Middle
East where he had served with great distinction with 70 Squadron, details of
his DFM being published in the London Gazette on 6 July 1943.

30-31 Aug   **26 OTU**   **Wellington X**   **HE500**   **Op: Special Task**
1943

Sgt K Knaggs	+
P/O R R F Durne	+
Sgt L M Lewis	+
Sgt P R Hogan	+
Sgt C Hayhurst	+
Sgt E Pursell	+

T/o Wing to bomb an ammunition dump in the Fôret d'Eperlecques N of St-Omer. Crashed at Rubrouck in the Department of Nord, 10 km NW of Cassel. P/O Burne is buried in Rubrouck Churchyard, while his five companions rest in Longuenesse (St-Omer) Souvenir Cemetery.

29 OTU   **Wellington III**   **BJ967**   **-F**   **Op: Special Task**

Sgt T A Wilder	+
Sgt A D Trotter	+
Sgt J Scott	+
Sgt A W Raggett	+
F/S A J Oakes	+
Sgt W H McDonald RAAF	+

T/o 2105 Bruntingthorpe similarly tasked. Ditched at approximately 2230, following a fire in the starboard engine, off Newhaven, Sussex. Only the pilot managed to get into the aircraft's dinghy and he was picked up at around 1030 on 31 August by an Air-Sea Rescue Walrus II HD908, captained by Sgt T Fletcher, and taken into Newhaven. His less fortunate crew are commemorated on the Runnymede Memorial. For further details of this dramatic rescue and other such similar stories, readers are urged to consult 'Another Kind of Courage' by Norman Franks and published by Patrick Stephens Ltd in 1994.

31 Aug   **16 OTU**   **Wellington III**   **BK263**   **Training**
1943   Sgt J P Dalton   T/o 0003 Upper Heyford but soon after becoming airborne an engine cut and the bomber was crash-landed at 0018, wheels retracted, near the airfield. Inadvertently, a member of the ground crew had isolated the port rear tank battery.

22 OTU   **Wellington X**   **HE556**   **Training**

Sgt C A Larson RCAF	inj
Sgt M Minett RCAF	inj

T/o Gaydon for a training exercise. Crashed and caught fire at Honeybourne airfield, where both of the injured were treated in the Station's Sick Quarters. On 26 February 1944, Sgt Minett's 419 Squadron Halifax failed to return from a gardening sortie in the direction of Kiel Bay (see Bomber Command Losses, Volume 5, page 106).

1 Sep   **18 OTU**   **Wellington III**   **BK445**   **Training**
1943

Sgt V H Wigmore	+
Sgt H Dean	+

T/o 1135 Finningley for a navigation exercise. During the flight, the fabric began peeling away from the mainplanes and the order to bale out was given. Sadly, only three were able to comply before the Wellington hit the ground at 1255 near West Feldom, NW of Richmond, Yorkshire. Sgt Wigmore rests in Highgate Cemetery, St. Pancras, Sgt Dean lies in Burton-upon-Trent Cemetery.

30 OTU   **Wellington X**   **HE222**   **-O**   **Training**
F/O F A Whitehead   T/o 2125 Hixon for a night navigation sortie. Partially abandoned, as ordered, after first the starboard and then the port engines lost power. F/O Whitehead then gamely tried to reach Seighford but his aircraft came down at 2230 near Lawrence Farm between Bishop's Offley and Eccleshall, 12 miles SSW of Stoke-on-Trent, Staffordshire.

2 Sep   **11 OTU**   **Wellington IC**   **R1451 TX-O**   **Training**
1943

F/S S G Rickersey RAAF	+
Sgt F W Nixon	+
P/O S M Johnston RAAF	+
F/S K G Fitzgerald RAAF	+
Sgt R J Clifford RAAF	+

T/o Westcott for a bombing exercise. Crashed at 2145 twixt Knightsbridge Farm and Model Farm to the N of Pyrton, a small village less than a mile N of Watlington, Oxfordshire. The four RAAF members of crew are buried in Oxford (Botley) Cemetery, while Sgt Nixon was taken to Northern Ireland and laid to rest in Galloon (St. Comgall) Church of Ireland Churchyard, Newtown Butler. Their aircraft had flown a total of 740.45 hours.

28 OTU   **Wellington IC**   **Z8870**   **Training**
Sgt J Rouse   T/o 2215 Wymeswold to practice night circuits and landings. After fifteen minutes of flying, Sgt Rouse discovered he was unable to lower the flaps and, thus, he forced-landed on the airfield with the undercarriage still retracted. Originally, the Wellington was thought to be repairable, but an inspection on 8 September consigned the bomber for scrap. Subsequently, this order was cancelled but was re-instated on 1 March 1944. However, it was not until 1 June 1944 that the airframe was officially removed from charge.

2 Sep	81 OTU	Whitley V	AD679		Training

2 Sep   **81 OTU**   **Whitley V**   **AD679**   **Training**
1943
Sgt W Hall   +   T/o 2015 Sleap in the company of eight other
Sgt A L Culley   +   aircraft, all tasked for a Bullseye exercise.
Sgt W Harrison   +   Two hours later, the bomber flew into the ground
Sgt I F W Pead   +   at Finch Lane, Bushey, Hertfordshire and burst
Sgt A C Strolin   +   into flames. All were taken to their home towns
                            for burial. It is thought the pilot became so
dazzled, when caught in searchlights, that in taking evasive action he exceeded
the safe limitations of the mainplanes.

2– 3 Sep   **22 OTU**   **Wellington III**   **HF645**   **Op: Special Task**
1943
P/O W I St. Johns RCAF   +   T/o 2204 Gaydon along with other aircraft drawn
P/O D C McDougall RCAF   inj   from the training units, and supported by PFF, to
Sgt L R G Dent RCAF   inj   bomb ammunition dumps in the Forêt de Raismes.
F/S W H Allan RCAF   +   While homebound at 17,000 feet, the port engine
F/O R W Wolfe RCAF   +   caught fire. While trying to extinguish the
                            blaze, control was lost and the bomber spun in
near Wantage in Berkshire. Those who perished were brought to Stratford-upon-
Avon Cemetery. P/O St. Johns RCAF and F/O Wolfe RCAF were Americans, the former
from Los Angeles and the latter from McCleary, Washington.

3 Sep   **16 OTU**   **Wellington III**   **BK264**   **Training**
1943
Sgt E W Hallett   T/o 2000 Upper Heyford for a Bullseye sortie.
Sgt Iliffe   inj   When the port engine failed, fifty minutes into
Sgt Nicholson   inj   the detail, the crew were ordered to bale out.
Sgt G J Clark   inj   Sgt Hallett then skillfully forced-landed the
                            Wellington on the Ot Moor ranges, NE of Oxford.
Sgt Clark was admitted to hospital having fractured one of his legs.

30 OTU   **Wellington III**   **X3564**   **–U**   **Training**
WO2 J W Chester RCAF   +   T/o Hixon for a night navigation flight. While
F/S G A Innes RCAF   +   over the Irish Sea, the port engine failed and
Sgt D G D Burnside RCAF   +   the crew headed for Jurby airfield on the Isle
Sgt L J Thorpe   +   of Man. With the runway in sight, the bomber
Sgt A R J Le Page RCAF   +   flew into the side of a cliff, roughly a mile
                            west of the airfield. The four Canadians were
buried in Jurby (St. Patrick) Churchyard, while Sgt Thorpe was taken back to
Werrington (St. John The Baptist) Churchyard, Peterborough. It can only be
assumed that the pilot lost his bearings at the crucial stage of his approach,
thereby losing control.

3– 4 Sep   **24 OTU**   **Whitley V**   **BD368**   **Op: Nickel**
F/S W W Massie RCAF   pow   T/o Honeybourne in the company of three other
F/S W J Prause RCAF   pow   aircraft and set course for the Orleans area of
Sgt R G Gillham RCAF   pow   France.
WO2 G P Halverson RCAF   pow
Sgt T O Mackay RCAF   pow

4 Sep   **22 OTU**   **Wellington III**   **HF683**   **Training**
1943
Sgt J G Stinson RCAF   T/o 2125 Gaydon for night circuits and landings
                            but veered from the runway and smashed its main
                            undercarriage.

23 OTU   **Wellington III**   **Z1739**   **Training**
Sgt W R Stewart RCAF   T/o 0010 Pershore for night circuit training.
P/O J C Hall RCAF   Five good circuits were flown but as the crew
F/S W H Wardell RCAF   prepared to go round again, the port engine cut.
Sgt W R Goodhue RCAF   inj   Seconds later, the bomber crashed through the
                            perimeter hedge and was damaged beyond repair.
Sgt Goodhue RCAF was taken to the local Station Sick Quarters, where he received
attention for quite severe lacerations to his forehead.

27 OTU   **Wellington III**   **X3727**   **Training**
F/S J E Richards RAAF   T/o 1844 Church Broughton for a night exercise.
                            On return to base, the flaps failed to fully
lower and on touch down at 2359 their difficulties were further exacerbated by
engine failure. Crashed and burnt out. Posted to 466 Squadron, F/S Richards
was killed during operations to Frankfurt in March 1944 (see Bomber Command
Losses, Volume 5, page 121).

5 Sep   **20 OTU A Flt**   **Wellington X**   **HE467**   **-N**   **Training**
1943   P/O D R Moon DFM   +   T/o 2132 Elgin but an engine cut and a minute
        Sgt S J Richardson   +   later the Wellington plunged into the ground,
        Sgt H E Rolfe   +   near the airfield, and exploded in flames. Two,
        Sgt T A Walkden   +   Sgt Richardson and Sgt Rolfe, were buried locally
        Sgt W E F Lavender   +   in Lossiemouth Burial Ground, while the others
        Sgt M P De Sachy   +   were claimed by their next of kin. P/O Moon had
                                            completed a tour of operations in the Middle East
with 148 Squadron, his DFM having been published on 5 February 1943.

        24 OTU   **Whitley V**   **Training**
        Sgt Kerr   T/o Honeybourne along with ten other aircraft,
                                            all tasked to carry out a Bullseye exercise.
While over South Wales, the starboard engine commenced misfiring and course was
set for Haverfordwest airfield in Pembrokeshire. On arrival here, a forced-
landing was made, which damaged the bomber beyond economical repair. According
to unit records, the serial was Z9314, but this is not supported by the entries
on Air Ministry Form 78.

        30 OTU   **Wellington III**   **Z1720**   **-M**   **Training**
        Sgt W Newton   +   T/o Hixon for a navigation exercise. Ditched
        Sgt J Dale   +   at 0832 off Aberdeen, the distance being quoted
                                            as 29 miles. The three survivors were picked
up at 2100 that same day. From their statements, it was deduced that weather
conditions along the route worsened and such was the static on the various radio
frequencies, no aid from this quarter was forthcoming. Thus, uncertain of his
position, it can only be assumed Sgt Newton considered ditching his best course
of action. Along with Sgt Dale, he is commemorated on the Runnymede Memorial.

5- 6 Sep   **29 OTU**   **Wellington III**   **BK442**   **Training**
1943   F/S I C Bertram RAAF   T/o 2354 Bitteswell for a night exercise. Landed
                                            at 0034, wheels up and with the starboard engine
on fire, in a field near the airfield. During April 1944, while flying Lancasters
with 115 Squadron, Sgt Bertram RAAF became a prisoner of war (see Bomber Command
Losses, Volume 5, page 175).

7 Sep   **81 OTU**   **Whitley V**   **BD257**   **-N**   **Training**
1943   F/O R W Browne   +   T/o 0020 Sleap but swung out of control and
        F/O E L Ware RCAF   +   travelling at high speed smashed into the control
        Sgt W D Kershaw   +   tower. On impact, the bomber exploded in a mass
        Sgt E Young   +   of smoke and flame. F/O Browne, the son of Major
        Sgt S Williams   inj   Theophilus Coxon Browne and Ethel May Browne of
                                            Rietandale in the Transvaal and F/O Ware RCAF
        Cpl N W Peate   +   are buried in Chester (Blacon) Cemetery. The
        ACW2 K M Ffoukles WAAF   +   others who died, including members of the control
        ACW2 V Hughes WAAF   +   tower staff, are buried in various cemeteries
        LACW A B Jowett WAAF   inj   across the country. Sgt Williams and the two
        ACW2 H Hall WAAF   inj   WAAFs, both of whom were from the station's
                                            meteorology section, were rushed to RAF Hospital
Cosford with severe burns. It will be recalled that as recently as 25-26 August,
an accident of similar nature had befallen the airfield control staff at Sleap
(see page 243), though on that occasion the outcome had not been so tragic.

7- 8 Sep   **12 OTU**   **Wellington III**   **BJ621**   **Training**
1943   Sgt W Shepherd   +   T/o 2153 Chipping Warden for a night navigation
        Sgt F G Wells   +   detail. Crashed 0030, with considerable force,
        Sgt G D H Morrow RCAF   +   at Eudon Mill near Bridgnorth, Shropshire. The
        Sgt W H Lawrence   +   two Commonwealth airmen and Sgt Lawrence lie in
        Sgt N L Wachter RAAF   +   Chester (Blacon) Cemetery, while the Runnymede
                                            Memorial perpetuates the names of Sgt Shepherd
                                            and Sgt Wells.

        29 OTU   **Wellington III**   **BK497**   **-O**   **Training**
        P/O G E Bilke   +   T/o Bruntingthorpe similarly instructed. Came
        Sgt J Baxter   +   down in the sea off the Pembrokeshire coast.
        F/S G D Scott RCAF   +   The two RCAF members of crew and Sgt Shephard
        Sgt C W Shephard   +   rest in Bath (Haycombe) Cemetery, the others
        Sgt G W J Hopkins RCAF   +   have no known graves.

8 Sep   **20 OTU**   **Wellington III** **HZ131**   **Ground**
1943   While having its oxygen supply replenished,
at Milltown, an explosion occurred and the bomber was wrecked.

9 Sep   **16 OTU**   **Wellington III** **DF668**   **Ground**
1943   At 0910, while undergoing a 50-hour (some
reports say a 100-hour) maintenance check at Barford St. John, petrol in a
drip tray ignited and set fire to the aircraft. At the Court of Inquiry, it
was mooted that a metal object may have fallen into the tray, causing a spark.

10 Sep   **27 OTU**   **Wellington III** **BK152**   **Training**
1943   F/O N G Stewart DFM RAAF   + T/o 2144 Lichfield for night dual circuits and
      F/S D J Fernance RAAF   + landings. At around 2245, the Wellington came
      Sgt E N Death RAAF   + into land on the Hixon runway but touched down
      F/S F C Stringer RAAF   + too far along the strip. The throttles were
      P/O T F Swinney RAAF   + opened and the bomber began to climb until,
      F/S A J Vickerman RAAF   + without any hint of trouble, it dived into a
                                   house less than a mile SW of the airfield. It
is thought likely that the flaps were raised in error for the undercarriage.
All are buried in Chester (Blacon) Cemetery. F/O Stewart RAAF had served in
the Middle East, gaining his award during a tour with 148 Squadron. Details
of this were published in the London Gazette on 16 February 1943.

11 Sep   **24 OTU**   **Whitley V** **LA786 FB-Z**   **Training**
1943   Sgt R V Long RCAF   T/o 2018 Long Marston but failed to become
      Sgt Cavanagh RCAF   inj airborne and at high speed ran off the runway
                                and ended up in a field. Sgt Cavanagh RCAF
was very seriously hurt, being admitted to hospital with a fractured spine.

13 Sep   **12 OTU**   **Wellington III** **BJ664**   **Training**
1943   F/L J E Fairchild   + T/o Chipping Warden for a navigation exercise.
      Sgt C S Walters   + At approximately 1545, the Wellington flew into
      F/L R T Bowen   + the vicinity of a violent thunderstorm. In the
      Sgt E Gates   + turbulent air, control was lost and the bomber
      Sgt E A Opie RCAF   + hurtled into the ground, W of the Craven Arms,
      F/S B Green   + near Aston on Clun, 9 miles NW of Ludlow in
      Sgt E Davies   + Shropshire. Four, including Sgt Opie RCAF,
      Sgt T Johnston   + were taken to Chester (Blacon) Cemetery and
                                  four were claimed by their next of kin. The
father of Sgt Gates, Harry Gates, held the Distinguished Conduct Medal.

14 Sep   **27 OTU**   **Wellington III** **BJ901**   **Air Test**
1943   Sgt E Hourigan RAAF   T/o 1508 Church Broughton for a pre-night
                                flying test. Returned to base thirty minutes
later but held off too high and bounced on landing. On its next arrival, the
Wellington promptly ground looped and ran through a hedge.

16 Sep   **14 OTU**   **Wellington IC** **L7897**   **Training**
1943   Sgt G G Runnals   T/o 1008 Husbands Bosworth for local flying.
                                Shortly before 1033, the air bomber reported
over the intercom that a cylinder head had just blown off and as he finished
his call a rather shaken navigator announced that the unit had come through the
side of the aircraft, narrowly missing him in the process. Unable to maintain
height, Sgt Runnals forced-landed about 2 miles S of the airfield. As the crew
scrambled to safety, the Wellington caught fire.

              14 OTU   **Wellington IC** **DV479**   **Training**
              Sgt K W McEweeney RAAF   T/o 1705 Husbands Bosworth for a cross-country.
                                        Landed at Welford in Berkshire but bounced quite
hard and an attempt was made to go round again. However, having lifted off the
runway, the bomber lost height and crashed 1840 near Welford Home Farm.

17 Sep   **10 OTU**   **Whitley V** **Z9471**   **Training**
1943   F/O M W Moore   + T/o 2348 Stanton Harcourt for a Bullseye detail
      Sgt H E Scarborough   + only to collide with another of unit's aircraft
      Sgt J G Boundy   + when some two miles SE of the airfield. Burials
      Sgt K C Blanch   + from both crews took place at Oxford (Botley)
      Sgt J R Grimmond   + Cemetery and at other locations around the
                                United Kingdom.

17 Sep 1943	**10 OTU** F/O L A Buck F/O B E Brown RCAF F/O J Gibson Sgt J D Arthur Sgt G W Clements	**Whitley V** + + + + +	**LA879**		**Training**

T/o 2350 Stanton Harcourt similarly tasked and lost in the manner described at the foot of the previous page. F/O Brown RCAF was the foster-son and nephew of Mrs U S Boisclair of Chicago.

	11 OTU Sgt A L Dickson RNZAF P/O Wilkes Sgt Anstruther	**Wellington IC** inj inj inj	**DV608 TX-R**	**Training**

T/o 1018 Oakley but at 150 feet the starboard engine cut. Sgt Dickson RNZAF made a valiant effort to fly round the circuit but two minutes later he struck high ground near the village of Brill. Sgt Anstruther was admitted to the Princess Mary's Hospital at Halton.

17-18 Sep 1943	**17 OTU** F/S N N Dunn RAAF Sgt J Donnachie P/O H Farrer RCAF Sgt R E Dolling Sgt J W Hallam Sgt H A Newnham RAAF	**Wellington X** + + + + + +	**HE324**	**Training**

T/o 2325 Silverstone for a night cross-country. Lost control, while in cloud, and crashed 0054 at East Burton Farm near Horwood, 5 miles SW from Barnstaple, Devon. Funeral arrangements for the three Commonwealth members of crew were handled by RAF Chivenor and their graves are located in Heaton Punchardon (St. Augustine) Churchyard. Sgt Donnachie was taken to Scotland and Cambusnethan Cemetery, Motherwell and Wishaw, while Welsh born Sgt Dolling rests in Llanelli Church Cemetery. Sgt Hallam is buried in Beeston and Stapleford (Beeston) Cemetery.

18 Sep 1943	**15 OTU** Sgt H P G Harris Sgt E D Huntley Sgt E J Cooke	**Wellington IC** + + +	**HX367**	**Training**

T/o Hampstead Norris for dusk solo circuits and landings. Crashed 2045 on high ground at Home Farm, a little under 2 miles SE of Pangbourne and, likely, near the western outskirts of Reading, Berkshire. Sgt Harris is thought to have emigrated to South Africa but had joined the Volunteer Reserve, his parents being noted as living in Chester. He is buried at Oxford (Botley) Cemetery, while the others rest in their home towns. At the Court of Inquiry, it was stated that the crew had been given permission to land, by Aldis lamp signal, but having acknowledged seemed to lose sight of the flare path.

21 Sep 1943	**24 OTU** Sgt G F Fielding RCAF	**Whitley V**	**AD697 TY-J**	**Training**

T/o Honeybourne as part of an eight strong force detailed for a Bullseye exercise. On nearing London, all were recalled (due to reports of enemy aircraft operating over the capital) and soon after turning back, Sgt Fielding RCAF called to say he was losing glycol from one of his engines. At circa 2300, he tried to land at Denham airfield in Buckinghamshire but overshot the runway and crashed. Later commissioned, Sgt Fielding RCAF was posted to 433 Squadron but was made a prisoner of war in the aftermath of the Schweinfurt raid in February 1944 (see Bomber Command Losses, Volume 5, pages 97 to 101). Very sadly, on his release from captivity and having returned to Canada, he died on 1 June 1945. He is buried in Nanaimo Cemetery in British Columbia.

21-22 Sep 1943	**12 OTU** Sgt R P Giles RAAF	**Wellington III**	**X3747**	**Training**

T/o 1950 Chipping Warden for a night navigation exercise. Returned to base at 0005, but overshot the runway and soon after crash-landed near Byfield, Northamptonshire, a village just over the border with Oxfordshire and about 9 miles NNE of Banbury. For most of the sortie the crew had experienced intermittent engine problems.

	12 OTU F/S K L Hart RAAF F/S W N Gould RCAF F/S L Sillito RCAF Sgt W G Denyer Sgt K Mackenzie Sgt R Cave	**Wellington III** + + + + + +	**BK200**	**-A**	**Training**

T/o 1950 Chipping Warden similarly tasked. On return to base at 0030, overshot the flare path and crashed in line with the runway. Four are buried in Banbury Cemetery, Sgt Denyer lies in Battersea (Morden) Cemetery, Merton and Morden, while Sgt Mackenzie was taken back to the Outer Hebrides where his funeral was held in Sandwick Cemetery, Stornoway on the Isle of Lewis.

22 Sep   **18 OTU**   **Wellington III**   **BK493**   **Training**
1943   P/O H C Jenner   T/o Finningley for a demonstration in feathering
         Sgt R Botham   inj   procedures. Lost power and wrecked 1547 in an
emergency, wheels up, landing at base having come
in too fast and with only fifteen degrees of flap selected.

         83 OTU   **Wellington X**   **LN530**   **Training**
         Sgt D L Spence   +   T/o Peplow but soon after becoming airborne the
         P/O A M McBride   +   starboard engine failed and the Wellington came
                                   inj   down at 1030 near Ellerton Hall, Sambrook, some
                                   inj   sixteen miles NE from the centre of Shrewsbury.
                                   inj   Sgt Spence is buried in Renfrew (Arkleston)
Cemetery, while P/O McBride, a fellow Scot,
lies in Dalziel (Airbles) Cemetery. Eyewitnesses state that the pilot seemed
to lose control as he tried to avoid flying into trees. This was the unit's
first serious accident and only its second since forming on 1 August 1943 (the
previous mishap occurring on 19 September and involving Sgt A Guilfoyle and
Wellington X HE830).

22-23 Sep   **11 OTU**   **Wellington IC**   **DV815 OP-E**   **Training**
1943   F/S A C Peake RAAF   inj   T/o 1956 Westcott for a night navigation sortie.
         Sgt F J Smith RAAF   inj   On return to base, F/S Peake RAAF spotted another
         Sgt K V A Holmes RNZAF   +   aircraft on the runway and elected to overshoot.
         Sgt H E C Nash   inj   While making a climbing turn to starboard, he
         Sgt E W Stafford   lost control at around 250 feet and crashed 0048
onto a wooded hillside, about a mile SE of the
airfield and not far from Waddesdon Manor. On impact, the aircraft caught fire.
Sgt Holmes RNZAF was laid to rest in Oxford (Botley) Cemetery. A record of the
"Proceedings of Court of Inquiry or Investigation" (RAF Form 412), which opened
on 25 September 1943 (kindly loaned by Errol W Martyn), shows that W/C C Gardner
of Headquarters Bomber Command was appointed President and F/L E Mirfin of 11 OTU
attended as a Member. Twelve witnesses were called, their ranks ranging between
Squadron Leader and Leading Aircraft Woman. The report runs to four pages and
was compiled, from the evidence, twixt 9 and 27 October 1943.

23 Sep   **15 OTU**   **Wellington IC**   **R1325**   **Training**
1943   W/O A H Johnson   +   T/o 1939 Harwell and while circling lost height
         F/O J E Leveroni   +   and crashed 1945 at Aldfield Farm , within the
         F/O J Suffield   +   circuit, and a mile SE of the village of East
         Sgt D S McDonald-Hunter   +   Hendred, Berkshire, bursting into flames. Of
         Sgt O Hunt   +   those who perished, F/O Leveroni of Glenageary,
         Sgt B Larkin   inj   Dublin, rests in Oxford (Botley) Cemetery, Sgt
McDonald-Hunter was buried at Harwell Cemetery
while the others were claimed by relatives. This Wellington had seen extensive
service with various OTUs and had logged a quite impressive 1204.25 flying hours.

         28 OTU   **Wellington IC**   **DV511**   **Ground**
                                           At around 0830, while parked in a hangar at
Wymeswold, a pedestal lamp was knocked over and fell into a drip tray. On
hitting the tray, the filament burst setting light to fuel residues. Before
any fire extinguishers could be brought to bear, the aircraft was well and
truly alight. Including flying with previous units, the Wellington (which had
been accepted on 20 August 1942) had amassed 1,018.50 flying hours.

         82 OTU B Flt   **Wellington X**   **HE265**   **-Y**   **Training**
         F/L W A Meyer DFC   inj   T/o 0957 Ossington with a No. 6 course crew.
         Sgt A G S Watkins   inj   While flying over Lincolnshire, the port engine
         Sgt J W Eunson   inj   began to misfire and it was decided to shut the
         Sgt W J Saxby   inj   motor down, feather the propeller, and head for
Skellingthorpe. These actions were successfully
accomplished at 1,500 feet and the undercarriage was pumped down, manually. On
nearing the runway, however, Flying Control fired off a red Verey flare as the
Wellington was erroneously approaching from downwind. F/L Meyer tried to overshoot but stalled and hit the ground at 1027, the impact soon being followed by
a fire. Posted to 97 Squadron, he was killed while on operations in March 1944
(see Bomber Command Losses, Volume 5, page 112). If, as is believed, Sgt Watkins
was commissioned, then he was lost on 13 September 1944 (with 166 Squadron) while
visiting Frankfurt (see the same volume, page 419).

23–24 Sep   **27 OTU**   **Wellington III**   **X3966**   **Op: Nickel**
1943   F/S G L Dowling RAAF   evd   T/o 1900 Lichfield and set course for the Orleans
        P/O W C Hawke RAAF   evd   region. Outbound, and while in the vicinity of
        Sgt E J Anderson RAAF   evd   Rouen, the crew observed two fighters, some way
        Sgt W Todd   evd   off and on the port side. Approximately ten
        Sgt F J Page   evd   minutes later, the Wellington was hit several
                                               times by flak. The enemy colours of the day
were fired, but the flak continued and further damage was caused. All leaflets
were jettisoned and after much difficulty, F/S Dowling RAAF was able to turn his
aircraft towards home. Fuel, however, was being lost at an alarming rate and a
strong smell of petrol was present inside the fuselage. With the gauges reading
almost zero, the order to bale out was given. All departed safely, landing near
Beauvais in the Department of Oise. In the summer of 1944, F/S Dowling RAAF was
posted to 76 Squadron and successfully completed an operational tour. His
favourite Halifax III was MZ516 MP-V 'Vera the Virgin' which, eventually, was lost
on 1-2 February 1945 (see Bomber Command Losses, Volume 6, page 57).

24 Sep   **22 OTU**   **Wellington III**   **DF634**   **Training**
1943   F/S G W Horborenko RCAF   T/o Gaydon for a cross-country. During the
        Sgt R F Guerrier RCAF   flight problems with the port engine were
                                               experienced. On regaining base at 1215, the
bomber was landed in almost zero wind conditions and, thus, it ran into the
overshoot area and was wrecked.

25 Sep   **14 OTU**   **Wellington IC**   **X9871**   **Training**
1943   Sgt S E Martin   T/o 0013 Market Harborough but due to premature
                                               retraction of the flaps, the bomber sank and hit
the ground. On 1 February 1944, Sgt Martin lost his life and he is buried in
Harrow (Harrow Weald) Cemetery.

        29 OTU   **Wellington X**   **JA448**   **Training**
        Sgt H J Wolff   +   T/o 0132 Bruntingthorpe for a night exercise but
        Sgt W D Gibby   +   before gaining sufficient height, the pilot began
        Sgt E S Smart   +   banking steeply. While doing so, the nose of the
        Sgt R R Townsend   +   aircraft dropped and at 0138 it plunged into a
        Sgt C A Farrell   +   field at Walton, 4 miles ENE of Lutterworth in
        Sgt G Meyrick   +   Leicestershire. Sgt Smart of Brixton was taken
        Sgt J Whitaker   +   to Oxford (Botley) Cemetery, while the rest were
                                               claimed by their next of kin.

26 Sep   **11 OTU**   **Wellington IC**   **T2884 OP-L**   **Training**
1943   Sgt J Dunman   T/o Westcott for a night cross-country, during
        Sgt H G Bright   +   which the starboard engine failed. For a while
                                               Sgt Dunman was able to maintain altitude, but
when at 2240 the lower cylinders partially detached from the port motor, he had
no option but to order everyone to bale out. Sadly, Sgt Bright (the tail gunner)
failed to leave the aircraft and his body was found amongst the wreckage at Park
Ground Farm, Castle Bytham, 12 miles SSE from Grantham, Lincolnshire. He rests
in Christchurch Cemetery.

        14 OTU   **Wellington IC**   **DV697**   **Training**
        F/S J W Woods RAAF   +   T/o 1504 Husbands Bosworth for a training detail.
        Sgt I W Ferguson   +   When the port engine developed a fault, the crew
        Sgt J M M Fraser RAAF   +   returned to base, approaching the runway from the
        P/O F P Moorby   +   downwind direction, Realising his mistake, the
                                               pilot opened up to go round again but at 600 feet
with the flaps and undercarriage fully extended, the bomber swung out of control
and crashed 1705, bursting into flames. Both Australians and Sgt Ferguson lie in
Oxford (Botley) Cemetery, while P/O Moorby is interred at Barton-under-Needwood
(St. James) Churchyard in Staffordshire.

        24 OTU   **Whitley V**   **Z9428**   **Training**
        F/S G M L'Hommedieu RCAF   +   T/o 1914 Honeybourne for a Bullseye exercise.
        Sgt W C Reid RCAF   +   Crashed 1945 near Stoke Orchard, 4 miles NNE of
        P/O R H O Mellor RCAF   +   Cheltenham, Gloucestershire. Three rest in Bath
        Sgt A V Andrews   +   (Haycombe) Cemetery, while Sgt Andrews and Sgt
        Sgt R B Morgan   +   Morgan lie in cemeteries in Scotland and Wales.
                                               Their skipper came from Sea Cliff, New York.

27 Sep 1943	**18 OTU**	**Wellington III**	**BJ645**	**Training**

F/O C Gozdz PAF   +   T/o Finningley for, it is believed, an exercise
Sgt S J Majewski PAF   +   in feathering procedures for at the Court of
Sgt J Duchaczek PAF   inj   Inquiry into the crash, which occurred at 1605
F/S E Formaniewicz PAF   +   at Everton, 7 miles NNW from Retford, it emerged
Sgt S L Piorek PAF   +   that the instructor had ordered his pupil to
feather the port airscrew. This he did, but
almost immediately the starboard engine cut. The effect of this sent the bomber
into a steep dive and it is thought the instructor lost control as he attempted
to restart the port engine. Those who died are buried in the Polish Plot at
Newark-upon-Trent Cemetery.

	19 OTU A Flt	**Whitley V**	**LA853 –D**	**Training**

Sgt D T W Cammies   +   T/o Kinloss for a cross-country detail. Crashed
Sgt E R Rogers   +   at approximately 0720 and burst into flames near
Sgt C A Hughes   +   Dishforth airfield in Yorkshire. Sgt Cammies is
Sgt J W Wallace RCAF   +   commemorated on the Runnymede Memorial; his crew
Sgt W S Robinson   +   rest in cemeteries both in England and Scotland.
Sgt R C Fowler   +   News of the accident was signalled to Kinloss
Sgt H Dickson   +   from No. 13 Group Inverness.

28–29 Sep 1943	**16 OTU**	**Wellington X**	**LN532 –V**	**Training**

Sgt R G Lees   +   T/o 2025 Upper Heyford for a Bullseye detail,
Sgt G Pearson   +   base-Worcester-Calne-VU4535-Poole-WQ225701-
F/S W F C Wisdom   +   Westminster Bridge-Conway-Peterborough-base.
Sgt N F Paice   +   Broke cloud, base 800 to 900 feet, and flew into
Sgt J E Frazer RAAF   +   the ground at around 0100 near Whittlebury Wood,
Whittlebury, 3 miles S of Towcester, Northampton-
shire. Sgt Paice and Sgt Frazer RAAF were buried in Oxford (Botley) Cemetery,
while their three companions were taken to their home towns.

	17 OTU	**Wellington X**	**HF600**	**Training**

Sgt E Atkinson   +   T/o 2020 Turweston for a Bullseye exercise. Lost
Sgt G E Cozens   +   control while orbiting a beacon and dived into
Sgt C G Braund   +   the ground at 0115, twixt 1 and 2 miles W from
Sgt K B Roberts   +   Wappenham, 13 miles SW of Northampton. Two, Sgt
Sgt A B Shanks RCAF   +   Roberts and Sgt Shanks RCAF lie in Oxford (Botley)
Sgt D Crosland   +   Cemetery, while the others were claimed by their
next of kin. Sgt Braund's mother had an unusual
first Christian name, Pretoria.

29 Sep 1943	**11 OTU D Flt**	**Wellington IC**	**W5724 , –C**	**Training**

F/S R F Hall RNZAF   inj   T/o Westcott for a cross-country detail but
Sgt Glover   inj   after encountering adverse weather on the route,
Sgt Scott   inj   the crew decided to terminate the sortie. Flying
Sgt J M Underwood RNZAF inj   at 2,000 feet, in cloud, the port engine began
Sgt W J Southern   inj   to misfire and soon afterwards flames could be
Sgt W H Evans RCAF   inj   seen spreading across the surfaces of the wing.
Skillfully, F/S Hall RNZAF set the Wellington
down, circa 1350, in a field at Harepath Farm, just to the W of Allington on the
Devizes to Alton Barnes road in Wiltshire. Sadly, Sgt Underwood RNZAF and Sgt
Evans RCAF died within a few hours of the accident and both are buried in Bath
(Haycombe) Cemetery. Sgt Southern, too, succumbed to his injuries within 24-
hours and he was taken to Ellesmere Port (Overpool) Cemetery. Interestingly,
unit records refer to the port engine, while other documents mention failure
of No. 6 cylinder on the starboard motor as a factor in this accident. The
Wellington had logged a total of 852.45 flying hours.

2 Oct 1943	**15 OTU**	**Wellington X**	**LN497**	**Training**

Sgt P M Lay   +   T/o 1101 Hampstead Norris for a cross-country.
Sgt K T Creamer   +   Ran into poor weather and in steadily worsening
Sgt L Nichol   +   visibility crashed 1226 into the side of a hill
Sgt D Postlethwaite   +   on Swindhope Common near Westgate, 16 miles SW
Sgt T B Churn   +   of Consett, Durham. Sgt Creamer of Edgeware in
P/O J R Brannan   +   Middlesex was taken to Harrogate (Stonefall)
Cemetery, while the rest are buried in their
home towns. It is thought likely the pilot was trying to establish his position.
In contrast to the previous bomber, Sgt Lay's aircraft had flown 15.50 hours.

2 Oct 1943	23 OTU	Wellington III	X3470	-D		Training

P/O W H Fuller RCAF + T/o 1937 Pershore for a night training exercise.
Sgt L A Pinchess RCAF + At 2135 the direction finding station at Sealand
F/O F J S Guppy RCAF + transmitted a fix and at the time the Wellington
F/O A F Bell RCAF + was more or less on course for its turning point
Sgt L Hockey + at the Skerries. Nothing further was heard, but
Sgt A J Copegog RCAF + the crew of another aircraft, operating off the
Pembrokeshire coast, report seeing a Wellington
falling into the sea. This crew immediately commenced searching for possible
survivors, but were unsuccessful. All are commemorated on the Runnymede Memorial.

23 OTU	Wellington III	Z1648		Training

Sgt F H Partridge RCAF + T/o 1617 Stratford-upon-Avon but it is believed
F/O J B J de Macedo RCAF inj the constant speed unit on the port engine
Sgt J W Dufton RCAF inj failed, jamming the propeller in fine pitch.
Sgt Partridge RCAF managed to fly round the
circuit but was slightly off line with his approach. While attempting to go
round again, with the unserviceable motor stopped, he lost height and crashed
at 1625, near the airfield. F/O de Macedo RCAF lost a leg and he died at 0400
the next day in Stratford-upon-Avon Hospital. Along with his skipper, he rests
in Pershore Cemetery. Sgt Dufton RCAF escaped relatively unscathed.

23 OTU	Wellington III	BJ667		Training

Sgt W R Stewart RCAF T/o 1840 Stratford-upon-Avon carrying 5 x 500lb
sand filled bombs. Soon after departing, the
port engine cut and the bombs were jettisoned. A strenuous effort was made to
pump the undercarriage down but on landing at 1925 the unit collapsed.

2- 3 Oct 1943	18 OTU	Wellington X	LN545		Training

F/S J Nalepa PAF T/o 1915 Finningley for a Bullseye sortie.
Crashed 0100 into a field some 3 miles E of the
airfield. At the Court of Inquiry it was established that, inadvertently, the
air bomber turned the fuel cock the wrong way. Eleven months later, on the 2nd
of September 1944, F/S Nalepa PAF was killed while flying Halifax II BB389 of
No. 1586 Special Duties Flight based at Brindisi in Italy.

3 Oct 1943	17 OTU	Wellington X	HE276		Training

F/S G Lamb + T/o 1901 Silverstone for a night navigation
Sgt J S Beach + exercise. It seems likely that the crew ran
Sgt R H J Hyde inj into difficulties for the Wellington crashed
Sgt A Longworth + at 2201, while approaching the base runway and
Sgt F P Smith RCAF + burst into flames. Sgt Smith RCAF was buried
Sgt J B Speake + in Towcester Cemetery (this is rather unusual
F/S H Smith DFM + in that by this stage of the war Commonwealth
Sgt R J Wells inj airmen were, in most cases, being taken to an
appropriate regional cemetery; in the case of
Sgt Smith this would have been Oxford (Botley)). The others were claimed by
their relatives. F/S Smith had served with 75 Squadron and details of his
award had been published in the London Gazette on 13 September 1940. Sgt Beech
had distinguished himself by being appointed a King's Scout and Senior Prefect
at Lymm Grammar School.

18 OTU	Wellington III	BK242		Training

Sgt T W H Dalziel + T/o 1840 Finningley for an evening detail.
Sgt W B Jarvie + Approached the runway, on one engine, at 2035
Sgt E Farrer + but for reasons that could not be determined,
Sgt M Cohen + decided to overshoot. Eyewitnesses report
Sgt L Lazarus + hearing the engine note increase but while
turning the nose pitched up and the bomber
plunged to the ground. All rest in cemeteries, both in England and Scotland.

3- 4 Oct 1943	19 OTU B Flt	Whitley V	Z9422	-N		Training

F/O E W Smith RCAF T/o 2223 Kinloss for night circuit training.
P/O A A McK Fraser Lost power and ditched 0053 in Findhorn Bay.
Sgt K W Newton P/O Fraser went on to fly Halifaxes with 296
F/O Stuart Squadron and was killed on 25 May 1945. He
F/S Leach rests in Grangemouth (Grand Sable) Cemetery.
Sgt Coffen A detailed account of the crews' rescue is
Sgt Mates reported in unit records.

6 Oct **19 OTU A Flt** **Whitley V** **LA792 UO–G** **Training**
1943   F/O C S Dallimore   +   T/o 1925 Kinloss for a night exercise. At 2047
  Sgt J E M Gess   +   F/O Dallimore called on the radio to say he was
  Sgt J G Kelly   +   returning to base as the port engine had failed,
  Sgt D Cawthorne   +   estimating his time of arrival as 2052. Flying
  Sgt W R Coster   +   Control immediately alerted the crash and rescue
  Sgt C J Haycock   +   sections and ordered all crews engaged in night
circuit training that if on the ground they were
to remain there until the emergency was over. The Sandra lights were switched on
and a call was made to nearby Lossiemouth asking for assistance, if necessary.
Sadly, all was to no avail and at 2230 it was announced the Whitley had crashed
about 400 yards NW of Kineachy Lodge, Boat of Garten, 18 miles NE of Kingussie,
Inverness-shire. On impact the bomber had exploded in flames. All are buried
in their home towns.

6– 7 Oct **26 OTU** **Wellington X** **HE572** **Training**
1943   F/O G R Balcombe RAAF   T/o 2225 Wing for a night cross–country. During
the flight a sump valve failed and the crew made
for Lichfield where an emergency landing was made at 0120. Unfortunately, soon
after doing so the Wellington caught fire and was destroyed. After converting to
Lancasters, F/O Balcombe RAAF joined 100 Squadron, only to be lost raiding Berlin
in mid–February 1944 (see Bomber Command Losses, Volume 5, page 77).

82 OTU **Wellington X** **LN291** **Training**
  Sgt D Y Bishop   T/o 2215 Ossington for a night sortie. On return
to base at around 0445, and while making a glide
approach, it is thought the carburettors iced up and the Wellington finished up in
the Clipston Forest on the E side of Mansfield and roughly 10 miles WSW from the
airfield. On 20–21 April 1944, Sgt Bishop's 625 Squadron Lancaster went down in
the sea off the coast of Holland (see Bomber Command Losses, Volume 5, page 175).

7 Oct **23 OTU** **Wellington X** **HE823** **Training**
1943   Sgt J G A G Meilleur RCAF   T/o 1859 Pershore carrying a full war load but an
engine cut and the Wellington hit an embankment,
smashing its main undercarriage in the process. No injuries reported but ten days
later Sgt Meilleur RCAF was killed, with his crew, during a night cross–country.

7– 8 Oct **21 OTU** **Wellington IC** **R1028** **Training**
1943   F/S J A Hazeldene RAAF   +   T/o 1856 Moreton-in-Marsh for an evening detail.
  Sgt A W Jones   +   Lost power from the port engine and at 2100, while
  Sgt H Cox   +   on finals to Little Rissington airfield, crashed
  Sgt J V Rees   +   into the back garden of the Lamb Inn at Great
  Sgt J A Johnson   +   Rissington, 16 miles ESE of Cheltenham. Of those
  Sgt J Smith   inj   who died, F/S Hazeldene RAAF was buried in Little
Rissington (St. Peter) Churchyard, while the rest
were recovered to their home towns. After his release from the service, Sgt Smith
emigrated to Canada but made a nostalgic return in 1988 to place a commemorative
wall plaque at the spot where he so nearly died over forty years previous. A
propeller blade also exists as a reminder to this tragedy.

8 Oct **20 OTU C Flt** **Wellington III** **X3662** **–B** **Training**
1943   F/S G F Smith RCAF   +   T/o Lossiemouth for a navigation sortie, base-
  F/S E M Anderson RCAF   +   Penrhos-Carlisle-Macduff-base. Crashed at circa
  P/O A W Howl RCAF   +   0600 off Dunvegan Head on the NW side of Skye.
  F/L J A Puttock   +   Hailing from Sherman in Texas, F/S Smith RCAF
  Sgt W J Sadler   +   and three of his crew are commemorated on the
Runnymede Memorial, while P/O Howl RCAF and Sgt
Sadler lie in Lerwick New Cemetery and Trondheim (Stavne) Cemetery respectively.

9 Oct **10 OTU** **Whitley V** **Z6976** **Training**
1943   Sgt J H Crane   T/o 1450 Stanton Harcourt with the intention of
carrying out a bombing exercise. However, as
the Whitley gathered speed, so a swing began to develop and the air bomber,
believing he could assist, advanced the starboard throttle. Unfortunately,
what had been a quite gentle swing now developed into a viscous turn and before
remedial action could be taken, the undercarriage gave way and the bomber came
to a stop close to the Watch Office. Graduating to Halifaxes, Sgt Crane was
killed on 25 May 1944, while serving with 640 Squadron (see Bomber Command
Losses, Volume 5, page 243). He is buried in Rheinberg War Cemetery.

9 Oct   **20 OTU**   **Wellington X** **HE283**   **Training**
1943   F/O R A L Young   + T/o 0940 Lossiemouth for a cross-country. While
         P/O P S G Thornton RNZAF   inj making an emergency landing, lost control and
         F/L R C Rawlings DFC RNZAF + crashed 1005 at Kirkby Hall, Kirkby Fleetham,
         F/O N J Furlong DFC   + some 5 miles WNW of Northallerton, Yorkshire.
         F/O C Seymour   + Those who died rest in various cemeteries. The
                                      sole survivor was admitted to Catterick Military
Hospital with severe facial burns and a multitude of cuts and abrasions. F/L
Rawlings RNZAF had recently completed a tour of duty with 158 Squadron, flying
at least twenty-two sorties in Halifax IIs. Tragically, for his parents, six
weeks previous, his younger brother, P/O Leslie McDonald Rawlings RNZAF, had been
killed when his 488 Squadron Mosquito NF.XII HK182 crashed minutes after taking
off from Drem in Scotland. Both brothers were cremated and their ashes laid
alongside each other in Cambridge City Cemetery.

        82 OTU   **Wellington X** **HE919**   **Training**
         W/O J D Rees   T/o 0243 Ossington for a night training detail.
         Sgt D E Aiken RCAF   Lost engine power and crashed 0347 in a field at
                                     Blyth, 6 miles NW of Retford, Nottinghamshire.
Subsequently commissioned, Sgt Aiken RCAF flew Lancasters with 44 Squadron until
his death in action, over France, in late June 1944 (see Bomber Command Losses,
Volume 5, page 300).

9-10 Oct **18 OTU**   **Wellington X** **LN583**   **Training**
1943   Sgt R Sharp   T/o 2040 Finningley for a night navigation
                                     flight. Became totally lost and though given
fixes that would have enabled them to reach Wymeswold, the crew were unable to
pinpoint their position. Thus, at 0245, with their fuel state dangerously low
all baled out leaving their aircraft to fall into the River Don between Barnby
Dun and Kirk Sandall, roughly 3 miles NE of Doncaster, Yorkshire.

12 Oct   **30 OTU**   **Wellington III** **BJ986** **-Q**   **Training**
1943   Sgt R F Mackrill   inj T/o Hixon for a flying detail, during which the
                             inj sleeve drive nuts on one of the engines sheared,
                             inj causing the motor to fail. At around 1705, the
                             inj Wellington came into land but overshot and flew
                             inj into telegraph wires about a mile away to the SW.
                                   By the spring of 1945, Sgt Mackrill was flying
Halifaxes with 298 Squadron. Sadly, he failed to return to Tarrant Rushton on
19 April 1945 and his grave can now be visited in the village of Vang in north-
western Jutland, Denmark. His service number indicates he joined the service,
at Uxbridge, shortly after the outbreak of war.

        82 OTU   **Wellington X** **HE201**   **Training**
         F/O J Coughlan DFM   + T/o 1448 Gamston but as the bomber climbed away,
         F/O H G Dayman RCAF   + the port engine cut, necessitating an immediate
         F/O H C McGavin RCAF   inj crash-landing. While doing so, the bomber flew
         WO1 R Tarling RCAF   inj into trees between Haughton Chapel and Bevercotes
         Sgt J A S MacGregor RCAF   inj some 5 miles SSE of Retford, Nottinghamshire.
         Sgt H D La Pointe RCAF   inj Both Canadians rest in Ollerton Cemetery, P/O
         P/O J Christie RCAF   + Christie's grave being in the Roman Catholic
                                    section. F/O Coughlan was taken back to Co. Cork
in the Irish Republic and buried in Kanturk Catholic Cemetery. He gained an
immediate DFM, Gazetted 11 May 1943, while serving with 166 Squadron, the
citation recording his skill in getting his badly damaged Wellington home
from an attack on Stuttgart. The injured were admitted to RAF Hospital Rauceby.
Sgt MacGregor died, in the service of 419 Squadron, on 28 December 1944 (see
Bomber Command Losses, Volume 5, page 522).

16 Oct   **26 OTU**   **Wellington III** **X3468**   **Training**
1943   F/O Mather   T/o Little Horwood for flying practice. Wrecked
         Sgt J Arbury   circa 1840 while landing at base.

17 Oct   **22 OTU**   **Wellington X** **HF669**   **Training**
1943   F/O C P Lundeen RCAF   inj T/o 1205 Wellesbourne Mountford intending to
         Sgt E L Heimpel RCAF   inj practice circuits and landings but the starboard
         Sgt Jarvie RCAF   inj engine cut and a minute later the Wellington was
                                   down, wrecked, near the direction finding hut
and Pit Farm on the western boundary of the airfield.

17 Oct　　**23 OTU**　　　**Wellington X**　**HE824**　**-H**　　　　　　**Training**
1943　　F/S J G A G Meilleur RCAF　　+　T/o 1830 Stratford-upon-Avon for a night cross-
　　　　　F/O J A L Morissette RCAF　　+　country. Presumed to have iced up before
　　　　　Sgt J J M P Marchessault　　+　crashing at 1909 on the S side of the Shrewton
　　　　　　RCAF　　　　　　　　　　　road and less than a mile W of Stonehenge on
　　　　　WO2 G Smith RCAF　　　　　+　Salisbury Plain. The crash and rescue services
　　　　　Sgt J A J Duhamel RCAF　　+　from nearby Boscombe Down attended the scene
　　　　　　　　　　　　　　　　　　and recovered the five bodies. All now rest
　　　　　in Bath (Haycombe) Cemetery. It will be recalled that F/S Meilleur RCAF had
　　　　　been involved in a take off crash earlier in the month (see page 254). I am
　　　　　extremely grateful to Norman Parker of Amesbury for sending precise details
　　　　　pertaining to the crash location.

　　　　　82 OTU C Flt　　**Wellington X**　**HE916**　**-B**　　　　　**Training**
　　　　　Sgt R E Kirkland RAAF　　　　　T/o 1920 Ossington for an evening navigation
　　　　　　　　　　　　　　　　　　　sortie. Crash-landed 2150 with both engines
　　　　　out of action, in a field, near Windrush airfield, Gloucestershire.

18 Oct　　**24 OTU**　　　**Whitley V**　**EB347**　　　　　　　　**Training**
1943　　F/O W J Caulfield RCAF　　+　T/o 2035 Long Marston for high-level bombing
　　　　　F/O G Hoopchuk RCAF　　　　+　practice. Crashed 2130 and burnt out at Old
　　　　　F/O J S Spencer RCAF　　　+　Manor Farm, Armscote, 7 miles SSE of Stratford-
　　　　　WO2 J G Sherk RCAF　　　　+　upon-Avon, Warwickshire. The four RCAF members
　　　　　Sgt K Reid　　　　　　　　+　of crew were buried in Oxford (Botley) Cemetery
　　　　　　　　　　　　　　　　　　while Sgt Reid was cremated at Newcastle-upon-
　　　　　Tyne (West Road) Crematorium. F/O Hoopchuk RCAF is described as a Metallurgist.

19 Oct　　**19 OTU**　　　**Whitley V**　**N1369 UO-U**　　　　　　**Ground**
1943　　　　　　　　　　　　　　　Damaged beyond repair after Anson I DJ104 XF-K
　　　　　of 19 OTU landed, at Kinloss, astride the fuselage. The Anson was removed from
　　　　　its precarious position and, following repairs, was returned to service wearing
　　　　　the combination XF-W. Later, it saw service with four other training units
　　　　　before being struck off charge on 15 January 1945. A photograph of this unusual
　　　　　accident appears on page 63 of 'The Anson File', compiled by Ray Sturtivant and
　　　　　published in 1988 by Air-Britain (Historians) Limited.

20 Oct　　**10 OTU**　　　**Whitley V**　**BD280**　　　　　　　　**Training**
1943　　F/S J R Burton RAAF　　　+　T/o 1840 Stanton Harcourt for a night cross-
　　　　　W/O I K Nicoll　　　　　+　country. When the port engine failed, the crew
　　　　　P/O L R V Sibley　　　　+　were obliged to make an emergency landing and
　　　　　Sgt D R Burton　　　　　+　while doing so at 2330 the bomber stalled as
　　　　　Sgt A E Smart　　　　　inj　F/S Burton RAAF tried to avoid a line of high-
　　　　　　　　　　　　　　　　　　tension cables. Out of control, it smashed into
　　　　　the ground at Vicarage Farm, a mile or so NNW from the village of Ivinghoe, six
　　　　　miles ENE of Aylesbury, Buckinghamshire. The Whitley was burnt out and of those
　　　　　who died, F/S Burton RAAF and W/O Nicoll were taken to Oxford (Botley) Cemetery
　　　　　and the others to their home towns in Buckinghamshire and Yorkshire respectively.

　　　　　11 OTU B Flt　　**Wellington IC**　**Z1066**　**-I**　　　　**Training**
　　　　　F/S J G Hudson RNZAF　　　　　T/o Westcott for a navigation exercise. At
　　　　　Sgt P M Constable　　　　　　approximately 0500, the crew baled out following
　　　　　Sgt W L Granbois RCAF　　　　a fire at 4,000 feet, leaving their aircraft to
　　　　　　　　　　　　　　　　　　come down at Duchy Farm, Methwold, Norfolk. At
　　　　　about 0540, Sgt Constable telephoned his unit from Southery, 6 miles WNW from
　　　　　Feltwell, to say that he was safe and by 0800 all five members of crew had been
　　　　　accounted for. Sadly, the three named above all died in 1944, while flying with
　　　　　514 Squadron (see Bomber Command Losses, Volume 5, page 182).

　　　　　12 OTU　　　**Wellington III**　**Z1717**　　　　　　　**Training**
　　　　　Sgt Z W C Dekkers　　　　+　T/o 2225 Chipping Warden for a night training
　　　　　Sgt D A R Colegate　　　+　flight. Overshot the airfield, climbed to around
　　　　　F/O W D Newel RCAF　　　+　a thousand feet, rolled over, and crashed 2254
　　　　　Sgt K J Gehrmann RAAF　　+　near Culworth, 16 miles SW of Northampton. On
　　　　　　　　　　　　　　　　　　hitting the ground, the bomber was engulfed in
　　　　　flames. Dutch born, Sgt Dekkers and Sgt Colegate rest in Banbury Cemetery, the
　　　　　two Commonwealth airmen are interred in Oxford (Botley) Cemetery, while Sgt Young
　　　　　lies in Binstead (Holy Cross) Churchyard. His brother, Sgt Kenneth Lincoln Young
　　　　　of the 1st Battalion Royal Sussex Regiment was killed in Italy on 13 July 1944,
　　　　　he is buried in Arezzo War Cemetery.

20 Oct   **17 OTU**   **Wellington X**   **HE298**   **Training**
1943   Sgt A R Taylor   T/o 1755 Silverstone for an evening flying
                                    detail. Crash-landed 1840 in a field, due to
loss of power, near Sulgrave, 16 miles SW from the centre of Northampton.

       29 OTU   **Wellington III**   **BK549**   **-N**   **Training**
       Sgt T R M Robertson   +   T/o 1833 Bruntingthorpe tasked with five other
       Sgt L Mortimer   +   crews to participate in a Bullseye exercise.
       Sgt C D Peary   +   Crashed, following an uncontrollable fire in
       Sgt S Fairhurst   +   the starboard engine, at 2253 near Basingstoke,
       WO2 L H Ramage RCAF   +   Hampshire. Sgt Robertson of West Nicholson in
       Sgt W E Hawksworth   +   Southern Rhodesia and WO2 Ramage RCAF are buried
                                      in Brookwood Military Cemetery, while the others
                                      were taken to their home towns.

21 Oct   **18 OTU**   **Wellington III**   **BK471**   **Training**
1943   Sgt M Solecki PAF   +   T/o 1917 Bircotes for an evening navigation
       F/L S K Alberti PAF   +   exercise. Soon after setting out, Sgt Solecki
       Sgt J Sawicki PAF   +   radioed to say he was returning to base, with
       F/S R Kot PAF   +   engine problems, and asked for permission to
       Sgt Z Maryknowski PAF   inj   land. Apparently, his situation must have
                                      worsened for at 1957 the Wellington came down
amongst trees about 2 miles to the N of the airfield and burst into flames.
The four who perished were taken to Newark-upon-Trent Cemetery. Accident
investigators sifting through the debris found a sheered split taper pin,
which normally secured the bevel gear wheel on the mixture control change
over spindle.

       20 OTU A Flt   **Wellington III**   **DF595**   **-Y**   **Training**
       F/S M Antifaev RCAF   +   T/o Lossiemouth for a night cross-country.
       F/S R M McEachern RCAF   +   Believed to have come down, circa 0320, in
       Sgt A McN Davidson   +   the Solway Firth. Two survivors were brought
       F/O M E O'Donoghue RCAF   +   ashore in an Air-Sea Rescue launch. The body
       Sgt Branford   of F/S McEachern RCAF was recovered and he now
       Sgt Snell   rests in Kirkwall (St. Olaf's) Cemetery, while
                                      the Runnymede Memorial perpetuates the names of
                                      the others who died.

       24 OTU   **Whitley V**   **EB348**   **Training**
       F/S W J Christie RCAF   +   T/o 1840 Long Marston for an evening cross-
       Sgt J H McMaster RCAF   +   country. While in the circuit of Waterbeach
       Sgt B W Burke RCAF   +   airfield, crashed 2215 at Kimpton Farm near
       WO2 W H Howson RCAF   +   Cottenham, 6 miles N of Cambridge where all
       Sgt W Paterson RCAF   +   are buried in the city's cemetery. This was
                                      the first all Canadian crew to lose their lives
while training at 24 OTU and it is noted that four shared the common Christian
name of William.

22 Oct   **14 OTU**   **Wellington IC**   **W5688**   **-O**   **Training**
1943   Sgt I Hayward   +   T/o 1940 Husbands Bosworth for bombing practice.
       Sgt H R Thompson RCAF   +   On return to base at 2005, and while coming in
       F/S P Norton RNZAF   +   from a north-westerly direction at 1,500 feet,
       Sgt D Clarke   +   the Wellington dived suddenly and crashed into
       Sgt H L Hembrough   +   Gumley Wood, bursting into flames. F/S Norton
                                      was taken to Oxford (Botley) Cemetery, but it
seems likely that relatives arranged the funeral of Sgt Thompson RCAF as he lies
in Yorkshire at Stockton-on-the-Forest (Holy Trinity) Churchyard. The rest of
the crew were claimed by their next of kin.

23 Oct   **15 OTU**   **Wellington IC**   **DV817**   **Training**
1943   Sgt S Cossey   +   T/o 1829 Harwell for a night cross-country,
       Sgt A J F May   +   base-Taunton-Bideford-Isles of Scilly-Skomer
       Sgt A Holloway   +   Island-Fishguard-Worcester-base-Odstone-base-
       Sgt C C Bishop   +   Taunton-base. Last fixed by Predannack when over
       Sgt G C Bangs   +   the Isles of Scilly. Probably came down in the
       Sgt W K Fraser   +   sea circa 2045. All are commemorated on the
                                      Runnymede Memorial.

24 Oct
1943

11 OTU	**Wellington IC**	**T2750**	**–H**	**Training**

F/S W A Watt RNZAF   T/o 2229 Oakley for a night cross-country but crashed soon afterwards, the Wellington taking light as the crew scrambled to safety. By the spring of 1944, F/S Watt RNZAF was flying Lancasters with 630 Squadron. On 11-12 May, he failed to return from an attack on a military camp at Bourg-Leopold in Belgium (see Bomber Command Losses, Volume 5, page 221).

14 OTU	**Wellington IC**	**DV839**	**–D** **Training**

F/S E G Reading RAAF   +   T/o 1845 Market Harborough for a night cross-
Sgt J G S Browne   +   country. Came down through cloud in order to
F/O R Hooper   inj   establish their position. While doing so, the
F/S L T Newton RAAF   +   rate of descent increased and though this was
Sgt W Buckley   inj   partially arrested, the Wellington hit the ground
                                          at about 2200, close to Wittering airfield in Northamptonshire. F/S Reading RAAF is buried in Ilford Cemetery (probably having been claimed by relatives), while F/S Newton RAAF rests, along with Sgt Browne and F/O Hooper (who died the following day from his injuries while being treated in Stamford and Rutland General Infirmary), in Cambridge City Cemetery. Sgt Buckley was initially treated in Wittering's Station Sick Quarters before being returned to Market Harborough. He was not too seriously hurt.

19 OTU D Flt	**Whitley V**	**BD386 ZV–S**	**Training**

Sgt L C Crowshaw   inj   T/o Kinloss for an evening flying detail. Came
P/O C F Knapp   +   down in the sea at 2159, less than a mile E of
Sgt S W Parr   +   Kirton Head and about 3 miles NNW of Peterhead
Sgt A Robertson   +   on the Aberdeenshire coast. Three of the crew
Sgt Phillips   baled out but fell into the sea and drowned.
Sgt Cranshaw   They are commemorated on the Runnymede Memorial.

25 Oct
1943

19 OTU D Flt	**Whitley V**	**LA881 ZV–I**	**Training**

F/S H R Hagstrom RAAF   T/o 2224 Forres and crashed almost immediately, coming down on the west side of the airfield and catching fire. Despite the severity of the crash, there are no reports of injury.

20 OTU	**Wellington III**	**HZ137** **Training**

Sgt P A Collins   +   T/o 2032 Milltown to practice night flying.
Sgt M W Hallam   +   Overshot the base runway at 2347 and came down
P/O W A White   +   in Innes Woods on the E side of the airfield.
Sgt L A Rother   +   Sgt Collins and Sgt Rother, the second named
Sgt Howson   inj   coming from Port of Spain, Trinidad, are buried
                                     in Lossiemouth Burial Ground, while the others who died were taken to their home towns. Sgt Howson was admitted to Dr. Gray's Hospital at Elgin.

26 Oct
1943

30 OTU	**Wellington X**	**HE696** **Training**

F/S T F Magee   inj   T/o Hixon for a flying detail. At 1700, the
                     inj   Wellington overshot the Burnaston runway and
Sgt A B Levene RCAF   +   crashed into a hangar. For some fifteen to
                     inj   twenty minutes previous to the accident, the
                                     crew had circled this Derbyshire airfield, but do not appear to have made any contact, either by radio or wireless. Although F/S Magee was a reasonably experienced pilot with 673 solo flying hours to his credit, only five of these had been logged on Wellingtons. Sgt Levene RCAF, who had married Theresa Levene of Orpington, Kent, rests in Stafford Cemetery. Prior to his joining the RCAF in January 1942, he had served since September 1940 with the Canadian army.

27 Oct
1943

11 OTU	**Wellington IC**	**R1790**	**–E** **Training**

F/S S C Corby RNZAF   +   T/o 1942 Westcott to practice night circuits
Sgt T B Tanner RNZAF   +   and landings. A number of successful circuits
Sgt R L Warren   +   were flown but at around 1955 the Wellington was
Sgt J S Buchan   +   observed to swing quite markedly to starboard on
Sgt Blount   inj   climb out and moments later it smashed into the
                                     tops of trees at Parrots Field, Wotton House, about a mile off the aerodrome and WNW of Wotton Underwood and burst into flames. Both New Zealanders were taken to Oxford (Botley) Cemetery, while Sgt Warren and Sgt Buchan lie in Twickenham Parochial Cemetery and Colinton Parish Churchyard, Southern Extension, respectively. Sgt Blount was taken to Halton Hospital.

27 Oct **12 OTU** **Wellington III** **DF613** **Training**
1943 Sgt O W Ray T/o 2203 Edgehill for an evening exercise. At
2243 the bomber was sighted in the funnels but
was not fully aligned with the flare path and while turning to make an adjust-
ment it struck the ground before Sgt Ray could level his wings. No one was
hurt and at first sight it was thought the damage was repairable. However,
upon closer inspection it was decided not to proceed and the airframe was
struck off charge having amassed 462.40 flying hours.

12 OTU **Wellington X** **HE860** **Training**
F/S T Black T/o 1620 Chipping Warden but the port engine
Sgt H Moncrieff RCAF failed and having left the runway, the bomber
ran through a hedge and was wrecked.

29 Oct **12 OTU** **Wellington III** **X3868** **Ground**
1943 Burnt out 1750 at Edgehill, while parked at
its dispersal. The cause of the fire could not be ascertained but the most
likely explanation put forward suggests a short in the electrical system.

31 Oct– **19 OTU C Flt** **Whitley V** **BD627 ZV-E** **Training**
1 Nov 1943 Sgt G H M Garner + T/o 1835 Kinloss for a night cross-country.
Sgt J W Mann + Flew into the waters of Spey Bay at approximately
F/O R V Lynch RCAF + 0020. Despite being very badly injured, Sgt Jones
Sgt R F Kincaid + managed to get into the aircraft's dinghy and,
Sgt Jones inj subsequently, was picked up by the trawler Emblem.
His four companions were less fortunate and their
names are perpetuated by the Runnymede Memorial. Twenty-two year old Sgt Garner's
wife was christened Calipso.

2 Nov **22 OTU** **Wellington III** **HZ113 XN-T** **Training**
1943 Sgt W M Bowyer inj T/o Wellesbourne Mountford to practice night
Sgt L E Hance inj circuits and landings. While so engaged, an
Sgt A J Taylor inj engine failed and reds were fired to signal that
Sgt G W Milne inj the crew were in trouble. At 2312, the bomber
was sighted but seemed to be rather too high
for a safe landing. Sgt Bowyer then attempted to overshoot but the Wellington
veered to the left and came down on Loxley Hill on the S side of the airfield.
Sgt Hance died from his injuries the next day and he lies in Greenwich Cemetery.

3– 4 Nov **24 OTU** **Whitley V** **AD675 TY-E** **Op: Nickel**
1943 F/L J L Kennedy RCAF evd T/o 1834 Honeybourne and set course for Orleans.
Sgt J H Upton RCAF evd Turned back with failing engines and abandoned
Sgt F W Forster RCAF evd in the vicinity of Courtalain (Eure-et-Loir),
WO2 G A Gauley RCAF evd some 26 km WNW of Châteaudun.
Sgt A E Spencer RCAF evd

4 Nov **26 OTU** **Wellington X** **HE872** **Air Test**
1943 Sgt J S Frisby inj T/o 1225 Llandbedr having landed here with
Sgt L Edwards inj instrument failure. Unfortunately, the tail
Sgt S J B Rowan inj trim was set too far forward and the bomber ran
Sgt D G Williams inj off the end of the runway and collided with an
Sgt J C Watts RAAF inj obstruction. LAC Jones, an electrician, had
Sgt N O'Hamley inj accompanied the crew for the purpose of the
Sgt R C Humpage + air test. Eighteen year old Sgt Humpage rests
LAC I W Jones inj in Newcastle-under-Lyne Cemetery, Staffordshire.

5– 6 Nov **29 OTU** **Wellington X** **LN551** **Training**
1943 P/O R A F Scrivener inj T/o 2130 Bruntingthorpe for a night navigation
P/O N A Smith inj exercise. Lost engine power and in marginal
Sgt G McDougall RCAF inj weather crash-landed 0300 at Naseby, 12 miles
Sgt F C Searle inj NNW of Northampton. Two, P/O Scrivener and Sgt
Sgt Brodenkamp inj Brodenkamp (he had enlisted either in Rhodesia
Sgt T R Clayton inj or South Africa) were admitted to the Leicester
Royal Infirmary, while the others were treated
in Station Sick Quarters Husbands Bosworth. On their recovery, five were destined
to lose their lives on bomber operations; P/O Scrivener, P/O Smith, Sgt Searle
and Sgt Clayton went down on the Mailly-le-Camp raid in May 1944, while serving
with 57 Squadron and later that same month Sgt McDougall RCAF was lost with 106
Squadron (see Bomber Command Losses, Volume 5, pages 206 and 216 respectively).

6 Nov
1943

26 OTU   **Wellington III**   **X3924**   **Training**

Sgt R B Main RCAF	inj	T/o 1918 Wing for an evening cross-country.
F/O D Potts RCAF	+	Collided in the air at 2208 with a Wellington
Sgt G A Hall	+	from 27 OTU Lichfield, both machines falling
Sgt M A Crimmins	+	near the main gate at Alconbury airfield in
Sgt S Edmondson	+	Huntingdonshire and not far from the village
Sgt J E Holbeck RCAF	+	of Abbots Ripton. At the time, Alconbury was

occupied by the United States Army Air Corps
and Sgt Main RCAF, who was thrown clear of the stricken Wellington, was treated
here for relatively minor injuries and soon discharged back to duty. Of those
who died, four were taken to Oxford (Botley) Cemetery, while Sgt Edmondson was
buried in his native Yorkshire at Barnsley Cemetery. F/O Potts RCAF was an
American from Paterson, New Jersey.

27 OTU   **Wellington III**   **X3637**   **Training**

P/O M E McKiggan RAAF	+	T/o 1940 Lichfield for an evening navigation
F/S F G Neville RAAF	+	detail. At approximately 2000, while flying
F/S J J Herbert RAAF	+	just below the base of cu nimbus cloud, hit a
P/O T T Jones RAAF	+	Stirling I R9192 of 1657 HCU Stradishall flown
F/S S S L La Frentz RAAF	+	by P/O D W Thomson RNZAF and F/O V L Scantleton
F/O D A McKechnie RAAF	+	of the RAAF. Out of control, the Wellington
F/O O I H Stoeckel RAAF	+	crashed at Raden Stock Farm, Little Walden some

two miles N of Saffron Walden, Essex. All seven
Australians were taken to Brookwood Military Cemetery. Meanwhile, the Stirling,
although damaged, managed to return to Stradishall where it was struck off
charge, though not until 12 June 1944.

27 OTU   **Wellington X**   **LN295**   **Training**

G/C P G Heffernan RAAF	inj	T/o Lichfield similarly tasked and collided
P/O L J Quaite DFM RAAF	+	with the Wellington described at the head of
P/O J F Parker RAAF	+	this page. G/C Heffernan RAAF, who commanded
P/O C G Finch RAAF	+	Lichfield, was admitted to RAF Hospital Ely,
Sgt A H Anderson RAAF	+	where he spent many weeks recovering from his
S/O K L Hughes WAAF	+	injuries. His crew, including S/O Hughes WAAF,

lie in Cambridge City Cemetery. P/O Quaite RAAF
had served with 460 Squadron, his DFM being Gazetted more then a month later on
10 December 1943. G/C Heffernan RAAF remained in the service and in 1953 was
awarded an OBE. He retired in the rank of Air Commodore in 1956 and died on
30 January 1996.

Note. It is believed this was the first, and only time, that three Wellingtons
from Bomber Command training establishments were lost through midair collisions
on the same night.

81 OTU   **Whitley V**   **Z9322**   **Training**

F/S J Knight RAAF	T/o 1515 Sleap but a swing developed, this
	being corrected. However, before reaching

flying speed the Whitley swung again and this time F/S Knight RAAF cut the
throttles but was unable to prevent his aircraft from crashing off the end
of the runway which, it is reported, was closed for the next three days.

6- 7 Nov
1943

15 OTU   **Wellington IC**   **Z9106**   **Training**

P/O A G McAlpine RAAF		T/o 1857 Hampstead Norris tasked to carry out a
P/O J W Erricker		Bullseye exercise. On return to base, the bomber
P/O F F Sait RCAF		was sighted flying at 1,000 feet and parallel to
Sgt W W Bright		the flare path. Then, while turning to port the
Sgt H Haire	inj	starboard engine surged and almost immediately
Sgt A Follett RCAF	+	the Wellington began to lose height. At this

juncture P/O McAlpine RAAF lost sight of the
flare path and when his port engine cut at 100 feet, he had no option but to
force -land 0155 straight ahead, hitting trees and a brick built garage at North
Heath, Chievely, 5 miles N of Newbury, Berkshire. Sgt Follett RCAF of Grand Bank,
Newfoundland, was buried in Oxford (Botley) Cemetery.

7 Nov
1943

30 OTU   **Wellington X**   **LN182**   **—A**   **Training**

P/O Rothchild RCAF	T/o Hixon for a night exercise. Wrecked at 2145
Sgt M J West	after crashing into the overshoot area on the
	south side of Cranage airfield, Cheshire.

7- 8 Nov **20 OTU C Flt** **Wellington III** **DF544** **-L** **Training**
1943 F/O H G Waugh   + T/o 1847 Lossiemouth for a navigation exercise.
      P/O W J Halfpenny   + Failed to return by its scheduled time of 0126.
      Sgt J Hodge   + Lost without trace. All are commemorated on the
      Sgt A F Peart   + Runnymede Memorial. Apart from the pilot, the
      Sgt J Rae   + crew matrix appears in the order that the names
      Sgt P Seager   + are published in the memorial registers.

8 Nov **27 OTU** **Wellington X** **LN586** **Training**
1943 F/S Dechastel RAAF   T/o Lichfield for a night cross-country. Landed
                                     at West Freugh, Wigtown but on touch down at 2119
      the port tyre burst, whereupon the undercarriage gave way, wrecking the bomber.

9 Nov **23 OTU** **Wellington III** **X3932** **-P** **Training**
1943 Sgt C R G Long RCAF   + T/o 1838 Pershore for an evening detail. Reported
      F/O H H Barton RCAF   + crashed 1940 at Lower Park Farm, Rowney Green,
      P/O G J Gallagher RCAF   + ten miles SSW from the centre of Birmingham. All
      P/O J H Magnes RCAF   + are buried in Pershore Cemetery. Sgt Long RCAF
      Sgt A J O'Neil RCAF   + was an American from Lomita Park in California.
                                     F/O Barton RCAF was a Bachelor of Arts graduate
      from the University of Western Ontario, London. His brother, P/O Thomas Granston
      Barton RCAF, was killed on Bomber Command operations on 29 July 1944, while with
      425 Squadron (see Bomber Command Losses, Volume 5, page 356).

81 OTU **Whitley V** **T4153** **Training**
      P/O E J Foulsham RAAF   T/o 1143 Sleap for dual flying but an escape
      P/O J R Marshall   hatch blew open, thus distracting the pilot.
                                     The instructor immediately took control but
      only closed one throttle and the Whitley promptly swung from the runway and
      lost its undercarriage.

11 Nov **21 OTU** **Wellington IC** **Z9103** **Training**
1943 F/S H C N Johnson RAAF   T/o 1805 Moreton-in-Marsh for a night cross-
      F/S L Tate RAAF   country. When the port engine failed, course
      Sgt L B Delahuny RAAF   was set for Chivenor on the north Devon coast.
      Sgt G Strachan RAAF   However, the crew were unsuccessful in sighting
      Sgt F C Ward RAAF   the airfield and at 2025 the Wellington ditched
                                     in Morte Bay between Baggy Point at the south
      end and Morte Point to the north and some 10 miles NW of Barnstaple. All got
      into the aircraft's dinghy and floated ashore, unharmed.

13 Nov **83 OTU** **Oxford II** **P8926** **Ferry**
1943 S/L K Stammers   T/o Peplow but became caught up in a severe
                                     snowstorm and while trying to find a suitable
      place to land, crashed at 1745 at Hollis Farm, Woods Favis, Shropshire.

13-14 Nov **20 OTU D Flt** **Wellington III** **DF544** **-V** **Training**
1943 P/O W C Bowen   T/o 1959 Lossiemouth for a night cross-country.
                                     At around midnight, the crew were advised to head
      for Leuchars in Fife as the weather in the Moray Firth area was deteriorating.
      En route, they encountered icing of such severity that the aircraft's windscreen
      glazed over completely and the air speed reading began to fluctuate as the pitot
      head tube froze. At approximately 0100 the Wellington was put down in the River
      Eden, not far from the diversion airfield.

14 Nov **10 OTU** **Whitley V** **AD688** **Training**
1943 F/S D Lawrence RAAF   T/o 2120 Abingdon for a night navigation sortie.
      Sgt R A Partridge   inj While flying at 13,500 feet the pitot head tube
      F/O H W Meldrum RNZAF   + iced up and after descending 3,000 feet control
      Sgt J W Bass   + was lost and the order to bale out followed. Only
      P/O H A Strange   + two managed to get clear before the Whitley hit
      Sgt H P G Harbour   + the ground at 2257, bursting into flames about
                                     a mile S of Winterbourne and some 3 miles NNW
      of Newbury, Berkshire. F/O Meldrum RNZAF and Sgt Harbour were taken to Oxford
      (Botley) Cemetery; Sgt Bass lies in Lambeth (Tooting) Cemetery, while P/O Strange
      is buried at Frogmore (Holy Trinity) Burial Ground, St. Albans. Sgt Partridge,
      meanwhile, was admitted to the Princess Mary's Hospital at Halton; it is thought
      he succumbed to his injuries and, if this is the case, he rests in Taunton (St.
      Mary's) Churchyard.

14 Nov
1943

20 OTU C Flt   **Wellington III**   **HF746**   **—B**   **Training**

| Sgt N F Grove | + | T/o Lossiemouth for night flying practice. |
| Sgt J H Rennie | + | Became caught out in a violent snowstorm and |

at circa 0030 the Wellington smashed into Ben Rinnes (S of the A95 road and roughly 5 miles WSW of Dufftown in Banff) and exploded in flames. Sgt Grove is buried in Evesham Cemetery (where many of his fellow OTU trainees from 22 OTU and 24 OTU rest), while Sgt Rennie was taken to Glasgow Western Necropolis.

15 Nov
1943

21 OTU   **Wellington IC**   **R1293**   **Training**

P/O W G Gilleland RAAF   T/o 1950 Enstone but the port engine cut and the bomber finished up 300 yards beyond the runway, where it caught fire. There are no reports of injury to the crew.

30 OTU   **Wellington X**   **LN223**   **—S**   **Training**

F/S E A Wheelhouse   T/o Hixon for a night cross-country. Abandoned circa 0130, due to icing, some 3 miles NNE from Bromyard, Herefordshire.

81 OTU   **Whitley V**   **Z6817**   **—J**   **Training**

F/O A G Dickie RCAF	T/o 2005 Tilstock as part of a six aircraft
P/O G F Horner	force tasked for a Bullseye exercise. During
Sgt W Manning	the flight, the crew encountered very severe
Sgt C Cockerell	icing which led to the pitch control levers
F/O J M Brand	freezing solid and it was while trying to shift
Sgt J Mensley	the starboard lever that P/O Horner inadvertently
Sgt S S Barnett	feathered the propeller. Soon afterwards, at

approximately 2110, the crew baled out leaving the Whitley to crash near Yateley, 4 miles NNE of Fleet, Hampshire. F/O Dickie later joined 100 Squadron, courageously sacrificing his own life in order to save those of his crew during a mining operation off Denmark in April 1944. Sgt Barnett, too, was destined to lose his life. Posted to 300 Squadron, he failed to return from Stettin on 29-30 August 1944 (see Bomber Command Losses, Volume 5, pages 164 and 405 respectively).

15-16 Nov
1943

28 OTU   **Wellington IC**   **Z8799**   **Training**

F/S J B Timperon RAAF	+	T/o 2250 Castle Donington for a Bullseye sortie.
Sgt G E Murray	+	Crashed 0240, possibly due to icing, on Anglezarke
Sgt E R Barnes	+	Moor, 3 miles N of Horwich, Lancashire. Five of
Sgt J B Hayton	+	the crew were claimed by their next of kin while
Sgt R S Jackson	+	F/S Timperon RAAF was buried in Chester (Blacon)
Sgt M Mouncey	+	Cemetery. This crash is mentioned in a number of

books concerned with memorials and the like for as long ago as June 1955, members of the Horwich Rotary Club erected a monument in memory of the crew.

16 Nov
1943

15 OTU   **Wellington IC**   **W5690**   **Training**

Sgt N R Templeman	+	T/o 2100 Hampstead Norris for a night exercise
Sgt J J H Littlejohns	inj	but almost immediately Flying Control received
F/S J Treadgold RAAF	+	an emergency call from the aircraft, requesting
Sgt J Stanley	inj	a priority landing. Thus, some ten minutes
Sgt K D Atwell RCAF	+	later eyewitnesses saw the Wellington execute

a very tight turn to port, losing height, and crash 200 yards S of Westridge (Westbusthay Farm is also quoted). Accident investigators probing the remains of the starboard engine found that the No. 1 cylinder head barrel had split. Those who died lie in Oxford (Botley) Cemetery.

21 OTU   **Wellington IC**   **DV918**   **Training**

F/S S H C Thrower RAAF	+	T/o 2010 Enstone only to crash ten minutes later
Sgt D W Pike	+	while going round the circuit, coming down at
F/O W R Matheson	+	Hookerswell Farm on the SE side of the village of
Sgt W D Cole	+	Little Tew, 9 miles SSW of Banbury, Oxfordshire.
Sgt Selby	inj	It is thought that the pilot may have been a

little premature in raising the flaps, thus losing valuable height while still close to the ground. He is buried in Oxford (Botley) Cemetery. The others who died rest in churchyards as far scattered as Devon, Yorkshire and the Isle of Lewis. It is noted that Sgt Cole had joined the air force, pre-war, as a Boy Entrant.

17 Nov   **10 OTU**   **Whitley V**   **LA882**   **Training**
1943   Sgt R Curnow   +   T/o 1042 Abingdon for a cross-country. While
         P/O M H Watson   +   over South Wales, the crew encountered a quite
         F/S W H Oakley RCAF   +   violent storm and at around 1435, the bomber
         Sgt G W W Crick   +   dived and smashed into the ground at New Inn
         Sgt I H Hill   +   Farm, St. Florence, 3 miles W of Tenby in
         Sgt L W Coleman   +   Pembrokeshire. F/S Oakley RCAF was taken
                                             to Bath (Haycombe) Cemetery, while the others
were claimed by their relatives. Accident investigators strongly suspect the
mainplanes were struck by lightning.

22 Nov   **10 OTU**   **Whitley V**   **BD227**   **Training**
1943   P/O H H Hancock   T/o 1050 Abingdon for a cross-country but the
                                             pilot decided to abort the sortie and return
to base after meeting adverse weather conditions. On regaining Abingdon, rain
was sheeting down and after landing at around 1130, the Whitley ran off the
runway and finished up, wrecked, astride an earth bank.

22-23 Nov   **82 OTU**   **Wellington X**   **LN601**   **-B**   **Op: Nickel**
1943   WO2 H W Johnson RCAF   +   T/o 2158 Desborough with the intention to drop
         F/O O G de Jongh   +   leaflets in the St. Nazaire region of France but
         P/O A Grant RCAF   +   having climbed to a mere 800 feet, the port
         F/S K R Fallowdown RCAF   +   engine failed and the Whitley plunged to the
         F/L J G Brassington   +   ground at Norwell Woods House near Kneeshall
         Sgt R J Wannell   +   Lodge. On impact, there was an explosion as
                                             the bomber went up in flames. The first four
named were buried in Ollerton Cemetery, while two were taken to their home towns.
F/L Brassington was the unit's Gunnery Leader. F/O de Jongh was born on 14 July
1917 at Smyrna (Izmia) Turkey. A close scrutiny of the port engine revealed
evidence to suggest that the locking ring on the propeller shaft failed, thus
allowing the blades to produce a reverse pitch effect.

24 Nov   **14 OTU**   **Wellington IC**   **DV435**   **Training**
1943   F/O D W A Stewart   T/o 1650 Market Harborough in the company of
         F/O J N Clark RNZAF   inj   two other aircraft, all detailed to carry out
         Sgt J Ould   inj   a Bullseye exercise. Abandoned circa 2115,
         Sgt J D Hall   +   after becoming so iced up that the controls
                                             were ineffective. It is reported that the
bomber came down near Shuttlegate, Derbyshire. Sgt Hall rests in Corbridge-
on-Tyne (Corbridge) Cemetery.

         23 OTU   **Wellington III**   **Z1682**   **Training**
         F/O K W Bolstad RCAF   +   T/o 0016 Pershore for a night cross-country.
         F/O R W H Budd RCAF   +   While flying in cloud, lost control and crashed
         P/O L F Cook RCAF   +   at 0235 at Holm Farm, Marston, on the northern
         P/O D A Dunlop RCAF   +   outskirts of Oxford. Five were taken back to
         F/O H R Beswick RCAF   +   Pershore for interment in the local cemetery,
         P/O T J Brehn RCAF   +   while F/O Beswick RCAF and P/O Brehn RCAF are
         P/O J L Gibault RCAF   +   commemorated on the Runnymede Memorial.

         30 OTU   **Wellington III**   **X3813**   **-A**   **Training**
         F/S J Parkinson   T/o 1537 Seighford only to collide with a hut
                                             on the airfield boundary.

25 Nov   **11 OTU**   **Wellington IC**   **DV836**   **Training**
1943   F/S A McR McLachlan RNZAF   T/o 1838 Westcott for an evening detail. Lost
         Sgt Hamilton   inj   its starboard propeller at 2238 and crash-landed
                                             near Manor Bridge, near the airfield. Posted to
115 Squadron, F/S McLachlan RNZAF failed to return from Trappes in late May 1944
(see Bomber Command Losses, Volume 5, page 249).

         26 OTU   **Wellington X**   **HE855**   **Training**
         Sgt D J Morley   +   T/o Wing for a navigation sortie. At 2235, some
         Sgt A E Ford   +   twenty minutes before it was due back at base,
         Sgt J H Ashcroft   +   Docking monitored a QDM signal intended for this
         F/S D J Conroy RAAF   +   aircraft. Nothing further was heard and all are
         F/S K J Page   +   commemorated on the Runnymede Memorial. It is
         Sgt G B Mould RCAF   +   believed that F/S Page joined the Volunteer
         Sgt L G Pullen   +   Reserve in 1937 as a trainee pilot.

25 Nov   **28 OTU**   **Wellington IC**   **DV771**   **Training**
1943

W/O R J Fryer	+	T/o 1905 Wymeswold for a night exercise. While
F/S F W Greenwell RAAF	+	nearing the airfield, at 2255, from the south,
Sgt R T McLean	+	the starboard engine burst into flames, sending
Sgt J V Curry	+	the bomber crashing into a field. Those who
Sgt A Macintyre	+	lost their lives (including P/O Emmerson who
Sgt N A Kenyon	+	died from his injuries on 28 November) were taken
P/O P Emmerson	inj	to various locations around the United Kingdom,
Sgt S S Hewitt	inj	either for burial or cremation. W/O Fryer had
		been involved in at least two serious accidents.

On 2 May 1941, he had been the captain of Wellington IC R3203, destined for the Middle East, when it ballooned on landing at North Front, Gibraltar and finished up in the sea. Then, on 28 November 1942, after being posted in to Wymeswold as a screened pilot, he had crashed on the airfield (see page 177).

25-26 Nov   **23 OTU**   **Wellington X**   **JA450**   **Training**
1943

Sgt J E J C Dubord RCAF	+	T/o 2108 Stratford-upon-Avon for night flying
F/S R F Morand RCAF	+	practice. When the starboard engine failed, the
F/S J J J J Vennes RCAF	+	pilot was unable to feather the propeller and at
F/S J B V Chevalier RCAF	+	2253, while in the circuit, the bomber came down
		out of control. All rest in Pershore Cemetery.

27 Nov   **16 OTU**   **Wellington III**   **BJ823**   **Training**
1943

Sgt J F Burton	+	T/o 0421 Upper Heyford for high-level bombing
Sgt R Hart	+	practice over the Preston Cape ranges. Twelve
Sgt D G James	+	minutes after setting forth, the Wellington
Sgt L Blunt	+	dived and crashed near Culworth, 16 miles SW
Sgt E McCarthy	+	from the centre of Northampton, exploding on
		impact. Sgt Burton of Urmston, Manchester, and

a Leaving Exhibitioner Sutton Valence School to Cambridge University, is buried in Oxford (Botley) Cemetery, as is Sgt McCarthy. Sgt Hart rests in Newcastle-upon-Tyne (West Road) Cemetery, Sgt James lies at Llanelli (Box) Cemetery and Sgt Blunt is interred in the extension to Prestwich (St. Margaret's) Churchyard.

28 Nov   **16 OTU**   **Wellington III**   **X3923**   **Training**
1943

S/L W E Allison DFC	+	T/o Upper Heyford for a night exercise, during
W/O V Kearney DFM	+	which a midair collision occurred at 2355, over
Sgt W Siddoway	+	Oxfordshire, with another of the unit's aircraft.
Sgt R W McLachlan RCAF	+	Debris from the two machines was scattered in the
Sgt E Cole	+	vicinity of Baynard's Green (on the NE side of
Sgt R J W Dhering	+	the airfield). Sgt McLachlan RCAF was taken to
Sgt W R Hemsley	inj	Oxford (Botley) Cemetery, while the others who
		perished were claimed by their relatives. W/O

Kearney had recently completed a tour of duty with 207 Squadron and details of his award had been published in the London Gazette on 11 June 1943.

        16 OTU   **Wellington X**   **HE904**   **Training**

W/O A J Lowman	inj	T/o Upper Heyford similarly tasked and destroyed
F/O D J Arneil RCAF	+	in the manner described above. Four were taken
F/O G A H Stevens DFC RCAF	+	to Oxford (Botley) Cemetery, F/S Slater rests at
F/S F V M Slater	+	Pinxton (St. Helen) Churchyard, Sgt Rose lies in
Sgt D G E MacNeil RCAF	+	New Kilpatrick (or Hillfoot) Cemetery, Scotland,
Sgt W Rose	+	and Sgt Buffham is buried in Nottingham Northern
Sgt R Buffham	+	Cemetery. Following a comparatively good run of
Sgt W H Sayres RCAF	+	two months of intense training without a serious
		accident, the unit had now lost three Wellingtons

and eighteen aircrew killed (plus two injured) in the space of forty-eight hours.

Note. The aircraft movement cards for the three aircraft concerned in these accidents show that they had been well utilised. The two Mk. IIIs had been accepted on 23 September and 27 September 1942 respectively and had logged, in order, 421.40 and 546.46 flying hours, while the Mk. X had flown 362.05 hours (its date of acceptance has been omitted).

29-30 Nov   **81 OTU**   **Whitley V**   **BD259**   **Op: Nickel**
1943   Sgt Curtis-Hayward   T/o 2030 Tilstock and set course for Versailles.
                                    Homebound, sparks and flames were seen coming
from the port engine. The crew tried to continue on one engine, but at 0130 they were obliged to force -land, in a marsh, not far from Lancing in Sussex.

30 Nov 1943	**14 OTU**	**Wellington IC**	**X9680**	**Training**

Sgt J A Macfarlane RCAF inj T/o Husbands Bosworth for a night detail. Came
Sgt A J C John inj down at 0305 at Orton, 1 mile SW of Rothwell in
Sgt J E Graham inj Northamptonshire. A fire broke out immediately
Sgt C Plant inj and Sgt John sustained very serious injuries.
Sgt D Penton inj Taken to RAF Hospital Ely, he died on 21 December
1943; his grave is in Norwood Cemetery. Sgt
Graham died within hours; he rests at Lockerbie (Dryfesdale) Cemetery. Their
skipper made a good recovery but, sadly, was killed on operations in the last
full month of the war in Europe (see Bomber Command Losses, Volume 6, page 156).
At the time of his death, he was serving with 61 Squadron.

2 Dec 1943	**18 OTU**	**Wellington X**	**LN186**	**Training**

F/O J G McCall T/o 1020 Bircotes for circuit practice. Wrecked
ten minutes later in a heavy landing. Progressing
to Halifaxes, F/O McCall went to 148 Squadron and was lost in Halifax II JP162/S
during a Special Operations Executive sortie from Brindisi, Italy, on 5 August
1944. He is buried in Poland at Krakow Rakowicki Cemetery.

4 Dec 1943	**24 OTU**	**Whitley V**	**AD674 FB–D**	**Training**

F/O Cresswell T/o 0837 Long Marston for a day exercise. On
F/O Calder RCAF return to base, at 1237, the undercarriage failed
P/O Mackeracher RCAF to lower properly and F/O Cresswell made a very
commendable landing on one wheel. As the aircraft
slowed, so it drifted off the runway and onto soft ground, being damaged beyond
reasonable repair. The failure of the unit was traced to a broken rubber hose
connection to the undercarriage jack.

5 Dec 1943	**22 OTU**	**Wellington III**	**DF739 DD–J**	**Training**

Sgt J Koresky RCAF inj T/o Gaydon for a night exercise. Crashed 0130,
while landing at base, and caught fire.

11 Dec 1943	**16 OTU**	**Wellington X**	**LN531**	**Training**

F/S E Leseberg RAAF + T/o 1728 Upper Heyford for a night cross-country.
Sgt E Harris + Emerged from cloud and crashed 2303 at the hamlet
Sgt V M Plahte RNAF + of Little Rollright, 3 miles NE from Chipping
Sgt H O Mitchell RCAF + Norton in Oxfordshire. F/S Leseberg RAAF and
Sgt F Nichols + his three Canadian colleagues, along with Sgt
Sgt B N Redmond RCAF + Nichols, were buried in Oxford (Botley) Cemetery
Sgt J Foote RCAF + (Sgt Plahte RNAF very likely accompanied them,
though it is thought he has since been taken back
to Norway), while Sgt Harris rests in Norfolk at Diss Cemetery. Sgt Mitchell's
younger brother, Sgt James Walton Mitchell RCAF, lost his life while flying with
415 Squadron on 21 August 1944 (see Bomber Command Losses, Volume 5, page 390).

	26 OTU	**Wellington III**	**BK440**	**Training**

F/S A Merridew + T/o 0645 Little Horwood for a navigation sortie.
Sgt S Wilson + Exploded 0800, or thereabouts, and crashed near
F/S N Doherty RAAF + Park Farm, Hindolveston, 8 miles ESE of Fakenham
Sgt E W Brown + in Norfolk. Five were taken to Cambridge City
Sgt W E Martin RCAF + Cemetery, while Sgt Brown is buried in Rushden
Sgt A W Ellis RCAF + Cemetery. In the years since this tragedy,
various items of debris have been recovered
from the fields and the more important pieces are now with the Norfolk and
Suffolk Aviation Museum at Flixton.

	82 OTU	**Wellington X**	**HE460 –A**	**Training**

Sgt H Di Domenico RCAF inj T/o Ossington for a night cross-country, during
Sgt W D Howlett RCAF inj which the air bomber was permitted to fly the
Sgt E H D Maguire RCAF inj Wellington. While he was so doing, at 9,000
Sgt J L Barber RCAF inj feet, the starboard engine cut. The captain
Sgt G E Ryan RCAF inj immediately took back the controls but was unable
Sgt W Young + to prevent a massive loss of height. As the
aircraft passed through 2,800 feet, he ordered
his crew to bale out but the first airman to reach the hatch called to say he
thought they had descended below the safety height. Thus, at 2303, a heavy
forced-landing was made at Bourne's Cottages, Snowshill, 12 miles NE from
Cheltenham, Gloucestershire, hitting a tree in the process. Sgt Young of
Drumaheagles, Ballymoney in Co. Antrim rests in Bath (Haycombe) Cemetery.

12 Dec
1943

12 OTU   **Wellington X** **LN187**   **Training**

Sgt Coyle   T/o Chipping Warden for an evening flying detail
Sgt J Whitehouse   inj which ended at 2245 with most of the crew taking
to their parachutes after the Wellington ran out
of petrol. Sgt Coyle, along with his wireless operator (he is not named),
remained in the aircraft and forced-landed at Chesterton Green, Warwickshire.
Meanwhile, Sgt Whitehouse (an air gunner) was taken to the Royal Leamington Spa
Hospital after sustaining serious leg injuries.

27 OTU   **Wellington III** **X3958**   **Training**

F/S D W Higgerson RAAF   inj T/o Lichfield for a navigation exercise which
took the crew over the Irish Sea. At 1315, they
landed at Ballyhalbert airfield in Co, Down, but downwind by mistake. Realising
he was going to run off the airfield, F/S Higgerson RAAF promptly retracted the
undercarriage. On coming to a halt, a fire broke out.

13 Dec
1943

23 OTU   **Wellington III** **BK213**   **Training**

Sgt F A Debeck RCAF   inj T/o 1105 Stratford-upon-Avon for an exercise
P/O J Zinkham RCAF   inj in cross-country flying. While over southern
P/O A R McIntyre RCAF   + England the port engine failed and at 1445 the
P/O J E E Winch RCAF   inj bomber touched down at Henstridge airfield in
Sgt J Basistuk RCAF   inj Somerset. Still travelling at speed, the bomber
Sgt J L P D Carrier RCAF inj ran off the runway and smashed into the bank of
the River Cale on the east side of the airfield.
P/O McIntyre RCAF is buried in Bath (Haycombe) Cemetery. Sgt Debeck RCAF frac-
tured his skill and it is thought all of the injured were pretty badly hurt.
Very sadly, shortly after being passed fit to resume flying, Sgt Carrier RCAF
was killed when his 1664 HCU Halifax V DG295 crashed on 16 March 1944, coming
down on the Strenshall bombing ranges. He is buried in Harrogate (Stonefall)
Cemetery. Although his Christian names hint at a French-Canadian connection,
it seems he was an American from Rumford, Maine.

18 Dec
1943

21 OTU   **Wellington IC** **DV808**   **Training**

W/O G W Roberts   T/o 1207 Moreton-in-Marsh for a cross-country
Sgt T Freeman   detail, part of which being routed over the North
Sgt P North   Sea between Flamborough Head and The Wash. Became
Sgt T Briggs   lost and in lowering visibility, force-landed at
Sgt A Mundell   around 1550 on a golf course some 5 miles from
Huddersfield, Yorkshire. W/O Roberts was later
commissioned and lost his life in a midair collision between his Anson I DG799
and an Oxford I NM482 on the approach to Halfpenny Green airfield on 30 May 1945
(both aircraft were on the strength of No. 3 Air Observers School at Bobbington).

23 OTU   **Martinet I** **HP383**   **Training**

P/O J H N Brousseau RCAF   T/o 1030 Stratford-upon-Avon for a fighter
LAC W T R Warne   inj affiliation task. Three hours later, in steadily
deteriorating weather and unable to locate an
airfield in the gloom, P/O Brousseau RCAF forced-landed 1340, wheels down, in
a field, only to have the misfortune to run into a hole and turn over.

20 Dec
1943

14 OTU   **Wellington IC** **X9823**   **Training**

Sgt M W Ling   T/o Market Harborough for a cross-country flight.
Sgt R L Meakin   Believed to have been partially abandoned before
Sgt F Carling   force-landing 1400, downwind, on Folkingham
Sgt Deane   airfield, Lincolnshire. At the time, Folkingham
Sgt R V Ind   inj was still under construction. Sgt Ind was taken
to RAF Hospital Rauceby with back injuries. He
recovered well and, eventually, went to 463 Squadron. On 19 July 1944, his aircraft was lost over France (see Bomber Command Losses, Volume 5, page 337). The
Wellington summarised here had initially seen service with 149 Squadron, since
when it had passed through the hands of two training establishments before being
accepted by 14 OTU as recently as 18 November. In total, it had amassed 716.25
flying hours.

14 OTU   **Wellington IC** **HD983** **-W**   **Training**

F/O J Lipton   T/o 1417 Husbands Bosworth for flying practice.
Sgt T S Smiley   Wrecked circa 1650, in an emergency landing
brought about by loss of power from the port
engine, at Desborough airfield in Northamptonshire.

20 Dec
1943

81 OTU		**Oxford II**	**V3555**	**Communications**
W/O F J Denham	inj			T/o Tilstock but encountered very severe air
P/O D A Baker	inj			turbulence and, shortly before 1448 when the
F/O Williams RCAF	inj			Oxford was forced-landed amongst trees at Great
P/O Guinn RCAF	inj			Bullamore Farm, Caerleon, just above Newport in
Sgt W R Waldron RCAF	inj			Monmouthshire, the buffeting caused one of the

engine cowls to break off. Three were admitted to Station Sick Quarters Llandow suffering from little more than shock, but W/O Denham sustained quite serious cuts to his lip and right thigh and he was treated at the Newport Army Reception Station. This was the last aircraft to be written off by the unit prior to its transfer to No. 38 Group. Meanwhile, Sgt Waldron RCAF was posted to 82 OTU and was killed during a training detail on 3-4 February 1944.

21 Dec
1943

14 OTU	**Wellington IC**	**T2738**	**Training**
F/S C W Kipper RCAF			T/o 2055 Market Harborough for night flying
Sgt Comen			practice. After losing the port propeller and
Sgt Millington			reduction gear, forced-landed 2205, wheels up,
Sgt Walker			on the airfield. Three baled out, as ordered,

but the tail gunner (he is not named) remained in the aircraft with his skipper.

22 Dec
1943

18 OTU		**Wellington X**	**HE681**	**Training**
P/O G Lewis	inj			T/o 1140 Bircotes for a cross-country. Lost

power from the port engine and force-landed at approximately 1535, wheels retracted, in a field 4 miles SW of Douglas on the Isle of Man.

27 OTU	**Wellington X**	**HE653**	**Training**
P/O W J B Murphy RCAF			T/o 1645 Lichfield only to fly into a flock

of birds, several bodies being impacted in and around the port engine. With the motor misfiring, the crew force-landed with the undercarriage retracted near the airfield. They had been in the air for less than a minute. On 15-16 July 1944, P/O (now F/L) Murphy RCAF and his 467 Squadron crew failed to return from Nevers (see Bomber Command Losses, Volume 5, page 331).

29 OTU		**Wellington X**	**LN160**	**Training**
Sgt H A S Russell	inj			T/o Bruntingthorpe for a night navigation detail.
Sgt C Wilkins	inj			While in flight, the driving dogs on the port
Sgt D Newby	inj			engine's oil pressure pump failed, leading to
Sgt R Thompson	inj			the unit being closed down. While preparing to
Sgt F Fraser	inj			make an emergency landing at Wigsley, the bomber

clipped a tree near the airfield and crashed at around 0640, heavily. All were taken to RAF Hospital Rauceby. Sgt Russell had enlisted in Rhodesia during 1940 and it is very much suspected that he was later commissioned as a F/O H A S Russell of Salisbury, Rhodesia, lost his life during a raid on Walcheren, with 44 Squadron, on 23 October 1944 (see Bomber Command Losses, Volume 5, page 460).

22-23 Dec
1943

15 OTU		**Wellington IC**	**W5714**	**Training**
F/O D E Raymond RCAF	+			T/o 1832 Hampstead Norris for a night navigation
F/S G A Hebblewhite RAAF	+			exercise. After midnight, a call for assistance
F/S A Lipshitz DFM	+			was made and the first class fix, which placed
Sgt C Griggs	+			the aircraft at 5002N 0646W, was acknowledged.
Sgt A C R Miles	+			At 0058, came a second call asking for urgent
Sgt F W Mittonette	+			help and a second class fix, 5000N 0650W, was

duly sent. This was not acknowledged and the final call came at 0121 with the aircraft's wireless operator holding down his key, the transmission gradually fading away. Thus, it is presumed the bomber came down west of the Scillies. Five are commemorated on the Runnymede Memorial but the body of F/S Lipshitz was recovered and he rests in Edmonton Federation Jewish Cemetery. Details of his DFM for outstanding service with 10 Squadron appeared in the London Gazette on 14 May 1943.

23 Dec
1943

10 OTU	**Whitley V**	**P4997**	**Training**
F/S G P Wylie RNZAF			T/o 1122 Stanton Harcourt for a cross-country

which ended at 1352, due to loss of power from the starboard engine, in a forced-landing near Swanton Morley airfield, Norfolk.

27 Dec
1943

17 OTU	Wellington III X3344	Training
F/O B F Gilmore RNZAF	inj	T/o 1030 Turweston for a training detail but the
F/S R G Ward RAAF	inj	crew returned to base at 1110 after experiencing

engine trouble. As the aircraft neared the runway, it was realised the undercarriage had failed to lower fully and while trying to overshoot, the Wellington lost height and came down near one of the airfield's dispersal pans, injuring the entire crew which is quoted as eight.

Note. The accident record card shows F/O Gilmore's service number as 412223. On page 216 of Errol Martyn's second volume of 'For Your Tomorrow' is reference to S/L Brian Montgomery Gilmour DFC RNZAF killed in action on Anzac Day 1944, while flying with 9 Squadron; his service number is quoted as 412224. Further details may be found in Bomber Command Losses, Volume 5, page 189.

28 Dec
1943

20 OTU B Flt	Wellington III X3805 —H	Training
P/O H W Boyd RAAF	+	T/o 1138 Lossiemouth but crashed four minutes
F/S J E Thomas RAAF	+	later when first the port and then the starboard
F/S J P O'Donnell RAAF	+	engines failed. Three are buried in Lossiemouth
Sgt K Dunkerley	+	Burial Ground; two, F/S O'Donnell RAAF and Sgt
Sgt W M Bridge	+	Dunkerley have no known graves, while Sgt Bridge
Sgt R Summers	+	rests at Salford (Agecroft) Cemetery.

28-29 Dec
1943

16 OTU	Wellington X HE431	Op: Nickel
W/C G F Rodney		T/o 1905 Upper Heyford, course being set for
Sgt L J Wood		France. Soon after crossing the French coast,

and flying at 16,000 feet, the Wellington was hit in the port engine (probably by flak) and both turrets were rendered unserviceable. After aborting the mission and jettisoning the leaflets over the Channel, the crew eventually regained the south coast. By this time, however, the bomber was flying in and out of increasing amounts of cloud and at around 2145, uncertain of their position, the crew took to their parachutes. It was later discovered their aircraft had crashed between 1 and 2 miles S of Finmere airfield in Buckinghamshire.

29 Dec
1943

11 OTU	Wellington IC Z1047	Training
F/L G R Gunn RNZAF		T/o 1430 Oakley for dual circuits and landings.
Sgt J D Kieller		Wrecked 1435 when the undercarriage folded up

after a very heavy arrival. F/L Gunn RNZAF had completed a tour of operations in the Middle East, where he had flown with 108 Squadron and 70 Squadron. By the late summer of 1944, he was flying Lancasters and commanding a flight at Mepal, home of 75 Squadron. On 17 September, he was mortally injured when his aircraft crashed at Hawkinge airfield in Kent (see Bomber Command Losses, Volume 5, page 428).

23 OTU	Wellington X HE366	Training
WO2 D L Snider RCAF		T/o 1014 Stratford-upon-Avon for a cross-country.

The return to base was not without incident, for on touch down the bomber ballooned badly and the throttles were immediately advanced in order to overshoot and go round again. While doing so, the port engine failed and though the propeller was feathered, the Wellington lost height on the crosswind leg and at 1509 crashed into a hut on the airfield. No one was hurt, but the fire that followed marked the end of the aircraft.

30 OTU	Wellington III X3883 —O	Training
Sgt F Collett	inj	T/o Seighford for a night exercise. Crashed at
Sgt J Whitehead	+	around 2140, following an uncontrollable fire in
P/O J W Lorrimore	+	the starboard engine, near Hoar Cross, 6 miles
Sgt H W Miller	+	to the NE of Rugeley, Staffordshire. The last
Sgt T B Joyce	+	two named are buried in Stafford Cemetery, while
Sgt E Dean	+	the others who died were claimed by relatives.

30 Dec
1943

18 OTU	Martinet I JN429	Training
F/O P R Street DFM	+	T/o 1600 Bircotes for a fighter affiliation
Sgt J M Holmes	+	sortie. Lost control at 1610 while making a

dummy attack and spun in from 500 feet about a mile W of Worksop, Nottinghamshire. F/O Street (he gained his DFM which was Gazetted on 23 March 1943 for service with 148 Squadron), is buried alongside his brother, Sgt Richard Street, in Great Berkhampstead (St. Peter) Church Cemetery, while Sgt Holmes rests in Scotland at Cathcart Cemetery.

| 30 Dec
1943 | **26 OTU**
W/O K G Tucker RNZAF
F/S A Migner RAAF
Sgt A A Sadler
Sgt J E Lane | **Wellington III** | **BK491**
+
+
+
+ | **Training**
T/o 1854 Little Horwood for a night flying
exercise but banked steeply and crashed 1855
at North End Farm near Thornborough, 4 miles
or so NW of the airfield and 3 miles E of
Buckingham. The two Commonwealth airmen |

and Sgt Sadler were taken to Oxford (Botley) Cemetery, while Sgt Lane is
buried in Hemel Hempstead Cemetery.

| 31 Dec
1943 | **21 OTU**
F/O C R Amos
Sgt T J Freeman
Sgt P North
Sgt T Briggs
Sgt A Mundell | **Wellington IC** | **X9666**
inj
+
inj
+
inj | **Training**
T/o 1005 Moreton-in-Marsh for bombing practice
combined with a navigation exercise. While over
the Welsh mountains, the Wellington flew into
cloud and began to ice over. Sighting water
through a gap in the overcast, F/O Amos dived
in order to try and establish his position. |

Unfortunately, he failed to realise that high ground, shrouded in mist, lay
between himself and the sea and at circa 1220 his Wellington, descending at
high speed, sliced into Ffrith Caenewydd, above Aberdovey, Merioneth and burst
into flames. F/O Amos was thrown through the windscreen, his terrible injuries
proving fatal. Miraculously, Sgt Mundell was not too badly hurt and he managed
to free a very gravely injured Sgt North. Meanwhile, as Edward Doylerush
reports in the second volume of 'No Landing Place', David Hughes, a King's Scout
and the brothers Alun and Lewis Jones had arrived at the scene and rendered
invaluable aid (David Owen Hughes of the 1st Dovey Group later received the
Scouts Bronze Medal for his part in the rescue) in tending to the injured.
F/O Amos, whose parents were of Delta Tigre, Buenos Aires, is buried in Towyn
Cemetery, while Sgt Freeman and Sgt Briggs were taken to their home towns in
Kent and Worcestershire respectively. It will be recalled that while flying
with W/O Roberts, four members of the crew had been involved in a very serious
crash on 18 December (see page 266).

Resumé. How different the outlook at the end of 1943, than twelve months
previous. The confidence referred to at the conclusion of the last review
had continued to build and everyone from the lowliest aircraftman to those
very senior officers on the Air Staff were only too aware that the bombing
campaign was beginning to show distinct signs of success. From spring to
mid-summer, Bomber Command had mounted an unprecedented assault on the
industrial towns of the Ruhr, followed by the near total destruction of
the port city of Hamburg and a timely strategic raid on the German rocket
research centre at Peenemünde on the Baltic coast. Now, as 1943 gave way
to the New Year, the infamous Battle of Berlin was at its height.

The cost in terms of human lives and resources had been staggering and
in our modern times of the twenty-first century it is, perhaps, difficult
to comprehend how the Command managed to survive such traumatic events. In
simple terms, casualties were hovering at, or just below, five percent per
raid. Thus, on average, squadrons were (on paper) being wiped out several
times a year. Looking at the tables for 1943 (as reported in Appendix 1 on
page 444 of Bomber Command Losses, Volume 4), the long established units
were all losing, on average, fifty or more of their aircraft. One example
will suffice; the returns from 78 Squadron reveal eighty-seven of their
Halifaxes lost or destroyed on operations, with a further four aircraft
written off in training accidents. To overcome such terrible casualties
demanded a high throughput of crews from the training establishments and
an equally efficient output from the aircraft manufacturing plants.

Thus, in 1943, the bomber OTUs reached their peak strength with, at the
end of the year, twenty-two such establishments in existence. During the
twelve months past, No. 13 OTU had transferred out of the Command's aegis
and No. 25 OTU had disbanded. Although two more units would form in the
year ahead, others would disband as the Command's requirements were met.
With the not inconsiderable input from the Americans, 'round-the-clock'
bombing was fast becoming the norm. The slimmest shafts of light that had
heralded the start of the year were now blossoming with each passing day
into the warm glow of victory.

| 1- 2 Jan | 28 OTU | Wellington IC | R1086 | | Op: Nickel |
1944

F/S T G Fuller RAAF   inj   T/o 1725 Wymeswold and set course for France.
Sgt K C Manders RAAF   inj   Caught fire after persistent overheating from
Sgt White   the starboard engine and crashed at around 2100
Sgt Caffyn   at Belney Farm, Southwick, 4 miles ENE from
Sgt L Anderson   inj   Fareham, Hampshire. Sgt Walmsley was taken
Sgt K E Walmsley   +   to Manchester Crematorium, where his name is
commemorated on panel 22.

| 2 Jan | 14 OTU | Wellington IC | Z1169 -J | | Training |
1944

Sgt B M Helps   T/o 1815 Market Harborough for a night detail
but when first the starboard and then the port
engines lost power, a crash was inevitable. This duly happened circa 1900 near
Middleton Lodge in Northamptonshire, the crew having successfully abandoned
the stricken Wellington.

| 82 OTU | Wellington III | BK387 | | Training |

WO2 E I Glass RCAF   +   T/o 1831 Ossington for an evening exercise in
F/O J J McHenry RCAF   +   navigation. Encountered mist and low cloud,
WO2 J E Dalling RCAF   +   crashing 2240 into high ground at Tewitt Hall
WO2 J Henfrey RCAF   +   Wood near the Lonely Grouse Inn and not far
Sgt N W Crawford RCAF   +   distant from Oakworth, 2 miles SW of Keighley
Sgt E Savage RCAF   +   in Yorkshire. All were taken to Harrogate for
burial in Stonefall Cemetery.

| 3- 4 Jan | 11 OTU | Wellington X | LN661 -E | | Training |
1944

F/S H W A Blackwood RNZAF +   T/o 2310 Westcott for a navigation exercise
Sgt R Miller RAAF   +   that involved the crew flying over the North
P/O H R Willis RNZAF   +   Sea. Lost without trace. All are commemorated
Sgt J H Jaeger   +   on the Runnymede Memorial.
Sgt L D May   +
F/S W H Hare RAAF   +
Sgt J J Body   +

| 4 Jan | 11 OTU | Wellington IC | Z8793 | | Training |
1944

W/O T K Paul RNZAF   +   T/o Westcott for a night cross-country. At
F/S A L Coulter RNZAF   +   approximately 0200, the bomber flew into a
Sgt E Clayton   +   barrage balloon cable and hurtled down out
Sgt C Estcourt RNZAF   inj   of control into Brockhurst Wood, alongside
Sgt V E Payne   +   Farnham Common and roughly 3 miles N of Slough,
F/S J O´Callaghan RNZAF +   Buckinghamshire. At the request of an aunt,
Mrs J C¹ Kjelgaard, W/O Paul RNZAF was buried
in his grandparents burial plot at Durham (St. Oswald´s) Burial Ground. The
others who perished were taken to Northwood Cemetery. After the war, a committee
headed by Colonel Millar, raised sufficient funds for the installation of a
magnificent stained glass window in the south side of St. John´s Church in
memory of those who died. This, and other events, are faithfully recorded in
'The Story of Farnham Royal and Farnham Common' by Duncan Stewart, published by
the author in 1995. On 24-25 May 1942, while serving with 207 Squadron, W/O
Paul had been very seriously injured in a Lancaster crash which claimed the
lives of four members of his crew (see Bomber Command Losses, Volume 3, page 98).
He had been serving as a pilot instructor at Westcott since 7 November 1943.

| 28 OTU | Wellington IC | X9754 | | Ground |

F/S J McLoughlin RAAF   Caught fire at 1325 and burnt out while starting
engines at Warmwell airfield, Dorset. First used
by 99 Squadron, the Wellington had progressed to 1483 Flight before being passed
to 30 OTU and thence to 28 OTU, the latter unit taking it over the previous
January, When destroyed, it had logged 917.50 flying hours.

| 6 Jan | 18 OTU | Wellington X | LN448 | | Training |
1944

P/O R Dubois RCAF   T/o 1325 Worksop for dual circuits and landings.
Sgt R H Jenkins   Bounced badly on completion of the first circuit
and having flown round again, touched down at
about 1330. However, the previous arrival had so damaged the undercarriage that
the unit folded up and as the bomber skidded to a stop, a fire broke out. After
completing his training and converting to Lancaster, Sgt Jenkins was posted to
101 Squadron at Ludford Magna. On 13 August 1944, he failed to return from a
raid on Russelsheim (see Bomber Command Losses, Volume 5, page 382).

6 Jan   **24 OTU**   **Whitley V** **BD283 TY-B**   **Training**
1944   P/O H R Jones RCAF   inj T/o 2030 Honeybourne for night circuits and
                             inj landings but the port engine failed and after
                             inj clipping some trees with its port wing, the
                             inj Whitley thudded back to earth in Saintbury
                             inj Gardens. Two of the injured were detained
                                  in RAF Hospital Evesham. An examination of
the failed motor revealed a fracture to the No. 4 inlet valve. On his recovery
and subsequent conversion to Halifaxes, P/O Jones RCAF joined 420 Squadron. On
8 June 1944, his aircraft was shot down while attacking Acheres marshalling
yards (see Bomber Command Losses, Volume 5, page 262).

8 Jan   **23 OTU**   **Wellington X** **LN241**   **Training**
1944   Sgt F W Dolter RCAF   T/o 1305 Stratford-upon-Avon to practice single-
                                  engined flying procedures. While so engaged,
the running motor cut and before recovery action could be taken, the bomber hit
a high-tension pylon and crashed 1519 at Palton Farm, Alderminster, 4 miles SSE
of Stratford-upon-Avon. Later commissioned, Sgt Dolter was posted missing from
operations while flying Halifaxes with 424 Squadron in May 1944 (see Bomber
Bomber Command Losses, Volume 5, page 242).

9 Jan   **16 OTU**   **Wellington X** **HE320**   **Training**
1944   P/O B W J Chenier RCAF   T/o 0125 Upper Heyford for bombing practice
    Sgt V G Bailey   + during which the starboard engine failed.
    Sgt L G Martin RCAF   + Abandoned circa 0155, except for the tail gunner
                                  and crashed at Moat Farm on the NE side of Ford,
between 3 and 4 miles SW of Aylesbury, Buckinghamshire. Sgt Martin RCAF was
taken to Oxford (Botley) Cemetery, while Sgt Bailey, whose body was discovered
lying beneath his fully deployed parachute, rests in Hornchurch Cemetery. It
is reported that Westcott despatched their Senior Medical Officer with an
ambulance, plus a fire tender and, later, a guard to the crash site.

11 Jan   **17 OTU**   **Wellington III** **BK333**   **Training**
1944   F/O E W Ward RCAF   + T/o 0100 Turweston tasked for night training.
    F/O K G Berry RCAF   + Crashed 0232, after the starboard engine cut as
    P/O G E Clode RCAF   + the Wellington approached the airfield from the
    Sgt R Dawson   + south-west. Of those who died, the four RCAF
    Sgt W E Shillito RCAF   inj members of crew were buried in Oxford (Botley)
    Sgt J J Golding RCAF   + Cemetery, while Sgt Dawson rests in Normacot
                                (Holy Evangelists) Churchyard at Stoke-on-Trent.
With P/O J N Cairney at the controls, this Wellington had been involved in a
minor flying accident on 27 August 1943.

14 Jan   **12 OTU**   **Wellington X** **LN246**   **Training**
1944   F/S R E Pellew RAAF   T/o 1005 Chipping Warden for flying practice.
                                  Within half-an-hour of departing, the port
engine was stopped and the propeller feathered. Immediately, the Wellington
began to lose height and despite increasing power on the starboard motor, it
was impossible to arrest the rate of descent. F/S Pellew RAAF then took steps
to restart the port engine but when he unfeathered the propeller, a violent yaw
developed and at around 1035 a forced-landing was carried out, in a field, some
four miles from Priors Marston, 12 miles ESE of Royal Leamington Spa. Posted
to 115 Squadron, he failed to return from Aulnoye on 18-19 July 1944 (see
Bomber Command Losses, Volume 5, page 335).

16 Jan   **19 OTU D Flt**   **Whitley V** **N1475** **-X**   **Training**
1944   F/L A R Dawes   T/o 2137 Forres for a night exercise but struck
    F/L B Osborne   a bank and crash-landed, smashing the under-
                                carriage. Initially placed in hand for repairs,
the airframe was struck off charge on the last day of the month.

17 Jan   **15 OTU**   **Wellington X** **LN506**   **Air Test**
1944   F/L L J Woolven   + T/o 1040 Harwell for a night flying test only
    F/S F Turner DFM   + to encounter extremely misty weather. Thus,
                                  at 1045, while trying to avoid some trees, the
pilot lost control and crashed on East Ginge Down, roughly 3 miles SW of the
airfield. F/L Woolven is buried in Bentley-with-Arksey New Cemetery, while
his wireless operator, who had gained his DFM with 83 Squadron (Gazetted on
15 October 1943), was taken for interment in Oxford (Botley) Cemetery.

20 Jan
1944

18 OTU	Wellington III	BK273		Training

F/O R H B Jennings + T/o 2025 Worksop for night conversion to type.
P/O R F Wade + At around 2050, after overshooting towards the
P/O C W O Sears + west and climbing to around 400 feet, a blade
Sgt P Downes + sheared from the starboard propeller and moments
Sgt K E D Sillatoe + later the nose dropped and the Wellington dived
into the ground's of Worksop College, roughly
three to 4 miles beyond the Chance lighting system and in line with the runway.
On impact came a large billow of flame as the aircraft disintegrated, spreading
debris over a wide area. All rest in various United Kingdom cemeteries.

21 Jan
1944

18 OTU	Wellington III	Z1733		Training

F/S R Bluett RNZAF inj T/o Worksop for a combined navigation/bombing
F/S R B Turvey inj sortie. Lost power from one engine and as a
Sgt J Alcock inj result of making too fast an approach, crashed
P/O R T H Ellis + at 1145 into a transformer hut, just off the
Sgt C A McFarlane inj airfield. A fire broke out almost immediately.
P/O Ellis rests at Neston Cemetery in Cheshire.

27 OTU	Wellington III	BJ652	—Z	Training

F/S L G Edmonds RAAF + T/o 2017 Church Broughton for a night cross-
F/O K J Perrett RAAF + country. At 2130, on the advice of the Met.
F/S J Kydd RAAF + Officer at No. 93 Group, Lichfield broadcast
F/S W T Barnes RAAF + a general message advising all aircraft to land
F/S F P Deshon RAAF + by 2330. This was not acknowledged by Z which,
Sgt T D Murton RAAF + nine minutes later, transmitted a wireless
signal advising its position as at Gainsborough.
Subsequently, the bomber, heading south, crashed at 2210 cutting a swathe through
trees before impacting onto a limestone outcrop, just below 700 feet above sea
level and on the western edge of Smerrill Dale, a mere 100 yards from Smerrill
Grange Farm, the farm being near the Derbyshire village of Middleton-by-Youlgrave.
Following a very difficult recovery operation, all were taken to Chester (Blacon)
Cemetery. I am indebted to Major General P B Cavendish CB OBE DL for advising me
of the precise crash location and for sending an Historical Summary of the events
that followed this terrible crash.

84 OTU	Wellington X	LN238		Training

F/O C L R Spooner RCAF + T/o 1405 Desborough for circuits and landings.
F/O H Hoyle + Twenty-five minutes later, the starboard motor
Sgt Dunmall inj cut and the Wellington crashed into a wood at
Sgt G C Ogilvie + Geddington Chase, Geddington, 4 miles SSE of
Corby, Northamptonshire. Of those who died (and
it is reported three crew members, who have not been identified, emerged from the
wreckage virtually unscathed), F/O Spooner RCAF lies in Oxford (Botley) Cemetery,
F/O Hoyle, a recipient of a Merit Badge from Lancashire County Constabulary, was
taken to Leyland (St. Andrew) Churchyard, while Sgt Ogilvie was cremated at
Edinburgh (Warriston) Crematorium. Their aircraft was the first to be written
off since the unit formed at Desborough on 1 September 1943.

23 Jan
1944

20 OTU D Flt	Wellington X	HE751	—A	Training

Sgt D J Hurley + T/o 1116 Lossiemouth for fighter affiliation
Sgt L W Gransden + training. Dived from 4,000 feet and crashed
Sgt D Sanderson + at 1130 on Elgin Golf Course. The two RCAF
F/S J Williams RAAF + airmen (Sgt Burton RCAF was an American from
Sgt G F Couse RCAF + Seattle in Washington State) lie in Lossiemouth
Sgt R W Burton RCAF + Burial Ground, while F/S Williams RAAF and his
three companions and buried elsewhere.

24 Jan
1944

14 OTU	Wellington X	LN948	—Y	Training

F/S R W Meeking inj T/o 1100 Market Harborough for a cross-country
Sgt L A Harbottle inj but after climbing to 1,000 feet, the starboard
F/O C D McKinley RCAF + engine failed and four minutes after departing,
Sgt N J Allen + the bomber was a mass of flames at Braybrooke,
Sgt G B Lawson + some 2 miles NW of Desborough, Northamptonshire.
F/S B McDonagh inj F/O McKinley RCAF is buried in Oxford (Botley)
Cemetery, while the others who died were taken
to their home towns. F/S McDonagh made a good recovery but, sadly, died while
serving with 619 Squadron when his aircraft was shot down over France (see Bomber
Command Losses, Volume 5, page 325). At the time he held the George Medal.

25–26 Jan **16 OTU** **Wellington III** **BK501** **Op: Granville**
1944 F/O J G Johnson RCAF + T/o Upper Heyford in the company of three other
Sgt J F Smith + aircraft, their assigned route being base-Rennes-
P/O N K Perry RCAF + Cherbourg-St. Malo-Granville and return. Presumed
Sgt P H Normanton + crashed in the sea off the west coast of the
Sgt G D Mitchell RCAF + Cherbourg peninsular. Two bodies, those of
Sgt W K Rodgers RCAF + P/O Perry RCAF, an American from Springfield,
Missouri, and Sgt Mitchell RCAF were washed
ashore near Lessay and both rest in the local communal cemetery. Their four
companions are commemorated on the Runnymede Memorial. On 10 August 1943, with
Sgt F Collis at the controls, their Wellington had suffered a minor accident.

26–27 Jan **10 OTU** **Whitley V** **Z9434** **Training**
1944 F/L J W S Skinner T/o 2115 Abingdon for a night cross-country.
Force -landed at around 0015, some 2 miles E of
Croughton airfield, Northamptonshire, after the port engine failed. In his
report, F/L Skinner stated that the oil pressure had dropped and, later, the
unit caught fire. This was followed by a drop in both boost and revs on the
starboard motor and though he picked up the flare path leading to Croughton,
his altitude was fast decreasing and, therefore, a crash-landing was his best
option. It is further noted that two members of crew were slightly injured.

27 Jan **18 OTU** **Wellington X** **HE983** **Training**
1944 Sgt M Mullins + T/o Worksop for bombing practice over the
Sgt J A Jefferson RCAF + Clayworth ranges. Lost control at 9,000 feet
Sgt W Roy + and crashed about a mile ESE of Lound, 3 miles
Sgt R J King + NNW of Retford, Nottinghamshire. Sgt Jefferson
Sgt G Prentice + was taken to Harrogate (Stonefall) Cemetery,
where so many of his fellow Canadians rest.
The others were claimed by relatives in the south and north of England.

82 OTU D Flt **Wellington X** **LN168** **-O** **Training**
F/L D H Perry RCAF T/o 1834 Gamston for a night exercise, which
was terminated early following loss of power
from the port engine. Having regained base, the Wellington was brought in,
its wheels still retracted, and crash-landed 1949, a fire breaking out as the
bomber skidded to a halt. Soon after this incident, F/L Perry RCAF converted
to Halifaxes and joined 427 Squadron. On 11-12 May 1944, he was shot down on
a visit to Boulogne (see Bomber Command Losses, Volume 5, page 220).

84 OTU **Wellington III** **X3392** **Training**
F/S M Hogan RAAF + T/o 1930 Desborough for an evening cross-
Sgt A Peat + country. Crashed 2004, following an in-flight
Sgt S G Tucker + fire, near Molesworth airfield, Huntingdonshire.
Sgt S T Dean + Both Commonwealth airmen and Sgt Dean were taken
Sgt D B Palmer + to Oxford (Botley) Cemetery, while the others
Sgt M H Graham RCAF + rest in cemeteries in their home towns.

84 OTU **Wellington X** **HZ484** **Training**
S/L J H Kirton + T/o 1855 Desborough similarly tasked. Crashed
F/O D E Blunt + circa 2245 near Manor House, Arthingworth, 13
F/O F W Jones + miles N from the centre of Nottingham. All rest
Sgt J Orr + in various United Kingdom cemeteries, two being
Sgt A L T Butler + interred locally at Desborough Cemetery. Three
days after the tragedy, a Court of Inquiry was
convened under the Presidency of S/L Albert William Tregidio Hills DFM, a pre-
war regular whose award had been promulgated as early as 31 May 1940. Also
appointed to serve was W/O R Black.

27–28 Jan **24 OTU** **Whitley V** **BD370** **Training**
1944 F/L L E Lynch RCAF T/o 2115 Honeybourne for a night navigation
exercise. At around midnight, the port oil
pressure gauge began to register an alarming drop in pressure and not long
afterwards, flames could be seen issuing from the unit. Sighting a flare
path, F/L Lynch RCAF made a valiant effort to save his aircraft but was obliged
to force -land at 0015, with the undercarriage still retracted, just short of
Lindholme's runway. For his skill in handling a potentially life threatening
situation, it was recommended that he should be officially commended.

28 Jan
1944
16 OTU   **Wellington III**   **BJ612**   **Training**
P/O N J McDonald RCAF   T/o Upper Heyford for an evening cross-country which involved the crew flying out over the North Sea. It was during this phase of the exercise that an unidentified aircraft approached the Wellington and opened fire. Prompt evasive action enabled the crew to make good their escape, but on regaining the East Anglia coast the port propeller went into fine pitch and power from the motor decayed. The crew managed to pump the undercarriage down but could not get the unit to lock. Thus on arrival at Little Snoring airfield in Norfolk, the wheels promptly folded up on touch down, damaging the bomber beyond economical repair.

29 OTU   **Wellington III**   **X3962**   **Training**
Sgt J Barrie   T/o 1215 Bruntingthorpe and set off on a cross-country flight. Returned to base at about 1700 but while approaching the runway, the starboard engine failed and the aircraft lost height, clipped a tree and crashed. The crew appears to have escaped injury. On 30 August 1943, only prompt action by the ground staff prevented this bomber from being destroyed by fire, while on the ground at Bruntingthorpe.

28-29 Jan
1944
30 OTU   **Wellington X**   **HE914**   **-O**   **Op: Nickel**
Sgt R C Drinkwater RCAF   inj   T/o Seighford and set course for France. While
                        inj   returning to base, the starboard engine failed. For the better part of an hour, Sgt Drinkwater coaxed his crippled aircraft towards the south coast but at circa 2125, with the port engine gradually losing power, he tried to reach Detling airfield in Kent but was obliged to force -land at Boxley Grange, Boxley, 3 miles NNE from the centre of Maidstone. It is not thought that anyone was seriously hurt.

29 Jan
1944
12 OTU   **Wellington III**   **Z1697**   **Training**
F/O H A Baker RCAF   +   T/o 1235 Chipping Warden for solo circuits and
F/O D MacNeill RCAF   +   landings. Dived into the ground at 1252 and
Sgt C J Pascoe   +   caught fire near Culworth, 16 miles SW from
Sgt H D Westley RCAF   +   Northampton. F/O Baker RCAF, a veteran of the "Thousand Bomber" raids of 1942, and his fellow Canadians were taken to Oxford (Botley) Cemetery, while Sgt Pascoe is buried in Northampton (Dallington) Cemetery. He had died, aged 21, practically within sight of his home.

30 Jan
1944
11 OTU C Flt   **Wellington X**   **JA139**   **-L**   **Training**
F/S J R Hendry   T/o 1450 Westcott for fighter affiliation
Sgt Pryke   inj   training. Crash-landed circa 1520 in a field, following a drastic power loss from the port engine, at Mursley, 8 miles ESE of Buckingham. Sgt Pryke sustained a broken leg and was admitted to the Princess Mary's Hospital at Halton.

22 OTU   **Wellington III**   **DF566**   **Training**
F/O L W Matthews DFM RCAF   +   T/o 1924 Wellesbourne Mountford for bombing
F/O G H Schlitt RCAF   +   practice. A mere six minutes later, a crew
F/O C W Pearce RCAF   +   from Honeybourne reported seeing a Wellington
P/O E A Davis RCAF   +   on fire in the air before it dived, steeply,
Sgt F A Nichols RCAF   +   and exploded at North Farm, Ladbroke, some
Sgt W A Hobson RCAF   +   eight miles SE of Royal Leamington Spa. All
Sgt C A Bannon RCAF   +   are buried in Stratford-upon-Avon Cemetery. F/O Matthews RCAF had flown at least 31 bombing operations with 150 Squadron, the citation for his award being published in the London Gazette on 13 April 1943.

31 Jan
1944
28 OTU   **Wellington IC**   **Z1067**   **Unknown**
Struck off charge on this date after being re-categorised. However, a search of the accident records cards between October 1943, when it was accepted by the unit, and the end of January 1944, reveals no recorded incidents.

3 Feb
1944
16 OTU   **Wellington X**   **LN400**   **Air Test**
F/O D W Probyn RCAF   +   T/o 1600 Upper Heyford for a night flying test
Sgt J Mawhinney   +   but having climbed to 200 feet, the starboard
Sgt H D Tomkins   +   engine faltered and the bomber spiralled back
Sgt W R Burke RCAF   +   to earth. Three lie in Oxford (Botley) Cemetery while Sgt Tomkins was claimed by his family.

3 Feb	**28 OTU**	**Wellington IC**	**N2764**	**Training**
1944	F/O J R Wilson			

T/o 2218 Wymeswold for a night cross-country but crash-landed two minutes later at Hoton, 3 miles north-east of Loughborough, Leicestershire. In his report, F/O Wilson stated he considered the engines were 'sluggish' from the outset. Subsequently, the airframe was adopted for training purposes and allotted the serial 3498M.

	28 OTU D Flt	**Wellington IC**	**Z1114 -T**	**Training**
	Sgt J M Stephens RCAF	+	T/o 1202 Castle Donington for a cross-country.
	Sgt E E Cowie RCAF	+	On return to base the port engine began to fail
	Sgt J H Casselman RCAF	+	and at 1742 the bomber overshot the runway and
	Sgt J A Webb	+	finished up, totally wrecked, in a field on the
	Sgt W R Stone RCAF	+	northern side of the airfield. Of those who
	Sgt J R Patterson RCAF	inj	died, four rest in Oxford (Botley) Cemetery,

while Sgt Webb lies at Blackpool (Carleton) Cemetery. Sgt Patterson RCAF recovered from his very serious injuries and, eventually, joined 12 Squadron. On 12 December 1944, now commissioned, he was killed on operations to Essen (see Bomber Command Losses, Volume 5, page 509).

	84 OTU	**Wellington X**	**HE749**	**Training**
	F/S C A Harrison RNZAF	+	T/o 1110 Desborough armed with live bombs and
	P/O C C Lumby	+	set out on a navigation task. At approximately
	Sgt H L Mein RCAF	+	1600 the Wellington, by now low on petrol, was
	F/O J Waring	+	seen closing on Worksop airfield but it seems
	Sgt J R Ballantyne	+	the pilot was not happy with his approach for
	Sgt K B Lewis	+	the engine note increased and the bomber began
	Sgt A E W Budden	+	to overshoot. However, the angle of attack was

quite steep and before levelling out the aircraft stalled, plunging to the ground with the port engine spluttering. On impact the bomb load exploded, scattering debris over a wide area. The two Commonwealth airmen were laid to rest in Harrogate (Stonefall) Cemetery, while the others were taken back to their home towns.

3- 4 Feb	**82 OTU**	**Wellington III**	**X3409**	**Training**
1944	Sgt A C Fisher	+	T/o 2012 Gamston for a Bullseye detail. It is
	F/S C D Jones RAAF	+	believed the last wireless exchange took place
	Sgt E H D Maguire RCAF	+	at 2322. Then, at 0026, eyewitnesses saw the
	Sgt J L Barber RCAF	+	Wellington diving at high speed, striking the
	Sgt W R Waldron RCAF	+	ground near the airfield and exploding. The

funeral services for the four Commonwealth airmen were held at Ollerton Cemetery, that for Sgt Fisher at Crystal Palace District Cemetery. It will be recalled that Sgt Waldron RCAF had been slightly injured in late December 1943, while training at 81 OTU (see page 267).

5 Feb	**24 OTU**	**Whitley V**	**LA929 FB-T**	**Training**
1944	F/O R N Wilson RCAF		T/o Long Marston for a navigation exercise.

On regaining base, at around 1550, the weather had deteriorated and F/O Wilson RCAF had great difficulty in lining up with the runway. Consequently, he touched down well beyond the threshold. With the perimeter fence fast looming into view, he swung the aircraft in order to stay within the confines of the airfield and, as he did so, the undercarriage gave way, causing irreparable damage.

	26 OTU	**Wellington X**	**JA455**	**Training**
	Sgt E T Bowe RAAF	inj	T/o Wing for a training exercise. Lost power
	Sgt J Corrigan	inj	while preparing to land and crashed into a wood
	Sgt J S Duguid RCAF	+	at Fox Covert, about midway between Wing and
	F/S W C Kinsman RAAF	+	Stewkley, Buckinghamshire. Those who died are
	Sgt B J O'Hare RAAF	inj	buried in Oxford (Botley) Cemetery.
	Sgt K L Pierce		

6- 7 Feb	**19 OTU C Flt**	**Whitley V**	**LA836 ZV-B**	**Training**
1944	Sgt D A Brooks	+	T/o 2015 Kinloss for a night navigation sortie.
	Sgt J A Brown	+	Reported by coastguards to have crashed in the
	F/S E J Lever RAAF	+	sea at 0150, some 3 miles off Lossiemouth on the
	Sgt J E Harling	+	Moray coast. Despite an extensive search, no
	Sgt R C Woods RCAF	+	bodies were recovered and all are commemorated
	Sgt A R Saunders	+	on the Runnymede Memorial. Sgt Brown held a

Bachelor of Arts degree, with Honours.

8 Feb	18 OTU	Wellington X	LN185	Training

8 Feb
1944

18 OTU   **Wellington X**   **LN185**   **Training**

Sgt R H Ramsey +   T/o 1810 Worksop for a night exercise involving
F/O J Riddell RCAF +   cooperation with Mosquito XIII HK374 flown by
Sgt A C Jones +   F/L A B Woods AFC and 2Lt Bugge of 85 Squadron.
Sgt R G Graves +   Tragically, the Mosquito crew misjudged their
Sgt J L Harrison +   closing speed and smashed into the tailplane of
Sgt W Varley +   the Wellington which fell away, out of control,
Sgt S G Johnson +   to crash at 2000 at Priors Leas, Southbourne,
Sussex. The Mosquito, which was operating from
West Malling, is reported to have crashed near Elmsworth in Hampshire, with fatal
consequences for its crew. F/O Riddell RCAF and Sgt Jones lie in the extension
to West Thorney (St. Nicholas) Churchyard, while the others were claimed by
their next of kin. By a strange coincidence, two OTU aircraft had been lost
following midair collisions with Allied night-fighters (see page 171 for details
of the 25 OTU tragedy) and in each case a member of the night-fighter crew had
graduated from Cambridge. F/L Woods is remembered by his fellow officers for
his decorative skills and help with mess refurbishments.

19 OTU A Flt   **Whitley V**   **Z6880**   **—M**   **Training**

Sgt C A Irvine +   T/o 0958 Kinloss for a navigation exercise.
Partially abandoned, circa 1130, after the port
engine failed at 9,000 feet, Blairgowrie Police later reporting that wreckage
had been found about a mile W of the town and that the five members of crew
who had parachuted were at their station awaiting an ambulance. Sgt Irvine
is buried in Barrow-in-Furness Cemetery.

10 Feb
1944

21 OTU   **Wellington IC**   **DV426**   **Training**

Sgt V Ansell inj   T/o Enstone for a practice bombing detail over
inj   the Radway ranges. While operating at 10,000
feet, the port engine failed and the pilot
decided to return to base, However, before he could accomplish his aims, the
starboard motor began to falter and at 1215 a forced-landing was made, wheels
up, in a field near Bampton, Oxfordshire.

30 OTU   **Wellington X**   **HF516**   **—K**   **Training**

Sgt W E Keeler   T/o Hixon for a bombing exercise. While making
Sgt A J Welstead inj   ready to land, the starboard engine cut and the
Wellington came down at 1944, short of the run-
way. Sgt Welstead was critically injured and he died the following day while
being tended in Stafford General Hospital. His grave is in Nunhead (All Saints)
Cemetery. An examination of the failed engine revealed a seized front big end
bearing.

84 OTU   **Wellington X**   **HF603**   **Training**

Sgt J M Gaston RCAF   T/o 1955 Desborough for a night cross-country
but returned to base after an hour. However,
the approach was much too high and touch down eventually came with the bomber
well down the runway. With insufficient room to stop, the Wellington raced
into the overshoot area and was damaged beyond repair.

10-11 Feb
1944

27 OTU   **Wellington X**   **HZ372**   **Training**

F/O N A Hallam RAAF   T/o 1840 Lichfield for a navigation sortie.
Ran low on fuel and when both engines failed
the Wellington was crash-landed at 0040, in a field, near Orton-on-the-Hill,
ten miles NW of Hinckley, Leicestershire. It is reported that one member of
the crew (six in total) required medical attention.

11 Feb
1944

21 OTU   **Wellington IC**   **X3215**   **Training**

F/S J F Martin RAAF +   T/o 1941 Moreton-in-Marsh for a Bullseye detail
Sgt L Purvis +   but it is thought an engine failed for a minute
Sgt J E Armitage +   later the bomber crashed into a tree on Black-
Sgt P H Earwaker +   downs between 3 and 4 miles NNW of the airfield
Sgt M Hole +   and about a mile WSW of Stretton-on-Fosse in
Sgt M J Breen +   Warwickshire. F/S Martin RAAF and two members
of his crew rest in Oxford (Botley) Cemetery,
Sgt Purvis is buried in Ealing and Old Brentford Cemetery (known locally as
South Ealing Cemetery), Sgt Hole rests at Deal Cemetery, while Sgt Breen was
taken back to the Republic of Ireland and interred in Naas (St. Corban's)
Catholic Cemetery, Co. Kildare.

12 Feb **12 OTU** **Wellington III** **BK248** **Training**
1944
F/S L M Sergeant RAAF + T/o 2042 Chipping Warden for a night bombing
Sgt H L Williams + practice sortie. At 2122, Flying Control
F/O R A J Vagg RCAF + called the aircraft, instructing it to land.
Sgt W L Pemberton + This message, which may not have been ack-
Sgt J J Gillis RCAF inj knowledged, was later repeated, but nothing
was known until 2300 when a report came through
to say that the burnt out remains of a bomber had been found at Fosters Booth
on Watling Street, some 9 miles NE of the airfield. Subsequently, it was learnt
that the crash had occurred at 2152 and that Sgt Gillis RCAF was in hospital
with a fractured right leg. Of those who perished, two were buried in Oxford
(Botley) Cemetery, Sgt Pemberton was laid to rest in Banbury Cemetery, while
Sgt Williams was taken back to Staffordshire and Tipton Cemetery. F/S Sergeant
of South Yarra, Victoria, had married Olive Sergeant of Edgeware, Middlesex.

24 OTU **Whitley V** **N1375** **Training**
P/O G G Moore RCAF T/o 1855 Honeybourne for night circuits and
landings. At 1925, made a good touch down
but almost immediately collided with another of the unit's Whitleys which,
unwittingly, had begun to taxi along the duty runway.

24 OTU **Whitley V** **Z6673 TY-C** **Training**
F/L R N Mathews DFC + T/o 1850 Honeybourne similarly tasked and
Sgt P B Eagles RCAF destroyed in the manner described above.
It transpired that there had been some confusion
between the Airfield Control Officer and the airmen stationed at the upwind end
of the runway regarding lighting and F/L Mathews was under the impression he had
been cleared to back-track. He is buried in Bath (Haycombe) Cemetery. His pupil,
Sgt Eagles RCAF, was unhurt and, later, he joined 426 Squadron. On 29 July 1944,
his Halifax was one of the twenty-six aircraft lost from an attack on Hamburg
(see Bomber Command Losses, Volume 5, pages 355-358).

24 OTU **Whitley V** **BD238** **Training**
Sgt Davies T/o 1820 Honeybourne for an exercise in night
F/S J W L Doherty RCAF navigation. Encountered very severe icing which
led to failure of the starboard engine. Wisely,
the crew took to their parachutes, leaving their aircraft to crash at 1935 near
Ledbury in Herefordshire.

13 Feb **15 OTU** **Wellington X** **LN658** **Training**
1944
Sgt H Chalton + T/o 1852 Harwell with the intention of flying
Sgt P T Parker + base-Taunton-Bideford-St. Mary's-Skomer Island-
Sgt I G Morgan + Fishguard-Worcester-base. At 2210, the crew
Sgt S Long + obtained a fix which showed they were more or
Sgt S Booth + less on track. Ten minutes later, the aircraft
was plotted as showing broad Identification
Friend of Foe emissions, after which nothing further was heard. Thus, all
are commemorated on the Runnymede Memorial.

14 Feb **22 OTU** **Wellington III** **HZ110** **Training**
1944
Sgt R W Shields RCAF + T/o Wellesbourne Mountford for night circuits
Sgt M J Craig RCAF + and landings, though, apparently, used the
WO1 A H Goodman RCAF + facilities at Snitterfield. Undershot and
Sgt T J Karaim RCAF + crashed 2226 near Cornyns Farm and caught fire.
All are buried in Stratford-upon-Avon Cemetery.
Although there are no indications as such, it is possible Sgt Craig RCAF served
under this name as his parents are shown as Phillip and Annie Krakoviski.

15 Feb **15 OTU** **Wellington III** **DF630** **Training**
1944
F/O D McCabe RCAF T/o 1145 Harwell for gunnery practice, eight
crew being aboard (in addition to the pilot).
Soon after clearing the circuit, the starboard engine failed completely and
when the port motor commenced misfiring, a forced-landing became inevitable.
Thus, at 1150, F/O McCabe RCAF set the Wellington down, wheels retracted, a
mile S of Chilton and 6 miles ESE from Wantage, Berkshire.

16-17 Feb **82 OTU** **Wellington X** **HE741** **Training**
1944
Sgt J A Phillis RCAF T/o 2210 Ossington for night training. Crashed
0025, due to double engine failure, at base.

20 Feb 1944	**26 OTU** F/S J S Wood	**Wellington X**	**HE479**	**Training**

T/o 2140 Wing for night circuits and landings only to suffer a runaway propeller. F/S Wood managed to climb to 300 feet, and feather the airscrew, but was unable to prevent the crash that ensued five minutes later, during which the Wellington caught fire.

21 Feb 1944	**23 OTU**	**Wellington III**	**BK506**	**Training**

F/S J C E F Rouleau RCAF   inj   T/o 1300 Stratford-upon-Avon for a cross-
F/O W L Tessier RCAF   country. Crashed 1520, after the port engine
P/O D G Decoste RCAF   inj   failed, at Cliburn, 5 miles SE of Penrith in
WO2 M Labelle RCAF   inj   Cumberland. Sgt Proteau RCAF is buried in
Sgt B A Reaume RCAF   inj   Chester (Blacon) Cemetery. This was the unit's
Sgt M P Proteau RCAF   +   last serious accident, prior to disbanding on 15 March 1944.

	27 OTU	**Wellington X**	**HE211**	**Training**

F/O N A Hallam RAAF   inj   T/o Lichfield for a night navigation detail.
Sgt J C Lee   inj   While letting down through cloud, the port engine failed and the Wellington crash-landed at around 0330, some 2 miles SW of the airfield. Sgt Lee sustained a broken leg, while for F/O Hallam RAAF it was his second serious crash in less than a month (see page 276).

22 Feb 1944	**24 OTU** P/O L W Frame RCAF	**Whitley V**	**Z9488**	**Training**

T/o 1907 Honeybourne tasked for an evening navigation exercise. To their alarm, the Whitley suddenly veered off the runway, ground looped and lost its under-carriage. In a statement, P/O Frame RCAF said he had anticipated a swing to port but when the Whitley went to starboard, he was caught quite unprepared.

23 Feb 1944	**18 OTU**	**Wellington III**	**BK156**	**Training**

F/S S Sarachman PAF   T/o Finningley for an evening navigation flight.
F/S M Grabowski PAF   While over Cumberland a fire broke out in the
P/O J J Zywicki PAF   starboard engine. The propeller was feathered
F/S W Cander PAF   and soon afterwards the blaze died away. Then
F/S W Korycko PAF   trouble broke out with the port motor and upon entering cloud, handling of the aircraft became quite difficult. At roughly 2100 a controlled ditching was carried out off Workington. P/O Zywicki PAF lies in the Polish Plot at Newark-upon-Trent Cemetery. Some records indicate this Wellington was written off during the course of a technical inspection at Finningley on 26 November 1943, after slipping off its jacks. However, the accident record card raised in respect of this incident shows that the damage was categorised as repairable at station level. Referring to Air Ministry Form 78, there are no indications of this work being carried out and on 1 March 1944, the card is annotated as struck off charge.

	21 OTU P/O A Calvert DFM	**Wellington IC**	**T2567**	**Training**

inj   T/o Enstone for a fighter affiliation exercise. On return to base, and while overshooting the runway at 1635, the port engine cut and the Wellington forced-landed in a field near the aerodrome. Very sadly, P/O Calvert was killed five weeks later when his Martinet trainer crashed near Bampton. Prior to his arrival on the unit, he had served in the Middle East with 37 Squadron, details of his award being published in the London Gazette on 3 March 1944.

23-24 Feb 1944	**84 OTU** Sgt Klunczny RCAF	**Wellington X**	**LN596**	**Op: Nickel**

T/o 1900 Desborough and set course for France. On the return journey, the port engine failed and though the crew were able to get the wheels down, they were not so successful with the flaps. Landed 0045 on, or near, Long Newnton airfield in Wiltshire and wrecked, due to the brakes not being effective on the damp surface.

24 Feb 1944	**14 OTU**	**Wellington IC**	**DV668**	**Ground**

Destroyed 1440 by fire at its dispersal pan on Market Harborough airfield when a person, or persons, unknown discharged the aircraft's Verey pistol inside the fuselage. Used first by 16 OTU, but on unit charge since 26 September 1942, the Wellington had accumulated a total of 736.55 flying hours.

24 Feb   **17 OTU**   **Wellington III   BJ655**   **Training**
1944   F/S D L Haynes RAAF   T/o 0300 Turweston for high-level bombing but
                                                    the engines laboured and the Wellington failed
to gain height. Retracting the wheels, F/S Haynes RAAF successfully force –
landed four minutes later without injury to himself or his crew.

          28 OTU   **Wellington IC   R1269**   **Training**
          Sgt J F Ross-Myring   T/o 1947 Castle Donington for night bombing
                                                practice. This detail was carried out, as
briefed, but on return to base the port engine failed and while trying to go
round again, the Wellington crashed at 2337, near the airfield.

          30 OTU   **Wellington X   HE903**   **Training**
          F/O E Ryan   +   T/o 1657 Seighford for a Bullseye exercise
          F/O W O Thompson   +   involving five of Seighford's aircraft and
          F/O C J Yates   +   two from Hixon. Emerged from cloud, in a steep
          Sgt D D Roblin   +   dive, and crashed 2222 at Ranton, near the air-
          Sgt D H Hearton   +   field and about 4 miles W of Stafford. F/O Yates
                                                was buried in Stafford Cemetery but F/O Thompson
was interred in Chester (Blacon) Cemetery, the others being taken to their homes
in England and Scotland. F/O Ryan's brother, Sgt George Ryan, died on 8 June
1942, while undergoing training at 10 OTU (see page 124). Both were aged 21 at
the time of their deaths.

29 Feb– **10 OTU**   **Whitley V   LA787**   **Op: Nickel**
1 Mar 1944 F/S R J Larner   +   T/o 1902 Abingdon and set course for France and
          Sgt R B Shuttleworth   +   the region around St. Quentin. Disappeared
          Sgt G W Smith   +   without trace. All are commemorated on the
          Sgt A E Jacks   +   Runnymede Memorial. Unusually, three members
          Sgt H J Prouten   +   of the crew were in their thirties, a quite
                                                senior age for aspiring operational airmen.
It is further observed that Sgt Smith had been a member of the pre-war Auxiliary
Air Force.

1 Mar   **84 OTU**   **Martinet I   MS803**   **Training**
1944   F/S J M Hewett   inj T/o 1950 Desborough to practice night-fighter
                                                tactics. Force –landed 2023, due to engine
failure, and hit a wall surrounding an airfield marker beacon, some 150 yards
off the perimeter.

1– 2 Mar **15 OTU**   **Wellington X   LN614**   **Training**
1944   F/S J V Avery   +   T/o 2226 Harwell for a night bombing exercise.
          F/S W R Goodwin   +   At 0146, the crew returned to base and having
          Sgt B H Pattenden   +   called on the radio requesting permission to land
          F/S D W Petitt RAAF   +   were given a "green" to do so. However, the
          Sgt G D Pearson   inj bomber then disappeared from view and it was
          Sgt H G Reason   +   daylight before wreckage was found at Lollingdon
                                                Hill Farm, near Cholsey, 3 miles SSW of Walling-
ford, Berkshire. F/S Goodwin was buried in Harwell Cemetery, while F/S Petitt
was taken to Oxford (Botley) Cemetery; the others who died being claimed by
relatives. This was the last fatal accident to befall the unit before it
disbanded thirteen days later. At the Court of Inquiry, it was felt that
a catastrophic electrical failure overtook the crew.

          28 OTU   **Wellington IC   DV948   –G**   **Op: Nickel**
          Sgt P H Allen   T/o 1900 Wymeswold and headed for France. It
                                                is likely that the crew were on the home leg
when trouble manifested itself, first with the starboard engine and then, as
the crew were combating the fire that had broken out in this motor, the port
engine took light and shed its propeller! Displaying remarkably good airmanship
for such a relatively inexperienced pilot, Sgt Allen succeeded in force –landing
at 2325 in a field near Cranfield airfield, Bedfordshire.

2 Mar   **14 OTU**   **Wellington IC   DV719**   **Training**
1944   Sgt J Bumford   T/o 1906 Market Harborough but abandoned seven
                                                minutes later, following a fire in the port
engine and left to crash at Weston-by-Welland, a Northamptonshire village, some
seven miles WNW of Corby and practically on the border with Leicestershire. It
was found that the No. 3 cylinder had failed.

3 Mar   **83 OTU**   **Wellington X** **LN164**   **Training**
1944   F/S J Graham   inj T/o 0227 Peplow but while climbing away, the
port engine failed. F/S Graham kept control
and, somehow, managed to get around the circuit though his altimeter was
registering less than 100 feet. Then, while on the crosswind leg, the bomber
suddenly veered through 180 degrees and crashed. It is believed that five
members of the crew were injured and, possibly, one succumbed to his wounds.

4 Mar   **11 OTU**   **Wellington X** **HE229 OP-D**   **Air Test**
1944   F/L A B Smith RNZAF   inj T/o 1403 Westcott but having climbed to a
    F/S West   inj mere 75 feet, the port engine stopped. The
    Sgt A F Bogan   + bomber immediately swung sharply to port and
crashed at Akeman Street Station. Sgt Brogan,
a pre-war regular who had trained as an engine fitter, came from Cork in the
Irish Republic. He is buried in Oxford (Botley) Cemetery.

18 OTU   **Wellington X** **LP240**   **Transit**
    Sgt W A Stewart   T/o 1525 Ossington for Finningley, which was
reached at 1600. On touch-down, the Wellington
ballooned back into the air and began to drift in the strong crosswind. Sgt
Stewart tried to go round again but before he could apply sufficient power,
the bomber hit the ground and was wrecked.

19 OTU B Flt   **Whitley V** **AD682** **-X**   **Training**
    F/S E R Parkes   T/o 0905 Kinloss for a cross-country, during
the course of which the crew encountered very
severe icing. Thus, at approximately 1055, the Whitley forced-landed near
Hillside Farm, Alves, a village roughly midway between Forres and Elgin.

20 OTU D Flt   **Wellington III** **HZ134** **-P**   **Training**
    F/S A G Robertson   inj T/o 1205 Milltown for a bombing exercise. Flew
    Sgt G H Bodsworth   + into cloud and while in the process of banking,
    F/S W S McIntyre USAAF   + on instruments, lost height and crashed 1215,
    Sgt F Cheney   inj possibly in the vicinity of Bin of Cullen, some
    Sgt S Smith   inj three miles ESE of Buckie, Banff. Those who
    Sgt A W Mills   + survived were taken to Seafield Cottage Hospital
at Buckie, where Sgt Cheney died from his wounds.
He was taken back to Yorkshire and laid to rest in Gomersal (St. Mary) Church-
yard, Spenborough. Sgt Bodsworth rests in Leicester (Gilroes) Cemetery, while
Sgt Mills was cremated at Manchester Crematorium. Their American colleague,
F/S McIntyre rests in Morton Parish Church Cemetery, Blackpool.

7 Mar   **18 OTU**   **Wellington X** **HE818**   **Training**
1944   P/O F R Bedford   + T/o 2015 Worksop for night circuit training.
    Sgt C R Whisk   + Overshot the runway, failed to climb above 600
    Sgt D W Tindell   + feet and crashed 2035, out of control, some
    Sgt R W Tunnicliffe   + six miles N of Worksop. P/O Bedford, who came
    Sgt C Cletheroe   inj from Lindfield in Sussex, rests in Harrogate
(Stonefall) Cemetery, while the others were
claimed by their next of kin. It is observed that Sgt Whisk of South Shields
was known to his family and friends as Peter.

8 Mar   **19 OTU C Flt**   **Whitley V** **Z9468** **-D**   **Training**
1944   F/S A W Meaden   inj T/o Kinloss for a night exercise which ended
    Sgt A J Shorter   inj at 2252 with the Whitley down in the Cromarty
    Sgt F Jones   inj Firth, off Alness, as a consequence of losing
    Sgt M A Harris   inj power from both engines. All were admitted to
    Sgt R L Evans   inj Station Sick Quarters at Alness suffering from
    Sgt D G Lockyer   inj the effects of shock and exposure. On 17 June
1944, fully recovered and fresh from their
Halifax conversion (where they were joined by Sgt R G Wells as their flight
engineer), they reported to 158 Squadron at Lissett and in the months that
followed completed a successful tour of operations. Interestingly, in 19 OTU
records, it is indicated that the crew were convinced they were flying in "G"
but this aircraft had been assigned to F/O Bounskill. This may be correct, but
at Lisset the crew flew most of their sorties in HX356 NP-G which bore the name
"Goofy's Gift". Prior to its loss in November 1944 (see Bomber Command Losses,
Volume 5, page 482), it survived 73 operations.

13-14 Mar   **11 OTU**   **Wellington X**   **HF480**   **-E**   **Op: Nickel**
1944

F/S G C Jamieson RNZAF	+
Sgt Mabbett	
Sgt J A Lancaster	+
Sgt Foard	
Sgt J T Mellish	+
Sgt W Blumire	+

T/o 1955 Westcott using call sign MZL E and set course for France. Having safely completed their primary objective, the crew then proceeded, as instructed, on a navigation exercise. While on this phase, the Wellington ran low on petrol and the crew called up Little Horwood and requested permission to make a precautionary landing. En route, having been given clearance, the engines began to splutter and the order to bale out was given. Only two were able to comply before the bomber dived to the ground at 0235, crashing amongst trees just short of Little Horwood´s runway and broke up. F/S Harrison RNZAF rests in Oxford (Botley) Cemetery, while the others who perished were taken to their home towns.

15 Mar   **11 OTU**   **Wellington X**   **LN660 KJ-O**   **Training**
1944

F/O J H S Lyon DFC RAAF	+
F/S D V R Francis RNZAF	+
F/O G H Gilbert RNZAF	+
F/O R Taylor	+
F/S G Hudson	+
Sgt R R Kemp	+
Sgt R D Barlow	+
F/S A F Goold RNZAF	+

T/o 2005 Westcott for a night cross-country. Crashed 2235 just to the E of Quainton, 6 miles NW from Aylesbury, Buckinghamshire, after flying into Stirling III EH989 WP-P of 90 Squadron (see Bomber Command Losses, Volume 5, page 117). The three RNZAF airmen are buried in Oxford (Botley) Cemetery, while the others rest in churchyards, both in England and Scotland. It is likely their Australian skipper was claimed by relatives as he lies in Berwickshire at Lennel Old Churchyard, Coldstream. During 1943, he served with 9 Squadron, flying many of his sorties in Lancaster III EE136 WS-R "Spirit of Russia", which went on to record 109 operational missions.

       12 OTU   **Wellington III**   **BJ696**   **Training**

F/O D L J Hill RCAF   T/o 1926 Chipping Warden for a night flying detail. Wrecked 2341, following a wheels up arrival at base, in the aftermath of which the bomber caught fire. It is indicated that two of the seven-man crew sustained minor injuries and both were removed to Halton for treatment. Accepted by the unit on 31 July 1942, this Wellington very nearly came to grief within a fortnight when, on 12 August, it was fired upon by a British convoy, sailing off Bridlington, shrapnel from one of the bursts entering the forward fuselage and mortally wounding the air bomber, Sgt Weston. Sgt Serger, the pilot, force -landed and his tail gunner, Sgt Lloyd, was admitted to Bridlington Lloyd Hospital with a compound fracture of the left radius and severe lacerations to his left knee and thigh.

16 Mar   **12 OTU**   **Wellington III**   **BK494**   **Training**
1944

F/S H R Hodge RCAF   T/o 1930 Chipping Warden for a night cross-country. Crash-landed at around 2235 at East Moor airfield, Yorkshire, after losing oil from the starboard engine.

       28 OTU   **Wellington IC**   **R1183**   **Training**

F/S A J Moseley RAAF	inj
Sgt W J Foxley	inj
F/S J N Gunnis RAAF	inj
Sgt A W H Rowley	+
Sgt E Small	inj

T/o 2319 Castle Donington for a night exercise but crashed within a minute of becoming airborne after the flaps dropped fully down, causing the nose to pitch up. With only 200 feet in hand, F/S Moseley RAAF was unable to retrieve the situation before his aircraft stalled and hit the ground. Sgt Small died from his injuries; as with Sgt Rowley he was taken back to his home town.

17 Mar   **17 OTU**   **Wellington III**   **BK352**   **Training**
1944

P/O R Dennis DFM	+
F/S P J Calder RAAF	+
F/S E W Baldwin RAAF	+
Sgt J J O Walters	+
F/S D S Robinson	+
Sgt T J Greenhill RAAF	+

T/o 0055 Turweston for night circuit training. Overshot 0105, coming down near Brackley airfield, and caught fire. Four rest in Oxford (Botley) Cemetery. P/O Dennis, whose award had been published in the London Gazette on 14 September 1943, following his tour of duty with 199 Squadron, is buried in Featherstone Cemetery, while Sgt Walters was taken to Marshfield (St. Mary) Churchyard.

       17 OTU   **Wellington X**   **HE915**   **Training**

F/O A C Ball   T/o 1445 Turweston for an air firing exercise. Ditched 1615, due to engine failure, some twenty miles S of Flamborough Head. Subsequently, the crew were picked up by the navy.

17 Mar **27 OTU** **Wellington III** **X3967**   **Training**
1944 F/S A R Dyer RAAF   T/o 2139 Church Broughton for a night exercise.
             At the third attempt to land, the bomber under-
shot the runway and crashed at 2334, a fire soon following. F/S Dyer RAAF was
posted (after converting to Lancasters) to 467 Squadron and was reported missing
from Bois de Casson on 2 August 1944 (see Bomber Command Losses, Volume 5, page
367). Accepted on unit strength on 8 October 1942, the Wellington had flown a
total of 739.20 hours.

19-20 Mar **14 OTU** **Wellington IC** **X9949** **-F**   **Training**
1944 P/O J E Furber   inj T/o 2010 Market Harborough for a night exercise
   P/O E Ferguson RCAF inj in navigation. On return to base, and while
   P/O W J Beugley RCAF inj circling to land, suffered total engine failure,
   Sgt H McKernan   inj crash-landing 0135 in the circuit near Little
   Sgt J L Peck RCAF   + Oxenden. Sgt Peck RCAF is buried in Brookwood
   Sgt Holyoak   Military Cemetery.

20 Mar **82 OTU** **Wellington X** **LN181** **-Z**   **Training**
1944 F/O C R Floyd RCAF + T/o Ossington for a night cross-country. Lost
   F/O R F Calnan RCAF + power from the port engine and upon entering
   P/O R N MacGillivray RCAF + cloud, went out of control and crashed twixt
   F/O D L Jacobs RCAF + 2250 and 2300 at Yardley Gobion, 11 miles SSE
   F/O M L Fullerton RCAF + from Northampton. All are buried in Brookwood
   Sgt L H Johnston RCAF + Military Cemetery. An engine and scraps of the
   P/O H C Millen RCAF + geodetic framework are held at Bletchley Park,
   F/O W J Mohring RCAF + while a memorial lectern has been dedicated at
            Yardley Gobion parish church.

21 Mar **20 OTU** **Wellington III** **X3545 ZT-N**   **Transit**
1944 F/S R E Cardona FFAF + T/o 2040 Leuchars with the intention of returning
   Lt F A Vandenabelle FFAF + to base, but failed to arrive. It is believed the
   Lt L A Lecomte FFAF + crew made their last wireless call at 2127.
   F/S M E Billot FFAF +
   F/S P Ambual FFAF   +
   Sgt M Bruneau FFAF   +

23 Mar **17 OTU** **Wellington X** **HE688**   **Training**
1944 F/O E N J Thomson RNZAF + T/o 1915 Silverstone for an evening cross-
   F/S B J Jones RAAF + country. Lost control, due to the port engine
   Sgt D L Watson RAAF + failing, and while trying to arrest the steep
   Sgt E P Moore   + dive the Wellington broke up and crashed 2105
   Sgt D G Stephens   + to the E of Little Beech Hill near Ellerbeck,
   Sgt B Woodhead   + about 4 miles ENE of Northallerton, Yorkshire.
            Funerals for the three Commonwealth members of
crew were conducted, at Harrogate (Stonefall) Cemetery, by The Church of England
padre from RAF Leeming. The others were taken to their home towns. Sgt Stephens
had, until recently, been a member of the Air Training Corps.

Note. A detailed account of the accident was submitted by Headquarters RNZAF
London to the Air Department in Wellington on 31 August 1944, paragraph B of
the report giving details of the sequence of the structural failure as the
Wellington plunged, almost vertically, from the sky. The report times the
accident as approximately 2105, but in a letter, dated 5 April 1944, written
to the pilot's mother, by the Officer Commanding RAF Silverstone, the crash
is said to have occurred "at 11 o'clock". I am, indeed, extremely grateful
to Errol Martyn for sending me a copy of this document.

22 OTU **Wellington X** **HF732**   **Air Test**
F/L G B Leddy DFC RCAF + T/o 1555 Sywell but veered out of control and
F/O W M Rawbone RCAF + ran at high speed into another of the unit's
P/O T W Dimma DFM RCAF + aircraft. The three RCAF members of crew were
LAC C W H Brook   inj taken to Brookwood Military Cemetery, while the
LAC O J McGowan   + others (LAC Brook succumbed to his injuries
AC2 S J Brandon   + three days later) were buried in their home
          towns. F/L Leddy RCAF had gained his DFC while
serving with 424 Squadron. He had already survived two flying accidents; a
ditching off the Italian coast in October 1943 and, the following month, a crash
in the desert. P/O Dimma RCAF had flown his operational tour with 408 Squadron
and details of his DFM had appeared in the London Gazette on 23 November 1943.

23 Mar **22 OTU** **Wellington XIV MP718** **Ground**
1944 Destroyed at Sywell in the manner described at
the bottom of the previous page. It is believed to have been the only Wellington
Mk. XIV written off at an OTU supported by Bomber Command.

26 OTU **Wellington X LP258** **Training**
W/C H A Simmons + T/o 1910 Wing for a night exercise. Later,
Sgt D M Smith RCAF + reports came through to say that the aircraft
F/O R E J Thornton + had crashed, circa 2320, about a mile NW from
Sgt E Crosland + Hardwick, 3 miles NW of Wellingborough. It seems
Sgt J W Day + control had been lost at around 4,000 feet as the
Sgt J Marsden + Wellington was descending through cloud. Thirty-
three year old W/C Simmons, whose service number
indicates he joined the service in the 1920s and who is described as a navigator,
is buried in Oxford (Botley) Cemetery, while Sgt Smith RCAF was taken to Brookwood Military Cemetery. The others rest in their home towns.

29 OTU **Wellington III X3337** **Training**
Sgt F D Galloway T/o Bruntingthorpe for high-level bombing, in the
course of which the port engine failed. Strenuous
efforts were made to pump down the undercarriage, but despite succeeding in
getting the wheels to lower, they would not lock and on touch down at 2225 on
Chipping Warden airfield the entire unit collapsed.

24 Mar **24 OTU** **Whitley V Z9514 FB-S** **Training**
1944 WO1 B W Smith RCAF T/o 0920 Long Marston for a bombing exercise but
swung off the runway. WO1 Smith RCAF managed to
correct the swing, bringing the Whitley back into a straight line. Then, without
warning, it veered sharply and as it did so, the undercarriage gave way.

24-25 Mar **18 OTU** **Wellington X LN229** **Training**
1944 F/S R Mansell T/o 1919 Finningley for a night training sortie.
Ran low on fuel and diverted to Lichfield, where
it landed at 0019. F/S Mansell's arrival, however, was somewhat heavy and the
Wellington bounced back into the air and then floated for some distance before
returning to the runway and smashing its undercarriage in the process.

25 Mar **28 OTU** **Wellington IC X9644** **Training**
1944 WO1 J F Winters RCAF T/o 1457 Castle Donington intent on carrying
out a practice bombing detail, but failed to
become airborne and the undercarriage was raised in order to stop within the
confines of the airfield.

25-26 Mar **28 OTU** **Wellington IC T2922** **Op: Nickel**
1944 T/o Wymeswold and head for France. Reported to
have been very badly shot about at the hands of a night-fighter and written off
after landing, wheels retracted, at base. This incident has not been recorded
in the unit's records and, thus, no crew details have come to light.

26 Mar **18 OTU** **Wellington III BK365** **Training**
1944 F/S R W Wright T/o 1020 Finningley for a cross-country. At
approximately 1430, the Wellington attempted
to land at Aberporth airfield in Cardiganshire, having lost power from its
starboard engine. Although F/S Wright managed to set his aircraft down on
the runway he was unable to prevent the bomber from running into the overshoot
area and finishing up some 20 yards off the aerodrome.

28 OTU **Wellington IC N2737** **Ground**
Cpl P Barker On completion of engine running at Wymeswold,
LAC Nicol Cpl Barker closed the port throttle and as he
did so, a sheet of flame erupted from the
exhaust and set light to the fabric surfaces beneath the wing. Although the
fire services were quickly to the scene, they were not able to prevent the
flames from engulfing the bomber completely. This particularly Wellington
had enjoyed a rather varied life, the Air-Britain serial register indicating
it had seen service at Hendon before being issued to 221 Squadron and thence
to 1 (Coastal) OTU and the Coastal Command Development Unit. It next transferred to Bomber Command control, passing through 23 OTU and 27 OTU before
ending its days at Wymeswold.

27 Mar **14 OTU** **Wellington IC** **R1669** **Training**
1944
F/S E K Ferguson RAAF   +   T/o 2049 Husbands Bosworth for night circuits
Sgt D McInnes   +   and landings. Two hours later, swung while on
Sgt D D Twomey   +   approach and dived into the ground near the
Sgt A J Spinks   +   airfield. Immediately upon impact there was
Sgt H T Tullett   +   an explosion as the bomber went up in flames.
Sgt T Longstaff   +   F/S Ferguson RAAF and Sgt Tullett are buried
in Oxford (Botley) Cemetery, while the others
were taken to their home towns. Accepted by the unit on 19 July 1943, this
veteran Wellington (the last of its type to be written off by 14 OTU) had
amassed 1208.00 flying hours since being delivered to service, initially
with 20 Operational Training Unit.

21 OTU **Martinet I** **MS641** **Training**
F/O A Calvert DFM   +   T/o 0845 Enstone for a fighter affiliation
detail. Shortly before 0915, the Martinet
was observed to break away from the target Wellington, roll onto its back and
dive into the ground at Bampton, 13 miles WSW from Oxford and not far distant
from Brize Norton airfield. F/O Calvert rests in Kersal (St. Paul) Churchyard
at Salford. It will be recalled that he had been slightly injured when his
Wellington had crashed, five weeks previous. For details on this, and for
notes pertaining to his award, please return to page 278.

27-28 Mar **20 OTU C Flt** **Wellington III** **DF604** **-C** **Training**
1944
F/S C J Warner   inj   T/o 2026 Lossiemouth for a night cross-country.
Sgt F Sefton   +   On return to base at 0030, and probably while
Sgt D E Telling   +   the fuel cocks were being manipulated, the
Sgt C C Crawley   +   starboard engine cut and the Wellington crashed
Sgt J G Fulton   +   into the Moray Firth. Search and Rescue:
Sgt J Gate   +

On the alarm being raised, local fishermen and
an Air-Sea Rescue launch began a search of the area. Eventually, one of the
fishing vessels, described as being steam driven, came across a piece of the
wing, upon which F/S Warner was lying. Putting into Lossiemouth harbour at
around 0740, the pilot was rushed to Dr. Gray's Hospital at Elgin, suffering
from facial cuts and exposure. Soon after, a second fishing boat recovered a
partially inflated dinghy and the unconscious bodies of the navigator and the
wireless operator. Both were taken to the same hospital as their skipper and
over the next three desperate hours, doctors and nurses tried to resuscitate
the two airmen. Sadly, their efforts were in vain and, thus, Sgt Sefton rests
in Deane (St. Mary) Churchyard while Sgt Crawley lies in St. Albans Cemetery.
The others who died are commemorated on the Runnymede Memorial.

28 Mar **24 OTU** **Whitley V** **BD214 TY-F** **Ground**
1944
After landing at Dunkeswell airfield in Devon
and being parked near the resident Liberators, it fell victim to an accidental
discharge from the guns of Liberator 32154. It seems that while being loaded
with ammunition, at around 1500, one of the gunners accidentally tripped the
foot pedal with the safety switch in the "off" position.

30 Mar **20 OTU A Flt** **Wellington III** **HZ128** **-D** **Training**
1944
F/L L H Ferry Twice MID   +   T/o 0901 Elgin for a bombing exercise. Lost
F/O J L Bell RCAF   +   a wing and at 1036 plunged into the waters of
F/O R W Ledger RCAF   +   Spey Bay. Search and Rescue:
Sgt R S Davis RCAF   +
Sgt L C Kilpatrick   +   An Air-Sea Rescue launch from Buchie recovered
Sgt G E Palmer   +   the bodies of the second pilot and the wireless
operator; both had sustained very severe head
injuries. After being taken to Dallyachy, they were conveyed by ambulance to
the morgue at Lossiemouth. Later, the body of F/L Perry was found on a beach
near Spey. He now rests in Wembley (Alperton) Burial Ground and it is noted
that he held a Certificate of Royal Society of Arts. F/O Bell RCAF is buried
in Lossiemouth Burial Ground, Sgt Kilpatrick was taken to Thirsk Cemetery and
his fellow Yorkshireman, Sgt Palmer, whose body was also recovered from the sea,
lies in Sheffield (Bungreave) Cemetery. F/O Ledger RCAF and Sgt Davis RCAF are
commemorated on panels 246 and 255 respectively of the Runnymede Memorial. Their
aircraft, which had been delivered from 33 MU at Lyneham, on 14 August 1943, had
chalked up a total of 400.50 flying hours.

| 1 Apr
1944 | 20 OTU A Flt | Wellington III | X3225 | –D | Training |

1 Apr 1944 — **20 OTU A Flt** — **Wellington III** — **X3225** –D — **Training**

F/S T R Cooke RAAF   +
Sgt J H Stafford   +
Sgt G W Lewis RCAF   +
Sgt G Hodgson   +
Sgt A E Robertshaw   +

T/o 1002 Elgin for a navigation task but failed to return by its allotted time. Later, the coastguard station on Colonsay reported seeing an aircraft falling into the sea, on fire, bearing 130 degrees and 6 to 7 miles towards Jura. Four have no known graves; Sgt Robertshaw rests in Dewsbury (Earlsheaton) Cemetery.

28 OTU C Flt — **Wellington IC** — **DV444** –D — **Training**

Sgt A R Harris

T/o 1230 Castle Donington for a bombing detail. While cruising at 9,000 feet, the port engine failed and the crew returned to base, arriving here at 1310. Having had no success in getting the wheels down, Sgt Harris made his approach but despite reducing power, the bomber floated and finished up in a field some 200 yards beyond the runway. This was the last Wellington of its Mk. to be written off in Bomber Command service. No record of its flying hours has been appended but before its issue to 28 OTU on 9 September 1942, the Wellington had served for a brief period with 23 OTU.

3 Apr 1944 — **10 OTU** — **Whitley V** — **BD377** — **Ground**

While hangared at Abingdon, undergoing a major technical inspection, a lamp fell into a drip tray and in the resultant fire that followed, the Whitley was burnt out. A time of 1030 is quoted on documents.

5 Apr 1944 — **11 OTU C Flt** — **Wellington X** — **LN482 OP–B** — **Training**

F/S N H Hewett RNZAF   +
F/S C J Mowat RNZAF   +
Sgt J A Freeman   +
P/O D McTeer   +
Sgt J R Dowling   +
Sgt E V Waller   +

T/o 1255 Oakley for a two-and-a-half hour cross-country. Lost control, while flying in cloud, and broke up circa 1230 to 1300 over fields on Poplars Farm, Rothersthorpe, 3 miles SW from Northampton. Both New Zealanders are buried in Oxford (Botley) Cemetery as is Sgt Dowling, a pre-war regular airman. The others were taken to their home towns. On 10 April 1994, a service of remembrance and dedication of a memorial to the crew was held at the church of St. Peter and St. Paul at Rothersthorpe, the service being attended by relatives of the crew, as well as by many local people. A report of this event appeared in RNZAFA News, published in 1995, and was submitted by Leith Mowat of Green Island, Dunedin. Earlier, during 1992, Robert Allen of the Northampton Airfields and Aircraft Research Group, led an excavation of the site and amongst the items brought to light was the propeller blade that now forms part of the memorial.

9–10 Apr 1944 — **10 OTU** — **Whitley V** — **BD271** — **Training**

F/O F W Newton   +
F/S D C Capewell   +
Sgt G L Pettitt   +
Sgt C P Cantlin   +
Sgt T A Regan   +
W/O T D Mayow   +
Sgt A Harnell   +

T/o 2300 Stanton Harcourt for a cross-country flight. It is thought likely that structural failure occurred as at around 0210 the Whitley dived to the ground and burst into flames at White House Farm, Brightwell, 2 miles WNW of Wallingford, Oxfordshire. All rest in various cemeteries scattered across England.

24 OTU — **Whitley V** — **Z9163 FB–O** — **Training**

Sgt F C Smith RCAF   +
Sgt T W Mechefske RCAF   +
F/O G J H Palsen RCAF   +
WO2 R F Schimmens RCAF   +
F/S R F C Reaume RCAF   +

T/o 2205 Honeybourne for a night navigation exercise. At 2219, QDY was obtained on the base direction finding, after which nothing further was heard. However, two crews operating from 11 OTU Westcott, flying at 10,000 feet saw, at 2315, yellow flares. Both aircraft came down to 6,000 feet and observed six reds being fired in position 5219N 0432W. Then, at 2328, a Wellington from 16 OTU, out from Barford St. John, saw oil burning on the water, the navigator plotting the position as 5223N 0435W. All are commemorated on the Runnymede Memorial.

10–11 Apr 1944 — **27 OTU** — **Wellington X** — **HE165** — **Op: Nickel**

F/S V K Gratton RAAF
F/S A V Pearson RAAF

T/o 2040 Lichfield and set course for Paris. Within the hour and while flying at 11,500 feet, the port engine cut and the crew turned for home. On reaching base, the undercarriage refused to lower and a crash-landing was made at 2142. No injuries were reported but the Wellington was damaged beyond repair.

11 Apr
1944

19 OTU C Flt   **Whitley V** **BD393 ZV-M**   **Training**
Sgt C A White   T/o 0910 Kinloss for a cross-country. While
                                  flying at 15,000 feet, the port engine failed
and course was set for Machrihanish, a naval air station towards the southern
end of Kintyre and about 4 miles WNW of Campbeltown. However, at 2,000 feet,
the Whitley struck an air pocket and though Sgt White applied full power, the
bomber sank into a field, just short of the runway. It is much suspected that
he converted to Halifaxes and was posted to 640 Squadron, gaining a commission.
If this proves to be the case, then he was lost, with his crew, over France on
25 August 1944 (see Bomber Command Losses, Volume 5, page 391).

22 OTU   **Wellington III** **BJ601 OX-S**   **Training**
Sgt D G Chance RCAF   T/o 1006 Wellesbourne Mountford for an exercise
Sgt Shaver   inj   in cross-country flying. When the port engine's
                                   oil pressure gauge registered a steady drop in
pressure, Sgt Chance RCAF closed the motor down. However, he then found it
impossible to feather the propeller and with his aircraft losing height, he
gave the order to bale out. This was accomplished at 1145, after which the
bomber came down in the vicinity of Rhayadet, Radnorshire.

29 OTU   **Martinet I** **JN427**   **Training**
F/L E A Loos DFC   inj   T/o 2150 Bruntingthorpe for a night fighter
                          inj   affiliation detail. On return to base at 2245,
                                   the engine failed as he approached the runway.
While attempting to stretch his glide, F/L Loos stalled and on hitting the
ground the Martinet flipped onto its back.

30 OTU   **Wellington X** **HF471 -D**   **Training**
P/O C H G Gale   +   T/o 2025 Hixon for a night cross-country. At
P/O F G Newell   +   approximately 2100, the Wellington came out of
Sgt R C Smith   +   the clouds, in a dive, and smashed into fields
Sgt R V Smith   +   at Sandhall Farm, on the E bank of the River
Sgt S Philip   +   Ouse and just over a mile SSW of the hamlet of
Sgt A G O'Connor   +   Skelton on the NE side of Goole, Yorkshire.
                                   All lie in various towns and villages scattered
across the United Kingdom. Sgt O'Connor's first Christian name was rather
unusual, Armel.

84 OTU   **Wellington X** **LN245**   **Training**
F/S R V Tubman RAAF   +   T/o 0457 Desborough for circuits and landings,
Sgt C W Massey   +   two of which were successfully completed. Then,
Sgt W A Bush   +   while nearing the threshold for the third time,
Sgt E R Farley   inj   the port engine stopped (a lack of petrol is the
                                   reason given) and the bomber came down in Glendon
Road, Rothwell, Northamptonshire. F/S Tubman RAAF was taken to Oxford (Botley)
Cemetery, Sgt Massey rests in Castle Donington Cemetery, while Sgt Bush lies in
Horsell (St. Mary) Churchyard. Sadly, having recovered well from his injuries,
Sgt Farley went to 44 Squadron and was killed on operations early in November
1944 (see Bomber Command Losses, Volume 5, page 478).

11-12 Apr
1944

21 OTU   **Wellington X** **LN737**   **Training**
Sgt L E Smith   T/o 2110 Moreton-in-Marsh for a night cross-
                                  country. While cruising over the North Sea,
the port engine failed and having put out an emergency call, the crew were homed
towards Middleton St. George. However, technical problems prevented the bomber
from landing and having flown onto nearby Croft, crashed 0033 through the perimeter fence, hitting the stump of a felled tree. A fire broke out but the five
members of crew scrambled to safety with only minor cuts and abrasions.

12-13 Apr
1944

24 OTU   **Whitley V** **AD683**   **Training**
Sgt J A Tease RCAF   T/o 2130 Honeybourne for a night cross-country.
                                  Overshot and crashed 0220, near the village of
Badsey, 2 miles ESE of Evesham, Worcestershire.

13 Apr
1944

22 OTU   **Wellington III** **DF598**   **Training**
Sgt R E Jones RCAF   T/o Wellesbourne Mountford for a night detail,
P/O Weber RCAF   during which a fire broke out in the starboard
Sgt Hyde RCAF   engine. Crash-landed 2237 at Sandtoft airfield
                                  in Lincolnshire.

15 Apr **11 OTU** **Wellington X LN505 -G** **Transit**
1944 F/S D Beaton T/o 1600 Marston Moor and set course for Westcott
landing here at around 1715. However, F/S Beaton
had allowed his speed to build up while nearing the threshold and as a result he
arrived at the end of the runway, still travelling at quite a pace. Realising he
would finish up in the overshoot area, he attempted to turn onto the perimeter
track but the bomber's momentum was such that the undercarriage gave way.

30 OTU **Wellington X HE465 -D** **Training**
F/L E J Bull + T/o 0006 Seighford for a night exercise but two
F/O S J Pugh + minutes later the bomber sliced into the side of
F/O R O'Neill + a hill at Swansmoor. Sgt Pocock was rushed to
Sgt A Whitehead + Stratford Infirmary where he died later in the
Sgt M C Pocock inj day. All were taken to cemeteries in England and
Wales. On 13 May 1943, while serving at 81 OTU,
F/L Bull had been injured in a Whitley crash (see page 219).

16 Apr **16 OTU** **Wellington X HE263** **Training**
1944 F/O K E Tingley T/o 0940 Barford St. John for a cross-country.
On completion of the sortie, and having come
down to 1,300 feet, the starboard engine stopped. At 800 feet, F/O Tingley
managed to feather the propeller but was unable to arrest the loss of height.
Selecting 40 degrees of flap and lowering the undercarriage, he turned towards
a field that he considered suitable for a forced-landing. At this point, the
propeller began to windmill. Raising the undercarriage, he dropped full flap
(his altimeter registering 50 feet as he did so) and crash-landed 1315 some 4
miles N of Banbury, Oxfordshire. As the Wellington slid to a stop, the starboard wing was ripped off.

19 Apr **28 OTU B Flt** **Wellington X MF200** **Training**
1944 F/O D H King + T/o 0250 Wymeswold for circuit training but
P/O D R Doyle + crashed fifteen minutes later at Normanton on
Sgt D Fretwell + Stour, Nottinghamshire and 3 miles NNW from
Sgt L E Garrod + Loughborough, Leicestershire after what had
seemed a normal take off. F/O King was a very
experienced pilot with 1,520 flying hours to his credit, though only thirty of
these had been logged on Wellingtons. Hailing from Christchurch in Hampshire,
he is buried in Burton-on-the-Wolds Church Cemetery. His crew were claimed by
their next of kin, both in the United Kingdom and the Republic of Ireland.

20-21 Apr **28 OTU** **Wellington X LN896** **Op: Nickel**
1944 F/O H J Brennan RCAF evd T/o Castle Donington and set course for northern
P/O A J Houston RCAF evd France. Last heard from when over Brest and fly-
Sgt E J Trotter RCAF evd ing on a south-westerly heading. It was assessed
Sgt J Kempson inj that the Wellington had less than an hour's fuel
Sgt R J Dickson RCAF evd remaining. Sgt Kempson is reported to have died
Sgt A Elder RCAF evd from his injuries on 25 April; he now rests in
Bayeux War Cemetery.

21 Apr **17 OTU** **Wellington X HZ412** **Training**
1944 Sgt W L Scott + T/o 1130 Turweston for high-level bombing. The
Sgt A W Sherry + detail was completed satisfactorily and at 1325
Sgt T H Stacey + Sgt Scott was seen, nearing the runway. Just as
Sgt N G Cailes + he was about to land, a red Verey flare soared
Sgt Cunnell inj into the sky. Eyewitnesses report hearing the
engine note increase as the bomber climbed away
but at around 250 feet a puff of smoke was seen, emitting from the starboard
engine. Almost immediately, the motor began to falter but with the flaps still
down, the Wellington continued to climb quite steeply, turning slowly to starboard before stalling and diving back to earth. Those who perished were taken
to their home towns for burial.

Note. This Wellington had been involved a in a serious crash, while on the
strength of 29 OTU, on 22 July 1943. Its pilot on that occasion had been
the late F/O John Howarth Heath RNZAF who died a month later, still in the
service of 29 OTU (see page 244). Since undergoing repairs, the Wellington
had arrived on 17 OTU as recently as 25 March. The number of flying hours
has not been entered on its movement card.

21 Apr   **30 OTU**   **Wellington III**   **BK347**   **–Q**   **Training**
1944   F/O E M Barrett   +   T/o 1040 Seighford for a navigation detail.
      F/L E Alderson   +   Strayed from track and in the prevailing cloudy
      Sgt P E Lomas   +   conditions failed to notice that the bomber was
      F/O R G C Brodie RCAF   +   flying perilously close to high ground. Thus,
      Sgt N Skirrow   +   at around 1615, it ploughed into moorland in
      Sgt R C Holmwood   +   the general vicinity of Whernside some 2,419
      Sgt Marks   inj   feet above sea level on the bleak North York-
shire moors. Amazingly, Sgt Marks escaped with
relatively minor injuries. His less fortunate colleagues were conveyed to
cemeteries scattered across the British Isles, F/O Barrett, a civil engineer
and rugby footballer who had played for Birkenhead Park, and F/O Brodie RCAF
being brought to Chester (Blacon) Cemetery. F/L Alderson, it is observed,
held a Bachelor of Science degree. The Wellington had served throughout its
active life with 30 OTU, being accepted as long ago as 30 December 1942. At
the time of the crash, it had logged 614.45 flying hours.

22 Apr   **11 OTU**   **Wellington X**   **JA128**   **–H**   **Training**
1944   F/S M J Irwin RNZAF   T/o 1020 Westcott for high-level bombing but
having raised the undercarriage, F/S Irwin RNZAF
noticed that the "red" warning lights were still glowing. After gaining height,
he put the undercarriage lever into the down position, but the "red" lights
remained on. He next tried using the emergency pump, but to no avail and in
the flapless landing that followed, the entire unit collapsed.

23 Apr   **10 OTU**   **Whitley V**   **P5015**   **Training**
1944   Sgt G E Colley   T/o 1230 Stanton Harcourt for a cross-country.
During the sortie, Sgt Colley noticed that the
undercarriage lever had become locked in the down position, but all indications
suggested the wheels had retracted. Continuing with the exercise, he was next
concerned with a faltering port engine and on regaining Stanton Harcourt he was
advised to land with the wheels up. However, while flying a right-hand circuit
the aircraft lost height and crash-landed at 1645, the crew escaping injury.

      22 OTU   **Wellington III**   **BK541**   **Training**
      Sgt J G M Savard RCAF   T/o 1026 Stratford-upon-Avon for a bombing
exercise. While returning to base, flying at
1,100 feet, the rev counter for the port engine indicated a loss of power and
at 1311, the pilot attempted to make a single-engined landing. In this he was
unsuccessful, the Wellington overshooting the runway and being damaged beyond
repair. After converting to Halifaxes, Sgt Savard RCAF went to 433 Squadron,
only to be killed in action on 17 August 1944 (see Bomber Command Losses,
Volume 5, page 388).

      28 OTU   **Wellington III**   **Z1621**   **Training**
      F/O M D Muggeridge RNZAF   T/o 1843 Wymeswold for circuits and landings
      F/S P McVerry RNZAF   but the boost pressure on the starboard engine
decayed. With the throttles closed, the bomber
sank rapidly and a minute after departing it force-landed straight ahead.

23–24 Apr   **19 OTU D Flt**   **Anson I**   **AX435**   **XF–S**   **Training**
1944   W/O M Drew   T/o 2209 Kinloss for a short night cross-
country. Caught in a downdraft and flew onto
high ground at 0044 near Carn na Cailliche, E of the road between Dallas to
the north and Upper Knockando to the south. At 0325, another Anson located
the stricken trainer and was able to ascertain all was well with its crew.

24 Apr   **21 OTU**   **Wellington X**   **LN878**   **Training**
1944   Sgt J G Bielby RAAF   +   T/o Moreton-in-Marsh for a navigation training
      Sgt M D D MacFarlane RAAF   +   exercise which involved the crew flying over
      Sgt J H Dunn   +   the North Sea. Last fixed at 1352 when eighty
      F/S E A Nayler RAAF   +   miles E of Hull. It is thought the Wellington
      Sgt W Lane   +   may have flown into cloud, losing control as a
consequence. All are commemorated on the
Runnymede Memorial. Sgt Beilby RAAF of South Brisbane in Queensland had
married Irene Joy Bielby of Terrace, British Columbia, Canada. His aircraft
had initially been issued to 15 OTU, but had been with its present unit since
4 March 1944. In total, it had accumulated 111.05 flying hours,

24–25 Apr   **12 OTU**   **Wellington III**   **BK542**   **Op: Sweepstake**

1944   F/S F C Coker   +   T/o Chipping Warden as part of a force, drawn
          Sgt C A Hargood   +   from the training units, to fly a diversionary
          Sgt F J Burton   +   sweep to within seventy-five miles of the enemy
          Sgt D A Barber   +   coast. Last heard on wireless at 2337, "Port
          Sgt A P Curran   +   engine unserviceable, losing height, position
                                               5424N 0630E". All are perpetuated on the panels
                                               of the Runnymede Memorial.

             16 OTU   **Wellington X**   **LP284**   **Op: Sweepstake**

     F/S F T Cross   +   T/o Upper Heyford similarly tasked. Last heard
          Sgt G W Hemming RCAF   +   at 0029 transmitting SOS. Section K responded,
          Sgt D E Lister   +   but received no acknowledgement. It is thought
          Sgt F W Hinton   +   the Wellington ditched in position 5342N 0254E.
          Sgt J W Cameron   +   All are commemorated on the Runnymede Memorial.
          Sgt M L Chaundy   +   Sgt Cameron was aged 18, Sgt Chaundy was a year
                                               older. They both came from Glasgow.

Note. Martin Middlebrook and Chris Everitt report in 'The Bomber Command War
Diaries' that a total of 165 OTU aircraft were employed, thus making this the
largest involvement of training unit aircraft since the "1,000 Plan" raids
of 1942. Principally, the objective was to induce the Luftwaffe to launch
its night-fighters, thus wasting valuable fuel stocks.

26 Apr   **30 OTU**   **Wellington III**   **DF640**   **–P**   **Training**

1944   F/O N A R Mousdell   +   T/o 0114 Hixon for night circuit training.
          Sgt E D Macdonald   +   Landed 0134 but bounced rather badly. The
          Sgt H D Purbrick   +   crew attempted to go round again, but their
                                               aircraft failed to gain height and flew into
a hill, 250 feet above sea level and known locally as Weston Bank, near the
airfield, bursting into flames on impact amongst some trees. F/O Mousdell of
Liverpool was laid to rest in Chester (Blacon) Cemetery, Sgt Macdonald rests
in the extension to Ennerdale (St. Mary) Churchyard, while Sgt Purbrick lies
in Yatton Keynell (St. Margaret) Churchyard. Their Wellington, while being
flown by F/O B A Mace RAAF, had been involved in a minor flying accident on
11 August 1943.

27 Apr   **26 OTU**   **Wellington III**   **X3340**   **Training**

1944   Sgt P A Beart   inj   T/o 0940 Little Horwood for solo circuits and
          Sgt S Henson   inj   landings. Shortly before 1100, the port motor
          Sgt N S Robson   inj   failed and having failed to land, crashed into
          Sgt J Duthie   inj   a field near Stony Stratford on the western
                                               side of Wolverton, Buckinghamshire.

28 Apr   **11 OTU**   **Wellington X**   **JA456 OP-M**   **Training**

1944   F/S T L Gardiner RNZAF   +   T/o Westcott for a night navigation sortie.
          Sgt A H Scott RNZAF   inj   While cruising at 15,000 feet over the Bristol
          Sgt S G Kingsmill   +   Channel, the port engine failed. Heading for
          Sgt Quadry   +   the nearby Pembrokeshire coast, the Wellington
          Sgt N L Taylor RNZAF   inj   arrived over Haverfordwest airfield where, at
          Sgt L E Laird RNZAF   +   2345, the crew attempted to land. Due to their
                                               unfamiliarity with the aerodrome, coupled with
the problem of having only one operating motor, they touched down some way
along the runway. Almost immediately, the bomber bounced back into the air
and then crashed into a ravine just beyond the airfield, bursting into flames.
Of those who died, both RNZAF fatalities were buried locally in Haverfordwest
(City Road) Cemetery, while the others were taken to their home towns. After
making a good recovery from his injuries, Sgt Scott RNZAF went on to fly with
75 Squadron. Sadly, on 4 November 1944, his Lancaster failed to return from
operations to Solingen (see Bomber Command Losses, Volume 5, page 473).

29 Apr   **11 OTU**   **Wellington X**   **LN843 OP-W**   **Training**

1944   F/S J Johnson   T/o Westcott for a night cross-country, during
          Sgt Ratter   inj   which the port engine failed as the Wellington
                                               flew at 15,000 feet. Losing height, and firing
off red distress flares, the crew were contacted by Moreton-in-Marsh, indicating
their runway was available. Thus, at 0017 the Wellington attempted to land but
finished up amongst some trees, not far from the airfield. Sgt Ratter was taken
to St. Hughes Hospital in Oxford.

30 Apr   **21 OTU**   **Wellington X**   **HE870**   **Training**
1944   F/S J H Bridgett RAAF   T/o 1150 Moreton-in-Marsh tasked for a fighter
affiliation exercise. On return to base at 1300
the Wellington overshot the runway and when both engines failed at 1,000 feet,
a successful forced-landing was made, E of the airfield, at Barton-on-the-Heath
some 5 miles S of Shipston-on-Stour, Warwickshire. One member of the five-man
crew is reported to have been slightly hurt. On 14 August 1943, when on the
strength of 23 OTU, this aircraft had been extensively damaged in a flying
accident. Its pilots on that occasion were Sgt S J Ouellette RCAF and F/L
R A Anderson RCAF (the former was killed while raiding Torino on 25 November
1943, with 142 Squadron). Following repairs, it saw service with 15 OTU before
being allotted to 21 OTU on 24 March. At the time of its destruction, it had
flown a total of 455.25 hours.

1 May   **10 OTU**   **Whitley V**   **P4962**   **Training**
1944   F/O A Beever   T/o 1330 Stanton Harcourt for a training detail.
       Sgt G Cooke   Crashed 1443, at base, following problems with
the hydraulic system. Although the undercarriage
lever had been placed in the down position, the wheels had failed to lower.

3 May   **30 OTU**   **Wellington III**   **DF622**   **-O**   **Training**
1944   Sgt K Sidwell   T/o 1114 Hixon for a day cross-country but soon
       F/L Gaunt   after becoming airborne the port airscrew began
       Sgt A B Howell   to overspeed. Aborting the exercise, the crew
headed for base, jettisoning most of their fuel
but on nearing the runway, the starboard engine cut and the Wellington came down
at 1132, just short of the airfield.

4 May   **19 OTU A Flt**   **Whitley V**   **Z9361 UO-F**   **Training**
1944   F/O J L Sneddon   T/o Kinloss for night training. At around 0240,
       F/S G W Dark   Flying Control reported a collision had occurred
       Sgt J A Reilly RCAF   between this aircraft and Whitley V BD385/Q of B
Flight. Despite sustaining considerable damage
to the tail section and rear turret, F/O Sneddon landed safely, though his aircraft was subsequently declared to be beyond economical repair.

       19 OTU B Flt   **Whitley V**   **BD385**   **-Q**   **Training**
       F/O A H Eastment   +   T/o Kinloss similarly tasked and destroyed in
       F/O T D Reilly AFM   +   the manner described above, coming down in very
       F/O A Duncan-Smith   +   boggy ground at Cullin Sands, W of Findhorn.
       P/O C J B Phillips   +   This made the recovery of the bodies extremely
       Sgt J T Cook   +   hazardous. By 0530, an Air-Sea Rescue launch
       Sgt R J Clayton   +   had been placed on standby to assist and it was
further reported that a number of civilians in
rowing boats were assisting the Medical Officer and others to get to the scene
of the crash. Eventually, all were brought out and five now rest in Kinloss
Abbey Burial Ground, while F/O Duncan-Smith was taken to Egham (St. Jude's)
Cemetery in Surrey.

       19 OTU A Flt   **Whitley V**   **LA838**   **-A**   **Training**
       F/S Lee   T/o Kinloss similarly tasked. At 0224, called
Flying Control to say that both engines had cut
while approaching the runway. A little under twenty minutes later, red Verey
flares were seen cascading in the direction of Kinloss Abbey and soon afterwards
the officer in charge of night flying reported that a Whitley had come down 300
yards W of Kinloss station and was partially blocking the Inverness to Elgin
line. Both stations were alerted to the danger. At about the same time, it
was announced the crew were safe.

Note. These three summaries have been written up from my interpretation of the
reports published in unit records, where only the aircraft's letter has been
appended against the name of the captain. I am aware, however, that other documents show F/O Eastment as flying in LA838.

6 May   **10 OTU**   **Whitley V**   **Z6798**   **Training**
1944   Sgt G Cooke   T/o 1535 Stanton Harcourt to practice single-
engined landings. Force-landed ten minutes
later after the port engine cut with the Whitley at 200 feet on climb out. This
was Sgt Cooke's second accident in less than a week (see this page).

6 May   **11 OTU**   **Wellington X**   **LP172 KJ–K**   **Training**
1944   Sgt S T Murphy   +   T/o 0040 Westcott for a five-hour navigation

Sgt C H Le Brun	+
F/O J C Ford	+
Sgt E G Rowe	+
Sgt R Gilmore RNZAF	+
Sgt J H Camp	+

exercise. During the flight, two wireless
messages were transmitted; the first at 0214
and the second at 0345. Fifty minutes later
the aircraft dived out of the cloud base and
crashed at Whittlebury, 3 miles S of Towcester
in Northamptonshire. Sgt Gilmore RNZAF and

Sgt Murphy,. who came from Manor Park in Essex, were taken to Oxford (Botley)
Cemetery, while the others were claimed by their next of kin.

7– 8 May   **29 OTU**   **Wellington X**   **LN646**   **Training**
1944   F/S K B Reid   T/o 2155 Bruntingthorpe for a night cross-
country. During the exercise, problems were
experienced with the port pitch control. On return to base at 0315, an attempt
was made to land without the help of flaps and as a result, the bomber finished
up, wrecked, in the overshoot area.

8 May   **83 OTU**   **Wellington X**   **LP568**   **Training**
1944   Sgt W T Cake   T/o 1500 Peplow with a crew of eight to practice

Sgt N L Pegg RCAF	inj
Sgt A O Wedin RCAF	+

cine camera gun and evasive flying tactics. Thus,
at around 1535, while engaged in a corkscrew type
manoeuvre, the starboard engine cut out and in
the ensuing forced-landing the Wellington clipped a tree and crashed into a field
on The Sydnall Farm, some 3 miles S from Market Drayton, Shropshire. Hailing from
Yreka, California, Sgt Wedin RCAF is buried in Chester (Blacon) Cemetery.

9–10 May   **30 OTU**   **Wellington III**   **BJ618**   **–T**   **Op: Nickel**
1944

F/L R C Thorn	evd	T/o Hixon and headed for the Orleans area of
Sgt J Russell	pow	France. Crashed at Selles (Eure), 6 km S of
Sgt P Rennick	evd	Pont-Audemer.
Sgt H M Harris	pow	
Sgt W H Stevenson	evd	
Sgt H Smith	evd	

10 May   **28 OTU**   **Wellington X**   **HE738**   **Training**
1944   Sgt H J Musselman RCAF   T/o 1220 Castle Donington for a cross-country.
While flying at 17,000 feet in the vicinity of
Aberystwyth the fuel gauges registered empty for the port main tank. The balance
cocks were turned on, but the engine cut and with height being lost, a forced-
landing was executed at 1520 approximately 12 miles E of Ponterwyd, the bomber
ending up in a gully, where it caught fire. Assuming the direction and distance
quoted to be correct, this would place the crash in Montgomeryshire, perhaps a
mile or so W of Tylwch.

12 May   **26 OTU**   **Wellington X**   **MS483**   **Training**
1944   W/O R F J Mansell   T/o 1440 Wing for a high-level bombing sortie.

W/C R N Cook

Having climbed to 10,500 feet, and while making
good progress with the detail, one of the bombs
detonated and set the aircraft on fire. The order to abandon was given and all
complied, though W/O Mansell reported that he was down to 4,000 feet before
making good his exit. Moments later, at around 1520, the bomber smashed into
the ground at Marsh Gibbon, 7 miles SSW of Buckingham. It is noted that W/O
Mansell had logged 1,130 flying hours, 1,057 of these on Wellingtons.

13 May   **10 OTU**   **Whitley V**   **Z9302**   **Training**
1944   S/L F K Bainbridge DFC   T/o 1003 Stanton Harcourt for P/O Dove´s end

P/O W B M Dove

of course flying test but at 200 feet the port
engine failed and the Whitley was forced-landed
one-hundred-and-fifty yards W of the airfield. The flight had lasted a mere
two minutes.

           28 OTU   **Wellington X**   **HE198**   **Training**
           F/L J H Woods RCAF   T/o 1140 Castle Donington but the run was
aborted after the crew heard a loud bang from
the port engine. As the bomber sped towards the airfield boundary, F/L Woods
smartly raised the undercarriage. However, the momentum was such that the
Wellington skidded through a hedge and, soon after coming to a stop, caught
fire. No one was seriously hurt.

14 May
1944

24 OTU　　　　　**Whitley V**　**N1436**　　　　　　　　　　**Training**

F/O L W Wright RCAF　　　　　　T/o 1135 Honeybourne for a cross-country. The bomber returned to base at 1735 but instead of landing, F/O Wright RCAF decided to overshoot, ordering his crew to take up positions as if for a ditching. With the engines on full power, the nose was raised and the undercarriage retracted. However, with 40 degrees of flap indicated and the tail trim fully forward, the Whitley lost flying speed. The throttles were then closed and a forced-landing made in line with the runway.

14-15 May
1944

82 OTU　　　　　**Wellington X**　**HE739**　**-H**　　　　　　　**Op: Nickel**

F/O K S Johnson RCAF	+	T/o Gamston and set course for Rennes. Ran out
F/O G S Oliphant RCAF	+	of fuel while returning to base and crashed into
Sgt J A Lanouette RCAF	+	trees at Thresby Park, Ollerton, 9 miles SSE of
WO1 J Tass RCAF	+	Worksop, Nottinghamshire. All are buried in
Sgt G K McLellan RCAF	+	Harrogate (Stonefall) Cemetery. F/O Oliphant
		was a Bachelor of Arts graduate from the
		University of Western Ontario.

15-16 May
1944

12 OTU　　　　　**Wellington X**　**LP155**　**-K**　　　　　　　**Op: Nickel**

F/O G D Coldwell-Horsfall	+	T/o Chipping Warden and headed for Brittany.
Sgt H Daly	+	Lost without trace. All are commemorated on
Sgt N C Rushton RCAF	+	the Runnymede Memorial. Oddly, F/O Coldwell-
Sgt K T James	+	Horsfall is also listed in the Allied air
Sgt R H Moyle	+	forces prisoner of war file. At forty-one,
Sgt N Walters	+	Sgt Rushton RCAF was well above the age normally
		associated with airmen training for operational

service in Bomber Command. Certainly, he was amongst the oldest Canadians to lose his life on active service.

26 OTU　　　　　**Wellington X**　**HF519**　　　　　　　　　**Training**

F/O A A Tilton RCAF	+	T/o 2240 Wing for a night navigation sortie.
F/O R W Bartlett RCAF	+	While attempting to let down through cloud, the
F/O D D G Bidwell RCAF	+	Wellington stalled at 10,000 feet and fell out
Sgt H W Ingleson RCAF	+	of control to crash 0101 about a mile NE of
Sgt D Sutcliffe	+	Llanrwst, Caernarvon and practically on the
Sgt R W Hare RCAF	+	border with Denbigh. The five RCAF airmen
		(F/O Bidwell was an American from Wells River

in Vermont) are buried in Chester (Blacon) Cemetery, while Sgt Sutcliffe was taken to Leeds (Hunslet New) Cemetery in Yorkshire.

17 May
1944

10 OTU　　　　　**Martinet I**　**JN284**　　　　　　　　　**Training**

| F/O D A Cass | + | T/o 1510 Abingdon for a fighter affiliation |
| | | duty. Eyewitnesses state that the Martinet |

climbed normally to about 250 feet before pulling up steeply, turning to port. Moments later, a wing dropped and the aircraft dived vertically into the ground a mere 800 yards E of the airfield. Visibility was clear but the surface wind was gusting to speeds of up to 30 knots. F/O Cass rests in Wembley (Alperton) Burial Ground.

29 OTU　　　　　**Wellington X**　**MF314**　　　　　　　　　**Training**

2Lt H A Whitcher SAAF	+	T/o 1125 Bruntingthorpe for a navigation detail
P/O F E W Mayhew	+	with a screened instructor, F/O Lance, two
F/O A C E Lance DFC	+	pupil pilots and a crew under training. Broke
F/O N Liddle	+	out of the cloud base, in a steep dive, and hit
F/O J J White	+	the ground at 1215 near Mendham, 11 miles WSW of
F/O H Moran	+	Beccles, Suffolk and practically on the border
Sgt D W Smith	+	with Norfolk. 2Lt Whitcher SAAF of Coldstream
Sgt F J Luxford	+	in the Cape Province was taken to Cambridge City
		Cemetery (he is the sole South African Air Force

casualty buried here), while the others were conveyed to their home towns.

18 May
1944

11 OTU　　　　　**Wellington X**　**HE318**　**KJ-F**　　　　　　**Training**

F/O R Kassler RNZAF		T/o 0015 Oakley for night dual circuits and
F/O R A Wilson		landings. The exercise progressed smoothly until
		around 0200 when F/O Wilson suspected a fire had

broken out in the port engine. F/O Kassler RNZAF assumed control but had to overshoot as his approach was too high. However, before he could complete a second circuit, the suspect engine stopped and he put the bomber down at 0207, crashing through a hedge and crossed the Oakley to Worminghall road.

19 May	17 OTU	Wellington X	LN606	Training

1944 W/O L W Brown   T/o 1154 Upper Heyford but a tyre burst and the
                                        Wellington promptly swung off the runway and on
to rough ground, which caused the bomber to porpoise. At first, it was thought
the damage was not too severe, but following a more detailed inspection the airframe was struck off charge on 31 July 1944.

22 OTU	Wellington III	BK396	Training

Sgt J A Brassard RCAF   inj T/o Wellesbourne Mountford for a cross-country.
Sgt Choquette RCAF   inj Wrecked in a forced-landing near Davidstow, some
WO1 Level RCAF   inj fifteen miles NNE of Bodmin.

82 OTU	Wellington III	BJ662	Training

Sgt G J Bradbury RCAF   inj T/o 1220 Peplow but almost immediately lost
F/O J E G Leblanc RCAF   inj power from the port engine. Sgt Bradbury RCAF
Sgt J J R Lanctot RCAF   inj made a valiant attempt to fly round the circuit
WO2 P N Leveille RCAF   inj but crashed 1225, heavily, near Child's Ercall,
Sgt O S T Clarke RCAF   inj five miles SSW from Market Drayton, Shropshire.
Sgt J R McKinnon RCAF   +   Sgt McKinnon RCAF rests in Harrogate (Stonefall)
                                  Cemetery. While on the strength of 12 OTU, this
Wellington had been badly shot about by a night-fighter while raiding Essen on
16-17 September 1942, the attack taking place some 32 km NNW of the target. In
the confusion, one member of the crew (F/S (later F/O) F O Bullen) baled out,
after which F/L J Simpson managed to fly the badly damaged machine back to East
Anglia and land at Docking airfield in Norfolk. From here his critically wounded
wireless operator, Sgt H H Welby, was admitted to Station Sick Quarters Bircham
Newton, where he died nine hours later. He was buried at Sprowston (SS Mary and
Margaret) Churchyard. Since its arrival on 7 June 1943 at 82 OTU, the Wellington
had been damaged on 30 August, its captain being the late Sgt R A J Bennett RCAF
(see Bomber Command Losses, Volume 5, page 50).

19-20 May	18 OTU	Wellington X	LP381	Op: Nickel

1944 Sgt J Pawlik PAF   +   T/o 2158 Worksop and headed for France. The
F/O Z Norski PAF   inj crew carried out their assigned task but at 0233
Sgt W Sledziewski PAF   inj while preparing to land flew into trees at Peak
Sgt Z Bukalo PAF   inj Hill, Carlton Road, about 2 miles N of the air-
Sgt P Pawlowski PAF   +   field. The two airmen who perished were buried
                                  in the Polish Plot at Newark-upon-Trent Cemetery.

83 OTU	Wellington III	BK463	Op: Nickel

F/O W E Hemingway   +   T/o Peplow for operations over northern France.
F/O W Norman   +   Crashed at Eps (Pas-de-Calais), 13 km NNW from
F/O H E Dinnage   +   St-Pol-sur-Ternoise, where all are buried in the
F/S W S Creber RAAF   +   local war cemetery. The last three named are
F/S H J W Stevens   +   identified as air gunners.
F/O R S Knapp RCAF   +
Sgt G D Cossins   +

22 May	82 OTU	Wellington III	BJ819	Training

1944 F/O J P Lee RCAF   T/o 1526 Ossington for a cine camera gun detail
                                        involving Spitfire I P7820 from 53 OTU. During
the exercise a collision occurred and both aircraft crash-landed in a field
close to Sturton Church near Leverton, 5 miles ENE of Boston, Lincolnshire.
From the evidence presented at the Court of Inquiry, it became clear that the
Wellington's crew owed their lives to the skill of their skipper, F/O Lee RCAF.
It was recommended that a "green" endorsement should be entered in his log book.

22-23 May	24 OTU	Whitley V	AD701 TY-B	Op: Nickel

1944 F/O D W Goodwin RCAF   +   T/o Long Marston and set course for the Alencon
F/O J Hong RCAF   +   region of France. All are buried in Bretteville-
F/O C B Wyckoff RCAF   +   sur-Laize Canadian War Cemetery. They were the
WO1 J G Jacques RCAF   +   last airmen to lose their lives from the unit in
Sgt J Hopper RCAF   +   a Whitley. Their aircraft had been taken on unit
Sgt W G Harris RCAF   +   charge on 6 September 1942 and had amassed a
                                  total of 652 flying hours. From unit records,
it seems six crews had been briefed for operations, all being assigned to a
variety of locations.

24 May
1944

20 OTU F Flt   **Wellington X**   **HE462**   **–U**   **Training**

Sgt R P Cummings RCAF	+	T/o Lossiemouth for a navigation exercise, base-
F/O W B Ernst RCAF	+	Montrose-Darlington-Hawes-base, estimated time of
F/O E H Widdes RCAF	+	arrival back at base, 1350. At 1129, the crew
Sgt R S Piers RCAF	+	transmitted a routine wireless message and from
Sgt J M Logelin RCAF	+	the single fix taken, the aircraft was placed in

the vicinity of Darlington. Nothing further was
heard and all are now perpetuated on the panels of the Runnymede Memorial.

25–26 May
1944

19 OTU D Flt   **Whitley V**   **EB384 ZV–U**   **Training**

F/O R F Edwards RCAF	+	T/o 2327 Kinloss for a fighter affiliation
F/O B H Dobesch RCAF	+	detail. Crashed 0015, probably due to very
Sgt N T Kester RCAF	+	severe icing, at Glen Esk in the Balmoral Forest
Sgt L N Gurden	+	area some 10 miles SW of Ballater. The five RCAF
Sgt T E R Donnelly RCAF	+	members of crew were buried in Fettercairn
Sgt J E Gray RCAF	+	Cemetery, while Sgt Gurden rests in Essex at

Romford Cemetery. It is likely the bodies were
recovered by a Mountain Rescue team that were ordered to move at 0200 from their
base at Montrose.

20 OTU E Flt   **Wellington X**   **ME553 JM–F**   **Training**

Capt R Richard FFAF	+	T/o 2220 Lossiemouth for a night cross-country.
Lt R Blot FFAF	+	Shortly before 0130, while flying at 15,000 feet,
Lt J Vles FFAF	inj	encountered very severe icing. A controlled
S/Lt A Pontin FFAF	+	descent was made to 7,000 feet but the situation
Sgt J Fischbach FFAF	+	failed to improve and the order to prepare to
Sgt J Foury-Lavergne FFAF	inj	abandon was given. However, before anyone left
Sgt G Allain FFAF	inj	the aircraft, a slight improvement in handling

was detected and Capt Richard FFAF forced-landed
on what he thought was an airfield. In reality, he was down at Bunker Hill about
a mile E of Consett, Durham. None of the injured were seriously hurt, Lt Vles
being returned to Lossiemouth within a few hours of the accident. The two air
gunners, however, sustained superficial burns and both were admitted to Shotley
Bridge Hospital. It is assumed that those who died have, since 1945, been
exhumed from their original graves (possibly at Harrogate (Stonefall) Cemetery)
and returned to France.

26 May
1944

20 OTU C Flt   **Wellington III**   **DF574**   **–F**   **Training**

P/O P A Boswell RCAF	inj	T/o 0933 Lossiemouth for a bombing exercise which
P/O Switzer RCAF		ended at 0950 with the crew ditching some 2 to 5
P/O Sloan RCAF		miles NW of Boars Head Rock after their starboard
Sgt Hendry RCAF	inj	engine cut while flying at 2,000 feet. No one was
Sgt Fritch RCAF		badly hurt and for a while after the incident the

tail of the wrecked aircraft could be seen pro-
truding above the surface. P/O Boswell RCAF eventually joined 76 Squadron and was
still on his first tour of operations when the war in Europe ended.

22 OTU   **Martinet I**   **JN428**   **Training**

F/O D G F Parker DFM RCAF	+	T/o 1625 Wellesbourne Mountford for a cine camera
		gun sortie. At 1645, while dog fighting at 1,000

feet, the Martinet flipped out of control and dived into the ground near Flint
Hall Farm, Wellesbourne. F/O Parker RCAF, whose DFM had been published in the
London Gazette on 1 October 1943, following a tour with 424 Squadron, is buried
in Stratford-upon-Avon Cemetery.

27 May
1944

22 OTU   **Wellington X**   **HE389**   **Air Test**

F/L R A G Tucker		T/o 1100 Wellesbourne Mountford. After climbing
		to 1,500 feet, both engines failed and at 1110

the Wellington crashed at Oldborough Farm on the SW side of the airfield. At
the Court of Inquiry it was stated that accident investigators had found both
propellers had slipped into fine pitch. An experienced pilot, F/L Tucker had
logged in excess of 1,750 hours flying, 1,570 of these hours being accumulated
on Wellingtons.

Note. The Wellington summarised had initially been issued to 466 Squadron
before being passed into the training role and issued to 23 OTU. Since 23
July 1943, it had been on the strength of 22 OTU and had, in total, flown
a creditable 815,15 hours.

27–28 May   **30 OTU A Flt**   **Wellington III**   **DF641**   **–T**   **Training**
1944

F/O C G Archibald RCAF	+	T/o 2235 Hixon in the company of eight aircraft
F/O R G Hills RCAF	+	tasked for a Bullseye detail. Last heard on
F/S J Rutter	+	wireless 30 minutes after departure. At 0035,
Sgt W O D Baird RCAF	+	with the bomber within 4 miles of its briefed
Sgt H Riley	+	track, the dinghy broke from its housing and
Sgt G W Mitchell RCAF	+	structural failure followed, debris falling
Sgt J R Pollon RCAF	+	about 5 miles SW of Ingham, Lincolnshire. The

five RCAF airmen rest in Harrogate (Stonefall) Cemetery (Sgt Pollon RCAF of Bethel, Manitoba was aged seventeen), F/S Rutter is buried in Bolton (Astley Bridge) Cemetery, while Sgt Riley was taken to Hatfield (Woodhouse) Cemetery.

28 May   **12 OTU**   **Wellington III**   **BK558**   **Air Test**
1944

W/O T W Black   T/o 1210 Chipping Warden. While flying at 3,000 feet, a fire was discovered beneath the navigator's table but despite prompt use of the extinguisher the flames continued to take a hold. The wireless operator (he is not named) then tried to smother the fire, using the canvas engine covers but was unsuccessful. While all this activity was going on, W/O Black was making all good speed towards base, where he landed safely, the entire crew vacating the Wellington without injury. The cause of the blaze was traced to an insecure joint in the aircraft's heating system.

14 OTU   **Wellington X**   **HE846**   **Training**

Sgt A C Strachan   inj   T/o 1023 Market Harborough with a crew of seven briefed for a fighter affiliation exercise. During the course of a combat manoeuvre at 4,000 feet, the port engine failed. With the propeller feathered, course was set for Bruntingthorpe where, at 1113, a wheels up landing was made. As the bomber skidded to a stop, a fire broke out and it is indicated that some of the crew received superficial injuries.

17 OTU   **Wellington III**   **X3445**   **Training**

F/S D G Haynes RAAF   T/o 2105 Turweston for high-level bombing. Returned to base at approximately 2315 but overshot after failing to line up with the runway. A second missed approach followed and it was while the crew were going around for the third time that the starboard engine cut. With little height in hand (300 to 350 feet is quoted), F/S Haynes RAAF had little option but to force –land. After coming to a halt, a fire broke out and the Wellington was destroyed.

28–29 May   **82 OTU**   **Wellington X**   **HE199**   **–J**   **Op: Nickel**
1944

WO2 D B Machum MID RCAF	+	T/o 2153 Ossington and set course for Nantes.
P/O C McFarlane RCAF	inj	While returning to base, and shortly after re-
Sgt J A Bugley RCAF	inj	gaining the south coast, came under anti-aircraft
Sgt W H McGuigan RCAF	+	fire from batteries in the Gillingham area of
WO1 L F Davey RCAF	+	Dorset. Hit, and partially abandoned before

crashing 0225 at Sweets Farm between the hamlets of Woodville and Stour Row, 4 miles SW of Shaftesbury. Those who died were taken to Brookwood Military Cemetery. Buried at Camp Hill Cemetery, Halifax, Nova Scotia is AC1 Ian Thompson Machum RCAF, brother of WO2 Machum RCAF, who died with P/O Robert William Allan Todd RCAF in a Harvard (3238 of 14 Squadron) crash near Aldergrove in British Columbia on 16 January 1943. The two injured airmen were taken to Shaftesbury Hospital; both are thought to have recovered.

82 OTU   **Wellington X**   **LN443**   **–C**   **Op: Nickel**

F/O D G W McKie RCAF	+	T/o 2140 Ossington similarly tasked. Lost in the
F/O C A Blackmore RCAF	+	manner described previously, crashing 0230 near
F/O L J Smith RCAF	+	Hazelbury Bryan, 4 miles SSW from Sturminster
Sgt A H Spinks RCAF	+	Newton, Dorset. All are buried in Brookwood
P/O W H Geddes RCAF	+	Military Cemetery.
Sgt B Gordon RCAF	+	

29 May   **24 OTU**   **Anson I**   **R9805**   **Training**
1944

P/O P Mudry RCAF   T/o Honeybourne for a solo flying detail. Came down, circa 1500, in a field in the vicinity of Bishop's Tachbrook, between 2 and 3 miles SSW from Royal Leamington Spa in Warwickshire.

30 May
1944

11 OTU   **Wellington X**   **LN741 TX-L**   **Training**

Lt V Vincent SAAF   inj   T/o Oakley to practice single-engined flying
F/O A A Whitman   inj   combined with solo circuit training. Shortly
Sgt Bayliss   before 1050, Lt Vincent SAAF found that he was
Sgt H G Colgate   +   unable to unfeather the starboard propeller and
                                 as he was losing height, he decided to make an
emergency landing at Finmere. However, en route the Wellington crash-landed at
Chetwode Grange on the S side of the London and North Eastern railway and five
miles SW of Buckingham. Sgt Colgate is buried in Heston and Isleworth Borough
Cemetery, Twickenham. F/O Whitman was gravely injured and he died on 8 October
1944; he rests in Brookwood Military Cemetery.

30-31 May
1944

30 OTU   **Wellington III**   **BJ597**   **-O**   **Op: Nickel**

F/O J F Boullier   T/o 2315 Hixon and set course for France. While
                             flying some 16 km W of Cherbourg, at 15,000 feet,
the starboard engine caught fire. Distress calls were broadcast but none were not
acknowledged and, eventually, the Wellington crossed the south coast (at 8,000
feet), continuing to seek assistance. The weather conditions were far from
ideal and at 0145, now down to 4,000 feet and with a thick blanket of cloud
beneath, the crew baled out, leaving their aircraft to crash at Bulkington,
four miles SW of Devizes, Wiltshire. Earlier in the year, on 21 January, while
engaged on a Bullseye with Sgt G L Rowe RCAF, this Wellington had landed with its
wheels retracted at Warmwell airfield in Dorset. Sgt Rowe RCAF went to the Far
East and was posted missing after his 99 Squadron Liberator VI KH360 ditched on
New Year's Day 1945, in the Gulf of Martaban off Kalegauk Island. His name is
inscribed on the Singapore War Memorial.

31 May
1944

12 OTU   **Wellington III**   **BK157**   **Training**

F/O D A Driver DFM   +   T/o 1005 Chipping Warden for a cine camera gun
F/S E Cotterell   +   detail, the crew comprising of the screened
F/S J H McGregor   +   pilot, two screened air gunners and four trainee
Sgt E W Blakeman   +   air gunners. After forty minutes of flying, F/O
Sgt J A Oliver   +   Driver made an evasive diving turn to port and
Sgt F J Pack   +   before he could level out, the port wing folded.
Sgt J H Nixon   +   Out of control, the bomber plunged to the ground
                             and burst into flames at Swalcliffe, 5 miles SW
of Banbury, Oxfordshire. F/O Driver had served in the Middle East with 104
Squadron and details of his award had been Gazetted on 9 July 1943. Along with
Sgt Blakeman, he is buried in Banbury Cemetery. The others all rest in burial
grounds scattered across the United Kingdom. F/S McGregor, who lies in Wick
Cemetery, lost his father Signalman Thomas McGregor Royal Naval Reserve in action
aboard HMS Laurentic on 25 January 1917; he is commemorated on the Portsmouth
Naval Memorial. It is further noted that Sgt Nixon, who was taken to Clough
Presbyterian Churchyard in Northern Ireland, had married Lily Mary Nixon of
Fulham in London.

1 Jun
1944

11 OTU   **Wellington X**   **LN743**   **Ground**

F/L E C Bulmer   +   Wrecked 0330 at its dispersal on Westcott air-
                             field when a 44 Squadron Lancaster I ME794 KM-V
exploded (see Bomber Command Losses, Volume 5, page 249). F/L Bulmer, a Flying
Control Officer, happened to be in the vicinity of the two aircraft when the
incident took place. He is buried in Hereford Cemetery.

2 Jun
1944

12 OTU   **Wellington III**   **X3823**   **Air Test**

F/O I F V Hawkins   T/o 1839 Edgehill and crashed out of control
F/O Dawes   inj   when the starboard engine cut with the bomber
                             two thirds of the way down the runway. The
pilot managed to arrest the resulting swing but when the brakes faded, he
raised the undercarriage in order to avoid running off the airfield. F/O Dawes,
his wireless operator, sustained painful cuts and abrasions to his right thigh
and right arm.

4 Jun
1944

16 OTU   **Wellington III**   **BK470**   **Training**

F/L P U Keel   +   T/o 0342 Barford St. John but failed to become
               inj   properly airborne and ended up amongst buildings
               inj   at Lovells Farm. F/L Keel of Denmark was taken
                             for cremation at Golders Green. On 8 January
1944, this Wellington had been involved in an overshoot accident at Barford St.
John (P/O A B Wheeler RNZAF) during which the port oleo had collapsed.

5 Jun   **27 OTU**   **Martinet I**   **HP384**   **Training**
1944   F/S G B McSweeney RAAF   +   T/o Lichfield for local flying,including circuits
           P/O A R Duel RAAF   +   and landings. F/S McSweeney RAAF was making his
                                             first flight in a Martinet, though he was a fully
qualified Wellington pilot. At 1610, his aircraft was seen to emerge from cloud,
in a spin, and without recovering strike the ground (MR 62/655478). Both airmen
were taken to Chester (Blacon) Cemetery. The CWGC register for the cemetery notes
P/O Duel's first Christian name as Allan, while the RAAF war museum register has
it as Allen. Both hailed from Queensland, the latter from Banyo and F/S McSweeney
from Holland Park.

Chapter Five

Peak Proficiency

6 June 1944 to 8 May 1945

It is a reasonable to say that the ultimate downfall of Adolf Hitler and the consequent misery inflicted upon the German people had its origins in the dark days of 1940, with the fall of France and the evacuation of the British Expeditionary Force from Dunkerque.

Between then and the successful Allied invasion of Normandy, the German armies had fought many outstanding battles, especially in North Africa and across the vast barren lands of the Soviet Union, though in each theatre of operations the initial promise of success had ended in abject failure.

Thus, by the summer of 1944, the generals in the German High Command were being forced to face the inescapable fact that defeat was inevitable. In bringing about this reversal of fortune, Bomber Command had played a very significant part.

Indeed, in the months preceding the landings, Bomber Command and the United States Army Air Corps had effectively reduced the rail services of the occupied countries to a mere shadow of its former self. Now, as the Allies fought to secure their slender bridgeheads and prepare for the battles yet to come, it was imperative to maintain the strength of a Command that was continuing to expand.

The mainstay of the Operational Training Units was now the Wellington; only 10 OTU at Abingdon and Kinloss based 19 OTU soldiered on with the venerable Whitley and both units would, in the autumn of 1944, change over to the Wellington.

In respect of flying accidents, these were much reduced from a year ago and with Bomber Command squadron strength peaking during the winter of 1944-1945, the opportunity to disband some of the units was taken. In fact, a gradual rundown had already started with the disbanding of 15 OTU and 23 OTU in mid-March 1944, followed in the October by the closing of 28 OTU, 83 OTU and 86 OTU, the latter having been formed in June 1944. Thus, at the end of 1944, nineteen establishments remained in existence. On New Year's Day 1945 16 OTU at Upper Heyford (satellite Barford St. John) gave up its Wellingtons in favour of Mosquitoes and before the cessation of hostilities in the May, two of the eighteen remaining Wellington – equipped units ceased operations.

As will be seen in the continuation of the summaries, the sheer demands of operational training continued to take its toll. But, as has been stated, the frequency and number of accidents decreased, a possible factor being the numbers of screened personnel arriving at the training units as the survival rates of operational crews increased over the grim days of 1942-1943 and the early part of 1944 when Bomber Command's losses were at their highest.

7 Jun	11 OTU	Wellington X	HE233		Training
1944	F/S K A Venn RAAF		inj		

T/o 1220 Oakley for circuits and landings. At 500 feet, following a normal departure, the starboard engine failed. Sgt Venn RAAF succeeded in feathering the propeller but was unable to keep the Wellington in the air and, thus, he force-landed at 1235. It is thought that all on board, five in total, received injuries of a relatively minor nature.

	82 OTU	Martinet I	MS870		Training
	F/O G Smith		+		

T/o 1440 Ossington in company with another aircraft to practice interceptions. At 1510, just as the second aircraft broke away from its attack, F/O Smith flew beneath a line of high-tension cables and smashed into a river bank near Burton upon Stather, five miles NNW from Scunthorpe, Lincolnshire. He is buried in Selby Cemetery.

	82 OTU	Wellington X	LN535		Ground

Wrecked 0334 at Gamston, after being struck by a 1667 HCU Halifax that was making an emergency landing. The Halifax, a Mk. V from Sandtoft, flown by P/O C H Henry RNZAF had developed a glycol leak in its port inner engine.

Note. The aircraft movement card raised for the Wellington shows that it was delivered to 48 MU at Hawarden on 26 August 1943, and thence to Gamston on 8 September. No details of its flying hours have been appended.

7- 8 Jun	**16 OTU**	**Wellington III**	**BK258**	**Training**

1944   F/S J H Molloy RNZAF   inj T/o 2240 Upper Heyford for a night cross-country
during which the Wellington suffered a complete
engine failure. This occurred at 11,000 feet and after six of the seven-man crew
had baled out, as ordered, F/S Molloy RNZAF carried out a forced-landing on high
ground near, it is believed, Llandinabo, some 10 miles NNE of Monmouth. Going
back to 16 February 1943, this Wellington was the subject of a fatal ground
accident at Hinton-in-the-Hedges. The tragedy occurred during a crew change
when the air gunner, Sgt Glenwood Alexander Taylor RCAF, walked into a still
rotating propeller. He is buried in Middleton Stoney (All Saints) Churchyard.

8 Jun	**17 OTU**	**Hurricane IIC**	**LF749**	**Training**

1944   W/O A L Terry RAAF   + T/o Turweston for a fighter affiliation duty.
Eyewitnesses report seeing the Hurricane per-
forming aerobatics, estimated at around 2,000 feet, when it dived steeply and
crashed 1229 at Boycott Farm, N of the A422 main road and on the SSW side of
Stowe Park, a large estate some 2 miles NW of Buckingham. W/O Terry RAAF rests
in Oxford (Botley) Cemetery. His aircraft was the first of its type to be
written off in the service of a Bomber Command Operational Training Unit.

9 Jun	**26 OTU**	**Wellington X**	**HE786**	**Ground**

1944   Burnt out 1655 at Wing when another of the
unit's Wellingtons crashed out of control, while landing from an air test.

	26 OTU	**Wellington X**	**HE854**	**Air Test**

F/O R F Huband   + T/o 1645 Wing for a standard night flying test
F/O H Wilkes DFM   + only to crash ten minutes later, bursting into
flames. In addition to the Wellington identified
above, the crash destroyed Tomahawk IIB AK116, which had been loaded on a "Queen
Mary" transporter and was parked near No. 4 hangar. It is reported that three
members of the ground staff died, though their names are omitted from the unit's
records. A year previous, F/O Huband (then a W/O) had been involved in a training
accident (see page 228). He was a very experienced pilot with 832 of his 1,314
flying hours being logged on Wellingtons. Known to his family and friends as
Dick, he rests in Fladbury (St. John The Baptist) Churchyard, while F/O Wilkes
is buried at Frampton-on-Severn (St. Mary) Churchyard. Notification of his DFM
(gained while flying with 150 Squadron in the Middle East) had appeared in the
London Gazette on 30 November 1943.

10 Jun	**21 OTU**	**Hurricane IIC**	**PG425**	**Training**

1944   F/O D Stevens   + T/o 1005 Moreton-in-Marsh for fighter affiliation
training. Flew into the ground 1112 at Long
Compton, 5 miles SSE of Shipston-on-Stour, Warwickshire. An Honours graduate
in Mechanical Sciences from Cambridge, F/O Stevens was cremated at Woking.

	30 OTU	**Wellington X**	**HE820**	**Training**

F/L A Maclean   + T/o 0935 Seighford for circuits and landings.
Sgt D Kelly   + At the Court of Inquiry it was stated that the
                 inj Wellington appeared to make a normal approach
                 inj at 1110 but did not touch down. It then rose
                 inj under full power to about 50 feet, banked to
port and flew into the ground. F/L Maclean,
who had recently commenced his training course, had a total of 1,798 flying
hours to his credit. He is buried in Scotland at Tobermory Cemetery, while
his fellow countryman, Sgt Kelly, rests in Edinburgh (Portobello) Cemetery.

11 Jun	**22 OTU**	**Wellington III**	**BK186**	**Training**

1944   F/O C Bouchard RCAF   T/o Stratford-upon-Avon for an evening detail.
During the sortie, the port engine cut out and
the crew were unable to pump the undercarriage down before a crash-landing was
made at 2212, after which the aircraft caught fire. On 14 May 1943, while on
the strength of 23 OTU, this Wellington had been involved in a fatal midair
collision with Spitfire IIA P8268 of 61 OTU, the fighter spiralling down to
crash 1 mile S of Long Stretton in Shropshire. Initially delivered to service
at 48 MU Hawarden on 25 August 1942, the Wellington had been issued to 23 OTU
on 18 September and saw almost continuous service until 30 December 1943, when
it underwent extensive maintenance. Allotted to 22 OTU on 11 March, it had
flown a total of 1,273.50 hours.

12 Jun	21 OTU	Wellington X	LN635	Training

12 Jun
1944

21 OTU   Wellington X   LN635   **Training**

F/S J M Gaddes RNZAF   T/o Moreton-in-Marsh for night bombing practice
Sgt G M Dilworth   inj   over the Radway ranges. Abandoned 0420 over the
F/S F N Chapman RAAF   inj   ranges, after a fire broke out in the bomb bay,
                                     and left to crash at Primrose Barn just a mile
west of Upper Tysoe and 4 miles NE of Shipston-on-Stour, Warwickshire. Of the
two airmen classified as injured, Sgt Dilworth sustained little more than a very
severe shaking accompanied by shock, but F/S Chapman RAAF was taken to hospital
with a broken leg.

Note. Quaintly, Upper Tysoe lies below Middle Tysoe with Lower Tysoe further
to the north. All three villages are close to the border with Oxfordshire.

13 Jun
1944

28 OTU   Wellington X   LP397   **Training**

F/O J Star   +   T/o 1447 Castle Donington for a cross-country.
F/O G D W Buchanan RCAF   +   Came out of the cloud cover, in a steep dive,
Sgt W C Davis RCAF   +   and crashed 1512 near the parish church at
Sgt J F Potts   +   Mayfield, a Staffordshire village close to
Sgt R J Taylor RCAF   +   the border with Derbyshire and about 3 miles
Sgt J J U Stevens RCAF   +   west of Ashbourne airfield. The four RCAF
                                     airmen rest in Brookwood Military Cemetery.
F/O Star of Yarmouth, Nova Scotia, lies in Nottingham Jewish Cemetery, while
Sgt Potts is at Shirley (St. John) Churchyard, Croydon. An investigation into
the crash could find no evidence of structural failure but the possibility that
the aircraft was struck by lightning could not be ruled out.

13-14 Jun
1944

11 OTU   Wellington X   LN172   —M   **Training**

F/S J B Marden RAAF   +   T/o 2325 Westcott for a night navigation detail.
Sgt R F Gray   +   Just after an hour into the flight, and possibly
Sgt N G Wakefield   +   while over the Irish Sea, a wireless message was
Sgt E Ankers   +   received advising that an engine had failed and
F/S R S Waring RNZAF   +   the crew were returning to base. At around 0140,
Sgt L Backhouse   +   an SOS signal was sent and it is believed that
Sgt J Key   +   soon afterwards the Wellington came down in
                                     Cardigan Bay (the SOS fixed the bomber at 5217N
0454W). Subsequently, all bodies were recovered and laid to rest in various
cemeteries across England and Wales.

14 Jun
1944

29 OTU   Wellington X   LN860   **Ground**

                                     While positioned on trestles, downwind of the
Wellington described in the next summary, became engulfed in flames and burnt
out at Bruntingthorpe airfield.

29 OTU   Wellington X   MS480   **Ground**

                                     At 0950 a fierce fire broke out in the region
of the starboard nacelle. Within a matter of seconds, the bomber was burning
with such intensity that the flames set light to the Wellington parked alongside (see above). At the time of the incident, both aircraft were undergoing
routine maintenance. It is thought that a pedestal lamp may have shattered,
igniting fuel vapour.

16 Jun
1944

22 OTU   Wellington X   HZ715   **Training**

P/O A D Cooper RCAF   +   T/o 1020 Stratford-upon-Avon for a combined
F/O F A Dixon RCAF   +   dual and cross-country exercise. While flying
F/L E Unterseher RCAF   +   in cloud, over the Lake District, smashed at
F/O D Titleman RCAF   +   1335 into the side of a hill identified in unit
Sgt G McC Anderson RCAF   +   records as Red Pike near Buttermere, 7 miles SW
F/O R E Simonson RCAF   +   of Keswick. All were brought back for interment
WO1 G R Coathup RCAF   +   in Chester (Blacon) Cemetery. Less than two
Sgt C McR Hodges RCAF   +   months previous, on 18 April to be precise,
                                     WO2 Clifford Harvey Coathup RCAF, brother to
WO1 Coathup RCAF, failed to return from operations to Noisy-le-Sec, while flying
with 427 Squadron (see Bomber Command Losses, Volume 5, page 172).

18 Jun
1944

28 OTU   Wellington X   MF537   **Training**

P/O H D Stevens RCAF   inj   T/o 1108 Castle Donington for a cross-country
                                     during which the air speed indicator failed.
At 1426 the Wellington landed at Penrhos in Caernarvon, but skidded into a hut
after the undercarriage was raised in order to stop inside the airfield.

19 Jun
1944

27 OTU   **Wellington III** BJ904   **Training**
F/S L K Maxwell RAAF   +   T/o 1055 Church Broughton for a cross-country.
Sgt A W Shiels RAAF   +   On return to base and while flying between 200
F/S R B Sterling RAAF   +   and 300 feet above the airfield, the port motor
P/O W G Moeller   inj   stopped after running out of fuel. Losing
Sgt W D Smout   inj   height rapidly, the Wellington crashed 1723
Sgt R C Schodde RAAF   inj   some 400 yards west of the aerodrome. Those
                                who lost their lives are buried in Oxford
(Botley) Cemetery. Sgt Schodde RAAF made a good recovery from his injuries
but was killed while serving with 460 Squadron in mid-March 1945 (see Bomber
Command Losses, Volume 6, page 138).

22 Jun
1944

10 OTU   **Whitley V** Z9466   **Training**
Sgt D T Waddington   T/o 1440 Stanton Harcourt for flying practice.
                                Crash-landed circa 1630 after overshooting the
runway, finishing up in a field. Sgt Waddington had experienced engine problems
and had made two single-engined approaches before coming to grief on his third
attempt to land safely.

22-23 Jun
1944

12 OTU   **Wellington X** HE989   **Training**
F/S Cann   T/o 2253 Chipping Warden for a night navigation
                                detail. While cruising at 6,000 feet, one of
the engines began to misfire and F/S Cann decided to land as quickly as possible.
At 0028 he touched down on Silverstone airfield, Northamptonshire, but his aircraft bounced and upon its second arrival, the undercarriage collapsed, a fire
breaking out soon after. F/S Cann's service number indicates he joined the air
force at Uxbridge within days of the outbreak of war.

23 Jun
1944

85 OTU   **Wellington X** LN589   **Training**
F/S F S Barnes   T/o 0045 Husbands Bosworth for an exercise in
Sgt B Hepworth   inj   night navigation. Became lost and crash-landed
Sgt S Cook   inj   circa 0650, breaking the undercarriage in the
                                process, at Hallbrook Farm, Aston, 2 miles E
of Stevenage, Hertfordshire. This was the unit's first serious accident since
forming eight days previous.

23-24 Jun
1944

28 OTU Det   **Wellington X** LN698   **Training**
Sgt D G Stuart   T/o 2217 Bircotes for a night cross-country.
                                Made too high an approach on return to base and
crashed 0347 while trying to go round again. This was the first of two serious
accidents involving the Bircote's detachment, which lasted from 20 June to 24
July 1944.

24 Jun
1944

82 OTU   **Wellington X** JA452   **Ground**
                                During oxygen recharging at Ossington, wrecked
when a cylinder exploded at 2210, starting a fierce blaze.

25-26 Jun
1944

29 OTU   **Wellington X** MF528   **Training**
Sgt T Spencer   T/o 2305 Bruntingthorpe for high-level bombing.
                                Encountered adverse weather and when the port
engine failed at 4,300 feet, Sgt Spencer (who hailed from Newfoundland) was
unable to maintain height. Ordering his crew to bale out, he began a controlled
descent with the intention of force -landing. However, at around 0115 when the
starboard motor stopped at 800 feet, he immediately took to his parachute, his
aircraft coming down 4 miles N of Thorney, a Nottinghamshire village some two
to three miles SW of Saxilby, Lincolnshire. Assuming the direction and distance
quoted to be correct, then the Wellington likely came down in Lincolnshire and
in the general vicinity of Stow Park, 2 miles WSW of Sturton by Stow.

27 Jun
1944

18 OTU   **Wellington III** Z1592   **Training**
Sgt G K Cameron RCAF   +   T/o 1335 Finningley for a cross-country. Caught
Sgt E A Crowe RCAF   +   fire in the air and crashed 1715 at Baner Farm,
Sgt G F Marchington RCAF   +   Middle Rasen and about a mile or so W of Market
Sgt G W Durham RCAF   +   Rasen in Lincolnshire. All rest in Harrogate
Sgt E Bunt RCAF   +   (Stonefall) Cemetery, their average age being
Sgt R S Cracknell RCAF   +   twenty. It is suspected all were in the early
                                stages of their training as it is unusual to
come across an entire RCAF crew of sergeant rank at this stage of the war.

29 Jun	22 OTU	Wellington III	HF641		Training

29 Jun 1944 — **22 OTU** — **Wellington III** — **HF641** — **Training**

F/O R J Andrews RCAF   +
F/O C E Stephen RCAF   +
F/O P W Tokar RCAF   +
Sgt W H Clark RCAF   +
Sgt J B Sollie RCAF   +
Sgt A H MacKimmie RCAF   +

T/o 1335 Wellesbourne Mountford for a navigation exercise. Struck by lightning and exploded 1720 over Roade, a little less than 6 miles SSW from Northampton. All were taken for interment in Brookwood Military Cemetery.

1 Jul 1944 — **14 OTU** — **Wellington X** — **LN689** — **Training**

F/O N S Toms RNZAF
Sgt J E G Cecile RCAF   inj
Sgt K A Atkinson   inj
Sgt J D Ballagh RCAF   inj
   inj
Sgt J R M Corman RCAF   +

T/o 1301 Husbands Bosworth with a staff pilot instructor to practice overshooting procedures. At around 1445, the port engine failed at 200 feet and the bomber immediately lost half of this precious height before F/O Toms RNZAF was able to arrest the descent and coax the bomber up to 500 feet. Then, while trying to make a climbing turn, the troublesome motor cut completely and at 1446 the Wellington hit a tree 2 miles N of Clipston, 6 miles WSW of Desborough, Northamptonshire. Sgt Corman RCAF is buried in Brookwood Military Cemetery. Sgt Cecile RCAF was admitted to Leicester Royal Infirmary.

3- 4 Jul 1944 — **24 OTU** — **Wellington III** — **BK251** — **Training**

F/O A S Woolaver RCAF   +
F/O R J Gray RCAF   +
P/O W A Tees RCAF   +
F/O E K Burleigh RCAF   +
Sgt L T Gabryelski RCAF   +
Sgt G A Jones RCAF   +
Sgt W Marshall RCAF   +

T/o 2253 Long Marston for a night cross-country. On return to base at approximately 0350, crashed into the station's bomb dump and caught fire. All are buried in Brookwood Military Cemetery. This was the unit's first major accident since re-equipping with Wellingtons.

4 Jul 1944 — **10 OTU** — **Whitley V** — **AD690** — **Training**

Sgt L Moore RCAF
P/O A E Cline RCAF
Sgt R L Joyce RCAF
Sgt C E Brown RCAF
Sgt C N Faulkner RCAF
Sgt R F McIntyre RCAF   inj

T/o 1150 Stanton Harcourt for a cross-country flight. Soon after setting out, and having climbed to 2,000 feet, Sgt Moore RCAF realised he was in close proximity to a large formation of twin-engined Dakota transports. In taking avoiding action, he lost height to around 1,300 feet, whereupon the starboard engine shed most of its coolant and caught fire. Over the next few minutes, he managed to feather the propeller and quell the blaze but as he approached the airfield the flames flared up again and a forced-landing was promptly carried out at 1210, in a field, some 3 miles S of the runway. At the Court of Inquiry, it was recommended that Sgt Moore's log book be suitably endorsed for his fine airmanship in the face of a difficult situation.

Note. When the officer who wrote the RAF Form 96(A) Message Form (Signal), advising the various authorities of the accident that had befallen the air-craft, he entered the serial as BD690 and, thus, this has resulted in both Whitley's, AD690 and BD690, being written off charge on this date.

4- 5 Jul 1944 — **82 OTU** — **Wellington X** — **HF485 —G** — **Op: Nickel**

F/L F L Burston RCAF   +
F/O G R Burston RCAF   +
F/O R V Doupe RCAF   +
F/O D G Bush DFC RCAF   +
Sgt O Miller RCAF   +
Sgt N S Hurder RCAF   +

T/o 2238 Ossington and headed for the Brest peninsular. It is understood that the crew crossed the French coast, but did not complete their assignment. On regaining the south coast crashed 0245, while attempting to force-land, with engine trouble, at Liverpool Farm near Honiton, Devon, striking a house in its final moments of flight. All are buried in Brookwood Military Cemetery. Very unusually, the crew included two brothers, both of whom were married. Along with F/O Doupe RCAF, they hailed from London, Ontario.

6 Jul 1944 — **19 OTU F Flt** — **Whitley V** — **N1354 XF-T** — **Training**

P/O W Newey

T/o 1611 Kinloss with a crew of ten, which included two Air Training Corps cadets. Nine minutes later, a distress call was received indicating the starboard engine had failed and a ditching was imminent. At 1650, it was advised that everyone was safe having been plucked from Findhorn Bay by the crew of a fishing boat owned by Sellar's Salmon Fisheries. P/O Newey was commended for his airmanship.

6 Jul
1944

21 OTU　　　　　　　　　**Martinet I**　JN299　　　　　　　　　　**Training**
W/O J T Patterson　　　　　　　　　T/o Moreton-in-Marsh for an exercise in night
　　　　　　　　　　　　　　　　　fighter affiliation. While flying at 1,000 feet
the engine commenced vibrating and not long after the propeller, along with its
reduction gear, sheared away. W/O Patterson skillfully forced-landed in a field
near Todenham, some 2 miles NE of the airfield, but was unable to prevent his
aircraft from turning over. He escaped relatively unharmed.

27 OTU　　　　　**Wellington III**　X3354　　　　　　　　　　**Training**
F/L J Burkhardt RAAF　　　　　　　　T/o 1205 Church Broughton with a screened pilot
F/O H G Johnson RAAF　　　　　　　　tasked for a dual cross-country but as the air-
　　　　　　　　　　　　　　　　　craft accelerated, the boost reading for the
starboard engine decayed and moments later, despite closing the throttles, the
Wellington swung off the runway and lost its undercarriage. This same bomber
had been damaged on 23 August 1943, its pilot then being P/O G M Haddern RAAF.

7 Jul
1944

26 OTU　　　　　　**Wellington X**　LP314　　　　　　　　　　**Training**
F/S J P S Dalton RAAF　　　+　T/o 0125 Wing for night circuit training. At
F/S W A Sheppard RAAF　　　+　approximately 0215, following the failure of
Sgt I A Checkley　　　　　　+　the starboard engine, the crew tried to make
　　　　　　　　　　　　　　　　a landing on the airfield. Initially, all went
well until the Wellington was nearing the runway when, at a height estimated
to have been no more than 250 feet, it swung violently and crashed. Both
Australians and Sgt Checkley (whose brother, Sgt Jack Ernest Checkley was
posted missing while flying Blenheims in the Western Desert with 203 Squadron
on 15 February 1942) are buried in Oxford (Botley) Cemetery.

7- 8 Jul
1944

17 OTU　　　　　　　**Wellington X**　HE325　　　　　　　　　**Training**
F/L J Shaw　　　　　　　+　T/o 2348 Turweston for a night exercise. Flown
Sgt W N Mitchell　　　　+　into at 0128 while at 1,000 feet by a Wellington
Sgt W E C Willett　　　+　from the same unit that had taken off six minutes
Sgt L W Barker　　　　　+　earlier. Both machines went down near Westbury,
Sgt C A Wyatt　　　　　　+　five miles WNW of Buckingham and on impact burst
Sgt H Kinchin　　　　　　+　into flames. Sgt Willett of Georgeham in Devon
　　　　　　　　　　　　　　　was buried at Towcester Cemetery, the rest being
taken to their home towns. It is noted that F/L Shaw, who is the sole service
burial in Benochy Parish Churchyard, was a history graduate from Caius College,
Cambridge.

8 Jul
1944

17 OTU　　　　　**Wellington III**　BK272　　　　　　　　　　**Training**
P/O C F Searles　　　　　+　T/o 0122 Turweston for local night flying and
F/O W Haraczay RCAF　　　+　lost in the manner described above. Similar to
F/O A G Corck RCAF　　　+　those who died in the other Wellington, funeral
Sgt P J Woods　　　　　　+　services were held at various churches across
Sgt R F Bradford　　　　+　the country, Sgt Woods of Hall Green, Birmingham
Sgt J B Lemon　　　　　　+　being cremated at Northampton and Counties
Sgt B Hadlow　　　　　　+　Crematorium, Milton.

9 Jul
1944

26 OTU　　　　　**Wellington III**　BJ795　　　　　　　　　　**Training**
P/O A W Canning　　　　inj　T/o 0053 Little Horwood for night circuit
　　　　　　　　　　　　　　training, including practice overshoots and
it was while so engaged at 0105 that the starboard engine cut with the bomber
at a mere 400 feet. In the ensuing forced-landing, the starboard wing clipped
a tree at Great Horwood, 4 miles ESE of Buckingham.

11 Jul
1944

10 OTU　　　　　　**Hurricane IIC**　MW346　　　　　　　　　**Training**
P/O R N H Walter　　　　　+　T/o 1710 Abingdon for fighter affiliation
　　　　　　　　　　　　　　　training. Eyewitnesses aboard the target Whitley
report seeing a Harvard formating with them, and then the Hurricane appeared,
carrying out an attack from the starboard beam. It then approached from the
starboard quarter and after passing beneath the bomber, pulled up vertically
before rolling onto its back and diving into the ground between the Oxfordshire
village of Nuneham Courtenay and the airfield at Mount Farm on the eastern edge
of Berinsfield. P/O Walter of Beckenham in Kent had been attached from 22 OTU.
He is buried in Stratford-upon-Avon Cemetery.

29 OTU　　　　　**Wellington III**　X3306　　　　　　　　　　**Training**
F/S N R Hooper RAAF　　　inj　T/o 1645 Bitteswell for an evening sortie. On
　　　　　　　　　　　　　　return to base at 1820, crashed and burnt out.

11–12 Jul **12 OTU**   **Wellington III** **BJ622**   **Training**
1944   Sgt J C Ridley RCAF   T/o 2305 Chipping Warden for night circuit
training. Landed 0030, wheels still retracted
and destroyed in the fire that followed. As a consequence of this accident,
six of the unit's aircraft that were engaged in night flying had to be diverted
to other airfields.

12–13 Jul **18 OTU**   **Wellington III** **Z1696**   **Training**
1944   W/O L Gawlowski PAF   + T/o 2245 Finningley for a night cross-country.
Sgt A Chmielowiec PAF   + Crashed 0230 in the circuit, about a mile SSW of
Sgt S T Hryniewiecki PAF + the airfield. All rest in Newark-upon-Trent
Sgt W Doda PAF   + Cemetery. Moments before the crash, the pilot
Sgt L Klepacki PAF   + had called Flying Control and had acknowledged
Sgt M Lewicki PAF   + an instruction to orbit at 900 feet.

13 Jul   **14 OTU**   **Wellington X** **LN509**   **Air Test**
1944   F/L A C Shilleto   + T/o 1515 Market Harborough for a standard night
W/O J Everett DFM   + flying test but fifteen minutes later collided
with another of the unit's Wellingtons, both
aircraft falling at East Farndon, 5 miles WNW from Desborough, Northamptonshire
and practically on the border with Leicestershire SW of Market Harborough. F/L
Shilleto, who had logged 1,079 of his 1,453 flying hours on Wellingtons, rests
in Brockenhurst (St. Nicholas) Churchyard. He had previously served with 29 OTU
and had been involved in a serious Tiger Moth crash on 5 July 1942 (see page 133).
His screened wireless operator had won an immediate DFM in March 1942, while
serving with 207 Squadron. Full details of his courageous actions were published
in the London Gazette on 7 April 1942; his grave is in Brighton (Bear Road)
Borough Cemetery and his service number indicates he was selected, at least,
for pilot training in the volunteer reserve in the late 1930s.

    14 OTU   **Wellington X** **LP627**   **Air Test**
F/L W D Browne DFC   + T/o 1525 Market Harborough with similar intent
W/O S P Edge   + and destroyed in the manner previously described.
F/L Browne is buried in Oxford (Botley) Cemetery,
while his screened wireless operator, W/O Edge, was taken to Wallasay (Rake Lane)
Cemetery in Cheshire.

14 Jul   **24 OTU**   **Wellington X** **HE381 TY–G**   **Training**
1944   F/O J A Thompson RCAF + T/o 1153 Honeybourne for circuits and landings.
W/O R Burns   + Spun and crashed two minutes later at Yerdly
Sgt J C Anderson RCAF + Farm on the E side of Long Crompton, 15 miles
F/S J W Johnston RCAF + SSE of Stratford-upon-Avon, Warwickshire. The
three RCAF members of crew (all shared a common
first name, John) were taken to Brookwood Military Cemetery, while W/O Burns was
buried in his native Scotland at Hawick (Wellogate) Cemetery. It is believed he
was the last Royal Air Force airman to be killed in service with 24 OTU. WO2
Eugene Huntley Johnston RCAF, brother of F/S Johnston RCAF, had died the previous
year, on 11 June, when his 415 Squadron Hampden had been involved in a midair
collision near Tain airfield in Scotland.

Note. Assuming the crash location details are correct, the crew had flown a
considerable way from the airfield circuit. Their Wellington, while on the
books of 23 OTU, had been slightly damaged on 17 August 1943. Its two pilots
on that occasion were F/L G F Smith and his pupil, Sgt B V Tedford RCAF, the
latter being killed on 22 November 1943, while flying with 434 Squadron (see
Bomber Command Losses, Volume 4, page 393).

15–16 Jul **30 OTU**   **Wellington X** **NC678 –Y**   **Training**
1944   Sgt D L Phillips RCAF inj T/o 2340 Seighford for night bombing practice.
F/O S D Mann RCAF   + Caught fire in the air over Staffordshire after
Sgt P C H Mullins RCAF + being struck by a flash bomb dropped from another
F/S J H Jones RCAF   + aircraft. The pilot ordered everyone to bale out,
Sgt J D D Watt   + reducing his airspeed in order to assist. Then,
believing all had complied, he took to his para-
chute, unaware that his crew had remained aboard. All perished as the Wellington
crashed 0135 near Huntingdon, 2 miles NNW from Cannock. The three Canadians were
buried in Chester (Blacon) Cemetery, while Sgt Wall was taken to Scotland and
laid to rest in Aberdeen (Allenvale) Cemetery.

16 Jul   **21 OTU**   **Wellington X**   **LN696**   **Ground**
1944   At approximately 1325, while having its fuel
drained into a bowser at Moreton-in-Marsh, the Wellington became engulfed in
flames and was totally destroyed.

17 Jul   **28 OTU**   **Wellington X**   **LP406**   **Training**
1944   F/O J E Thompson   +   T/o 0052 Wymeswold to practice bombing over the
      F/O J Michalec RCAF   +   nearby Ragdale ranges. At 0107, while over the
      F/O F P O Weary RCAF   +   range, the Wellington went into a dive from
      Sgt F V Davis   +   which it failed to recover. On hitting the
      Sgt W A Lewin   +   ground, there was a huge explosion. The two
      Sgt W L O´Connor   +   RCAF officers were taken to Brookwood Military
                                     Cemetery, while the others were claimed by their
next of kin. The last three named are identified as air gunners.

17-18 Jul   **28 OTU Det**   **Wellington X**   **LP296**   **Training**
1944   F/O J E Burton   T/o 2222 Bircotes for night circuit training
      W/O O R Herbert   during which the wind changed direction. At
                                     0233 the Wellington touched down, out of the
wind and as a result ran beyond the runway. The pilot decided to swing the
aircraft but as he did so, the undercarriage collapsed.

18 Jul   **27 OTU**   **Wellington X**   **MF584**   **Training**
1944   F/S J S Walker RAAF   T/o 1830 Lichfield for bombing practice. Within
                                     half-an-hour of departure, the starboard engine
began to vibrate so alarmingly that before it could be shut down, it literally
fell out of its frame. Calmly, F/S Walker RAAF ordered his crew to jump and
moments after he had followed them through the escape hatch, the Wellington
crashing into Sack Lane, Woodlands near Marchington, 3 miles SE of Uttoxeter
in Staffordshire. Subsequently, the young Australian was praised for his good
crew drills.

19 Jul   **84 OTU**   **Wellington X**   **LN967**   **Training**
1944   Sgt R W Gillian   T/o 2300 Desborough tasked for a Bullseye detail
                                     but as the speed built up, an escape hatch blew
out. Sgt Gillian immediately closed the throttles and braked hard, but he was
unable to prevent his aircraft from running into an obstruction.

22 Jul   **20 OTU G Flt**   **Wellington X**   **HZ262**   **-H**   **Training**
1944   F/S A J Grigg RAAF   +   T/o 1153 Lossiemouth for a fighter affiliation
      F/S E W O´Dwyer RAAF   +   exercise. At approximately 1230, the Wellington
      F/O A Sunter   +   was sighted, flying at an estimated 2,500 feet,
      F/S D B Barry RAAF   +   over the local golf course when the starboard
      Sgt A G Pring   +   wing suddenly came off. Totally out of control,
      Sgt J Kirk   +   the bomber plunged into Lossiemouth harbour.
                                     Search and Rescue:

      Cpl M Lucas WAAF   Cpl Lucas WAAF, a nursing orderly, happened to be
      Mr H Woodcock   +   visiting the Stotfield Hotel and saw the aircraft
                                     hit the sea, about 250 yards from the shore.
Without hesitation, she ran to the water´s edge and, fully clothed, began swimming
towards the wreckage. At the time a moderate swell was running and a considerable
amount of seaweed was present, threatening to trap her at any moment. With total
disregard for her own safety, Cpl Lucas pressed on and was the first to reach the
terrible scene. There she remained until joined by other helpers and was able to
identify two of the crew that had come to the surface. Then, satisfied that no
one was alive, she struck off to aid a civilian (probably Harold Woodcock) who
was in difficulties. Again, she rendered aid until others arrived to assist. Near
exhausted, she swam the remaining few yards to safety. For her unstinting efforts
Cpl Lucas was recommended for the British Empire Medal. The three Australians lie
in Lossiemouth Burial Ground, the others being buried in their home towns at
New Shildon, Newton Poppleford and Newbattle cemeteries respectively.

22-23 Jul   **27 OTU**   **Wellington X**   **MF654**   **Training**
1944   F/O W R Martin RAAF   T/o 2319 Lichfield for a dual night navigation
      F/S G W Henry RAAF   flight. When the port engine failed, the crew
                                     headed for Valley airfield on Anglesey, but
were unable to lower the flaps beyond 20 degrees. Thus, on landing at 0020
the bomber ran beyond the runway and the undercarriage was deliberately raised.

22-23 Jul   **83 OTU**   **Wellington X**   **MF504**   **Training**
1944   F/O R W Purves RCAF   inj   T/o 2110 Peplow for a night navigation detail.
                                  Returned to base at 0325 and crashed, after an
engine failed as tanks were changed in the circuit, on the runway, a fire soon
breaking out.

23 Jul   **83 OTU**   **Wellington X**   **LP567**   **Training**
1944   Sgt L R Carter RCAF   +   T/o 2330 Peplow for a night navigation sortie.
       F/O W D Watson RCAF   +   Crashed in the sea off the coast of Wales,
       Sgt W L Blunt RCAF   +   after losing all wireless contact. Five bodies
       Sgt G H Van-Every RCAF   +   were recovered and taken to Chester (Blacon)
       Sgt R A Johnson RCAF   +   Cemetery, while panel 255 of the Runnymede
       Sgt L K Beattie RCAF   +   Memorial perpetuates the name of Sgt Johnson.

23-24 Jul   **30 OTU**   **Wellington III**   **X4002**   **-D**   **Training**
1944   F/S F Searsby RAAF   inj   T/o 2254 Hixon on a special Bullseye sortie.
       F/O G Dyson   inj   While cruising at 7,000 feet, over East Anglia,
                                    the port engine began to misfire. As the power
fell away, the crew transmitted a series of distress calls but the sole response
was so weak and with total cloud cover beneath, the order to abandon was given.
All seven did so and the Wellington fell at around 0020 at Limes Farm, Bunwell,
five miles SSE of Wymondham, Norfolk. American servicemen from Old Buckenham
were requested to assist.

24 Jul   **30 OTU**   **Wellington III**   **HF727**   **Ground**
1944   Burnt out 1745 while having the oxygen supply
changed at Hixon. By a strange coincidence, this Wellington had been seriously
damaged by fire when, on 13 January 1944, the port engine had burst into flames
while starting up at Milltown (Sgt G R Short 20 OTU). Only prompt action by the
fire services had prevented the bomber from being totally destroyed. Following
repairs in works, it had been delivered to Hixon on 5 June and when written off
had flown a total of 248.45 hours.

24-25 Jul   **22 OTU**   **Wellington III**   **HF610**   **Training**
1944   F/O A Macleod RCAF   T/o 2238 Wellesbourne Mountford tasked for a
                                    Bullseye exercise. Reported to have been damaged
beyond repair after landing 0552 at Snitterfield airfield, Warwickshire, the
starboard undercarriage having failed to lock in the down position.

27 Jul   **83 OTU**   **Hurricane IIC**   **PG536**   **Training**
1944   F/O H Morrison   +   T/o 1135 Peplow for a training flight. An hour
                                    and five minutes later, while in cloud, collided
with a 41 OTU Hurricane IIC LF327 flown by F/O W H Skelton RCAF. Both fighters
crashed at Peplow Grange, Peplow, 11 miles NE of Shrewsbury. F/O Morrison is
buried in Faslane Cemetery. Of his 640 solo flying hours, around 200 had been
logged on type. F/O Skelton RCAF had flown 111 hours on Hurricanes and had
amassed 1,494 hours overall. He rests in Chester (Blacon) Cemetery. By a quirk
of near coincidence, his second Christian name was Hugh, while F/O Morrison had
been Christened Hew.

29-30 Jul   **22 OTU**   **Wellington X**   **LN869**   **Training**
1944   F/O J J D Belanger RCAF   +   T/o 2220 Stratford-upon-Avon for a "Flashlight"
       F/O R L Cuzner RCAF   +   exercise. The crew had been given permission to
       Sgt J L Moreau RCAF   +   land when, at 0340, it crashed into a wood at
       Sgt J A M Dauplaise RCAF   +   Coombe Farm, about 3 miles SE of the airfield.
       Sgt J M O Martin RCAF   +   The cause of the accident was attributed to an
       Sgt J J P Dion RCAF   inj   engine bursting into flames at a critical stage
                                    of the approach. Those who perished are buried
                                    in Stratford-upon-Avon Cemetery.

30 Jul   **27 OTU**   **Wellington X**   **LP437**   **Training**
1944   F/S J L Stephens RAAF   +   T/o 0120 Lichfield for night bombing practice.
       F/S R K Bolger RAAF   +   Stalled, while in the circuit, and crashed 0410
       F/S J H Normyle RAAF   +   at Doxey Wood Farm, Thorney Fields Lane. On
       Sgt H A Smyth RAAF   +   impact the aircraft burst into flames. All are
       Sgt E H Beatson RAAF   +   buried in Chester (Blacon) Cemetery.

       Note. It is thought the Wellington was carrying a sixth member of crew; so far
his name has not come to light.

30–31 Jul   **12 OTU**   **Wellington X**   **NC452**   **Training**
1944

F/L W J Timperley	inj	T/o 2207 Chipping Warden for a dual night cross-
F/S A C Lockyer RNZAF	inj	country with a screened pilot. Force -landed
Sgt C S A Johnston	inj	at 0047, with the wheels retracted, in the air-
		field circuit after the navigator inadvertently

switched off the fuel supply while changing tanks. F/S Lockyer RNZAF went on
to fly Lancasters with 550 Squadron and was killed when his aircraft was shot
down by an enemy intruder on 17 March 1945 (see Bomber Command Losses, Volume 6,
page 136).

31 Jul   **10 OTU**   **Whitley V**   **Z6499**   **Training**
1944

F/O L J Eggby	T/o 0115 Stanton Harcourt but swung out of
Sgt R B Knight RNZAF	control. In the ensuing crash, the undercarriage
	was smashed and the port wing was very severely

damaged. This particular Whitley had seen extensive service with the unit,
participating in the St. Eval detachment of 1942-1943. While at St. Eval, it
had been damaged in a landing accident on 24 December 1942. Sgt Knight RNZAF,
meanwhile, converted to Lancasters and died on 9 February 1945, while serving
with 630 Squadron (see Bomber Command Losses, Volume 6, page 73).

           12 OTU   **Wellington III**   **BK455**   **Training**

W/O T Davies	+	T/o 1502 Edgehill for an initial dual sortie.
F/O C W Warren	+	At 1518, eyewitnesses saw the bomber stall at
F/S P H Walden	+	one hundred feet and upon hitting the ground,
Sgt A D Marks	+	it rolled onto its back and began to burn
Sgt D J Roberts	+	fiercely. All are buried at various locations
		in England and Wales.

1 Aug   **14 OTU**   **Wellington X**   **LN511**   **Training**
1944

Sgt W F Baty	inj	T/o 1709 Market Harborough briefed to practice
	inj	overshoot procedures. All went well until 1849
	inj	when, having overshot, the starboard engine cut
	inj	at 500 feet. Sgt Baty feathered the propeller,
	inj	but was unable to regain the airfield, his air-
		craft coming down on the N side of the circuit

near the village of Church Langton. The impact was severe and he was taken to
the Leicester Royal Infirmary with a fractured left forearm and serious cuts
to his face.

           18 OTU   **Wellington X**   **HE993**   **Training**

P/O W Grubski PAF	+	T/o Finningley for a night flying exercise.
Sgt S Korol PAF	+	While orbiting Ashbourne airfield, lost control
Sgt Z Lasko PAF	+	and side slipped into the ground. All rest
Sgt T Krzensinski PAF	+	in the Polish section at Newark-upon-Trent
Sgt A J Jankowski PAF	+	Cemetery. They were the last all PAF crew
Sgt M Gutowski PAF	+	to be killed while training at 18 OTU.

3 Aug   **18 OTU**   **Wellington III**   **X3541**   **Training**
1944

Sgt S Sewemyn PAF	T/o 1530 Finningley for a navigation detail.
	At approximately 1710, the crew attempted to

land at Hell's Mouth Landing Ground in Caernarvon but overshot and finished
up in a cornfield, part of the bomber impacting into a brick wall.

           82 OTU   **Wellington III**   **X3937**   **Air Test**

F/O P J Helyar	T/o 1016 Ossington and crashed 1110 on return
	to base, a fire breaking out soon afterwards.

5 Aug   **27 OTU**   **Wellington III**   **Z1667**   **Training**
1944

F/S J G Fleming RAAF	T/o 1157 Lichfield for a navigation exercise
	during which the port engine failed as the

aircraft cruised at 4,000 feet. Four baled out, as ordered, and the bomber
was force -landed 1327, wheels up, near Jurby airfield on the Isle of Man.

           86 OTU   **Wellington X**   **HE821**   **Training**

WO1 W D Murdie RCAF	+	T/o 1355 Gamston for a cross-country. Lost power
P/O L M Brehaut RCAF	+	at 800 feet, stalled and crashed at Henny Moor
F/O W W Cooper RCAF	+	Farm, Creswell, 9 miles ENE of Chesterfield in
Sgt J R Clarke RCAF	+	Derbyshire. All rest in Harrogate (Stonefall)
Sgt J J Lee RCAF	+	Cemetery. This was the unit's first write off.

5- 6 Aug **24 OTU** **Wellington X** MF596 **Training**
1944 F/O G Retallick RCAF T/o 2205 Honeybourne for a high altitude night
cross-country. At 17,000 feet, the port engine
failed and soon after the starboard motor cut. Abandoned 0140 and left to crash
near Burrington, 7 miles SW of South Molton, Devon. RAF Winkleigh was tasked to
assist in the collection of the crew and mount a guard on the wreckage.

7 Aug **30 OTU** **Wellington X** JA533 —W **Training**
1944 W/O A D Groome T/o 1415 Seighford with a crew of nine, tasked
F/L McKinnon for a cine camera gun exercise. On return to
F/L G A Kirby base, and while in the airfield circuit, the
port engine caught fire. W/O Groome managed
to reach the runway, landing at 1500. Then, with the flames spreading along
the port wing he braked hard and ordered his crew to be ready to abandon the
aircraft as quickly as possible. All did so in the moments before the bomber
came to a stop. F/L Kirby, the Wellington's wireless operator, is related to
Dr. Robert Kirby, author of the definitive work on the Manchester, which was
published by Midland Publishing in 1995.

8 Aug **30 OTU** **Wellington X** LN588 —Y **Training**
1944 F/O G C Rogerson T/o 0945 Seighford for fighter affiliation
training but was obliged to abandon the detail
following partial hydraulic failure. On regaining base, the Wellington overshot
the runway and crashed at 1010, smashing the undercarriage in the process.

9 Aug **28 OTU** **Hurricane IIC** LF313 **Air Test**
1944 F/S F M Clarke RAAF T/o 1226 Peterborough but the engine cut and an
emergency landing was made, wheels up, near the
airfield. The Hurricane had recently undergone unspecified repairs and was
making its first flight on completion of this work.

9-10 Aug **30 OTU** **Wellington X** HE828 —E **Op: Nickel**
1944 F/S Jolly T/o Seighford in the company of five other aircraft and set course for France. At some stage
during the operation, the bomber was hit by flak. Control was maintained but at
around 0230, soon after crossing the south coast, all six members of crew baled
out, leaving their Wellington to come down at Burl Farm, SW of the hamlet of
Holywell, 11 miles NNW of Dorchester. Prior to assembling at the naval air
station at Yeovilton to await transportation back to Seighford, two of the crew
were taken to Warren Hill Camp for medical treatment.

10 Aug **10 OTU** **Whitley V** Z9474 **Air Test**
1944 W/O A O Page T/o 1657 Stanton Harcourt but while making a
climbing turn at 500 feet, the port engine cut.
Maintaining control, W/O Page returned to base and crash-landed 1705, with the
Whitley's undercarriage and flaps retracted.

20 OTU B Flt **Wellington X** MF551 —R **Training**
Sgt D N Lawrence inj T/o 0042 Elgin for a night solo exercise.
Sgt Williams inj Burnt out at 0207 after undershooting the
Sgt Smith inj runway and smashing into trees. Three escaped
Sgt Jones inj with only superficial injuries, but Sgt Williams
was admitted to hospital with one of his legs
badly fractured.

11 Aug **24 OTU** **Wellington X** LP618 **Training**
1944 F/L S M Bruce RCAF T/o 2155 Honeybourne with the intention of
F/S H G Round RCAF + carrying out a night bombing sortie over the
Sgt L H Fraser RCAF + Longdon ranges. Tragically, at 2303 a midair
Sgt L M Lysak RCAF + collision occurred, involving another of the
Sgt L C Lamb RCAF + unit's aircraft, and the Wellington spun down
Sgt G O Prime RCAF + to crash near Upton-upon-Severn, 5 miles SE of
Sgt A E Kidney RCAF + Great Malvern, Worcestershire. Those who died
were taken to Brookwood Military Cemetery.
Quite miraculously, F/L Bruce RCAF managed to parachute to safety, despite
the fact that the collision had removed one of the bomber's wings and the
resultant spin was extremely vicious.

11 Aug	24 OTU	Wellington X	MF591	Training

1944

F/O W W McSween RCAF
P/O McGuire RCAF
P/O J Shwaikoski RCAF   +
Sgt Scott RCAF
Sgt Fullerton RCAF

T/o 2138 Honeybourne similarly tasked to the
crew described at the foot of the previous page
and involved in the same incident. The impact
of the collision threw P/O Shwaikoski RCAF out
of the aircraft (he lies in Brookwood Military
Cemetery), but F/O McSween RCAF managed to
retain control and crash-landed at Defford, his Wellington being wrecked in
the process. No one was hurt but as a precaution, on being brought back to
Honeybourne, they were kept under observation in the Station's Sick Quarters.

	30 OTU	Wellington III	DF612 -T	Training

P/O N E Burton
F/S J H Player

T/o 1455 Hixon to practice single-engined
landings. During the demonstration, the bomber
landed heavily and bounced. The pilot commenced
going round again, but on the downwind leg it was realised that the flaps and
undercarriage had been severely damaged. Flying Control were informed of their
predicament and moments later the starboard engine failed and smoke was reported
to be billowing inside the fuselage. Feathering the propeller, the aircraft was
landed at 1515, on the airfield, the five members of crew escaping injury. Their
skipper, P/O Burton was a Rhodesian who had logged 1,048 flying hours, 618 of
these on Wellingtons.

11-12 Aug	30 OTU	Wellington III	BK562 -R	Training

1944

F/O P W Clifton
W/O J W J Butler   +
Sgt W S Owens   +
Sgt D E Townsend   +

T/o 2230 Seighford for a night cross-country.
During the sortie, and having flown into some
cloud, the artificial horizon indicator failed.
Within seconds the gyros began to spin and at
0236, by now partially abandoned, the aircraft
crashed onto a tennis court at Wilford, on the banks of the River Trent, in the
south-east suburbs of Nottingham. The three who died were taken to their home
towns in England and Scotland.

12 Aug	12 OTU	Wellington X	LN446	Training

1944

F/S J D Forbes RNZAF   inj
P/O L S R Smith RCAF   inj
Sgt W R Malvern   inj
Sgt R Fuller   inj
Sgt R Johnson   inj
Sgt A A Jolly   +

T/o 2134 Chipping Warden for a Bullseye detail.
About an hour into the flight, the starboard
engine failed and while trying to reach Worksop
airfield the Wellington crashed 2249, heavily,
just short of the runway. Sgt Jolly is the sole
service burial in Dowsby (St. Andrew) Churchyard.

13 Aug	14 OTU	Wellington X	LN281	Training

1944

F/O N Owen DFC   +
Sgt E M Roberts   +
P/O S J Guiver   +
Sgt W M Thomas   +
Sgt L Wilson   +
Sgt R McCudden   +
Sgt P R Stafford   +
Sgt G R Raby   inj

T/o 1545 Market Harborough for a cross-country
exercise, the crew including a staff pilot and
navigator as instructors. Stalled and crashed
circa 1930, after the starboard engine failed,
four miles N of Melton Mowbray, Leicestershire,
a fire breaking out immediately. Nineteen year
old Sgt Raby, an ex-Air Training Corps cadet,
was rushed to the Leicester Royal Infirmary
suffering from severe burns to his hands and
face. Thankfully, he survived. His fellow airmen rest in cemeteries scattered
across the United Kingdom. F/O Owen was the uncle of Raymond Glynne-Owen who,
over many years of dedicated research has collated much valuable historical
data in respect of 207 Squadron and has published several books relating to
his subject.

	26 OTU	Wellington X	HE172	Training

F/S J Cameron RAAF   inj

T/o 2327 Wing but lost an engine and swerved
violently off the runway and ended up in the
vicinity of the bomb dump. On 20 August 1943, while on the strength of 17 OTU
and with Sgt G Pryer RAAF at the controls, this Wellington had been very badly
damaged in a flying accident. Following repairs in works, it was allocated to
26 OTU on 12 April 1944, and when written off had flown a total of 538.25 hours
which included an initial spell of operational service with 429 Squadron based
at East Moor in Yorkshire. It is believed F/O Cameron RAAF survived the war
and returned to Australia.

13 Aug   **28 OTU**   **Wellington X**   **LN987**   **Training**
1944   P/O M L Matkin RCAF   T/o 1105 Wymeswold for circuits and landings.
Touched down at 1150, but the brakes failed and to avoid running off the airfield, P/O Matkin RCAF raised the undercarriage. No one was hurt, but his aircraft was a write off. Although not disbanded until mid-October 1944, this was the last major accident to befall the unit. Sadly, P/O Matkin RCAF was killed early in 1945 when his 514 Squadron Lancaster failed to return from Wanne-Eickel (see Bomber Command Losses, Volume 6, page 52).

13-14 Aug   **10 OTU**   **Whitley V**   **BD221**   **Training**
1944   Sgt M Kinsella   inj   T/o 2155 Abingdon for a cross-country flight.
      Sgt D G A Owen   inj   Force-landed 0210, following loss of power
      Sgt J T Heath   inj   from the port engine (this was caused by the
      Sgt C C Corfield   inj   flame traps burning out), near some cross roads
      Sgt H A Morris   inj   at West Aston and not far distant from Keevil
      Sgt J Western   inj   airfield in Wiltshire, where the crew were
hoping to make an emergency landing. In his report, Sgt Kinsella said he lost sight of the flare path while trying to set the altimeter. Sgt Western was badly concussed and he was taken to a military hospital at Shaftesbury in Dorset.

14 Aug   **12 OTU**   **Wellington X**   **HE754**   **Training**
1944   F/S A C Lockyer RNZAF   T/o 2209 Chipping Warden for a "Flashlight"
sortie. While flying at 15,000 feet in the Bristol area, the port engine failed. Heading for nearby Castle Combe, the captain ordered his crew to bale out. Five promptly departed, after which he crash-landed 2325 on this Wiltshire airfield, ending up in the overshoot area where the Wellington caught fire. It will be recalled that F/S Lockyer had been involved in a serious crash at the end of July 1944 (see page 307 for details pertaining to this incident and his subsequent fate).

20 OTU A Flt   **Wellington III**   **HF816**   **-A**   **Training**
      P/O P L B Paterson   +   T/o Lossiemouth for an evening cross-country.
      Sgt J M Downey   +   Dived 2230 at very high speed and smashed into
      Sgt H Todhunter   +   the ground, exploding not far from Nethy Bridge
      Sgt S Fraser   +   some 5 miles SSW of Grantown-on-Spey, Moray.
      P/O D H Rankin   +   P/O Paterson, who may have come from Lancashire,
      Sgt R A G Bailey   +   was buried in Elgin New Cemetery, Sgt Fraser of
Auldearn in Nairn rests in Lossiemouth Burial Ground, while the others were claimed by relatives in England and Northern Ireland. P/O Rankin was a Member of the British Ornithological Union; he was by profession a Pharmaceutical Chemist. Sgt Downey's aircrew trade is described in the cemetery register as 'flight engineer', while Sgt Bailey was an ex-member of the Air Training Corps.

82 OTU   **Wellington X**   **HE428**   **Training**
      P/O R H Wintle   T/o 1000 Ossington for a navigation detail. On
      F/L J F Hadley RCAF   return to base, both fuel cocks were turned off,
inadvertently, resulting in both engines cutting and necessitating a forced-landing at 1525 in a field near Egmanton, 8 miles SSE of Retford, Nottinghamshire. F/L Hadley RCAF was later posted to 428 Squadron and was killed on operations to Hildesheim in March 1945 (see Bomber Command Losses, Volume 6, page 144).

15-16 Aug   **19 OTU A Flt**   **Anson I**   **NK424**   **-R**   **Training**
1944   F/O J H Watson   T/o 2200 Kinloss for a night navigation detail.
Returned to base at 0026, crossing the boundary at 300 feet and flying quite fast. Thus, on touch down (which was made without the assistance of flaps) the Anson careered off the end of the runway, losing its undercarriage and inflicting such severe damage to the port main spar that repairs were deemed to be inappropriate. This was the last major accident to befall an Anson trainer at a Bomber Command Operational Training Unit.

16-17 Aug   **19 OTU A Flt**   **Whitley V**   **BD236 UO-A**   **Training**
1944   F/S T A O'Halloran   T/o 2145 Kinloss for a night cross-country.
Crash-landed 0036 at Lossiemouth after the starboard engine failed and, accidentally, the Verey pistol had been discharged. It is strongly suspected that F/S O'Halloran was commissioned, losing his life in April 1945 with 115 Squadron (see Bomber Command Losses, Volume 6, page 152).

16–17 Aug   **82 OTU**   **Wellington III**   **BJ790**   **Op: Nickel**
1944   P/O J E Verge RCAF   inj   T/o 2114 Ossington and set course for Gien.
      P/O W A Sage RCAF   Presumed abandoned and crashed behind Allied
      P/O J A Roth RCAF   lines. All are described as "safe", though
      Sgt S Ratsoy RCAF   P/O Verge RCAF broke a leg on landing and was
      Sgt J H Feeley RCAF   admitted to hospital.
      Sgt E D Dykes RCAF

17 Aug   **14 OTU**   **Wellington X**   **LN600**   **Training**
1944   W/O R W Meeking   T/o 2107 Market Harborough in the company of
                                          three other aircraft, all tasked for Bullseye
duties. During the course of the detail, the port engine began to run rough
and on several occasions cut out completely. Then, at 2307, while preparing
to land the motor stopped again and in the ensuing emergency landing the bomber
ran into the overshoot area and was very badly damaged, although it was not
officially declared a write off until five days later.

      19 OTU   **Whitley V**   **LA819**   **Ground**
                                          Caught fire 0905 at Forres. The accident
followed an engine clean, during which petrol was used as a cleaning agent.
A technician was then ordered to carry out a magneto test and it was while
disconnecting the generator that a spark ignited the residues of fuel vapour.

      26 OTU   **Martinet I**   **JN285**   **Ground**
      W/O H J Siveratch   At 2345, while awaiting clearance for take off
                                        from Little Horwood, the Martinet was struck
from behind by a motor transport vehicle. Neither W/O Silveratch, or his
passenger were hurt. Responsibility for the accident was deemed to lie with
the driver of the vehicle.

18 OTU   **17 OTU**   **Wellington X**   **HE502**   **Training**
1944   F/O W J Lambert   T/o Turweston for a cross-country. While
                                          flying over eastern England at 15,000 feet,
the port engine failed. Course was set for Grimsby airfield, but the crew
were unable to get the undercarriage to lock down. Thus, on touch down at
around 1400, the unit collapsed and as the bomber slid to a halt, a fire
broke out. All six members of crew vacated the aircraft without injury.

19 Aug   **16 OTU**   **Martinet I**   **HP390**   **Air Test**
1944   P/O D B Woodhead RNZAF   +   T/o 1636 Upper Heyford but at approximately
                                          one-hundred-and-fifty feet the engine cut.
P/O Woodhead RNZAF was observed to bank away from nearby Upper Heyford village
and, having clipped two trees, crash to the ground. Barely sixty seconds had
elapsed since he had begun his take off roll. He is buried in Oxford (Botley)
Cemetery.

23 Aug   **20 OTU D Flt**   **Wellington X**   **HE415**   **–P**   **Training**
1944   P/O F W Maw RCAF   +   T/o 0030 Lossiemouth for a bombing detail,
      F/O R Greavison RCAF   +   which was scheduled to be completed by 0545.
      F/O S L Braaten RCAF   +   Search and Rescue:
      Sgt R Gough   +
      Sgt H P Veregin RCAF   +   At 0605 the first search was organised. During
      Sgt J F Yacko RCAF   +   the morning the Air-Sea Rescue unit at Buchie
                                        radioed at 1130 to say they had recovered an
empty dinghy from Spey Bay and was continuing to search for possible survivors.
Eventually, two of the Canadians were recovered; both now rest in Lossiemouth
Burial Ground. On 19 November 1944, the body of Sgt Gough was washed ashore
and he was interred at Swadlincote District (Church Gresley) Cemetery. The
Runnymede Memorial commemorates F/O Braaten RCAF and both air gunners.

      24 OTU   **Wellington X**   **MF520**   **TY–G**   **Training**
      F/S J L Murray RCAF   +   T/o Honeybourne for an evening cross-country.
      F/O J M Rinahan RCAF   +   Lost control in cloud and after recovering the
      Sgt W S Paton RCAF   +   engines failed and the bomber broke up and came
      Sgt Hobbs RCAF   down at 2215 at Nornea Farm, Stuntney on Middle
      Sgt Jones RCAF   Fen some 2 miles SE of Ely, Cambridgeshire. The
      Sgt A D Daniels RCAF   +   two survivors were cared for in Station Sick
      Sgt R C Green RCAF   +   Quarters at Witchford, while those who died
                                        were interred at Brookwood Military Cemetery.

23 Aug   **83 OTU**   **Wellington X**   **JA453**   **—X**   **Training**
1944

P/O E Hartstein	+	T/o 2036 Peplow for a night navigation sortie.
P/O D H Skelton RCAF	inj	Lost power from the starboard engine and, at
Sgt F E Simons	+	around 2330, crash-landed some 6 miles S of
Sgt R Lindahl RNAF	+	Aberporth airfield in Cardiganshire. Of those
	inj	who lost their lives, P/O Hartstein rests in
	inj	Willesden Jewish Cemetery, Sgt Simons is buried

at Erdington (St. Barnabas) Churchyard, while
it is likely Sgt Lindahl RNAF has been taken to Bergen in Norway, where he was
born on 26 October 1906. P/O Hartstein's brother, P/O Phillip Hartstein (a
Pathfinder pilot serving with 7 Squadron) had been killed over Germany on 8-9
October 1943 (see Bomber Command Losses, Volume 4, page 352).

23-24 Aug   **10 OTU**   **Whitley V**   **BD215**   **Training**
1944

F/S R B Knight RNZAF		T/o 2049 Stanton Harcourt for a night cross-
Sgt J Montague		country. Returned to base at circa 0210 but
Sgt N E A Sharpe		made a heavy landing. Opening the throttles,
Sgt J Lamont RNZAF		F/S Knight RNZAF attempted to go round again
Sgt L Young		but the port engine cut and upon its second
Sgt S L Cameron	inj	arrival, the bomber swung and finished up in

a quarry 200 yards beyond the runway. It was
the last Whitley to be written off by the unit, now in the process of taking
on Wellingtons. Furthermore, it will be recalled that Sgt Knight RNZAF had
been involved in a nasty crash on the last day of July (see page 307 for
details and a note on his fate, which also involved the crew here summarised).
He had already narrowly escaped death during his training in New Zealand and
his parents had already suffered a terrible blow when they were informed that
his brother, F/S Jack Muir Knight RNZAF had died while flying Corsairs in the
Pacific with 19 Squadron RNZAF (see page 270 of the second volume of Errol
Martyn's 'For Your Tomorrow').

25-26 Aug   **12 OTU**   **Wellington X**   **LN293**   **Op: Diversion**
1944

W/O J R Harvey RNZAF	+	T/o 2010 Chipping Warden for operations over
Sgt D M Paterson RCAF	+	Normandy. Strayed from track while returning
Sgt F S Martin	+	to base and at 0146 dived into the ground at
Sgt W E Hankin	+	Uplands Lane, Keynsham, 5 miles SE from the
Sgt D D Evans	+	centre of Bristol. W/O Harvey RNZAF had married
Sgt A Blewett	+	Hazel Harvey of Carlisle and he lies in Carlisle

(Dalston Road) Cemetery. Sgt Paterson RCAF from
Toronto was probably claimed by a relative as he is buried in Kingston-upon-
Thames Cemetery. The others were taken to their home towns, both air gunners
being interred in Wales (they were ex-Air Training Corps cadets).

83 OTU   **Wellington X**   **HF517**   **Op: Diversion**

F/O E F K Michielsen	+	T/o Peplow similarly tasked. Crashed 0125 after
P/O R S Junor		colliding in the air with another of the unit's
P/O J G Sutherin	+	aircraft, both machines coming down at Prestwood
Sgt J E Clarke	+	five miles NNE of High Wycombe, Buckinghamshire.
Sgt J Butterfield	+	F/O Michielsen was born at Padang in the Dutch
Sgt G I Callow	+	East Indies (though his parents address is shown

as Den Hague). He rests in Brookwood Military
Cemetery, while those of his crew who died were taken to their home towns. The
three Sergeants were aged nineteen, Cornishman, Sgt Callow being an ex-Air
Training Corps cadet. P/O Junor passed away on Christmas Eve 1990.

83 OTU   **Wellington X**   **MF589**   **Op: Diversion**

F/O E O Smith RCAF	+	T/o Peplow similarly tasked and lost in the
F/O V H Bolton RCAF	+	manner described previously. All five Canadians
F/O N E Cousins RCAF	+	were taken to Brookwood Military Cemetery, while
Sgt J J Poston	+	Sgt Poston is buried in Liverpool (Anfield)
Sgt J C McMurtrie RCAF	+	Cemetery. F/O Bolton RCAF was the son of Capt
Sgt R J Sander RCAF	+	Henry L Bolton and Florence Catherine Bolton of
		Hamilton, Ontario. An extremely well researched
Mr Holt	inj	account of this terrible crash has been prepared
Mrs Holt	inj	by Derek Sadler and a copy has been lodged with
		the Buckinghamshire Record Office. Thus, it is

through being given a sight of this research that I can report that Mr and Mrs
Holt received burns while escaping from their cottage and having to cross a newly
tarred road ablaze with aviation fuel.

26 Aug **17 OTU** **Wellington X** **LP340** **Training**
1944 F/S C D Pauline RAAF T/o Turweston for a night cross-country, during
which the port engine stopped at 12,000 feet,
obliging the crew to put their aircraft down at 0100 in Cardigan Bay (5243N
0047W being quoted as the position) and take to their dinghy. Having survived
this alarming experience, it is sad to report that F/S Pauline RAAF was killed
during operations to Lutzkendorf on 14-15 March 1945 (see Bomber Command Losses,
Volume 6, page 126). At the time he was serving with 57 Squadron.

30 OTU **Wellington X** **HE224** **Training**
F/S R E George T/o 2225 Hixon for night circuits and landings.
From one such arrival, the Wellington ballooned
back into the air and finished up on, or near, a railway embankment.

28 Aug **18 OTU** **Wellington X** **LP208** **Training**
1944 F/L J V W McDonald T/o 2200 Finningley tasked for a Bullseye detail.
While cruising at 16,000 feet, it became necessary
to stop the port engine. Radio calls for assistance brought no response and the
crew began to make a controlled descent. A flare path was sighted but before at
that point the starboard engine caught fire. Very skillfully, F/L McDonald came
down from 2,000 feet and forced-landed at 2330, by which time the flames had
spread over most of the airframe. It is believed he was at Hardwick Park Landing
Ground in Derbyshire which, between 1 October 1941 and September 1943, was used
as a satellite by 27 and, occasionally, by 51 Maintenance Units.

19 OTU **Whitley V** **Z6739 00-G** **Training**
F/S P G Caddy RAAF + T/o 0231 Kinloss for practice bombing and cross-
F/S R Yabsley RAAF + country flying. Lost without trace. All are
Sgt J Crawford + commemorated on the Runnymede Memorial. Sgt
Sgt J A B Finch + Finch was the son of the Revd Laurence Finch
Sgt R E Tibbles + and Gertrude Finch, nephew and ward of Phyllis
Sgt H F Truffet + S R Finch of St. David's, Pembrokeshire.

29 Aug **12 OTU** **Wellington III** **BJ917** **Training**
1944 F/L L I Falber inj T/o 1414 Edge Hill for dual circuit training,
F/L H R J Jansen the crew comprising of a screened pilot and
two pupil pilots. Landed 1434 but caught fire
as it reached the end of the runway. The blaze, which took hold quickly, was
centred near the main spar and, wisely, the crew decided to make good their
exit. No one was badly hurt, though F/L Falber, the screened pilot, injured
an ankle as he left the aircraft. It is noted that F/L Jansen, a Dutchman,
had accumulated 1,120 hours of flying experience, though only five of these
had been at the controls of Wellingtons.

29-30 Aug **21 OTU** **Wellington III** **BJ970** **Op: Sweepstake**
1944 W/O J F Dell + T/o 2215 Enstone as part of a force of ninety-
Sgt W J Stephens + three aircraft drawn from the training units with
Sgt J Rogers + instructions to fly over the North Sea towards
Sgt D T Evans + the enemy coast before turning for home. Lost
Sgt F P Sharpe + without trace. All are commemorated on the
Sgt J J Starsmore + Runnymede Memorial.

21 OTU **Wellington X** **HE444** **Op: Sweepstake**
F/S F I Griffin RAAF + T/o 2216 Enstone similarly tasked. Lost without
Sgt R D Kempthorne + trace. All are commemorated on the Runnymede
Sgt C C Grego + Memorial.
F/S G J K Laidler RAAF +
Sgt D C McLachlan +
Sgt R Whittle +

21 OTU **Wellington X** **LN895** **Op: Sweepstake**
F/S F G Lewis RAAF inj T/o 2220 Moreton-in-Marsh similarly tasked. Hit
Sgt J K Lowe by "friendly" anti-aircraft fire off Cromer and
F/S D A Sharpe RAAF at 0300 crash-landed with an unserviceable star-
F/S D Middleton RAAF board engine at East Kirkby, Lincolnshire. As
Sgt K D Weightman inj the bomber slowed, it hit a dispersal hut on the
Sgt Pascoe airfield, The two injured airmen were taken to
RAF Hospital Rauceby, while the others were
treated for shock in Station Sick Quarters at East Kirkby.

30 Aug	14 OTU	Wellington X	LN394	Training

F/O R L Chambers RCAF	+	T/o 0110 Market Harborough for circuit practice.
F/O B Deane-Freeman RCAF	+	Twenty-five minutes into the exercise, the crew
F/O D A Gordon RCAF	+	flew into a high-tension pylon and crashed near
Sgt T S Diggin	+	the railway sidings at Welham, about 4 miles NE
Sgt R C Pegg RCAF	+	of Market Harborough, Leicestershire. The four
Sgt J Martin RCAF	inj	Canadians who died lie in Brookwood Military

Cemetery, while Sgt Diggin was taken back to
the Republic of Ireland and buried in Kilahenny Catholic Cemetery, Co. Kerry.
Sgt Martin RCAF was treated in his local Station Sick Quarters.

19 OTU	Whitley V	AD712 ZV-L	Training

Sgt F L Frank RCAF	+	T/o 0933 Kinloss for a navigation detail. Dived
F/O J W Tucker RCAF	+	out of cloud and disintegrated 1106, burning
Sgt G H Barr RCAF	+	debris being scattered to the E of Stirling.
Sgt R M Dickie RCAF	+	All are buried in Cadder Cemetery, the two air

gunners being aged 19 and 18 respectively. It
is further noted that Sgt Frank's first Christian name matched his surname.

86 OTU	Wellington X	HE485	Training

F/O L E Chapman RCAF	+	T/o 0447 Gamston for a night exercise but an
F/O G W Davidson RCAF	+	engine overspeeded and the Wellington crashed
F/O W S Ross RCAF	+	two minutes later at Haughton Hall, Bothamsall
P/O M Kram RCAF	+	some 5 miles SSW of Retford, Nottinghamshire.
F/O P P Loszchuk RCAF	+	All rest in Harrogate (Stonefall) Cemetery.

This was the second, and last, major accident
suffered by the unit (both had proven fatal and both had involved all Canadian
crews) before disbanding on 15 October 1944.

31 Aug	21 OTU	Wellington III	BK135	Training
1944				

F/S A D McIntyre RAAF	+	T/o 1025 Moreton-in-Marsh for a cross-country.
Sgt P Henshall	+	Flew into an electrical storm and at 1042 dived
Sgt T E Rhodes	+	out of the clouds to crash at Odstone Farm near
Sgt S D Gingold	+	Ashbury, 9 miles WSW of Wantage, Berkshire. The
Sgt D G Grant RAAF	+	two Australians were taken to Oxford (Botley)
Sgt B Sandall	+	Cemetery, while the others are buried in their
Sgt R Davidson	+	home towns in England and Scotland.

31 Aug-	22 OTU	Wellington III	DF737	Training
1 Sep 1944				

F/O W C Miller RCAF	+	T/o Gaydon for a night navigation exercise
F/O J K Reid RCAF	+	that involved the crew with flying part of
Sgt F D Bristow RCAF	+	the route over the North Sea. Lost without
F/O N E P Douglas RCAF	+	trace. All are commemorated on the Runnymede
Sgt D McLean RCAF	+	Memorial.
Sgt C Jutzi RCAF	+	
Sgt M G Casey RCAF	+	

1 Sep	82 OTU	Wellington III	Z1661	Training
1944				

P/O H M Wilton RCAF		T/o 2235 Ossington for a night cross-country
F/L R W Andres RCAF		but was obliged to make an early return when

the port engine failed as the aircraft flew
at 10,000 feet. Emergency drills were followed to the letter but the undercarriage refused to lock in position. Consequently, when the bomber landed
at 2250, the entire unit gave way. One of the six-man crew received slight
injuries. While being flown by Sgt McQueen on 31 August 1943, this aircraft
had been involved in a minor flying accident. When written off, the airframe
had accumulated 611.00 hours in the air.

4- 5 Sep	84 OTU	Wellington X	HF570	Training
1944				

P/O R E Byrne RAAF	+	T/o 2110 Desborough tasked for a navigation
Sgt W J Barnett	+	sortie. Returned to base at around 0205 and
Sgt E Brisbourne	+	while in the process of descending from 3,000
	inj	to 2,000 feet in the airfield circuit, the
	inj	starboard engine failed and in the ensuing
	inj	emergency landing the aircraft hit a tree
		and caught fire. P/O Byrne RAAF rests in

Oxford (Botley) Cemetery, Sgt Barnett lies in Wales at Sarn Cemetery, while
Sgt Brisbourne was taken to Much Wenlock Cemetery.

5 Sep	21 OTU	Wellington III	BK138	Ground

1944

P/O R J Taylor
F/S M H Sisley RAAF

Lost control while taxying at 2235 towards the duty runway at Enstone. The Wellington was proceeding down a gentle slope when control was lost and the bomber ended up, wrecked, in a ditch. There were no injuries amongst the eight-man crew that had been briefed for a combined night bombing and fighter affiliation exercise.

6- 7 Sep	27 OTU	Wellington III	BK252	Training

1944

F/S A L Currie RAAF	+
F/S R F Newnham RAAF	inj
Sgt R W McDougall RAAF	inj
F/S R A Groves RAAF	+
F/S R J Heal RAAF	inj
F/S T E Hennesey RAAF	inj

T/o 2058 Church Broughton for a night cross-country during the course of which the port engine ceased to function. Aborting the sortie, the crew returned to base but overshot their first approach and it was while attempting to go round again that the bomber yawed violently and crashed 0018 some 2,000 yards NW of the airfield. A fierce fire broke out, more or less on impact. Both Australians are buried in Oxford (Botley) Cemetery.

7 Sep	17 OTU	Wellington X	HE982	Training

1944

F/S A A South	+
Sgt P A Anderson	inj
Sgt D S Norman	+
Sgt D Sheen	+
Sgt R R Hesketh	+
Sgt D J Fortune	inj

T/o 2307 Silverstone to practice night circuits and landings. Overshot at 2353, climbed steeply and then dived to earth, bursting into flames. Three were buried in Towcester Cemetery, while the others were claimed by their next of kin, including Sgt Anderson who died within 48 hours.

7- 8 Sep	14 OTU	Wellington X	MF562	Training

1944

P/O C M Campbell DFC	+
F/L J A Jayes	+
P/O R A Green	+
Sgt R H Moorcroft RCAF	+
F/S N Dixon DFM	+
Sgt J Phillips	+
Sgt J Retallick	+
Sgt J H Brierley	+

T/o 2120 Market Harborough for a dual night navigation detail. Dived and crashed 0020 a little under a mile E of Keyham, 5 miles ENE from Leicester. Sgt Moorcroft RCAF was laid to rest in Brookwood Military Cemetery, while the others were taken to their home towns. F/S Dixon had completed a tour of operations with 514 Squadron, details of his award having been published in the London Gazette as recently as 8 August 1944.

8 Sep	29 OTU	Wellington III	BK552	Training

1944

F/O D De V Clarke	+
P/O H J Holmes	+
Sgt D E Manning	+
Sgt C Taylor	+
F/S T D Potter RAAF	+
Sgt N E Walker	+
Sgt J S A Nicholson	+

T/o 1120 Bruntingthorpe for a cross-country. Iced up, while flying in cloud and dived at 1330 from 1,500 feet into the ground at Maesbury Road near Oswestry, Shropshire. F/O Clarke of South Africa, F/S Potter RAAF and Sgt Nicholson rest in Chester (Blacon) Cemetery, Sgt Manning lies in the Irish Republic at Malahide (St. Andrew) Church of Ireland Churchyard, while the others are buried in various English cemeteries. Sgt Wallace Bennett Blakely RCAF, an air bomber, died in this aircraft on 29 December 1943, when it was struck, at Bitteswell, by Wellington III X3872 (F/O A C Shilleto and Sgt E Cook), neither aircraft being seriously damaged.

9 Sep	19 OTU C Flt	Whitley V	Z9427 ZV-A	Training

1944

Sgt J P Nelson RCAF

T/o Kinloss for a glider towing detail, at night. During the flight, the starboard engine began to misfire and a precautionary landing was made at Great Orton airfield in Cumberland. While taxying under the direction of ground staff, the Whitley collided with another aircraft that had been parked near the Glim lights.

10-11 Sep	14 OTU	Wellington X	MF439	Training

1944

F/O H A Pickersgill RCAF

T/o 2110 Market Harborough for a night cross-country, which was completed by around 0200. While circling base, awaiting his turn to land, F/O Pickersgill RCAF noticed that the revs on his port engine were fluctuating and as the aircraft commenced the downwind leg, the starboard motor cut. Requesting permission for a priority landing, he turned towards the runway only to have his flight path obstructed by another bomber. Miraculously, he managed to turn inside this aircraft and arrived at high speed on the runway, ending up in a field beyond the airfield.

| 11 Sep | **19 OTU B Flt** | **Whitley V** | **LA835** | **—Y** | **Training** |

1944   Sgt O M Munro RCAF   T/o 0240 Kinloss with the intention of making his night conversion to type, but a swing developed and while trying to regain control by using the engines, Sgt Munro inadvertently closed the wrong throttle. Moments later, the undercarriage collapsed.

| | **22 OTU** | **Wellington III** | **DF735** | | **Training** |

P/O A E Smith RCAF   T/o 1014 Gaydon for a bombing detail. Flying at 5,000 feet, the port engine failed and the crew returned to Gaydon but crashed 1334 amongst trees after failing in its attempt to land. At first it was thought the aircraft could be repaired but on 29 September 1944, the airframe was struck off charge.

| 12 Sep | **10 OTU** | **Wellington X** | **NC551** | | **Training** |

1944   W/O D M Bacon   T/o Abingdon for a training exercise. Its return to base was rather dramatic. At 1602 W/O Bacon undershot his approach and the port elevator struck an oil drum that was being used as a marker for a runway under construction. The force of the impact jammed the controls and though the bomber was seen to climb to about fifty feet, it soon lost flying speed and stalled back to the ground. This second arrival resulted in a badly twisted fuselage, a smashed port tailplane and starboard oleo, while serious damage was done to both propellers, port nacelle, bomb beams and doors. This was the unit's first serious accident since converting to Wellingtons.

| | **83 OTU** | **Wellington X** | **HE459** | **—F** | **Training** |

F/O D W Hill RCAF   T/o 0153 Peplow for night bombing practice. Forced-landed 0347, following loss of power from the port engine, near the airfield. Prior to this emergency landing, five members of the crew had taken to their parachutes (as ordered). Not long after this incident, F/O Hill RCAF converted to Lancasters and joined 166 Squadron. On 20-21 February 1945, he failed to return from Dortmund (see Bomber Command Losses, Volume 6, page 82).

| 13 Sep | **11 OTU** | **Wellington X** | **HE227** | **—A** | **Training** |

1944   F/S Hamilton RNZAF   T/o 2115 Westcott but the boost dropped and being unable to correct the swing to starboard, F/S Hamilton RNZAF found himself off the airfield and in a field near the direction finding site, having crossed the main Aylesbury to Bicester road.

| | **18 OTU** | **Wellington X** | **LP642** | | **Training** |

Sgt R H Chittam RCAF   inj   T/o 2055 Finningley for a night exercise. When the port engine cut at 15,000 feet, and being unable to obtain any response to their emergency calls, the crew baled out circa 2340, leaving their aircraft to crash at Longridge in West Lothian and some 22 miles WSW of Edinburgh.

| | **20 OTU E Flt** | **Wellington X** | **MF730** | **—D** | **Training** |

W/O C A Winch   +   T/o 2105 Lossiemouth for a night cross-country.
Sgt E H Pitty   +   Exploded 2233 and plunged into the sea 3 miles
Sgt J C Berry   +   west of Duntulm Castle on the northern tip of
Sgt F Dobbie   +   Skye. Five are commemorated on the Runnymede
Sgt P Crozier   +   Memorial, while Sgt Smith is buried in Bradford
Sgt A D Smith   +   (Bowling) Cemetery.

| | **24 OTU** | **Wellington X** | **MF554** | | **Training** |

F/O J G Clothier RCAF   T/o 0925 Honeybourne for a navigation detail. Wrecked 1230 while trying to land at Skipton-on-Swale airfield, Yorkshire, with an unserviceable port engine. This was the first of two serious accidents in September, involving F/O Clothier RCAF.

| 13-14 Sep | **27 OTU** | **Wellington X** | **HE180** | | **Training** |

1944   F/S R A Swift RAAF   inj   T/o 2255 Lichfield for a night navigation detail. At approximately 0040, the bomber touched down halfway along the 1,000 yards runway at Ternhill airfield in Shropshire, having being obliged to make an emergency landing with a badly overheating starboard motor. Realising he would not be able to stop, F/S Swift RAAF raised the undercarriage and skidded into the overshoot area, where a fire broke out.

16 Sep	21 OTU	Wellington X	LN429	-Q		Training

1944
F/O W J Hicks RAAF
F/O J H Clarke
Sgt R Clifton
Sgt D Tuffnel
Sgt L Grimwood
Sgt C Birch
Sgt R W Drewett

T/o Enstone for night circuit training. Struck at 0055 by another of the unit's aircraft and totally destroyed in the fire that followed.

	21 OTU	Wellington X	LN771		Training

F/O P J Temple   inj
F/S J C Ladd   inj
Sgt N R Luker   inj

T/o Enstone similarly briefed and destroyed in the circumstances described in the previous summary. Sgt Luker died from complications brought about by smoke inhalation; he is buried in Tunbridge Wells Cemetery. Four other members of crew escaped unharmed. I am indeed grateful to Ron Drewett for supplying details of this unfortunate crash.

18 Sep	12 OTU	Wellington X	LP625		Training

1944
F/S Crabtree RAAF
Sgt L H Kilby   +
F/S R D Jones RAAF   +
                         inj
                         inj

T/o 2024 Chipping Warden for a night cross-country. While in flight, an engine caught fire and a distress call was broadcast. At 2139 the Wellington crash-landed on Colerne airfield in Wiltshire, but careered off the runway and collided with a 409 Squadron Beaufighter VIF MM882 and a Mosquito NF.30 MT456 belonging to 488 Squadron, wrecking both. By now totally out of control, the Wellington finished up amongst some huts near one of the dispersal areas. Sgt Kilby is buried in Cardiff (Cathays) Cemetery, while F/S Jones RAAF was taken the few miles to Bath (Haycombe) Cemetery at Englishcombe.

	27 OTU	Wellington X	LP436		Training

F/S L D Southwood RAAF   +
F/O E C Buckland RAAF   +
F/S D Fletcher RAAF   +
F/S D R McDonald RAAF   +
F/O J M Ruglen RAAF   +

T/o 2240 Lichfield for night bombing training. Dived from 6,000 feet, pulled up sharply and stalled 2320 into trees about 4 miles W of the airfield. All are buried in Chester (Blacon) Cemetery. Three, F/S Fletcher RAAF and both officers were just nineteen years of age.

21 Sep	14 OTU	Wellington X	LN876		Training

1944
W/O J E Birch

T/o 1115 Market Harborough for flying practice. Shortly before 1135, the starboard engine cut and although the propeller was feathered, the blades continued to windmill. The resultant drag caused the Wellington to lose height and with a forced-landing imminent, W/O Birch jettisoned most of his petrol and put the bomber down in a field at Theddingworth, Leicestershire and practically on the border with neighbouring Northamptonshire.

23-24 Sep	24 OTU	Wellington X	LP494 FB-Z		Training

1944
P/O E J Kennedy RCAF   +
F/O I T Cromb RCAF   +
Sgt J W Irwin RCAF   +
Sgt E La D Dunn RCAF   +
Sgt B A Skebo RCAF   +

T/o 1920 Long Marston on a night navigation exercise, base-Peterborough-Thirsk-Filey-a point over the sea-Wells-Priors Hardwick-Radway-base. Contact was made with the Wellington in position 5415N 0250E but at 0120 the crew were reported overdue. Search and Rescue:

Early on 24 September and again the following day, six of the unit's aircraft carried out an extensive search, but without making any sightings. Subsequently, it was thought likely the Wellington had gone down in the sea some 68 miles NNE of Wells-next-the-Sea on the Norfolk coast. All are perpetuated on the panels of the Runnymede Memorial.

24 Sep	85 OTU	Wellington X	LP826		Training

1944
Sgt A H Wilton   +
Sgt C J Rowlands   +
Sgt J D Shykoff RCAF   +
Sgt S F Coleman   +
Sgt F C Saunders   +
Sgt C Harper   +
Sgt T W Jones   +

T/o 1935 Husbands Bosworth for an evening cross-country. Dived steeply and broke up circa 2330 some 6 miles N of Northampton. Sgt Shykoff RCAF was taken to Brookwood Military Cemetery, while the others rest in burial grounds in England, Wales and Scotland.

26 Sep	24 OTU	Wellington X	MF516	Training

26 Sep 1944 **24 OTU** **Wellington X** **MF516** **Training**

F/O J G Clotheir RCAF
F/L Board
P/O Gillies
Sgt Matthews   inj
Sgt Kidston
Sgt Badstead   inj

T/o 0946 Honeybourne to practice high-level bombing. Returned to base at around 1255 and while orbiting at 1,200 feet the pilot asked one of the air gunners to switch on the nacelle tanks. Unfortunately, in doing so he mistook the 'C' cocks for the 'N' cocks and moments later both engines spluttered and died. Thus, at 1258, the Wellington crash-landed on the west side of the airfield. The two injured airmen were admitted to Station Sick Quarters, though neither suffered major injuries. It will be recalled that F/O Clothier RCAF had been involved in a serious accident thirteen days previous (see page 316). By the spring of 1945, he was flying Halifaxes with 432 Squadron and while returning from a raid on Chemnitz in early March, his aircraft was shot down by coastal defence guns sited near Walton on the Naze in Essex (see Bomber Command Losses, Volume 6, page 113).

30 OTU **Wellington X** **LN711** **Training**

F/O J S Walker RAAF

T/o 2218 Seighford for night circuit training but as the Wellington lifted from the runway, the starboard engine cut. A short circuit was executed, but the crew overshot their approach and crashed, damaging the aircraft beyond repair. A mere two minutes had elapsed since the start and unforeseen end of the exercise.

28 Sep 1944 **11 OTU** **Wellington X** **LP825** **Training**

F/O D M Lloyd   inj
W/O G A Davies RNZAF   inj

T/o 1935 Oakley for dual bombing practice. Returned to base early, after requesting an emergency landing. On touch down at 2045, the Wellington bounced and though the pilot managed to open the throttles, he was unable to prevent his aircraft from flying into a tree, before tangling with some power lines. A fire broke out and W/O Davies RNZAF, an ex-Merchant Navy sailor, was very seriously burned. Taken to RAF Hospital Halton, he died the following day. His grave is in Oxford (Botley) Cemetery.

29 OTU **Wellington X** **LP342** **Training**

F/S A J Cantwell RAAF   +
Sgt J E Conchie   +
Sgt C R Collop   +
Sgt M Woodhead   +
F/S J N Smith RAAF   +
Sgt N Graham   +

T/o 1925 Bruntingthorpe for an evening cross-country. Came apart, while in a dive, and crashed 1715 at Branton near Finningley airfield. Four are buried in Harrogate (Stonefall) Cemetery, Sgt Woodhead was cremated at Birmingham Municipal Crematorium, while Sgt Graham was taken to Gress Old Churchyard, Stornoway on the Isle of Lewis. His is the sole air force grave, the others being the resting place for six local sailors.

2 Oct 1944 **19 OTU C Flt** **Whitley V** **P5102 ZV-H** **Training**

F/S R W G Henry RCAF   +
Sgt J W Fraser RCAF   +
F/O J F Muir RCAF   +
Sgt T Huddleston   +
Sgt T S Buchkowski RCAF   +
                                    inj

T/o 1857 Forres and crashed two minutes later after banking and flying into trees near the airfield. The four Canadians were buried in Kinloss Burial Ground, while Sgt Huddleston was taken to Whicham (St. Mary) Churchyard. In his statement, the air gunner (he is not named) considered it likely that an engine had failed as he heard the pilot remark that he was losing power.

3 Oct 1944 **26 OTU** **Wellington X** **LP254** **Training**

F/S W N Sievers RAAF

T/o 1025 Wing tasked for a fighter affiliation sortie but in the gusting wind, the pilot lost control and having veered to the right, off the runway, the Wellington crashed into trees just beyond the perimeter track.

4 Oct 1944 **19 OTU C Flt** **Whitley V** **Z6491 ZV-M** **Training**

Sgt N Gorrie RCAF   inj

T/o 1437 Forres for a fighter affiliation sortie but after climbing to a mere 30 feet, the port engine stopped. Reacting with commendable speed, Sgt Gorrie RCAF closed both throttles, raised the undercarriage and crash-landed straight ahead, though he had the misfortune to be injured when a fragment of broken propeller blade came into his cockpit.

4 Oct
1944

82 OTU	Wellington III	Z1691	Training

F/S G Noble RCAF   + T/o Ossington for a cross-country. At around
Sgt Z Wasserman RCAF   + 1400, while flying over Worcestershire, the
F/O R G Campbell RCAF   + bomber entered cumulus cloud and soon afterwards
Sgt G E Opie RCAF   + broke up, scattering wreckage over a wide area
F/S G A MacLeod RCAF   + between Badsey, 2 miles ESE of Evesham and the
F/S F E Thistle RCAF   + village of Mickleton, just inside the border
with Gloucestershire. The bulk of the smashed
aircraft, however, was recovered from Norton Hall, a mile W of Mickleton. All
were interred in Brookwood Military Cemetery.

6 Oct
1944

17 OTU	Wellington X	ME996	Training

F/S D F McKindlay   T/o 0925 Silverstone but before becoming fully
airborne the undercarriage was raised. Sinking
back onto the runway, the Wellington slid at high speed and when finally coming
to a stop, it caught fire. None of the seven-man crew were hurt.

11 Oct
1944

19 OTU A Flt	Wellington X	NC721 −F	Training

F/O G W Lucas DFC   + T/o 2004 Kinloss for dual circuit training, at
F/S L Brewer   + night. While in the circuit at 2009, collided
F/S W H Lillywhite   + with Wellington X LP781/X of B Flight, piloted
Sgt D R Sharman   + by F/S McHarg. Out of control, the A Flight
Sgt F A White   + machine went down into Burghead Bay, thus
becoming the first of its type to be written
off by the unit, now in the process of giving up its venerable Whitleys. F/S
McHarg landed safely, his aircraft little damaged. Despite an extensive search
by launches from No. 7 Marine Craft Unit, based at Burghead, no survivors were
found and all are commemorated on the Runnymede Memorial.

12 Oct
1944

14 OTU	Wellington X	JA475	Training

F/S L J Stott   + T/o 1420 Market Harborough for a solo cross-
Sgt C W West   + country. Encountered a violent electrical
Sgt I D W Fletcher   + storm (at the time the Wellington was flying
Sgt G Moreman   + twixt 4,000 and 6,000 feet) and crashed 1445
Sgt K L Hilton   + just to the S of Guilsborough, 9 miles NW of
Sgt R A Ellis   + Northampton. Two rest in Oxford (Botley)
Cemetery, while the others were claimed by
their next of kin. Sgt Hilton had only recently joined the service, after
service with the Air Training Corps.

21 OTU	Wellington X	LN693	Training

F/S H J Maddalena RAAF   + T/o 1058 Moreton-in-Marsh briefed for a five-
Sgt F J W Rawlings   + hour navigation exercise. Dived into the ground
Sgt H Allport   + at 1543 from around 800 feet, near the airfield.
F/S D V White RAAF   + Both Australians are buried in Oxford (Botley)
Sgt J E Peck   + Cemetery, while the others rest in their home
Sgt R A Dowling   + towns.

30 OTU	Wellington X	MF698	Training

P/O D J White RAAF   + T/o Hixon for a night navigation detail which
W/O J R Gibson RAAF   + involved the crew flying over the Irish Sea.
F/S R G Kingsley RAAF   + Last heard transmitting, by wireless, at 0338.
F/S W M Schafer RAAF   + All are commemorated on the Runnymede Memorial.
F/S A R Telford RAAF   +
Sgt H Glasper   +

83 OTU	Wellington X	HE700	Training

P/O J C Hubble   + T/o 0125 Peplow for a night cross-country.
F/S T R T Gooding   + After acknowledging a recall signal, sent due
Sgt P N Gent   + to worsening weather conditions, the aircraft
Sgt E Evans   + spun out of the cloud base and crashed 0530
Sgt J E Maddocks   + into a plough field at Narnerley Farm, Stoke
Sgt J L Doveton   + Grange, just to the W of Ternhill airfield and
three miles SW of Market Drayton, Shropshire.
Two, Sgt Gent and Sgt Maddocks, were taken to Chester (Blacon) Cemetery, while
the others rest in the their home towns. This was the last major accident re-
ported from the unit, which disbanded fourteen days later.

13 Oct	**24 OTU**	**Wellington X**	**NC650**	**Training**
1944	F/S A R Wilde RCAF	+		T/o Honeybourne for flying practice. Lost

Sgt C C W Woodford RCAF	+	control and crashed onto a railway line, near
F/O R D Matthew	+	the airfield. It seems likely that relatives
Sgt H H Cleghorne RCAF	+	of F/S Wilde RCAF of London, Ontario, arranged
Sgt S W Wells RCAF	+	his funeral as he is buried in Goose Green
Sgt Hannon RCAF	inj	(St. Paul) Churchyard, while the others who
		perished were taken to Brookwood Military

Cemetery. Sgt Hannon RCAF was treated in Station Sick Quarters for head wounds.

14–15 Oct	**16 OTU**	**Wellington III**	**BK466**	**Training**
1944	F/S H H Candles	inj		T/o 2230 Barford St. John for an exercise in

night navigation. Returned to base at around
a quarter-to-one and having received permission to land seemed to be making a
good approach on the north side of the airfield. Then, at sixty feet and with
a mile to go before touch down, the port engine cut. Skillfully, F/S Candles
managed to overshoot and coax his crippled machine up to 400 feet, at which
point the starboard engine failed him. Losing height rapidly, the Wellington
collided with a tree.

15 Oct	**18 OTU**	**Wellington X**	**HE289**	**Training**
1944	Sgt W Karpinski PAF			T/o 0036 Finningley for a combined exercise

Sgt J Gajda PAF		in night bombing and cross-country flying.
Sgt H Furmanski PAF		When an engine failed, the crew tried to get
Sgt P Kulagowski PAF	+	rid of their bomb load but were only partially
Sgt J Soltys PAF		successful. Thus, having made an emergency
Sgt J Szyc PAF		wheels up landing at 0440 on Kelstern airfield
		in Lincolnshire, during which the Wellington

caught fire, there was an explosion. The crew, meanwhile, had vacated the
burning aircraft but Sgt Kulagowski PAF had the tragic misfortune to be killed
in the blast, becoming the last Polish Air Force fatality at 18 OTU. He rests
in Newark-upon-Trent Cemetery where three-hundred-and-twenty-nine of his fellow
Polish airmen are buried.

	29 OTU	**Wellington III**	**BK555**	**Training**
	F/S C M Lever RAAF	inj		T/o Bruntingthorpe for a cross-country. Ran
				out of fuel, due to faulty manipulation of the

fuel cocks, while approaching the runway and damaged beyond repair in the crash
that followed at 1715.

16 Oct	**12 OTU**	**Wellington X**	**LN536**	**Training**
1944	S/L A L Vipan	+		T/o 1915 Chipping Warden for a night cross-

F/L D J Falconer	+	country detail. Caught fire in the air and
Sgt W H Chappell	+	crashed 2245 at Yardley Hastings, 7 miles ESE
Sgt V S Wright	+	of Northampton. S/L Vipan, an experienced
Sgt P N Hewitt	+	pilot with 1,140 solo hours to his credit (but
Sgt H D Hudson	+	slightly less than fifty of these on type) is
		buried in Cambridge City Cemetery. A pre-war

regular officer, he is believed to have left the service for a short while
before being recalled from the reserve. His crew rest in churchyards scattered
across the United Kingdom. F/L Falconer was a Bachelor of Commerce.

	14 OTU	**Wellington X**	**MF518**	**Training**
	F/S A Woods	+		T/o 1952 Market Harborough for solo circuits

Sgt E E Mann	+	and landings practice but within three minutes
Sgt T Shaw	+	the Wellington was down, and on fire, amongst
Sgt S Burnside	+	trees at Marston Trussell. Eyewitnesses say
Sgt R E Taylor	+	the bomber seemed to go out of control, in the
Sgt G W F Wall	+	circuit, while flying at 500 to 600 feet. Sgt
		Shaw was taken to Oxford (Botley) Cemetery,

while his five companions rest in cemeteries both in England and in Scotland.

	27 OTU	**Wellington III**	**X3719**	**Training**
	F/S H G Payne RAAF			T/o 1655 Church Broughton for his first solo on
				type only to have the misfortune to suffer an

engine failure while downwind at 1,000 feet. Showing good presence of mind,
F/S Payne RAAF made his approach but decided to overshoot and go round again.
However, due to haze he had great difficulty in keeping the runway in sight and
his second attempt to land ended in a crash, injuring one of the crew.

16 Oct
1944

30 OTU		**Wellington III**	**X3357**	**-P**	**Training**

F/S P E B Vallender RAAF   +   T/o 1800 Hixon for a solo evening navigation
F/O P J Castle RAAF   +   detail. At 2141, transmitted by wireless
P/O R C Parker RAAF   +   requesting a course to steer. Nine minutes
F/O W P Heatley RAAF   +   later, the bomber collided with trees and
F/O G B Sandilands RAAF   +   crashed at Ingestre Park on the SW side of
the airfield. All are interred in Chester
(Blacon) Cemetery. F/O Sandilands RAAF of Uralla, New South Wales, had wed
Dorothy Mary Sandilands of Victoria, British Columbia, Canada.

17 Oct
1944

19 OTU		**Whitley V**	**AD685 XF-J**		**Training**

F/O K Reed RCAF   +   T/o 1901 Kinloss for an evening cross-country.
F/O W D Wall RCAF   +   Exploded in the air, at 2135, while flying at
Sgt L J Olmstead RCAF   +   12,000 feet, debris falling in and around the
Sgt E W Leivers   +   harbour at Seaham, Durham. The five RCAF airmen
P/O J F Dowding RCAF   +   were taken to Harrogate (Stonefall) Cemetery,
P/O A L Sunstrum RCAF   +   while Sgt Leivers rests at Derby (Normanton)
Cemetery. A lethal mixture of severe turbulence
and icing are believed to have brought about the destruction of the last Whitley
to be lost in Bomber Command service. P/O Dowding RCAF was just seventeen years
of age, thus being one of the youngest officers to lose his life in World War II.

24 OTU		**Wellington X**	**LP610**		**Training**

F/O N C Dumont RCAF   +   T/o 1850 Honeybourne for an evening navigation
F/S R C Orrock RCAF   +   sortie. While cruising at 15,000 feet, over the
Sgt E J Post RCAF   +   sea, lost control and came down in Veryan Bay
on Cornwall's south coast, 11 miles NE from
Falmouth. In the final moments of flight, three members of the crew managed
to bale out and were saved. Their less fortunate companions are commemorated
on the Runnymede Memorial. By an awful quirk of coincidence, Sgt Prost RCAF
was the second Canadian to die that evening before reaching his eighteenth
birthday, both perishing within a few minutes of each other.

29 OTU		**Wellington III**	**X3879**		**Training**

F/S J L Thomson RAAF   inj   T/o 0925 Bitteswell for high-level bombing.
Wrecked 1115 in an attempted forced-landing,
near the airfield, brought about by loss of power from the starboard engine.

83 OTU		**Wellington X**	**HE589**		**Unknown**

Struck off charge this day, reported as burnt
though, as yet, no accident report has been traced.

19 Oct
1944

29 OTU		**Wellington X**	**LP332**		**Training**

F/S T C Moore RAAF   inj   T/o Bruntingthorpe for a night exercise. Iced
F/S R J Manly RAAF   +   up and crashed 0245, breaking up as it dived,
Sgt M J Pill   +   near Castle Donington airfield, Leicestershire.
Sgt C A Jackson   +   F/O Manley RAAF, whose father was Dr. Richard
Sgt T P Eastwood   +   Arthur Manley of Malvern, Victoria, and three
Sgt K R Geen   +   others were taken to Oxford (Botley) Cemetery,
while Sgt Eastwood is buried in Mellor Methodist
Chapelyard. In a statement prepared for the Court of Inquiry, F/S Moore RAAF
said he was flying in cloud and was attempting to turn onto a reciprocal heading
when he lost control, the Wellington rolling onto its back and falling away in
an inverted dive.

29 OTU		**Wellington X**	**MF527**		**Training**

F/S W P Sharp RAAF   T/o 1220 Bruntingthorpe for a navigation sortie.
Shortly before 1635, the port engine failed and
while trying to land at Upper Heyford in Oxfordshire, the Wellington overshot the
runway and crashed at Somerton, 6 miles NW of Bicester.

24 Oct
1944

18 OTU		**Wellington X**	**LP844**		**Weather Test**

P/O W H Wright DFC RCAF   +   T/o 1858 Worksop but crashed three minutes later
P/O D N Phillips   +   after stalling at low altitude. P/O Wright RCAF
Sgt J N Corlett   +   rests in Harrogate (Stonefall) Cemetery, the
Sgt K Hounslow   inj   others being taken to their home towns. Sgt
Sgt R J Winters   inj   Corlett's brother, F/S Geoffrey Scott Corlett
RNZAF, died in action on 3 August 1943, while
flying with 75 Squadron (see Bomber Command Losses, Volume 4, page 256).

25 Oct	10 OTU	Martinet I	JN655	Transit

1944   Sgt D Melville   T/o 0928 Stanton Harcourt with the intention of
                                returning to Abingdon but was obliged to force-
land, two minutes later, in a field some 2 miles NE of the airfield after the
engine cut out at around 650 to 700 feet. Sgt Melville was unhurt.

	30 OTU	Hurricane IIC	LF170	-P	Training

       F/O A V Browne RAAF   +   T/o 1440 Seighford but fifteen minutes later
                                      crashed into a tree near the Officers' Mess.
Married to Edna Edith Browne of Morton in Cheshire, F/O Browne RAAF is buried
in Wallasey (Frankby) Cemetery, Hoylake.

27 Oct	30 OTU	Wellington III	BK146	-A	Training

1944   Sgt W B Pollock   T/o 2025 Hixon for a night cross-country but as
                                 the bomber accelerated, the starboard engine cut.
Sgt Pollock immediately closed the throttles and raised the undercarriage, his
aircraft skidding wildly to a stop. Moments later, the photoflash flare went
off and the Gee set exploded, the crew making good their escape.

28 Oct	12 OTU	Wellington X	HF465	Training

1944   F/S L J Timperley   +   T/o 0913 Chipping Warden for a cross-country.
        Sgt D S H Wilson   inj   Lost control while descending through cloud and
        P/O C F Holmes   +   at 1223 the Wellington disintegrated, throwing
        Sgt L E Harrison   +   clear the navigator. Most of the debris fell
        Sgt J D Milne   +   near Bridgemere, a village close to the Cheshire-
        Sgt R Whitely   +   Shropshire border and roughly 6 miles SE from
        Sgt A F Baker   +   Nantwich. F/S Timperley is buried in Chester
                                      (Blacon) Cemetery, while the others who lost
their lives were taken to their home towns. It is noted that Sgt Baker, the
sole service burial in Tisbury (St. John The Baptist) Churchyard, was aged 35.

	19 OTU B Flt	Wellington X	NC554	-S	Training

        F/L I MacLeod   +   T/o 0802 Kinloss for a bombing exercise. While
        Sgt G Charles   +   operating at 6,000 feet, the port engine failed
        Sgt Oxtoby   inj   and the crew returned to base. F/L MacLeod made
        Sgt Booth   inj   a good approach but, on touch down at 0924, had
        Sgt Whyte   inj   the misfortune to balloon back into the air.
        Sgt Worrell   inj   Opening up the throttles, he tried to make a
                                      second circuit but crashed, wheels down, into
Findhorn Bay, his aircraft turning over as it struck the water. He is buried
in Cumbernauld Cemetery, while Sgt Charles rests in Rhosllanerchrugog (or Rhos)
Cemetery in Denbighshire.

29 Oct	20 OTU C Flt	Wellington X	HE439	-G	Training

1944   F/O A Hunter   inj   T/o 0929 Lossiemouth for a navigation exercise.
        S/Lt P A Lefebvre FFAF   Force-landed 1212, after the starboard airscrew
                                      sheared, 1 mile from Gairlochy, at the southern
end of Loch Lochy and 8 miles NE from Fort William, Inverness-shire. The force
of the landing rendered F/O Hunter unconscious.

30 Oct	21 OTU	Wellington X	NC649	Training

1944   F/S L D Moran RAAF   +   T/o 1800 Moreton-in-Marsh for a night cross-
        Sgt R M Sinclair   +   country. While in the process of letting down
        F/O W P C Finlayson   +   through cloud the Wellington is believed to
        Sgt J S Allan   +   have stalled for at 2335 it crashed, out of
        Sgt D G Talbot   +   control and burst into flames at Donnington
        Sgt D Pratt   +   Farm near Stow-on-the-Wold, Gloucestershire.
        Sgt W H Plunkett   +   F/S Moran RAAF is buried in Oxford (Botley)
                                      Cemetery, while his crew rest in churchyards
                                      scattered across England and Scotland.

3 Nov	20 OTU D Flt	Wellington X	LP415	-O	Ground

1944   Burnt out 1430 at Lossiemouth, while being
refuelled. Forty-five minutes earlier, it had completed a navigation detail.

	21 OTU	Wellington X	LN847	Training

        F/O J V Evans RNZAF   T/o 1959 Moreton-in-Marsh for dual circuit
        F/S J R Carroll RAAF   training but went out of control, skidded and
                                      crashed, the undercarriage being retracted.

4 Nov	12 OTU	Wellington X	HE806	Training

4 Nov
1944

12 OTU   Wellington X   HE806   Training

F/L T Dudding RNZAF   inj   T/o 1744 Chipping Warden for a dual night
F/O D F Law   navigation exercise. Crash-landed 1954, after
                                   the starboard engine failed on the approach to
base. As the crew made their exit, F/L Dudding RNZAF nursing a fractured wrist,
a fire broke out. F/O Law was killed on 3 May 1945; he is buried in Aberdeen
(Springbank) Cemetery, Peterculter. Two days previous to the accident, here
summarised, the Wellington, with F/S Wales at the controls, had forced-landed
at Chipping Warden with an unserviceable starboard engine.

6 Nov
1944

12 OTU   Wellington X   LP460   Training

Sgt R G Hann   T/o 1819 Edgehill for a high-level bombing
                                   exercise. Burnt out 2034, after crashing short
of the base runway, the crew of five escaping unscathed.

19 OTU B Flt   Wellington X   MF551   -W   Training

F/O C A Kirkham   inj   T/o 0945 Kinloss for dual instruction. Quite
P/O A R Billis   inj   early on in the sortie, the starboard engine
F/O G T Collins   inj   failed and caught fire. Attempting to land
                             inj   back on the airfield, the bomber stalled and
                             inj   crashed 1008, under a mile to the north-east.

7 Nov
1944

12 OTU   Wellington III BJ584   Ground

                                   At 1140, while being worked on at Edgehill,
a spark from one of the propeller pitch control leads ignited petrol vapour.
An electrician working on the aircraft escaped unhurt.

27 OTU   Wellington X   LN953   Training

F/O R Marks RAAF   T/o Lichfield with a crew of nine for air
F/S H F Payne RAAF   gunnery practice. Landed 1135, on Doncaster
                                   aerodrome but on the wet grass the aircraft's
brakes were ineffective and while swinging to avoid an obstruction, the undercarriage collapsed. No one was hurt but the Wellington was beyond repair.

8 Nov
1944

27 OTU   Wellington X   JA343   Training

Sgt J S Hood RCAF   +   T/o 1935 Church Broughton for a night exercise
Sgt H L Fernstrom RCAF   +   but twenty minutes later dived into the ground
Sgt J F Gazzard RCAF   +   about a mile SSW of the airfield. Five rest in
Sgt A White RAAF   +   Chester (Blacon) Cemetery, while Sgt Williams
Sgt W J Drozdiak RCAF   +   was taken to Cornwall and interred at Liskeard
Sgt B I Williams   +   (St. Martin) Churchyard.

82 OTU   Hurricane IIC PG578   -H   Training

P/O W W E Anderson RCAF   +   T/o 1630 Ossington and reported crashed in
                                   Ferry Road, W of Sculthorpe airfield, Norfolk.
P/O Anderson RCAF is buried in Brookwood Military Cemetery.

82 OTU   Wellington X   HE787   -P   Training

F/O L Pappas RCAF   T/o 1816 Ossington for an exercise in dual
F/O A P Jensen RCAF   flying. Wrecked 2150 in a landing accident at
                                   base. Eyewitnesses say the Wellington arrived
over the threshold with its left wing low and upon touching down bounced back
into the air. Its second arrival followed moments later, this time the bomber
swung sharply to port and caught fire. F/O Jensen RCAF progressed to Halifaxes
and was posted to 408 Squadron. While attacking Hamburg on 8-9 April 1945, his
aircraft was shot down near Heidenau (see Bomber Command Losses, Volume 6,
page 157).

8- 9 Nov
1944

20 OTU   Wellington X   LP660   Training

F/S P G D Dowling   inj   T/o 2030 Lossiemouth for the pilot's first solo
Sgt R B Jowatt   inj   cross-country, at night. All went well until
Sgt J H Moseley   inj   the crew returned to base at 0105 and prepared
F/O W Morrice   inj   to land. Approaching the runway, the starboard
Sgt G R Blishen   inj   engine failed and almost straight away the port
Sgt A F Jeffrey RCAF   inj   motor commenced to vibrate quite alarmingly and
Sgt A Robinson   inj   before the aircraft could reach the airfield, it
                                   flew into the ground. F/O Morrice was critically
injured and he died at 0130 in the ambulance taking him to hospital. He rests in
Aberdeen (Allenvale) Cemetery.

9 Nov	82 OTU	Wellington X	LP840	Training

1944

F/O R P Willison RCAF	+	T/o 1124 Ossington to dump explosives off
F/O T McL Young RCAF	+	Prestatyn on the North Wales coast. At 1614,
P/O A Rosen RCAF	+	the Wellington emerged from the cloud base, in
Sgt J A A Giroux RCAF	+	a steep dive, and crashed at Woodhouse near
Sgt D Goodwin RCAF	+	Queens Head, Oswestry, Shropshire. All lie

in Chester (Blacon) Cemetery. F/O Young RCAF was a Bachelor of Arts graduate from the University of British Columbia. It is noted in 'They Shall Grow Not Old' that the aircraft's tail gunner 'missed' boarding the aircraft.

10 Nov	20 OTU C Flt	Wellington X	LP682	-L	Training

1944

S/C N J Chatain FFAF		T/o 1736 Lossiemouth for a night cross-country

and was soon swallowed up in cloud. Icing conditions were severe and at 1851 the crew were obliged to bale out, leaving the Wellington to crash some 15 miles S of Killin, Perthshire.

13 Nov	12 OTU	Wellington X	HE750	Unknown

1944

Reported to have been destroyed by fire on this date.

84 OTU	Wellington X	LN401	Training

Sgt C D Patterson		T/o 1110 Desborough for a cross-country. At

approximately 1405, while cruising at 20,000 feet, both engines began to misfire. A descent through cloud was initiated and while doing so, the pitot head tube iced over. On emerging from the overcast, the crew sighted Hutton Cranswick airfield (in Yorkshire). With both engines continually spluttering, Sgt Patterson headed towards the runway but as he neared the threshold, the Wellington clipped a totem pole and crashed. No one was hurt, but the bomber was deemed beyond economical repair.

17 Nov	24 OTU	Wellington X	LP355 FB-S	Training

1944

WO1 W H Cyples RCAF	+	T/o 0144 Honeybourne for night circuit practice
F/S R L Melville RCAF	+	but lost control and flew into high-tension
F/S D J Spence RCAF	+	cables and crashed at Abbey Farm, Willersey
Sgt H A Stock RCAF	+	some 5 miles ESE of Evesham, Worcestershire.

All are buried in Brookwood Military Cemetery. F/S Melville RCAF was the son of Brigadier James Learmonth Melville of Ottawa.

18 Nov	84 OTU	Wellington X	LN639	Training

1944

F/S D F Stroud	inj	T/o 1855 Desborough for night bombing practice.
	inj	Wrecked 2015 after swinging at high speed off
	inj	the runway and hitting Wellington X LN234, also

of the unit. F/S Stroud died from his injuries within twenty-four hours and he is buried in Oxford (Botley) Cemetery. The second Wellington was not too badly damaged and, following repairs, was put back into service.

20 Nov	14 OTU	Wellington X	HF484	-B	Training

1944

Sgt J B Dobbie		T/o 1250 Market Harborough for a cross-country.

After encountering adverse weather conditions, the crew made a precautionary landing at the Royal Aircraft Establishment at Farnborough but in the pouring rain their Wellington skidded off the runway and was damaged beyond repair.

14 OTU	Wellington X	LN428	Training

F/S J G Lamb	+	T/o 1125 Market Harborough similarly tasked.
F/S E R Southern	+	Crashed 1455, from a high speed dive, near
Sgt S E Witz	+	Lilleshal, roughly midway between Oakengates
Sgt B Kelly	+	and Newport in Shropshire. Five were taken to
Sgt D W H Hall	+	Chester (Blacon) Cemetery (where their graves
Sgt W B Forsyth	+	are marked by special type C headstones); Sgt

Forsyth lies in Wallsend (Holy Cross) Cemetery.

Note. Some reports, concerning the Wellington here summarised, locate the crash at Red House Inn, Brockton, 6 miles SSE from Oakengates but this is not supported by the information reported in unit records.

20 Nov
1944

| 22 OTU | Wellington X | LN460 | | Training |

P/O D McK Roy RCAF + T/o 1847 Gaydon for an evening cross-country.
F/S F Knowles RCAF + While flying between 6,000 and 9,000 feet, a
Sgt A A Cameron RCAF + fire broke out in the starboard nacelle. The
extinguisher was activated, but had little or
no effect and as the blaze spread, P/O Roy RCAF ordered his crew to bale out.
Sadly, only three were able to get clear before the Wellington crashed at 1912
near Buckland Farm, Aston Somerville, 4 miles SSE of Evesham, Worcestershire.
It is likely F/S Knowles RCAF was claimed by relatives, as he is buried in
Lancashire at Denton Cemetery, while his two fellow Canadians were laid to
rest in Stratford-upon-Avon Cemetery. Following their funerals, only one more
RCAF airmen was buried here, namely F/S Gordon Brasset Stevens RCAF who walked
into a rotating propeller on 14 April 1945.

| 22 OTU | Wellington X | MF505 | | Training |

P/O J W Nezan RCAF T/o 1830 Stratford-upon-Avon similarly tasked.
Late in the exercise, the starboard engine began
to misbehave and the crew were ordered to divert to Gaydon but in the event they
arrived at Wellesbourne Mountford and crashed 2230, after overshooting the runway. No one was hurt but the Wellington was deemed to be a write off.

| 22 OTU | Wellington X | MF509 | | Training |

P/O C Hamel RCAF + T/o 1926 Stratford-upon-Avon similarly tasked.
F/L W J Allison RCAF + Shortly before 2050 the crew radioed, seeking
Sgt J R R Villeneuve RCAF + permission to descend below the cloud base as
Sgt J P E Burke RCAF + they were experiencing engine problems. This
Sgt J A E Groulx RCAF + was their last contact, for shortly afterwards
Sgt J L U G Du Sablon RCAF + their aircraft smashed into the Brecon Beacons
(Scrihy Giedd being quoted in some reports).
All are buried in Chester (Blacon) Cemetery.

| 30 OTU | Wellington X | LP569 | | Ground |

Burnt out at 1125 in a hangar fire, at Hixon.

22 Nov
1944

| 17 OTU | Wellington X | MF705 | | Training |

F/S P D Jones T/o 0815 Silverstone for a cross-country, during
which the port engine failed. Then, having lost
height to around 8,000 feet, the starboard motor began to falter. Thus, at 1145
the bomber came down amongst trees at Ashby St. Ledgers, 4 miles N of Daventry,
Northamptonshire. One airman from the six-man crew is reported to have been
slightly injured. F/S Jones joined the air force in 1941, either in Rhodesia
or South Africa.

24 Nov
1944

| 12 OTU | Master II | DL475 | | Training |

W/O R C Macpherson RNZAF T/o 1552 Chipping Warden for dual training.
F/O C R Henderson RAAF Sometime later, with the engine misfiring,
the trainer touched down on Kelmscott Relief
Landing Ground in Oxfordshire, overshot the landing area and crashed into a
hedge. The day previous, it had been advised that Kelmscott was closed to
flying, owing to the waterlogged state of the ground. It was the first of
two Masters written off at a Bomber Command OTU.

| 12 OTU | Wellington X | NA783 | | Training |

F/S T Keenay + T/o 1705 Chipping Warden for a night navigation
Sgt R P St. Leger + exercise. At around 2110, the inhabitants of
F/O J H Povey + Litchborough, 8 miles SW of Northampton, were
Sgt H Daniel + alerted by the sound of a low flying aircraft
Sgt D R Puttick + circling the area. Then came the sound of a
crash as one of the bomber's wingtips dug into
the ground. All are buried in cemeteries scattered across the United Kingdom.

25 Nov
1944

| 12 OTU | Wellington X | LN242 | | Training |

Sgt R M High + T/o 2055 Chipping Warden for a night cross-
F/S A D Springett + country but at 300 feet the port engine cut
Sgt E F Isterling + and seconds later the bomber scythed through
F/O G Smith + the tops of trees along the Welsh Road before
Sgt J Heap + dropping into a field, its momentum being hardly
Sgt J R Robinson + slowed as it careered through the garden wall at
Sgt J C Carlyle + Manor Farm, Upper Boddington. Search and Rescue:

25 Nov	Mrs E M Tester	+	Owned by Mr S Brooks, Manor Farm (or Manor House
1944	Miss C Tester	+	as it is referred to in the Banbury Advertiser's
	Mstr M Tester	+	edition for 29 November 1944) was a sixteenth
	Mr S H Brooks	inj	century building, comprising of two wings. One
	Mrs Brooks		of the wing's was rented by LAC Roy Tester, who
	Miss H Brooks		had been posted to Chipping Warden and who, on
			the night of the accident, was on duty at the

airfield. Within seconds of the impact, the wing housing the Tester family was
ablaze, and though the flames quickly spread to the remainder of the house, the
owner, his wife and daughter, Hilary, escaped almost unscathed, though Mr Brooks
sustained very painful burns to his right forearm as he tried to gain entry to
that part of the building which had taken the full force of the crash. Within
the next few minutes, he (Mr Brooks) was joined by his nephew, Mr F T Brooks,
Sgt Montague Smith, an airmen living in the village and members of the National
Fire Service crews from both Brackley and Banbury. Their efforts were to no
avail and over the next three harrowing days, the remains of the two Tester
children, aged three and two respectively, were recovered from the mass of
debris carried into the cellar; very sadly, nothing could be found of their
mother, who is remembered for her fine singing voice and cheerful willingness
to, in the words of the Banbury Guardian report, place her accomplishments at
the disposal of any good cause. As recounted, her husband was on duty and the
news of this terrible tragedy was conveyed to him by Upper Boddington's Rector,
the Revd W T Gibbings, whose church had been slightly damaged by bits of aircraft that had been thrown through the air. Of its crew, F/S Springett from
Worthing was buried in Banbury Cemetery, while the others were taken to their
home towns.

Note. I am indebted to Eric Kaye of Epwell, author of 'The Story of RAF Edgehill',
for securing newspaper clippings from both the Banbury Advertiser and Banbury
Guardian, and for delving even further into his own records for information pertaining to this very tragic accident.

22 OTU	**Wellington X**	**LP579**	**Training**

F/O E G Paquette RCAF   T/o 2220 Stratford-upon-Avon for a night cross
country. While cruising at 19,000 feet, the
pilot noticed that his engine revolutions were fluctuating and this was followed
by sustained rough running. Attempted to land 2345 at Colerne airfield but had
the misfortune to overshoot and crash through a wall bordering the aerodrome.

27 Nov	**26 OTU**	**Wellington X**	**LP659**	**Training**

1944   F/O K W Skeates   T/o 1125 Wing but swung badly and though the
bomber climbed into the air, a crash quickly
followed, by which time F/O Skeates had managed to retract the undercarriage.

30 Nov	**24 OTU**	**Welllington III**	**BK402**	**Training**

1944   F/O A S Robertson RCAF   T/o 1523 Honeybourne with a crew of eight,
tasked to carry out cine camera gun practice.
At 1545, and flying at just 800 feet, both engines began to misfire. Regaining
the airfield, F/O Robertson's approach was baulked by another aircraft and in
the wide circuit that ensued, he force -landed between Stanton and Snowshill,
two north Gloucestershire villages, 7 miles SSE from Evesham, Worcestershire.

82 OTU		**Wellington X**	**LN167**		**Training**
F/O J G McC Rowe RCAF	+				T/o 1050 Ossington for practice bombing. At
F/O J A Smallwood RCAF	+				approximately 1130, the port engine burst into
F/O J R G Farlette RCAF	+				flames and while banking at low level, the air-
Sgt S L W McCron RCAF	+				craft fell out of control and crashed at Crow
Sgt G C Morris RCAF	inj				Park Farm, Sutton on Trent, 11 miles SE from
					Retford, Nottinghamshire. Four were killed

outright and Sgt Morris RCAF lived but for a few hours. All are buried in
Brookwood Military Cemetery.

2 Dec	**16 OTU**	**Master II**	**DL470**	**Training**

1944   W/O C J Grant RCAF   T/o Upper Heyford for practice flying on type.
Landed at 1600 and, having turned off at the
runway's intersection, found himself heading towards a B-17 Flying Fortress.
Swerving to the right, the Master's starboard wing smashed into a contractor's
mud-scraping machine. At the time of the accident, the pilot was taxying into
the sun, which was low on the horizon.

5 Dec   **11 OTU**   **Wellington X**   **LN226**   **-Y**   **Training**
1944

F/S J T Elder RNZAF	inj	T/o 2023 Oakley for night circuits and landings.
P/O R J Marsh RNZAF	inj	At 2043, while approaching runway 21, the bomber
Sgt Kemp	inj	was observed to pull up, sharply, stall and dive
F/S O Dixon RNZAF	inj	wing first into the ground, cartwheeling as a
F/S N T Sandiford RNZAF	inj	result. All were taken to St. Hugh's Hospital
F/S L N Scrimshaw RNZAF	inj	in Oxford, where P/O Marsh RNZAF died. He lies
		in Oxford (Botley) Cemetery. At the Court of

Inquiry evidence was presented that suggested at least two members of the crew had reported that both engines were on fire, but their fears were not borne out by the findings of the accident investigation team. At best, it was thought, they had seen a very bright exhaust glow, or possibly sparks emitting from the exhaust stubs.

       22 OTU   **Wellington X**   **NC967**   **Training**

F/S P A M Jobin RCAF	+	T/o 1024 Wellesbourne Mountford for a navigation
Sgt J J P O Berlinguette	+	exercise. Crashed at 1149, while enveloped in
RCAF		cloud, at Westacott Farm, Inwardleigh, 3 miles
F/O J L G Dumas RCAF	+	north-north-west of Oxehampton, Devon. All are
F/S J L M Dube RCAF	+	buried in Brookwood Military Cemetery.
Sgt G A Chevrier RCAF	+	
Sgt J L N Savard RCAF	+	

       84 OTU   **Wellington X**   **LN231**   **Training**

Sgt N P Hitchcock	+	T/o Desborough for a navigation sortie which,
Sgt L Knighton	+	for part of the route, took the crew out over
Sgt P I Spencer	+	the North Sea. Last made contact, by wireless,
Sgt A Robertson	+	at 2103. All are commemorated on the Runnymede
Sgt T F Green	+	Memorial. Sgt Green had recently served with
Sgt R H Beer	+	the Air Training Corps. Weather in the exercise
Sgt J Bruce	+	area was, according to crews of other aircraft,
		fine and should have presented no problems.

7 Dec   **24 OTU**   **Wellington X**   **LP876**   **Training**
1944

F/O S E Leppert RCAF	+	T/o 2148 Honeybourne for night circuit training
F/O F C Bull RCAF	+	and crashed four minutes later at Kifts Gate
Sgt G L Warthe RCAF	+	Court near Mickleton, 7 miles NNW of Moreton-
Sgt J L Rheaume RCAF	+	in-Marsh, Gloucestershire. The resultant blaze
Sgt S E Cross RCAF	+	was clearly visible from Honeybourne's Watch
		Office. All were taken to Brookwood Military
		Cemetery. Their average age was twenty-one.

8 Dec   **11 OTU**   **Wellington X**   **LN845**   **-C**   **Training**
1944

F/S C R Wagstaffe RNZAF   T/o 1955 Westcott for a night cross-country. Reported to have landed, roughly 2200, at Stratford-upon-Avon airfield, touching down at least a third of the way along the duty runway, which featured a downhill gradient. This, combined with a light wind, caused the aircraft to run off the airfield and finish up with its nose overhanging the rail line. Not long afterwards, the local Station Master chartered an engine and proceeded along the track, in order to assess the situation. Unfortunately, upon reaching the scene, the driver of the locomotive was too late in applying the brakes and ran into the Wellington, which, until this point, had only been lightly damaged.

9 Dec   **21 OTU**   **Wellington III**   **BJ782**   **Training**
1944

F/S J A Hay RAAF	+	T/o 1820 Moreton-in-Marsh for a night cross-
Sgt A Barker	+	country. At sometime prior to 2145, the
Sgt J H Bell	+	starboard engine caught fire at 5,000 feet.
Sgt R G Clements	+	Unable to establish their precise position,
Sgt W Robinson	+	the crew broadcast a number of distress calls
Sgt W H Donaldson		and as a result were given a course that would
		take them to Barford St. John. Eyewitnesses

here saw the Wellington in the circuit, losing height, but as it entered the funnels the engine note increased as if the crew were intending to overshoot. However, after crossing the airfield, it dived suddenly and came down on a railway embankment on the ENE side of the aerodrome, near the village of Adderbury and burst into flames. Those who died rest in cemeteries across England and in Northern Ireland. Sgt Donaldson escaped with little more than severe shock, for which he was treated in the local Station Sick Quarters.

10 Dec 1944	**26 OTU** Sgt H Hill RCAF	**Wellington X**	**MF195**		**Training** T/o 2115 Wing for a night cross-country but having climbed to 11,500 feet, the port engine

failed and the exercise was abandoned. Returned to base, the port airscrew
feathered, and crash-landed 2210 with the wheels still retracted. A fire broke
out and one member of the six-man crew was slightly injured.

12 Dec 1944	**12 OTU** Sgt H Maunsell	**Wellington III**	**X3459**	inj	**Training** T/o 2042 Edgehill for night circuit training but almost immediately the starboard engine

began to overspeed. Sgt Maunsell managed to stop the motor and feather its
propeller but at 2047, he crashed just short of the threshold. A Rhodesian
by birth, it is not thought that his injuries were of a serious nature.

17 Dec 1944	**17 OTU** Sgt G A C Caton Sgt J Hartley Sgt R G Miller Sgt W Kennedy Sgt R P H Fernie Sgt M E Griffiths	**Wellington X**	**LP306**	+ + + + + +	**Training** T/o 1354 Turweston for local flying practice. Crashed 1404, off a starboard turn, after over- shooting the runway and attempting to go round again. All are buried in various United Kingdom churchyards.

18 Dec 1944	**22 OTU** F/L W F Scott AFM RCAF F/L P A C Maeder RCAF F/O G E B Forbes RCAF Sgt C E Anderson RCAF Sgt S S Galvin RCAF Sgt J C Smart RCAF	**Wellington X**	**NC494**	+ + + + + +	**Training** T/o Wellesbourne Mountford for a night cross- country. Dived into the ground at 0043, near Chipping Warden airfield in Oxfordshire. All were interred in Brookwood Military Cemetery.

	27 OTU F/S J M Irvine RAAF F/S A M McPhail RAAF F/S G T Miller RAAF F/S R D Westphal RAAF Sgt M T Dower RAAF	**Wellington X**	**HZ533**	+ + + + inj	**Training** T/o 1955 Church Broughton for night circuits and landings practice. Got into trouble between 200 and 400 feet, after overshooting the runway, and crashed close to the local railway line. Those who perished were laid to rest in Chester (Blacon) Cemetery.

31 Dec 1944	**14 OTU** F/O G K Hathersich F/O B A Day F/O R B Sharp	**Wellington X**	**LN973**	-S	**Training** T/o 1935 Market Harborough for a night dual check. Landed five minutes later with the wheels still retracted. After sliding to a halt, a fire broke out.

Resumé. So ended the last full year of the war, and as will be noted from
the last two entries, the Operational Training Units had operated for close
on a fortnight without a major accident. In total, only thirteen aircraft
had been written off during December 1944, a far cry from the same period
twelve months previous when twenty-nine major accidents had been reported
and, overall, 1944 had been a less traumatic year for the training units.

This improvement is all the more noteworthy, bearing in mind the increase
in operational activity in the run-up to D-Day. In the five months leading
up to the invasion, the Operational Training Units flew 911 Nickel sorties
(eleven such missions were made during the night of 2-3 June, thus bringing
the overall total to 922) plus a further 324 operational sweeps towards the
enemy coast; the latter being flown on two separate nights in April 1944.
An unknown number of sweeps had been flown in February and March, on these
occasions the crews had joined up with their colleagues in the Heavy Conversion Units.

In the wake of the landings, Nickel operations decreased; with intense
nightly air activity over France throughout the month of June, operations
of this type were suspended but 100 missions were flown in July and ninety-
four were mounted in August. However, operational sweeps over the North Sea
were conducted on a fairly regular basis throughout the second half of the
year and, as has been observed in the summaries, these sweeps were intended
to induce a response from a Luftwaffe anxious to preserve dwindling stocks
of aviation fuel. Losses to the training establishments from these raids
had been relatively slight and, it would seem, that on most occasions their

objectives had had the desired effect. Now, with a New Year ready to dawn, an end to nearly six years of unremitting effort from Bomber Command was in sight. Nonetheless, the strength of the training arm had to be maintained and of the nineteen Operational Training Units that were in existence at the start of 1945, only two would disband ahead of Germany's unconditional surrender at midnight on 8 May.

2– 3 Jan   **19 OTU B Flt**   **Wellington X**   **NC716**   **–O**   **Training**
1945   F/S R C Fayers   + T/o Kinloss for night navigation exercise.
Sgt A H Brown   + At 2150, a general recall signal was trans-
Sgt J Busk   + mitted, due to worsening weather conditions.
W/O J H Diffley   + Failed to make any wireless calls after 2200
Sgt J N Wheldon   + and at 0200 was presumed lost. All are per-
Sgt J E Muldowney DFM   + petuated on the Runnymede Memorial. Prior to
his posting to Kinloss, Sgt Muldowney had
flown in Lancasters with 101 Squadron, based at Ludford Magna. Details of
his award had been published in the London Gazette on 2 June 1944. Rather
surprisingly, he had not been promoted beyond the rank of Sergeant.

4 Jan   **10 OTU**   **Wellington X**   **LP729**   **Training**
1945   F/S F C Haglund RNZAF   + T/o 1110 Abingdon for a cross-country detail,
W/O N W Harnett   + climbing to 17,000 feet. While cruising at
Sgt W A George   + this height, the starboard engine failed and
F/S M H Walton RNZAF   + altitude could no longer be maintained. It
F/O B A Hogg RNZAF   + is believed the crew were heading for Wheaton
Sgt C D Wong   + Aston airfield in Shropshire when, at 1245,
F/S J R Gammon   inj   the bomber dived into the ground at Church
Eaton, 6 miles SW from Stafford. Of the six
who lost their lives, F/S Haglund RNZAF, F/O Hogg RNZAF, W/O Harnett from
Twillgate, Newfoundland and Sgt Wong of Kingston, Jamaica rest in Chester
(Blacon) Cemetery. Sgt George is buried in Reading (Henley Road) Cemetery,
while funeral arrangements for F/S Walton RNZAF were likely handled by his
United Kingdom relatives as he lies in New Shildon (All Saints) Churchyard.
According to details kindly supplied by Stephen King, F/S Gammon owes his
life to Police Constable Poole, who was one of the first to reach the scene.

11 OTU   **Wellington X**   **HE740**   **Training**
F/S M Reece RNZAF   + T/o 1910 Westcott for a training sortie but
Sgt I P H Smith   + fifteen minutes later dived from around 5,000
F/S A G Bolger RNZAF   + feet, out of cloud, and crashed at Marston,
F/S D W McLennan RNZAF   + seven miles NNW of Aylesbury, Buckinghamshire.
Sgt R B Price   + Five were taken to Oxford (Botley) Cemetery,
Sgt J A Wenham   + while Sgt Wenham rests in Maidstone Cemetery.

22 OTU   **Wellington III**   **BJ832**   **Training**
F/O V Thygeson RCAF   T/o 1000 Wellesbourne Mountford for an air
firing exercise, during which it was necessary
to stop and feather the port engine. On return to base, in lowering visibility,
the crew overshot the runway and finished up in a field.

22 OTU   **Wellington X**   **MF508**   **Training**
WO1 L J A Connolly RCAF   T/o 1000 Wellesbourne Mountford for practice
bombing. When the elevators jammed, the crew
were obliged to take to their parachutes, leaving the Wellington to dive in
from 8,000 feet and crash circa 1230 near Wigginton, 6 miles SW of Banbury
in Oxfordshire.

5 Jan   **16 OTU**   **Mosquito B.25**   **KB443**   **Training**
1945   F/L W A Moore   + T/o 1905 Upper Heyford for a night navigation
F/S A Sinclair   + detail. F/L Moore has no known grave; his nav-
gator lies in Glasgow (Riddrie Park) Cemetery.
This was the first Mosquito to be lost from the unit, which until the turn of
the year had been a Wellington equipped establishment. On paper, at least,
16 OTU disbanded on 1 January 1945, but reformed immediately as a light-bomber
training unit upon the redesignation of No. 1655 (Mosquito) Training Unit.

29 OTU   **Wellington III**   **BJ909**   **Training**
F/S D I Savage RAAF   + T/o 1915 Bruntingthorpe for high-level bombing
F/S K S F Allen RAAF   + practice. On return to base the local weather
F/S L W Cann RAAF   + had deteriorated to the point where the pilot
F/S M W Milne RAAF   + was unable to pick up the funnel lights and
F/S C J Nolan RAAF   + while trying to establish his position, flew
Sgt R J Leeson RAAF   inj   into the ground at 2330 near Kimcote, 3 miles
east-north-east of Lutterworth, Leicestershire.
Those who died were taken for burial in Oxford (Botley) Cemetery. It is reported
that Sgt Leeson RAAF was very seriously injured.

5 Jan
1945

82 OTU   **Wellington X** **LP841**   **Training**

F/O J C McLeod RCAF	+
F/O E E Fernandez RCAF	+
F/O L J Robillard RCAF	+
Sgt E A Bishop RCAF	+
Sgt R Eden RCAF	inj

T/o 1943 Ossington for a night exercise but stalled and crashed two minutes later at Laxton, nineteen miles NNE from Nottingham. In the last seconds of flight, the bomber collided with high-tension cables and burst into flames. Those who perished lie in Brookwood Military Cemetery. At the Court of Inquiry, it was suggested that the flap lever may have been left in neutral, thus allowing the flaps to creep down.

6 Jan
1945

24 OTU   **Wellington X** **HE633**   **Training**

F/O J N Beatty RCAF

T/o 1500 Honeybourne but the port engine cut at twenty feet and the Wellington was forced-landed straight ahead. Soon after coming to a stop, a fire broke out.

8 Jan
1945

10 OTU   **Wellington X** **HE328**   **Training**

W/O Niezrecki PAF

T/o Abingdon for flying practice. Landed at 1900, whereupon the undercarriage collapsed, both propellers sustaining severe damage. Deemed to be worth repairing, the Wellington was taken to Gatwick but on 18 June 1945, all work ceased and the airframe was struck off charge on 4 July 1945. This was the only serious accident to befall the Polish Flight, which had been operating from Abingdon since early December 1944.

21 OTU   **Wellington X** **LN612**   **Training**

P/O W C Norman RAAF
F/O Howley RAAF
F/S Callinan RAAF
P/O Casteley RAAF
F/S Poole RAAF
Sgt Hutchinson RAAF

T/o Moreton-in-Marsh for a night cross-country. At 0046, after loss of power from both engines, force-landed a mile E of Gaydon airfield in Warwickshire. Prior to the emergency landing, four of the crew took to their parachutes. All were detained for twenty-four hours in Station Sick Quarters at Moreton-in-Marsh.

30 OTU   **Wellington X** **HE853** **-B**   **Training**

Sgt R K M Lewis	+
F/S R W Mitchell RAAF	+
Sgt C W Woods	+
Sgt T S McLoughlin	+
Sgt T R W Vincent	+

T/o Hixon for a navigation exercise. At 1416 Bristol transmitted a fix, 5153N 0443W and this was acknowledged. Nothing further was heard and all are commemorated on the Runnymede Memorial.

30 OTU   **Wellington X** **LN166** **-G**   **Training**

F/S L J Porter RAAF	+
Sgt M F Maclean	+
Sgt J S Wright	+
Sgt E S Parrett	+
Sgt C Wade	+
Sgt L T Meadows	+

T/o 1035 Hixon for a high-level bombing detail. Broke up in flight and crashed 1130 at Burton's Lane, Eccleshall, 6 miles NW of Stafford. Most were taken to their home towns, but F/S Porter from Ipswich in Queensland is buried in Chester (Blacon) Cemetery, while Sgt Meadows of Barras Heath, Coventry, was laid to rest in Stafford Cemetery. He had transferred from the navy to the air force in March 1943.

10 Jan
1945

17 OTU   **Wellington X** **HE832**   **Training**

S/L A Mac C Stott	inj
Sgt W J Rose	inj
Sgt B M Lloyd	inj
Sgt D A Ottaway	+
Sgt W R Pike	+

T/o 1720 Turweston for an evening cross-country. On emerging from cloud, the crew found themselves in the midst of very heavy snow showers and at 2130, having failed to see the rising ground beneath, crashed into a hill 670 feet above sea level at Park Corner, a mile NNW of Nettlebed, Oxfordshire. Sgt Ottaway is buried in Esher (Cobham) Cemetery, while Sgt Pike rests at Poole (Branksome) Cemetery.

20 OTU   **Hurricane IIC** **PG529**   **Training**

W/O J Butterworth   +

T/o 2107 Lossiemouth for fighter affiliation practice, at night. Crashed 2122, following a midair collision with Wellington X HE490, at Crowford's Farm, nearly 3 miles east of Lhanbryde, a village on the main Elgin to Keith road. W/O Butterworth, who is buried in Heywood Cemetery, is believed to have closed on the bomber in order to make a positive identification and misjudged his speed. Of his 560 hours of solo flying experience, 107 had been logged on Hurricanes.

10 Jan	20 OTU	Wellington X	HE490		Training
1945	F/O B A Read DFC		+		T/o Lossiemouth similarly tasked and destroyed

10 Jan **20 OTU** **Wellington X** **HE490** **Training**
1945
F/O B A Read DFC + T/o Lossiemouth similarly tasked and destroyed
F/O R Moyes + in the manner outlined at the foot of the page
F/S E E Thurston + previous. F/O Read, one of the unit's screened
Sgt K C Campin + pilots, rests in Lossiemouth Burial Ground, his
Sgt N C Swingler + crew being taken to churchyards across the
Sgt J Downie + United Kingdom.
F/S R J Vincent +

11 Jan **20 OTU B Flt** **Wellington X** **LR140** **-U** **Training**
1945
W/O J A R Bertlin + T/o 2115 Lossiemouth for night circuits and
Sgt A A O'Brien + landings. At about 2320, according to one of
Sgt P Stimpson + the screened instructors, observing the night
Sgt L R Woods + flying, the engine note decreased and from a
W/O F B Kershaw + height estimated between 200 and 300 feet, the
Wellington dived into the sea some 500 yards
off the airfield. Both air gunners were found, a week later, washed onto one
of the local beaches, and the sea also gave up the body of Sgt O'Brien. On
12 April 1945, Sgt Stimpson's remains were found near Lossiemouth. Three
were taken to their home towns, W/O Kershaw was buried in Lossiemouth Burial
Ground, while W/O Bertlin's name is perpetuated on the Runnymede Memorial.
W/O Kershaw's service number indicates he was called up in July 1939 under
the provisions of the Royal Air Force Volunteer Reserve Military Training Act.

13-14 Jan **17 OTU** **Wellington X** **HE856** **Training**
1945
F/S A G Humphrey + T/o 1820 Silverstone for a night cross-country
Sgt G C Edwards + during which the crew were advised not to land
Sgt R Davies + back at base, due to lowering visibility. Thus,
Sgt V L Goddard + while trying to locate an airfield in the south
Sgt W R Askew + of the country, they crashed circa 0330 into
Sgt J Done inj trees on high ground (700 feet above sea level)
near Bayardo Farm, Milton, west of the Pewsey to
Malborough road and not far from Overton Heath airfield, Wiltshire. Sgt Goddard
of Portloe in Cornwall was taken to Upavon Cemetery, while the others who died
were claimed by their next of kin.

14 Jan **11 OTU** **Wellington X** **LN403 OP-V** **Training**
1945
F/L H Tricks DFM + T/o 1335 Westcott for flying practice. While
F/S N S Shaw RNZAF + approaching runway 07, the bomber was seen to
Sgt L J Tarr + turn away and crash 1644 near Wotton Underwood
F/S H A Purvey + Railway Station on the London and North Eastern
F/S B L Ireland RNZAF + Railway, a shade under 8 miles WNW of Aylesbury
F/S J Hollingsworth + in Buckinghamshire. Both New Zealanders rest in
Sgt Brown inj Oxford (Botley) Cemetery, while the others who
P/O Dickie inj died were taken to their home towns. Amazingly,
both air gunners escaped the inferno with only
minor injuries. F/L Tricks gained his DFM in the Middle East, while serving
with 148 Squadron, details being published on 5 February 1943. In a statement,
P/O Dickie was of the opinion the controls had suddenly jammed.

26 OTU **Wellington X** **MF116** **Training**
F/O N Chobaniuk RCAF + T/o 1805 Wing for an evening cross-country.
Sgt L G Good + Shortly before 2340, the pilot made a distress
Sgt J S Gunn + call before crashing at Holt Farm, Sketchley,
Sgt J W McMurdo RCAF + on the S side of Hinckley, Leicestershire. Both
Sgt J Thompson + Canadians rest at Chester (Blacon) Cemetery,
Sgt C D Parker + Sgt Gunn lies at Oxford (Botley) Cemetery, while
the others were claimed by their relatives.

14-15 Jan **27 OTU** **Wellington III** **X3465** **Op: Sweepstake**
1945
F/O K E Cranley RAAF inj T/o Lichfield as part of a force comprising of
F/O G Thompson RAAF inj one hundred-and-twenty-six aircraft, all drawn
F/O J Hann RAAF inj from training units, tasked to fly over the
F/O J Reuter RAAF inj North Sea as a diversionary ploy. Encountered
F/O E Minns RAAF inj bad weather and on return crashed 2358 and was
F/O E R Peace RAAF + burnt out while attempting to land at Wymeswold.
F/O Peace RAAF is buried in Oxford (Botley)
Cemetery. From Koonya, Tasmania, he was the last RAAF airman to die in an air
crash while undergoing training at Lichfield.

14-15 Jan   **30 OTU**   **Wellington X** **LP828**   **Op: Sweepstake**
1945   F/O P N Hickman   T/o 1620 Hixon tasked similarly to the crew
                                    described at the bottom of the previous page.
Abandoned, out of fuel, circa 0020 and left to crash onto tennis courts at
Wilford, S of the River Trent and on the south-west side of Nottingham. Although
given instructions to divert (the airfield is not named), the crew had failed to
find a gap in the cloud cover.

           30 OTU   **Wellington X** **LP830** **—M**   **Op: Sweepstake**
           F/S D Hudson   T/o 1630 Hixon similarly tasked. Abandoned at
                                      approximately 0030, crashing in the Arnold area
of Nottingham. As Brian Walker has been able to discover, one airman caught a
bus from Arnold into the city, complete with his rolled up parachute, while
another was rescued by a local farmer after being caught up in the branches of
a tree bordering the Henry Mellish Grammar School rugby football ground. It is
unfortunate that unit records are devoid of details pertaining to both crews.

17 Jan   **29 OTU**   **Wellington X** **NC706**   **Training**
1945   F/S A T O´Reilly RAAF   + T/o 0310 Bruntingthorpe for a night cross-
           F/S B A Atkinson RAAF   + country. Stalled and crashed 0730 at Walton
           F/S B T Devall RAAF   + on the S side of the airfield. Eyewitnesses
           F/S R P Quinn RAAF   + say the starboard engine had failed, but the
           F/S R J White RAAF   + airscrew was windmilling, thus causing excessive
                                        drag. All rest in Oxford (Botley) Cemetery.
F/S O´Reilly RAAF hailed from Queensland, while his crew came from New South
Wales (F/S Atkinson and F/S Devall), Queensland and Victoria respectively.

21 Jan   **85 OTU**   **Wellington X** **ME883**   **Training**
1945   W/O G W Barnard   inj T/o 1820 Husbands Bosworth for a Bullseye
                               inj detail. While flying in the London area,
           F/O R T Shaw RCAF   inj the elevator control torque tube snapped and
                                      the bomber went down, rapidly. W/O Barnard
was able to maintain some semblance of control as his crew baled out, before
the Wellington crashed 2112 in Beaconsfield Road, Slough, Middlesex.

22 Jan   **22 OTU**   **Wellington III** **HF609**   **Training**
1945   WO1 B D Cathcart RCAF   T/o 1756 Gaydon for night high-level bombing
                                      practice. Returned early to base, with the
port engine stopped, and wrecked 1824 after overshooting the runway. This
particular Wellington had been quite seriously damaged in an accident early
in September 1943. On that occasion, Sgt V R Hawkes RCAF was at the controls.

27 Jan   **18 OTU**   **Wellington X** **HE687**   **Training**
1945   F/O D G Marshall RCAF   T/o 1740 Finningley for an evening navigation
                                      exercise, which ended when the Wellington came
down at 2105 in the Irish Sea, off Maughold Head on the north-eastern side of
the Isle of Man. In his report, F/O Marshall RCAF stated that the starboard
engine twice cut out, but on each occasion he was able to restore power. Then,
both motors failed, flames and sparks being seen by his crew, and he had no
option other than to alight in the sea. This was the last major accident to
befall the unit, which disbanded three days later.

28 Jan   **16 OTU**   **Mosquito XX** **KB157**   **Training**
1945   F/L J McP Richardson RAAF + T/o 1056 Barford St. John for practice flying.
           F/L L A Butcher DFC   + At 1241, the port engine cut at 200 feet as the
                                      pilot banked to port in the circuit, causing
the Mosquito to spin to the ground. F/L Richardson RAAF lies in Oxford (Botley)
Cemetery, F/L Butcher rests in Newcastle-upon-Tyne (Byker and Heaton) Cemetery.

31 Jan   **19 OTU A Flt**   **Wellington X** **LP786**   **Training**
1945   F/S G D O´Connor RCAF   + T/o 1822 Kinloss for a night navigation detail.
           F/O D A Spice RCAF   + Last heard from at 1918 in a position plotted as
           F/O D L Dewart RCAF   + being WSW of Grantown-on-Spey. Roughly 5 minutes
           F/O W M Howard RCAF   + later, witnesses say they heard the whine of
           Sgt E A Wilson RCAF   + aero engines followed by a thud and searing
           Sgt J Stevenson   + flash of light out over the sea. All are per-
                                      petuated on the Runnymede Memorial.

2- 3 Feb   **14 OTU**   **Wellington X**   **LN838   —R**   **Training**
1945   F/O D McKay   +   T/o 2050 Husbands Bosworth for a night cross-
          F/O J Henderson   +   country. At approximately 0130, the aircraft
          F/S A L Phillips   +   dived into the ground and exploded near Flore
          Sgt S A Hall   +   some 7 miles WSW of Northampton. All were taken
          Sgt P J Riley   +   for burial, or in the case of F/S Phillips,
          Sgt C S Martin   +   cremation, in their home towns.
          Sgt R F Sorrell   +

3 Feb   **26 OTU**   **Wellington X**   **HE574**   **Training**
1945   F/L J P Gillespie   inj   T/o 0055 Wing for night circuit practice. Came
                                       down ten minutes later at Hurdlesgrove Farm on
          the A413, a little over a mile N of Whitchurch, 4 miles or so NNW from Aylesbury
          in Buckinghamshire.

          85 OTU   **Wellington X**   **LP640**   **Training**
          F/O L A Harvey   T/o 0920 Husbands Bosworth for high-level
                                       bombing. However, it is reported the aircraft
          was cruising at 2,000 feet when the starboard engine failed and at 1130, the
          crew crash-landed while trying to get down on Market Harborough airfield.

4 Feb   **16 OTU**   **Mosquito III**   **LR529**   **Training**
1945   F/O D Jackson   +   T/o 2250 Barford St. John for a night solo
                                       but within five minutes the port engine began
          to overspeed. All efforts to stop the motor and feather the propeller failed
          and F/O Jackson crashed while flying a right-hand circuit, coming down 3 miles
          west of the airfield. He is buried in Whitley Bay (Hartley South) Cemetery.

5 Feb   **14 OTU**   **Wellington X**   **ME978   —J**   **Training**
1945   F/O B A Day   T/o 1215 Husbands Bosworth for a navigation
          Sgt P W Harris   +   detail. Flew into cloud, becoming heavily iced
                                       up, and abandoned circa 1525. The wreckage of
          the bomber was soon cleared from Blease Farm, Knutsford, Cheshire but the body
          of Sgt Harris lay undiscovered for three weeks. He is buried in Kirk Sandall
          (St. Oswald) Churchyard. Nearby is the grave of a fellow Operational Training
          Unit trainee, P/O Murray, who died on 6 November 1942 (see page 172). It is
          further observed that Sgt Harris was the unit's last fatality.

          16 OTU   **Mosquito B.25**   **KB469**   **Training**
          F/L J F Marshall DFC AFC   T/o 1500 Barford St. John for a solo flight.
                                       As the bomber gathered speed, a quite gentle
          swing to port developed and it was while corrective measures were being taken
          that the Mosquito veered sharply to starboard and ground looped, the under-
          carriage folding as a consequence. F/L Marshall was not without experience
          having logged at least 1,840 flying hours, but only one of these had been at
          the controls of a Mosquito.

7 Feb   **29 OTU**   **Wellington X**   **HE286**   **Training**
1945   F/S J C Kinnon RAAF   T/o 2030 Bruntingthorpe for night circuits and
          Sgt R Kneale   landings. Fifteen minutes into the sortie, and
                                       while at 200 feet, going round again, the star-
          board engine cut. Calmly, F/S Kinnon RAAF forced-landed, straight ahead, near
          Gilmorton on the western side of the airfield. While on the strength of 27 OTU,
          this Wellington had been seriously damaged in a forced-landing near Peterborough
          on 21 January 1944. On that occasion it was being flown by S/L E A Hudson RAAF.

11 Feb   **29 OTU**   **Wellington X**   **JA457**   **Training**
1945   F/S J C Kinnon RAAF   T/o 0140 Bruntingthorpe to practice single-
          F/S Baker   inj   engined flying. F/S Kinnon RAAF (see above
                                       for his previous mishap) climbed to 3,000 feet
          and stopped the port engine. Immediately, the bomber began to lose height and
          when his attempts to restart the motor failed, he had little option but to
          force -land at 0210 near Shearsby in the airfield circuit.

13-14 Feb   **11 OTU**   **Wellington X**   **LP396   —H**   **Training**
1945   F/L A K Heaton   T/o 2235 Oakley for practice bombing. Due to
                                       both engines cutting, F/L Heaton forced-landed
          at approximately 0110, in a field, some 500 yards short of the base runway.

16 Feb
1945

20 OTU   **Wellington X**   **LN453**   **Training**

W/O C H R Mortimer   T/o 1910 Lossiemouth for night flying practice
P/O A G Phillips   inj   but when smoke began to billow forth from the
                                 aircraft's wireless equipment, the crew made
a prompt return to base. Landed 2000, but swung sharply, collapsing the port
undercarriage leg. P/O Phillips was the wireless operator and it is not clear
if his injuries were sustained in the air, or when the Wellington crashed in
the process of landing.

19 Feb
1945

29 OTU   **Hurricane IIC**   **LF741**   **Training**

F/O D C Gordon RAAF   T/o Bruntingthorpe for a flying exercise. At
                                 around 1710, F/O Gordon RAAF attempted to land
in a crosswind and without the aid of flaps. Relatively inexperienced with only
eighteen of his 601 flying hours flown in Hurricanes, he finished up in a ditch
beyond the runway.

20 Feb
1945

16 OTU   **Mosquito XX**   **KB365**   **Training**

F/O M P Floyd   T/o 1910 Barford St. John tasked for a night
                                 cross-country, but swung to port and slid to
                                 a stop, less its undercarriage.

25 Feb
1945

17 OTU   **Wellington X**   **HE994**   **Training**

P/O J Creevy   T/o 0113 Turweston for a night cross-country.
                                 Climbed to 7,000 feet, at which height the
port engine failed. Having feathered the propeller, the crew attempted to
land, at 0158, at Little Horwood but overshot the runway. No one was hurt
but the Wellington was declared damaged beyond repair.

27 Feb
1945

20 OTU   **Wellington X**   **LN453**   **Training**

F/O C F Last   +   T/o 2132 Lossiemouth for a night exercise but
P/O S J Carthy DFC   +   three minutes later the pilot called over the
P/O K R Tatham   +   radio, 'Coming straight in to land on a wide
W/O W E Fielder   +   circuit'. At 2137, with its port motor stopped,
Sgt A A Pardoe   +   the Wellington dived onto civilian property in
Sgt J Mellor   +   the vicinity of Lossiemouth harbour. Amazingly,
Sgt C M Ormond   inj   Sgt Ormond escaped with only superficial burns
                                 and minor abrasions. Three were interred at
Lossiemouth Burial Ground and three were claimed by their next of kin.

1 Mar
1945

12 OTU   **Wellington X**   **PF839**   **Training**

P/O L Hampson   inj   T/o 0231 Edgehill for night flying practice
                                 but failed to climb and hit the ground, upwind
of the runway. It was discovered that the flaps had dropped into the fully
down position. P/O Hampson fractured several ribs.

24 OTU D Flt   **Wellington X**   **MF538**   **Training**

F/O W A Leslie RCAF   +   T/o 1159 Honeybourne with a screened pilot for
F/O F Scott RCAF   +   flying practice. Crashed 1244 near Evesham in
Sgt A C Thoms RCAF   +   Worcestershire. All are buried in Brookwood
WO1 G D McVicar RCAF   +   Military Cemetery. F/O Scott RCAF came from
Sgt E J Cooper RCAF   +   Tucker's Town on Bermuda. It is believed the
                                 elevators failed, causing structural failure
                                 of a sudden and catastrophic nature.

2 Mar
1945

16 OTU   **Mosquito III**   **RR281**   **Training**

F/L H A P Payntg RCAF   T/o 1805 Upper Heyford for single-engined
F/O L J Porter RNZAF   inj   flying practice, during which the starboard
                                 engine was shut down. Crash-landed, after
overshooting the runway, coming down on Wickham Hill, Oxfordshire.

26 OTU   **Wellington X**   **JA131**   **Training**

F/O G A Larder   T/o 2000 Wing for bombing practice but abandoned
                                 twenty-five minutes later after the crew reported
smoke and fire inside the fuselage. However, when accident investigators examined
the wreckage, they could find no evidence to support the crew's assertions. Thus,
it was thought they had mistaken the flickering reflections from the upper identification light for flames, but as to their reports of smoke, this could not be
satisfactorily explained.

4 Mar 1945	**29 OTU** F/S G P Handly RAAF	**Wellington X**	**LN178**	**Training**

T/o 0335 Bruntingthorpe for flying practice. A little before 0435, the port engine failed and, inadvertently, the crew pumped down full flap in mistake for the undercarriage. With the Wellington displaying a tendency to enter a spiral dive, F/S Handly RAAF promptly forced-landed at Shearsby in the airfield's circuit.

10 Mar 1945	**16 OTU** F/L J C Blair	**Mosquito III**	**LR526** +	**Training**

T/o 2148 Upper Heyford for solo night flying practice. Lost control, while approaching the runway at 2210, and dived into the ground. The wreckage was not discovered until daylight. Spread over an acre, it was lying approximately 8,000 yards from the threshold of the 280/100 runway. F/L Blair was taken home to Northern Ireland and buried in Mallusk Cemetery. He had flown at least 1,543 hours, but only three on type.

	16 OTU P/O J G Howell DFC F/L A S J Fardell	**Mosquito III**	**RR287** + +	**Training**

T/o 2250 Barford St. John for night dual circuit training but lost power and flew into trees some 3,000 yards from the airfield. P/O Howell rests in Ipswich Cemetery; he had recently married Ann Dallas Howell (née Fraser) of Inverness. F/L Fardell is buried in Petersfield Cemetery.

13 Mar 1945	**29 OTU** F/O K E Holt RAAF	**Wellington X**	**LP402**	**Training**

T/o 1140 Bruntingthorpe for a cross-country. When the oil pressure dropped on one engine to below 60lb per square inch, F/O Holt RAAF shut down the unit and landed 1550 at North Killingholme airfield in Lincolnshire. His arrival, however, was too far down the runway and to avoid running beyond the perimeter, he deliberately raised the undercarriage.

19 Mar 1945	**20 OTU**	**Wellington III**	**BJ989**	**Unknown**

Reported written off on this date, though no accident card has been traced. Accepted at Lossiemouth on 2 September 1943, its movement card has been annotated to show 1,815.10 flying hours.

19-20 Mar 1945	**19 OTU B Flt** P/O R T Knowles	**Wellington X**	**NC614**	**-T**	**Training**

T/o 2305 Kinloss for a night navigation sortie during which the port engine failed as the aircraft cruised at 5,000 feet. In trying to get the undercarriage to lower, the crew used up all the emergency air bottles, but without any success. Thus, at around 0145, P/O Knowles called on the radio, "I am landing at Charterhall". Ten minutes later, Flying Control were advised by Charterhall that the bomber had forced-landed on their Winfield satellite, and had caught fire.

20 Mar 1945	**16 OTU** W/O D Little	**Mosquito XX**	**KB125**	**Air Test**

T/o 1535 Barford St. John for a standard night flying test. Landed 1555, heavily, and swung off the runway, coming to a halt with the starboard oleo leg collapsed.

21 Mar 1945	**29 OTU** F/S C E Cooper RAAF	**Wellington X**	**NA917**	**Training**

T/o 1115 Bruntingthorpe to practice single-engined flying procedures. While going round the circuit, for a second time on one engine, lost height and force-landed circa 1515, near the airfield.

24 Mar 1945	**16 OTU** F/O P B Jackson RAAF	**Mosquito B.25**	**KB523**	inj	**Training**

T/o 1935 Barford St. John for an evening cross-country, but having climbed to 9,000 feet, the engines began to cut in and out. Aborting the exercise, the crew returned to base but were obliged to force-land 1952, wheels still retracted, in a field at Milcombe on the western side of the airfield and just over a mile from the runway. F/O Jackson RAAF was quite badly hurt.

25-26 Mar 1945	**12 OTU** W/O O J Mann	**Wellington X**	**LP435**	**Training**

T/o 2250 Edgehill for a high-level bombing detail. Force-landed 0030 on Wellesbourne Mountford airfield having experienced serious problems with the aircraft's hydraulic system. No one was injured, but the aircraft was a write off.

26 Mar **27 OTU** **Wellington X** **NA901** **Training**
1945   F/O A J Bolitho RAAF   T/o 1145 Church Broughton for a navigation
                                      exercise, but while accelerating swung off
the starboard side of the runway, finishing up with a smashed undercarriage.
As the crew vacated the wreck, so the Wellington caught fire.

27 Mar **12 OTU** **Wellington X** **NC973** **Training**
1945   F/S Thompson   inj T/o 0044 Edgehill for night circuit training.
                                    Drifted off the centre line and while going
round again at 0124, flew into the windsock, crashed and burst into flames.
F/S Thompson was badly injured, but his crew escaped with little more than a
very bad fright.

2 Apr **29 OTU** **Wellington X** **LN159** **Training**
1945   F/O R G Watts DFC RAAF   + T/o Bruntingthorpe for air gunnery, the crew
  F/S W K Dever   + comprising of a screened pilot, two screened
  Sgt N Langford   + gunnery instructors and six trainee air gunners.
  Sgt M Musgrave   + Collided with a tree and crashed some 4 miles SW
  Sgt C E Grevett   + of the airfield. F/O Watts RAAF rests in Oxford
  Sgt S H C Stagg   inj (Botley) Cemetery. F/S Dever, one of the two
  Sgt Adams   inj gunnery instructors, is buried in Prescot (St.
  F/S McDermott   inj Mary) Churchyard, also in Lancashire, at Hindley
                                    Cemetery, lies Sgt Langford, while Sgt Musgrave
was taken to Scarborough (Woodlands) Cemetery. Sgt Grevett is the sole Second
World War burial at Lower Gravenhurst (St. Mary) Churchyard, while Sgt Stagg,
who died the next day from his injuries, rests in Sittingbourne and Milton
(Sittingbourne) Cemetery. It was the unit's last major accident prior to
disbanding on 27 May 1945.

3 Apr **16 OTU** **Mosquito III** **RR291** **Training**
1945   F/L H R Moody   inj T/o 1635 Upper Heyford for a combined exercise
  F/L T S Morgan   inj in dual circuit flying and single-engined
                                    overshoots. It was while practising the latter
that the crew got into difficulties, finding it impossible to maintain height
on climb out. Thus, at 1740, with the wheels retracted, the Mosquito was
force -landed at Little Tew, 4 miles ENE of Chipping Norton, Oxfordshire.
Both pilots were experienced, though it would seem that F/L Morgan (who was
was seriously injured) was receiving his initial instruction on type.

4 Apr **20 OTU** **Wellington X** **NC428** **Training**
1945   F/L J R Vallance   inj T/o 1145 Lossiemouth for dual circuits and
  Sgt H M C Labulle FFAF   landings. During the detail, the starboard
                                    engine cut at 3,500 feet. After feathering
the propeller, F/L Vallance attempted to re-start the motor, but discovered
the airscrew had jammed. Unable to maintain his height, he was obliged to
ditch at 1200, in the Moray Firth, some 3 miles N of Kinloss airfield. All
were brought safely ashore.

5 Apr **16 OTU** **Mosquito XX** **KB193** **Air Test**
1945   F/L J Stark   T/o 1530 Upper Heyford for a night flying test.
                                    Wrecked 1600, in an emergency landing at base,
after the starboard engine failed at 6,000 feet, F/L Stark electing to make a
direct approach to the runway, rather than attempt to go round the circuit.

      24 OTU **Wellington X** **MF644** **Training**
      P/O G D Dickie RCAF   + T/o Honeybourne for a four-hour night cross-
      F/O W McD Hunt RCAF   + country and was due to return to base at 2345.
      F/O E F W Mitchell RCAF   + Lost without trace. All are commemorated on
      F/S R H Bruce RCAF   + the Runnymede Memorial. It is, however, very
      F/S C C MacDonald RCAF   + likely the Wellington descended into the North
      Sgt R L McCaskill RCAF   + Sea as six months later a wallet identified as
                                      belonging to Sgt McCaskill RCAF was found in a
      fishing net by the crew of a North Sea trawler.

6 Apr **16 OTU** **Mosquito XX** **KB343** **Training**
1945   F/O H M George   T/o 1600 Barford St. John for bombing practice
                                    but swung out of control, coming to a stop with
                                    its undercarriage broken.

6 Apr 1945	**26 OTU**	**Wellington X**	**HE928**	**Training**
	F/L D L Wix DFC	+	T/o 1316 Wing for high-level bombing practice	
	Sgt R J Borland	+	over the Hogshaw ranges. While letting down	
	Sgt A Brierley	+	through cloud, collided with another of the	
	F/S V A Thompson	+	unit's aircraft. Both Wellingtons broke up,	

scattering debris over an elongated triangle bordered by Mount Pleasant to the west, the hamlet of Sandhill and Verney Junction on the London Midland Scottish railway to the east and Middle Claydon to the south. All three locations were within 3 miles or so WSW of Winslow in Buckinghamshire. F/L Wix is buried in Shinfield (St. Mary) Church Cemetery, Sgt Borland rests in Manchester Southern Cemetery, Sgt Brierley was cremated Rochdale Crematorium, while F/S Thompson was taken home to Northern Ireland and interred at Ballymena New Cemetery.

	26 OTU	**Wellington X**	**LN540**	**Training**
	F/L M L Hore DFC RNZAF	+	T/o 1451 Wing and lost in the circumstances	
	Sgt D J Rowson	+	previously described. F/L Hore RNZAF was taken	
	Sgt E W Jennings	+	to Oxford (Botley) Cemetery, while the others	
	Sgt F E Jordan	+	were claimed by their next of kin. During	
	W/O J Muir DFM	+	December 1943, this aircraft had been on the	
	Sgt M G B James	+	strength of 16 OTU and while on a flight off	
	Sgt E E Barfoot	+	the Yorkshire coast, on the 21st, became iced	

up and dropped out of control. The order to bale out was given and Sgt William Roderic Christien RCAF complied. Moments later the pilot regained control and, with the rest of the crew, returned to base. Sadly, no trace was found of their rear gunner and his name is now commemorated for perpetuity on panel 186 of the Runnymede Memorial. W/O Muir had recently completed a tour of operations with 51 Squadron, details of his award having been published in the London Gazette on 14 November 1944.

7- 8 Apr 1945	**21 OTU**	**Wellington III**	**BK133**	**Training**
	F/S J K Vickers RAAF	+	T/o Moreton-in-Marsh for night circuits and	
	F/S A G S Brunskill RAAF	+	landings. Crashed 0055, due to loss of engine	
	F/S J W Newcombe RAAF	+	failure, at Great Rollright, 10 miles SW of	
	W/O C H Harrison RAAF	+	Banbury, Oxfordshire. All rest in Oxford	
	F/S E C Graebner RAAF	+	(Botley) Cemetery. F/S Graebner RAAF was	
	F/S J R Thomas RAAF	+	the son of the Revd Rudolph Graebner and	

Doris Graebner of Perth. This was the last Wellington of its Mk. to be lost from a Bomber Command Operational Training Unit. No flying hours total has been appended, but it had been allotted to Moreton-in-Marsh 16 May 1944. Throughout its service life, the Wellington had flown on training units; 17 and 24 Operational Training Units being noted.

9 Apr 1945	**27 OTU**	**Wellington X**	**ME881**	**Training**
	F/O S E Bourke RAAF		T/o Lichfield carrying a crew of eight, the	
			air gunners having been briefed for an air	

firing exercise. Returned to base at 1710, but while downwind the port engine cut and the crew were unable to get the starboard undercarriage to lock in the down position. Thus, at 1714, the Wellington ended up, wrecked, in the over-shoot area of the airfield.

12 Apr 1945	**84 OTU**	**Wellington X**	**LN237**	**Training**
	F/S F Sanderson		T/o 1300 Desborough for flying practice. Crash-	
			landed 1510, at base, after the port engine's	

throttle jammed in the fully open position. This particular Wellington had been delivered to the unit, ex-works, on 26 September 1945, but its record of hours flown have not been appended to the movement card.

16 Apr 1945	**11 OTU**	**Wellington X**	**LP609 -E**	**Training**
	W/O W Erskine	+	T/o Oakley for flying practice. Collided in	
	F/S J P Redpath RNZAF	+	the funnels area at 0038 with another of the	
	F/S C W Burt RNZAF	+	unit's aircraft, both Wellingtons coming down	
	F/S G T Matthews RNZAF	+	about 2 miles NNE of the airfield and in the	
	F/S A C Hope	+	general direction of Borstall. Three lie in	

Oxford (Botley) Cemetery, W/O Erskine rests at Cambuslang (Westburn) Cemetery, while F/S Hope was taken to Liverpool (Toxteth Park) Cemetery.

16 Apr   **11 OTU**   **Wellington X**   **LP651**   **Training**
1945

F/O C R Baker DFC RNZAF	+
F/O J A P Nicholls	+
Air Medal USA RNZAF	
F/O J A Millar RNZAF	+
F/O D J Dickson RNZAF	+
F/S S Fernyhough RNZAF	+
F/O W W Ford	+
F/S E D Hitchins RNZAF	+

T/o 0030 Oakley and destroyed eight minutes later in the manner reported at the foot of the previous page. In the last few seconds before impact, Flying Control at Oakley had radioed the crew, ordering them to overshoot. All six New Zealanders lie in Oxford (Botley) Cemetery, while F/O Ford was taken home to Scotland and interred in Glasgow (Riddrie Park) Cemetery. This was last substantial loss of life amongst the RNZAF airmen undergoing training at the unit.

     11 OTU   **Wellington X**   **NA782**   **-R**   **Training**
F/O M Wilson
F/L V L Cole

T/o Oakley for dusk dual practice. Overshot the base runway at 2135 and ended up, wrecked, in a ditch after the brake lever jammed in the off position.

18 Apr   **12 OTU**   **Wellington X**   **LP286**   **Training**
1945

F/S W J Hillier	+
Sgt H Mairs	+
Sgt A G Grant	+
Sgt J B Egan	+
Sgt P McGowan	+
Sgt P V Birch	inj

T/o 1238 Chipping Warden for a cross-country. Returned to base, in the wake of starboard engine failure, but failed to land off the first attempt. Going round again, the bomber stalled and crashed 1403 into Edgcote Park on the south-east side of the airfield, catching fire immediately. Those who perished rest in cemeteries across the United Kingdom. It is noted that Sgt McGowan, buried in Banbury Cemetery, came from Kiltyclogher, Co. Leitrim in the Irish Republic.

19 Apr   **22 OTU**   **Wellington X**   **HZ363**   **Training**
1945   F/O J F Tees RCAF

T/o 1115 Wellesbourne Mountford only to crash-land two minutes later following total loss of power from the starboard engine at a crucial stage of the climb out. Displaying commendable skill, F/O Tees RCAF managed to retract the undercarriage and lift his crippled aircraft sufficiently to clear a line of trees that lay in his path. His Wellington had come close to being written off, while on the strength of 27 Operational Training Unit, in a serious accident on 5 August 1943. On that occasion, Sgt Page RAAF had been at the controls. Following repairs, it had arrived at Wellesbourne Mountford on 4 May 1944.

     30 OTU   **Hurricane IIC**   **MW347 TN-A**   **Training**
F/O C Koder

T/o 1503 Gamston but the engine cut and a wheels up landing was effected two minutes later, in a field, near the aerodrome and in line with the runway.

19-20 Apr   **16 OTU**   **Mosquito B.25**   **KB495**   **Training**
1945   W/O C G Johnson

T/o 2200 Barford St. John for a night cross-country. Wrecked circa 0120 in a landing mishap, at base, the undercarriage being deliberately raised in order to stop within the confines of the airfield.

20 Apr   **19 OTU C Flt**   **Wellington X**   **LP760**   **-H**   **Training**
1945

F/O A G Matthews	+
F/O E Rawlinson	+
F/O R E Williams RCAF	+
Sgt V P Dias	+
Sgt J D Pulham	+
Sgt W Gourlay	+

T/o 1152 Kinloss for a cross-country which, at 1240, ended in scenes of terrible devastation in the vicinity of Bank Head Farm, Humble, some eight miles SSW of Haddington in East Lothian. Eyewitnesses report the Wellington cruising at around 5,000 feet when the overcast sky was lit by a flash, followed by an explosion and debris raining down (accident investigators concluded that the outer section of the starboard wing sheared away). Three were buried in cemeteries in the Haddington area and three were taken south to rest in their home towns. This was the unit's last fatal accident in five years of operational training.

23 Apr   **12 OTU**   **Wellington X**   **LN549**   **Training**
1945
F/O A Duckworth
F/O M P Floyd

T/o 0020 Edgehill but clipped one of the unit's Wellingtons, parked at its dispersal. Ordered to head for Woodbridge in Suffolk, the crew duly arrived here at 0150, their aircraft being wrecked in the ensuing crash-landing.

23 Apr
1945

12 OTU   **Wellington X**   **LN710**   **Ground**

Damaged beyond repair at Edgehill, in the manner described at the foot of the page, previous.

25 Apr
1945

11 OTU   **Wellington X**   **HE417**   **—C**   **Training**

F/O J B Newton   T/o 1555 Oakley but the port engine cut out at one-hundred feet. F/O J B Newton turned away to port, to avoid rising ground, but was unable to complete the circuit before force -landing at 1557 near Waterstock, 4 miles W of Thame, Oxfordshire.

26—27 Apr
1945

85 OTU   **Wellington X**   **NA798**   **Training**

F/L S B Dalmais   T/o 2140 Husbands Bosworth for a night cross-coun try. Encoun tered very adverse weather and before the crew could find a suitable airfield on which to land, all were closed to flying operations. Still in thick cloud at 8,000 feet, the five airmen baled out at 0410, leaving their aircraft to crash near Whittlesey, Cambridgeshire.

27 Apr
1945

16 OTU   **Mosquito III**   **LR531**   **Training**

WO1 G J M Robertson RCAF   T/o 1710 Barford St. John for solo circuit practice. All went well until around 1740 when the port engine stopped at 400 feet. WO1 Robertson RCAF feathered the propeller and force -landed in the airfield circuit.

26 OTU   **Wellington X**   **LN708**   **Training**

W/O R Bereton   T/o 0155 Little Horwood for night circuits and landings. Crash-landed 0225, wheels retracted, at Redfield on the NW side of Winslow, 6 miles SE of Buckingham. The cause of the accident was attributed to failure of the port engine.

1 May
1945

12 OTU   **Wellington X**   **HE822**   **Training**

F/S K Tregoning RAAF   T/o 0843 Chipping Warden detailed for high-level bombing practice. Crashed 0945, while making a forced-landing with the undercarriage down, at Wardington, a shade over 4 miles north-east of Banbury, Oxfordshire. This was the last serious accident reported from the unit, which disbanded on 22 June 1945.

2 May
1945

10 OTU   **Hurricane IIC**   **LF700**   **Training**

F/O G F Ockenden RCAF   T/o Abingdon with the intent of flying a night sortie. After being instructed to carry out an overshoot, F/O Ockenden RCAF had the Hurricane's engine fail him at 400 feet, leaving him with no other option but to force -land, wheels up, in a field near the airfield.

17 OTU   **Wellington X**   **HE351**   **Unknown**

Reported damaged on this date, and though handed over to a repair team, it seems little work was done. Thus, on 19 September 1945, the Wellington was struck off charge.

20 OTU   **Wellington X**   **HE535 A1—S**   **Training**

Sgt L R Piget FFAF   inj   T/o 1040 Lossiemouth for a navigation detail. Ditched 1525, due to loss of power from the starboard engine, in the Moray Firth off Burghead, 8 miles NW of Elgin.

4 May
1945

84 OTU   **Hurricane IIC**   **PG581**   **Training**

F/O R E Ashcroft   T/o 1455 Desborough for a fighter affiliation exercise. Landed 1550 but while taxying to its dispersal, F/O Ashcroft's attention was distracted by the presence of one of the unit's crew coaches. Thus, he failed to see, until it was too late, that he was heading towards a fuel bowser. In the collision that followed, the Hurricane's undercarriage collapsed. This was the last major incident at a Bomber Command Operational Training Unit before the cessation of hostilities four days later.

Chapter Six

Running Down

9 May 1945 to 15 March 1947

On the first day of peace in Europe, Bomber Command still boasted seventeen Operational Training Establishments. Before the turn of the year, twelve of these units had ceased to exist, such was the rapid rundown of the Command. During 1946, two more units laid up their training syllabuses, leaving 16 OTU at Cottesmore (the headquarters of this unit having been domicile here since early March) to take care of the Command's Mosquito needs while Wellington training was maintained at Swinderby and Finningley, the headquarters of 17 OTU and 21 OTU respectively.

Then, on 15 March 1947, a restructuring of the training requirements took place and as at this date, 16 OTU disbanded in order to provide aircraft and support staff for the newly formed 231 Operational Conversion Unit and 204 Advanced Flying Training School.

Both units continued to use Cottesmore and it is unlikely that the air and ground crews that made up these new establishments were conscious of any great changes to the daily round of flying training.

Similarly, at Swinderby and Finningley, the new units were designated 201 Advanced Flying Training School and 202 Advanced Flying Training School, the latter absorbing the former at the beginning of December 1947, still using Wellington Mk. Xs.

It is now generally acknowledged that the contribution made by Bomber Command to the overall victory in 1945, was significant and to this end the input from the Operational Training Units also deserves due recognition for without the expertise, dedication and sheer hard work of instructors and trainees alike, the operational effectiveness of the Command would have been much the poorer.

As will have been seen from the hundreds of summaries reported in this volume, many fell in the course of their training or sustained very serious injuries. Few, however, failed to achieve the exacting standards required and it is to their everlasting memory and those of their colleagues who paid with their lives that this volume is dedicated as a testament to their courage.

10 May 1945	14 OTU	Hurricane IIC	MW341	Ground

F/O G M Buchanan RNZAF — Experienced brake trouble while taxying at Market Harborough and at 1525 the propeller sliced into a van, driven by LACW Hunstsman. Although not badly hurt, she was treated in the local Station Sick Quarters for bruising to her ribs and shock. The Hurricane was deemed to have been damaged beyond repair, though the airframe was retained for training purposes, the serial 5311M being applied.

11 May 1945	16 OTU	Mosquito XX	KB123	Training

F/O G E Warriner RCAF — T/o 1755 Barford St. John for practice bombing. Flew through a violent hailstorm, which had a marked effect on the aircraft's performance. Landing 1925, at high speed, the Mosquito ran into the overshoot area and was wrecked.

24 OTU		Wellington X	LP404	Training
F/O M A East RCAF	inj			
F/L A J Allen RCAF	inj			
Sgt F O Coles RCAF	inj			
F/O R J Delderfield RCAF	inj			
F/S N E Brown RCAF	inj			
F/O G J Hay RCAF	+			

T/o 2133 Honeybourne for a night navigation exercise. While flying over East Anglia at 15,000 feet, the starboard engine failed. An attempt was made to land at Langham airfield in Norfolk, but the Wellington overshot the runway and crashed 2323 into the nearby village. No one on the ground was hurt, though the roofs of three cottages were damaged and the local Young Men's Christian Association building was wrecked. An hour earlier and the story would have been very different as the building was then thronged with service personnel from the nearby airfield. It is also related that a Mr Sexton, living in one of the houses that lost its roof, was quite ill and that very morning had had his bed brought downstairs in order to ease the work of his wife, who was nursing him. Meanwhile, F/O Hay RCAF who died when the tail unit broke away, was taken to Brookwood Military Cemetery. This was the last serious accident reported by the unit ahead of disbandment on 24 July 1945.

15 May
1945

27 OTU	Wellington X	PG259	Training

F/O D R Britton RNZAF   T/o 2130 Church Broughton for a dual navigation
W/O D M Fimmell RNZAF   sortie. Within the next hour, fluid from the
aircraft's hydraulic system began to leak and
the crew decided to terminate their exercise and return to base. Upon reaching
Church Broughton, at 2243, it was impossible to lower the undercarriage and in
the ensuing wheels up arrival, the flash bomb exploded, setting light to the
Wellington. There are no reports of injuries amongst the seven-man crew.

18 May
1945

10 OTU	Wellington X	NC686	Training

F/O R F Angell   T/o 2201 Abingdon but the port engine lost
power and F/O Angell found it impossible to
gain height. While struggling to fly round the circuit, he came down beside
the waterworks at the corner of Wootton Road and Boars Hill. No one was hurt
but the Wellington was extensively damaged and repairs were deemed unadvisable.

30 OTU	Wellington X	NA718 BT-O	Air Test

F/O R F Thompson   +   T/o 1120 Gamston but something went terribly
LAC D F Dryden   +   wrong and in a desperate effort to glide back
to the airfield, the Wellington stalled and
crashed 1140 at Bank Haughton Farm, 3 miles from the runway. F/O Thompson,
a pilot with over 1,100 hours flying experience (782 of these hours on type),
is buried in Newcastle-upon-Tyne (Byker and Heaton) Cemetery, while LAC Dryden
was taken home to Scotland and interred at Paisley (Hawkhead) Cemetery. It was
the unit's last major accident before disbanding on 12 June 1945.

19 May
1945

16 OTU	Mosquito XX	KB208	Training

F/L J C Crawford   T/o 1045 Barford St. John for the pilot's first
solo on type. At 1140, he arrived back over the
threshold, but flared out too high and his arrival on the runway was severe
enough to smash the undercarriage.

20 May
1945

20 OTU	Wellington X	NC594 A1-W	Air Test

F/O R A Rickard   +   T/o 0952 Lossiemouth but from eyewitness accounts
F/O D P R Cameron   +   was in trouble from the start. For approximately
Sgt C G W Mawby   +   five minutes, the Wellington circled with one of
its engines misfiring; then, while approaching
Mrs J Flood   +   from the direction of the sea, it dived and came
Mstr Flood   +   down onto a block of municipal housing in Church
Mstr Flood   +   Street, Seatown on the E side of Lossiemouth.
Mstr Flood   +   The destruction was terrible; the top floor of
Mstr Flood   +   the building, which housed three families, took
Mstr D Flood   +   the full impact, killing Mrs Flood and four of
Mrs E Allan   +   her sons immediately. In the same instant, Mrs
Miss V Allan   +   Allan, a widow, and her adopted daughter, died.
From the floor below, Mr John Flood and his
daughter Jeannie, aged eleven, were about to prepare breakfast. Dropping his
little girl to safety in the garden below, Mr Flood managed to find his youngest
boy, David, but just as he reached the open window there was an explosion and the
little chap was literally blown from his arms, while he was catapulted out of the
building and was barely hurt. From the ground floor, Mrs John Stewart and her
three children escaped uninjured. F/O Rickard, a screened pilot, was cremated
at Manchester Crematorium, his screened wireless operator, F/O Cameron, lies in
Edinburgh (Morningside) Cemetery, while Sgt Mawby is buried in Ealing and Old
Brentford Cemetery, Ealing. I am indebted to Edinburgh Libraries and Information
Services for providing photocopies of The Scotsman newspaper that carried an
account of this awful tragedy.

22 May
1945

26 OTU	Wellington X	LP863	Training

F/S R St. J T Crawford   +   T/o Wing for high-level bombing over the Odstone
Sgt G S Watts   +   ranges. Broke up 1255, after diving steeply, and
Sgt J K Roche   +   crashed near Baunton, 2 miles N of Cirencester,
Sgt B P Van Noey   +   Gloucestershire. It is thought that the pilot,
W/O W R Martin   +   who was taken to Northern Ireland and buried in
the extension to Carnmoney Cemetery, lost control
while flying in cloud. W/O Martin, too, lies in Northern Ireland at the main
Carnmoney Cemetery, while Sgt Roche rests in the Irish Republic at Killorglin
Cemetery, Co. Kerry. Sgt Watts was cremated at Enfield Crematorium, while Sgt
Van Noey is interred at Walthamstow (Queen's Road) Cemetery in Essex.

24 May   **21 OTU**   **Hurricane IIC PG495 UH-S**   **Training**
1945   F/O L J Tiso   T/o 1003 Moreton-in-Marsh with the intent of
                                              carrying out a fighter affiliation detail, but
a glycol leakage obliged him to make an early return. His approach, however,
was rather fast and after overshooting the runway, the Hurricane finished up
in a chicken farm, owned by Mr Eric Rolph, on the south side of the main road
between Moreton-in-Marsh and Chipping Norton.

26 May   **17 OTU**   **Wellington X LN445**   **Training**
1945   F/O K G Kelly RAAF   inj   T/o Turweston but the port engine cut and the
              Sgt F H Ennis   inj   bomber flew into a tree, crashed 0525 and caught
              W/O A C Shankland   inj   fire at Whittlebury, 3 miles S of Towcester in
              F/O D W H Furber   +   Northamptonshire. F/O Furber rests in Uley
              Sgt R C Develin   +   (St. Giles) Churchyard, while Sgt Develin was
                                                 taken home to Co. Waterford in the Irish Republic
and laid to rest at Tramore (Christchurch) Church of Ireland Churchyard. Those
who survived were treated at the Princess Mary's Hospital at Halton.

28 May   **17 OTU**   **Wellington X HE226**   **Training**
1945   W/O E C Cole   +   T/o 1420 Turweston for a cross-country. While
              Sgt J Mann   +   flying in total cloud cover, struck a hill,
              F/S A J Griffiths   +   1,400 feet above sea level, and crashed circa
              Sgt J Duncan   +   1550 at Gill House on Bycliffe Moor near the
              Sgt H H Rawnsley   +   hamlet of Conistone and some 3 miles N from
                                                 Grassington, Yorkshire. W/O Cole of Kingswood
in Surrey was buried in Harrogate (Stonefall) Cemetery, while his crew were
taken to their home towns. Unusually, two, F/S Griffiths and Sgt Rawnsley,
were members of the pre-war Auxiliary Air Force. It is believed the crew,
uncertain of their position (they were 38 miles west of their turning point),
had decided to come down through the overcast in the hope of establishing a
good pinpoint. Their Wellington, prior to its arriving on the unit on 29 March
1944, had undergone repairs from an accident sustained while at 12 Operational
Training Unit on 3 September 1943, Sgt R W Crane RAAF being the pilot.

                    22 OTU   **Wellington X HE871**   **Training**
              WO1 J W Duncan RCAF   +   T/o 1005 Wellesbourne Mountford for a cross-
              F/O A H Handley RCAF   +   country, from which it failed to return. It
              F/S F T Gidilevich RCAF   +   is believed the aircraft entered a large bank
              F/S W E Algar RCAF   +   of cu. nimbus cloud, iced up and fell into the
              Sgt J R Isabelle RCAF   +   St. Georges Channel. Six Wellingtons conducted
                                                 an extensive search on 29 May, but without any
success; thus, all are commemorated on the Runnymede Memorial. Sgt Isabelle RCAF
served as Morin. This was the unit's last reported loss and a little under two
months later, on 24 July 1945, 22 Operational Training Unit disbanded.

8 Jun   **11 OTU**   **Wellington X LN690   -Q**   **Training**
1945   F/O A A Kingsbury RNZAF   +   T/o 1235 Westcott for a navigation sortie,
              Sgt C J H Lister   +   base-York-Flamborough Head-5413N 0236E-Wells-
              Sgt P R J Kingham   +   Gooderstone-Northampton-base. Last heard on
              Sgt R F Atkins   +   wireless at 1405, the signal being interrupted.
              Sgt G C H Lauener   +   A fix taken plotted the Wellington's position
                                                 as 5410N 0041E. All, their average age was 20,
are commemorated on the Runnymede Memorial. From known weather conditions in
the exercise area, it is thought the crew may have entered cu. nimbus cloud,
losing control as a consequence.

10-11 Jun   **20 OTU D Flt**   **Wellington X NC791   -P**   **Training**
1945   Sgt J B F Caurcoul FFAF   T/o 2155 Lossiemouth for a combined night
                                                 navigation and bombing detail. While over
the ranges, a bomb from another aircraft smashed into the starboard wing,
damaging the aileron and hydraulics. Maintaining control, Sgt Caurcoul FFAF
regained Lossiemouth, making a wheels up landing at 0207. Shortly after this,
the Wellington caught fire.

12 Jun   **16 OTU**   **Mosquito XX KB200**   **Training**
1945   F/L K L Kilner   inj   T/o Upper Heyford and headed for the Preston
                                                 Capes bombing range. Became hopelessly lost
and eventually force-landed on Terschelling in the Dutch Frisian Islands.
It is reported that both members of crew were quite seriously injured.

1 Jul   **16 OTU**   **Mosquito III**   **W4053**   **Training**
1945   F/O W J Mepham DFC   +   T/o Barford St. John for a demonstration in
Lt(A) W G Addison-Scott RNVR +   single-engined flying procedures. Landed at
1555, but at high speed. Eyewitnesses saw
the pilot deliberately retract the undercarriage, just moments before the
Mosquito crashed head-on against a tree. F/O Mepham is buried in Crystal
Palace District Cemetery, while Lt(A) Addison-Scott of Kinloss in Moray, and
attached from HMS Goldcrest, lies in Hampshire at Haslar Royal Naval Cemetery,
Gosport. It is believed he was only the second naval airman to be killed at a
Bomber Command Operational Training Unit, the first being Midshipman Mortimer
who lost his life five years previous, whilst being trained at 12 Operational
Training Unit (see page 22). Coincidentally, both had been given the name
George as their second Christian name.

2 Jul   **16 OTU**   **Mosquito XX**   **KB223**   **Training**
1945   F/O J Howard   T/o 1435 Barford St. John for the pilot's first
solo on type, but swung badly. F/O Howard closed
the throttles, but as the Mosquito lost speed its undercarriage collapsed.

5 Jul   **16 OTU**   **Mosquito B.25**   **KB496**   **Training**
1945   W/O S Dennis   T/o 1440 Barford St. John for a cross-country.
Returned to base at 1752, but on touch down, the
Mosquito veered to the left and ended up with a broken undercarriage. W/O Dennis
had joined the pre-war Volunteer Reserve and had amassed 1,080 solo flying hours,
nineteen of these on type.

11 Jul   **10 OTU**   **Wellington X**   **LP873**   **Training**
1945   F/O R L Walters   +   T/o Stanton Harcourt for a night navigation
F/S J E Fivash   +   detail. Presumed to have lost control, while
F/O M E P Tardif   +   in cloud, crashing circa 0125 at Kineton, six
Sgt J Grant   +   miles WNW from Stow-on-the-Wold, Gloucestershire.
Sgt B W Kelly   +   Wellesbourne Mountford was tasked with recovering
the bodies, after which they were claimed by next
of kin in England and Scotland.

        10 OTU   **Wellington X**   **NC714**   **Training**
W/O R M Morrison   +   T/o Stanton Harcourt similarly tasked. Crashed
F/S N D Rendle   +   at approximately 0115 at Walton Grange, Much
Sgt N Hooley   +   Wenlock in Shropshire. Eyewitnesses reported
Sgt S Williams   +   that the Wellington was on fire, in the air,
Sgt A J Franklin   +   before it hit the ground. F/S Rendle and Sgt
Franklin were laid to rest in Chester (Blacon)
Cemetery, while the others were taken to their home towns. In the years that
have followed this tragic event, a plaque has been mounted beneath a Memorial
Clock in the Guildhall at Much Wenlock inscribed with their names, along with
those of the United States Army Air Force and Canadians who lost their lives
in this area of Shropshire.

        10 OTU   **Wellington X**   **NC715**   **Training**
F/O E E Ritson   T/o 1122 Abingdon but swung gently to starboard.
This was immediately corrected, though it was
quite apparent that the engines were rather sluggish, even when the throttles
were fully advanced. Aborting the take off, F/O Ritson raised the undercarriage,
just as the Wellington ran beyond the end of the runway, and came to a stop in
soft ground some one hundred-and-fifty yards distant.

13 Jul   **11 OTU**   **Wellington X**   **LN844**   **-G**   **Training**
1945   F/O J W Heames   T/o Westcott for a night cross-country during
F/O P Smith   inj   which the starboard engine failed. Diverting
F/O S E Jones   inj   to Bottesford airfield in Leicestershire, the
P/O R G Nelson   inj   crew were nearing the runway at 0025 when the
F/O C W Tiplady   inj   port engine cut. The ensuing crash was followed
W/O L Wild   inj   by a fire, but all managed to scramble to safety
Sgt H R Grant   before the bomber was fully engulfed.

        20 OTU   **Wellington X**   **NA937**   **Training**
F/O H Smith   T/o 1240 Lossiemouth for a cross-country. While
flying at 2,000 feet, the port engine caught fire
and at 1500, a crash-landing was made in a field near Catfoss in Yorkshire.

27 Jul   **21 OTU**   **Wellington X**   **NA833**   **Training**
1945   F/O W Webley RAAF   T/o 2145 Moreton-in-Marsh for a night cross-country but within an hour the port engine had lost power and the crew headed for Fairwood Common airfield in Glamorganshire. Touch down, without the aid of flaps, came at 2250 and almost immediately the undercarriage collapsed, followed by a fire which destroyed the Wellington.

23 Aug   **16 OTU**   **Mosquito XX**   **KB194**   **Training**
1945   F/O G M Proctor DFC RNZAF   +   T/o 2046 Barford St. John for a night navigation
      F/O K L Kelly DFC RNZAF   +   sortie. It is believed F/L Proctor RNZAF lost control, after entering cloud for at 2104 the Mosquito broke up and crashed at Heath Farm, Great Rollright, 10 miles SW of Banbury in Oxfordshire. Both officers were taken to Oxford (Botley) Cemetery. They were well experienced, having served together (in the same crew) on 619 Squadron, chalking up 34 and 36 operational sorties respectively. Their deaths were the last from the RNZAF at a Bomber Command Operational Training Unit.

28 Aug   **11 OTU**   **Wellington X**   **PG394**   **—M**   **Training**
1945   F/S C A Jones   +   T/o Westcott for a night cross-country. Seen
      F/S L N Smith   +   in a steep dive, emerging from cloud, from which
      Sgt G N Lawrence   +   it failed to recover before plunging into the
      Sgt D S Price   +   waters of Lyme Bay off the Dorset coast. All
      Sgt M A Taylor   +   were recovered and taken for burial (cremation in the case of Sgt Lawrence) at cemeteries both in England and Wales. They were the last fatalities from 11 Operational Training Unit which disbanded, without further serious incident, on 18 September 1945.

Note. The above loss represents the last Bomber Command Operational Training Unit casualties of the Second World War. Furthermore, it was the last bomber to be lost during the period covered by the war, 3 September 1939 to 2 September 1945 (to all intents and purposes, fighting had ceased in the Far East in mid-August 1945).

3 Sep   **26 OTU**   **Wellington X**   **LP657**   **Training**
1945   F/O P L Huygens   +   T/o 2221 Wing for the pilot's first night
      F/S S C Jessup   +   navigation exercise. Crashed 2311, flying
      Sgt N Smith   +   into the ground at Map Reference 64/679422.
      Sgt C B Allen   +   All were claimed by their next of kin. Their
      Sgt D J Wright   +   deaths were the first Bomber Command casualties of the 'new peace'. Sgt Smith was a Member of the Pharmaceutical Society and Sgt Wright had been an Air Training Corps cadet.

12 Sep   **26 OTU**   **Wellington X**   **JA113**   **Training**
1945   W/O B Aves   T/o 2035 Wing for dual night circuits and
      S/L P M Proctor   landings. While being flown by S/L Proctor, an engine failed as the Wellington entered the funnels in readiness to land on runway 17. Unable to maintain height, he crash-landed at 2043, in a field, some 200 yards short of the threshold. Both pilots had logged over a thousand hours each, solo, and had flown Wellingtons for well in excess of a hundred hours.

24 Sep   **16 OTU**   **Mosquito XVI**   **PF485**   **Air Test**
1945   F/L C Batten DFC   +   T/o 1406 Upper Heyford for an acceptance test
      ACW1 G D Harris WAAF   +   during which one of the engines shed most of its coolant. Returned to base at 1431 and while trying to land in a strong gusting crosswind, stalled and cartwheeled into a stubble field. As the bomber went end-over-end, so it broke up and burst into flames. F/L Batten rests in Alfriston (St. Andrew) Churchyard, his being the sole service grave here for the Second World War. His nineteen year old WAAF passenger, ACW Harris, from Trethomas in Monmouthshire, is interred at Oxford (Botley) Cemetery.

18 Oct   **17 OTU**   **Hurricane IIC**   **MW350**   **Ferry**
1945   W/O W H Allchin   inj   T/o 1440 Turweston and set course for Kirkcudbright. As he flew northwards, weather conditions deteriorated and while trying to establish his position the Hurricane ran out of fuel. Selecting a suitable field, W/O Allchin made a good approach, but on force-landing at 1635, his aircraft flipped onto its back. As it was to prove, he was not far from his intended destination.

8 Nov
1945
10 OTU   **Wellington X   NA952**   **Training**
W/O D W R Thompson   T/o 1706 Stanton Harcourt intending to fly a
                                   solo evening navigation exercise, but, having
run two-thirds of the way along the runway, the starboard engine lost power.
This caused the bomber to swing violently and moments later, as W/O Thompson
was in the process of retracting the undercarriage, the port oleo clipped a
Nissen hut. No one was hurt, but an examination of the aircraft revealed very
serious distortion to the fuselage, sufficient to warrant the airframe being
declared a write off.

26 Nov
1945
26 OTU   **Wellington X   NC654**   **Training**
F/L C Cannell   T/o 1934 Wing for an exercise in high-level
                                   bombing. Not long after departing, an engine
caught fire and the crew aborted the sortie and headed for base. Nearing the
runway, F/L Cannell had the misfortune to collide with a tree, some 700 yards
from the threshold. In the ensuing crash, at 1957, the Wellington continued
to burn, but there are no reports of serious injuries.

8 Dec
1945
26 OTU   **Hurricane IIC   MW351**   **Training**
F/O C R Castleton   T/o 0930 Wing for fighter affiliation training.
                                   After twenty minutes, the Hurricane's engine
failed and a forced-landing was made, in a plough field, close to the airfield.

13 Dec
1945
26 OTU   **Wellington X   NC446**   **Training**
F/O C Fenwick DFC   +   T/o 1855 Wing for a night cross-country. At
W/O L R Waterson   +   approximately 2210, the bomber dived to earth
Sgt D E Richards   +   at Home Farm, Brimpton, some 5 miles ESE from
P/O I Castle   +   Newbury, Berkshire. F/O Fenwick was taken to
F/S C C F Gillespie   +   Cadoxton-Juxta-Neath (SS Cattwg and Illtyd)
F/S R S Winter   +   Churchyard, Blaenhonddan and buried in a joint
Sgt B A J Timms   +   grave with his brother (though no details of
                                   their parents are recorded), Second Officer
David Fenwick of the Merchant Navy who lost his life on 29 January 1940 aboard,
or while serving with, the London registered steam-ship Stanburn. His crew are
at rest in various cemeteries across the United Kingdom.

18 Jan
1946
16 OTU   **Mosquito XVI   PF495**   **Training**
Sgt N P Kerarul   T/o 1130 Upper Heyford for familiarisation on
                                   type. Landed at 1415, but swung off the runway
and came to a stop, wrecked, with its undercarriage smashed.

17 OTU   **Wellington X   LR125**   **Training**
Sgt N C Brunning   +   T/o 0950 Silverstone for a cross-country. Broke
F/O G S Button   +   up at 1045, while flying in cloud, and crashed
F/S W S Kinnair   +   near Corwen, 11 miles NE of Bala, Merioneth. It
Sgt L T Crabb   +   is thought likely that the pitot head froze over
Sgt A F Butler   +   leading to loss of control. F/S Kinnair of St.
                                   John's Wood, London, was taken to Harrogate
(Stonefall) Cemetery, while the others are buried in their home towns.

30 Jan
1946
21 OTU   **Wellington X   LP875**   **Training**
F/O H Annable   T/o 1951 Moreton-in-Marsh to practice single-
F/O C R Bluemell   inj   engined landings. At 2150, while approaching
F/O J A Turner   inj   the runway, the Wellington stalled and came down
Sgt A Wells   inj   amongst some trees. A strong and gusting cross-
F/O D V Anderson   inj   wind was a contributory factor.
Sgt J A Neston

5 Feb
1946
10 OTU   **Wellington X   NC725**   **Training**
F/O G F Burt   T/o Abingdon for a navigation detail. During
                                   the exercise, the oil pressure reading on the
starboard engine dropped alarmingly and F/O Burt decided to make a precautionary
landing at East Moor in Yorkshire. However, his arrival speed was high and in
order to prevent his aircraft from overrunning the airfield, he retracted the
undercarriage. No one was hurt, but the Wellington was damaged beyond repair.

18 Feb
1946
16 OTU   **Mosquito XVI   PF507**   **Training**
P/O A A Cruetzmeyer FFAF   T/o 0925 Upper Heyford for solo flying. Landed
                                   at 0943, only to ground-loop in the crosswind.

18 Feb 1946	**21 OTU** F/O T H James Sgt Telford F/S Soall F/O Errington F/S Jones	**Wellington X**	**PG150**	**Training**

T/o 1815 Moreton-in-Marsh for a night cross-country. Wrecked 2156, on return to base, after swerving off the runway.

7 Mar 1946	**21 OTU** F/O S E Judd W/O K H Shepherd Sgt Turton Sgt Gregory Sgt Kew	**Wellington X**	**PG392**	**Training**

inj inj

T/o 2045 Moreton-in-Marsh for dual circuits and landings. Fifteen minutes into the detail, the port engine failed and with the Wellington heading towards the perimeter fence, F/O Judd promptly raised the undercarriage.

19 Mar 1946	**17 OTU** F/O J Oldham P/O R C Cripps F/O E D Beaumont P/O A F Rigby Sgt F W Bunning	**Wellington X**	**NC444**	**Training**

inj inj inj inj inj

T/o 1317 Silverstone for circuit training, combined with single-engined flying practice. Lost power from the starboard engine and while trying to complete the circuit, crashed 1414 and caught fire. This was the last serious incident reported from the unit, which, a year later, was redesignated No. 201 Advanced Flying School.

26 Mar 1946	**16 OTU** P/O G De Thorey FFAF	**Mosquito XVI**	**PF492**	**Training**

T/o 1650 Cottesmore for solo circuits and landings. Touched down at 1725, but veered to starboard and while trying to correct the situation, the Mosquito turned sharply in the opposite direction, breaking its undercarriage as a result. This was the unit's first serious accident since moving to Cottesmore at the beginning of the month.

30 Mar 1946	**16 OTU** Lt de Verneilh FFAF	**Mosquito III**	**HJ870**	**Training**

T/o 0945 Cottesmore for solo circuits and landings. Landed at 1050, but ballooned back into the air and upon its second arrival, the undercarriage gave way.

2 Apr 1946	**16 OTU** Lt R M J Duvillard FFAF	**Mosquito XVI**	**RV317**	**Training**

T/o 1415 Cottesmore for solo circuits and landings. Wrecked at 1425, following the loss of the undercarriage as the bomber swerved to port on touch down.

14–15 May 1946	**16 OTU** F/O W J O Morrison	**Mosquito XVI**	**RV363**	**Training**

T/o 2125 Cottesmore for a night cross-country and bombing detail. Returned to base at 0105 in weather conditions described as marginal. After landing, the Mosquito ran off the end of the runway and is reported to have turned over in the overshoot area, apparently without causing any serious hurt to its crew.

17 May 1946	**16 OTU** W/C G L B Hull DFC	**Mosquito III**	**TW108**	**Training**

+ T/o 2200 Cottesmore for solo night circuits and landings. An hour later, W/C Hull called Flying Control to advise he was trying to extinguish a fire that had broken out in the starboard engine. Soon after making this call, it was reported he had crashed, with fatal consequences, amongst trees at Bellamore's Farm near Goadby Marwood, 5 miles NNE of Melton Mowbray, Leicestershire. Described in the cemetery register for Oving (All Saints) Churchyard, Buckinghamshire as a 'pupil pilot', W/C Hull had at least 1,500 hours of flying experience to his credit, though only ten of these were on type. His parents are shown as living in the town of Retreat, Cape Province, South Africa.

3 Jul 1946	**16 OTU** F/O D F Cook	**Mosquito XVI**	**PF538**	**Training**

T/o 1108 Cottesmore intent on carrying out a cross-country and bombing exercise. However, as the Mosquito accelerated, a swing to port developed and F/O Cook applied full opposite rudder. As he did so, the aircraft went out of control and slid, sideways, to a halt, minus its undercarriage.

22 Jul
1946

16 OTU   **Mosquito XVI** **PF540**   **Training**

P/O A Hutchinson   T/o 1345 Cottesmore for solo circuits and landings, P/O Hutchinson being relatively inexperienced with only 117 solo hours to his credit, four of these being on type. As he reached flying speed, the Mosquito swung, whereupon he cut the throttles and raised the undercarriage. The resultant high speed slide was sufficient to damage his aircraft beyond repair.

31 Jul
1946

21 OTU   **Wellington X** **LP920**   **Training**

F/O R Broadbent   T/o 0005 Moreton-in-Marsh for a night cross country. While carrying out the detail, the Wellington's hydraulic system failed and after returning to base, and landing at 0410, the bomber overran the runway and tipped onto its nose. Although the damage caused was slight, no repairs were carried out and after languishing for the better part of six months, the airframe was struck off charge on 4 February 1947.

23 Aug
1946

10 OTU   **Wellington X** **LP451**   **Training**

F/L A M Dow   T/o 2030 Abingdon for dusk circuit training.
W/O E Coleman   The first circuit was completed satisfactorily, but as the pupil pilot accelerated to go round again, the Wellington veered to the left. This was duly corrected, but almost immediately the bomber began to drift towards the starboard side of the runway. At this point F/L Dow, the screened pilot, took control but though he was able to bring the aircraft back onto the centre line, he had insufficient airspeed to effect a safe departure. Consequently, he raised the undercarriage and the Wellington slid to a stop, in the overshoot area. This was the last serious incident reported from the unit ahead of disbanding on 10 September 1946.

6 Sep
1946

21 OTU   **Wellington X** **PG135**   **Training**

F/O D J Ferdinando   + T/o Moreton-in-Marsh for a low-level night
F/L K G J Gratton   + exercise in navigation. Lost control at 0315,
F/S R Dunn   + coming down at Long Compton in Warwickshire,
Sgt W B Greatrix   + some 5 miles ENE from its place of departure.
Sgt D E Robinson   + F/O Ferdinando and his ex-Air Training Corps cadet air gunner, Sgt Robinson, are buried in Oxford (Botley) Cemetery, while their three companions were claimed by their next of kin. This was the last major tragedy to overtake the unit and it was the last Wellington to be written off from such a training establishment.

9 Sep
1946

16 OTU   **Mosquito XVI** **PF601**   **Training**

F/L A S Holgate   inj T/o 1615 Cottesmore for solo circuits and landings but swung out of control and wiped away its undercarriage. As the propeller blades made contact with the runway, a fragment from the starboard airscrew pierced the cockpit canopy, severely injuring F/L Holgate.

7 Oct
1946

16 OTU   **Mosquito XVI** **RV361**   **Training**

W/O G C Dalgarno   T/o 1010 Cottesmore for a combined navigation and practice bombing exercise. Returned to base at 1210, but as a consequence of applying the brakes rather sharply, the Mosquito swung off the runway and lost its undercarriage.

5 Nov
1946

16 OTU   **Mosquito III** **RR289**   **Training**

F/L C G Jones   T/o Cottesmore for dual practice in single-
F/L C G Lewis   engined landings. Following an overshoot of the runway, failed to maintain height and, thus, forced-landed with the wheels retracted.

22 Nov
1946

16 OTU   **Mosquito III** **VA874**   **Training**

W/O G C Dalgarno   T/o 2100 Cottesmore for the pilot's first night solo on type. Wrecked sixteen minutes later in a landing accident. Since his previous crash (see this page), W/O Dalgarno had added a further fourteen hours of solo flying on type, bringing his total to twenty-two. His accident was the penultimate loss suffered by the unit and, as will have been observed by the number of summaries featuring Mosquitoes, it seems that it was not the easiest of aircraft for trainee pilots to master.

28 Nov	16 OTU	Mosquito III	RR293	Training

1946   F/L M H G MacLucas   +   T/o 2136 Cottesmore for dual night circuits
W/O D A Clark   +   and landings. While so engaged, the weather
in the area took a marked turn for the worse
with visibility being much reduced. Therefore, it is assumed that the crew
lost sight of the runway and while trying to establish their position, they
flew into the ground, at approximately 2150, between a mile and 2 miles N of
the airfield. F/L MacLucas of Weston-super-Mare was buried in Bath at Haycombe
Cemetery, while W/O Clark, who hailed from Kenton near Harrow, was laid to rest
in Brookwood Military Cemetery. Both were very experienced pilots, the former
with close on 1,300 flying hours recorded and the latter with at least 917 hours
of flying behind him, though only twenty of these had been at the controls of
Mosquitoes. This was the last major accident reported from a Bomber Command
Operational Training Unit.

**ROYAL AIR FORCE
BOMBER COMMAND LOSSES
of the SECOND WORLD WAR**

W R Chorley

**THE BOMBER COMMAND
WAR DIARIES** – An Operational
Reference Book: 1939-1945

Martin Middlebrook & Chris Everitt

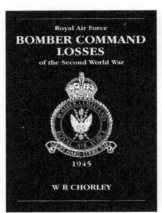

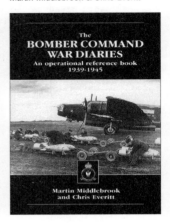

**We hope you enjoyed
this book . . .**

Midland Publishing titles are edited
and designed by an experienced and
enthusiastic team of specialists.

Further titles are in preparation and
we always welcome ideas from
authors and readers for books they
would like to see published.

In addition, our associate company,
Midland Counties Publications,
offers an exceptionally wide range of
aviation, spaceflight, astronomy,
military, naval and transport books
and videos for sale by mail-order
around the world.

For a copy of the relevant catalogue,
or to order further copies of this
book, and any of the titles mentioned
on this and the final page, please
write, telephone, fax or e-mail to:

Midland Counties Publications
4 Watling Drive, Hinckley, Leics,
LE10 3EY, England

Tel: (+44) [0]1455 254 450
Fax: (+44) [0]1455 233 737
E-mail:
midlandbooks@compuserve.com
Web site:
www.midlandcountiessuperstore.com

This highly acclaimed series identifies,
on a day-by-day basis, the individual
aircraft, crews and circumstances of
each of the 10,000+ aircraft lost in the
European Theatre of Operations during
the Second World War.

Appendices include loss totals by
squadron and aircraft type each year;
Group loss totals; Squadron bases,
bomber OTU losses by unit and type,
PoWs, escapers and evaders etc.

This series is an ideal complement
to *Bomber Command War Diaries*.

Available in 234 x 156mm sbk format:

Volume 1: 1939-40
Details 1,217 aircraft losses; 160pp
0 904597 85 7   **£9.95**

Volume 2: 1941
Details 1,515 aircraft losses; 224pp
0 904597 87 3   **£12.95**

Volume 3: 1942
Details 2,035 aircraft losses; 318pp
0 904597 89 X   **£15.95**

Volume 4: 1943
Details 3,100 aircraft losses; 494pp
0 904597 90 3   **£18.95**

Volume 5: 1944
Details 3,537 aircraft losses; 576pp
0 904597 91 1   **£19.95**

Volume 6: 1945
Details 1,080 aircraft losses; 224pp
0 904597 92 X   **£14.95**

Some books acquire the 'classic'
status without really deserving it.
Others become classics and don't
need to advertise the fact.

Bomber Command War Diaries is
firmly in the latter category – essential
reading matter for anyone interested in
Bomber Command and its campaigns
during the Second World War.

Bomber Command War Diaries
provides a concisely worded review of
each raid and its background.
Operational statistics provide unit and
group sorties against aircraft lost –
which range from 1% through to 18%.

Copiously indexed, this is a
balanced testament to Royal Air Force
Bomber Command, its men and its
rationale.

This Midland Publishing edition
includes a revised appendix on the
aircrew survival rates from shot down
British bombers, plus minor
amendments and observations, but
essentially *Bomber Command War
Diaries* continues to be what it has
always been, an icon in aviation
publishing – the essential classic.

Softback
234 x 156 mm, 808 pages
65 b/w photographs
1 85780 033 8   Available
£19.95

The Airspeed AS.10 Oxford, a three-seat advanced trainer, served the British and Commonwealth Air Forces throughout the war and until retirement in 1954. Over 8,500 were built. N4720 is representative of the Armstrong Siddeley Cheetah-engined turretless Mk.II that served with all but two of the bomber OTUs, in a pilot training and support role. P.H.T. Green collection

The Armstrong Whitworth AW.41 Albemarle was developed as a recce-bomber, but only ever saw use as a glider tug or special transport, though a few were employed at two of the bomber OTUs. P1475, a Mk.I series II, delivered around the end of 1941, served in a transport role with 511 Squadron and survived until SoC (struck off charge) in August 1947. P.H.T. Green collection

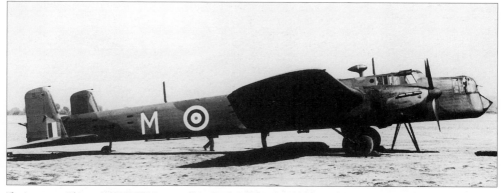

The Armstrong Whitworth AW.38 Whitley was a front-line bomber in the early years of the war. It also served with distinction in Coastal Command, as a glider tug for the airborne forces, and it equipped four of the bomber OTUs. N1503, a Mk.V, was eventually damaged in a heavy landing at 10 OTU Stanton Harcourt on 24th April 1941. MAP/ P.H.T. Green collection

The Avro 652A Anson undertook general recce duties with Coastal Command early in the war, but was employed as a trainer and light transport for most of its career. Cheetah-engined, the type served in large numbers with 19 of the bomber OTUs. Mk.I K6190 was with 27 OTU Lichfield when forced to land just off the airfield on 7th September 1941. P.H.T. Green collection

The Avro 679 Manchester was a great disappointment as a front-line bomber, due to frequent engine failures, but with new wings and four Merlin engines it found fame as the Lancaster. The Manchester served with ten Bomber Command squadrons, but with only one OTU, No.25 at Finningley. L7427 is an 83 Squadron Mk.I, seen circa March 1941. P.H.T. Green collection

The Boulton Paul Defiant was initially successful as a day 'turret' fighter, but when compromised it was re-roled as a night-fighter. It was also used at Air Gunnery Schools, and Air Rescue units. Over 1,000 were built; 290 were converted or built for target towing duties and as such were used by 22 of the bomber OTUs. This example is a Mk.I. P.H.T. Green collection

The Bristol 142 Blenheim light bomber outpaced the biplane fighters when introduced in 1937. The Mk.IF night-fighter variant featured a ventral gun pack with four Brownings. Four bomber OTUs employed the Mk.I, two of them in substantial numbers. L6680 served with 13 OTU, but collided with a Wellington, landing at Chipping Warden, 31st July 1941. P.H.T. Green collection

The Blenheim Mk.IV superseded production of the Mk.I in 1939 and served in the front-line until replaced by Bostons and Mosquitoes in 1942. L8795, a Mk.IV of 13 OTU, belly-landed at Launton near Bicester, after engine failure on 10th May 1940. It wears the code EP-B of 104 Squadron, which joined with 108 Squadron to form 13 OTU in April 1940. P.H.T. Green collection

The DH.82A Tiger Moth is one of the best-known elementary training aircraft. Total production in Britain, Canada, Australia and New Zealand exceeded 7,000. It was used as a 'hack' for communications at 18 of the bomber OTUs. This representative example, Mk.II R4922, saw service with No.7 Elementary Flying Training School, at Desford, Leics. P.H.T. Green collection

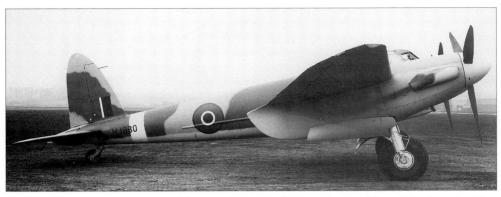

The de Havilland DH.98 Mosquito was one of the outstanding aircraft of WWII, serving in the fighter, PR, bomber and training roles. It was used as a major type at two bomber OTUs and in a support role at three others. It superseded the Blenheim and gradually supplanted the Beaufighter and Havoc. Illustrated is Mk.III HJ880, in March 1943. P.H.T. Green collection

The Fairey Battle three-seat light bomber was obsolescent at the start of WWII, but stayed in front-line service until September 1940. It was employed in considerable numbers by two bomber OTUs, and in four others in a support role. This in-works shot is of a 12 OTU machine with 52 Squadron codes (one of the units that amalgamated to form 12 OTU). P.H.T. Green collection

The Handley Page HP.52 Hampden, along with the Whitley and Wellington, carried out Bomber Command's early WWII raids on Germany. The Hampden was used in substantial numbers by three of the bomber OTUs. Mk.I P1174, 'JS-G' of 16 OTU, later served with 5 OTU, with whom it was written-off following a forced landing on Skye, 16th August 1942. P.H.T. Green collection

The Handley Page Hereford was a variant of the Hampden, differing from the latter in that it was powered by Napier Dagger engines instead of Bristol Pegasuses. The Hereford was mainly used as a bomber crew trainer by 14 and 16 OTUs. L6070 'GL-A2' was a 14 OTU machine, photographed in July 1940, just two months after the type joined the unit. P.H.T. Green collection

Various fighter aircraft were employed by nearly all the bomber OTUs, albeit in small numbers, for fighter affiliation (gunnery practice). 21 OTU's Hurricane Mk.IIc PG495 'UH-S' suffered a glycol leak on 24th May 1945, overshot its emergency landing at Moreton-in-Marsh, and ended up in a chicken farm on the other side of the A44 Oxford to Evesham road. Eric Kaye collection

The Miles Master two-seat advanced trainer served in a support role at most of the bomber OTUs, either as the M.19/Mk.II (Bristol Mercury radial) or M.27/Mk.III (P&W Wasp Junior engine) variant. This example, an M.9/Mk.Ia with a R-R Kestrel engine, got into difficulties when serving with 61 OTU, a fighter OTU formed at Histon in June 1941. P.H.T. Green collection

The Miles M.25 Martinet was designed from the outset as a two-seat target tug based on the Master trainer, powered by a Bristol Mercury engine. It served with Air Gunnery Schools and Anti-Aircraft Co-operation Units, and like the Master, was employed by all the Bomber OTUs. This anonymous TT Mk.I was photographed at St Merryn in 1946. P.H.T. Green collection

The Miles M.14A Magister (or 'Maggie') was a popular low wing two-seat trainer that equipped many elementary flying schools. They also served as 'comms hacks' with dozens of other units, including 11 of the bomber OTUs. L5958 is seen here while with 108 Squadron at Bicester. Control was lost at Abingdon on 28th November 1940, when with 10 OTU. P.H.T. Green collection

The Vickers Wellington night bomber, with a crew of six, undertook the majority of operations against Germany in the early stages of WWII. The Mk.I had Pegasus XVIII engines, Vickers nose and tail turrets and a Nash & Thompson ventral gun turret. L4236 of 15 OTU stalled-in at Harwell, 22nd April 1940, and is seen on a 'Queen Mary' trailer on 18th May. P.H.T. Green collection

The Wellington IA had Nash & Thompson turrets in lieu of the Vickers nose and tail types, and saw service with three bomber OTUs whereas the Mk.I served with only two. N2980, a 20 OTU Lossiemeouth Mk.IA, ditched in Loch Ness, 31st December 1940. Salvaged in September 1985, it is seen under restoration at Brooklands Museum in November 1992. P.H.T. Green collection

Large numbers of the 2,685 Wellington Mk.ICs built in the early part of WWII went on to equip at least 15 of the bomber OTUs. In this variant the ventral turret was replaced by beam guns and enlarged main wheels that still protruded when retracted. L7850 'VB-Y' of 14 OTU crash-landed in Exton Park, near Cottesmore, 2nd December 1942. P.H.T. Green collection

The Wellington Mk.II (Merlin X) and Mk.III (Hercules engines) followed the IC into service in 1941. The Mk.II (400 built) only served with one bomber OTU, but the Mk.III (1,519 built) equipped all but one (No.81 Ashbourne). Mk.III BK347 'BT-Z' heads this line-up at 30 OTU Hixon; it later crashed (as 'Q') into Whernside hill, Yorks, on 21st April 1944. P.H.T. Green collection

Although the Wellington Mk.IV (220 built with P&W Twin Wasps) served at 18 OTU, the Mk.XVIII with 15 OTU and the Mk.XIII with 29 OTU, all the bomber OTUs received a complement of Mk.Xs – the last bomber variant. This Mk.X, LN710, is seen when with 27 OTU. It was hit by LN549 on 22nd/23rd April 1945, while parked with 12 OTU at Edgehill. P.H.T. Green collection

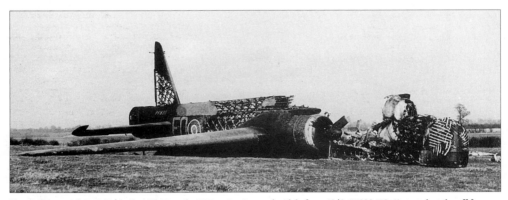

The Wellington Mk.X (3,804 built, with Hercules XVI engines) served widely from 1943. PF839 'FQ- ?' started a take-off from 12 OTU Edgehill during the night of 1st/2nd March 1945, but full flap crept on and although the aircraft hopped over the hedge at the end of the runway, it belly-landed in the next field. The crew escaped before fire broke out. Eric Kaye collection

The Westland Lysander is well known for its Army Co-operation duties and SOE flights into occupied Europe, however it also served with distinction on Air Rescue duties and as a target tug. All the bomber OTUs appear to have had an allocation of Lysanders of various Mks for target towing and/or general support duties. L4698, a Mk.I, was with 2 Squadron in August 1938, though it later served with 23 OTU. It was eventually struck off charge on 23rd July 1943. P.H.T. Green collection

Appendix 1

Operational Training Unit Bases April 1940 to March 1947

6 Group	Abingdon, Berkshire	8 Apr 40 –	11 May 42	Headquarters
			11 May 42	Redesignated 91 Group
10 OTU	Abingdon, Berkshire	8 Apr 40 –	11 May 42	Headquarters
	Jurby, Isle of Man	6 Apr 40 –	10 Sep 40	C Flight
	Stanton Harcourt, Oxfordshire	3 Sep 40 –	11 May 42	Satellite
	Mount Farm, Oxfordshire	23 Jul 41 –	12 Feb 42	Satellite
11 OTU	Bassingbourn, Cambridgeshire	8 Apr 40 –	20 Dec 41	Headquarters
	Jurby, Isle of Man	8 Apr 40 –	28 Jul 40	Detachment
	Steeple Morden, Cambridgeshire	Dec 40 –	11 May 42	Satellite
	Tempsford, Bedfordshire	20 Dec 41 –	18 Feb 42	Headquarters
	Bassingbourn, Cambridgeshire	18 Feb 42 –	11 May 42	Headquarters
12 OTU	Benson, Oxfordshire	8 Apr 40 –	16 Aug 41	Headquarters
	Penrhos, Caernarvon	8 Apr 40 –	9 Dec 40	Detachment
	Mount Farm, Oxfordshire	Aug 40 –	23 Jul 41	Satellite
	Thame, Oxfordshire	Sep 40 –	Dec 40	Detachment
	Chipping Warden, Oxfordshire	16 Aug 41 –	11 May 42	Headquarters
13 OTU	Bicester, Oxfordshire	8 Apr 40 –	15 Jul 40	Headquarters
	Weston-on-the-Green, Oxfordshire	8 Apr 40 –	15 Jul 40	Reserve Landing Ground
			15 Jul 40	Transferred 7 Group
14 OTU	Cottesmore, Rutland	8 Apr 40 –	15 Jul 40	Headquarters
	Stormy Down, Glamorgan	May 40 –	7 Jun 40	Detachment
	Pembrey, Carmarthen	7 Jun 40 –	Jun 40	Detachment
			15 Jul 40	Transferred 7 Group
15 OTU	Harwell, Berkshire	8 Apr 40 –	15 Jul 40	Headquarters
			15 Jul 40	Transferred 7 Group
16 OTU	Upper Heyford, Oxfordshire	8 Apr 40 –	15 Jul 40	Headquarters
	Weston-super-Mare, Somerset	May 40 –	Jul 40	Detachment
	Brackley, Northamptonshire	Jun 40 –	15 Jul 40	Satellite
	Croughton, Northamptonshire	Jun 40 –	15 Jul 40	Satellite
			15 Jul 40	Transferred 7 Group
17 OTU	Upwood, Huntingdonshire	8 Apr 40 –	15 Jul 40	Headquarters
	Squires Gate, Lancashire	Apr 40 –	Jun 40	Detachment
			15 Jul 40	Transferred 7 Group
18 OTU	Hucknall, Nottinghamshire	15 Jun 40 –	7 Nov 40	Headquarters
	Bramcote, Warwickshire	7 Nov 40 –	11 May 42	Headquarters
	Bitteswell, Leicestershire	30 Jun 41 –	11 May 42	Satellite
19 OTU	Kinloss, Moray	27 May 40 –	11 May 42	Headquarters
	Forres, Moray	25 Jan 41 –	11 May 42	Satellite
	Brackla, Nairn	7 Jan 42 –	11 May 42	Satellite
20 OTU	Lossiemouth, Moray	27 May 40 –	11 May 42	Headquarters
	Elgin, Moray	30 Jun 40 –	11 May 42	Satellite
21 OTU	Moreton-in-Marsh, Gloucestershire	21 Jan 41 –	11 May 42	Headquarters
	Edgehill, Warwickshire	21 Oct 41 –	11 May 42	Satellite
22 OTU	Wellesbourne Mountford, Warwickshire	14 Apr 41 –	11 May 42	Headquarters
	Stratford-upon-Avon, Warwickshire	5 Jul 41 –	11 May 42	Satellite
23 OTU	Pershore, Worcestershire	1 Apr 41 –	11 May 42	Headquarters
	Defford, Worcestershire	25 Sep 41 –	11 May 42	B Flight
27 OTU	Lichfield, Staffordshire	23 Apr 41 –	11 May 42	Headquarters
	Tatenhill, Staffordshire	Aug 41 –	11 May 42	Satellite

7 Group	Brampton Grange, Huntingdonshire	15 Jul 40	-	1 Sep 41	Headquarters
	Winslow Hall, Buckinghamshire	1 Sep 41	-	11 May 42	Headquarters
				11 May 42	Redesignated 92 Group
13 OTU	Bicester, Oxfordshire	15 Jul 40	-	11 May 42	Headquarters
	Weston-on-the-Green, Oxfordshire	15 Jul 40	-	1 Nov 40	Reserve Landing Ground
	Hinton-in-the-Hedges, Northamptonshire	1 Nov 40	-	11 May 42	Reserve Landing Ground
14 OTU	Cottesmore, Rutland	15 Jul 40	-	11 May 42	Headquarters
	Woolfox Lodge, Rutland	13 Dec 40	-	1 Aug 41	Satellite
	Saltby, Leicestershire	1 Aug 41	-	11 May 42	Satellite
15 OTU	Harwell, Berkshire	15 Jul 40	-	25 Jul 41	Headquarters
	Hampstead Norris, Berkshire	Sep 40	-	11 May 42	Satellite
	Mount Farm, Oxfordshire	25 Jul 41	-	12 Feb 42	Headquarters
	Harwell, Berkshire	12 Feb 42	-	11 May 42	Headquarters
16 OTU	Upper Heyford, Oxfordshire	15 Jul 40	-	Mar 42	Headquarters
	Brackley, Northamptonshire	15 Jul 40	-	11 May 42	Satellite
	Croughton, Northamptonshire	15 Jul 40	-	11 May 42	Satellite
	Catfoss, Yorkshire	Jul 40	-	22 Oct 40	Detachment
	Barford St. John, Oxfordshire	Mar 42	-	11 May 42	Headquarters
17 OTU	Upwood, Huntingdonshire	15 Jul 40	-	11 May 42	Headquarters
	Polebrook, Northamptonshire	Jan 41	-	Jun 41	Satellite
	Warboys, Huntingdonshire	17 May 41	-	11 May 42	Satellite
24 OTU	Honeybourne, Worcestershire	15 Mar 42	-	11 May 42	Headquarters
25 OTU	Finningley, Yorkshire	1 Mar 41	-	11 May 42	Headquarters
	Balderton, Nottinghamshire	14 Jun 41	-	14 Nov 41	Satellite
	Bircotes, Nottinghamshire	14 Nov 41	-	11 May 42	Satellite
26 OTU	Wing, Buckinghamshire	15 Jan 42	-	11 May 42	Headquarters
	Cheddington, Buckinghamshire	15 Mar 42	-	11 May 42	Satellite
29 OTU	North Luffenham, Rutland	21 Apr 42	-	11 May 42	Headquarters
91 Group	Abingdon, Berkshire	11 May 42	-	14 Apr 47	Headquarters
10 OTU	Abingdon, Berkshire	11 May 42	-	20 Mar 44	Headquarters
	Stanton Harcourt, Oxfordshire	11 May 42	-	20 Mar 44	Satellite
	St. Eval, Cornwall	4 Aug 42	-	23 Jul 43	Detachment
	Stanton Harcourt, Oxfordshire	20 Mar 44	-	16 Nov 44	Headquarters
	Abingdon, Berkshire	16 Nov 44	-	10 Sep 46	Headquarters
	Stanton Harcourt, Oxfordshire	16 Nov 44	-	23 Nov 45	Satellite
11 OTU	Bassingbourn, Cambridgeshire	11 May 42	-	28 Sep 42	Headquarters
	Steeple Morden, Cambridgeshire	11 May 42	-	28 Sep 42	Satellite
				28 Sep 42	Transferred 92 Group
				15 Jun 45	Returned 91 Group
	Westcott, Buckinghamshire	15 Jun 45	-	18 Sep 45	Headquarters
	Oakley, Buckinghamshire	15 Jun 45	-	18 Sep 45	Satellite
12 OTU	Chipping Warden, Oxfordshire	11 May 42	-	15 Jun 42	Headquarters
	Gaydon, Warwickshire	13 Jun 42	-	15 Jun 42	Satellite
				15 Jun 42	Transferred 93 Group
17 OTU	Silverstone, Northamptonshire	15 Jun 45	-	28 Oct 46	Headquarters
	Turweston, Buckinghamshire	15 Jun 45	-	15 Dec 45	Satellite
	Swinderby, Lincolnshire	28 Oct 46	-	15 Mar 47	Headquarters
18 OTU	Bramcote, Warwickshire	11 May 42	-	1 Sep 42	Headquarters
	Bitteswell, Leicestershire	11 May 42	-	1 Sep 42	Satellite
				1 Sep 42	Transferred 93 Group
				20 Oct 44	Returned 91 Group
	Finningley, Yorkshire	20 Oct 44	-	30 Jan 45	Headquarters
	Bircotes, Nottinghamshire	20 Oct 44	-	15 Nov 44	Satellite
	Worksop, Nottinghamshire	20 Oct 44	-	2 Dec 44	Satellite
19 OTU	Kinloss, Moray	11 May 42	-	26 Jun 45	Headquarters
	Forres, Moray	11 May 42	-	22 Oct 44	Satellite
	Brackla, Nairn	11 May 42	-	27 Apr 44	Satellite
	Abingdon, Berkshire	24 Jun 42	-	28 Jun 42	Detachment
20 OTU	Lossiemouth, Moray	11 May 42	-	17 Jul 45	Headquarters
	Elgin, Moray	11 May 42	-	24 Jun 45	Satellite
	Stanton Harcourt, Oxfordshire	26 May 42	-	3 Jun 42	Detachment

91 Group Continued

20 OTU	Snaith, Yorkshire	24 Jun 42 - 28 Jun 42	Detachment
	Elsham Wolds, Lincolnshire	28 Jul 42 - 29 Jul 42	Detachment
	Elsham Wolds, Lincolnshire	10 Sep 42 - 12 Sep 42	Detachment
	Milltown, Moray	14 Jun 43 - Jun 45	Satellite
21 OTU	Moreton-in-Marsh, Gloucestershire	11 May 42 - 25 Nov 46	Headquarters
	Edgehill, Warwickshire	11 May 42 - 12 Apr 43	Satellite
	Enstone, Oxfordshire	12 Apr 43 - 11 Aug 45	Satellite
	Honeybourne, Worcestershire	11 Aug 45 - 6 Oct 45	Satellite
	Enstone, Oxfordshire	6 Oct 45 - 1 Dec 45	Satellite
	Finningley, Yorkshire	25 Nov 46 - 15 Mar 47	Headquarters
22 OTU	Wellesbourne Mountford, Warwickshire	11 May 42 - 24 Jul 45	Headquarters
	Stratford-upon-Avon, Warwickshire	11 May 42 - 15 Nov 42	Satellite
	Elsham Wolds, Lincolnshire	27 May 42 - 3 Jun 42	Detachment
	Wing, Buckinghamshire	27 May 42 - 3 Jun 42	Detachment
	Gaydon, Warwickshire	1 Sep 42 - 24 Jul 45	Satellite
	Stratford-upon-Avon, Warwickshire	15 Mar 44 - 15 Dec 44	Satellite
23 OTU	Pershore, Worcestershire	11 May 42 - 15 Mar 44	Headquarters
	Defford, Worcestershire	11 May 42 - 18 May 42	B Flight
	Bourn, Cambridgeshire	27 May 42 - 3 Jun 42	Detachment
	Oakington, Cambridgeshire	27 May 42 - 3 Jun 42	Detachment
	Stradishall, Suffolk	27 May 42 - 3 Jun 42	Detachment
	Stratford-upon-Avon, Warwickshire	16 Nov 42 - 15 Mar 44	Satellite
	Valley, Anglesey	Dec 42 - Dec 42	Detachment
26 OTU	Wing, Buckinghamshire	15 Jun 45 - 4 Mar 46	Headquarters
	Little Horwood, Buckinghamshire	15 Jun 45 - 30 Nov 45	Satellite
27 OTU	Lichfield, Staffordshire	11 May 42 - 1 Sep 43	Headquarters
	Tatenhill, Staffordshire	11 May 42 - Oct 42	Satellite
	Wing, Buckinghamshire	27 May 42 - 3 Jun 42	Detachment
	Church Broughton, Derbyshire	Aug 42 - 1 Sep 43	Satellite
		1 Sep 43	Transferred 93 Group
		14 Feb 45	Returned 91 Group
	Lichfield, Staffordshire	14 Feb 45 - 22 Jun 45	Headquarters
	Church Broughton, Derbyshire	14 Feb 45 - 8 May 45	Satellite
30 OTU	Gamston, Nottinghamshire	2 Feb 45 - 12 Jun 45	Headquarters

92 Group	Winslow Hall, Buckinghamshire	11 May 42 - 15 Jul 45	Headquarters
11 OTU	Westcott, Buckinghamshire	28 Sep 42 - 15 Jun 45	Headquarters
	Oakley, Buckinghamshire	28 Sep 42 - 15 Jun 45	Satellite
		15 Jun 45	Returned 91 Group
12 OTU	Chipping Warden, Oxfordshire	15 Nov 42 - 22 Jun 45	Headquarters
	Turweston, Buckinghamshire	28 Nov 42 - 1 May 43	Satellite
	Edgehill, Warwickshire	12 Apr 43 - 7 Jun 45	B & C Flights
13 OTU	Bicester, Oxfordshire	11 May 42 - 1 Jun 43	Headquarters
	Hinton-in-the-Hedges, Northamptonshire	11 May 42 - 23 Aug 42	Reserve Landing Ground
	Finmere, Buckinghamshire	11 May 42 - 1 Jun 43	Reserve Landing Ground
	Turweston, Buckinghamshire	1 Oct 42 - 28 Nov 42	Reserve Landing Ground
14 OTU	Cottesmore, Rutland	11 May 42 - 1 Aug 43	Headquarters
	Saltby, Leicestershire	11 May 42 - 10 Sep 43	Satellite
	Husbands Bosworth, Leicestershire	28 Jul 43 - 15 Jun 44	Satellite
	Market Harborough, Leicestershire	1 Aug 43 - 24 Jun 45	Satellite
15 OTU	Harwell, Berkshire	11 May 42 - 15 Mar 44	Headquarters
	Hampstead Norris, Berkshire	11 May 42 - 15 Mar 44	Satellite
16 OTU	Barford St. John, Oxfordshire	11 May 42 - 15 Dec 42	Headquarters
	Brackley, Northamptonshire	11 May 42 - 18 Jul 42	Satellite
	Croughton, Northamptonshire	11 May 42 - 18 Jul 42	Satellite
	Hinton-in-the-Hedges, Northamptonshire	18 Jul 42 - 2 Apr 43	Satellite
	Upper Heyford, Oxfordshire	15 Dec 42 - 1 Jan 45	Headquarters
	Barford St. John, Oxfordshire	15 Dec 42 - 1 Jan 45	Satellite
	Upper Heyford, Oxfordshire	1 Jan 45 - 1 Mar 46	Headquarters
	Barford St. John, Oxfordshire	1 Jan 45 - 26 Nov 45	Satellite
	Cottesmore, Rutland	1 Mar 46 - 15 Mar 47	Headquarters
17 OTU	Upwood, Huntingdonshire	11 May 42 - 17 Apr 43	Headquarters

92 Group Continued

17 OTU	Warboys, Huntingdonshire	11 May 42 -	5 Aug 42	Satellite
	Steeple Morden, Cambridgeshire	14 Jan 43 -	4 May 43	Satellite
	Silverstone, Northamptonshire	17 Apr 43 -	15 Jun 45	Headquarters
	Turweston, Buckinghamshire	3 Jul 43 -	15 Jun 45	Satellite
			15 Jun 45	Transferred 91 Group
24 OTU	Honeybourne, Worcestershire	11 May 42 -	15 Nov 42	Headquarters
	Long Marston, Gloucestershire	27 May 42 -	15 Nov 42	Satellite
			15 Nov 42	Transferred 93 Group
	Honeybourne, Worcestershire	14 Feb 45 -	27 Jul 45	Headquarters
	Long Marston, Gloucestershire	14 Feb 45 -	24 Jul 45	Satellite
25 OTU	Finningley, Yorkshire	11 May 42 -	1 Feb 43	Headquarters
	Bircotes, Nottinghamshire	11 May 42 -	1 Feb 43	Satellite
26 OTU	Wing, Buckinghamshire	11 May 42 -	15 Jun 45	Headquarters
	Cheddington, Buckinghamshire	11 May 42 -	3 Sep 42	Satellite
	Little Horwood, Buckinghamshire	3 Sep 42 -	26 Aug 44	Satellite
	Little Horwood, Buckinghamshire	16 Oct 44 -	15 Jun 45	Satellite
			15 Jun 45	Transferred 91 Group
28 OTU	Wymeswold, Leicestershire	16 May 42 -	15 Jun 42	Headquarters
			15 Jun 42	Transferred 93 Group
29 OTU	North Luffenham, Rutland	11 May 42 -	24 May 43	Headquarters
	Woolfox Lodge, Rutland	1 Aug 42 -	3 Jun 43	Satellite
	Bruntingthorpe, Leicestershire	6 Nov 42 -	30 Jan 43	Satellite
	Bruntingthorpe, Leicestershire	24 May 43 -	27 May 43	Headquarters
	Bitteswell, Leicestershire	1 Jun 43 -	1 Nov 44	Satellite
84 OTU	Desborough, Northamptonshire	1 Sep 43 -	14 Jun 45	Headquarters
	Harrington, Northamptonshire	6 Nov 43 -	26 Mar 44	Satellite
85 OTU	Husbands Bosworth, Leicestershire	15 Jun 44 -	14 Jun 45	Headquarters
93 Group	Lichfield, Staffordshire	15 Jun 42 -	7 Jul 42	Headquarters
	Egginton Hall, Derbyshire	7 Jul 42 -	14 Feb 45	Headquarters
12 OTU	Chipping Warden, Oxfordshire	15 Jun 42 -	15 Nov 42	Headquarters
	Gaydon, Warwickshire	15 Jun 42 -	6 Sep 42	Satellite
			15 Nov 42	Transferred 92 Group
18 OTU	Bramcote, Warwickshire	1 Sep 42 -	27 Mar 43	Headquarters
	Bitteswell, Leicestershire	1 Sep 42 -	7 Feb 43	Satellite
	Finningley, Yorkshire	25 Jan 43 -	27 Mar 43	Satellite
	Nuneaton, Warwickshire	7 Feb 43 -	27 Mar 43	Satellite
	Finningley, Yorkshire	27 Mar 43 -	20 Oct 44	Headquarters
	Bircotes, Nottinghamshire	27 Mar 43 -	20 Oct 44	Satellite
	Doncaster, Yorkshire	Jun 43 -	Jun 43	Satellite
	Worksop, Nottinghamshire	1 Sep 43 -	20 Oct 44	Satellite
			20 Oct 44	Returned 91 Group
24 OTU	Honeybourne, Worcestershire	15 Nov 42 -	14 Feb 45	Headquarters
	Long Marston, Gloucestershire	15 Nov 42 -	14 Feb 45	Satellite
			14 Feb 45	Returned 92 Group
27 OTU	Lichfield, Staffordshire	1 Sep 43 -	14 Feb 45	Headquarters
	Church Broughton, Derbyshire	1 Sep 43 -	14 Feb 45	Satellite
			14 Feb 45	Returned 91 Group
28 OTU	Wymeswold, Leicestershire	15 Jun 42 -	6 Jun 43	Headquarters
	Castle Donington, Leicestershire	1 Jan 43 -	15 Oct 44	Satellite
	Ossington, Nottinghamshire	6 Jun 43 -	18 Jun 43	Headquarters
	Wymeswold, Leicestershire	18 Jun 43 -	15 Oct 44	Headquarters
	Bircotes, Nottinghamshire	20 Jun 44 -	24 Jul 44	Detachment
30 OTU	Hixon, Staffordshire	28 Jun 42 -	2 Feb 45	Headquarters
	Seighford, Staffordshire	16 Sep 42 -	28 Oct 44	Satellite
			2 Feb 45	Transferred 91 Group
81 OTU	Ashbourne, Derbyshire	10 Jul 42 -	1 Sep 42	Headquarters
	Tilstock (Whitchurch Heath) Shropshire	1 Sep 42 -	1 Jan 44	Headquarters
	Sleap, Shropshire	26 Jan 43 -	1 Jan 44	Satellite

93 Group Continued

82 OTU	Ossington, Nottinghamshire	1 Jun 43 - 9 Jan 45 Headquarters
	Gamston, Nottinghamshire	1 Jun 43 - 28 Aug 43 Satellite
	Bircotes, Nottinghamshire	28 Aug 43 - 5 Oct 43 Satellite
	Gamston, Nottinghamshire	5 Oct 43 - 15 Jun 44 Satellite
83 OTU	Childs Ercall (Peplow) Shropshire	1 Aug 43 - 28 Oct 44 Headquarters
86 OTU	Gamston, Nottinghamshire	15 Jun 44 - 15 Oct 44 Headquarters

Supplementary notes in respect of formation and disbandment of Operational Training Units.

Unit	Formed	Disbanded	Remarks
10 OTU	8 Apr 40 at Abingdon from 4 Group Pool comprising of 97 Squadron and 166 Squadron	10 Sep 46	Principal equipment Whitley, Wellington from Jun 44 Codes: EL JL RK UY ZG
11 OTU	8 Apr 40 at Bassingbourn from 215 Squadron and Station Headquarters Bassingbourn	18 Sep 45	Principal equipment Wellington Codes: KJ OP TX
12 OTU	8 Apr 40 at Benson from 1 Group Pool and 52 Squadron, 63 Squadron and C Flight 12 Squadron	22 Jun 45	Principal equipment Battle, Wellington from Dec 40 Codes: FQ JP ML
13 OTU	8 Apr 40 at Bicester from 2 Group Pool comprising of 104 Squadron and 108 Squadron		Principal equipment Blenheim; transferred 1 Jun 43 to 70 Group Codes: AT EV FV KQ OY SL UR WO XD XJ
14 OTU	8 Apr 40 at Cottesmore from 185 Squadron	24 Jun 45	Principal equipment Hampden, Wellington from Sep 42 Codes: AM GL VB
15 OTU	8 Apr 40 at Harwell from 3 Group Pool comprising of 75 Squadron and 148 Squadron	15 Mar 44	Principal equipment Wellington Codes: EQ FH KK
16 OTU	8 Apr 40 at Upper Heyford from 5 Group Pool comprising of 7 Squadron and 76 Squadron	1 Jan 45	Principal equipment Hampden, Wellington from Apr 42
	1 Jan 45 at Upper Heyford from 1655 Mosquito Training Unit	15 Mar 47	Principal equipment Mosquito Codes: GA JS XG
17 OTU	8 Apr 40 at Upwood from 35 Squadron and 90 Squadron	15 Mar 47	Principal equipment Blenheim, Wellington from Apr 43 Codes: AY JG WJ
18 OTU	15 Jun 40 at Hucknall	30 Jan 45	Principal equipment Battle, Wellington from Nov 40 Codes: EN VQ XW
19 OTU	27 May 40 at Kinloss	26 Jun 45	Principal equipment Whitley, Wellington from Aug 44 Codes: UO XF ZV
20 OTU	27 May 40 at Lossiemouth	17 Jul 45	Principal equipment Wellington Codes: AI HJ JM MK XL YR ZT
21 OTU	21 Jan 41 at Moreton-in-Marsh	15 Mar 47	Principal equipment Wellington Codes: ED SJ UH
22 OTU	14 Apr 41 at Wellesbourne Mountford	24 Jul 45	Principal equipment Wellington Codes: DD LT OX XN
23 OTU	1 Apr 41 at Pershore	15 Mar 44	Principal equipment Wellington Codes: BY FZ WE

Unit	Formed	Disbanded	Remarks
24 OTU	15 Mar 42 at Honeybourne	24 Jul 45	Principal equipment Whitley, Wellington from Apr 44 Codes: FB TY UF
25 OTU	1 Mar 41 at Finningley	1 Feb 43	Principal equipment Hampden, Wellington Codes: PP ZP
26 OTU	15 Jan 42 at Wing	4 Mar 46	Principal equipment Wellington Codes: EU PB WG
27 OTU	23 Apr 41 at Lichfield	22 Jun 45	Principal equipment Wellington Codes: BB UJ YL
28 OTU	16 May 42 at Wymeswold	15 Oct 44	Principal equipment Wellington Codes: LB QN WY
29 OTU	21 Apr 42 at North Luffenham	27 May 45	Principal equipment Wellington Codes: NT TF
30 OTU	28 Jun 42 at Hixon	12 Jun 45	Principal equipment Wellington Codes: BT KD TN
81 OTU	10 Jul 42 at Ashbourne		Principal equipment Whitley: transferred 1 Jan 44 to 38 Group Codes: EZ JB KG
82 OTU	1 Jun 43 at Ossington	9 Jan 45	Principal equipment Wellington Codes: BZ KA TD 9C
83 OTU	1 Aug 43 at Childs Ercall	28 Oct 44	Principal equipment Wellington Codes: FI GZ MZ
84 OTU	1 Sep 43 at Desborough	14 Jun 45	Principal equipment Wellington Codes: CO CZ IF
85 OTU	15 Jun 44 at Husbands Bosworth	14 Jun 45	Principal equipment Wellington Codes: 9P 2X
86 OTU	15 Jun 44 at Gamston	15 Oct 44	Principal equipment Wellington Codes: unconfirmed but possibly BZ

Unit	Additional remarks
10 OTU	2 Dec 44 absorbed Polish Flight from 18 OTU, this element disbanding on 4 Jun 45
13 OTU	Briefly absorbed 1655 Mosquito Conversion Unit, prior to transfer to 70 Group but this element was reclaimed by Bomber Command on 1 Jun 43
18 OTU	Initially formed to train Polish Air Force crews for Battle squadrons; continued as the principal Polish Air Force training unit until transfer of the Polish Flight to 10 OTU on 2 Dec 44
81 OTU	On transfer to 38 Group, continued to use the Whitley as a glider tug trainer
82 OTU	Upon disbandment, personnel posted to form 23 Heavy Glider Conversion Unit
86 OTU	Upon disbandment, personnel posted to assist in the formation of Heavy Glider Conversion Units

Note.   The structure of the foregoing appendix has been taken from Royal Air Force Flying Training and Support Units, compiled by Ray Sturtivant, John Hamlin and James J Halley, published by Air-Britain (Historians). To these three eminent historians, I am exceedingly grateful.

Appendix 2 (Part 1)

Operational Training Unit Losses April 1940 to March 1947

Unit	Type	Op	Trg	Ea	Grnd	Misc	Unkn	Total
10 OTU	Hurricane IIC		2					2
	Magister I		1					1
	Martinet I		1			1		2
	Anson I		4			1		5
	Wellington X		10					10
	Whitley II		1					1
	Whitley III		3	1		1		5
	Whitley V	63	77		2	7	1	150
11 OTU	Martinet I		1					1
	Anson I		2					2
	Wellington I		13	1			1	15
	Wellington IA	1	6	2			1	10
	Wellington IC	14	64	4	3	2		87
	Wellington X	1	26		1	2		30
12 OTU	Battle I		28			1		29
	Lysander III		1					1
	Martinet I		2					2
	Master II		1					1
	Anson I		3					3
	Wellington I						1	1
	Wellington IA		1					1
	Wellington IC	7	15	1		1	1	25
	Wellington III	5	36		2	2		45
	Wellington X	2	20		1		1	24
13 OTU	Battle I		1					1
	Tutor		1					1
	Albemarle				1			1
	Anson I		1				2	3
	Blenheim I		18			1	1	20
	Blenheim IV		61		2	3	1	67
14 OTU	Hurricane IIC				1			1
	Anson I		9		1	1		11
	Hampden I	11	70	1	2	1		85
	Hereford I		3			2		5
	Oxford I		2			2		4
	Oxford II		1					1
	Wellington IC		36		2			38
	Wellington II		1					1
	Wellington X		17			2		19
15 OTU	Defiant I		1					1
	Martinet I		1					1
	Anson I		3					3
	Wellington I		18	3	1		3	25
	Wellington IA		2	2			1	5
	Wellington IC	9	56		1	3	2	71
	Wellington III		3					3
	Wellington X		3			1		4
16 OTU	Magister I					1		1
	Martinet I					1		1
	Master II		1					1
	Anson I		5	1		1		7
	Hampden I		78	1	1	2		82
	Hereford I		4					4
	Mosquito III		12					12
	Mosquito XVI		9			1		10
	Mosquito XX		8			2		10
	Mosquito B.25		5					5

Unit	Type	Op	Trg	Ea	Grnd	Misc	Unkn	Total
16 OTU	Wellington IC	12	3				1	16
	Wellington III	3	29		2	1		35
	Wellington X	2	5			1		8
17 OTU	Hurricane IIC		1			1		2
	Lysander TT						1	1
	Magister I		1					1
	Anson I		3					3
	Blenheim I		13	1	1	1	1	17
	Blenheim IV		79		2	1	1	83
	Wellington III		9					9
	Wellington X		23				1	24
18 OTU	Battle		1					1
	Magister I			1				1
	Martinet I		1					1
	Anson I		3					3
	Wellington I		2	1				3
	Wellington IA		2					2
	Wellington IC	4	21	1	1		2	29
	Wellington III		18		1			19
	Wellington IV		2	1				3
	Wellington X	2	16			2		20
19 OTU	Lysander III		1					1
	Magister I					1		1
	Anson I		8					8
	Wellington X		7					7
	Whitley III		1					1
	Whitley IV		14				1	15
	Whitley V	1	89		2	1		93
20 OTU	Hurricane IIC		1					1
	Magister I		1					1
	Anson I		8					8
	Wellington I		4					4
	Wellington IA		10		1		2	13
	Wellington IC	3	61		2	1		67
	Wellington III		13		1	1	1	16
	Wellington X		23		1			24
21 OTU	Hurricane IIC		2					2
	Martinet I		2					2
	Anson I		5	1	1		1	8
	Wellington IC	8	66	1	2	4		81
	Wellington III	1	3		1			5
	Wellington X	2	16		1			19
22 OTU	Martinet I		1					1
	Anson I			1	1			2
	Wellington I				1			1
	Wellington IC	14	32		2	1	1	50
	Wellington III	2	36		1			39
	Wellington X		22			2		24
	Wellington XIV				1			1
23 OTU	Martinet I		1					1
	Wellington IC	7	17		2	2		28
	Wellington III	3	31		1	3	1	39
	Wellington X		7					7
24 OTU	Anson I		3					3
	Wellington III		2					2
	Wellington X		16					16
	Whitley V	10	41		3	2		56
25 OTU	Anson I		5					5
	Hampden I		18					18
	Manchester I		2					2
	Wellington IC	6	22	1			1	30
	Wellington III	4	7					11
26 OTU	Defiant I					1		1
	Hurricane IIC		1					1
	Martinet I				1			1
	Wellington IC	11	18		1			30
	Wellington III		16		1			17
	Wellington X	1	27		1	2		31

Unit	Type	Op	Trg	Ea	Grnd	Misc	Unkn	Total
27 OTU	Martinet I		1					1
	Anson I		1			1		2
	Wellington IA		2					2
	Wellington IC	8	15	1	2		2	28
	Wellington III	3	29			2		34
	Wellington X	1	22					23
28 OTU	Hurricane IIC					1		1
	Moth Minor						1	1
	Wellington IC	7	21		5	1	1	35
	Wellington III		1					1
	Wellington X	1	9					10
29 OTU	Hurricane IIC		1					1
	Lysander TT		1					1
	Martinet I		1					1
	Tiger Moth					1		1
	Wellington IC	1	2					3
	Wellington III	3	30					33
	Wellington X	1	17		2			20
30 OTU	Hurricane IIC		2					2
	Lysander II				1			1
	Wellington IC		2					2
	Wellington III	5	22		1	1		29
	Wellington X	5	22		1	1		29
81 OTU	Oxford II					1		1
	Whitley V	1	20					21
82 OTU	Hurricane IIC					1		1
	Martinet I		2					2
	Wellington III	1	6		1	1		9
	Wellington X	5	17		2			24
83 OTU	Hurricane IIC		1					1
	Oxford II					1		1
	Wellington III	1						1
	Wellington X	2	8				1	11
84 OTU	Hurricane IIC		1					1
	Martinet I		1					1
	Wellington III		1					1
	Wellington X	1	11					12
85 OTU	Wellington X		5					5
86 OTU	Wellington X		2					2
	Total	255	1916	27	71	82	36	2387

Appendix 2 (Part 2)

Supplementary data in respect of operational losses from the Operational Training Units.

Unit	Type	Bombing	AS Patrol	ASR	Nickel	Sweep	Total
10 OTU	Whitley V	9	53		1		63
11 OTU	Wellington IA				1		1
	Wellington IC	12			2		14
	Wellington X				1		1
12 OTU	Wellington IC	7					7
	Wellington III	2			2	1	5
	Wellington X				1	1	2
14 OTU	Hampden I	11					11
15 OTU	Wellington IC	7			2		9
16 OTU	Wellington IC	12					12
	Wellington III	1		1	1		3
	Wellington X				1	1	2
18 OTU	Wellington IC	4					4
	Wellington X				2		2
19 OTU	Whitley V	1					1
20 OTU	Wellington IC	3					3
21 OTU	Wellington IC	5			3		8
	Wellington III					1	1
	Wellington X					2	2
22 OTU	Wellington IC	14					14
	Wellington III	1			1		2
23 OTU	Wellington IC	6			1		7
	Wellington III	3					3
24 OTU	Whitley V	5			5		10
25 OTU	Wellington IC	6					6
	Wellington III	3			1		4
26 OTU	Wellington IC	11					11
	Wellington X	1					1
27 OTU	Wellington IC	6			2		8
	Wellington III				2	1	3
	Wellington X				1		1
28 OTU	Wellington IC			1	6		7
	Wellington X				1		1
29 OTU	Wellington IC	1					1
	Wellington III	1			2		3
	Wellington X				1		1
30 OTU	Wellington III				5		5
	Wellington X				3	2	5
81 OTU	Whitley V				1		1
82 OTU	Wellington III				1		1
	Wellington X				5		5
83 OTU	Wellington III				1		1
	Wellington X					2	2
84 OTU	Wellington X				1		1
	Total	132	53	2	57	11	255

Appendix 2 (Part 3)

Supplementary data in respect of losses, by type, from the Operational Training Units.

Type (Single-engined)	Op	Trg	Ea	Grnd	Misc	Unkn	Total
Battle I		30			1		31
Defiant I		1			1		2
Hurricane IIC		12		1	3		16
Lysander TT		1				1	2
Lysander II				1			1
Lysander III		2					2
Magister I		3	1		2		6
Martinet I		15		1	2		18
Master II		2					2
Moth Minor						1	1
Tiger Moth					1		1
Tutor		1					1
Total		67	1	3	10	2	83

Type (Twin-engined)	Op	Trg	Ea	Grnd	Misc	Unkn	Total
Albemarle				1			1
Anson I		63	3	3	4	3	76
Blenheim I		31	1	1	2	2	37
Blenheim IV		140		4	4	2	150
Hampden I	11	166	2	3	3		185
Hereford I		7			2		9
Manchester I		2					2
Mosquito III		12					12
Mosquito XVI		9			1		10
Mosquito XX		8			2		10
Mosquito B.25		5					5
Oxford I		2			2		4
Oxford II		1			2		3
Wellington I		37	5	2		5	49
Wellington IA	1	23	4	1		4	33
Wellington IC	111	451	9	23	15	11	620
Wellington II		1					1
Wellington III	31	292		12	11	2	348
Wellington IV		2	1				3
Wellington X	26	351		10	13	3	403
Wellington XIV				1			1
Whitley II		1					1
Whitley III		4	1		1		6
Whitley IV		14				1	15
Whitley V	75	227		7	10	1	320
Total	255	1849	26	68	72	34	2304

A full revision of the losses that feature in this series will be presented in Volume 8.

Appendix 3

Operational Training Unit Evaders April 1940 to May 1945

Retained at the Public Record Office Kew are a series of papers officially referred to as the Escape Reports. Grouped under the class reference, WO208, these fascinating reports describe in some detail the evasion of Royal Air Force, Commonwealth and Allied airmen, principally from those areas of Europe where the Wehrmacht dominated, while a few pertain to aircrew who parachuted into Germany itself, and yet avoided capture.

Some made their way to freedom practically unaided, but the majority were helped in one way or the other by those men and women, who at tremendous risk, were willing to give aid where ever possible. Some belonged to the various agencies, established soon after the fall of France in 1940, but it should be emphasised that most were ordinary citizens who performed a quite extraordinary task and in many cases paid with their lives when the enemy caught up with their activities.

Listed below are the references concerning the years covered by this volume, plus additional material considered helpful.

Royal Air Force

Name	Date	Unit	Serial	Target/Duty	Reference
F/L R C Thorn	9-10 May 1944	30 OTU	BJ618	Nickel	3321 (-)2153
Sgt J B R Black	31- 1 Aug 1942	24 OTU	BD347	Düsseldorf	3310 (-)855
F/S B Evans DFM	30-31 May 1942	15 OTU	R1791	Köln	3310 (-)809
Sgt B C Reeves	11-12 Jun 1943	30 OTU	BK559	Nickel	3315 (-)1506
Sgt P Renwick	9-10 May 1944	30 OTU	BJ618	Nickel	3322 (-)2217
Sgt W H Stevenson	9-10 May 1944	30 OTU	BJ618	Nickel	3321 (-)2191
Sgt W Todd	23-24 Sep 1943	27 OTU	X3966	Nickel	3317 (-)1634
Sgt A J Whicher	31- 1 Aug 1942	24 OTU	BD347	Düsseldorf	3310 (-)835

Royal Australian Air Force

P/O G Silva	31- 1 Aug 1942	24 OTU	BD347	Düsseldorf	3310 (-)834
Sgt R J Collins	30-31 May 1942	15 OTU	W5586	Köln	3309 (-)792
F/S G L Dowling	23-24 Sep 1943	27 OTU	X3966	Nickel	3316 (-)1548

Royal Canadian Air Force

F/L J L Kennedy	3- 4 Nov 1943	24 OTU	AD675	Nickel	3317 (-)1658
Sgt H E De Mone	1- 2 Jun 1942	16 OTU	DV763	Essen	3309 (-)778
WO2 G A Gauley	3- 4 Nov 1943	24 OTU	AD675	Nickel	3318 (-)1708
Sgt A E Spencer	3- 4 Nov 1943	24 OTU	AD675	Nickel	3320 (-)2009
Sgt J H Upton	3- 4 Nov 1943	24 OTU	AD675	Nickel	3319 (-)1898

Note. The three 24 Operational Training Unit evaders, in the wake of the Düsseldorf raid on 31 July - 1 August 1942, were assisted by Comete. Following his return to the United Kingdom, F/S B Evans of 15 Operational Training United was recommended for a Mentioned in Despatches.

Appendix 4

Operational Training Unit Prisoners April 1940 to May 1945

Information concerning airmen who were taken prisoner of war is principally confined to a single document, namely AIR20 2336, which is held at the Public Record Office Kew.

Edited in March 1945, the names of most of the airmen taken into captivity during the period covered by this volume are listed. Similar to the preceding appendix, data considered useful has been added to the tables. The names of the camps, reported here by the system of codes used in AIR20 2336, appear at the end of the appendix.

Royal Air Force

Name	Date	Unit	Serial	Target/Duty	Camp	Number
F/L A G Allen	31- 1 Aug 1942	23 OTU	X9917	Düsseldorf	M&MN	25667
F/O F O Bullen	16-17 Sep 1942	12 OTU	BJ662	Essen	L3	6458
F/O D H Cochran	8- 9 Oct 1942	10 OTU	AD671	AS Patrol	L3	727
F/O E J Cooper	25-26 Jun 1942	12 OTU	DV951	Bremen	L3	465
F/L M E S Dickenson	13-14 Sep 1942	11 OTU	X3169	Bremen	L1	704
F/O J L Dowdeswell	31- 1 Aug 1942	23 OTU	X9917	Düsseldorf	L3	595
F/O G T Freeman	22-23 Jun 1943	30 OTU	HE527	Nickel	L3	1652
P/O C J Frith	31- 1 Aug 1942	25 OTU	DV829	Düsseldorf	L3	705
F/L J Hamilton	31- 1 Aug 1942	25 OTU	DV439	Düsseldorf	L3	597
F/L J B Harper	30-31 May 1942	15 OTU	W5586	Köln	L3	374
F/L C G Hughes	30-31 May 1942	25 OTU	L7802	Köln	L3	375
F/L G T Hunt	13-14 Sep 1942	11 OTU	X9744	Bremen	L3	687
F/L R F Jessop	1- 2 Jun 1942	25 OTU	DV434	Essen	L3	549
F/L T J J Lee	14 Jun 1943	10 OTU	BD220	AS Patrol	L3	1600
F/L F Lowe	28-29 Jul 1942	16 OTU	R1450	Hamburg	L3	600
F/L W L Merryfield	16-17 Sep 1942	10 OTU	P4931	Essen	L3	714
S/L R A Nicholson	13-14 Sep 1942	11 OTU	X9744	Bremen	L3	688
F/L T E P Ramsay	30-31 May 1942	14 OTU	P2116	Köln	L3	382
F/L E J Seaman	10-11 Sep 1942	16 OTU	R1297	Düsseldorf	L3	686
F/L M T C Shields	31- 1 Jul 1942	23 OTU	X9917	Düsseldorf	L3	25160
F/L A W Thompson	31- 1 Jul 1942	24 OTU	Z9512	Düsseldorf	L3	
F/L R Van Toen	25-26 Jun 1942	10 OTU	BD201	Bremen	L3	39675
F/L G W Walenn	10-11 Sep 1941	25 OTU	N2805	Training	L3	3776
Twice MiD						
F/L P P L E Welch	31- 1 Aug 1942	25 OTU	DV439	Düsseldorf	O4C	610
F/S H J D G Adams	11-12 Jun 1943	30 OTU	BK559	Nickel	357	53
W/O J Akehurst	13-14 Sep 1942	11 OTU	X3169	Bremen	344	27152
F/S R Baker	30-31 May 1942	25 OTU	L7802	Köln	L3	391
Sgt D W Bartholomew	11-12 Jun 1943	30 OTU	BK559	Nickel		
W/O P Bell	25-26 Jun 1942	19 OTU	Z6730	Bremen	L3	308
W/O B Bing	10-11 Sep 1942	16 OTU	T2606	Düsseldorf	344	26995
W/O R A Booth	1- 2 Jun 1942	25 OTU	DV434	Essen	L3	485
W/O E E Brocklehurst	31- 1 Aug 1942	23 OTU	X9917	Düsseldorf	344	25162
W/O L L Brown	25-26 Jun 1942	19 OTU	Z6730	Bremen	L3	310
W/O F A A Browne	10-11 Sep 1942	16 OTU	R1297	Düsseldorf	344	27022
W/O J H Bulford	30-31 May 1942	11 OTU	R1065	Köln	L3	398
W/O H J Camden	25-26 Jun 1942	12 OTU	DV951	Bremen	L3	313
W/O D W Caswell	30-31 May 1942	26 OTU	DV709	Köln	L3	12677
W/O R Charlesworth	6- 7 Aug 1941	11 OTU	Z8807	Nickel	4B	66
F/S L W Chatterton	25-26 Jun 1942	12 OTU	DV951	Bremen	344	25106
W/O R S Davey	13-14 Sep 1942	11 OTU	X3169	Bremen	344	27009
Sgt J Dawson	10-11 Jun 1943	24 OTU	BD442	Nickel	4B	222472
W/O A S Day	30-31 May 1942	11 OTU	R1065	Köln	L6	404
W/O F Dean	10-11 Sep 1942	16 OTU	T2606	Düsseldorf	344	27159
W/O L H Dean	8- 9 Oct 1942	10 OTU	AD671	AS Patrol	344	27193
Sgt J H Dew	13-14 Sep 1942	22 OTU	HD991	Bremen	344	27131
W/O P A Edwards	10-11 Sep 1941	25 OTU	N2805	Training	L6	9655
Sgt D Dunkley	30-31 May 1942	11 OTU	R1065	Köln		

Name	Date	Unit	Serial	Target/Duty	Camp	Number
F/S K G D´arcy	21 Sep 1942	10 OTU	Z6795	AS Patrol		
W/O C N Ellis	8- 9 Oct 1942	10 OTU	AD671	AS Patrol	344	27187
F/S F J R Eminson	13-14 Sep 1942	10 OTU	BD275	Bremen	L6	813
F/S P N Faber	10-11 Sep 1942	16 OTU	R1297	Düsseldorf	344	26991
W/O J M Forster	1- 2 Jun 1942	16 OTU	DV763	Essen	L6	500
F/S R J Franklin	22-23 Jun 1943	30 OTU	HE527	Nickel	357	135
W/O F D Garrett	8- 9 Oct 1942	10 OTU	AD671	AS Patrol	344	27216
F/S W Gilroy	22-23 Jun 1943	30 OTU	HE527	Nickel	357	145
F/S G T Graves	14 Jun 1943	10 OTU	BD220	AS Patrol	L3	150
F/S F G Greensides	30-31 May 1942	25 OTU	L7802	Köln	L3	411
W/O J F Grier	21 Sep 1942	10 OTU	Z6795	AS Patrol	344	27154
F/S C E Gunning	4- 5 Mar 1943	28 OTU	Z1109	Nickel	344	27642
W/O R A Hale	25-26 Jun 1942	19 OTU	Z6730	Bremen		
W/O G McB Harris	25-26 Jun 1942	10 OTU	BD201	Bremen	344	24990
Sgt H M Harris	9-10 May 1944	30 OTU	BJ618	Nickel	L3	4913
W/O R J Harvey	10-11 Sep 1942	16 OTU	DV775	Düsseldorf	344	27110
W/O J E Hatton	30-31 May 1942	15 OTU	W5586	Köln	L3	39660
W/O L Hedley	10-11 Sep 1942	26 OTU	DV703	Düsseldorf	344	27100
W/O W Henderson	25-26 Jun 1942	19 OTU	Z6730	Bremen	L6	323
W/O R Higham	30-31 May 1942	11 OTU	R1065	Köln	L3	414
W/O R Hill	30-31 May 1942	15 OTU	W5586	Köln	L3	415
W/O F G Hillyer	30-31 May 1942	26 OTU	DV740	Köln	L6	508
W/O F R Hindle	30-31 May 1942	15 OTU	W5586	Köln	L3	417
W/O C H Homer	25-26 Jun 1942	12 OTU	DV951	Bremen	344	25107
W/O F T Hooper	16-17 Sep 1942	11 OTU	DV612	Essen	344	27103
W/O T Humphery	6- 7 Aug 1941	11 OTU	Z8807	Nickel	4B	61
W/O C L Humphrys	14-15 Oct 1941	15 OTU	R1275	Nickel	357	24365
W/O N F James	16-17 Sep 1942	11 OTU	DV612	Essen	M&MN	27096
Sgt O M Jameson	13-14 Sep 1942	11 OTU	X9744	Bremen	344	27016
W/O H C M Jarvis	13-14 Sep 1942	11 OTU	X3169	Bremen	344	27010
W/O J T Johnston	13 Oct 1942	10 OTU	BD290	AS Patrol	L6	831
F/S R J A Johnstone	1- 2 Jun 1942	25 OTU	DV434	Essen	L3	329
W/O S Jolly	13-14 Sep 1942	10 OTU	BD275	Essen	344	27044
W/O I G Keiller	21 Sep 1942	10 OTU	Z6795	AS Patrol	344	27181
W/O E Lockwood	10-11 Sep 1942	16 OTU	R1297	Düsseldorf	344	26993
W/O J Longden	16-17 Sep 1942	11 OTU	DV612	Essen	344	27129
F/S G C Loveday	4- 5 Mar 1943	28 OTU	Z1109	Nickel	344	27723
W/O G C Maddams	31- 1 Jul 1942	23 OTU	X9917	Düsseldorf	344	25161
F/S P Martin	10-11 Sep 1942	16 OTU	T2606	Düsseldorf	344	27056
W/O K P E Monk	30-31 May 1942	22 OTU	R1714	Köln	L3	515
W/O J N Morgan	26-27 Jun 1943	21 OTU	X9667	Enemy Action	L4	42700
W/O J G Moriarty	25-26 Jun 1942	10 OTU	BD201	Bremen	L3	340
W/O R V C Oliver	30-31 May 1942	25 OTU	L7802	Köln	L3	519
W/O N R Parson	25-26 Jun 1942	10 OTU	BD201	Bremen	L3	347
W/O D J Paul DFM	30-31 May 1942	15 OTU	R1791	Köln	L4	39731
F/S J G Perfect	11-12 Jun 1943	30 OTU	BK559	Nickel	357	41
W/O W A Platt	10-11 Sep 1941	25 OTU	N2805	Training	357	9616
W/O S J Pryor	6- 7 Aug 1941	11 OTU	Z8807	Nickel	4B	59
W/O L R Read	30-31 May 1942	25 OTU	L7802	Köln	L1	440
W/O R O Riddle	13-14 Sep 1942	11 OTU	X9744	Bremen	344	27024
W/O D Riley	31- 1 Jul 1942	21 OTU	X9983	Düsseldorf	344	25134
F/S R H Roskell	4- 5 Mar 1943	28 OTU	Z1109	Nickel	344	27660
Sgt J Russell	9-10 May 1944	30 OTU	BJ618	Nickel	357	3831
F/S G R Simmons	25-26 Aug 1943	22 OTU	HF628	Nickel	4B	222642
W/O L E Sparks	6- 7 Aug 1941	11 OTU	Z8807	Nickel	4B	84
W/O G B Spenceley	1- 2 Jun 1942	11 OTU	DV767	Essen	L3	360
W/O S C Stevens	10-11 Sep 1941	25 OTU	N2805	Training	L6	9656
F/S J Tweddle	13-14 Sep 1942	10 OTU	BD275	Bremen	L1	856
F/S L Waterson	10-11 Sep 1942	16 OTU	T2606	Düsseldorf	344	27011
W/O W White	28-29 Jul 1942	16 OTU	R1450	Hamburg	344	27046
W/O B C Whittle	30-31 May 1942	25 OTU	L7802	Köln	L3	453
W/O M W E Wild	13-14 Sep 1942	11 OTU	X9744	Bremen	8B	27104

Royal Australian Air Force

Name	Date	Unit	Serial	Target/Duty	Camp	Number
F/O W C Hawke	23-24 Sep 1943	27 OTU	X3966	Nickel	L3	2618
F/L T L Walker	10-11 Sep 1941	25 OTU	N2805	Training	L3	3774
W/O A J Benson DFM	14 Jun 1943	10 OTU	BD220	AS Patrol	L3	86
W/O E F Collins	31- 1 Aug 1942	14 OTU	N9062	Düsseldorf	L3	42898
W/O W S Harrison	10-11 Sep 1942	16 OTU	R1297	Düsseldorf	344	26994

Name	Date	Unit	Serial	Target/Duty	Camp	Number
W/O R C Mackenzie	6- 7 Aug 1941	11 OTU	Z8807	Nickel	4B	73
W/O C B P Nind	13-14 Sep 1942	10 OTU	BD275	Bremen	344	27028
W/O D G Oxenham	10-11 Sep 1942	16 OTU	T2606	Düsseldorf	344	26987
F/S A F Rees	16-17 Sep 1942	25 OTU	BJ969	Essen	344	27101
W/O R L Rennick	14 Jun 1943	10 OTU	BD220	AS Patrol	L3	232
W/O N F Wallace	13-14 Sep 1942	27 OTU	W5709	Bremen	344	27026
W/O D A G Watkins	1- 2 Jun 1942	21 OTU	W5618	Essen	L3	452
W/O N S Whiting	31- 1 Jul 1942	14 OTU	N9062	Düsseldorf	344	25150

Royal Canadian Air Force

Name	Date	Unit	Serial	Target/Duty	Camp	Number
F/L E W Bell	28-29 Jul 1942	22 OTU	X3201	Hamburg	L3	25111
F/O W J Clough	1- 2 Jun 1942	25 OTU	DV434	Essen	L3	546
F/L W L Kell	16-17 Sep 1942	10 OTU	P4931	Essen	L3	709
F/O S G King	25-26 Jun 1942	11 OTU	R1078	Bremen	L3	290
F/L A Kingsley	14 Jun 1943	10 OTU	BD220	AS Patrol	L3	1656
F/L P W Langford	28-29 Jul 1942	16 OTU	R1450	Hamburg	L3	710
F/O W H Mitchell	25-26 Aug 1943	22 OTU	HF628	Nickel	L3	2536
F/L W J Shaver	13-14 Sep 1942	22 OTU	HD991	Bremen	344	27135
WO2 E T Beal	1- 2 Jun 1942	16 OTU	DV763	Essen	L6	484
WO2 K C Bonter	10-11 Sep 1942	16 OTU	DV775	Düsseldorf	344	27156
WO2 R Carlson	13-14 Sep 1942	14 OTU	L4109	Bremen	344	27023
WO2 J D Carmichal	13 Oct 1942	10 OTU	BD290	AS Patrol	L4	807
WO2 E J Christian	21 Sep 1942	10 OTU	Z6795	AS Patrol		
WO2 P F B Creech	13 Oct 1942	10 OTU	BD290	AS Patrol	L4	878
WO2 M O Edwards	16-17 Sep 1942	23 OTU	X3799	Essen	344	27172
WO2 H J Elliott	1- 2 Jun 1942	12 OTU	X3203	Essen	L3	408
Sgt F W Forster	3- 4 Nov 1943	24 OTU	AD675	Nickel	4B	269844
WO2 W A Gammon	8- 9 Oct 1942	10 OTU	AD671	AS Patrol	344	27194
WO2 J A Gartlan	13-14 Sep 1942	26 OTU	X9786	Bremen	344	27143
Sgt R G Gilham	3- 4 Sep 1943	24 OTU	BD368	Nickel	4B	222699
WO2 G P Halverson	3- 4 Sep 1943	24 OTU	BD368	Nickel	4B	222707
WO2 H G P Hart	21 Sep 1942	10 OTU	Z6795	AS Patrol	344	27180
WO2 H J Lafortune	1- 2 Jun 1942	12 OTU	X3203	Essen	L3	427
WO2 N W Levasseur	25-26 Jun 1942	20 OTU	T2723	Bremen	344	24977
Sgt T O Mackay	3- 4 Sep 1943	24 OTU	BD368	Nickel	4B	222735
WO2 N E McGowan	31- 1 Jul 1942	14 OTU	P1185	Düsseldorf	344	25131
WO2 J J Makarewicz	25-26 Jun 1942	19 OTU	Z6730	Bremen	4B	337
F/S W W Massie	3- 4 Sep 1943	24 OTU	BD368	Nickel	4B	222744
WO2 J H Morrison	31- 1 Aug 1942	14 OTU	P5322	Düsseldorf	344	25121
WO2 T F Needham	13-14 Sep 1942	14 OTU	L4109	Bremen	344	27113
WO2 J A Nugent	1- 2 Jun 1942	25 OTU	DV434	Essen	L3	345
WO2 A E Parr	16-17 Sep 1942	23 OTU	X3799	Essen	344	27146
WO2 J Pierce	28-29 Jul 1942	22 OTU	X3201	Hamburg	344	25110
F/S W J Prause	3- 4 Sep 1943	24 OTU	BD368	Nickel	4B	222763
WO2 A Restno	16-17 Sep 1942	10 OTU	P4931	Essen	344	27153
WO2 W C Roach	8- 9 Oct 1942	10 OTU	AD671	AS Patrol	344	27232
F/S C C Simonson	16-17 Sep 1942	10 OTU	P4931	Essen	344	27182
WO2 G C Thomson	25-26 Jun 1942	20 OTU	T2723	Bremen	344	25645
WO2 M H Treanor	13 Oct 1942	10 OTU	BD290	AS Patrol	L4	853
WO2 S Valensky	31- 1 Aug 1942	25 OTU	DV439	Düsseldorf	344	25682
WO2 D J Veasey	31- 1 Aug 1942	25 OTU	DV439	Düsseldorf	344	25142
F/S J A Walker	6- 7 Aug 1941	11 OTU	Z8807	Nickel	4B	60
WO2 W C Warren	28-29 Jul 1942	22 OTU	X3201	Hamburg	344	25140

Royal New Zealand Air Force

Name	Date	Unit	Serial	Target/Duty	Camp	Number
F/L M N Aicken	1- 2 Jun 1942	12 OTU	X3203	Essen	L3	281
F/L N J Mundell	21 Sep 1942	10 OTU	Z6795	AS Patrol	L3	92
W/O L A Death	16-17 Sep 1942	10 OTU	P4931	Essen	344	27183
W/O G H Dow	13-14 Sep 1942	11 OTU	X3169	Bremen	M&MN	27018
W/O T A Guthrie	30-31 May 1942	11 OTU	R1065	Köln	L3	412
W/O W N Hollands	25-26 Jun 1942	11 OTU	R1078	Bremen	L4	325
W/O G B Russell	31- 1 Aug 1942	14 OTU	N9062	Düsseldorf	344	25132

Polish Air Force

Name	Date	Unit	Serial	Target/Duty	Camp	Number
F/L K Boratynski	25-26 Jun 1942	18 OTU	DV765	Bremen	L3	2154
W/O W Kowalik	25-26 Jun 1942	18 OTU	DV765	Bremen	L3	332
F/S J Laudan	25-26 Jun 1942	18 OTU	DV765	Bremen	L6	534

Name	Date	Unit	Serial	Target/Duty	Camp	Number
W/O A Pozorski	25-26 Jun 1942	18 OTU	DV765	Bremen	L3	350
Sgt C Rajpold	25-26 Jun 1942	18 OTU	DV765	Bremen		

Note. Very sadly, having survived the trauma of being shot down and captured, five of the airmen listed in this appendix died whilst in captivity.   Three, F/O Cochran, F/L Walenn and F/L Langford RCAF, were involved in the mass break out from Sagan in March 1944 and, following their recapture, were summarily executed by the Gestapo. A few months later, on 5 July 1944, F/L Thompson was shot and killed, while almost a year previous, the death of Sgt Rajpold PAF occurred (he is buried in Berlin's 1939-1945 War Cemetery).   The ashes of the first three named are interred at Poznan Old Garrison Cemetery, while F/L Thompson lies in the Commonwealth plot of Malbork Cemetery, Poland. Five others have no details appended against their entries; W/O Hale is known to have been repatriated, arriving aboard the Letitia in Liverpool on 2 February 1945, and it is assumed the rest, too, arrived home before the end of the war in May 1945. Astute readers of AIR20 2336 will come across the name of F/O G D Coldwell-Horsfall, reported missing from a Nickel sortie flown by 12 Operational Training Unit on 15-16 May 1944. His entry is erroneous (hence the omission of his name from the preceding table) for, tragically, he is presumed to have perished along with the rest of his crew and all are commemorated on the panels of the Runnymede Memorial.

Camp	Location	Camp	Location
L1	Stalag Luft Barth Vogelsang	04C	Oflag Saalhaus Colditz
L3	Stalag Luft Sagan and Beleria	4B	Stalag Mühlberg (Elbe)
L4	Stalag Luft Sagan and Beleria	8B	Stalag Teschen
L6	Stalag Luft Heydekrug	344	Stalag Lamsdorf
M&MN	Marlag ind Milag Nord Westertimke	357	Stalag Thorn

Appendix 5

Operational Training Unit Internees April 1940 to May 1945

Within the papers of WO208, referred to in my introduction to Appendix 3, are reports from airmen who were interned in the neutral countries. For those who found themselves, temporarily, guests of General Franco, their sojourn on Spanish soil invariably ended with deportation to Gibraltar from whence by sea or air (usually the latter) they were returned to the United Kingdom.

Regarding the twenty-four internees, mentioned in this volume, all belonged to 10 Operational Training Unit and their brief Iberian adventures came about during the

period of their detachment to St. Eval for anti-submarine duties over the Bay of Biscay and convoy protection work in the Western Approaches.

All, I believe, eventually returned home following internment in Spain and, I assume, all owe their lives to the keen sight of the Spanish fishermen who plucked them from the hostile waters into which they had been unceremoniously pitched.

Despite these dire circumstances, their numbers are practically double that of their colleagues who evaded capture.

Royal Air Force

Name	Date	Unit	Serial	Duty	Reference
P/O F L Perrers	11 Dec 1942	10 OTU	Z9437	AS Patrol	3312 (-)1095
P/O R Price	17 May 1943	10 OTU	BD260	AS Patrol	3313 (-)1238
Sgt D S Aird	22 Aug 1942	10 OTU	Z6645	AS Patrol	3310 (-)878
Sgt S J Barnett	17 May 1943	10 OTU	BD260	AS Patrol	3313 (-)1241
Sgt T A Berwick	22 Aug 1942	10 OTU	Z6645	AS Patrol	3310 (-)877
Sgt J Clapperton	11 Dec 1942	10 OTU	Z9437	AS Patrol	3312 (-)1046
Sgt F J Crowe	11 Dec 1942	10 OTU	Z9437	AS Patrol	3312 (-)1097
Sgt E D W Davis	22 Aug 1942	10 OTU	Z6645	AS Patrol	3310 (-)873
Sgt G F Dimmock	30 May 1943	10 OTU	Z9440	AS Patrol	3313 (-)1286
Sgt D A Jones-Ford	22 Aug 1942	10 OTU	Z6645	AS Patrol	3310 (-)874
Sgt D P P Hurst	22 Aug 1942	10 OTU	Z6645	AS Patrol	3310 (-)875
Sgt R B Newton	11 Dec 1942	10 OTU	Z9437	AS Patrol	3312 (-)1098
Sgt J H Pike	17 May 1943	10 OTU	BD260	AS Patrol	3313 (-)1242
Sgt G O Sharpe	17 May 1943	10 OTU	BD260	AS Patrol	3313 (-)1240
Sgt L O Slade	30 May 1943	10 OTU	Z9440	AS Patrol	3313 (-)1282
Sgt J Vaughan	22 Aug 1942	10 OTU	Z6645	AS Patrol	3310 (-)876
Sgt G W Vines	30 May 1943	10 OTU	Z9440	AS Patrol	3313 (-)1285
Sgt W Walpole	11 Dec 1942	10 OTU	Z9437	AS Patrol	3312 (-)1047
Sgt H A Weber	17 May 1943	10 OTU	BD260	AS Patrol	3313 (-)1239
Sgt J F White	11 Dec 1942	10 OTU	Z9437	AS Patrol	3312 (-)1096
Sgt L Whitworth	17 May 1943	10 OTU	BD260	AS Patrol	3313 (-)1243
Sgt W F Wicks	30 May 1943	10 OTU	Z9440	AS Patrol	3313 (-)1284

Royal Canadian Air Force

Name	Date	Unit	Serial	Duty	Reference
P/O B A Russell	30 May 1943	10 OTU	Z9440	AS Patrol	3313 (-)1281
Sgt W J Wood	30 May 1943	10 OTU	Z9440	AS Patrol	3313 (-)1283

Appendix 6

Kinloss Log

Throughout the many hours spent researching Unit Operations Record Books, I was struck by the lack of detail in respect of aircraft accidents. For example, Lossiemouth failed to report any losses from the resident unit for the better part of two years, while the early entries in Benson's records are more concerned with the work of the Photographic Reconnaissance Unit than that of the resi-

dent Operational Training Unit. It would be the autumn of 1940 before the unit thought it worth mentioning the demise of some of their Fairey Battles!

However, there were occasions when units did describe events in reasonable detail and the following notes, by no means complete, have been taken from the records compiled by 19 Operational Training Unit at Kinloss.

Page 189   Whitley V   N1469:

0003   Aircraft in area of airfield, waiting for QGH.

0030   Contacted station direction finding and was about to be given first QDM when transmissions ceased. Unable to contact aircraft on any frequency.

1005   Aircraft came up on base frequency. Position approximately 4 to 5 miles east of Loch Dallas. Air-Sea Rescue crew called and Air-Sea Rescue Anson prepared.

1030   Air-Sea Rescue Anson took off. Dallas Police contacted and requested to organise local search.

1130   Air-Sea Rescue Anson landed, having located "1469", 57.30N 03.20W, approximately 3 miles west-north-west from Archiestown.

Page 253   Whitley V   Z9422:

0053   Crash reported by crash tender crew, who witnessed aircraft firing off red Verey lights.

0055   P/O Elcock requested to fire Verey lights over area of crash site.

0058   Air-Sea Rescue launch, Findhorn Police and local fishermen requested to make a search of the shore and in-shore waters.

0128   Air-Sea Rescue Anson (airborne) reports difficulty in getting flares to ignite and, thus, will return to base. Whitley H of C Flight (F/O Chisholm) dropping flares.

0159   Air-Sea Rescue Anson landed. Air-Sea Rescue launch having difficulty entering Findhorn Bay without aid of lights. Sandra lights illuminated and placed horizontally over Bay entrance.

0235   Findhorn Police boat report recovering crew from dinghy, All safe.

Addendum

Since preparing the overall structure of this volume, additional information has been unearthed in respect of some of the material summarised.   Thus, the notes that follow will
enhance this data, which is identified by the page number and unit.

Page 29   17 OTU   Blenheim I   L8610:

Sixty years on, to the day, a memorial service for the crew was held on the
bleak hillside at Garn Wen. Mr Ken Clark of Abersychan and Garndiffaith Local
History Group, was the prime instigator of this service, which was conducted
by Father Ron Jefford, vicar of Abersychan.   In attendance were the sisters of
two of the deceased crew, Mrs Brenda King whose brother was Sgt Bertie Wilson,
and Mrs Clare Jeffries, younger sister to Sgt John November. The solemn service
was marked by a single fly past of a Hawk jet, which overflew the gathering at
high speed at precisely 1045. A full account of this event was reported in the
Pontypool Free Post.

Page 30   10 OTU   Anson I   R3304:

Omitted from unit records, further details of this loss have been discovered
which identifies the crew as:

Sgt C F Gibbons   Sgt A White was the sole fatality. Hailing from
Sgt F H Abbott   Heanor in Derbyshire, he rests in Northern Ireland
Sgt Zalsberg   at Newtownards (Movilla) Cemetery. The rest of the
Sgt A White   crew escaped unharmed, all being picked up by His
Sgt R H White   Majesty's Yacht Virginia.

Page 44   21 OTU   Wellington IC   T2712:

The pilot of this aircraft, W/C N G Mulholland DFC, was a regular officer
whose name appears on an accident card raised for a minor flying accident
on 8 January 1940, in respect of 148 Squadron Wellington I L4282 damaged at
Kidlington following a flight from Harwell. On 15 February 1942, he was the
captain of an Overseas Aircraft Delivery Unit Wellington IC (DV539) reported
missing in the final stages of its transit to the Middle East. Interestingly,
his entry in the Commonwealth War Graves Commission register for Catania War
Cemetery in Sicily shows his unit as 458 Squadron which, according to records,
was still based in the United Kingdom at Holme-in-Spalding Moor, though preparing for Middle East service, an embarkation party departing on 20 March 1942.

Page 58   10 OTU   Whitley V   Z6667:

Sgt Sanderson, who is buried at Middlesbrough (Acklam) Cemetery, lost his
father, Lieutenant-Commander Percy George Sanderson RN (Retd) Chief Engineering
Officer in the steamship Warlaby (registered in West Hartlepool) on 12 February
1941. Lieutenant-Commander Sanderson has no known grave and his name is perpetuated on panel 116 of the Tower Hill Memorial, on the south side of the
garden of Trinity Square, close to The Tower of London.

Page 62   19 OTU   Whitley IV   K9033:

The wireless operator was Sgt G Carman RNZAF (not Carmen as reported) and, as
Errol Martyn has been able to advise, he was lost on operations to Hüls during
September 1941, while flying with 78 Squadron. Details of his death are shown
in Volume 1 of 'For Your Tomorrow', pages 141 and 142, and on page 139 of Bomber
Command Losses, Volume 2. Born at Catfield in Norfolk, his parents had gone
out to New Zealand in 1914.

Page 100   20 OTU   Wellington IC   N2825:

Sgt Clark's parents, Henry and Ethel Clark of Lancaster, suffered the loss
of a second son, Kenneth (a Craftsman in the Royal Electrical and Mechanical
Engineers), who died in Italy on 13 November 1945. He is buried in Milan War
Cemetery.

Page 109   10 OTU   Whitley V   AD706:

Sgt Mott's brother, Sgt Geoffrey Seaby Hayen Mott, was posted missing in action
after his 58 Squadron Whitley failed to return from operations to Hamburg on
30 November - 1 December 1941. Along with the entire crew, he is commemorated
on the Runnymede Memorial (see Bomber Command Losses, Volume 2, page 197).

Page 165   29 OTU   Wellington III   X3705:

Since the completion of the text, the crew has been identified as:

F/S H Hyde	No one was badly hurt, but three, Sgt McCrae RCAF,
Sgt W E McCrae RCAF	Sgt Coxall and Sgt Sutherland, required medical
Sgt E E P Coxall	attention.
Sgt J Sutherland	
Sgt Gibson	
Sgt Adams	
Sgt Clark	

Page 170   10 OTU   Whitley V   Z9217:

As indicated, details of the crew were omitted from unit records. However,
an examination of other official documents reveal their names to be:

F/S J McCubbin	The sole fatality was Sgt MacKenzie, who sustained
Sgt G C MacKenzie	a compound fracture to one of his legs. This, com-
Sgt B J Sherry	bined with the trauma of being forced down into the
Sgt K J Dagnall	sea and the effects of the exposure that followed,
Sgt A M Smith	led to his death. Aged nineteen, and from Edinburgh,
Sgt C A Stewart	he is commemorated on panel 88 of the Runnymede
	Memorial. The others are described as "safe".

There are no indications as to where the Whitley ditched but it is presumed
the crew were rescued by an allied vessel.

Page 179   14 OTU   Wellington IC   DV929:

Unusually, the name of F/O William Francis Rielly is omitted from the registers
produced by the Commonwealth War Graves Commission. Although he was an American
from Youngstown, Ohio, his service number indicates he was a member of the Royal
Air Force (Volunteer Reserve) and, for this reason, I would have expected his
details to be published. His RCAF air gunner, Sgt Gladish, also hailed from
the United States, his home town being given as Girardeau in Missouri.

Page 191   10 OTU   Whitley V   Z6464:

The crew of the Liberator (239230) have been identified as:

Maj B C Martin USAAF	From the meticulous records kept by Hans de Haan, and
1Lt W H Bagley USAAF	generously shared, it is known that four were either
1Lt E E Haskell USAAF	killed outright, or died soon afterwards from their
2Lt W A Krozel USAAF	injuries. All were initially laid to rest in the
S/Sgt M L Halsey USAAF	American plot at Brookwood Military Cemetery, but
S/Sgt T J O'Toole USAAF	since 1945, their bodies have been exhumed
T/Sgt H A Sullenberger USAAF	and reinterred as follows:
T/Sgt J R Lowry USAAF	
Sgt J W Mansfield USAAF	Maj Martin to his hometown in the State of Montana.
Sgt A W Lundy USAAF	1Lt Haskell to his hometown in the State of Ohio and
	T/Sgt Lowry to his hometown in the State of Iowa.
	1Lt Bagley, has been taken to the United States
	Military Cemetery at Madingley on the western out-
	skirts of Cambridge, where he lies in plot F, row 6,
	grave 30.

Page 199   81 OTU   Whitley V   Z6496:

The five injured members of crew were:

Sgt A C Best
Sgt A Hockney
Sgt J G Waugh
Sgt W Wisby
Sgt W T Martin

Page 200   81 OTU   Whitley V   LA769:

Additional to the two names identified are:

Sgt N E Legge   It is indicated that Sgt Legge, Sgt Sheppard and
P/O Todd   Sgt Webb were injured.
Sgt E Sheppard
Sgt Bucklitach
Sgt J L Webb

Page 201   30 OTU   Wellington X   HE466:

Ten months previous, on 24 April 1942, P/O Thorogood´s younger brother,
Sgt Herbert John Thorogood, had been killed during air operations near Snaith
airfield in Yorkshire (see Bomber Command Losses, Volume 3, page 76). Both
are buried in Romford Cemetery, Essex.

Page 206   29 OTU   Wellington III BK390:

When this bomber crashed into Eastern Road, Coates, at least four civilians
lost their lives:

Mr S G Fletcher   Sgt McDougall, the Wellington´s tail gunner, was
Mrs P Fletcher   taken to RAF Hospital Ely.
(child) Fletcher
Mrs M King

Page 211   26 OTU   Wellington III BJ879:

The loss of this aircraft, and its crew, is commemorated in an article by
Leslie Smith in October 2001 Newsletter of Bomber Command Association. The
water tower, referred to in the summary as belonging to Little Horwood, was
at Mursley and from the two photographs that accompany Leslie Smith´s article,
it has been rebuilt and a memorial plaque, perpetuating the names of the crew,
was unveiled on 8 May 1995. In the form of a disc, the plaque was donated by
Anglian Water Services Limited and incorporates the title of Mursley Parish
Council. Of particular interest, the article traces the service life and
achievements of the pilot, P/O Dint DFM, who died a mere six weeks after
celebrating his twentieth birthday. Posted to 26 Operational Training Unit
in June 1942, on completion of a tour of operations with 150 Squadron, he had
undergone an intensive course in flying instruction at 7 Flying Instructors
School at Upavon, before returning to Wing and his untimely death.

Page 213   81 OTU   Whitley V   LA768:

Sgt Findlay´s brother, F/O Brian Findley, was killed on active service with
227 Squadron . Operating out of Biferno, Italy, his Beaufighter failed to
return on 26 January 1944. He is buried in Greece at Phaleron War Cemetery.

Page 214   10 OTU   Whitley V   P4989:

Since preparing the summary, details of the remainder of the crew have come
to light:

P/O J Verney
Sgt R W Cumbers
Sgt Bishop
Sgt Cough
Sgt Culey

Page 225   28 OTU   Wellington IC   DV613:

The crew of this aircraft comprised of:

Sgt J W Shearer   Sgt Fulthorpe of Ely, Glamorgan was the sole fatality
Sgt C Broomfield   and he is commemorated on panel 150 of the Runnymede
Sgt N F Worsnup   Memorial.
Sgt D Naylor
Sgt C T Akers RAAF
Sgt R Fulthorpe

Page 229   29 OTU   Wellington X   HE372:

The four members of crew, all of whom being injured, have been identified as:

Sgt H C G Piper   Please note the amendment to Sgt Piper's initials.
P/O T G Wilson
Sgt J Clark
Sgt A Fraser

Page 230   12 OTU   Wellington III   BJ965:

The crew of this Wellington is now known to have comprised of:

F/O F S Taylor   Additional to the death of F/O Taylor, the rest of
P/O G M Roberts   the crew sustained injuries of varying severity.
Sgt D Rainton
Sgt W J Matthews RCAF
Sgt Menzies
Sgt E J Warren RAAF

Page 232   27 OTU   Wellington III   BJ713:

Full details of the crew are:

F/L L J Simpson RAAF   Sgt Edwards was critically injured and he died soon
P/O W N T Russell RAAF   after the crash. Aged twenty, he is the sole service
P/O C E Neath   burial from the Second World War in Alderford (St.
P/O Sigmont   John The Baptist) Churchyard, Norfolk.
F/S Davies
Sgt Hall
Sgt Purcell
Sgt L E Edwards

Page 236   28 OTU   Wellington IC   DV455:

Complete crew details for this Wellington, plus the identities of the three
civilians who perished, are as follows:

Sgt F Chase RCAF   Sgt Jepson, the son of Capt Reginald Jepson and Edith
Sgt F T Gwarpney RCAF   Jepson, is buried at Derby (Nottingham Road) Cemetery.
Sgt R A B Jepson   Through the kind auspices of Anglesey County Record
Sgt Wilcox   Office, and in particular the help provided by Mrs
Sgt Greenwood   Anne Venables, I am able to report that Dr Chill was
Dr M W Chill   aged sixty-four, his wife was aged thirty, while Mrs
Mrs M Chill   Scott was Mrs Chill's mother. It is presumed they
Mrs M L Scott   all shared the family house. Furthermore, details
                         of this awful tragedy are reported in a book concerning
                         aircraft accidents in Gwynedd by Roy Sloan.

Page 236   24 OTU   Anson I   DJ242:

Crew details are reported as:

P/O K F Smith   All were injured, though (it is believed) not too
Sgt W R Boucher   severely. Three, Sgts Boucher, Radbourne and Bracken,
Sgt A B Radbourne RCAF   lost their lives in late November 1943, while raiding
Sgt W D Bracken   Berlin with 428 Squadron (see Bomber Command Losses,
P/O T L Mayfield   Volume 4, page 392).

Page 241   27 OTU   Wellington X   MS475:

Crew details for this aircraft are:

Sgt D O Glindening RAAF   Please note the correction to the name of the pilot.
Sgt J G Carl RAAF   All were injured.
Sgt B G Dillon RAAF
Sgt L E Welldon RAAF
Sgt R J Coventry RAAF

Page 248   24 OTU   Whitley V   LA786:

The crew of this Whitley has been identified as:

Sgt R V Long RCAF   The sole injury concerned the tail gunner.
P/O Young
Sgt Treleaven
Sgt Hailey
Sgt W J Cavanagh RCAF

Page 256   10 OTU   Whitley V   BD280:

W/O Nicoll, whose parents were the Revd Peter Hill Nicoll and Margre Vivien
Nicoll of Garvoch in Kincardineshire, lost his elder brother, Sgt James Vivian
Kenealy Nicoll on 9 April 1943. He is buried in Benghazi War Cemetery, Libya.

Page 258   19 OTU   Whitley V   BD386:

Since setting the parameters for the page, I have learnt that P/O Knapp was
a Scholar of New College, Oxford and he graduated with a Bachelor of Arts
degree.

Page 303   29 OTU   Wellington III   X3306:

The crew has been identified as:

F/S N R Hooper RAAF   All required medical attention for their injuries.
Sgt G H Pearce
F/O J T Costello RAAF
Sgt J E Bailey

RAF FIGHTER COMMAND LOSSES OF THE SECOND WORLD WAR

Norman Franks

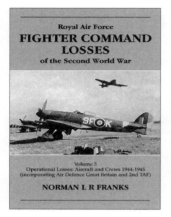

BRITISH AIRFIELD BUILDINGS 2: EXPANSION & INTER-WAR PERIODS

Graham Buchan Innes

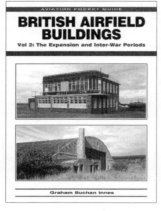

BOMBER COUNTY
A History of the RAF in Lincolnshire

Terry Hancock

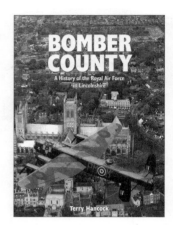

Following the Battle of France and the retreat through Dunkirk, Britain stood alone awaiting the inevitable onslaught from Germany. At the forefront of the UK's defence was Fighter Command and it was their Hurricanes, Spitfires, Blenheims and Defiants that became the world-famed 'Few' that managed to repulse the Luftwaffe in 'The Battle of Britain' during the summer of 1940.

Germany's failure to overcome the RAF and their decision to attack Russia allowed Britain to consolidate, rebuild, go on the offensive, and after D-Day, battle across Europe to the bitter end.

Fighter Command, ADGB and 2nd TAF lost over 5,000 aircrew between 1939 and 1945. This work examines on a day-to-day basis the sacrifices made by these men during the desperate years of the war. The reasons and circumstances for the losses are given as crucial campaigns are enacted.

Available in 234 x 156mm sbk format:

Volume 1: 1939-41
Details 1,000 aircraft losses; 168pp
40 b/w pics 1 85780 055 9 **£12.95**

Volume 2: 1942-43
Details 1,800+ aircraft losses; 156pp
53 b/w pics 1 85780 075 3 **£12.95**

Volume 3: 1944-45
Details c.2,450 acft losses; 200pp
83 b/w pics 1 85780 093 1 **£14.95**

Airfield buildings are a constant source of fascination to enthusiasts and historians. Those who welcomed the author's first volume, *British Airfield Buildings of the Second World War*, will welcome this second book on the subject, which focuses primarily on the period from 1935 to 1939, when the government responded belatedly to the rise of Hitler and the threat he posed to Britain's inadequate air defences.

The book includes a handful of First World War and post-First World War buildings as well as some wartime temporary designs for comparison. The great majority of photographs are in colour and as with the first volume, there is an illustration of a surviving example of each type of building, along with its location and details of its former use etc.

This invaluable pocket-sized guide deals with a wide variety of buildings, including hangars, barrack blocks, maintenance buildings, guard houses, mess buildings, fuel stores etc, right down to the humble latrines.

Softback
184 x 120 mm, 128 pages
approx 250 colour photographs
1 85780 101 6 Available
£8.95

A third, totally revised, updated and re-designed version of a perennial favourite. Lincolnshire – forever 'Bomber County' because of the many RAF Bomber Command bases dotted about its flat landscape – is undoubtedly one of England's premier counties when it comes to military aviation. This rich history dates back to the days of the RNAS and RFC when rudimentary airfields were constructed during the First World War, through the RAF's night bombing offensive of the Second World War and on to the V-Force. But the 'bomber' tag relates only part of the county's aviation history, for the RAF's time in Lincolnshire has also included a strong training element, which continues to this day; a front-line contribution to air defence of the UK; and a reputation as 'NATO Central' thanks to the comings and goings at RAF Waddington during air combat training.

For this new edition, most of the photographs are new. Maps of the bases' locations are included, as is a comprehensive Station-by-Station appendix featuring all the units based at over 150 airfields during nearly 90 years of aviation history.

Softback, 280 x 215 mm, c160 pages
c150 b/w and colour photos
1 85780 129 6 May
c£17.99